Security: A Multidisciplinary Normative Approach

International Humanitarian Law Series

VOLUME 26

The International Humanitarian Law Series is a series of monographs and edited volumes which aims to promote scholarly analysis and discussion of both the theory and practice of the international legal regulation of armed conflict.

The series explores substantive issues of International Humanitarian Law including,

- protection for victims of armed conflict and regulation of the means and methods of warfare
- questions of application of the various legal regimes for the conduct of armed conflict
- issues relating to the implementation of International Humanitarian Law obligations
- national and international approaches to the enforcement of the law and
- the interactions between International Humanitarian Law and other related areas of international law such as Human Rights, Refugee Law, Arms Control and Disarmament Law, and International Criminal Law.

The titles in this series are listed at the end of this volume.

Security: A Multidisciplinary Normative Approach

Edited by

Cecilia M. Bailliet

MARTINUS
NIJHOFF
PUBLISHERS

LEIDEN • BOSTON
2009

On the cover: A man on a donkey looks up at a passing Eufor patrol from the Polish contigent near Iriba in eastern Chad on March 13, 2009, two days before the end the European force (EUFOR) mandate in the country. The European Union will keep more than 2,000 peacekeepers in Chad and the Central African Republic after United Nations troops take over. EUFOR, comprised of around 3,200 soldiers drawn from 14 countries, began a year-long mission a year ago to protect refugees from Sudan's strife-torn Darfur region, as well as people displaced by the rebel insurgency in Chad and the northern CAR. UN Resolution 1861 also extended the mandate of the UN Mission in the Central African Republic and Chad (MINURCAT) for one year until March 2010 in order to ensure the security and protection of civilians in the two countries. AFP PHOTO / PHILIPPE HUGUEN

This book is printed on acid-free paper.

Library of Congress Cataloging-in-Publication Data

Security : a multidisciplinary normative approach / edited by Cecilia M. Bailliet.
p. cm. – (International humanitarian law series ; v. 26)
Includes index.
ISBN 978-90-04-17296-8 (hardback : alk. paper)
1. International law. 2. Humanitarian law. 3. National security–Law and legislation. 4. Environmental law, International. I. Bailliet, Cecilia.

KZ3410.S43 2009
341.7'2–dc22

2009023159

ISSN 1389-6776
ISBN 978 90 04 17296 8

PRINTED IN THE NETHERLANDS

For little Helena, whose fear of rising seas impeded her sleep and revealed to me how the new generation views security.

C.M.B.

Table of Contents

Foreword

Arne Willy Dahl

Since times immemorial, man has sought security. When our distant ancestors roamed about the savannah it did not make much difference whether the threat came from lions or competing tribes. More recently, the concept has been divided into safety, which is about threats from natural causes or harm inflicted unintentionally, and security, which is about harm caused deliberately by human beings.

Although the end result may be the same, we tend to look upon security threats with more concern than safety threats. As a participant in the ordinary traffic on the roads or in the streets in Norway (irrespective of whether I am a driver, a passenger or a pedestrian), I run a risk of about one in 10,000 of losing my life in an accident throughout the course of one year. This is a kind of risk that we all run and which few of us are concerned about. Enforcing strict speed limits would mean that a typical trip by car would take ca. fifteen or thirty minutes more and could probably reduce the risk to close to zero. It appears that this would, however, be a too high price to pay for safety on the roads.

The risk of becoming a murder victim is (at least in Norway) substantially lower; maybe by a factor of five or ten. We abhor murders. Each case is treated very seriously and is likely to result in grave punishments for the perpetrators. From time to time discussions flare up as to whether certain persons should be locked up for life to prevent them from repeating such acts.

If we move further to the risk of becoming the victim of a terrorist attack, we could probably add a couple of additional zeros after the comma; although spectacular events like the terrorist attack on the World Trade Centre in 2001 make the statistics peak in particular years. We expect our governments to make substantial efforts to reduce security risks posed by terrorist activities and we accept delays and inconveniences at airports and other places for the same purpose.

Collectively we accept (at least so far) a grave long-term safety risk to our own or our children's well-being or even lives posed by global warming, which is unintentional, although it is man-made. We do not, however, accept security risks posed by foreign states that might occupy our territory, cut off the supply of important resources, such as oil, or do other nasty things against us. While it is disputable whether we might be willing to spend one single per cent of our gross domestic product to reduce carbon dioxide emissions in order to avert global warming, many states are willing to spend ten times as much on military security measures.

The bottom line is: We want security. We want it for objective reasons, but even more for subjective grounds. We dislike accidents and natural disasters, but abhor deliberate infliction of damage, suffering and death. Maybe the security threats have a moral and emotional dimension that safety threats do not possess. If you stumble and fall, you may bang your head and that is not good. Nevertheless, it feels worse if someone beats you on your head; in spite of the fact that the resulting physical consequences may be identical.

Although it may at times be irrational, our demand for security has to be accepted. But we must look upon it critically; in particular, when we place burdens on others in the name of our own security. In some situations our own demand for security can be at the expense of the security of other people. In other situations, it can even be said that measures taken to increase our own security generate distrust and response from others that ultimately reduces our own security – like the nuclear arms race.

This book discusses a number of aspects of security, some general, and others more specific. Although the field has been given a broad coverage, there are probably vast numbers of aspects and special cases that could be added. It is therefore my hope that this book will spur further discussion and academic work on these questions that are so important for us.

Introduction

Cecilia M. Bailliet

Security is an all-encompassing term of art which is subject to diverse interpretations and understandings. It envelops notions of protection against transnational threats including: terrorism, organized crime, narco-trafficking, refugee movements, environmental disasters and degradation, state failure, ethnic strife, poverty, infectious diseases, inter-state conflict, internal conflict, and proliferation of nuclear, chemical and biological weapons.

In the recent period, the University of Oslo has recruited researchers to address various aspects related to the field of security, e.g. International Public Law, International Criminal Law, International Humanitarian Law, Refugee Law, Human Rights, Environmental Law, and Ethics. All researchers have identified the need to explore issues pertaining to the legitimacy of practices pursued in their respective fields pursuant to the evolution of national, regional, and international norms and institutions seeking to maintain security.

The papers in this collection were presented at a conference titled "Security: A Multidisciplinary Normative Approach" held at the University of Oslo on 16–17 October 2008. We sought to stimulate dialogue between researchers from different fields who do not normally address security with security practitioners in order to promote new discourses on the interpretation and application of this norm. As an initiative, the papers explore a variety of security issues and scenarios, but are not fully exhaustive, rather calling for additional research and debate.

Participants were encouraged to address the normative evolution of the notion of security. Specifically, they were asked to explore whether there are there normative gaps in our understanding of security in each of the respective fields of law, ethics, etc. Is there a lack of clarity/vagueness? Alternatively, is there normative overlap or congruity between the notions of security in each arena?

Similarly, they were asked to compare the interpretation of normative standards pertaining to security at the international, regional and national levels. Is the context of various authorities rendering decisions pertaining to the recognition/response to security situations one which complicates the interpretation of the term? Further, what is the legitimacy of the institutions creating security related norms? What effect do these norms have on persons or areas beyond the traditional jurisdiction of the institution?

The security debate also raises the issue of state sovereignty/non-intervention. Does our obligation towards human security, sometimes expressed as the "responsibility to protect", justify an increase in military interventions? Is this applicable only to failed states, or also to repressive states, states that are incapable of securing their citizens basic needs, or states that fail to contain non-state actors from attacking a citizenry? How should combatant status and obligations be understood when military personnel fight under the aegis of 'protection'? In response to the increased importance of non-state or private actors in conflict and security operations, we invited reflection on the special normative conundrums resulting from their participation.

Further, we wished to explore how one measures the legitimacy of the application of the principle of security, as well as the legitimacy of the enforcement mechanisms. Human security means protecting vital freedoms. But appeals are commonly made to security as an alleged justification for setting fundamental freedoms aside. The conference sought to address the problem that appeals to security contain moral dilemmas, not least exemplified in the ongoing "war on terror". Can security for political collectives justify setting aside the fundamental rights of individuals, such as liberty and privacy? The notion of human security seems to encompass such values, whereas the narrower concept of state security seems, at least in practice, to conflict with it. Is the concept of security a normatively ambiguous term covering radically different and irreconcilable phenomena, or is there a common normative source from which all the various types of security are derived?

Finally, the identification of individuals and groups of individuals claiming rights to security (e.g. women exposed to violence) as well as exhibiting the power to impact the security of other individuals or even states, challenges the paradigms by which the right to security and the duty not to impinge upon the security of others is altered.

Part I addresses the development of the concept of security within the international legal framework. *Marco Sassòli* confronts the use and abuse of the term "security"; both for the purpose of justifying the use of force under the UN Charter (ius ad bellum) and for restricting the rights of victims of armed conflicts under international humanitarian law (ius in bello). Additionally, he discusses the obligations of belligerents to protect the "security" of war victims. He calls for a restrictive interpretation of the term "security" in order to address physical violence against persons or property and limiting the mandate of the UN Security Council.

Marco Odello contemplates the emergence of newly identified threats to international peace and security according to the UN and international regional organisations. He concludes that the regional organisations have adopted wider definitions that may challenge UN control over security issues. He also examines the interface between human security and state security and advocates greater engagement by national and international judicial bodies to address inconsistencies.

Part II embarks upon review of the evolution of international humanitarian law. *Ulf-Petter Häußler* identifies the normative gaps emerging from the doctrinal war and peace divide, and confounded by the diversification of contemporary threats to international peace and security. Specifically, this is characterized by the expansion of transitional authorities/peacekeeping missions, employment of private contractors, and engagement of non-governmental armed groups and terrorists. Further complications are due to a lack of review bodies. He suggests that the application of general principles of international humanitarian and human rights law is sufficient to close the normative gaps.

Matthew V. Ezzo & Amos Guiora tackle the issue of the "voluntary human shield" as representing the primary dilemma facing today's soldier. Uncertain whether the civilians standing in the vicinity of a legitimate military target are "voluntary", the soldier must make enormously critical and complicated operational decisions. While international law requires minimal collateral damage, attacking legitimate targets is the essence of lawful operational counterterrorism. Determining whether the civilian is a "voluntary human shield" manifests the tension between the security of the soldier and the security of the individual.

Kjetil Mujezinovic Larsen asserts that the existence of legal obligations upon participating states in international peace operations for the removal and destruction of anti-personnel mines and explosive remnants of war remains contentious. He examines the relationship between international humanitarian law (in particular the Anti-Personnel Mine Ban Convention) and human rights law (specifically the "right to life"). He calls for further normative development.

Gro Nystuen describes the process behind the adoption of the treaty banning cluster munitions in 2008. She discusses the scope of application of the principle of distinction to these weapons and the impact of the M-85 Report. Nystuen explains that a partnership between civil society and governments generated sufficient political capital to ensure emergence of the new law addressing a key reclamation of human security.

Part III confronts conflicting defintions of security within the realm of Ethics and Democracy. *Lene Bomann Larsen* offers consequence-based and principled reasons against legalization of 'private soldiers'. She explores whether it is permissible to be a mercenary and whether it is acceptable for States to use mercenaries. Examination of the motivation of the soldiers and their representative function as instruments of the State is conducted in order to demonstrate the incompatibility of conflicting aims with the sovereign interest of the State.

Cecilia M. Bailliet presents a case study of Colombia's targeted strike against FARC leader Raúl Reyes in Ecuador in 2008. Examination is made of the institutional debates within the OAS and Rio Group addressing the articulation of a new norm: "The Responsibility to Prevent Terrorism". It is suggested that UN Security Council Resolution 1373 has prompted the articulation of juridical innovations that promote an international state of exception based on an inverted concept of security. This negatively affects the international rule of law, as it pierces the veil of sovereignty and further impacts the interpretation of protection duties under humanitarian law, human rights, and refugee law.

Christopher Kutz discusses the conflicts between democracy and security. Democracy is generally considered to support international peace and security. Yet democracy is also linked to insecurity. For example, cases involving alleged lack of democracy have resulted in increased interventions. Democratic processes have also resulted in restrictions on civil liberties and civil strife. Kutz seeks to reconcile the competing demands of democracy by exploring the shift from national security to human security, the pairing of human security with democratization, the impact of globalisation, and the ensuing legitimation discourse.

Larry May strikes at the core of the security debate by identifying the rights of habeas corpus and non-refoulement as key components of global procedural justice. He addresses tensions between the notions of human and state security; pursuing an historical approach which takes the reader back to the Magna Carta when considering detention at Guantanamo Bay. May proposes the normative principle of visibleness as a counter to arbitrary exercise of detention powers.

Naomi Cahn examines six US reports measuring state fragility and asserts that the evaluation is often devoid of gender equity assessment. She demonstrates the relationship between women's security (including their legal, social, political and economic status) and state security. Cahn identifies gender equity as a useful indicator of state security and calls for gender mainstreaming in order to reduce state fragility.

Part IV addresses the global challenge of environmental security. *Christina Voigt* confirms the effects of climate change as posing a significant security threat, specifically in the form of environmental migration. She discusses the normative concept of peace and security in the UN Charter and its relationship to climate change. The mandate of the Security Council to impose sanctions, "legislate", condemn state actions or inactions, or request an advisory opinion from the ICJ is also examined. Nevertheless, recognition is made of the need for political consensus.

Jo Stigen and Ole Kristian Fauchald continue the discussion of environmental security and the UN Security Council by characterising environmental issues as "conflict drivers". These may be characterised as a "threat to the peace, breach of the peace or act of aggression", according to the UN Charter, Article 39. Although they note that the Security Council has only rarely addressed environmental issues, they recognize arguments in favour of expanding its mandate to be an effective protector of the environment.

Part V concludes the collection by presenting contemplations on the divide between security practitioners and academics. *Sean Kanuck* describes how multiple voices (including foreign policy makers, military commanders, intelligence analysts, academics, journalists, NGOs, and others) apply different priorities and value judgments when addressing issues pertaining to international law. He explains how practitioners are negatively affected by collection of imperfect information, time constraints and risk assessments. This is combined with uncertainty and professional duties, creating a gap between practitioners and academics when discussing security. He calls for a collaborative and strategic approach to international law that would create more enforceable rules.

In conclusion, the diverse papers confirm a state of normative flux and evolution which complicates the understanding and application of the term "security". It behoves further reflection within international and national institutional forums, academia, as well as among practitioners.

I wish to extend my appreciation to the Norwegian Ministry of Defence for its financial support of the conference upon which this publication is based. I also wish to thank the editorial staff at Brill for their top assistance. The chapters have been written by the individual authors, hence they were not required to conform to a uniform style or format.

Part I

The Overarching Security Framework in International Law

Chapter 1

The Concept of Security in International Law Relating to Armed Conflicts

Marco Sassòli[*]

International law regulates the relations between States; to an increasing extent, the relations between States and individuals; and to a still limited and controversial extent, the behavior of individuals, even when it cannot be attributed to a State. Armed conflicts cause problems at all three of these levels. The notion of security appears on at least the first two of these levels.

On the first, inter-state level, armed conflicts are the most traditional and the most comprehensive threat to the security of a State. Security threats can justify an armed conflict and security reasons may justify a State taking action that would normally be incompatible with its obligations during armed conflicts.

On the second level, armed conflicts constitute the most extreme threat to the security of individuals. In an armed conflict, the security of the State may justify certain interferences with the rights of persons affected by said conflict, but States also have obligations to protect the security of such persons. It is therefore appropriate to analyze how the concept of security is used in the international law relating to armed conflicts.

Many treaties of the international law relating to armed conflicts use the term security, but interestingly enough (and as we will see, symptomatically) none of these treaties define the term.

War is regulated by two distinct and completely separate branches of international law: the *ius ad bellum*, prohibiting and exceptionally authorizing the use of force, and the *ius in bello*, regulating, mainly for humanitarian purposes, that use of force.

Today, the use of force, *i.e.* the launching of an armed conflict, is prohibited by a peremptory rule of international law.[1] The *ius ad bellum* has turned into *ius contra bello*, which is today mainly codified in the UN Charter. There are two exceptions to the prohibition of the use of force between States: individual and collective self-defense, which is not the launching of an armed conflict but rather the reaction to

* The author would like to warmly thank his research assistants, Ms. Eleanor Grant and Ms. Julia Grignon for their valuable research and for having revised this text.

1 See Art. 2 (4) of the UN Charter.

Cecilia M. Bailliet (ed.), Security: A Multidisciplinary Normative Approach.
Printed in The Netherlands. ISBN 978 90 04 17296 8. pp. 7–22.

an armed attack, and armed conflicts launched (according to the letter of the UN Charter)[2] – or (in international reality) authorized – by the UN Security Council "to maintain or restore international peace and *security*". As for non-international armed conflicts, it is inherent in the concept of the modern State that the government has the monopoly on the lawful use of force. Individuals are prohibited under the domestic law of all States – although not by international law – from launching armed conflicts against their government.

As for *ius in bello*, or in more modern terminology, international humanitarian law (IHL), it applies independently of whether an armed conflict is lawful or unlawful under *ius ad bellum* (or launched in violation of the domestic law of the State affected by a non-international armed conflict) never mind what the causes claimed by or attributed to the parties to the conflict may be. The laws on how force may be used apply equally to all parties to a conflict, regardless of the legitimacy of the initial use of force.[3] The treaties of IHL distinguish between international and non-international armed conflicts, the latter being governed by less detailed and less protective rules. As for customary IHL, a recent comprehensive study undertaken under the auspices of the International Committee of the Red Cross (ICRC) found that there is a large body of customary rules, the majority of which purportedly apply to both international and non-international armed conflicts.[4]

I. The Concept of Security in General

As the concept of security is not defined in the relevant treaties (*i.e.*, the UN Charter and the Geneva Conventions[5] and Additional Protocols[6] which codify most of IHL) its meaning must be determined through the interpretation of every provision in which it appears. This must be done in accordance with the ordinary meaning of

---

2 See Art. 42 of the UN Charter.

3 This distinction is re-affirmed in the fifth preambular paragraph of *Protocol [No. I] Additional to the Geneva Conventions of 12 August 1949 relating to the Protection of Victims of International Armed Conflicts*, 8 June 1977, 1125 *UNTS* 3 – 434. See also Christopher Greenwood, "The Relationship Between *jus ad bellum* and *jus in bello*", 9 *Review of Int'l Studies* (1983) 221; Marco Sassòli, "*Ius ad bellum* and *Ius in Bello* – The Separation between the Legality of the Use of Force and Humanitarian Rules to be Respected in Warfare: Crucial or Outdated?", in: Michael N. Schmitt *et al.* (eds.), *International Law and Armed Conflict: Exploring the Faultlines, Essays in Honour of Yoram Dinstein*, Nijhoff, Leiden/Boston, 2007, pp. 242–264; Henry Meyrowitz, *Le principe de l'égalité des belligérants devant le droit de la guerre*, Pédone, Paris, 1970.

4 Jean-Marie Henckaerts and Louise Doswald-Beck (eds.), *Customary International Humanitarian Law*, Cambridge University Press, Cambridge, 2005.

5 *Convention [No. I] for the Amelioration of the Condition of the Wounded and Sick in Armed Forces in the Field*, 12 August 1949, 75 *UNTS* 31–83; *Convention [No. II] for the Amelioration of the Condition of the Wounded, Sick and Shipwrecked Members of Armed Forces at Sea*, 12 August 1949, 75 *UNTS* 85–133; *Convention [No. III] relative to the Treatment of Prisoners of War*, 12 August 1949, 75 *UNTS* 135–285; *Convention [No. IV] relative to the Protection of Civilian Persons in Time of War*, 12 August 1949, 75 *UNTS* 287–417.

6 Protocol I, *supra* note 3; *Protocol [No. II] Additional to the Geneva Conventions of 12*

the term, taking into account the object and purpose, the context of the treaty and of the rest of international law, and subsequent practice of States.[7] Scholarly writings on this concept are very rare.[8] In order to determine the ordinary meaning of the term, which derives from the Latin "*se-cura*", "*sine cura*", i.e., without concern, referring to a dictionary definition may be useful. For "security", the "security of the nation's citizens" is mentioned and explained with the terms "safety, freedom from danger, protection, invulnerability,"[9] and the "security of the children/jewels", is explained by "safety, freedom from danger, invulnerability, protection, safekeeping, shielding".[10] In these definitions, the relationship between security and safety is apparent. "Safety" is defined as "the state of being safe; exemption from hurt or injury; freedom from danger".[11] In English, "security" seems to refer to threats by deliberate human behavior, while "safety" to threats from natural causes or human negligence. Such a distinction is however not very practical in view of new, e.g. biological, threats and we will see that it is not made in other official UN languages.

On the international level, during the cold war era, a UN Group of experts defined security (in the context of disarmament discussions) as:[12]

> ... a condition in which States consider that there is no danger of military attack, political pressure or economic coercion, so that they are able to pursue freely their own development and progress. International security is thus the sum of the security of each and every State [...] accordingly international security cannot be reached without full international co-operation. However, security is a relative rather than an absolute term. National and international security need to be viewed as matters of degree.

In discussions on international law, *e.g.* in the context of collective security, when defining what is meant by the security of the State, writers distinguish between an

---

August 1949, and relating to the Protection of Victims of Non- International Armed Conflicts, 8 June 1977, 1125 *UNTS* 609 – 699.

7 See Art. 31 of the Vienna Convention on the Law of Treaties, general rule of interpretation.

8 I was only able to find Stephan Verosta, "Der Begriff 'Internationale Sicherheit' in der Satzung der Vereinten Nationen", in: René Marcic *et al.* (eds.*), Internationale Festschrift für Alfred Verdross zum 80. Geburtstag*, Wilhelm Fink Verlag, München/Salzburg, 1971, pp. 533–547.

9 "security, *n.*" *The Oxford Paperback Thesaurus*, edited by Maurice Waite, Oxford University Press, Oxford, 2006, *Oxford Reference Online*. Oxford University Press, online: ⟨http://www.oxfordreference.com/views/ENTRY.html?subview=Main&entry=t24.e11327⟩.

10 "security, *n.*" *The Oxford Paperback Thesaurus*, compiled by Betty Kirkpatrick, Oxford University Press, Oxford, 2000, p. 726; see also: "safety, *n.*" The Oxford Paperback Thesaurus, p. 713.

11 "safety, *n.*" The Oxford English Dictionary, 2nd ed., Clarendon Press, Oxford, 1989, Volume XIV Rob-Sequyle, pp. 358–361; see also: "security, *n.*" The Oxford English Dictionary, Volume XIV Rob-Sequyle, pp. 853–855.

12 See the report by a group of governmental experts set up to carry out a comprehensive

objective and a subjective element of security.[13] In my view, this distinction may equally be applied to the security of persons. Hans Kelsen writes: "Security is the condition of being protected against, or not exposed to a danger. It is an objective condition of man which, rightly or wrongly, man assumes to exist. The effect of this assumption is a certain state of mind which may be described as freedom from fear, the fear of a danger."[14] The objective element is the absence of, or protection against a threat. Some see it as being embodied in the mechanisms, procedures and instruments aiming at stable, peaceful, ordered and predictable relations.[15] Such security can only be guaranteed by the collective to which the State or the individual belongs.[16] The subjective dimension is the perception of the security situation, which may or may not correspond to the objective situation. Respect for international law is crucial to international security from both a subjective and an objective view point.[17] Depending on the absent, existing or perceived threat, international security, like peace (as we will discuss later), has economic and social aspects, thus going beyond military threats which have traditionally been the focus of international law.[18] As shown elsewhere in this volume, what Kelsen calls freedom from fear[19] is extended to freedom from want by certain adepts of the concept of "human security".

II. Security Threats as a Justification for the Use of Force under the UN Charter

The United Nations was created as a collective security organization. The organization's first purpose is peace,[20] i.e. to avoid international armed conflicts. The drafters of the UN Charter understood however that to achieve this aim, the absence of war

---

study of concepts of security, requested by UN General Assembly Resolution 38/188 H of 20 December 1983, submitted by the UN Secretary-General as Report A/40/553 of 26 August 1985, *Study on Concepts of Security*, p. 10. This group distinguished the following concepts of security: balance of power; deterrence; equal security (between super-powers and the blocs of the cold war); collective security; neutrality; non-alignment; peaceful co-existence; common security (*Ibid.*, pp. 12–22).

13 Mirko Zambelli, *La constatation des situations de l'article 39 de la Charte des Nations Unies par le Conseil de Sécurité*, Helbing&Lichtenhahn, Genève, Bâle, Munich, 2002, pp. 161–162; Rüdiger Wolfrum, "Article 1", in: Simma (ed.) *The Charter of the United Nations, A Commentary*, Oxford University Press, New York, 1995, p. 51. See also *UN Study on Concepts of Security, supra* note 12, p. 11.

14 Hans Kelsen, *Collective Security under International Law*, Government Printing Office, Washington D.C., 1957, p. 1.

15 Serge Sur, *Relations internationales*, 4th ed., Montchrestien, Paris, 1995, pp. 439–441.

16 Verosta, *supra* note 8, 536.

17 See *UN Study on Concepts of Security, supra* note 12, pp. 58–60.

18 See Kelsen, *supra* note 14, p. 1 and *UN Study on Concepts of Security, supra* note 12, pp. 23 and 28.

19 The concept of freedom from fear first appeared in the Atlantic Charter, reproduced as Annex 2 in: Leland M. Goodrich and Edvard Hambro, *Charter of the United Nations: commentary and documents*, 2nd ed., World Peace Foundation, Boston, 1949.

20 Mohammed Bedjaoui, "Article 1 (Commentaire général)", in: Jean-Pierre Cot, Alain

was not sufficient. They therefore included economic and social development and the universal respect of human rights among the purposes of the organization.[21] One of the main organs of the UN is the Security Council. Apart from references to that organ, the term "security" is used 29 times in the UN Charter. Nonetheless, except for rules that have lost their practical importance,[22] security always appears together with peace in the phrase "international peace and security". Under the Charter, international peace and international security are today seen as equivalents.[23] Originally, it might have been that security was the narrower concept and it was widened to cover all aspects of peace, a development which has been confirmed by the emergence of the concept of "human security".[24] Others consider that peace was initially the narrower concept and security also covered positive aspects of peace.[25]

An armed attack constitutes a breach of international peace and security, which the Security Council must take measures against in order to restore the peace.[26] The State victim of an armed attack may however also, individually of collectively, use force in self-defense. Under the text of the Charter, all other instances of the use of force between States must be decided by the UN Security Council. Unlike individual States, the Security Council may decide – and in practice authorize – the use of force for a much wider variety of situations than armed attacks: to maintain or restore international peace and security. The use of the term "maintain" implies that the Council may and must also act preventively, including by authorizing the use of force before the State threatening international peace and security has used force. The Council determines, according to Article 39 of the Charter, the existence "of any threat to the peace, breach of the peace or act of aggression". The fact that here and only here the term peace is not accompanied by the term "security" is probably of no importance, because the article then goes on to direct the Council to "decide what measures shall be taken to maintain or restore international peace and security". In recent resolutions, the Security Council has regularly classified situations as threats to international peace *and security*[27] and taken measures under Chapter VII, even though Art. 39 of the Charter does not use the term "security" in this context. In both its determination of the situation and its decision as to what measures should be

Pellet and Mathias Forteau (eds.), *La Charte des Nations Unies, Commentaire article par article*, 3rd ed., Economica, Paris, 2005, pp. 314–315.

21 See Preamble and Art. 1 of the UN Charter.

22 Art. 73 on non-self-governing territories and Arts. 76, 83 and 84 on the trusteeship system.

23 In the index of Commentaries to the UN Charter, the entry "security" refers the reader to "peace" (see Cot/Pellet/Forteau, *supra* note 20, p. 2290).

24 Dan Henk, "Human Security: Relevance and Implications", Parameters 35:2 (2005), pp. 92–106. See also already *UN Study on Concepts of Security, supra* note 12, pp. 4, 23, 28 and 55 (adopting a broad concept of security without yet using the term "human security").

25 Verosta, *supra* note 8.

26 Art. 39 of the UN Charter.

27 See *e.g.* SC Res. 1556 (2004), preambular para. 21 (on Sudan).

taken, the Council has a wide discretion, however it is not above the law.[28] In practice however, there is no court or other organ capable of reviewing the legality of UN Security Council resolutions and Member States are under an obligation to comply with Security Council resolutions adopted under Chapter VII of the UN Charter.[29]

In its practice, the Security Council has increasingly extended the concept of threats to international peace and security. It is obvious that inter-State conflicts are the prime example of such a threat. The first non-international armed conflict to be classified as such a threat was the Congo crisis in 1961.[30] This practice has continued, with the internal armed conflicts in the former Yugoslavia, Iraq and Somalia as well as a great number of other conflicts right up to the current crisis in Sudan, being considered a threat to international peace and security. Often without making a clear distinction with the conflict itself, serious violations of IHL[31] committed in such armed conflicts have been considered as threatening international peace and security. The main evidence for the fact that the Security Council considered such violations as threats distinct from the conflict itself is the resolutions creating the international criminal tribunals for the former Yugoslavia and Rwanda (ICTY and ICTR), as the statutes of those tribunals only allowed them to prosecute war crimes and crimes against humanity, not crimes against peace.[32] Prosecutions could therefore not possibly prevent or put an end to the conflicts themselves, but only the violations of IHL committed during them. More recently, the Council has also classified serious violations of Human Rights[33] and, according to some interpreters even the (non-democratic) nature of some regimes[34] as being threats to international peace, without clarifying whether the violations or regime alone, or only their possible repercussions beyond the borders of the affected State constituted the threat. In the cases of South Africa and Rhodesia, the denial of a people's right to self-determination was considered as threatening international peace, although in those cases the threat was

28 ICTY, *Prosecutor v. Tadic, Decision on the Defence Motion for Interlocutory Appeal on Jurisdiction*, Appeals Chamber, 2 October 1995, para. 39.

29 Arts. 25 and 103 of the UN Charter. See International Court of Justice, *Order of 14 April 1992*, in the Case *Questions of Interpretation and Application of the 1971 Montreal Convention arising from the Aerial Incident at Lockerbie (Libyan Arab Jamahiriya v. US)*, ICJ Reports, 1992, p. 126.

30 SC Res. 161 (1961).

31 See for references Pierre d'Argent, Jean d'Aspremont Lynden, Frédéric Dopagne and Raphaël van Seenberghe, "Article 39", in: Cot/Pellet/Forteau (eds.), *supra* note 20, pp. 1155–1157, with references.

32 See SC Res. 827 (1993) and 955 (1994) and their annexes.

33 The Security Council first hinted at this in SC Res. 917 (1994) with regard to the situation in Haiti. The following resolutions expressly mention human rights considerations as among the reasons for taking action under Chapter VII of the UN Charter: SC Res. 1264 (1999), SC Res. 1272 (1999), SC Res. 1289 (2000), SC Res. 1341 (2001), SC Res. 1497 (2003), SC Res. 1509 (2003), SC Res. 1556 (2004), SC Res. 1577 (2004). See generally Zambelli, *supra* note 13, pp. 270–279 and also the suggestions in *UN Study on Concepts of Security*, *supra* note 12, pp. 37 and 38.

34 Zambelli, *supra* note 13, pp. 279–280.

never clearly separated from the parallel risk of trans-border repercussions.[35] Despite the fact that general international law does not contain disarmament obligations and does not prohibit the possession of nuclear weapons, the Security Council has considered, in the case of several countries,[36] and on one occasion even generally,[37] that the proliferation of weapons of mass destruction constitutes a threat to international peace and security. International terrorism was initially only considered as threatening international peace and security when the acts or omissions could be attributed to a certain State.[38] It is only since the attacks of 11 September 2001 that terrorism has been seen as a threat to international peace and security independently of any State involvement.[39]

As early as in 1992, the Security Council meeting at the level of Heads of State and Government considered that: "The absence of war and military conflicts among States does not in itself ensure international peace and security. The non-military sources of instability in the economic, social, humanitarian and ecological fields have become threats to international peace and security."[40] In 2004, the *High-level Panel on Threats, Challenges and Change* put the situation as follows:[41]

> Any event or process that leads to large-scale death or lessening of life chances and undermines States as the basic unit of the international system is a threat to international security. So defined, there are six clusters of threats with which the world must be concerned now and in the decades ahead:
>
> - Economic and social threats, including poverty, infectious diseases and environmental degradation
> - Inter-State conflict
> - Internal conflict, including civil war, genocide and other large-scale atrocities
> - Nuclear, radiological, chemical and biological weapons
> - Terrorism
> - Transnational organized crime

35 See the very nuanced analysis by Zambelli, *supra* note 13, pp. 203–209. For a more blunt account, see: *UN Study on Concepts of Security, supra* note 12, p. 29.

36 See the practice summarized in Pierre d'Argent *et al., supra* note 31, pp. 1159–1162, and most recently SC Res. 1718 (2006) in relation to the Democratic People's Republic of Korea and SC Res. 1696 (2006), SC Res. 1737 (2006) and SC Res. 1747 (2007) in relation to Iran.

37 The SC President's statement of 31 Jan 1992 (S/23500) refers to the proliferation of weapons of mass destruction as being a threat to international peace and security generally rather in relation to a particular country.

38 See the practice summarized in Pierre d'Argent *et al., supra* note 31, pp. 1162–1163.

39 SC Res. 1368 (2001); 1373 (2001); 1455 (2003); 1526 (2004); 1566 (2004); 1611 (2995); 1617 (2005); 1618 (2005); 1624 (2005); 1735 (2006); 1787 (2007).

40 UN Doc. S/23500 of 31 January 1992, *Statement of the President of the SC made on behalf of the members of the Council.*

41 *A more secure world: our shared responsibility, Report of the High-level Panel on Threats, Challenges and Change*, UN doc. A/59/565, 2 December 2004, p. 12.

Such a wide understanding of international security corresponds – or, as some would argue, constitutes a return[42] – to a positive and structural concept of peace. Following groundbreaking research by Johan Galtung, distinguishing between personal and structural violence, peace conceived as the absence of violence can be seen as a narrow concept of negative peace meaning the absence of personal violence. It can and should however also have a wider meaning as the absence of structural violence, for which social justice is a positively defined condition.[43] The wide understanding suggested by the *High-Level Panel* also corresponds to the idea of "human security," brought to the forefront in recent years, which nevertheless remains highly controversial among UN member States.[44]

In the context of the UN Charter, a wide understanding of the notion also has significant structural and institutional implications, which demonstrate the inherent dangers. "[A] threat to international peace and security may be almost anything, as far as the [Security Council] reaches the required majority to pass a resolution."[45] The only body within the United Nations which is able to make decisions which are binding on States is the Security Council, and it may only do so under Chapter VII of the Charter, after classifying a threat as a threat to international peace and security. This is, in present-day general international law, the only vertical element in a fundamentally horizontal, self-applied international legal system. The Security Council acting under Chapter VII is the embryo of a law enforcement system of the international community. Admittedly it is still weak, dominated more by real power structures than by the rule of law, marked by inherent double standards and a crying absence of due process, but in existing international law there is no alternative when decisions binding all States have to be taken.[46] Because of its unique ability to take binding decisions and despite widespread criticism by scholars and some States, the Council has recently also taken legislative action.[47] It has adopted a small international crim-

---

42 Pierre d'Argent *et al.*, *supra* note 31, p. 1155; Pierre-Marie Dupuy, "Sécurité collective et organisation de la paix", Revue générale de droit international public 97 (1993), p. 623; Marco Odello, "Commentary on the United Nations' High-Level Panel on Threats, Challenges and Change", *Journal of Conflict and Security Law* 10 (2005) 231, at 235.

43 See in particular Johan Galtung, "Peace Research: Past Experiences and Future Perspectives", in: *Essays in Peace Research*, vol. I, Copenhagen, 1975, 244 at 251–253; Johan Galtung, "Violence, Peace and Peace Research", Journal of Peace Research (1969) 167, at 168 and 183. For international law, this was concretized by Bert V. Röling, *Einführung in die Wissenschaft von Krieg und Frieden*, Neukirchener Verl., Neukirchen, 1970, pp. 87–91.

44 See S. Neil MacFarlane and Yuen Foong-Khong, *Human Security and the UN: A Critical History*, (Bloomington: Indiana University Press, 2006), p. 10.

45 Odello, *supra* note 42, at 237.

46 On the advantages of Security Council action against "new" threats to international security, including a discussion of their legitimacy, see Allen S. Weiner, "The Use of Force and Contemporary Security Threats: Old Medicine for New Ills?", *Stanford Law Review* 59 (2006) 415 at 482–495.

47 See, for a discussion, Paul C. Szasz, "The Security Council Starts Legislating", American Journal of International Law 96 (2002), pp. 901–905; José E. Alvarez, "Hegemonic International Law Revisited", American Journal of International Law 97 (2003), pp. 874–878; Stefan Talmon, "The Security Council as World Legislature", American Journal of International Law 99 (2005), pp. 175–193; Axel Marschik, "The Security Council as World

inal code on the fight against international terrorism, laying down new obligations of all States in the field of repression of international terrorism and judicial cooperation in this field.[48] It thus avoided the long treaty-making process needing the formal consent of all those to be bound or the long, mysterious and cumbersome customary process that is subject to manipulation and leads to vague results always subject to controversy. Those who criticize such action remained remarkably silent when the Council took another inherently legislative[49] action, creating the International Criminal Tribunals for the Former Yugoslavia and Rwanda.[50]

In addition, a wide understanding of international peace and security has institutional consequences. By classifying an economic, social, humanitarian or ecological problem as a threat to international peace and security, the Council moves it from the field of action of the more "democratic" UN General Assembly, to which it belongs under the UN Charter, to that of the Council.[51] However, only the use of force in the form of armed conflicts, genocide and widespread and serious human rights violations physically threatening persons need urgent action, which is the strength of the Security Council, while realization of comprehensive peace and human security need long-term action, based upon wide consultation and consensus.[52] In addition, such a shift of decisions on human security subjects them to the veto power of a permanent member of the Security Council,[53] bars in practice any legality control,[54] and moves the matter concerned out of the field of "matters falling essentially within the domestic jurisdiction of a state."[55] The High-Level Panel significantly does not clarify whether the Security Council would "be allowed to use its powers, including the use of force, to deal with all new threats."[56]

Legislator? Theory, Practice and Consequences of an Expansion of Power", *IILJ Working Paper 2005/18*, Institute for International Law and Justice, New York University School of Law, online: http://www.iilj.org/research/documents/2005.18Marschik.pdf, and the discussion by Jürg Lindenmann in Yves Sandoz (ed.), *Actes du Colloque international, Quel droit International pour le 21e siècle? Neuchâtel, 6–7 mai 2005*, Bruylant, Bruxelles, 2007, pp. 52–55.

48 SC Res. 1373 (2001).

49 Under International Human Rights Law, a tribunal must be "established by law" (see, *e.g.*, Art. 14 (1) of the International Covenant on Civil and Political Rights, 999 *UNTS* 171).

50 SC Res. 827 (1993) and 955 (1994).

51 Under Art. 24 of the UN Charter the Council has "primary responsibility for the maintainance of international peace and security", while under Art. 10, the General Assembly discusses any question or matter within the scope of the Charter.

52 Dupuy, *supra* note 42, pp. 623–624.

53 Art. 27 (3) of the UN Charter.

54 See *supra* note 29, and the nuanced and comprehensive discussion by Zambelli, *supra* note 13, at 333–413.

55 Art. 2 (7) of the Charter reads: "Nothing contained in the present Charter shall authorize the United Nations to intervene in matters which are essentially within the domestic jurisdiction of any State or shall require the Members to submit such matters to settlement under the present Charter; but this principle shall not prejudice the application of enforcement measures under Chapter VII."

56 Odello, *supra* note 42, at 245.

The most serious problem resulting from a wide understanding of security under the UN Charter is that a threat to international peace and security does not only authorize the Security Council to take binding decisions, but also to authorize the use of force, *i.e.* to confer the *ius ad bellum* and to initiate armed conflicts. Parallel to its extension of the concept of threats to international peace and security described above, the Security Council has indeed also extended the kind of threats for which it authorized, when no permanent member objected, the use of force.[57] This is probably a major reason for the reluctance of countries of the South, always afraid of outside interventions under new guises, towards the entire concept of "human security".[58] Many countries of the South, including the largest democracy of the world, India, perceive Security Council authorized humanitarian intervention not as protecting "human security", but as a major threat to their own security.[59]

In my view, the use of force cannot be authorized against economic and social threats, poverty, infectious diseases and environmental degradation. It is however difficult to find a legal reason for such a limitation. Some authors write that the use of force to counter environmental threats would be disproportionate, contrary to the peaceful spirit of environmental law and counterproductive.[60] These are not very objective standards. How can one be confident, at the time of authorizing it, that the use of force to counter human rights violations (as seen above a growing practice of the Security Council) will cause only suffering proportionate to the threat and not lead to even more serious human rights violations, taking the unpredictable and uncontrollable development of an armed conflict into account? Both International Humanitarian Law and International Human Rights Law, the violation of which has already led the Security Council to authorize the use of force, are they too not marked by a peaceful spirit? A limitation to violent threats could however be based upon the wording of Art. 42 which reads: "Should the Security Council consider that measures provided for in Article 41 [on non-military sanctions] would be inadequate or have proved to be inadequate, it may take such action by air, sea, or land forces as may be necessary to maintain or restore international peace and security. [...]" One could argue that the use of force is never necessary to maintain or restore this aspect of international peace and security, or the concept of security itself could be limited to violent threats. I would however not go so far to consider that the concept of "peace" (which is as seen above an equivalent to "security") is in the entire Chapter VII limited to the absence of organized use of force between States.[61] In conformity with

57 For some statistics, see Charlotte Ku, "When can Nations go to War? Politics and Change in the UN Security System", Michigan Journal of International Law 24 (2003) 1077 at 1082–1087.

58 See MacFarlane and Foong-Khong, *supra* note 44, p. 10.

59 See e.g. Ramesh Thakur and Dipankar Banerjee, "India: democratic, Poor, Internationalist", in: Charlotte Ku and Harold Jacobson (eds.), *Democratic Accountability and the Use of Force in International Law*, Cambridge University Press, Cambridge, 2003, p. 204.

60 Alexandra Knight, "Global Environmental Threats: Can the Security Council Protect our Earth?", *New York University Law Review* 80 (2005) 1549 at 1563.

61 Jochen Abr. Frowein, "Article 39", in: Bruno Simma (ed.) *The Charter of the United Nations, A Commentary*, Oxford University Press, New York, 1995, p. 608.

the Security Council practice described above, not only violent threats against States should qualify, but also violent threats against persons.

III. The Concept of Security in International Humanitarian Law

The treaties of International Humanitarian Law (IHL) use the term "security" 40 times. The term is however not defined in the treaties, nor is it defined in the Commentaries published by the ICRC to the Geneva Conventions and the Additional Protocols.[62] As explained below, these Commentaries nevertheless provide some examples which may help to understand the outer limits of the concept. The term "security" serves two completely different purposes in IHL.

Most often, the term relates to the security of the State and is used in provisions allowing a State to restrict certain rights of people affected by armed conflicts or of international control mechanisms, or to take certain measures. The ICRC Commentaries mention that the term gives the State concerned a wide discretion,[63] but should be invoked only in exceptional cases[64] and only in good faith.[65] The broadest case is Article 5 of Convention IV, which allows general derogations from rights protected by that Convention. Those are however circumscribed in that civilians suspected of activities hostile to the State may be deprived of substantive rights (on a belligerent's own territory) or communication rights (in occupied territories), but

62 Jean S. Pictet (ed.), *The Geneva Conventions of 12 August 1949: Commentary, IV, Geneva Convention relative to the Protection of Civilians in Time of War*, ICRC, Geneva, 1958 [hereafter: *ICRC Commentary, Convention IV*], p. 56, explains: "The idea of activities prejudicial or hostile to the security of the State, is very hard to define." *Ibid.*, p. 257 he states: "It did not seem possible to define the expression 'security of the State' [in Art. 42 of Convention IV, *supra* note 5] in a more concrete fashion." Astonishingly, in one instance the ICRC Commentaries consider that "[t]he expression 'for reasons of security' should [...] be considered to be self-explanatory" (Yves Sandoz, Christophe Swinarski & Bruno Zimmermann (eds.), *Commentary on the Additional Protocols of 8 June 1977 to the Geneva Conventions of 12 August 1949*, ICRC, Martinus Nijhoff Publishers, Geneva/Dordrecht, 1987, p. 754).

63 Jean S. Pictet (ed.), *The Geneva Conventions of 12 August 1949: Commentary, III, Geneva Convention Relative to the Treatment of Prisoners of War*, ICRC, Geneva, 1960 [hereafter: *ICRC Commentary, Convention III*], p. 478 (on "interests of national security" used in Art. 103 of Convention III, *supra* note 5); *ICRC Commentary, Convention IV, supra* note 62, p. 207 (on "measures of security in regard to protected persons as may be necessary as a result of the war" used in Art. 27 (4) of Convention IV, *supra* note 5); *Ibid.*, p. 257 (on when the "security of the Detaining power makes [an internment of an enemy national] absolutely necessary" under Art. 42 (1) of Convention IV, *supra* note 5).

64 *ICRC Commentary, Convention III, supra* note 63, p. 492 (on "interest of State security" used in Art. 105 (5) of Convention III, *supra* note 5); *ICRC Commentary, Convention IV, supra* note 62, p. 218 (on "security considerations" used in Art. 30 (2) of Convention IV, *supra* note 5); *Ibid.*, p. 367 (on when "imperative reasons of security" allow an occupying power to intern protected persons under Art. 78 (1) of Convention IV, *supra* note 5).

65 *ICRC Commentary, Convention III, supra* note 63, p. 596 (on "measures which the Detaining Powers may consider essential to ensure their security" used in Art. 125 (1) of Convention III, *supra* note 5).

only if the exercise of such rights by the individual would be prejudicial to the security of the State.[66]

In five instances the term "security" refers to the security of persons, which belligerents must protect. For this purpose, the treaties more frequently use the term "safety". The latter term must however be an equivalent to security, as treaties drawn up in several authentic languages – such as the Geneva Conventions and the Additional Protocols – must be presumed to have the same meaning in each of those texts.[67] The equally authentic French and – concerning the Additional Protocols – Spanish versions use indifferently the terms "sécurité" or "seguridad" for "security" and for "safety" in the English version. Those two terms can therefore not have a different meaning. There are however exceptions to these uniform translations, which lack objective explanation. On the one hand, terms other than "sécurité" or "seguridad" are sometimes used for safety[68] and "safety" is twice used for the security of belligerents, once translated by "sécurité"[69] and once by "sureté".[70]

As for customary international law, it does not, by definition, use terms but prescribes conduct. State practice and *opinio juris* show however that certain conduct normally prohibited is exceptionally admissible for reasons related to certain interests of the State. States also have certain obligations to protect victims of war from certain threats and if such a threat does materialize, a State may be allowed not to comply with certain general prohibitions. In the recent ICRC study attempting to define the rules of customary IHL and to put them into writing after ten years of analyzing State practice (mainly in the form of official declarations and statements), the term "security" is only used in one rule. It appears in the provision on the prohibition of forcible transfers of civilians: "unless the security of the civilians involved [...] so demand."[71] In the same context, if displacements are admissible, measures to protect *inter alia* the "safety" of the civilians concerned must be taken[72] and such persons have a right to return in "safety."[73] Beyond that, one may confidently assume that where universally ratified treaties such as the Geneva Conventions or widely ratified treaties such as the Additional Protocols foresee security as a limit to certain

66 In any case, Art. 5 (3) of Convention IV, *supra* note 5, prescribes an underogable right to humane treatment and a fair and regular trial.

67 Art. 33 (3) of the Vienna Convention on the Law of Treaties.

68 Art. 19 (2) of Convention I, *supra* note 5, and Art. 12 (4) of Protocol I, *supra* note 3, formulate the obligation to situate medical establishments so that attacks on military objectives cannot imperil their "safety" with the terms "mettre ces établissements ... en danger" and "las pongan en peligro".

69 Art. 15 (4) of Protocol I, *supra* note 3, concerning limitations of movement for medical personnel.

70 Art. 78 of Convention IV, *supra* note 5, (concerning safety measures taken by an occupying power).

71 Henckaerts and Doswald-Beck, *supra* note 4, Rule 129 (A) and (B), which correspond to Art. 49 of Convention IV, *supra* note 5, and Art. 17 of Protocol II, *supra* note 6.

72 *Ibid*, Rule 131.

73 *Ibid.*, Rule 132.

obligations or a responsibility towards certain persons, this must also be valid for the corresponding customary obligations.

With regard to the security or safety of persons,[74] establishments or installations,[75] or aircraft,[76] which must be respected and/or protected by belligerents, or which absolves them from certain obligations or prohibitions,[77] such terms are never qualified by additions. Even in peace-time, such individual security can never be absolutely guaranteed.[78] This is even more difficult in wartime and it can therefore only imply an obligation of means, not an obligation of result.

Conversely, when the security of the State is referred to as a reason permitting a State to derogate from normal IHL obligations,[79] qualifying terms are often added to restrict such exceptions. Sometimes a measure must be necessary for (and not only justified by) security reasons[80] or "a grave emergency involving an *organized* threat to the security of the Occupying power" must exist.[81] A belligerent may intern on its own territory "protected" (i.e. mainly enemy) civilians only when its security "makes it absolutely necessary"[82] and an occupying power may do so only for "imperative reasons of security."[83] The first term seems to be more restrictive, but according to the logic of IHL, a State has more leeway on its own territory than on territory it occupies and therefore the two wordings are probably equivalent. The obligation on Protecting Powers to take into account "imperative necessities of security"[84] or the possibility to refuse individual relief consignments for "imperative reasons of security"[85] falls, in my view, into the same category, as in all those cases it is not sufficient for security reasons to merely exist, the elements of necessity or imperativeness indicate that they can only be taken into account if there is no alternative solution. When provisions allow States to subject the activities of relief societies to measures they "consider essential to ensure their security", the State has more room to maneuver, as the judgment is clearly for them to make. This is equally and perhaps even more so the case where the provision adds: "or to meet any other reasonable need."[86]

---

74 Art. 26 of Convention II, *supra* note 5; Arts. 20 (2), 46 (3), 47 (1) and (2) and 51 (2) of Convention III, *supra* note 5; Arts. 14, 36 (1), 49 (2) and (3), 51 (2) and 127 (2), (3) and (4) of Convention IV, *supra* note 5; Arts. 12 (4), 41 (3) and 78 (1) of Protocol I, *supra* note 3; Arts. 4 (3)(e), 5 (2)(c) and (4), and 17 (1) of Protocol II, *supra* note 6.

75 Art. 19 (2) of Convention I, *supra* note 5, and Art. 51 (2) of Convention IV, *supra* note 5.

76 Arts. 25, 27 (2) and 31 (2) of Protocol I, *supra* note 3.

77 Art. 49 (5) of Convention IV, *supra* note 5, and Art. 17 (1) of Protocol II, *supra* note 6.

78 Verosta, *supra* note 8, 537.

79 Art. 8 of Conventions I and II, *supra* note 5; Arts. 8, 18, 37, 103, 105 and 125 of Convention III, *supra* note 5, Arts. 5, 9, 26, 27, 30, 39, 42, 62, 63, 64, 75, 78, 93, 142 of Convention IV, *supra* note 5; Arts. 15 (4), 45, 63, 64, 71 and 74 of Protocol I, *supra* note 3.

80 Art. 27 of Convention IV, *supra* note 5.

81 *Ibid.*, Art. 75 (my highlighting).

82 *Ibid.*, Art. 42.

83 *Ibid.*, Art. 78.

84 Art. 8/8/8 and 9, respectively, of Conventions I–IV, *supra* note 5.

85 Art. 62 of Convention IV, *supra* note 5.

86 Art. 125 of Convention III and Art. 142 of Convention IV, *supra* note 5.

Sometimes only some aspects of security may be taken into account. Pre-trial confinement of prisoners of war in cases where a soldier of the detaining power would not be confined is only admissible "if it is essential to do so in the interests of national security."[87] "National security" restricts the exception in the sense that the mere security of the camp or the guards is not sufficient. Where IHL refers to "military security", only the security of the armed forces may be taken into account, which is logical in occupied territories,[88] where an occupying power may only be present with armed forces and take measures only for their security.

In other instances, exceptions can be justified by reasons larger than security, such as "national interest."[89]

Exceptions for military reasons, "imperative military reasons",[90] military necessity, action which is "absolutely necessary for military operations,"[91]imperative military necessity or even "unavoidable military necessity"[92] are in my view related to a consideration different from security. On the one hand, military operations are not always related, justified by or necessary for the security of the State or of individuals, on the other hand such exceptions only cover threats consisting of hostilities against persons or objects belonging to the armed forces.

All of the above still does not clarify the limits and meaning of "security". In my view, the object and purpose of the treaties in which the term appears and the context of the provisions indicate that the meaning must be limited to the defense against physical threats to persons or property. Such threats may however also result indirectly from the individual conduct against which security is invoked. The ICRC Commentaries to the Conventions may be used to further the discussion on this necessary link to acts of physical violence. Article 5 of Convention IV allows for derogations in cases where individuals are engaged in activities hostile to the security of the State, including, according to the ICRC Commentary, espionage and intelligence.[93] However, in my opinion, this is only the case if the latter relates to military action or military objectives, not to peace-time activities e.g. industrial espionage. Similarly, cases in which the "security of the Detaining power makes [an internment of an enemy national] absolutely necessary" under Article 42 (1) of Convention IV include, according to the ICRC Commentary, "subversive activity carried out inside the territory of a Party to the conflict or actions which are of direct assistance to an enemy Power", including membership "of organizations whose object is to cause

87 Art. 103 of Convention III, *supra* note 5.

88 E.g. in para. 2 of the aforementioned Art. 5 of Convention IV, *supra* note 5, which allows for derogations from communication rights in occupied territories only when "absolute military security so requires."

89 *Ibid.*, Art. 35 allowing belligerents to prohibit the departure of enemy nationals, which includes economic reasons (*ICRC Commentary, Convention IV*, *supra* note 62, p. 236).

90 *Ibid.*, Art. 49 (5).

91 Justifying under *ibid.*, Art. 53, destruction of property.

92 Art. 11 (2) of the 1954 *Hague Convention for the Protection of Cultural Property in the Event of Armed Conflict* of 14 May 1954, 249 U.N.T.S. 240–357.

93 *ICRC Commentary, Convention IV*, *supra* note 62, p. 56.

disturbances, or [...] by other means such as sabotage or espionage."[94] However I believe that the final intended result in all such cases must be the facilitation of acts of violence. Finally, Article 18 (5) of Convention III, permits a detaining power to withdraw articles of value from POWs "only for reasons of security" and the ICRC Commentary explains that this concerns articles of value which might be used to bribe guards.[95] Such bribing involves neither violence against those bribed or other guards nor against the Detaining Power. At worst, it would allow POWs to escape and then rejoin the fighting, which constitutes a threat of violence. Such an indirect and rather remote threat is however difficult to accept as a threat of violence. Otherwise, even providing shoes, chocolate reserves or language training could be prohibited for security reasons and an individual engaged in political propaganda could be covered by derogations.[96]

A limitation to physical threats would also explain why safety and security are equivalents in IHL, as evidenced by authentic texts of the treaties in languages other than English. If economic, political, social and environmental threats were included in the security reasons which allow a State to derogate from its obligations concerning war victims, which were adopted precisely for situations of armed conflict, such derogations would become the rule rather than the exception. Provisions such as Article 35 of Convention IV allowing belligerents to prohibit the departure of enemy nationals for reasons of "national interest", which includes economic and manpower problems, would be unnecessary.[97]

As for the security or safety of persons which must be guaranteed by belligerents, if it encompassed all aspects of human security, the detailed provisions on means of existence, employment, hygiene and public health, relief, food, clothing, respect of property, public welfare and procedures and reasons admissible for depriving a person from his or her freedom would not have been necessary.

IV. Conclusion

Leaving aside larger discussions about "human security" and the need for a wider concept of "security", the term must be limited to violent physical threats for both *ius ad bellum* and for *ius in bello*. In law, definitions do not exist to confirm philosophical truths or to prove that all problems are interlinked, they are used for a normative purpose, *i.e.* to determine when certain rules apply, which has specific legal effects. The terminology used in law is therefore often different from that used in social sciences, the media, or political discussions. In both *ius ad bellum* and *ius in bello*, the term "security" makes rules applicable which are only adequate to meet threats involving physical violence against persons or property, while in both branches other terms are used in rules dealing with other threats to human security in the widest sense, which set out more appropriate consequences and procedures. In *ius ad*

94 *Ibid.*, p. 258.

95 *ICRC Commentary, Convention III, supra* note 63, p. 170.

96 Which is excluded by *ICRC Commentary, Convention IV, supra* note 62, p. 56.

97 *Ibid.*, p. 236.

bellum this limited understanding is also necessary because of important institutional implications a wider understanding would have. The UN Security Council is not qualified to become the World government and World legislator (unchecked by any judiciary), which deals with all the problems of the World.

Chapter 2

International Security and International Organisations: Considerations under International Law

Marco Odello

I. Introduction

Issues of international security have received wide attention by international relations and political science scholars, in particular since the end of the Cold War.[1] International lawyers have devoted most of their analysis to the concept of collective security,[2] mainly within the terms of the United Nations (UN) Charter[3] and in the context of the right of states to use force (jus ad bellum and jus contra bellum).[4] Specifically, that means the provisions concerning the use of force in case of threat and actual armed attack arising from one or more states against one or more other states. Quite limited scrutiny has addressed legal issues related to a broad concept of international security.[5] In the last ten years, international concerns *vis-à-vis* newly identified

1 Barry Buzan, Ole Waever, and Jaap de Wilde, *Security: A New Framework for Analysis* (Boulder, Colo: Lynne Rienner Pub., 1998); Michael T. Klare and Yogesh Chandrani, eds., *World Security: Challenges for a New Century*, 3rd ed. (New York: St. Martin Press, 1998); Ronnie D. Lipschutz, ed., *On Security*, (New York, Columbia University Press, 1995); David Dewitt, David Haglund, and John Kirton, *Building a New Global Order*, (Toronto, Oxford, New York: Oxford University Press, 1993); Barry Buzan, "New patterns of global security in the twenty-first century", *International Affairs* 67, no. 3 (1991): 431–451.

2 Hans Kelsen, "Collective Security and Collective Self-Defense Under the Charter of the United Nations", *Am. J. Int'l L.*, 42, no. 4 (1948): 783; Danesh Sarooshi, *The United Nations and the Development of Collective Security: The Delegation by the UN Security Council of Its Chapter VII Powers* (Oxford: Oxford University Press, 1999); Nigel D. White, "On the Brink of Lawlessness: The State of Collective Security Law", *Ind. Int'l & Comp. L. Rev.* 13, no. 1 (2002): 237–251; Erika de Wet, *The Chapter VII Powers of the United Nations Security Council* (Oxford: Hart Publishing, 2004).

3 "Charter of the United Nations," 26 June 1945, 59 Stat. 1031, T.S. 993.

4 Christine Gray, *International Law and the Use of Force*, 2nd ed. (Oxford: Oxford University Press, 2004).

5 Among the recent works see Martin Trybus and Nigel D. White, eds., *European Security Law* (Oxford: Oxford University Press, 2007).

Cecilia M. Bailliet (ed.), Security: A Multidisciplinary Normative Approach.
 ISBN 978 90 04 17296 8. pp. 23–45.

international threats to international security show new developments both within the UN and some international regional organisations (IROs), and may need new analysis from the legal point of view.

In the contemporary structure of international relations, international security seems not to be limited to the control and possible reactions to the threat of the use of force, as originally foreseen by the UN at the end of World War II. Collective security linked the concept of security to the survival of states, and to the threat and use of force among states.[6] During the last decade, some other issues have been considered as possible threats to international security. They include the fight against terrorism and organised crime, the control over weapons of mass destruction, environmental threats, widespread violations of human rights, environmental issues, etc.[7]

This means that the traditional concept of collective security, as a means available to states for dealing with threats to international peace and security has been stretched. This raises the question whether the established forms of collective security, accepted under the UN Charter, cannot be considered suitable to deal with the various international threats to security. Therefore, it seems that newly identified threats to international security pose some relevant questions to the meaning and boundaries of collective security. This evolution necessarily includes the analysis of the possible impact of legal rules that can be applied by and to states in dealing with identified threats. This approach focuses mainly on the security of states, as the major actors of the international system. Nevertheless, the security of states should be matched nowadays with important limitations based on the rules of international law, including the law of armed conflict, regulating the use of force and its conditions, and in particular international human rights law that have acquired a growing influence in the structure of the contemporary international legal system.

In the specific attempt to identify the concept and limits of international security under international law, the concept of human security,[8] linked to developments in international human rights law, represents a possible relevant evolution in international law and politics. The 1994 *Human Development Report* tried to deal with the concept in the following terms:

"*(I)t focuses directly on human beings* – respecting national sovereignty but only as long as nation-states respect the human rights of their own people".[9]

This means that state sovereignty is linked to the protection of fundamental rights, shifting the pure interest of states towards the protection of people and individuals, with some possible relevant implications for the structure of international law.

---

6 See Tarcisio Gazzini, *The Chaging Rules on the Use of Force in International Law* (Manchester: Manchester University Press, 2006); Gray, *International Law and the Use of Force*, note 4 above.

7 See Elke Krahmann, ed., *New Threats and New Actors in International Security* (New York: Palgrave, 2005).

8 UNDP, *The Human Development Report* (New York: Oxford University Press, 1994). See also Benjamin J. Goold and Liora Lazarus, eds., *Security and Human Rights* (Oxford: Hart, 2007).

9 UNDP, *The Human Development Report*, ibid., 14.

Dealing with security issues should be regarded as a complex activity that takes into full consideration the security of states and the security of persons. States allegedly try to ensure their security with the aim of protecting their own population, but sometimes this aim seems to be abused and fundamental rights of people not taken in due consideration. The two concepts of state's security and human security should be seen as two faces of the same medal, interlinked by the relevant rules of international human rights law and by international humanitarian law, when applicable.[10]

Starting briefly from the concept of security under the UN system, and taking into account relevant documents and practice within the universal organisation, the present chapter shall try to focus its analysis on documents elaborated by regional organisations. It will identify the possible content and definition of threats to international peace and security, taking into consideration the main IROs and international documents which make reference to international security. This first analysis should try to provide a clarification of the concept of threats faced by the international community.

Once the different issues and possible answers suggested by the relevant organisations have been considered, the chapter shall explore some problems that the formulation of an expanded concept of international security may pose to the existing regulation of collective security law and human rights obligations, within the context of general international law. In particular, the possible implications and problems concerning the aims and structure of international legal rules will be addressed. Since the adoption of the Universal Declaration on Human Rights in 1948,[11] the effects of this relevant and pervasive area of international law are still in the process of being realised.

The UN and other IROs, as international subjects, act within the general framework of international law. They contribute to the definition and implementation of international rules. At the same time, the relationship between regional and universal legal rules and the consistency of measures adopted will be addressed. The intention is to support the construction of a more effective international law and the strengthening of international security with a human face. This topic will identify the issues that trigger collective security measures and the feasible measures to deal with threats to international threats to peace and security. In this context, recent developments concerning the evaluation of UN measures and their implementation will be considered.

It should be kept in mind that the analysis of this chapter will focus on general issues of international security in the framework of international law. It shall not deal with specific issues of either national or international security, even if national security issues are strictly related to international security activities. Nor shall it deal with more specific operational issues and practical implications of security, as in the case of security operations and security forces that are discussed in other chapters of this book.

---

10 See Marco Sassóli, chapter 1 in this volume.

11 UN, "Universal Declaration of Human Rights", G.A. res. 217A (III), U.N. Doc A/810 at 71 (1948).

II. International Security and the United Nations

Issues related to international security have to be addressed in the framework of international legal rules. The first question is what is meant by international security and threats to international security.[12] In this section a brief analysis of the basis of international legal rules related to international security will be pursued by examining the identification of threats to international security. Traditional international law dealt mainly with the security of states, as the only subjects of international law.[13] The classic international law based on the sovereignty of states and the territorial integrity, including the principle of inviolability of borders, made the survival of states the exclusive aim of international security. This issue was examined by the International Court of Justice in relation to the possible use of nuclear weapons in an advisory opinion in 1996. The Court affirmed that in general the use of nuclear weapons can be seen as unlawful, but that "in view of the current state of international law, and of the elements of fact at its disposal, the Court cannot conclude definitively whether the threat or use of nuclear weapons would be lawful or unlawful in an extreme circumstance of self-defence, in which the very survival of a state would be at stake."[14]

Threats to international security seem limited to the survival of the state as an independent political and territorial entity. For the (strict) majority of judges in the International Court of Justice, even the use of nuclear weapons and their terrible and widespread effects on both the people and the environment seem to be justified when the survival of the state is at risk. An issue that clashes with international rules and principles concerning the protection of human life and the environment, and even more established rules of international humanitarian law which prohibit the use of means and methods of warfare with indiscriminate effect.[15] The idea of a prevailing state's interest could be justified if states' security would prevail over the survival of individuals, and if security threats were only related to the use of force by states, mainly under the form of military aggression.[16] The same human rights instruments recognise the possibility of derogations from certain international obligations when the 'survival of the state is at stake'.[17] These are the so-called situations which lead

12 On the concept of security in international law see Marco Sassóli, chapter 1 in this volume.

13 See Antonio Cassese, *International Law*, 2nd ed. (Oxford: Oxford university Press, 2005) chapter 2.

14 ICJ, *Legality of the threat or use of nuclear weapons*, Advisory Opinion of 8 July 1996, *I.C.J. Reports 1996*, 226, para. 105(E), 266; see also Eric David, "The Opinion of the International Court of Justice on the legality of the use of nuclear weapons", *Int'l Rev. Red Cross* 316 (1997): 21–34; Laurence Boisson de Chazournes and Philippe Sands, eds., *International Law, the International Court of Justice and Nuclear Weapons* (Cambridge: Cambridge University Press, 1999).

15 See the Dissenting Opinions attached by judges Schwebel, Oda, Shahabuddeen, Weeramantry, Koroma and Higgins to the Avisory Opinion, ibid.: 311–593. See also the special theme Methods of Warfare, *Int'l Rev. Red Cross*, no. 864 (2006); Ingrid Detter, *The Law of War*, 2nd ed. (Cambridge: Cambridge University Press, 2000), chapters 7 and 8.

16 UN GA Res. 3314 (XXIX), UN GAOR 29th Sess., Supp. No. 31 (1974).

17 See Article 4 of the "International Covenant on Civil and Political Rights," G.A. res. 2200A (XXI), 21 U.N. GAOR Supp. (No. 16) at 52, U.N. Doc. A/6316 (1966), 999 U.N.T.S. 171.

to the declaration of states of emergency, but even in those exceptional and extreme cases, the state concerned is still bound by some procedural and legal obligations and some core human rights obligations would apply.

The link between security and peace, that ensures the survival of the state, is expressed in article 39 of the UN Charter, where it refers to measures of collective security against threats to the peace, breach of the peace and acts of aggression. Collective security measures, adopted under the procedures of the UN Charter, also leave the right for individual states to use their inherent right to self-defence under article 51 of the UN Charter, clearly a right related to the case of armed attack by another state.[18]

The UN has used the powers provided by the Charter to identify threats to international peace and security, and situations which led to a breach of the peace. They included interstate conflict, risks related to internal conflict situations,[19] humanitarian crisis,[20] protecting safe areas for the civilian population caught in an internal conflict,[21] but also restoring the overthrown democratic regime of Haiti, and the Libyan lack of cooperation in handling two suspects of terrorism.[22] The means used to address them have ranged from the use of multinational forces, under the peacekeeping operations framework and in some cases, the use of sanctions, and other means, particularly under anti-terrorism provisions that shall be discussed later in this chapter.

The inter-state concept of international law seems to have shifted to take into consideration other subjects of international law, in particular due to the developments of international human rights law and principles. This last element brings to our consideration the concept of human security that has tried to focus the attention on the needs of people at least as a parallel issue to state security. In this context it should be considered that international law is showing a trend to a more humanised legal system of norms,[23] an issue that will be addressed in the following parts of this chapter, jointly with the main work and actions by international organisations.

III. Regional Organisations and the Concept of Security

There are different ways how states establish types of institutional cooperation, which may take the form and structures of international organisations.[24] If the UN and its related agencies are considered as universal organisations, for the purposes of this paper, IROs are identified by a limited membership, generally including

18 Yoram Dinstein, *War Aggression and Self-defence*, 4th ed. (Cambridge: Cambridge University Press, 2005); Gray, *International Law and the Use of Force*, note 4 above, chapter 4.

19 In the case of the situation of East Timor, see UN, SC Res. 1264 (1999).

20 In the case of Operation Restore Hope in Somalia, UN, SC Res. 794 (1992); in the case of Rwanda, UN, SC Res. 929 (1994).

21 In the case of Bosnia and Herzegovina, UN, SC Res. 836 and 844 (1993).

22 UN, SC Res. 748 (1992) and 883 (1993).

23 Theodor Meron, *The Humanization of International Law* (Leiden: Martinus Nijhoff, 2006).

24 Dapo Akande, *International Organizations*, in Malcom Evans, *International Law*, 2nd ed. (Oxford: Oxford University Press, 2006); Nigel D. White, *The Law of International*

geographically contiguous states.[25] A wide variety of organisations fall within these parameters. Most of existing IROs developed after the end of the II World War. They were foreseen as elements of the developing new international order within the general framework of the UN Charter, in particular under Chapter VIII. Therefore, many regional organisations, or specialised organisations, were established as part of the security concerns of limited groups of states.

Despite the different theoretical backgrounds related to the nature of international organisations (IOs),[26] it is part of the justification of IOs to be functional entities, which means they have to pursue certain objectives on the basis of their specific aims and purposes, through the procedures defined in their constitutive documents. Some organisations had clearly defensive or military purposes, which could be defined as security purposes in a strict sense, such as the Warsaw Pact[27] and the North Atlantic Treaty Organisation (NATO).[28] Other organisations, such as the European Communities, established in the 1950s, had other functional aims, such as the control of coal and steel (ECSC) market, the production of atomic energy (Euratom), and the Economic Community (EEC) with more general purposes for the establishment of an European common market.[29] All the mentioned organisations, despite their original limited objectives, were part of the establishment of closer and more friendly relations among the founding (and potential) member states. The idea of United States of Europe was formulated by Winston Churchill,[30] and retaken by other politicians such as Robert Schumann and Altiero Spinelli, as part of security concerns, to limit the possibility of conflicts among European states that had caused two world wars.

Due to the limits and purposes of this paper, reference shall be made to the major regional organisations. They include the European Union (EU), the Organisation of American States (OAS), the NATO, the Organisation for Security and Co-operation in Europe (OSCE), the Council of Europe (CoE), and the African Union (AU). These organisations are particularly relevant due to the fact that they have developed both policy and legal documents related to security, and have adopted specific measures dealing with security concerns.

Organizations, 2nd ed. (Manchester: Manchester University Press, 2005); Henry G. Schermers and Niels M. Blokker, *International Institutional Law: Unity within Diversity*, 4th ed. (Leiden: Martinus Nijhoff, 2004).

25 Clive Archer, *International Organizations*, 3rd ed. (London: Routledge, 2001), 45–49.

26 White, note 24 above, chapter 1.

27 "The Warsaw Security Pact", 14 May 1955, *American Foreign Policy 1950–1955*, Basic Documents, Vol. 1 (1957). The Pact was officially terminated in Prague in 1991.

28 "The North Atlantic Treaty," Washington D.C., 4 April 1949, *American Foreign Policy 1950–1955*, Basic Documents, Vol. 1 (1957).

29 See Paul Craig and Grainne de Burca, *European Law*, 4th ed. (Oxford: Oxford University Press, 2008), chapter 1.

30 On 19 September 1946, Winston Churchill, former British Prime Minister, gave a speech at the University of Zurich in which he invited the European countries to form a United States of Europe, at http://www.ena.lu/; Wendell R. Mauter, "Churchill and the Unification of Europe", *The Historian* 61, no. 1 (1998): 67–84.

Regional organisations have developed and expanded their powers and fields of activity over the past sixty years. A clear example is provided by the European Communities that merged and developed into the EU.[31] The three pillars structure of the EU now include many issues that were not foreseen in the original treaty of Rome, such as the Common Foreign and Security Policy (CFSP), Justice and Home Affairs (JHA) including the judicial cooperation in civil and criminal matters, common migration and asylum policy, fight against drug and human trafficking, organised crime and terrorism. These forms of cooperation have developed not only legal and policy documents but also specific bodies and activities such as Europol, the European Police College (CEPOL), and the European Agency for the Management of Operational Cooperation at the External Borders (FRONTEX).

Nevertheless, the expansion of powers and activities in the different areas have to comply with other international obligations, and in this context the reference to fundamental rights[32] as a set of common legal background of all member states becomes an important development in European law. All those issues are related to a broad concept of security, in this case to the concept of European regional security, which should be linked to other European institutions, in particular the Council of Europe and the European Convention on Human Rights,[33] but also to the other main regional organisation, the OSCE.[34]

If international organisations can play different roles, the main assumption in this study, as discussed by the reformist scholars on international relations, and in particular by the so-called functionalist school, is that by creating specific institutional links among member states, all types of organisations encourage co-operative relations among members, and decrease the level of conflict between members.[35] In a broad sense, this can be considered a general aim of security for the members of the organisation, achieved through the means of co-operation through technical and political common objectives.

Despite the possible different scopes and aims of member states of international organisations and their actual role, international law plays an important part in this context. International organisations are often based on international treaties. Organs and institutions of organisations have powers defined by the treaties and often they rely on concepts of international law, such as implied powers, and legal personality. Being legal persons, international organisations are subject to international legal rules, at least to the rules of general international law, including the general principles

31 EU, "Consolidated versions of the Treaty on the European Union and of the Treaty Establishing the European Community," *Official Journal* C 321E, 29 December 2006.

32 EU, "Consolidated versions of the Treaty on European Union and the Treaty on the Functioning of the European Union," *Official Journal* C 115, 9 May 2008, Art. 21.2(b); and "Charter of Fundamental Rights of the European Union," *Official Journal* C 303, 14 December 2007.

33 Council of Europe, "Convention for the Protection of Human Rights and Fundamental Freedoms," Rome, 4 November 1950, *CETS* no. 005.

34 Marco Odello, "The Organization for Security and Co-operation in Europe and European Security Law," in *European Security Law*, in Trybus and White, eds., note 5 above.

35 White, note 24 above, 9–13; Archer, note 25 above, 54.

of international law, *jus cogens*[36]and obligations *erga omnes*.[37] The main purpose of this work is to analyse some developments of international organisations in the framework of international law, as the legal order of the international community, because new development regarding international security should be framed within the limits of international legal principles and rules. Accepting the opposite position would create more fragmentation of the international legal order,[38] with consequent uncertainty and therefore insecurity in international legal and political relations among different subjects of the international community.

IV. New Threats to Security and International Organisations

In this section the concept of international security in the UN and some IROs will be addressed. Both types of organisation show a trend that includes and addresses several interrelated threats to international security, moving forward from the more traditional interstate conflict, and including new possible actors and areas of concern that may affect international security.

A. *The United Nations*

The UN Charter refers to the maintenance of international peace and security as one of the main purposes of the organisation. This meaning of security, as already mentioned, refers mainly to the threat and use of force by states. But since the adoption of the concept of human security, and the end of the Cold War with the military and ideological threat on both sides of the world, other issues have been included in the concept of international security, without a proper systematic approach in terms of UN powers and functions.

A series of documents have addressed the issue of international and collective security in the UN system. The most relevant and recent document is this area is

36 "Vienna Convention on the Law of Treaties," U.N. Doc A/CONF.39/27 (1969), 1155 U.N.T.S. 331, Articles 53 and 64. Robert Kolb, "Jus cogens, entagibilité, intransgressibilité, dérogation 'positive' et 'négative,'" *Revue Générale de Droit International Public*, 109, no. 2 (2005): 305–330.

37 ICJ, *Barcelona Traction, Light and Power Company, Ltd. Case* (Merits), *Belgium v. Spain*, Judgement of 5 February 1970, *ICJ Reports 1970*, 3. See also Maurizio Ragazzi, *The Concept of International Obligations Erga Omnes* (Oxford: Oxford University Press, 1997); Paolo Picone, "La distinzione tra norme internazionali di "jus cogens" e norme che producono obblighi 'erga omnes,'" *Rivista di diritto internazionale*, 1 (2008): 5–38.

38 Since the year 2002 the UN International Law Commission has developed a study on the issue of "Fragmentation of International Law". See the final report in UN, GA, *Report of the International Law Commission*, Official Records, Sixty-first session, Supplement no. 10 (A/61/10), 2006. See also Mario Prost and Paul Kingsley Clark, "Unity, Diversity and the Fragmentation of International Law: How Much Does the Multiplication of International Organizations Really Matter?'" *Chinese Journal of International Law*, 5, no. 2 (2006): 341–370; Martti Koskenniemi, "Fragmentation of International Law: Difficulties Arising from the Diversification and Expansion of International Law," *Report of the Study Group of the International Law Commission*, UN Doc. A/CN.4/L.682, 13 April 2006.

the 2004 High-Level Panel Report,[39] which endorsed "a *broader, more comprehensive concept* of collective security: one that tackles new and old threats and addresses the security concerns of all States – rich and poor, weak and strong".[40] The panel identified six specific areas of threats:

1. Interstate conflict;
2. Poverty, infectious disease and environmental degradation;
3. Internal violence, including civil war, genocide, ethnic cleansing and state failure;
4. Weapons of mass destruction, including chemical, biological, radiological and nuclear weapons;
5. Terrorism; and
6. Transnational organized crime.

Compared to the traditional concept, these threats to international security are already broader. In particular, the Panel recognised the interrelationship between threats to international security, which makes the circumscription to state borders quite an absurd concept.

This wider concept was already mentioned in some other documents, such as the 2000 Millennium Declaration, and during the 2003 UN General Assembly to address different challenges to the peace that could lead to the UN reform.[41] The 2005 World Summit Declaration[42] has stressed that "peace and security, development and human rights are the pillars of the United Nations system and the foundations for collective security and well-being", and that "development, peace and security and human rights are interlinked and mutually reinforcing.[43] In other parts of the same declaration there are references to food security,[44] and even in the section concerning collective security it is affirmed that member states are committed "to work towards a security consensus based on the recognition that many threats are interlinked, that development, peace, security and human rights are mutually reinforcing".[45] More recently the relationship between women, peace and security has also been addressed.[46]

Another relevant document that shows this trend in the UN system is the 2005 report In Larger Freedom by Kofi Annan,[47] which considers that "[T]he notion of

39 UN, *High-Level Panel on Threats, Challenges and Change, A more secure world: our shared responsibility*, UN Doc. A/59/565, 2 December 2004.

40 Ibid., note by the Secretary General, para. 5 (original italics).

41 For more details see Marco Odello, "Commentary on the United Nations' High-Level Panel on Threats, Challenges and Change," *Journal of Conflict & Security Law* 10, no. 2 (2005): 237.

42 UN, GA Res. 60/1, UN Doc. A/RES/60/1, 24 October 2005.

43 Ibid., para. 9.

44 Ibid., para 46.

45 Ibid., para. 72.

46 UN, SC Res. 1325 (2000) and 1820 (2008); UN Doc. S/PRST/2008/39, 29 October 2008.

47 Kofi Annan, *In Larger Freedom: Towards Development, Security and Human Rights for All*, Report of the Secretary General, UN Doc. A/59/2005, 21 March 2005.

larger freedom also encapsulates the idea that development, security and human rights go hand in hand".[48] This concept is further clarified in the following statement framed in the section on collective security:

> The threats to peace and security in the twenty-first century include not just international war and conflict but civil violence, organized crime, terrorism and weapons of mass destruction. They also include poverty, deadly infectious disease and environmental degradation since these can have equally catastrophic consequences. All of these threats can cause death or lessen life chances on a large scale. All of them can undermine States as the basic unit of the international system.[49]

Finally, these concepts have been further stressed in the document on the Responsibility to Protect,[50] elaborated by the International Commission on Intervention and State Sovereignty. This document endorses the idea that state sovereignty[51] implies the responsibility of individual states to protect fundamental rights of the population under their control, and in case of failure, the international community has a responsibility to act, even by the extreme remedy of force. Therefore, human security implies a duty for all states to protect the fundamental rights of people under their jurisdiction, and the sovereignty rights can be overcome by other states in case of flagrant violation of human rights and human security.

B. *Regional Organisations*

Several regional organisations have adopted documents defining what they understand to be threats to security. They include NATO's *Alliance's Strategic Concept* (1999);[52] the EU's *A Secure Europe in a Better World: European Security Strategy* (2003); the OAS' *Declaration on Security in the Americas* (2003); and the OSCE's *Common Purpose: Towards a More Effective OSCE* (2005). All the mentioned documents identify threats that go far beyond the use of force by one or more states against another state. Since 1975 the OSCE has developed a wider concept of international security, which includes disarmament, human rights, democracy, minority issues, economic, and environmental concerns.[53]

---

48 Ibid., para. 14.

49 Ibid., para. 78.

50 International Commission on Intervention and State Sovereignty, *The Responsibility to Protect*, 2001, at http://www.iciss.ca/pdf/Commission-Report.pdf.

51 Ibid., paras. 2.7–2.10; Ramesh Thakur, *The United Nations, Peace and Security: From Collective Security to the Responsibility to Protect* (Cambridge: Cambridge University Press, 2006), 251–257.

52 NATO, *The Alliance's Strategic Concept*, adopted by the Heads of State and Government at the meeting of the North Atlantic Council, Washington, 23–24 April 1999, at http://www.mde.es/ficheros_fi/concepto.pdf.

53 The documents include: *The London Declaration* (6 July 1990), *The Rome Declaration* (8 November 1991), *The Madrid Declaration* (8 July 1997), *The Washington Declaration* (23–24 April 1999), and the *Prague Summit Declaration* (21–22 November 2002). See also

If security, as a general aim, can be considered a relevant component leading to the establishment of international organisations, what this work tries to clarify is how international security issues have been identified and shaped by international regional organisations in more specific terms. This will be done by briefly looking at some IROs, and the analysis should provide a better picture of security concerns that have been included in the evolution of selected IROs.

The case of the OSCE is quite paradigmatic for our purposes, as the concept of security is already included in the name of the organisation. Also, the importance of this organisation is relevant for our study, as the concept of security adopted in its constituent and further documents envisages a wide set of security issues. In the 1975 Helsinki Final Act,[54] the constitutive document of the OSCE, the idea of security was very much linked to peace, and threats were founded on the security of states. The Cold War confrontation between East and West European states and the respective super power's allies was particularly relevant for the purposes of the OSCE. Conflict prevention and distension in international relations was a central factor, when the two blocks were also parties to military alliances, NATO and the Warsaw Pact.

A variety of documents and policy papers, and specific institutions have been developed in the framework of the OSCE to deal with security concerns. They range from the 1975 Helsinki Summit Final Act, the constitutive document of the CSCE, to the Charter for European Security, adopted at the Istanbul Summit in 1999.[55] The comprehensive debate on security within the OSCE led to identify a series of issues that would define the broad concept of security in the wide European context. The 1999 Charter for European Security[56] has widened the concept of security defined in the Helsinki Act and in subsequent documents. It recognised that 'threats to security can stem from conflicts within States as well as from conflicts between states' and for that reason both types of conflicts 'represent a threat to the security of all OSCE participating states'.[57] International terrorism, organised crime and drug trafficking 'represent growing challenges to security', and are linked to the 'destabilising

Lionel Ponsard, "The dawning of a new security era?", *NATO Review* (Autumn 2004); Lord Robertson, "Change and continuity", *NATO Review* (Winter 2003): 2–6; Marco Odello, "The Organization for Security and Co-operation in Europe and European Security Law," in Trybus and White, eds., note 5 above; Marco Odello, "Thirty Years After Helsinki: Proposals for OSCE's Reform," *Journal of Conflict and Security Law* 10, no. 3 (2005): 435–449.

54 CSCE, *Final Act*, Helsinki, 1 August 1975, 14 ILM (1975) 1292.

55 Other relevant documents including security issues are: the 1990 Paris Summit, the 1992 Helsinki Summit, the 1994 Budapest Summit, the 1996 Lisbon Summit. Also relevant for the discussion of the concept of security in the area of OSCE, see Follow-up Meeting 1980–1983, *Concluding Document*, Madrid, 11 November 1980 to 9 September 1983, The Security Model Discussion 1995–1996, *Report of the Chairman-in Office to the Lisbon Summit Review Meeting*, Lisbon 1996. The Istanbul Summit, 18–19 November 1999, adopted a *Final Declaration* and a *Charter for European Security*, OSCE Istanbul Summit, *Istanbul Documents 1999*, Cm 4560, January 2000.

56 OSCE, *Istanbul Documents 1999*, ibid.

57 Ibid., para. 2.

accumulation and uncontrolled spread of small arms and light weapons'.[58] Acute economic problems and environmental degradation are related to the already existing areas of co-operation in the fields of economy, science and technology.[59] These issues are not supposed to derogate the existing ones. They add further elements to the areas of co-operation among states within the OSCE in the effort of providing security. The broad sense of security within the OSCE is expressed in the following terms in Paragraph 9 of the Charter:

> We will build our relations in conformity with the concept of common and comprehensive security, guided by equal partnership, solidarity and transparency. The security of each participating state is inseparably linked to that of all others. We will address the human, economic, political and military dimensions of security as an integral whole.

The most recent document concerning the definition of security has been adopted in the form of Follow-up Decisions taken at the Maastricht Ministerial Council in December 2003.[60] It makes reference to the areas mentioned before, and also stresses its attention on the economic and environmental dimensions of security.[61]

Apart from the policy documents adopted by states, a series of institutions and activities dealing with the broad security concerns. The leading institutional organ in the area of Human Dimension is the Office for Democratic Institutions and Human Rights (ODIHR), created in 1991, but recognition of the importance of minority rights for the purposes of security[62] led to the creation of the High Commissioner on National Minorities (HCNM) in 1992.[63] The ODIHR deals with four main areas: assistance of democratic processes, monitoring the implementation of OSCE Human Dimension in participating states, co-operation with intergovernmental and non-governmental organisations, and integration of the Human Dimension into the security activities of the OSCE.[64]

Activities include the so-called Long-term Missions that could take the form of peace-keeping operations with broad aims that include negotiation powers, institutional building activity, and human rights monitoring.[65] They are based on co-

58 Ibid., para. 4.

59 Ibid., para. 5.

60 OSCE, Ministerial Council, *OSCE Strategy to Address Threats to Security and Stability in the Twenty-First Century*, Maastricht 1–2 December 2003.

61 Ibid., Part I, paras. 5 and 14.

62 Reference to minority rights was included in the 1999 Vienna Document. On the importance of minority issues for security see Li-Ann Thio, "Developing a 'Peace and Security' Approach Towards Minorities' Problems," *International & Comparative Law Quarterly* 52, no. 1 (2003): 115–150.

63 CSCE, *1992 Helsinki Summit*, Decisions, chapter II, para. 1.

64 The mandate of the ODIHR is included in several documents, in particular the 1990 *Charter of Paris for a New Europe*, the 1992 *Helsinki Follow-up Documents*, the 1993 Rome Council Meeting, and the 1994 Budapest Review Conference.

65 CSCE, 1992 Helsinki Summit Decisions, Chapter III, *Early warning, conflict prevention and crisis management (including fact-finding and rapporteur missions and CSCE peace-keeping)*, paras. 17–56.

operation agreements between the OSCE and member states usually within the framework of existing mechanisms, such as the ODIHR, the HCNM, and other programs, such as election monitoring, mainly within the area of Human Dimension.[66]

NATO and the EU have developed legal tools regarding European security issues and defence matters. They are the European Security and Defence Identity (ESDI) within NATO, and the European Security and Defence Policy (ESDP) in the case of EU.[67] As far as NATO is concerned, mention should be made to the 1991 Alliance Strategic Concept,[68] to the 1997 Madrid Declaration,[69] to the 1999 Strategic Concept,[70] and to the 2002 Prague Summit Declaration.[71] Within the EU, reference should be made to the European Security Strategy presented by Solana in 2003.[72] Solana's document identifies new key threats 'which are more diverse, less visible and less predictable' than the traditional attacks on state sovereignty. They include terrorism, proliferation of arms of mass destruction, regional conflicts, state failure, and organised crime.[73]

The same EU, as an international economic organisation, has developed new interests and activities in the field of international security, in particular since 2003 with the adoption of the European Security Strategy.[74] This document identifies terrorism, proliferation of weapons of mass destruction, regional conflicts, state failure, and organised crime as the main threats for European security. The EU has established working relationships with NATO in the field of security and peacekeeping

66 See Allan Rosas and Timo Lahelma, "OSCE Long-Term Missions", in *The OSCE in the Maintenance of Peace and Security*, ed. Michael Bothe, Natalino Ronzitti and Allan Rosas (The Hague/London/Boston: Kluwer Law International, 1997).

67 On these specific issues and their relationships see Fabien Terpan, "EU-NATO Relations: Consistency as a Strategic Consideration and a Legal Requirement", in Trybus and White, eds., note 5 above.

68 NATO, *The Alliance's Strategic Concept*, agreed by the Heads of State and Government participating in the meeting of the North Atlantic Council Rome, 8 November 1991, at http://www.nato.int/docu/basictxt/b911108a.htm.

69 NATO, *Madrid Declaration on Euro-Atlantic Security and Cooperation*, issued by the Heads of State and Government, Madrid, 8 July 1997, at http://www.nato.int/docu/pr/1997/p97-081e.htm.

70 NATO, *The Strategic Concept of the Alliance*, approved by the Heads of State and Government participating in the meeting of the North Atlantic Council in Washington D.C. on 23 and 24 April 1999.

71 NATO, *Prague Summit Declaration*, issued by the Heads of State and Government participating in the meeting of the North Atlantic Council in Prague on 21 November 2002.

72 EU, *A secure Europe in a better world: European Security Strategy*, document proposed by Javier Solana and adopted by the Heads of State and Government at the European Council in Brussels on 12 December 2003, published by the European Institute for Security Studies, Paris, at http://www.iss-eu.org/solana/solanae.pdf.

73 Ibid., 6–9.

74 Ibid. See also Vincent Kronenberger and Jan Wouters, *The European Union and Conflict Prevention* (The Hague: TMC Asser Press, 2004); Jess Pilegaard, ed., *The Politics of European Security*, (Copenhagen: Danish Institute for International Studies, 2004); Carl C. Hodge, ed., *Redefining European security* (New York, London: Garland Pub., 1999).

on the basis of the so-called Berlin Plus Agreement.[75] The Berlin Plus arrangements refer to a series of agreements concluded by NATO and the EU between December 2002 and March 2003 which allow the EU to carry out operations using NATO assets and capabilities, provide the basis for NATO-EU cooperation in crisis management by allowing EU access to NATO's collective assets and capabilities for EU-led operations. The Berlin Plus agreements have been used to establish the Operation Concordia in the Former Yugoslav Republic of Macedonia[76] and EUFOR Althea Mission in Bosnia and Herzegovina (BiH).[77]

The OAS adopted a declaration at the level of Heads of State and Government in 2003,[78] which identified the following threats, apart from the traditional ones:

- Terrorism, transnational organized crime, the global drug problem, corruption, asset laundering;
- Illicit trafficking in weapons, and the connections among them;
- Extreme poverty and social exclusion of broad sectors of the population, which also affect stability and democracy. Extreme poverty which erodes social cohesion and undermines the security of states;
- Natural and man-made disasters, HIV/AIDS and other diseases, other health risks, and environmental degradation;
- Trafficking in persons;
- Attacks to cyber security;
- The potential for damage to arise in the event of an accident or incident during the maritime transport of potentially hazardous materials, including petroleum and radioactive materials and toxic waste; and
- The possibility of access, possession, and use of weapons of mass destruction and their means of delivery by terrorists.[79]

The AU, in the process of reform from the Organisation for African Unity, established a new organ, the Peace and Security Council of the African Union since 2003,[80] which

75 NATO/EU, Berlin Plus Agreement, adopted on 17 March 2003, and based on the NATO Washington Summit of Heads of State and Government, 23–25 April 1999, *An Alliance for the 21st Century*, at http://www.nato.int/docu/pr/1999/p99-064e.htm. For further information on the Berlin Plus Agreement and the relationship between the EU and NATO, see Gerrard Quille "What does the EU agreement on Operational Planning mean for NATO?", *NATO Notes*, vol. 5, no. 8, (December 2003): 6–15; Martin Reichard, *The EU-NATO Relationship: A Legal and Political Perspective* (Aldershot: Ashgate, 2006).

76 The Operation was launched on 31 March 2003 on request by the government of the Former Yugoslav Republic of Macedonia (EU, Council, Joint Action 2003/92/CFSP, 27 January 2003).

77 EU, Council, Joint Action 2004/569/CFSP, 12 July 2004.

78 OAS, *Declaration on Security in the Americas*, doc. OEA/Ser.K/XXXVIII, CES/DEC. 1/03 rev.1, 28 October 2003.

79 Ibid., para 4(m). For an analysis, see: Marco Odello, "International Security in the Western Hemisphere: Legal and Institutional Developments," *Anuario de Derecho Internacional* 21 (2005): 379–411.

80 AU, "Protocol Relating to the Establishment of the Peace and Security Council of the African Union," adopted in Durban, South Africa, 10 July 2002, entered into force on the 26 December 2003.

does not expand on the concept of threats to security and seems to adopt a quite traditional concept of security related to either inter-state or intra-state violence. Nevertheless Article 4(h) of the new African Union Act[81] provides the right of intervention for the AU in its member states, to prevent a "serious threat to legitimate order". That opportunity looks like a shift from the interest to protect human security to the protection of established governments in Africa. This power also raises some possible problems concerning the authorization of the use of force by the UN Security Council to intervene in the states of the region.

This short survey of a selection of international organisations demonstrates that several documents include many threats to international security, ranging from the traditional regional conflicts, proliferation of weapons of mass destruction, terrorism, and transnational criminal organisations, to environmental degradation and damages, illegal immigration, massive flows of people, infectious diseases and pandemics such as HIV/AIDS, etc.[82]

V. Security, Human Rights and International Law

Most international organisations have drafted their constitutive documents on the basis of the UN Charter. As a result, it is not uncommon to find opening references to human rights protection and compliance with international law in their constitutions or in relevant policy documents. At this stage it may be relevant to understand how international law and human rights can be relevant in the definition and clarification of threats to international security, and identify some problems, limitations and gaps concerning the possible actions by international organisations in the area of international security.

A. *Collective Security, Human Rights and Human Security*

As briefly mentioned before, traditional collective security was foreseen as a tool for states to deal with threats to their survival.[83] The essential feature of this element was the use of force and the threat of using force by states. Despite the general prohibition on the use of force by states, under Article 2(4) of the UN Charter, states retained, under the UN Charter the right to self-defence, and to react militarily to the use of force by other states. Under the ideal structure of the UN Charter, the international community would intervene to solve international crisis, and restore peace. The shifting and expanding of international threats to security, as seen before, may mean that states and international organisations perceive wider and more complex forms of threats to their security.

---

81 AU, "Constitutive Act," Lomé, 11 July 2000, at http://www.africa-union.org/root/au/AboutAu/Constitutive_Act_en.htm. See Ademola Abass and Mashood A. Baderin, 'Towards effective collective security and human rights protection in Africa: An assessment of the Constitutive Act of the new African Union', *Netherlands International Law Review* 49 (2002): 1–38.

82 See Krahmann, note 7 above.

83 See note 2 above.

At this stage, it may be relevant to clarify which forms and which means can be used by states to deal with new threats to both national and international security, as there may be disagreements on the possible use of force and other means by states and international organisations. These means should be framed under the principles and rules of international law. In particular, they should be included within the framework of international human rights law, as part of the obligations of states, and within the scopes of international organisations' mandates under their constitutions. If the concept of collective security had a clear meaning in international law, one would infer that, in spite of the fact that new threats to security are now identified, it may still be used in the sense of a collective action by states to deal with the different threats. The problem in this case is that collective security has a meaning related to the use of force by states, under specific regulations, foreseen by the UN Charter. But during the last decade, security has been link also to human rights and fundamental freedoms of individuals, under the concept of human security.

Human rights concerns and related legal instruments have expanded since the creation of the UN and the adoption of the 1948 Universal Declaration of Human Rights. Reference to human rights was very limited in the UN Charter due to the lack of international definitions of those rights.[84] Nowadays, after six decades since the definitions offered by the Universal Declaration, the international human rights system is clearer and provides a set of general principles, rules, bodies and mechanisms.[85] These elements should be kept in mind when interpreting the UN Charter, and other international documents, including the constitutions of other international organisations. Furthermore, the development of human rights standards has influenced in some forms the interpretation and application of many areas of law, both international and national. Nevertheless, there are reactions to this interpretative phenomenon and states seem reluctant to afford a wider 'humanisation of international law', an issue that will be discussed in the later part of this paper.[86]

The shifting of international attention from state survival to broader issues of international security has been stressed by the introduction of the concept of human security in the 1990s.[87] The issue received significant attention by the Commission on Human Security which delivered its report in 2003.[88] This evolution is due to the growing relevance of international human rights law in international relations. Human security focuses on the well being of persons more than on states as

84 See UN Charter, Preamble and Arts. 1(3); 13(1)(b); 55(c); 62(2); 68; 76(c).

85 See Dina Shelton, *Remedies in International Human Rights Law*, 2nd ed. (Oxford: Oxford University Press, 2005).

86 See Meron, note 23 above.

87 Since the 1990s the concept of human security has been included in the United Nations language, see: UNDP, *The Human Development Report*, note 8 above; UN, GA Res. 55/2, 8 September 2000, adopted by the Millennium Summit, New York, 6–8 September 2000. See also UN, *Report of the Secretary General*, UN doc. A/53/948, 10 May 1999; Kofi Annan, *We the Peoples: The Role of the United Nations in the 21st Century* (New York: United Nations, 2000).

88 Commission on Human Security, *Human Security Now*, (New York, 2003), at: http://www.humansecurity-chs.org/finalreport/FinalReport.pdf.

abstract geo-political entities.[89] The fundamental issue is that respect and promotion of human right within states would contribute to the broader international security. This relationship between international peace and security, peaceful relations among states and respect for human rights and fundamental freedoms was shortly stated in Article 1 of the UN Charter at the end of the II World War. An issue also analysed by international political scientists, such as Professor Barry Buzan, and that now seems to get further consideration at both political and institutional levels.[90]

B. *The Role of International Law*

International law has become a difficult subject to define.[91] Traditionally identified as a set of rules regulating states' relations; now, international law includes a wider range of subjects, such as international organisations, individuals and other groups, under the development of international rules related to human rights, humanitarian law and criminal law. International human rights law is playing an important role in the shaping of contemporary international law. As international law should be seen as a system of norms regulating a composite international community, the fundamental norms developed at international level should be applicable to its subjects. As international law includes international human rights law, it is therefore important to consider the limitations that this area of law can impose on states, on the UN and other IROs. Not looking at international law in this comprehensive might lead to the so-called phenomenon of fragmentation that may imply serious inconsistencies and possible dangerous gaps in the international legal system.[92]

This issue has been partly addressed by the UN Secretary General in a recent report on the relationship between the UN and IROs in the maintenance of international peace and security.[93] The document provides guidelines for the co-operation between the UN and IROs, but still does not clarify the legal structures and obligations of each organisation in the operational aspects of security. For instance, in the human rights section (Report, para. 81) there is a general reference to the importance of human rights components in peacekeeping, support for IROs in mainstreaming international human rights instrument and institutional capacity, and developing a strategy for the promotion and protection of human rights, with particular reference to the African Union. These issues should be better analysed to understand the relevance of human rights in the activities of both the UN and IROs.

Furthermore, the Report focuses on strategies within Chapter VIII of the UN Charter, but does not consider the most complex issue of powers under Chapter VII,

89 Ibid., 2. Cfr. Bertrand G. Ramcharan, *Human Rights and Human Security* (The Hague: Martinus Nijhoff, 2002), 4.

90 Barry Buzan, *People, States and Fear*, 2nd ed. (Harlow: Pearson, 1991).

91 That may be the reason why several manuals on international law do not even try to provide a definition of this area of law.

92 On fragmentation of international law see note 38 above.

93 UNSC, *Report of the Secretary-General on the relationship between the United Nations and regional organizations, in particular the African Union, in the maintenance of international peace and security*, UN Doc. S/2008/186, 7 April 2008.

related to the use of force by the UN and the powers by IROs. As already evidenced in the past, during the 1999 NATO bombing of Yugoslavia,[94] and later formulated in the recommendation by the High-Level Panel on Threats, Challenges and Change,[95] that authorisation from the Security Council should in all cases be sought for regional peace operations.[96] These examples show some relevant gaps within the international system in the fields of human rights protection and use of force by the UN and by IROs.

An additional issue, that can be linked to the mentioned topics, concerning both human rights and use of force, can be the relevance of rules of international humanitarian law (IHL), and the rights of humanitarian intervention. IHL has been often considered a separate branch of international law from human rights law. Nevertheless, states and international organisations, when using force and sending troops under different mandates to foreign countries, should act under the general principles and customary rules of IHL. A matter that took a long time to be clarified within the UN, and that finally was included in the form of the UN Secretary-General Bulletin.[97]

As many rules of IHL have reached the status of customary international law, the main rules related to the use of force should be considered part of the core system of international law, in closer relationship with human rights law.[98] IROs, and the UN, should be more careful in defining their policies and setting their priorities in the light of these fundamental rules of international law.

Some examples show that there are trends, rather marginal though, towards the need of considering the international legal system in a more consistent way with general principles and rules of international law. One of the cases can be the shifting in the UN sanction system to apply targeted sanctions, to avoid widespread and indiscriminate sufferings for the general population of the sanctioned state.[99] Another example can be the developing recent practice of forms of humanitarian occupation or democratic reconstruction under international supervision of states that have been affected by protracted or massive violations of human rights.[100] Democratic

---

94 See Ruth Wedgwood, "NATO's Campaign in Yugoslavia," *The American Journal of International Law* 93, no. 4 (1999): 828–834.

95 UN, *High-Level Panel on Threats, Challenges and Change*, note 39 above.

96 See Marten, Zwanenburg, "Regional Organisations and the Maintenance of International Peace and Security: Three Recent Regional African Peace Operations," *Journal of Conflict and Security Law* 11 (2006): 483–508; Odello, "Commentary on the United Nations' High Level Panel on Threats, Challenges and Change," note 41 above.

97 UN, *Secretary-General's Bulletin*, ST/SGB/1999/13, 6 August 1999.

98 On the relationship see Roberta Arnold and Noëlle Quénivet, eds., *International Humanitarian Law and Human Rights Law* (Leiden: Martinus Nijhoff, 2008).

99 Annan, *In Larger Freedom*, note 47 above, paras. 109–110.

100 See Gregory H. Fox, *Humanitarian Occupation* (Cambridge: Cambridge Univesity Press, 2008); Ulf Häußler *Ensuring and Enforcing Human Security. The Practice of International Peace Missions* (Nijmegen: Wolf Legal Publishers, 2007); Carsten Stahn, *The Law and Practice of International Territorial Administration: Versailles to Iraq and Beyond* (Cambridge: Cambridge University Press, 2008).

institutions and protection of human rights seem to prevail on the rights of the sovereign state and the principle of non-intervention in internal affairs, at least in selected cases such as Bosnia, Kosovo, East Timor and Eastern Slavonia.

IROs should also go through a process of clarifying their position regarding the respect of international law. Considering that many states are parties to regional systems for the protection of human rights, they might show more attention to the enforcement and international obligations related to human rights. Interesting developments in this sense come from the case law of the European Court of Human Rights (ECtHR). The 2008 judgment of *Saadi v. Italy*[101] reaffirmed the 1999 case of *Chahal v. United Kingdom*[102] in reasserting the importance of the respect of human rights and the rule of law in case of torture linked to security concerns.

Also relevant issues were raised on the relationship between European Court of Justice and the blacklisting of alleged terrorist individuals and associations. The cases of *Yusuf* and *Kadi* [2005], of *Ayadi* and *Hassan* [2006] and more recently the case of *Kadi and Al Barakaat*[103] have addressed the compatibility of actions by international organisations and the respect of *jus cogens* norms and other fundamental rights, such as the right to property and to fair hearing.[104] The ECJ clarified that point asserting that:

"the obligations imposed by an international agreement cannot have the effect of prejudicing the constitutional principles of the EC Treaty, which include the principle that all Community acts must respect fundamental rights, that respect constituting a condition of their lawfulness which it is for the Court to review in the framework of the complete system of legal remedies established by the Treaty".[105]

The ECJ has therefore annulled some secondary norms of European Law that were considered not in conformity with general obligations of international law.[106] In these cases, the relationship between different legal orders, universal and regional, and the hierarchy of states' and institutional obligations were addressed by the ECJ. On the one side it may be true that the regional courts may not have jurisdiction in

---

101 ECtHR, *Saadi v. Italy*, no. 37201/06, Judgment of 28 February 2008, at: http://cmiskp.echr.coe.int/tkp197/view.asp?action=html&documentId=829510&portal=hbkm&source=externalbydocnumber&table=F69A27FD8FB86142BF01C1166DEA398649.

102 ECtHR, *Chahal v. The United Kingdom*, no. 70/1995/576/662, Judgment of 15 November 1996, 23 EHRR 413.

103 ECJ, *Yassin Abdullah Kadi and Al Barakaat International Foundation v. Council and Commission*, Judgment (Grand Chamber) of 3 September 2008, Joined Cases C-402/05 P and C-415/05 P, OJ C 36, 11.02.2006. OJ C 48, 25 February 2006.

104 Ibid., para. 371.

105 Ibid., para. 285.

106 EC, Council Regulation no. 881/2002 of 27 May 2002 imposing certain specific restrictive measures directed against certain persons and entities associated with Usama bin Laden, the Al-Qaeda network and the Taliban, and Council Regulation no. 467/2001 prohibiting the export of certain goods and services to Afghanistan, strengthening the flight ban and extending the freeze of funds and other financial resources in respect of the Taliban of Afghanistan, in so far as it concerns Mr Kadi and the Al Barakaat International Foundation, ibid.

deciding cases involving the UN and based on the UN Charter. This is due to the fact they do not have jurisdiction on the UN organs and pursuant to article 103 of the UN Charter, which states: "In the event of a conflict between the obligations of the Members of the United Nations under the present Charter and their obligations under any other international agreement, their obligations under the present Charter shall prevail". On the other side it may also be true that the UN Charter does not stand beyond international law, but rather under the principles and rules of that legal system, as the Charter is an international treaty, regulated by international law, and the organisation is a subject of international law. A further question is whether national judges may consider the conformity of international organisations' decision with fundamental rules of international law, as those rules bind not only the state, but the state's authorities and their national organs as well.

By looking at international law as a more comprehensive and holistic system of law, the possible inconsistencies of the system might be better identified by the co-operation or action of different judicial bodies. National, regional and international judicial bodies, assisted by other international actors, such as NGOs and academics would be able to identify gaps and contradictions of the law.

VI. Conclusion

At this stage, international lawyers should consider if the evolution of the concept of threats to peace and security, the widening of the concept of collective security and the related activities need a better clarification of their limit and regulations under international law.

If there is an expanded notion of threats to international peace and security, collective security may not be restricted to international actions related to the threat and the use of force by states against another State. Threat to states' security can lead to the use of collective actions, including the use of force, as far as an international threat is identified by the competent international body, both at regional and universal level, but also as it is perceived by individual States which could try to invoke the right to self-defence. The obvious risk in this case is a possible proliferation of the use of force to address international threats, with a menace for the principle established by the UN Charter under Article 2(4) and the primary responsibility of the UN for the maintenance of international peace and security, including the authorization of the use of force by states[107] and by other international organisations.[108]

The positive side of this development could be the clarification of legal justifications for international actions, in particular under the umbrella of human security and the protection of fundamental human rights. The fact that the protection of human rights is an essential issue under new international security provisions, might provide better legal justifications for enforcement actions in cases of massive violations of human rights, or to re-establish the international responsibility of states to protect the rights of people under their respective jurisdictions, and the role of

107 UN Charter, Article 39.

108 UN Charter, Article 52.

the international community to ensure and supplement that responsibility. The responsibility to protect linked to the concept of human security might better guarantee the protection of fundamental rights of the people concerned, by reshaping some general principles like state sovereignty.[109]

But the wide list of threats to international security also makes it difficult to move from the narrowly defined concept of collective security to include broadly defined issues, from environmental protection, to migration, from transnational crime, including terrorism, to HIV/AIDS, etc. If the protection of the survival of the state was the core element of traditional collective security, the broad range of issues under consideration makes almost impossible to define a specific area where the use of force is allowed and the international community should act with all available means. By looking at regional and universal documents mentioned before, almost everything has become a matter of international security.[110] How is it possible to define the areas of concern and the limits of international actions?

It may be difficult to reshape fairly clearly defined legal categories, as in the case of collective security. Established rules and procedures have an appeal because they provide some 'security' in relations among states, due to the fact that they are recognisable, established and widely shared by those who use them. But it is also difficult not to consider and clarify the legal implications of the evolution of the concept of international security mentioned before. The legal significance may still be quite limited, but it should be stressed the fact that parallel legal criteria should be applied to specific situations by the organs of international organisations when dealing with international security matters. In a way, the UN Security Council and other IROs have already expanded the notion of threats to international security. Documents with identified threats to international security in a way provide more legal certainty and justification for future decisions by IOs concerning threats to international security. Furthermore, the concerted identification of threats to security in the context of different IOs provides a more democratic consensus by the international community than a decision taken by the fifteen members of the Security Council.

Another positive outcome of this definitional process may be the clarification of the difference between threats to the peace, breach of the peace and more general threats to security. Threats to the peace and breach of the peace could be limited to the case of armed conflict and aggression, and the wider list of possible threats to international security that are not necessarily linked to the use of force by states could be defined in a different way. To limit the risk of an expanded and unclear use of security threats it could be suggested a change in the terminology by adopting a semantically similar concept to security, for instance 'safety', that could incorporate threats which do not involve the use of force among states, leaving the concept of collective security to more limited cases related to the use of force. Nevertheless, the concept of human security has been already defined and used for more than ten years, and the Security Council has identified threats to international peace and security

109 Sorpong Peou, "The UN, Peacekeeping and Collective Human Security: From *An Agenda for Peace* to the Brahimi Report," *Internantional Peacekeeping* 9, no. 2 (2002): 51–68.

110 Odello, "Commentary on the United Nations' High-Level Panel on Threats, Challenges and Change," note 41 above, 237.

in several contexts not always linked to the use of force by states, as mentioned before. Furthermore, collective security can refer to collective actions to deal with international security, which may have different types of outcomes.

Fundamental legal issues are involved by an expanding concept of collective security. They include for instance the definition and demarcation of the concepts of state sovereignty, aggression, use of force, humanitarian action, etc. Documents adopted by international organisations are still quite vague in the clarification of legal limits to the international collective action. The UN *High-Level Panel Report* is an example. The *Report* considers that to build a credible system of collective security three elements are considered necessary, effectiveness, efficiency, and equity. These criteria may provide political and managerial guidelines, but they do not provide practical legal rules for international action. The rules may evolve through the practice of states or the adoption of documents that clarify the limits and concepts of international security. In this area, IROs should contribute to the clarification of the powers in relationship to the UN and to their members under international law.

There may be other implications linked to the development of international actions addressing security issues. In particular, the fact that IROs have endorsed their own wider concept of threats to security means that the UN Security Council, and the UN in general, might lose control over some relevant issues related to international security. Depending on the circumstances of each case, this may be considered either as a positive or as a negative outcome. When the UN is unable to intervene and deal with a specific security issue, regional organisations may act for the sake of international security, at least when regional security concerns are involved.[111] The risk is that the UN might lose importance, and groups of states, under the form of regional organisations or *ad hoc* alliances, could intervene without the required authorization, in particular to use force, as foreseen by the UN Charter. It is true that most regional organisations formally recognise the principles enshrined in the UN Charter, but it is also unclear when the use of force is subject to the authorisation by the Security Council, apart the case of self-defence under Article 51. Another possible negative outcome could be the potential contraposition of IROs in case of conflicting security interests, with a much higher risk for international peace and security.[112] This is why it might be relevant that IROs and the UN clarify the terms of their co-operation and functions in more explicit ways when dealing with the use of force.

International law has a fundamental role to provide the basic standards for the security of relations among actors of the international community. Legal rules are mainly defined for the peaceful coexistence and co-operation of all members of the

---

111 See UNSC, Presidential Statement, UN Doc. SC/8984, 28 March 2007; UN, SC, *Report of the Secretary-General on the relationship between the United Nations and regional organizations, in particular the African Union, in the maintenance of international peace and security*, note 93 above.

112 The AU has called on the UN Security Council to suspend the International Criminal Court's indictment of Sudanese President Omar Hassan al-Bashir for Darfur war crimes, after the UN Security Council referred the matter to the ICC through resolution 1593 (2005). AU, Peace and Security Council, Communiqué, 142nd meeting, PSC/MIN/Comm (CXLII) 21 July 2008.

international community. Therefore, the definition of threats to international security through the process of consultation conducted by international organisations can be welcomed as a means of interpretation of international legal terms. IROs also may play a relevant role in the assessment of international actions either by states or by international organisations, such as the UN. In the process of clarification and identification of new threats, IOs should properly address the legal implications of this evolution and clarify the limits of international action. The role of regional human rights bodies and courts could provide a legal control over the protection of fundamental rights in dealing with international security issues. If institutional bodies within IROs do not make clear their limits, national and international judicial bodies would be left to clarify the legal boundaries of their actions under international law. To leave gaps and grey zones in the international legal system could be misused by some international actors, with the risk of creating more insecurity in the long term and in the system of international relations for the international community than some of the identified threats.

Part II

Approaching Security through the Application of International Humanitarian Law: A Review of Normative Gaps

Chapter 3

General Principles of International Humanitarian and Human Rights Law: A Tool to Overcome the War-and-Peace Divide in International Law

Ulf Häußler[*]

I. Preliminary Remarks & Introduction

In recent years, the international law discourse has experienced a renaissance of the notion of 'normative gaps', that is, the well-known argument that certain situations are not covered by the existing rules – those codified as well as those developed in pertinent jurisprudence. Claiming the existence of a normative gap implies that a new rule is needed. Lawyers are used to both making such claims and making proposals as to the content of the desired new rule. However, as a matter of legal policy, in international law they frequently rely on the traditional presumption in favour of sovereignty. In doing so they allege that the 'normative gap' can be filled by a state's sovereign government action without there being any pertinent principles and rules of international law. As this line of argument may create the impression that there is a legal vacuum it is in conflict with the usual characteristic of a legal order to be comprehensive. Accordingly, claims that a normative gap exists may cause uncomfortable feelings because they reflect the assertion, made by some states, that they still possess certain exclusive sovereign prerogatives vis-à-vis other states in their international relations – whose exercise is frequently perceived as an expression of unilateralism. The conduct of international organisations and the activities of non-governmental actors[1] are not immune against the occurrence of 'normative gaps', either.

---

* At the time of writing, the author was the Legal Advisor, Joint Command Special Operations (Germany). The views expressed do not necessarily correspond with the official position of the German Federal Government, the Federal Ministry of Defense, or the German Armed Forces.

1 It seems to be more appropriate to speak of non-governmental rather than non-state actors if only because, strictly speaking, international organisations are non-state actors, also.

Cecilia M. Bailliet (ed.), Security: A Multidisciplinary Normative Approach.
© *2009 Koninklijke Brill NV. Printed in The Netherlands.* ISBN *978 90 04 17296 8. pp. 49–90.*

Many 'normative gaps' have been invoked with respect to the principles and rules of international law governing the use of force. This is in part due to the fact that the traditional categories of war and peace are no longer paradigmatic in the manner they used to be in classical international law. Accordingly, unclarities have emerged both concerning the question of whether the use of force is lawful or (at least) legitimate in certain circumstances, and concerning the question what force may actually be used in the course of a lawful or legitimate operation. These unclarities are capable of being exploited in a manner running counter to the values fundamental to the existing rules or the prevailing policy perception of what the future rules should be. Buzzwords such as robust peace missions, international terrorism, targeted killings, the Proliferation Security Initiative (PSI), UN sanctions against individuals, dual use nuclear facilities, Guantánamo Bay, Abu Ghraib, private security contractors, "ISAF complicity in Afghan torture", child soldiers, voluntary and involuntary human shields, and asymmetric and terrorist warfare indicate the broad range and complexity of the challenges involved. On that basis, participants in any discourse concerning normative gaps and associated legal vacuums must bear in mind that they participate in a process of refining and developing the international law in force, and that they assume, whether or not they admit it, whether or not they possess the necessary capabilities and legitimacy, an active, and avantgardist, role in that process.

This chapter aims to contribute to the critical reflections of the avantgarde refining and developing international law. To that end, it will first analyse and categorise the variety of normative gaps identifiable in relation to the maintenance or restoration of international peace and security in contemporary international law. Second, it will discuss the relationship between normative gaps and the war-and-peace divide. Then, third, it will assess the effect of new approaches to maintaining and/or restoring international peace and security on the growth or shrinking of normative gaps. The fourth section of this chapter is dedicated to an analysis of the key mechanism that has evolved in this field, namely, transitional authority to maintain and restore international peace and security. Finally, section five will demonstrate how transitional authority can be prevented from degenerating to the level of arbitrary power-brokering: that is, by way of requiring that its exercise respect and ensure general principles of international humanitarian and human rights law in such a manner as strikes an appropriate balance between the international community's shared interest that international peace and security be ensured or, if necessary, enforced, and the shared interest of all affected individuals that they benefit from rather than become victims of this effort.

II. Developing Categories of Normative Gaps in International Law

Lawyers are used to dealing with normative gaps because that is what they do on a frequent basis. Some of them even watch out for normative gaps because identifying and operationalising them is a fairly effective method of legal reasoning. It facilitates tailoring legal rules to individual cases involving situations beyond the range of precedent, using such methods as analogy, induction, and deduction. This specific capability, however, is also the source of one inherent danger of dealing with normative gaps: once identified, they are prone to be used in unconventional ways, sometimes even with a view to deliberately exploiting them (though exploitation oftentimes occurs in a camouflaged manner). This phenomenon is even more likely to occur in international law for two reasons. On the one hand, the principle of non-intervention might tempt certain actors to try and convert (on the basis of a claim of state sovereignty or an international organisation's implied powers) such normative gaps as they happen to identify into areas removed from any accountability towards, or control by, the international community. On the other hand, the sometimes fragmentary character of codifications and case-law, and the limited nature of judicial enforcement of the law in force have repeatedly tempted certain actors to draw as many benefits as possible from situations to which the arm of the law does not reach out with the same strength as with respect to a stable state's domestic affairs.

Normative gaps can occur in relation to the actions of states and international organisations, and the activities of non-governmental actors. Nevertheless, this chapter suggests that, for the purposes of a systematic analysis, normative gaps should preferably be categorised with a view to their exploitability and associated effects on the international legal order. This chapter will discuss normative gaps associated with:

- The broader range of multilateralism for which no comprehensive set of rules exists in international law;
- Different obligations under, and/or interpretations of, existing international law; and
- The mismatch of obligations and related enforcement mechanisms.

A. *Normative Gaps Associated with Extended Multilateralism*

In recent years, multilateralism in the field of the maintenance and restoration of international peace and security has frequently taken the shape of robust peacekeeping and comprehensive peace-building. Both phenomena require a different role of international organisations involving, in particular, the exercise of transitional authority. The scope of transitional authority covers means and measures pertaining to the full range of public authority, viz. ranging from the use of force to institution-building, if state-building. There is no uniform legal basis for the exercise of transitional authority by international organisations and its subsidiary organs or equivalent bodies; both non-consensual and consensual legal acts of different character – in particular international agreements and secondary legislation of international organisations – are an option. Finally, notwithstanding the broad range of authority entrusted in peace missions responsible for robust peacekeeping and/or comprehensive peace-building it is as of yet unclear what the position of these missions towards the armed conflict they are supposed to bring to an end or any other armed conflict on-going in an area of operations might be. Contending that their actions transcend the classical concept of what parties to an armed conflict, occupation regimes, or national governments are usually doing only highlights the openness of related questions; it does not provide an answer. As a result, normative gaps associated with extended mutilateralism trigger, on the one hand, expectations concerning the question what action should be taken multilaterally[2] and, on the other hand, the search for minimum standards concerning the limits of such action warranted from a legal perspective.

2 From that perspective, the efforts to develop the responsibility to protect as a source of

B. *Normative Gaps Associated with Different Legal Obligations*

No two states or international organisations have identical obligations under international law; the position of non-governmental actors is even less clear. The reasons for this diversity in obligations under international law are manifold; some of them are inherent in legal principles and rules, others relate to the factual situations to which the law might or might not be applicable.

i. Normative Gaps Inherent in Legal Principles and Rules

Different positions concerning the applicability, and interpretation and application of existing legal principles and rules are abundant. Many states are not parties to even such international agreements as may be considered fundamental to the international legal order. Under the *res inter alios acta* principle, they need not abide by the rules contained in such agreements in their capacity as international treaty law. However, even if parties to the same international agreement, states might interpret its terms differently; the same is true with respect to obligations stemming from customary international law or rooted in general principles of international law. The legal position of international organisations poses an even bigger challenge. Many international agreements are open to signature by states only; this is particularly true for treaties in the fields of international humanitarian and human rights law. Not being parties to much international treaty law, international organisations will be more likely to have obligations stemming from custom or rooted in general principles; yet few cases have been adjudicated from which related guidance can be derived. Finally, defining the obligations of non-governmental actors under international law is yet more difficult. To bind on non-governmental actors, the sources of international law from which obligations shall be derived must be self-executing and directly applicable. Hitherto, only few rules of universal application related to the maintenance and restoration of international peace and security have been considered elevated to that status. Most of them pertain to international humanitarian law; by way of contrast, international human rights law lacks, as a matter of principle, similar direct horizontal applicability (viz. applicability in legal relationships between subjects whose legal personality derives from private law).

Moreover, the conduct of some non-governmental actors does not fit in existing sets of rules and/or is based on different premises than those underlying these rules. Key examples comprise international terrorist groups and their members, non-governmental armed groups which do not qualify as legitimate liberation movements

---

guidance for decision-making in the United Nations Security Council is a response to a normative gap. Namely, the normative gap associated with the fact that the Security Council has chosen to intervene in some cases, that it has abstained from intervening in others, and that it has intervened with rather different robustness in rather similar situations. Nothing has unveiled this normative gap, which had been growing ever since the international community's failure to prevent the genocide in Rwanda and the acts of genocide in Srebrenica, more clearly than Operation Allied Force, NATO's intervention aimed at preventing the ethnic cleansing of Kosovo in 1999.

and their members, and certain private security contractors and their personnel, all of whom might or might not be taking a direct part in hostilities. It is interesting to note that non-governmental armed groups (in particular international terrorist groups) show a certain disinterest in, or reluctance to rely on, international humanitarian law by way of e.g. claiming status – the claim typically made by liberation movements in the context of de-colonisation and eventually endorsed by Article 1(4) of GP I.

Turning now to international organisations, attention has already been drawn to their inability to become parties to many relevant international treaties. It does not make a difference if some, or all, of their member states are parties to a particular treaty. The tempting theorem that they may have succeeded in their members' treaty obligations has never been supported by practice. Practice demonstrates (as paradigmatically indicated by the adoption of the United Nations Secretary-General's Bulletin on the "Observance by United Nations forces of international law[3]") that the obligations of international organisations under international law are genuine in nature and reinforce the independence of their legal personality. As a result, international organisations may decide to adopt uniform rules governing their subsidiary organs' action or chose an ad-hoc approach instead; and they may make such rules transparent or withhold them from access by the general public.[4]

Finally, normative gaps associated with the conduct of states may be the consequence both of reluctance to subscribe to new rules – in particular those contained in newly adopted codifications[5] – and of efforts initiated by lobby groups to extend the scope of application of existing rules to conduct hitherto not covered by them. Assessing the obligations of states does not get easier if rescue is sought in customary international law as highlighted by the fact that states have not applauded in unison when the International Committee of the Red Cross released its study on the

---

3 UN document SG/SGB/1999/13 dated 06 August 1999.

4 For example, NATO by and large confines its public statements concerning the legal framework of its operations to highlighting that it considers NATO forces under its political direction and control bound to comply with the spirit of relevant international humanitarian law. See the reference to and explanation of Standardization Agreement (STANAG) No. 2449 "Training in the Law of Armed Conflict" dated 29 March 2004 "NATO/PfP Unclassified" in my book *Ensuring and Enforcing Human Security* (2007), at 73 (footnote 230).

5 For instance, related normative gaps may arise from the fact that the obligations under GP I are broader in scope than their counterpart under GCs III & IV both with respect to the situations covered and the conduct of hostilities and associated actions, and that GP II obligations are more detailed than those deriving from common Article 3 of GCs I–IV. Abstention from e.g. the Genocide Convention, the Convention on the Prohibition of the Development, Production, Stockpiling and Use of Chemical Weapons and on their Destruction (Chemical Weapons Convention, 1993), the Convention on the Prohibition of the Use, Stockpiling, Production and Transfer of Anti-Personnel Mines and on their Destruction (1997), the newly signed Convention on Cluster Munitions (2008), and certain Protocols to the Convention on Prohibitions or Restrictions on the Use of Certain Conventional Weapons Which May Be Deemed to Be Excessively Injurious or to Have Indiscriminate Effects (1980) results likewise in different obligations under international treaty law and hence helps grow normative gaps.

existing rules of customary international humanitarian law.[6] There is no need to say that existing international treaty law is not spared from dispute concerning its scope of applicability and actual interpretation and application. The controversy concerning the extraterritorial application of international and regional human rights treaties is the key example of this phenomenon.

ii. Normative Gaps Related to Factual Situations

Factual factors capable of contributing to the emergence of normative gaps comprise the occurrence of new policies and technologies not covered by existing sets of rules, and the complexity of situations characterised by a melange of multiple armed conflicts and the presence of actors exercising transitional authority without being party to either any, or at least all of these armed conflicts.

As regards new policies and technologies, both 'zero casualty warfare'[7] and asymmetric warfare involve major challenges for the maintenance or restoration of international peace and security. Zero casualty warfare benefits from, *inter alia*, new Command Information Systems (CIS) technology which permits better access to the battlefield, new Electronic Countermeasures (ECM) technology which permits better access to adversary CIS, and new data management technology which permits better processing of information concerning adversary personnel, assets, and Tactics, Techniques and Procedures (TTPs). International humanitarian law as it stands is not concerned with any related limitations. Asymmetric strategies, oftentimes resorted to by non-governmental armed groups which do not qualify as legitimate liberation movements, amount to a fourth generation of warfare which deliberately ignores certain existing rules – like e.g. the principle of distinction – which were devised with the third generation of warfare in mind.

Complex factual situations involve similarly huge challenges for the maintenance or restoration of international peace and security. Without prejudice to the details pertaining to theatres like e.g. Afghanistan, Somalia, the Democratic Republic of the Congo, Iraq, or the occupied Palestinian territories, one and the same geographical area can be affected by multiple conflicts some of which have an international nature while others have a non-international nature, some are within the ambit of a United

6 The Initial response of U.S. to ICRC study on Customary International Humanitarian Law with Illustrative Comments dated 03 November 2006 – available at http://www.state.gov/s/l/2006/98860.htm (visited 11 August 2008) to Jean-Marie Henckaerts & Louise Doswald-Beck (eds), *Customary International Humanitarian Law*, Volume 1, Rules (2005); is but one example.

7 The notion of 'zero casualty warfare' refers to the attitude of military commanders that they will not expose their subordinates to unnecessary risks, attitude which tends to increase the danger to civilians. However, although an aim that experts in the law of armed conflict would heartily endorse, it is impossible to fight a war with neither own nor civilian casualties. Reducing casualties to the maximum extent that the exigencies of armed conflict will allow is contingent on factors like due target verification including the exercise of such care as reasonable in the circumstances, especially in light of the time available for making a decision. Cf. APV Rogers, Zero-casualty Warfare, in *International Review of the Red Cross* No. 837, at 165–181 (2000).

Nations Security Council Resolution while others are not, and the actors involved in these conflicts may comprise one or more non-governmental armed groups (including, as the case may be, international terrorist movements and/or private security contractors), one or more state governments, and one or more international organisations. Oftentimes, there is no true consensus concerning the legal nature of the situation in theater, and the obligations resting on the various actors are similarly controversial.

It is hardly surprising that all these unclarities provide fertile ground for the growth of various normative gaps.

C. *Normative Gaps Tantamount to Enforcement Gaps*

The international community has dealt with a lack of mechanisms for enforcing obligations under international law in a variety of cases. World War II was followed by judicial enforcement of international humanitarian law, yet the example set by the International Military Tribunals at Nuremberg and Tokyo was not followed suit by the international penal tribunal envisaged by Article VI of the Genocide Convention. As a result, prior to the establishment of the ICTY and ICTR, the ICC, the SC-SL, and the Extraordinary Chambers in Cambodia there was no international judiciary which had jurisdiction over genocide, crimes against humanity, and war crimes. The existence of the *ad hoc* tribunals and the referral of the situation in the Darfur province of the Sudanese Islamic Republic since 01 July 2002 to the Prosecutor of the International Criminal Court (UNSCR 1593 (2005)) illustrate that the adoption of the ICC Statute has not entirely closed that normative gap. In addition, a similar normative gap might be considered to exist with respect to human rights because no international judicial enforcement body for gross violations of human rights amounting to serious crimes exists.[8] Thus far, only such human rights violations as have occurred during armed conflict and come within the ambit of genocide, crimes against humanity, and war crimes, have been adjudicated.[9]

Apart from enforcement gaps associated with genocide, crimes against humanity, and war crimes, and (maybe) gross violations of human rights unrelated to armed conflict, there might also be an institutional deficit resulting from the absence of review bodies for e.g. operational detentions conducted by international peace missions entrusted with transitional authority and claims cases arising from the conduct of such missions.[10] Moreover, the practice of international organisations, in

8 See UN GA Resolution 60/147 entitled "Basic Principles and Guidelines on the Right to a Remedy and Reparation for Victims of Gross Violations of International Human Rights Law and Serious Violations of International Humanitarian Law" (21 March 2006).

9 Arguably, certain newly developed international crimes like e.g. the criminalisation of certain cases of sexual violence as both crimes against humanity and war crimes – Articles 7(1)(g) and 8(2)(b)(xxii)/(2)(e)(vi) of the ICC Statute – build upon jurisprudence which sought to close a normative gap tantamount to an enforcement gap concerning particularly heinous violations of human rights committed in the course of conduct of hostilities as part of a plan or policy or on a large scale.

10 See my paper 'Regional Human Rights vs. International Peace Missions: Lessons Learned from Kosovo', in *Journal of International Law of Peace and Armed Conflict* 2007, 238

particular the United Nations, might be tantamount to nourishing normative gaps, namely those concerning political enforcement of legal obligations, because their responses to serious crises involving threats to international peace and security including human security of individuals prone to be victimised should the threats materialise, are arbitrary and insufficient.

III. Normative Gaps and the War-and-Peace Divide

The war-and-peace divide is a remnant of classical international law which continues to influence the perception of many basic co-ordinates of the international legal order, the interpretation and application of international law, and the analysis of the practice of states and international organisations. However, international legal history has revealed that the war-and-peace divide is dysfunctional; namely that it aggravates the exploitability of normative gaps and that it is a key facilitator of the adverse effects generated by normative gaps in relation to the legal aspects of the use of force. Accordingly, the current international legal order has been devised in order to overcome the war-and-peace divide. Yet, its interpretation and application has been breathing much of the classical spirit since its inception after World War II.

As a doctrinal approach, the war-and-peace divide used to enable states to distinguish between the legal orders applicable on the diplomatic floor and on the battlefield, respectively. It also enabled states to distinguish (hitherto during war and now during all kinds of international armed conflict) between areas under their effective control coming under (military or civil) occupation government and areas governed in the usual constitutional fashion (though subject to such adjustments as warranted by war-time emergency). However, the classical war-and-peace divide is in itself no longer congruent with the foundations of international law. The UN Charter contains, in its preamble, the pledge of all "peace-loving states" (Article 4 of the UN Charter) "to save succeeding generations from the scourge of war". In the same vein, the prohibition of the threat or use of force by virtue of Article 2(4) of the UN Charter and equivalent customary international law[11] aims at abolishing international armed conflict. Accordingly, the war-and-peace divide has lost much of its significance as a doctrinal means to facilitate the determination of applicable law in the contemporary international legal order. The responses to violations of the prohibition of the threat or use of force confirm this assessment: they rely on different criteria than those derived from the war-and-peace divide. They envisage action by the international community not only to restore international peace and security in cases of a breach of the peace, an act of aggression, or if an armed attack has occurred, but also with

---

at 243 sq. Note that operational detentions do not only occur in NATO peacekeeping theatres but also, as some sources indicate, e.g. in the framework of MONUC. The European Court of Justice's judgment of 03 September 2008 in *Kadi* – Joined Cases C-402/05 P and C-415/05 P – indicates that no similar institutional deficit exists within the EU.

11 In the *Nicaragua* case, the International Court of Justice has characterised the prohibition of the threat and use of force in international relations as both *jus cogens* and customary international law (judgment of 27 June 1986 – Case *Concerning Military and Paramilitary Activities in and Against Nicaragua* – at paras 188–190).

respect to any threat of the peace, that is, to maintain international peace and security. Chapters VI and VII of the UN Charter demonstrate beyond ambiguity that from the Charter's perspective, the war-and-peace divide is no longer the starting point of legal analysis: neither Chapter is based upon an implied premise that would render its application contingent on an assessment of whether the situation fits within one of the classical categories of war and peace.[12] Article 33 of the UN Charter does not preclude measures aimed at the stabilisation of an endangered, or the conclusion of a, cease-fire or armistice – agreements pertaining to the state of war. Rather, the obligation of the parties to as dispute to "seek a solution by … peaceful means" under the Charter "continues to exist even after armed activities have begun between them".[13] In a similar manner, Article 39 of the UN Charter is not averse to a determination of a threat to the peace while no declaration of war has been issued and no armed attack has occurred either, followed by an authorisation of the use of force under Article 42 of the UN Charter on the basis of an assessment that "measures not involving the use of armed force" (as per by Article 41 of the UN Charter) "would be inadequate or have proved to be inadequate". This interpretation is supported by the position that the criteria "threat to the peace or breach of the peace" do not "presuppose an actual or potential violation of international law".[14]

The contemporary international legal order has overcome the war-and-peace divide for good reasons. Both as a doctrinal concept and as an approach guiding state practice it had (in awkward alliance with other doctrinal concepts of the classical era) left individuals exposed to arbitrary exercise of power in a zone removed from the ambit, or shielded against the effective application and enforcement of international law. In that respect, the effects of World War II on the international legal order are remarkably different from those of World War I. Both World Wars had been fought under the same principles and rules concerning the conduct of hostilities on land yet while World War I witnessed a comparably small ratio of approximately 10 % civilians among its dead, World War II reversed the civil-military ratio, causing a civilian death toll of approximately 90 %. During World War I, civilians were, by and large, effectively banned from the scenes of combat; World War II brought the battlefield into civilian quarters in almost all its theaters. At first sight, the civilian death toll of World War I confirmed the approach demonstrated by the sporadic nature of the rules concerning the protection to civilians and their rights in Section II on "Hostilities" of the 1907 Hague Regulations, viz. that the realities of war still reflected, as proclaimed by the preamble of the St. Petersberg Declaration (1868), the principle "[t]hat the only legitimate object which States should endeavour to accomplish

12 Chapter VI of the UN Charter is triggered in the case of "any dispute, the continuance of which is likely to endanger the maintenance of international peace and security" (Article 33 of the UN Charter), Chapter VII of the UN Charter may be invoked if the Security Council determines "the existence of any threat to the peace, breach of the peace, or act of aggression" (Article 39 of the UN Charter).

13 Christian Tomuschat, in Simma (ed.), *Charter of the United Nations*, 2 ed (2003), Article 33 at para 14.

14 Jochen Abr. Frowein & Nico Krisch, in Simma (ed.), *Charter of the United Nations*, 2 ed (2003), Article 39 at para 9.

during war is to weaken the military forces of the enemy".[15] Accordingly, the war-and-peace divide easily survived World War I; the legal terminology representing it as a thought model is omnipresent in the Covenant of the League of Nations and many other important legal instruments agreed upon in the 1920s.

The devastating effects of the awkward alliance formed by the war-and-peace divide, the reluctance to protect the rights of the human person in peace and war, and the principle of non-intervention in domestic jurisdiction were yet to come. While the lack of protection of a state's own nationals was reconcilable with the approach towards international law prevailing at the time, the side-effects of the war-and-peace divide jointly with the principle of non-intervention which enabled states to deprive, during armed conflict, foreign nationals of the minimum standards under the law of occupation and the rules governing the status of foreigners, respectively, were not acceptable.[16] World War II practice has demonstrated that states were nevertheless ready to exploit existing enforcement gaps and generate new normative gaps watering down their substantial obligations (by way of e.g. forcing civilians, both own and foreign nationals, into statelessness, or by way of declaring entire enemy populations hostile) in the intent to enable themselves to persecute individuals on a large scale up to and including (*inter alia*) the wars of annihilation against South East Asian and Eastern European civilian populations and German and Japanese cities, ethnic cleansings (including after the closure of hostilities), and, at its worst, the genocide perpetrated on the Jews of Europe. As a "total war" inflicted upon the international community by totalitarian regimes, World War II had brought to light the ugly effects that the synergy between the war-and-peace divide, the reluctance to protect rights of the human person in international law, and the principle of non-intervention in domestic jurisdiction could possibly generate.

Apart from having been discredited by the events of World War II, the war-and-peace divide has proved disconnected from practical realities in most crises and conflicts since. It is increasingly hard to assess the true legal nature of contemporary conflicts. If, accordingly, the war-and-peace divide fails to provide substantial guidance concerning the nature of a conflict situation it is *a fortiori* incapable of assisting in determining the legal order governing both the conduct of hostilities and the exercise of transitional authority in conflict theaters. This assumption is supported by the recent practice of states and international organisations with respect to conflict and

---

15 It is beyond the scope of this chapter to discuss what lessons learned from colonial warfare, including the 1899–1902 Anglo-Boer War (aka the South African War) and the 1904–1907 Herero War could (and should) have made the policy-makers of the classical era reconsider their approach. The fact is that it never happened.

16 Prior to the adoption of the provisions concerning the protection of foreign nationals in the territory of a party to a conflict (Articles 35–46 of GC IV), "enemy aliens" could only rely on the rules governing the status of foreigners; the Hague Regulations do not address this issue. The state of war did not render irrelevant the rules governing the status of foreigners because their essence is an integral part of the "protection and the rule of the principles of the law of nations, as they result from the usages established among civilized peoples, from the laws of humanity, and the dictates of the public conscience" (see the preamble of Hague Convention IV Respecting the Laws and Customs of War on Land (1907)).

crisis management. Where the United Nations Security Council determined that the situation in a state or particular area poses a threat to international peace and security it has – provided the necessary political will and availability of capabilities – tailored its response so as to counter the threat effectively. As a result, the assessment of the threat rather than the legal nature of the situation in which the threat has grown is the key factor for determining what measures are considered adequate for maintaining or restoring international peace and security. The resulting threat-based and mission-tailored mandates do not reflect the categorisations deriving from the war-and-peace divide. They combine an authorisation of the use of force and a genuine, mission-specific set of rules governing the actual use of force, that is, operational planning and execution of operations.[17] Where threats are similar, mandates are also similar regardless of whether the situations at issue are governed by e.g. an (at the time) underinclusive peace treaty or a cease-fire agreement.[18] As a result, contemporary mandates demonstrate more pragmatism than the war-and-peace divide could ever digest. Accordingly, the international community is moving away from the war-and-peace divide's undesired effects. The criterion established by the UN Charter instead, the notion of threat to international peace and security, permits more flexible decision-making with respect to both the question of whether the use of force should be authorised and the question to what principles and rules it should be subject.

IV. Security: New National and International Approaches

The end of the Cold War has not brought as much of a peace dividend to the international community as expected; rather it has unveiled just how troubled and insecure many areas in the world are. Many of these troubles and insecurities were known yet few determined efforts were made to resolve them due to the ideological deadlock prevailing at the time. However, driven *inter alia* by the euphoria caused by the downfall of many a communist dictatorship, the United Nations, NATO, the EU, ECOWAS, the AU (previously the OAU), and many individual states have started to devise an increasingly proactive approach towards challenges to international peace and security. (By way of contrast, the new ASEAN Treaty adopted in 2007 is fairly

17 To that end, the Security Council defines the responsibilities and tasks of an international peace mission entrusted with transitional authority entailing the use of force, or the purposes for which force may be used.

18 The mandates of IFOR (later succeeded by SFOR and still later by NHQ Sarajevo and EUFOR ALTHEA) in Bosnia and Herzegovina and KFOR in Kosovo are pretty similar although in Bosnia and Herzegovina formal peace had been restored between the major belligerents (yet not with regard to the variety of non-governmental armed groups which were not parties to the Dayton Agreement) whereas in Kosovo the Military-Technical Agreement between the International Security Force ("KFOR") and the Governments of the Federal Republic of Yugoslavia and the Republic of Serbia of 9 June 1999 had established no more than a cease-fire – which was not even binding upon the Kosovo Liberation Army whose future was only determined by the Undertaking of Demilitarization and Transformation of the UCK concluded between COMKFOR and the Commander of the UCK of 21 June 1999. NATO practice is based on the same approach; the organisation has adopted one single strategic OPLAN for both its Balkans missions.

more restrictive.) As a key result, the notion of "international security" is on the move – it might in fact have become a separate heading for action taken in particular by the UN Security Council.[19]

The broader understanding of the concept of international security relies on the premise that there are more situations requiring a response involving an authorisation of the use of force than hitherto identified. However, it is unlikely that the said premise implies a need for an increasingly use of force-driven approach to be taken by states. As observed by the High-level Panel on Threats, Challenges and Change, their record can hardly be said to be force-averse.[20] Moreover, contemporary state practice demonstrates that certain remnants of the pre-World War II legal order concerning the *jus ad bellum* and those rooted in the combinative effect of the war-and-peace divide and the principle of non-intervention must yet be removed.[21]

At the same time, however, the panel's observations indicate that to be effective the UN Charter's approach towards banning the use of force depends on more than enhanced adherence by states. Prudent exercise by the Security Council of its powers is equally important. However, the Security Council's increasing preparedness to use the legal framework designed to overcome the war-and-peace divide and to prevent the adverse effects of related normative gaps and associated legal vacuums is not an insurance policy against normative gaps and associated legal vacuums. Rather, the creativeness demonstrated both by the Security Council in adopting mandates for the maintenance and/or restoration of international peace and security and by states and international organisations in their implementation or the adoption of other action serving an equivalent purpose, have created new normative gaps. Part of this surprising consequence derives from the fact that much of the fast-evolving post-Cold War practice both within and outside the variety of international organisations dedicated to the maintenance or restoration of international peace and security sought to reconcile the irreconcilable: more and stronger multilateralism on the one hand and determined, powerful plurilateralism[22] on the other hand.

---

19 See my paper 'Enforcing the Rule of Law: Military Contributions to Comprehensive Security', in: 8 *New Zealand Armed Forces Law Review* (2008) pp. 47–71.

20 As observed the High-level Panel on Threats, Challenges and Change, state practice involves too many rather than too few cases where force was used: –

> For the first 44 years of the United Nations, Member States often violated these rules and used military force literally hundreds of times, with a paralysed Security Council passing very few Chapter VII resolutions and Article 51 only rarely providing credible cover.
> UN document A/59/595 at para 186.

21 The panel has noted that: –

> in seeking to apply the express language of the Charter, three particularly difficult questions arise in practice: first, when a State claims the right to strike preventively, in self-defence, in response to a threat which is not imminent; secondly, when a State appears to be posing an external threat, actual or potential, to other States or people outside its borders, but there is disagreement in the Security Council as to what to do about it; and thirdly, where the threat is primarily internal, to a State's own people.
> UN document A/59/595 at para 187.

22 In my view it is wrong to characterise e.g. Operation Iraqi Freedom as a unilateral (scilicet

Many aspects of this development were in fact more likely to grow rather than shrink normative gaps. This is because they involve the creation of new legal bases for the exercise of public authority, new practical approaches towards exercising such authority, and the need to interpret and apply, for the first time, various newly adopted law-making international treaties. There are landmark changes in the development of robust peace missions, the concept of human security and the responsibility to protect, new conflict realities such as the fighting against "combat rebels"[23] under the headings of counter-insurgency and counter-terrorism,[24] new tactical realities of "three-block war", outsourcing of combat-related activities to private security contractors, increasing numbers of child soldiers in some theaters of war, and the creation of an international criminal judiciary. At the same time, the written part of the international legal order has undergone significant changes.[25] Moreover, the interpretation of certain treaty regimes adds such dynamism to them as their framers may never have envisaged. In particular, as far as the interpretation and application of existing international human rights treaty law is concerned, two big themes have been attracting the interest (and in some cases activism) of justices and members of human rights treaty bodies for more than a decade now. They are namely the extraterritorial application of human rights treaties to the conduct of states in general and their security sector agencies (including the armed forces) in particular, and the applicability of human rights treaties to the conduct of international organisations which are not parties thereto, while some or all of their members are. By contrast, many jurisprudential innovations in the field of international humanitarian law can be traced back to policy decisions embodied in the ICTY and ICTR Statutes.

Most of these new developments breathe a spirit of enhanced humanitarianism. It should not be surprising that this spirit does not only purport to eradicate a variety of practices from the repertoire of those waging armed conflict. It also generates an expectation that the international community steps in with preventive and, should the need arise, repressive measures against those failing to abide by the new principles

---

U.S. only) operation given the participation of 46 states. Cf. Center for Law and Military Operations (CLAMO), Legal Lessons Learned From Afghanistan and Iraq, Vol. I, at 21 including n. 102.

23 This phrase relates to the "membership approach" concerning the question of when individuals not belonging to legitimate armed forces take a direct part in hostilities. As an alternative to the membership approach, the question of whether an individual participates directly in hostilities is assessed on the basis of individual fighting situations.

24 For instance, one major question related to the fight against Al Qaeda terrorism is whether its nature is that of a series of one-incident wars or a series of battles in a long war.

25 Apart from the adoption of the law-making treaties referred to earlier (supra footnote 5), the entry into force of the Protocols Additional to the 1949 Geneva Conventions, signed on 8 June 1977 for many European states in the late 1980s and early 1990s (cf. my book Ensuring and Enforcing Human Security (2007), at 16) and the adoption of new treaty law in the fields of international humanitarian and human rights law, namely the Optional Protocol on the involvement of children in armed conflict and the International Convention for the Protection of All Persons from Enforced Disappearance, all have a direct impact on the exercise of public authority in the field of maintenance and/or restoration of international peace and security.

and rules. As a result, it is fairly likely that the Security Council will be expected to play its new role as an active provider rather than a moderator of international peace and security. Doing so will most probably involve an increasing number of cases where transitional authority is bestowed upon international peace missions.

V. Transitional Authority to Maintain and Restore International Peace and Security

Transitional authority is authority entrusted in an entity not established by the constitution of a state which this said entity may exercise vis-à-vis governance institutions and individuals (up to and including the general public) in a specified area, and for a not open-ended period of time. Whether an entity is called a transitional authority (like e.g. UNTAC[26] and UNTAET[27]), a Transition Assistance Group[28] or a peacekeeping force[29] is immaterial to the nature of its actual authority.

The concept of transitional authority is not static. Neither is it linked to a particular kind of entity nor does it purport a specific scope of authority. The common denominator of different examples of transitional authority is its similarity to supranational authority. Yet, the entities possessing transitional authority are usually less institutionalised than those possessing supranational authority. Further, transitional authority as such is, unlike supranational authority, not meant to prevail for an indefinite period of time. The key similarity between transitional authority and supranational authority lies within the fact that it extends over governance institutions and individuals. Moreover, it stems from a source external to the constitutional law which governs these institutions and individuals domestically. Accordingly, an act conferring transitional authority limits the sovereign rights of the state affected. However, notwithstanding this similarity, the exercise of transitional authority does not transform the entity exercising it (or the legal person to whom its acts are attributable under international law) into a supranational entity, organisation or legal person.

The flexible nature of the concept of transitional authority is also reflected by the broad variety of acts conferring transitional authority. Entities entrusted with

26 The United Nations Transitional Authority in Cambodia (1992–1993) was established pursuant to UNSCR 745 (1992) to ensure the implementation of the Agreements on a Comprehensive Political Settlement of the Cambodia Conflict of 23 October 1991. See also the Report of the Secretary-General on Cambodia dated 19 February 1992 (UN document S/23613).

27 The United Nations Transitional Authority in East Timor (UNTAET) was established on 25 October 1999 in accordance with UNSCR 1272 (1999).

28 The United Nations Transition Assistance Group (UNTAG) was established by UNSCR 435 (1978) for the task of supervising and controlling free elections in Namibia. See also UNSCRs 629 and 632 (1989) and UN document S/20412 of 23 January 1989.

29 In my view, robust peacekeeping forces may use force (beyond self-defence) and other means or measures of coercion for the purpose defined by their mandate and as long as their mandate extends *ratione temporis* are entrusted with transitional authority to do so. The fact that this authority may be limited to matters of security and the security sector is without prejudice to its nature as transitional authority. For a different view see Marten Zwanenberg's review of my book *Ensuring and Enforcing Human Security*, in *The Military Law and The Law of War Review* Vol. 48 (2008) p. 477.

transitional authority may be established by an international organisation possessing sufficient powers to do so. This may be according to the organisation's own right,[30] delegated authority,[31] or via an agreement with the state, or states affected.[32] A state,

---

30 To date, the United Nations is the only international organisation which possesses the power to establish an entity – as a subsidiary organ (Article 7(2) of the UN Charter) – and to entrust it with transitional authority – in accordance with Chapter VII of the UN Charter – of its own right.

It remains to be seen whether the AU will use the option, under Articles 7(1) and 4(h) of its Constitutive Act, to decide by two-thirds majority on the exercise of –

> the right of the Union to intervene in a Member State pursuant to a decision of the Assembly in respect of grave circumstances, namely war crimes, genocide and crimes against humanity

(cf. http://www.africa-union.org/root/au/AboutAu/Constitutive_Act_en.htm – visited 08 August 2008). To date, the AU has only approved peace missions in a consensual manner.

31 NATO and the EU, while empowered to establish peace missions as subsidiary organs (or equivalent entities), lack the power to entrust them with transitional authority of their own right, respectively. They may, however, use delegated Chapter VII authority for that purpose if so authorised by the UN Security Council.

32 The following examples demonstrate that such agreement can be expressed in various ways.

At United Nations level, the most important example is UNIFIL. Established as a classical Chapter VI peacekeeping mission, UNIFIL has been entrusted with transitional authority by virtue of UNSCR 1701 (2006). Unlike in the cases of other missions, the Security Council has not invoked Chapter VII of the UN Charter – even though it has determined that the situation in Lebanon poses a threat to international peace and security. As a result, the transitional authority entrusted in UNIFIL is based upon the agreement composed of the consent of the Lebanese Government expressed in its unanimous decision of 07 August 2006 to request the assistance of additional UNIFIL forces (see the preamble of UNSCR 1701 (2006) and the decision approving of this request, of the United Nations embodied in para 11 of UNSCR 1701 (2006)).

NATO has deployed a series of peacekeeping forces entrusted with transitional authority to Macedonia, namely Operations ESSENTIAL HARVEST (22 August – 23 September 2001), AMBER FOX/Task Force FOX (23 September 2001–15 December 2002), and ALLIED HARMONY (16 December 2002 – 31 March 2003). The relevant agreements were composed of requests made by the then Macedonian President Trajkovski and decisions made by the North Atlantic Council approving that forces be deployed as requested. On the initial request see the Statement by the North Atlantic Council dated 20 June 2001 as per NATO Press Release (2001) 093 (available online at: http://www.nato.int/docu/pr/2001/p01-093e.htm). In a similar manner, agreement was reached between Macedonia and the EU, which took over from NATO and deployed EUFOR CONCORDIA (31 March – 15 December 2003).

The AU and ECOWAS (cf. Article 58(2)(f) of the Treaty of ECOWS as implemented by the Protocol relating to the Mechanism for Conflict Prevention, Management, Resolution, Peacekeeping and Security – http://www.iss.co.za/af/RegOrg/unity_to_union/pdfs/ecowas/3ECOWASTreaty.pdf and http://www.iss.co.za/af/regorg/unity_to_union/pdfs/ecowas/ConflictMecha.pdf – both visited 08 August 2008) have also deployed consent-based peacekeeping forces entrusted with transitional authority. As the constituent acts of both organisations require, as a matter of principle, decision-making by consensus, the affirmative vote of the state or states affected are sufficient to express the consent necessary to create an agreement under international law. If the clauses permitting decision-making by two-thirds-majority are applied (see Article 7(1) and 4(h) of the Constitutive Act of the

or a coalition of states, may establish an entity entrusted with transitional authority by, or in accordance with, an international agreement with the state, or states affected, or upon request by the state, or states affected, as endorsed the United Nations Security Council.[33] The UN Security Council may not only delegate authority or endorse an affected state's request but also endorse, by virtue of a Chapter VII resolution, any other agreement if it deems doing so necessary in order to maintain or restore international peace and security. All relevant Chapter VII resolutions afford recognition *erga omnes* to both the entity and the scope of its transitional authority. By way of contrast, in the absence of a Chapter VII authorisation or endorsement, the agreement forming the constituent act of an entity with transitional authority has *inter partes* effects only.

Entities possessing transitional authority may be subsidiary organs of an international organisation or an entity *sui generis* linked to the state, or coalition of states, that has/have established it. The scope of transitional authority is usually defined in the conferring act, and, as the case may be, subsequent acts amending, supplementing, or replacing it, including relevant international agreements. As indicated, the international mandates of entities entrusted with transitional authority frequently attach a definition of responsibilities and tasks to the authorisation to use force, and detail the purposes for which force may be used such as mission accomplishment, ensuring the mission's freedom of movement, protection of the mission's personnel and assets (force protection). Some mandates limit the use of force to self-defence.

The exercise of transitional authority is usually governed by instruments implementing the conferring act such as the Operation Plans (OPLANs) of military peace missions which contain specific guidance concerning the use of force in attached Rules of Engagement (ROE).[34] OPLANs are supplemented by Standing Operating Procedures (SOPs), Commander's Directives, and similar instruments. Unlike the international mandate, none of these instruments has a clearly defined legal nature. In particular, they cannot in and of themselves be perceived as secondary legislation of an international organisation; they are not equivalent in nature to administrative by-laws or directives, either. Frequently, moreover, they lack one key characteristic of legislation, viz. transparency. Classified as they usually are, they are not published in a government gazette or official journal of an international organisation. At the same time, however, they represent a long-standing history of quasi-legislative and

---

African Union and Articles 7 and 9 of the ECOWAS Mechanism for Conflict Prevention, Management, Resolution, Peacekeeping and Security), the consent to those provisions entailed in the ratification of the quoted instruments will suffice.

33 For example, UNSCR 1386 (2001) authorised the establishment of ISAF on the basis of the request for a UN mandate contained in para 3 of Annex I to the Bonn Agreement of 01 December 2001.

34 ROE are defined as:

> Directives issued by competent military authority which specify the circumstances and limitations under which forces will initiate and/or continue combat engagement with other forces encountered.
>
> NATO Glossary of Terms and Definitions – NATO document AAP-6 (2008) at 2-R-10 (definition adopted 01 January 1973).

quasi-judicial powers specific to military operations. Even though these powers are no longer considered unfettered in present days, the notion as such has prevailed. This is indicated, for instance, in the provisions of GC IV acknowledging, and at the same time limiting the powers of an occupying power to amend legislation[35] and engage in the administration of justice.[36] It is also evident in the U.S. Supreme Court's judgment concerning the authority of the President of the United States of America in his capacity as Commander-in-Chief of the U.S. Forces to establish military commissions for the purpose of trying crimes committed in the course of hostilities.[37] As a result, even though different from legislative enactments proper, OPLANs, and in any event such policy decisions approving them as taken by principal organs of an international organisation or, as the case may be with respect to coalition operations, a ministry of defence or cabinet of a state, can be assimilated to legislation from a legal perspective.[38]

If the Security Council confers transitional authority, it usually authorises the use of "all necessary means" or "all necessary measures" to fulfil the mandate.[39] With respect to situations the Security Council has characterised as threatening international peace and security, either authorisation[40] covers the use of the full spectrum of armed force: provided that such use of force can reasonably be characterised as 'necessary'.[41] On that basis, the number and characteristics of legal relationships within which maintaining and restoring international peace and security may justify limita-

35 As demonstrated by *a contrario* analysis of Article 64 of GC IV.

36 Cf. Articles 70–73 of GC IV.

37 The U.S. Supreme Court's judgment of 29 June 2006 – case no. 05–184 – *Hamdan v. Rumsfeld* – 548 U.S. ____ (2006) = 126 S.Ct. 2749 (2006) contains a detailed analysis of the history of the authority to establish military commissions.

38 Cf. my book *Ensuring and Enforcing Human Security* (2007) at 126 discussing the notion of "legal order" with respect to NATO decision-making in matters of operational detention.

39 The authorisation of "all necessary means" or "all necessary measures" is implemented differently at different levels of a command and control structure. The usual decision-making processes at the political-strategic and military-strategic levels involve two key aspects of relevance in the present context. On the one hand, policy-makers and military leaders define the strategic end-state in more detailed terms than the international mandate. On the other hand, they determine what means or measures may become necessary at subordinate levels to reach that end-state. Arguably, as a whole, these aspects reflect a quasi-legislative value judgment as to what can legitimately be considered necessary to maintain and/or restore international peace and security in the theater of operation. – By way of contrast, operational and tactical level military commanders may choose from the options made available to them on the basis of their assessment of the situation in determining what means or measures they deem necessary to achieve a concrete and direct military advantage within an individual field level operation.

40 The phrases are used interchangeably: Christine Gray, *International Law and the Use of Force*, 3 ed (2008) at 264 sq.; cf. my book *Ensuring and Enforcing Human Security* (2007) at 85.

41 Using a means or measure is 'necessary' if its military necessity as per international humanitarian law can be established. In the present context, fulfilling the mandate is the military advantage which must not be excessive if weighed against the expected collateral damage or collateral effects caused by the planned use of a particular means or measure.

tions of rights of the human person has changed. However, unlike in states' domestic legal orders there is less sophistication concerning the legal bases of such limitations in international law. The UN Charter only contains the fairly broad phrase "international peace and security"; related practice is still too topical to be a source of added legal certainty.[42]

VI. Transitional Authority vs. Rights of the Human Person

The foregoing indicates that there is a normative gap concerning the protection of the rights of the human person affected by limitations implemented to maintain or restore international peace and security. Contemporary international law is no longer sympathetic to the concept of sovereign prerogatives; it is not sympathetic to unfettered transitional authority, either. However, albeit supporting the protection of the rights of the human person, limits of transitional authority must reflect the fact that this kind of authority is supposed to cover determined action against violence unleashed by non-governmental armed groups in an unprecedented scale. This is contrary to the long-established consensus that only states, international organisations, and – under GP I – legitimate liberation movements may resort to the use of force, in well defined circumstances and subject to limits defined by law.

A. *Assessing the Challenge*

Contemporary international law considers sovereign prerogatives vis-a-vis other members of the international community the exception rather than the rule, and – given states' sovereign equality – it militates against the idea that prerogatives other than those associated with permanent membership in the Security Council can prevail. The UN Charter has outlawed the hitherto paradigmatic sovereign prerogative to go to war. Many other international treaties seem to confirm the international legal order's dislike of sovereign prerogatives: notably those pertaining to international humanitarian law limit the prerogative to conduct hostilities with no matter what means, measures and methods, and those pertaining to international human rights law limit the prerogative to treat individuals within a state's jurisdiction and on its territory in a manner exposing them to unfettered power. Nevertheless, certain situations have remained beyond the scope of existing treaty law – be it *ratione personae*, *ratione materiae*, *ratione loci*, or *ratione temporis*. This phenomenon occurs in particular where the development of the international legal order has not kept path with, or got disconnected from, evolving practical realities. It may also occur where states and/or international organisations attempt to transform the legal order by way of innovative, if unconventional techniques which rely on the quasi-informal process of actively generating new customary international law rather than on the

42 To date, the Security Council has tackled such situations as full inter-state war, civil warfare and/or strife, war crimes, ethnic cleansing, international terrorism, perhaps also proliferation of weapons of mass destruction, and (looking at the various sanctions regimes) certain economic activities linked thereto. Some of these categories are rooted in government activities, others in private individuals' activities, and further ones involve both.

formalised process of seeking multilateral consent for a codification project from the outset. Apart from that, (albeit contemporary international law has not ceased to prohibit violence by non-governmental actors against international organisations and their personnel, and states and their citizens) the international community faces a "reintroduction of a form of private war".[43] Arguably, the violent practices of non-governmental armed groups which, if effected by states or international organisations, were clearly incongruent with relevant international treaties, upset the very premises of the international legal order.[44]

As demonstrated, the UN response to these phenomena involves the establishment of robust peace missions entrusted with transitional authority. The example of post-occupation Iraq indicates that the United Nations is also ready to authorise similar crisis response missions conducted by parties to the closed armed conflict. The international community may also consider relying on non-military means and measures for the purpose of maintaining or restoring international peace and security yet still authorise the exercise of transitional authority. Many enforcement measures not involving the use of force may both limit the sovereignty of the state affected and authorise limitations of the rights of its citizens and/or inhabitants. Apart from economic sanctions – whose effects on rights of the human person are by and large indirect in nature – sanctions regimes like in the counter-terrorism field, the establishment of transitional administrations or judicial organs, and referrals to the International Criminal Court, all involve the exercise of authority on behalf of the international community vis-à-vis both affected states and individuals.

The range of possible cases of the exercise of transitional authority points at the need to define appropriate limits of transitional authority conferred on states and/or international organisations, even if short of the full spectrum of armed force. Moreover, there is likewise a need to supplement international criminal law by a human rights-based framework capable of facilitating the prosecution of illicit violent activities of non-governmental armed groups.

B. *Developing the Limits of Transitional Authority*[45]

Many rights of the human person form part of the universally recognised minimum considered indispensable for the purposes of a comprehensive protection of the individual against abuse of public authority. Nevertheless, the proper source from

43 Kenneth Watkin, 'Controlling the Use of Force: A Role for Human Rights Norms in Contemporary Armed Conflict', in *American Journal of International Law* Vol. 98 (2004) p. 34.

44 As noted by Watkin, ibid.:

> Groups that rely on the benefits of globalization and technological advances to conduct operations across international borders are threatening the maintenance of international order.

45 This passage draws from my paper,'Inhalt, Schranken und Durchsetzung des Habeas Corpus-Rechts in der Praxis internationaler Friedensmissionen', in: Dieter Weingärtner (ed.), *Streitkräfte und Menschenrechte*, Baden-Baden (2008), p. 105 sqq.

which their binding force can be derived must be identified in order to establish with what precise content they apply to individual cases. No less than five sources of rights of the human person vis-à-vis entities exercising transitional authority can be considered, namely

- Domestic human rights law of the state on whose territory an operation is conducted;
- Domestic human rights law of the state whose troops conduct an operation;
- Customary international law deriving from the Universal Declaration of Human Rights (1948);
- Regional and/or universal international human rights treaty law; or
- International Humanitarian Law, in particular the Hague Regulations, GCs I–IV, and GPs I & II.

The following analysis will examine the applicability of these sources to the exercise of transitional authority; it will focus on the legal position of international organisations to which the exercise of transitional authority can be attributed rather than the troop contributing states.

i. Receiving State Human Rights Law

International organisations and their subsidiary organs are not bound by the domestic human rights law of the state on whose territory they conduct an operation. If the operation is mandated by a Chapter VII UNSCR, it takes precedence (Article 25 of the UN Charter) over any domestic law including constitutional law (Article 27 of the Vienna Convention on the Law of Treaties). The same is true if the mandate is based on consent unless provided otherwise in the relevant international agreement.[46] In particular, if Status of Forces Agreements (SOFAs)[47] require respect for local law, they confirm that domestic law does not apply *ipso jure*. Such provisions

46 The mandate of the Regional Assistance Mission to Solomon Islands (RAMSI) established under the auspices of the Pacific Islands Forum provides that both the Participating Police Force and the Participating Armed Forces "shall exercise the powers, authorities and privileges exercised by members of the Solomon Islands Police Force"; moreover, it renders the exercise of transitional authority by RAMSI subject to Solomon Islands constitutional human rights law.

For the quote see Articles 5(8) and 6(4) of the Agreement between Solomon Islands, Australia, New Zealand, Fiji, Papua New Guinea, Samoa and Tonga Concerning the Operations and Status of the Police and Armed Forces and Other Personnel Deployed to Solomon Islands to Assist in the Restoration of Law and Order and Security dated 24 July 2003, respectively; for the assessment concerning Solomon Islands human rights law see Nori v Attorney General [2006] SBHC 134; HCSI CC 172 of 2005 (Civil Case Number 172–05; 04 April 2006), at para 15(4), per Palmer CJ – available for download at http://www.paclii.org/sb/cases/SBHC/2006/134.html (last visited 06 March 2008). For further details and references cf. my paper "Enforcing the Rule of Law: Military Contributions to Comprehensive Security", in: 8 New Zealand Armed Forces Law Review 47–71 (2008).

47 A SOFA defines the status of a force deployed on foreign territory, the authority which the force may use, the status of the members of the force and accompanying personnel (personal or functional immunity from jurisdiction), claims procedures, and other

create an obligation on the part of the lead organisation to issue such direction and guidance as deemed appropriate to reconcile the respect requirement with the exigencies of mission accomplishment.

ii. Sending State Human Rights Law

Unless provided otherwise, the human rights law of troop contributing states will usually govern all matters for which a troop contributing State retains exclusive responsibility. This addresses, in particular, those concerning the internal administration of its contingent, including disciplinary and criminal matters. Generally speaking, a troop contributing State's domestic human rights standards can only be made applicable to extraterritorial cases if they involve the exercise of the State's own public authority. As a rule, the broader the executive prerogatives in matters of foreign affairs, the more unlikely that there will be recognition of extraterritorial applicability of domestic human rights standards vis-à-vis nationals of third States. It follows that troop contributing States' domestic human rights standards are not only incapable of generating a general principle of extraterritoriality; but also that they are *a fortiori* so incapable with respect to missions conducted under the operational control of an international organisation based on an international mandate entrusting transitional authority in the mission.[48]

relevant issues. Examples comprise the UN Model SOFA – UN document A/45/594 dated 09 October 1990, Appendix 2 to Annex 1A to the Dayton Agreement, and the Joint Declaration by the Special Representative of the Secretary-General in Kosovo and COMKFOR on the status of KFOR and UNMIK and their personnel, and the privileges and immunities to which they are entitled on 17 August 2000 (subsequently implemented by virtue of UNMIK Regulation 2000/47 in a manner equivalent to the domestic implementation of international agreements).

48 NATO respects that its members may have to abide by their respective constitutional law in decision-making on NATO peace missions in the North Atlantic Council (NAC). The NATO Strategic Concept 1999 provides that: –

> Taking into account the necessity for Alliance solidarity and cohesion, participation in any such operation or mission will remain subject to decisions of member states in accordance with national constitutions.
>
> The Alliance's Strategic Concept 1999 at para 31 (NATO document NAC-S(99)65 – http://www.nato.int/docu/pr/1999/p99-065e.htm – visited 06 December 2007.)

Arguably, the quoted passage is without prejudice to the implementation of NAC decisions. – Apart from that, Article 27 of the Vienna Convention on the Law of Treaties precludes that NATO Member States, all of whom are also members of the United Nations, may rely on their domestic law, including constitutional human rights law, to absolve themselves from obligations under a Chapter VII mandate as implemented by a NAC decision approving a strategic OPLAN including the Rules of Engagement attached to it, and the approval of target sets and effectors.

iii. Customary International Law deriving from the Universal Declaration of Human Rights

Unlike the Universal Declaration of Human Rights, which some OPLANs and SOPs quote as an instrument applicable as a matter of policy, practice has not yet considered customary international law deriving from it binding upon international peace missions. Considering that customary international law deriving from the Universal Declaration of Human Rights has emerged in the practice of states it is not *eo ipso* applicable to the exercise of authority by international organisations. There is, moreover, no practice on which to rely in support of the assumption of such applicability. Not even the United Nations applies the Universal Declaration of Human Rights in matters governed by its internal law.[49] Rather, the UN Secretary-General includes human rights-based standards in direction and guidance issued to peace missions or in a generalistic manner.[50] NATO practice is similar.[51]

iv. Regional and/or Universal International Human Rights Treaty Law

Human rights treaties have been concluded both at regional and universal level; specific international courts and treaty bodies review pertinent state reports and individual cases. Although human rights treaty bodies, international human rights courts and the International Court of Justice have assessed the extraterritorial exercise of public authority by armed forces in certain communications and case-law, their approach towards the applicability of human rights treaty law bears little relevance with respect to the exercise of transitional authority by international peace missions. In particular, the relevant judgments of the European Court of Human Rights[52] and the Advisory Opinion on the Legal consequences of the construction of a wall

49 The UN General Assembly has the power to adopt internal law of the organisation with binding force. The UN Staff Regulations are the key example for the General Assembly's reluctance to implement human rights in its legislative acts; the United Nations and International Labour Organization Administrative Tribunals have not challenged this approach.

50 See, for instance, the Bulletin "Special measures for protection from sexual exploitation and sexual abuse" (UN document SG/SGB/2003/13).

51 For instance, the NATO Policy on Combating Trafficking in Human Beings implements human rights standards governing the protection from sexual exploitation or violence as a matter of policy. On the NATO Policy on Combating Trafficking in Human Beings see my book *Ensuring and Enforcing Human Security*, at 82; Roberta Arnold, 'The NATO Policy on Human Trafficking: Obligation to Prevent, Obligation to Repress', in: id (ed) *Law Enforcement Within the Framework of Peace Support Operations* (2008), pp. 351–379. The policy is reproduced ibid at 297–304.

52 The judgment of 23 February 1995 – application no. 15318/89 – *Loizidou v. Turkey* (preliminary objections) dealt with acts of public authority in Northern Cyprus attributed to Turkey in its capacity as occupying power. In the judgment of 12 May 2005 – application no. 46221/99 – *Öcalan v. Turkey*, the Court reviewed the arrest of PKK leader Abdullah Öcalan by Turkish security forces in Kenya. Finally, the judgment of 16 November 2004 – application no. 31821/96 – *Issa v. Turkey*, brought a strike conducted by Turkish military in Northern Iraq under its scrutiny.

in the Occupied Palestinian Territory[53] address the conduct of states; none of the impugned acts of public authority was rooted in an international mandate entrusting transitional authority in a peace mission. The same is true for the leading case assessed by the Inter-American Commission of Human Rights in 1999.[54]

The only relevant case so far is *Behrami & Saramati*, adjudicated by the European Courts of Human Rights in 2007.[55] However, the Court determined that it lacked jurisdiction to deal with this case. Accordingly, the case contains no guidance as to the applicability of human rights treaty law to the conduct of international peace missions entrusted with transitional authority. The same is true for the Human Rights Committee's position which is unlikely to amount to subsequent practice in the application of the treaty which establishes the agreement of the parties regarding its interpretation (Article 31(3)(b) of the Vienna Convention on the Law of Treaties).[56] First, the Human Rights Committee has relied on imprecise reasoning in support of its position concerning extraterritoriality vis-à-vis the states parties to the Covenant on Civil and Political Rights.[57] In particular, it has summarised the essence of Article 2

53 The Advisory Opinion of the International Court of Justice of 09 July 2004 assessed measures taken by Israel to increase its protection against asymmetric threats which reduce the accessibility of certain parts of the territory occupied following the six days war.

54 Report No. 109/99 dated 29 September 1999 – case no. 10951 – *Coard et al v. The United States of America* is deals with challenges brought by individuals detained by U.S. forces in the course of the intervention in Grenada (1983) against the detention as such and the conditions of detention. Albeit it opined on the matter before it from a human rights perspective, the Inter-American Commission considered the U.S. intervention to protect Grenada from a communist putsch an armed conflict (Report No. 109/99 at para 44).

55 Judgment of the European Court of Human Rights of 02 May 2007 – case no. 71412/01 – *Agim Behrami and Bekir Behrami v. France* and case no. 78166/01 – *Ruzhdi Saramati v. France, Germany and Norway*. The matter of Behrami concerned the allegation that French KFOR troops had, by not removing unexploded ordnance (although doing so had been necessary and obligatory), caused the death of Mr Behrami's son. Mr Saramati had challenged his detention by KFOR.

56 The Human Rights Committee contends that:

> the enjoyment of Covenant rights is not limited to citizens of States Parties but must also be available to all individuals, regardless of nationality or statelessness ... This principle also applies to those within the power or effective control of the forces of a State Party acting outside its territory, regardless of the circumstances in which such power or effective control was obtained, such as forces constituting a national contingent of a State Party assigned to an international peace-keeping or peace-enforcement operation.

General Comment No. 31 – Nature of the General Legal Obligation Imposed on States Parties to the Covenant – UN document CCPR/C/21/Rev.1/Add. 13, at para 10. The Human Rights Committee has not examined whether the Covenant on Civil and Political Rights binds upon international organisations or whether the actions taken by armed forces contributed to peace missions entrusted with transitional authority should be attributed to the international organisations in whose respective chain of command the missions in question are integrated.

57 The Human Rights Committee has misquoted the International Court of Justice's dictum concerning the "rules concerning the basic rights of the human person" which apply *erga*

of the Covenant in a manner disrespectful of the wording of the said article.[58] This method of reasoning does neither afford credibility to the assertions based on it nor support these assertions in a cogent manner. Second, turning to practice, the efforts made by the Human Rights Committee to mobilise support for its position by way of requesting certain states to make declarations endorsing it[59] has been of limited success.[60]

The practice of international organisations is equally unlikely to support the emergence of customary international human rights law based on the application of the Covenant on Civil and Political Rights – despite the Human Rights Committee's related efforts. Following a suggestion made by the representative of Serbia, the Human Rights Committee has requested UNMIK to submit a report on the human

---

omnes. General Comment No. 31, at para 2. The relevant judgment of the International Court of Justice (Barcelona Traction, judgment of 05 February 1970 – ICJ Rep. 1970, 3) discussed *jus cogens* (at para 33) in a generalistic manner, referring, by way of example, to "the outlawing of acts of aggression, and of genocide, as also … the principles and rules concerning the basic rights of the human person, including protection from slavery and racial discrimination" (at para 34).

58 According to its Article 2, the Covenant applies to "all individuals within its territory and subject to its jurisdiction". By way of contrast, the Human Rights Committee considers it applicable to "all persons who may be within their territory and […] all persons subject to their jurisdiction" or "who may find themselves in the territory or subject to the jurisdiction of the State Party". Both quotes, which are contained in para 10 of General Comment No. 31, modify the nexus between the territorial and jurisdictional criteria established by the wording of the Covenant.

59 See the Concluding Observations responding to Germany's fifth periodic report dated 30 March 2004 (UN document CCPR/CO/80/DEU), at para 11, and the Concluding Observations concerning Belgium dated 12 August 2004 (UN document CCPR/CO/81/BEL), at para 6.

60 The Federal Republic of Germany has maintained that:

> Wherever its police or armed forces are deployed abroad, in particular when participating in peace missions, Germany ensures to all persons that they will be granted the rights recognized in the Covenant, insofar as they are subject to its jurisdiction.
>
> Germany's international duties and obligations, in particular those assumed in fulfilment of obligations stemming from the Charter of the United Nations, remain unaffected.

On this declaration see Dieter Weingärtner, in: *id.* (ed.), *Streitkräfte und Menschenrechte*, Baden-Baden (2008), pp. 83–90, and my book *Ensuring and Enforcing Human Security* (2007) at 77.

The Human Rights Committee claims that Italy has subscribed to its position. See the Concluding Observations responding to Italy's fifth periodic report dated 24 April 2006 (UN document CCPR/C/ITA/CO/5), at para 3. Note, however, that neither Italy's periodic report dated 19 March 2004 (UN document CCPR/C/ITA/2004/5; see para 7 on Article 2 of the Covenant) nor the letter by Italy's Ministry of Foreign Affairs responding to the Human Rights Committee's list of issues (UN document CCPR/C/84/L/ITA) support this claim. In any event, there are further states that have expressly refused to do so. Cf. Norbert Berthold Wagner, Zu den Grenzen des Menschenrechtsschutzes bei Auslandsfriedenseinsätzen deutscher Streitkräfte, in *NZWehrr* 2007, p. 2 including further references.

rights situation in Kosovo.[61] In its report, UNMIK has emphasised that it is under no obligation stemming from the Covenant.[62] It follows that UNMIK, being one subsidiary organ of the United Nations, has expressly denied the Human Rights Committee, another subsidiary organ of the United Nations, the power as of law to review its conduct. Things might, however, be different within the EU.[63]

That notwithstanding, the Human Rights Committee has continued to pursue its own legal policy agenda. Not having been able to receive declarations endorsing its position e.g. by several NATO Member States, it seized the opportunity to discuss certain aspects of the practice of NATO's peacekeeping force in Kosovo, KFOR, in the course of reviewing UNMIK's human rights record. In doing so, it demonstrated once again its preparedness to resort to questionable methods of reasoning in support of untenable positions.[64]

---

61 See the report on the 2383th meeting of the Human Rights Committee on 19 July 2006 at para 3 (UN document CCPR/C/SR.2383/Add. 1 – http://www2.ohchr.org/english/bodies/hrc/hrcs87.htm – visited 07 December 2007).

62 UNMIK has maintained that:

> In submitting this report on the human rights situation in Kosovo since June 1999 to the Human Rights Committee (HRC), the United Nations Interim Administration in Kosovo (UNMIK) is acting under the authority granted to it under United Nations Security Council resolution 1244 (1999) (UNSCR 1244).

Para 1 of Part II of the Report submitted by UNMIK (UN document CCPR/C/UNK/1). Moreover, UNMIK has maintained, in its submissions concerning Article 4 of the Covenant, that it is not a party thereto:

> The procedure for derogation set forth in Article 4 does not apply to UNMIK because it is not a State Party to the International Covenant on Civil and Political Rights (ICCPR).

Para 6 of Part II of the Report submitted by UNMIK (UN document CCPR/C/UNK/1).

63 See the European Court of Justice's judgment of 03 September 2008 in *Kadi* – Joined Cases C-402/05 P and C-415/05 P.

64 In my view, the Human Rights Committee has exceeded its competence in discussing KFOR detentions. UNMIK had not addressed KFOR detentions in its submissions concerning Article 9 of the Covenant, demonstrating thus that it neither considered these detentions attributable to it nor itself responsible for them. The Human Rights Committee, apparently building on the report submitted by Amnesty International: United Nations Interim Administration Mission in Kosovo (UNMIK): Briefing to the Human Rights Committee: 87th Session, July 2006 (AI document EUR 70/007/2006), has noted –

> with concern that criminal suspects have been arrested solely under a detention directive of the Commander of KFOR and under executive orders of the Special Representative of the Secretary-General (SRSG) without being brought before a judge promptly and without access to an independent judicial body to determine the lawfulness of their detention.
>
> Para 17 of the Concluding Observations concerning UNMIK dated 25 July 2006 (UN document CCPR/C/UNK/CO/1).

While this statement reveals that the Human Rights Committee blurred the distinction between KFOR operational detentions and KFOR support to criminal law enforcement, this has not been the only case of imprecision in the discussion of KFOR detentions. The Human Rights Committee has also included a reference to an outdated COMKFOR

The practice of NATO and the Council of Europe with respect to access of the latter's Committee for the Prevention of Torture (CPT) to KFOR detention facilities in Kosovo confirms that human rights treaty law does not create obligations on the part of international organisations which are not parties thereto. NATO has maintained that, not being a party to the European Convention on Human Rights and the European Convention for the Prevention of Torture, it is not bound by these conventions. It has authorised KFOR to allow the Council of Europe's Committee for the Prevention of Torture access to places where persons are detained by KFOR with a view to examining the treatment of detainees. NATO has reserved its right, to be exercised by a high-ranking KFOR officer, to ensure that no such visit interferes with military operational requirements.[65] The co-operation between NATO and the Council of Europe is hence based on a *sui generis* arrangement which creates a procedure supportive of the prevention of torture or inhuman and degrading treatment, and responsive to the exigencies of military operations. It demonstrates that NATO, which had never doubted the peremptory nature of the universal ban on torture, takes the rights of the human person seriously although it does not contemplate the idea of being bound by human rights treaties to which it is not a party.

One final consideration concerning extraterritorial applicability of international human rights treaty law can be derived from Article 29 of the Vienna Convention on the Law of Treaties. This article provides that "[u]nless a different intention appears from the treaty or is otherwise established, a treaty is binding upon each party in respect of its entire territory". This provision, while primarily confirming that states may not unilaterally limit the applicability *ratione loci* of international treaties to

---

Detention Directive (UN document CCPR/C/UNK/CO/1, *ibidem*), apparently by way of copy-and-paste from the report submitted by Amnesty International (AI document EUR 70/007/2006 at 34) where the same mistake occurs. Moreover, it seems that the Human Rights Committee has not invited NATO to present its own point of view concerning the practice of KFOR (cf. my book Ensuring and Enforcing Human Security at 142 sqq.).

Even worse, the Human Rights Committee has turned a blind eye on UNSCR 1244 (1999) which contains separate mandates for KFOR and UNMIK (paras 7–9 and 10–11, respectively) and has established them as equal partners. The United Nations has confirmed this separateness and equality in its submissions of the to the European Court of Human Rights in *Behrami & Saramati* (judgment of the European Court of Human Rights of 02 May 2007 – cases no. 71412/01 and 78166/01, at paras 118 sqq.), following the practice represented by the SRSG/COMKFOR Joint Declaration (*supra* n. 47); the preamble of UNMIK Regulation 2000/47 expressly confirms that the regulation was adopted "[f]or the purpose of implementing, within the territory of Kosovo, the Joint Declaration".

65 The conditions of access and examination defined by the NATO letter are different from those contained in the Agreement between the United Nations Interim Administration Mission in Kosovo and the Council of Europe on technical arrangements related to the European Convention for the Prevention of Torture and Inhuman or Degrading Treatment or Punishment dated 23 August 2004 – http://www.cpt.coe.int/documents/scg/2004-08-23-eng.htm (visited 28 January 2008). For an assessment see my paper 'KFOR: Current Legal Issues', in *Journal of International Law of Peace and Armed Conflict* (2007) p. 26 sq.

which they are parties to parts of their territories, also supports the presumption that a treaty is not binding upon a state party beyond its territory unless intended otherwise. This is but one more reason why international human rights treaty law must be held to be essentially territorially rather than extraterritorially applicable.

v. International Humanitarian Law

No international organisation is party to any treaty pertaining to international humanitarian law. As far as possible to establish, the resulting lack of obligations under international humanitarian law on the part of international organisations has hardly been questioned. Nevertheless, NATO and the United Nations require that troops operating under their political direction and control respect the principles of international humanitarian law.[66] Related policies require implementation of relevant principles in pertinent OPLANs and subordinate instruments.

VII. General Principles of International Humanitarian and Human Rights Law

By conclusion *ad interim*, the foregoing analysis demonstrates that neither international treaty law nor customary international law addressed at states wields binding force on international organisations including peace missions under their political direction and control. As a result, the key remaining source of legal obligations on the part of international organisations are general principles of international law (Article 38(c) of the ICJ Statute). In order to respond to practical realities, and to conform to the premises underlying the mandates of international peace missions entrusted with transitional authority, this refers to comprehensive general principles of international law that can be induced from relevant rules of both international humanitarian law and international human rights law.

The following considerations will demonstrate that inducing general principles of international humanitarian and human rights law fits harmoniously within contemporary international law doctrine. The history of the development of both international humanitarian law and international human rights law under the auspices of the UN Charter supports this approach; practice does not back compelling counter-arguments. Accordingly, it is methodologically sound to interpret the legal bases of the exercise of transitional authority, particularly those based upon Chapter VII of the UN Charter, so as to have integrated, albeit implicitly, appropriate limits deriving from general principles of international humanitarian and human rights law.

The methods of interpretation in international law attach little weight to arguments based on the drafting history of written sources.[67] However, the development of the protection of the rights of the human person by post-World War II interna-

66 STANAG No. 2449 "Training in the Law of Armed Conflict"; Bulletin on the "Observance by United Nations forces of international law" (UN document SG/SGB/1999/13).

67 In particular, "the preparatory work of the treaty and the circumstances of its conclusion", being "supplementary means of interpretation" only, are subsidiary to "the ordinary meaning to be given to the terms of the treaty in their context and in the light of its object

tional law indicates what criteria determine the relevance of written sources for the induction of general principles limiting the exercise of transitional authority. This development is characterised *inter alia* by the desire of states to spare human beings from the kind and degree of suffering likely to be caused by warfare but also by genocide, crimes against humanity, and war crimes committed in a manner exploiting normative gaps associated with on-going hostilities. Apart from the prohibition of the threat and use of force, which puts a ban on wars of aggression in particular (Articles 2(4), 39 sqq., and 51 of the Charter of the United Nations), the international community has outlawed the activities typical for genocide, crimes against humanity, and war crimes in a two-step process – yet initially limited, with the exception of genocide, to times of war.[68] Relevant prohibitions – whose implementation by criminal law is mandatory under all relevant international humanitarian law treaties with respect to grave breaches – limit the exercise of authority in the territory of a belligerent including any foreign territory brought under the effective control of its armed forces (occupation). These prohibitions focus on the conduct of armed forces and related policy decision-making. By adopting the Geneva Protocols in 1977, the international community demonstrated that it had not abandoned the approach underlying international humanitarian law that this branch of international law shall govern the exercise of public authority by armed forces deployed extraterritorially.

Reaching common ground was more difficult for states in respect of international protection of human rights. The Universal Declaration of Human Rights was adopted as a non-binding General Assembly Resolution (cf. Article 10 of the UN Charter); no earlier than in 1966 were the Covenant on Civil and Political Rights and the Covenant on Economic, Social, and Cultural Rights adopted. States decelerated the process of codification *inter alia* in light of concerns rooted in the non-intervention principle. These concerns illustrate that the assumption that the protection of human rights comes within the domestic jurisdiction of states – that is, matters having a legal nexus to their own territories – used to be states' lowest common denominator.[69]

---

and purpose", and to the practice of its interpretation and application (cf. Articles 31 and 32 of the Vienna Convention on the Law of Treaties).

68 Relevant prohibitions are contained in the Genocide Convention and GCs I–IV. While all four Geneva Conventions tackle war crimes, GC IV in particular tackles such activities as may result in genocide or crimes against humanity. GP I has supplemented GCs I–IV with respect to war crimes resulting from attacks against the civilian population and attacks causing excessive incidental loss of civilian life or damage to civilian objects.

69 This approach is even more visible in the rules of international law governing decolonisation. The Declaration Regarding Non-Self-Governing Territories (Articles 73 and 74 of the UN Charter) did not render the exercise of public authority prior to decolonisation subject to human rights as demonstrated by its rather weak language (cf. Ulrich Fastenrath in Simma, Charter of the United Nations, 2 ed (2003), Article 73 at para 18: "… legal guarantees are couched in very vague terms …"). The definition of the international trusteeship system's purpose, viz. –

> to encourage respect for human rights and for fundamental freedoms for all without prejudice as to race, sex, language, or religion, and to encourage recognition of the interdependence of the peoples of the world

(Article 76(c) of the UN Charter) is equally insufficient to place binding human rights

The early practice of the Council of Europe and its Member States who had codified regional human rights treaty law in 1950 is likewise unsympathetic to extraterritorial application of the European Convention on Human Rights, that is, to the exercise of public authority in colonies and continued League of Nations mandates. The context and purpose of the provisions governing the territorial scope of applicability of the European Convention on Human Rights demonstrate that to apply beyond the mainland territory of a state party a declaration of that state is necessary.[70] As a result, any extension of the territorial scope of applicability of the European Convention on Human Rights to areas not under the full sovereignty of one or more of the states parties is, as a matter of principle, incongruent with the Convention.

This brief overview reaffirms that international law generally differentiates between the exercise of public authority by armed forces on foreign territory which it renders subject to international humanitarian law,[71] and the exercise of public authority in states' mainland territories which it renders subject to international human rights law. As indicated, the only exception is the Genocide Convention which does not distinguish either on account of whether a situation can be characterised as armed conflict or peace (see Article I of the Genocide Convention), or whether it might be considered within the domestic jurisdiction of the state concerned. At the same time, the Genocide Convention demonstrates that the spheres covered by international humanitarian law and international human rights law, respectively, can overlap and that a legal framework likewise overlapping these spheres can be devised. There is no practice pertaining to other *de facto* overlaps of the spheres of international humanitarian law and international human rights law indicating the opposite.

---

obligations on the authority exercising the administration of a trust territory (administering authority), viz. "one or more states or the Organization itself" (Article 81 of the UN Charter). Contrary to a view sometimes discussed, the obligation to encourage respect for human rights and for fundamental freedoms for all entails an obligation to include human rights provisions in trusteeship agreements concluded in accordance with Article 75 of the UN Charter rather than to actually afford such respect. This notwithstanding, no trusteeship agreements contained a comprehensive bill of rights. Cf. Rauschning in Simma, *Charter of the United Nations*, 2 ed (2003), Article 76 at paras 32 sqq.

70 Article 56 (then Article 63) of the European Convention on Human Rights provides that states parties *may* "declare by notification … that the … Convention shall … extend to all or any of the territories for whose international relations it is responsible". Some former colonial powers have not made such declarations any earlier than in 1974 (France), 1979/1986 (the Netherlands), and 2004 (the United Kingdom). See the list of declarations, reservations and other communications at http://conventions.coe.int.

71 As far as situations involving hostilities are concerned, international human rights law is particularly inept to govern the exercise of authority by armed forces on its own because it is not based on reciprocity. As observed with respect to conflict yet capable of generalisation, its "[a]pplication to only one party to the conflict, the State, may be considered as contradicting a basic principle of humanitarian law, according to which both parties to the conflict have equal rights and duties". Liesbeth Zegveld, 'The Inter-American Commission on Human Rights and International Humanitarian Law: A Comment on the Tablada Case', in *IRRC* vol. 38 (1998) p. 511 at n. 21 (available at: http://www.icrc.org/web/eng/siteengo.nsf/html/57JPGB – visited 11 July 2008). Indeed human rights law "is designed to function in peacetime, contains no rules governing the methods and means of warfare, and applies only to one party to a conflict". Watkin, supra note 43 at 30.

As a result, the approach inferring general principles of international humanitarian and human rights law which cover situations where – speaking in the terms of the war-and-peace divide – armed conflict (the sphere of international humanitarian law) and peace (the sphere of international human rights law) are indistinguishable, is based on the same pragmatic premises as Chapters VI and VII of the UN Charter, and the Genocide Convention. Inferring general principles is the same method as applied for the step-by-step development, within European Community Law, of human rights protection for "market citizens" (as citizens of the European Union used to be called).[72] This method does not facilitate arbitrary rule-making because there are substantial minimum requirements for deriving rules from general principles. Relevant criteria can be borrowed from the jurisprudence of the European Court of Human Rights. Its case-law indicates that the transfer of authority to international organisations does not cause human rights concerns if the relevant organisation is considered to protect fundamental rights, as regards both the substantive guarantees offered and the mechanisms controlling their observance, in a manner which can be considered at least equivalent to that for which the Convention provides[73] – that is, in the present context, what such written international humanitarian and human rights treaty law and instruments as used for the purpose of induction provide.

---

72 The European Court of Justice, having established that Community Law is an independent source of law and supranational in nature, has determined that there are unwritten human rights which bind upon Community organs, and which derive from general principles of Community Law. In *Stauder*, the European Court of Justice has upheld a provision of Community Law holding that it "contains nothing capable of prejudicing the fundamental human rights enshrined in the general principles of Community Law and protected by the Court". Judgment of 12 November 1969 – case no. 29/69 – *Stauder v. Stadt Ulm* – 1969 ECR 419 = 1969 Danish Special Edition 107, at para 7. The court has confirmed this judgment subsequently, e.g. in the judgment of 17 December 1970 – case no. 11/70 – *Internationale Handelsgesellschaft v. Einfuhr- und Vorratsstelle für Getreide und Futtermittel* – 1970 ECR 1125 = 1970 Danish Special Edition 235, at para 4.

According to the Court, these human rights result from the constitutional traditions common to the Member States. The other Community organs have implicitly subscribed to the Court's jurisprudence since the Joint Declaration by the European Parliament, Council and the Commission concerning the protection of fundamental rights and the ECHR (OJ 1977 C 103 at 1), codifying it in Article 6(2) of the Treaty on European Union: –

> The Union shall respect fundamental rights, as guaranteed by the European Convention for the Protection of Human Rights and Fundamental Freedoms signed in Rome on 4 November 1950 and as they result from the constitutional traditions common to the Member States, as general principles of Community law.

Eventually, they adopted the Charter of Fundamental Rights of the European Union (OJ 2000 C 361 at 1).

73 Judgment of the European Court if Human Rights of 30 June 2005 – application No. 45036/98 – *Bosphorus Hava Yollari v. Ireland*, at para 155. The court observed, *ibidem*, that –

> By "equivalent" the Court means "comparable"; any requirement that the organisation's protection be "identical" could run counter to the interest of international cooperation pursued.

A. *A Note on Non-Governmental Violence*

General principles of international humanitarian and human rights law can also supplement international criminal law as a human rights-inclusive framework facilitating the international criminal prosecution of illicit violent activities of non-governmental armed groups. The capability of international humanitarian law to create direct horizontal obligations on the part of individuals without express implementation by legislation at state level can be extended to all general principles of international humanitarian and human rights law no matter what rule is key to their induction, that is, they are capable of tackling the whole range of gross violations of human rights committed by non-governmental actors involved in illicit violence. As the examples of the *ad hoc* tribunals and the referral of the situation in the Darfur to the Prosecutor of the International Criminal Court demonstrate, international criminal prosecution is not contingent on the existence of written definitions of crimes prior to their commission for the purposes of the *nullum crimen sine lege* and *nulla poena sine lege* principles. It rather follows the example of common law where definitions of crimes can derive from a practice demonstrating the illegality of certain activities and a legal consensus confirming their punishability. However, a detailed discussion of an adaptation of the concept of common law crimes to international criminal prosecution would exceed the scope of the present chapter.

B. *Alternative Approaches*

Relying on general principles of international humanitarian and human rights law is not the only possible approach to ensure the protection of rights of the human person in conflict and other situations involving the exercise of transitional authority. Apart from the point of view that human rights treaties apply to non-parties and in situations not covered by their object and purpose, there is also a view which amounts to the assertion that if short of constituting hostilities, the exercise of transitional authority would – like situations short of constituting hostilities to which international humanitarian law would apply on the basis of the classical categorisation[74] – be guided by a 'law enforcement paradigm' as opposed to an 'armed conflict paradigm'. Supporters of this position draw attention to the different proportionality tests governing the use of force under international humanitarian law and international human rights law.[75] Their key concern is the protection of the right to life in targeting. While international humanitarian law weighs the direct and concrete military advantage against incidental loss of human life and incidental damage, international human rights law weighs the public and private interests supporting certain action against the interests of the individuals affected, including the interest to have one's substantive rights procedurally safeguarded. As a result, individuals targeted as members of a non-governmental armed group party to hostilities and/or because of their own participation in individual fighting situations would enjoy less protec-

74 See the discussion of the situation in occupied territory and during non-international armed conflict by Nils Melzer, *Targeted Killings in International Law* (2008), at 155–175.

75 Ibid at 175–176.

tion under the auspices of an 'armed conflict paradigm' than under the auspices of a 'law enforcement paradigm'. Non-kinetic offensive operations may generate similar concerns with respect to the protection of many other rights of the human person.[76]

The supporters of the 'law enforcement paradigm' derive this theorem from human rights law and consider it to be modified by international humanitarian law with respect to hostilities.[77] However, it is hard to trace such a 'law enforcement paradigm' in international law. In any event, even if international human rights treaty law were capable of being interpreted in light of a 'law enforcement paradigm', this paradigm – not being part of "the terms of the treaty" and not representing agreement concerning "its object and purpose" (Article 31(1) of the Vienna Convention on the Law of Treaties), either – might at best have the character of a "supplementary means of interpretation" (Article 32 of the Vienna Convention on the Law of Treaties). It would, in particular, fail to be a "subsidiary means for the determination of rules of law" (Article 38(d)) of the ICJ Statute). Severed from the binding elements of international human rights law, it would not, accordingly, be part of human rights law in its capacity as *lex generalis* vis-à-vis international humanitarian law.

It is, accordingly, wrong to contemplate the "Potential Relevance of International Humanitarian Law for the Law Enforcement Paradigm"[78] where the relevance of the 'law enforcement paradigm' for international humanitarian law cannot be demonstrated.

On a separate note, like any other case of non-written limitations of sovereign authority, the limitation by the asserted 'law enforcement paradigm' would have to withstand the test for the emergence of customary international law. In this it utterly fails. It seems impossible to demonstrate that the existing practice of many states to limit the authority available under international humanitarian law represents *opinio juris* concerning the legally binding force of such human rights provisions as the limits allegedly reflect. On the contrary, it is not unusual that ROE or SOPs limit the use of force for political-strategic and/or military-strategic reasons. For instance, detaining and interrogating a targeted individual with a view to putting him or her on trial rather than killing him or her[79] may not only secure access to mission-essential information but also serve the strategic aim to demonstrate that perpetrators will be brought to justice not only for the acts committed against the detaining force but, *a fortiori*, also for those committed against their fellow nationals. Similar considerations apply to investigation requirements and payment of (in particular: *ex gratia*)

76 Cecilia M. Bailliet, 'War in the Home': An Exposition of Protection Issues Pertaining to the Use of House Raids in Counterinsurgency Operations, in *Journal of Military Ethics*, Vol. 6, (2007) pp. 173–197. The paper discusses jurisprudence concerning law enforcement in order to derive criteria for assessing the lawfulness and legitimacy of visit operations in Iraq.

77 Melzer, supra note 74 at 89–90.

78 Ibid at 140 (paragraph heading).

79 Cf. the judgment of the Supreme Court of Israel of 23 Kislev 5767 (13 December 2006) – HCJ 769/02 – *The Public Committee against Torture in Israel v. The Government of Israel*, at para 40.

compensation following a kinetic strike against a targeted individual[80] – there can hardly be credible justification without investigation, and compensation paid may prevent the family members of a legitimately targeted individual from such victimisation as would generate (additional) psychological support for the cause of the non-privileged belligerent group to which the individual belonged. Accordingly, the application of less harmful means than killing and investigation/compensation represent one aspect of the uniform effort to achieve the strategic end-state of a given operation rather than a 'law enforcement paradigm'. Associated ROE- or SOP-based limits on the use of force do not represent a practice reflecting *opinio juris* concerning obligations under international law.

One further criticism of the 'law enforcement paradigm' derives from its ignorance towards the status of non-governmental armed group as parties to hostilities. As a theorem rooted in human rights law it shares its lack of reciprocity. Accordingly, the proportionality test associated with the 'law enforcement paradigm' is inept to govern situations which either involve hostilities or in whose respect the use of all necessary means or measures is authorised. It is in any event doubtful whether resorting to a 'law enforcement paradigm' duly implements the International Court of Justice's characterisation of international humanitarian law as a *lex specialis* vis-à-vis international human rights law.[81] This *dictum* implies that, as observed by the Supreme Court of Israel, "[w]hen there is a gap (lacuna) in [international humanitarian] law, it can be supplemented by human rights law".[82] International humanitarian law is not *per se* concerned with law enforcement and does not, accordingly, suffer from a related gap which would trigger the *lex generalis*. Hostilities are not a matter of law enforcement at all. During occupation, international humanitarian law differentiates between responses to threats to the occupying forces representing paramilitary or military capabilities and law enforcement proper which continues to be a responsibility of civilian government agencies. Transitional authority addresses threats representing paramilitary or military capabilities, as well – otherwise the Security Council would determine that a situation poses a threat to law enforcement rather than to international peace and security. Consequently, the 'law enforcement paradigm' is insufficient to govern the exercise of transitional authority including the use of force or any other authority justifying responses to threats representing paramilitary or military capabilities.

Rejecting the assertion that international humanitarian law suffers from a law enforcement gap does not, however, imply that authority justifying responses to threats representing paramilitary or military capabilities is immune against normative gaps. As discussed, existing legal instruments address only part of the changing realities of crisis and conflict. While international human rights law might by now

80 Ibid.

81 Advisory Opinion of 08 July 1996 on the *Legality of the Threat or Use of Nuclear Weapons*, at para 25, and Advisory Opinion of 09 July 2004 on the *Legal Consequences of the Construction of a Wall in the Occupied Palestinian Territory*, at paras 105–106.

82 Judgment of the Supreme Court of Israel of 23 Kislev 5767 (13 December 2006) – HCJ 769/02 – *The Public Committee against Torture in Israel v. The Government of Israel*, at para 18.

depict more clearly what interests of the human person deserve protection international humanitarian law has not lost its ability to tell anyone employing armed forces – be it civilian superiors or military commanders – how the protection of such interests of the human person can be factored into military planning and the execution of deliberate offensive operations. As a result, an interactive manner[83] of applying international humanitarian and human rights law is the logical response to the contemporary way of addressing threats to international peace and security. It reflects the incapability of the categories concerning the applicability of international humanitarian and human rights law hitherto derived on the basis of the war-and-peace divide. As demonstrated, many situations posing a threat to international peace and security do not fit in these classical categories on account of their factual complexity, and conferring transitional authority including the authority to use force does neither require an assessment of the situation on the basis of these categories nor has any such authorisation recently been based on such assessment.

Relying on general principles of international humanitarian and human rights law is no more than the method of interactive application with respect to situations for which no written legal sources exist. Accordingly, this method does not generate less protection with respect to the conduct of international organisations than the interactive application of international humanitarian and human rights customary and treaty law to cases concerning the conduct of individual states. One example for the ability of interactive application to close normative gaps occurring in relation to a new factual development of contemporary military operations concerns such rights of the human person as are affected by non-kinetic operations. Counter-insurgency and counter-terrorism and, on a more general note, "three-block war", involve operations not relying on effects generated by kinetic energy, namely visits to houses which are thereupon searched with a view to obtaining information by way of questioning the individuals and exploiting the documents and tangible assets present at the location where the operation is conducted. In light of the purpose of such operations, namely to neutralise para-military or military threats associated with the location where they are conducted, their effects on the individuals affected are significantly more intense than the effects of e.g. peace-time police raids. However, international humanitarian law contains rudimentary rules governing such military operations only whereas the human rights-based rules applicable to police raids are not reciprocal and hence unfit for situations where the probability of hostile engagements is high. Accordingly, while international humanitarian law is underinclusive of the rules necessary to strike an equitable basis between mission accomplishment and the protection of the rights of the individuals affected by a visit operation, international human rights law is overinclusive of protection in particular for such members of non-governmental armed groups as may be present in the location where the operation is conducted and willing to engage the force conducting it. Interactive application – of relevant treaties where states take action and of equivalent rules derived from general

83 Cf. Robert Kogod Goldman, 'International Humanitarian Law: Americas Watch's Experience in Monitoring Internal Armed Conflicts', 9 *Am. U. J. Int'l L & Pol* 49/51 (1993) (as quoted by Kenneth Watkin, supra note 43.)

principles of international humanitarian and human rights law where (particularly) international organisations exercise transitional authority – avoids either undesired effect.

The rights of the human person most likely to be affected by a visit operation are property, privacy (including family life), the protection of one's home, the protection of life and limb, and freedom of religion.[84] All these rights are protected by various rules of international humanitarian law albeit not in a fully coherent manner, and by rules of international human rights treaty law. For the purposes of devising an appropriate legal framework governing visit operations, these rules must be reviewed with a view to inferring the general principles they give effect to (or, as the case may be, with a view to identifying their shared substance). The substantial standards of protection developed on that basis must then be linked up with the specific mechanisms for controlling the effects of deliberate offensive operations in order to provide the necessary procedural safeguards during planning and execution of visit operations. The enclosed Collateral Effects Estimation Guidelines – which represent a theater-unspecific adaptation of an existing document – demonstrate how general principles of international humanitarian land human rights law (or, more generally speaking, interactive application) reconcile the protection of the rights of the human person with the exigencies of mission accomplishment.

VIII. Conclusion

Contemporary threats to international peace and security are as diverse as they are manifold. They defy categorisation in the classical manner, and they are dealt with in an unorthodox way for that very reason. Accordingly, if based on thought models rooted in classical international law, any legal assessment of the threats and the responses to them will lack accuracy. The UN Charter has devised a new pragmatic approach, leaving the discredited war-and-peace divide behind, towards the challenges faced by the international community. The Security Council has started to give effect to this approach, eventually taking its role of provider of international peace and security seriously. In doing so, it has frequently conferred transitional authority on entities it deemed fit to address a threat. Its practice lacks, however, clarity with respect to the limits of transitional authority inasmuch as it entails the power to impose limitations on the rights of the human person. In the absence of relevant international treaty-law, general principles of international humanitarian and human rights law can prevent the emergence of normative gaps in the exercise of transitional authority whose exploitation would run counter the object and purpose of the UN Charter and might undermine the success of the international community's determined effort to bring international peace and security to everyone.

84 See the discussion by Bailliet, supra note 76 which has inspired the enclosed Collateral Effects Estimation Guidelines.

Collateral Effects Estimation Guidelines for Sensitive Site Exploitations, Cordon and Search Operations, and Comparable Operations

1. *General Remarks*

Under normal circumstances, it is difficult, if impossible, to prevent adverse effects on the rights of individuals present in sites potentially linked to unfriendly forces during the execution of non-kinetic operations. For the purpose of these guidelines, non-kinetic operations comprise deliberate offensive operations not involving the pre-planned use of mortar, artillery, bombs, or similar ammunitions whose effects are generated by kinetic energy released by an explosion.

Depending on the details of the operation, the following rights of the human person are liable to be adversely affected:

- property rights concerning the site in question and any tangible objects apprehended therein or in the vicinity thereof,
- privacy rights of the individuals present in the site in question or its vicinity,
- the right to protection of one's home, if, and to the extent that, buildings affected by the operation are used as accommodation by human beings and that the individuals present in such buildings are not just guests of the rightful owner,
- the right to protection of life and limb of any individual present in the site in question, and
- the freedom of religion of any individual present in the site in question.

2. *Legal Framework*

a. Throughout the execution of an operation, the on-scene commander is personally responsible for the adherence of his/her subordinates to the relevant principles of international humanitarian and human rights law. As far as kinetic operations are concerned, the relevant balancing of the military advantage expected and the harm caused to civilians and/or civilian objects is part of the Collateral Damage Estimation (CDE) to be conducted in accordance with relevant theater Standing Operating Procedures. To date, Collateral Effects Estimation for the purposes of non-kinetic operations is not governed by Standing Operating Procedures.

b. The military Commander responsible for the planning of an individual field level operation must assess and balance the expected concrete and direct military advantage operation, and its possible adverse effects on the rights of affected individuals (collateral effects). He/She is obligated to implement the necessary precautions in the operation plan / concept of operations / operation order to prevent the possible collateral effects from being excessive in relation to the expected direct and concrete military advantage. Should excessive collateral effects occur, the operation must not be executed, or, if its execution is on-going, suspended.

c. In the course of execution, the on-scene commander must re-assess and re-balance the expected concrete and direct military advantage operation, and its possible collateral effects, taking due account of the development of the situation. Should he/she conclude that the collateral effects actually occurring are excessive in relation to the direct and concrete military advantage expected by the operation, he/she must suspend the further execution of the operation.

d. Collateral effects are excessive if they clearly lack the proportionality[1] in relation to the direct and concrete military advantage expected by the operation in accordance with the value judgment of the military commander responsible for the operation.[2]

3. *Purpose*

The following guidelines aim to summarise the legal aspects of collateral effects estimation in the framework of non-kinetic operations against sites potentially linked to unfriendly forces with a view to enhancing legal and practical certainty concerning the adherence to such principles of international humanitarian and human rights law as are relevant for such operations.

1. The assessment of the expected concrete and direct military advantage of a non-kinetic operation against a site potentially linked to unfriendly forces should rely on, *inter alia*, the following effects, which can be considered advantageous from a military perspective:
   - any expected collection of information,
   - any expected collection of intelligence, and
   - any expected effects of the collection of such information and/or intelligence (or the possibility thereof), in particular on the future conduct of unfriendly forces.
2. The collection of information and/or intelligence shall be considered an advantageous effect of an operation if the information and/or intelligence meets one of the following non-conclusive criteria:
   - it is related to at least one unfriendly forces' member's positive identification as an individual taking a direct part in hostilities, the pattern of life permitting to distinguish him or her from individuals not so taking part in hostilities, or the proof of evidence of such unfriendly forces' member's non-compliant activities, and can hence be used in the course of targeting in accordance with relevant theater Standing Operating Procedures;
   - it contributes to a better understanding of unfriendly forces military or paramilitary capability, such as:
     - unfriendly forces networks (including the position of individuals within such networks),

1 Gerhard Werle, *Völkerstrafrecht* [International Criminal Law] (2 ed. 2007), at para 1164; cf. Jean Pictet (ed.), *Commentary of the Additional Protocols of 8 June 1977 to the Geneva Conventions of 12 August 1949* (1987), at para 1979.

2 Cf. Knut Dörmann, *Elements of War Crimes under the Rome Statute of the International Criminal Court* (2003), at pp. 164–165.

    - unfriendly forces TTPs (including the co-operation or co-ordination of unfriendly forces activities and/or operations with LPBs, IAGs, and organised crime),
    - unfriendly forces supply chains and routes,
    - unfriendly forces personnel recruitment activities and processes/procedures,
    - unfriendly forces training and exercise activities and processes/procedures, or
    - unfriendly forces weapons and ammunitions storage sites,
  - it contributes to a better understanding of the use, by unfriendly forces, of the site targeted by the operation (e.g. as a temporary command post, operating base, retreat area, and/or logistics base), or
  - it is not incapable of contributing to improving own forces' operational success and/or weakening unfriendly forces in any other way.

  The responsible military commander may expect that a planned operation generates advantageous effects on the basis of at least being able to either apprehend tangible assets or conduct the tactical questioning of individuals present in the site targeted by the operation, in order to collect information and/or intelligence of the kind at issue.

3. The assessment of the concrete and direct military advantage expected by an individual field level operation must take into account the entirety of the militarily advantageous or, as the case may be, disadvantageous, effects of such operation in relation to the Centers of Gravity:
  - at tactical level,
  - at operational level (multinational and national), and
  - at strategic level (multinational and national).[3]

  The weight of the concrete and direct military advantage expected by an individual field level operation in the course of balancing with possible collateral effects should be assessed with a view to the nature, extent, and sustainability of the operation's expected effects on:
  - on-going and future own forces operations,
  - unfriendly forces conduct, and
  - from an information operations perspective.

  The concrete and direct military advantage expected by an individual field level operation shall be considered as having significant weight if it entails the likely prevention of any development of the situation causing an increased threat level to own forces, the verification or falsification of existing information/intelligence of operational value, and/or the collection of new information/intelligence of operational value.

---

3 From a strategic level perspective, the notion of "center of gravity" is defined as:

> Characteristics, capabilities or localities from which a nation, an alliance, a military force or other grouping derives its freedom of action, physical strength or will to fight.

NATO Glossary of Terms and Definitions – NATO document AAP-6 (2008) at 2-C-3 (definition adopted 25 September 1998).

4. The following aspects of the situation must be assessed with a view to determining what collateral effects a non-kinetic operation against sites potentially linked to unfriendly forces will possibly cause:
   - concerning the rightful owner of a site targeted by an operation: is he/she an individual belonging to unfriendly forces or has no link of his to unfriendly forces been established?
   - concerning the buildings on the site: what is their actual use, in particular, are they being used as living quarters?
   - concerning the buildings on the site used as living quarters: how many individuals with and without a link to unfriendly forces, and of those without such link, how many women and children, use the buildings in question as their permanent domicile?
   - concerning the individuals present in the buildings without using them as their permanent domicile: how many individuals with and without a link to unfriendly forces, and of those without such link, how many women and children, are usually present in these buildings and must hence be expected to be present at the planned time of execution?

   If, and to the extent that, individuals and objects in the vicinity of the site targeted by the operation are liable to be more than insignificantly affected, related aspects must be made part of the assessment of the situation. Effects shall be considered insignificant if, *inter alia*, if e.g. a blocking force limits freedom of movement for the duration of the operation within a specified perimeter around the site targeted by the operation.
5. In assessing what collateral effects will possibly be caused by a non-kinetic operation, the competent commander shall take the intensity of the limitations of all relevant rights of the human person by the operation. Mere nuisances are below the threshold of collateral effect.
6. In particular, the following rights of the individuals affected by the operation shall be considered in the course of collateral effects estimation.
   - **property rights concerning the site in question and any tangible objects apprehended therein or in the vicinity thereof**

     The following shall be considered *low intensity limitations*:
     - possible minor damage to the site or tangible objects therein which does not render them unusable or does render them unusable for a short period of time only, or for such limited period of time as the rightful owner will need to repair them by way of, *inter alia*, minor construction work, or
     - the temporary apprehension of any tangible objects found in the site for the duration of the operation, as defined by the presence of own forces on-scene, with or without the consent of the rightful owner or the person exercising *de facto* control over such objects.

     The following shall be considered *medium intensity limitations*:
     - possible damage to the site or tangible objects therein which render them unusable for a considerable period of time and/or will require repair by specifically trained construction workers, or
     - the temporary apprehension of any tangible objects found in the

site for the duration of the operation, as defined by the presence of own forces on-scene, if such apprehension can only be implemented forcefully.

The following shall be considered *high intensity limitations*:
  - possible damage to the site or tangible objects therein which render them permanently unusable, or the destruction thereof, or
  - the apprehension of any tangible objects found in the site followed by their being removed from the site for such purposes as INTEL gathering, document exploitation, or the use as evidence.

The assessment that a limitation shall be considered as of high intensity may include a comparison of the possible effects with those of a kinetic operation.

Documentation of the state of the site and any tangible objects contained therein prior to, during, or after the execution phase of an operation is without prejudice to the assessed intensity of possible limitations.

- **the right to protection of one's home**

  The possible entry into a building used as living quarters including the assessment and, as the case may be, apprehension of tangible objects found therein, shall be considered a *low intensity limitation* if it:
  - will not exceed a short period of time, or
  - is consented by the individuals using the building in question as their domicile.

  The method of entry into a building affects its owner's property rights rather than the right to protection of the home.

  The possible entry into a building used as living quarters including the assessment and, as the case may be, apprehension of tangible objects found therein, shall be considered a *medium intensity limitation* if it:
  - will not exceed a short period of time but is not consented by the individuals using the building in question as their domicile, or
  - is executed against the resistance of the individuals using the building in question as their domicile yet without using force against these individuals.

  The possible entry into a building used as living quarters shall be considered a *high intensity limitation* if it:
  - is executed, including the assessment and, as the case may be, apprehension of tangible objects found in the building in question, against the resistance of the individuals using it as their domicile, including the use force against one or more of these individuals for mission accomplishment, or
  - involves the removal of one or more of these individuals from the building in a forceful manner, in particular if such removal occurs during the assessment and, as the case may be, apprehension of tangible objects found in the building.

  The act of assessing and, as the case may be, apprehending tangible objects found in a building includes the documentation of these measures with appropriate means and methods.

- **privacy rights**
  The following shall be considered *low intensity limitations*:
  - documenting the identity, and the presence during the execution phase, of the individuals affected by the operation, or
  - the possibility of interfering with the usual daily routines of the individuals affected by the operation, provided that such interference does not have an impact on personal hygiene, health, or meals.

  It shall be considered as a *medium intensity limitation* if the possibility of interfering with the usual daily routines of the individuals affected by the operation involves delayed personal hygiene, health, or meals.
  Additionally, any interference with routine sleeping periods at night shall be considered a *medium intensity limitation.*
  Possible interferences with the usual daily routines of the individuals affected by the operation shall be considered *high intensity limitations* if they:
  - affect the personal health of the individuals in question, or
  - prevent the individuals in question from taking care of their personal hygiene or having their meals throughout the execution phase of the operation.

  Additionally, any case of entering rooms which are designated for the exclusive use by women and/or children; or which carry cultural sensitiveness according to an on-scene situational assessment (e.g. rooms designated for religious purposes such as routine prayers), shall be considered a *high intensity limitation.*
- **the right to protection of life and limb**
  It shall be considered a *low intensity limitation* if the individuals affected by the operation may suffer from self-inflicted minor irritations of their physical well-being such as surface injuries (e.g. small scratches or small haematomas).
  The following shall be considered *medium intensity limitations*:
  - irritations of the physical well-being by way of binding or cuffing of hands, or
  - surface injuries (e.g. small scratches or small haematomas) caused by the use of force for mission accomplishment, unless they are the causal result of the injured person's resistance against a legitimate measure.

  Any injury going below surface and caused by the use of force for mission accomplishment shall be considered a *high intensity limitation.*[4]

---

4 The above is without prejudice to the right to use deadly force, i.e. "force intended or likely to cause death, or serious injury resulting in death" as defined by MC 362/1

- in self-defence, including extended self-defence – under international law – including and where the need to defend is the direct result of measures aimed at mission accomplishment, or
- in any other case self-defence, including extended self-defence, in particular as per the definition in relevant national criminal law.

- **freedom of religion**
  As a matter of principle, any limitation of freedom of religion, in particular interferences with Islamic prayer times[5] or any other prayer and/or meditation practices, *are high intensity limitations.*

7. For the purpose of balancing, all possible collateral effects shall be assessed as a whole. The possible collateral effects of an operation shall not automatically be considered of high intensity solely for the reason that the adverse effects on one right of the human person by the operation are of high intensity.
8. The responsible military commander shall reach his/her value judgment on the basis of a continuous assessment of the situation, taking into account if the following groupings of individuals are present in the site targeted by the operation as a whole, in an identifiable part thereof, or in an individual room:
   - individuals linked to unfriendly forces only, or
   - individuals not linked to unfriendly forces only, or
   - both individuals linked and not linked to unfriendly forces.

   His/her value judgment shall be based on the balancing of:
   - his/her assessment of the expected concrete and direct military advantage, and
   - his/her assessment of possible collateral effects (limitations of rights of the human person).

In addition to the factors discussed above, the on-scene commander shall also consider the tactical dynamics prior to, and during, the execution phase of the operation in assessing the expected concrete and direct military advantage and possible collateral effects.

5 Although Islamic prayer times are not specifically defined they can be estimated at a high probability. Estimated prayer times are webpublished at: http://www.islamicfinder.org/.

Chapter 4

A Critical Decision Point on the Battlefield – Friend, Foe, or Innocent Bystander

*Matthew V. Ezzo & Amos N. Guiora**

Captain James Smith reported to the Battalion Command Post outside of Kabul, Afghanistan. He was anxious to receive the next mission for India Company. Captain Smith and his men had been actively engaging al Qaeda supported militants over the past 2 weeks. They had successfully conducted raid operations against militant compounds near the Afghanistan and Pakistan border. On each occasion, the militants were caught off-guard and therefore had little opportunity to offer resistance.

Captain Smith sat in the Command Post listening to the latest intelligence reports from the Battalion Intelligence Officer. The intelligence reports indicated an unusually large amount of activity from the local civilian population in and around suspected militant strongholds. Captain Smith noted this as the Battalion Commander stepped into the tent to issue the operations order for the next day. India Company was to conduct an early morning raid on a suspected militant compound near the southeastern Afghanistan and Pakistani border. Unmanned aerial vehicles provided imagery that indicated that the militants were consolidating and re-grouping in a large clay and brick enclosed compound at the base of Hill 402.

India Company was to seize the objective by force and consolidate on the compound so that follow-on forces could conduct a thorough search of the compound for weapons caches and any other valuable intelligence. Captain Smith left the Command Post confident about his mission and anxious to brief his subordinates.

Captain Smith and his men infiltrated to the objective under the cover of darkness and reached the compound about an hour before their pre-dawn, coordinated attack.

* Mr. Ezzo previously was employed by the U.S. Department of the Navy working on anti-terrorism and force protection warfare requirements. He is currently an assistant prosecuting attorney in Cuyahoga County Ohio. Mr. Guiora is currently Professor of Law, SJ Quinney College of Law, The University of Utah. The opinions and content expressed in this article are exclusively those of Mr. Ezzo and Prof. Guiora. They do not represent the views of the Department of Defense or the Department of the Navy. The authors would like to thank Mr. Jeffrey Lowe (J.D. expected, S.J. Quinney College of Law, May 2009) for his significant research and editing contributions. In addition, the authors would like to thank the participants at the "Security: A Multidisciplinary Approach Conference", Institute for International and Public Law, The University of Oslo, October, 2008 for their thoughtful insights and commentary both during and after the paper was presented. Those comments contributed both to changes in this paper and will lead to additional papers on similar issues.

Cecilia M. Bailliet (ed.), Security: A Multidisciplinary Normative Approach.
 ISBN 978 90 04 17296 8. pp. 91–115.

As Captain Smith and some of his subordinate leaders were conducting a visible reconnaissance of the compound using their night vision devices, they begin to notice a group of women and elderly men starting to walk the perimeter of the compound about an hour before dawn ... just when the attack was supposed to launch.

The women and elderly men appeared to be unarmed, but seemed to be walking the perimeter of the compound in a fashion normally associated with sentries walking their post. Captain Smith received a call on the radio from the Battalion Commander asking him to launch the attack as planned, as the follow-on forces were on their way. Captain Smith knew he was at a critical decision point ... were these people walking the perimeter of the compound innocent civilians or were they working with the militants and therefore legitimate targets?[1]

I. Introduction

We come to this article from different – yet ultimately similar – professional backgrounds. One of us, Matt Ezzo, was a United States Marine Corps infantry officer who served in various company level leadership positions. During his time in the Marine Corps, Mr. Ezzo led Marine Corps infantry units during security operations in the Republic of Haiti and various operations in Kosovo and Albania. Amos Guiora served for 19 years in the Israel Defense Forces and had command responsibility for the development of an interactive video based on international law, Israeli law and the IDF code teaching junior commanders an 11 point code of conduct with respect to a civilian population in "armed conflict short of war".

We write this article based on our mutual conviction that a (perhaps the) significant challenge facing military commanders in operational counter-terrorism is the requirement to distinguish between innocent civilians and combatants. In the context of operational counter-terrorism, we define combatants as individuals who threaten innocent civilians and soldiers alike. However, we do not argue that an individual who kills a soldier is a terrorist, as terrorism is acts only against civilian targets.

A combatant in the terrorism paradigm is not a soldier, as he/she does not meet the four-part Geneva Convention requirement (bear arms openly, follow the rules of war, belong to a chain of command and wear insignia). In terms of dress, the civilian is indistinguishable from the combatant. Therein lies the dilemma facing the commander who must decide *quickly* if the person before him/her represents a threat.

The rules of war boil down to one central principle: the need to distinguish combatants from noncombatants. As stated in a previous article by Amos Guiora,

> What concerns us is how the contemporary army prepares itself for today's war, which is fundamentally different from yesterday's war. That difference relates to the core question of whom is the soldier fighting; who is the enemy? Contemporary

---

1 This scenario is fictitious, but is meant to serve as a potential real-world situation for junior commanders on today's battlefields. This scenario should be kept in mind as you read this article regarding the critical strategic, operational and legal decisions that junior commanders must assess and ultimately make regarding human shields. Human shields are a very real threat on today's battlefield. Identifying whether they are there voluntarily or not is an important assessment that a junior commander may have to make before he decides to engage an enemy force. That issue is the essence of our paper.

> armed conflict does not and will not take place on the vast battlefields of the past; rather, it will occur in the back alleys of Groznyy, Nablus and Mosul. The soldier will not be facing another soldier wearing a uniform with insignia, carrying his weapon openly, and serving in a unit with a clear chain of command. In the contemporary combat arena, the combat is far more complicated, complex, and ambiguous than in traditional warfare for two primary reasons. Increasingly, combat will occur in urban centers and not on a battlefield, and civilians will be very much present.[2]

The requirement to distinguish between combatants and civilians is rooted in and articulated by international law, which soldiers are obligated to act in accordance with. Unlike traditional war in which soldiers fought soldiers and tanks attacked tanks, the post 9/11 world is characterized by the "unseen enemy in the dark shadows of the back alleys". The blurring of who is and who is not a combatant on today's battlefield puts a tremendous strain on battlefield commanders actively engaged in the day-to-day fight.

The commander does not want to harm innocent civilians. Neither does the commander want to place the lives of those under his command in further danger by failing to engage who he perceives to be the enemy. Soldiers are by nature in "harm's way"; there is no need to exacerbate that "harm". The security of the unit versus the security of the perceived civilians is the crux of the issue.

Turning perception into reality is what we seek to address. There will likely never be a fail proof solution to determining who is and who is not a combatant in today's asymmetric battlefield environment.[3] However, there should always be a rational framework to rely on and use as a means to assess what the realities on the ground truly are. The security of soldiers and the security of civilians are *the* competing interests at the heart of the assessment.

What increasingly complicates the commanders' dilemma in determining the status either of the individual standing before him, or the shadow he believes to be a person in the near-by alley, is what we describe and define as "voluntary human shields". Our term refers to a civilian who *voluntarily*[4] places himself between the

---

2 See Amos N. Guiora, 'Teaching Morality in Armed Conflict – The Israel Defence Forces Model' in *Jewish Political Studies Review*, Vol. 18 No. 1–2 at 3 (Spring 2006).

3 As suggested by conference participants, the dilemmas we address in this paper are not new; rather issues of battlefield morality and conduct have confronted military commanders through the ages. While that is unarguable, we do suggest that the "post 9/11 world" presents different and unique challenges to nation-states by non-state actors. While this is our working proposition we understand it is a "point in contention" amongst conference participants and others. To that end, one of us (Guiora) will more fully address this issue in a forthcoming project.

4 A term we define as: A person not compelled by another's influence, who acts without compulsion and on his or her own initiative; See also *Black's Law Dictionary* (8th ed., West 2004) Voluntary – 1. Done by design or intention ⟨voluntary act⟩. 2. Unconstrained by interference; not impelled by outside influence; See also *Merriam-Webster Online* (Voluntary – **1**: proceeding from the will or from one's own choice or consent **2**: unconstrained by interference: SELF-DETERMINING **3**: done by design or intention: INTENTIONAL ⟨*voluntary* manslaughter⟩ **4**: of, relating to, subject to, or regulated by the will ⟨*voluntary* behavior⟩ **5**: having power of free choice **6**: provided or supported by voluntary action ⟨a *voluntary*

soldier and the armed combatant. We have chosen to address this issue for multiple reasons: commanders demand clear criteria regarding the status of those in the "zone of combat";[5] the innocent civilian must be protected; international law demands the soldier be trained in distinguishing between the innocent and non-innocent and the community supporting terrorist organizations must know that the truly innocent will be protected (to the greatest extent possible).

It is our thesis that the innocent civilian requires protection from two sources: the military unit that may mis-identify him and categorize him as a threat and from the terrorist organization that has pushed him into the line of fire. In addition, it is our conviction that commander's must clearly define to their soldier's who presents a threat. That threat definition is directly related to our assertion that without mission definition – particularly in operational counter-terrorism – soldiers will invariably engage those who should not be engaged. The absolute requirement to define the mission is directly related to the obligation of the commander to define "who is the enemy".[6] Whether a human shield is voluntary or involuntary is perhaps one of the most important and complicated aspects of the "zone of combat" in the post 9/11 world.

History provides some insight on the impact human shields have on the decisions made on today's battlefield. Commanders are required to examine an extraordinarily broad range of factors in seeking to determine whether an individual is a "voluntary" human shield. They must do so – necessarily – in a matter of seconds. In assessing the threat presented, the commander's "tools" must consist, at a minimum, of the following factors:

- Intelligence information
- Analysis of the conduct of the specific individual
- Battlefield circumstances at the relevant time
- Commander's prior experience
- Conduct of individuals in the surrounding area
- Known tendencies of the enemy
- Public's likely reaction to potential collateral damage

These tools must be integrated into the battlefield assessment calculus from the operational warning order and continually updated up to and including the units' consolidation on the objective and through any subsequent follow-on operations.

We seek to integrate formal intelligence assessment tools into all levels of operational planning that will specifically address the issue of human shields. If the intel-

organization⟩ 7: acting or done of one's own free will without valuable consideration or legal obligation.) Available at: http://www.m-w.com/dictionary/voluntarily (last viewed 25 January 2008).

5 The term refers to the location of a terrorist attack and highlights its flexibility; unlike the set-piece battle field of yesterday, the "zone of combat" includes a just hijacked commercial airliner, a shopping center under attack and an alley in Mosul where American forces are under fire.

6 See Guiora, Amos N. and Martha Minow, 'National Objectives in the Hands of Junior Leaders: IDF Experiences in Combating Terror', in *Countering Terrorism in the 21st Century*, (James JF Forest ed.) Westport, CT: Praeger Security International, 2007.

ligence points to voluntary human shields, then that young leader on today's battlefield, like Captain Smith in our fictional scenario above, can conduct an informed assessment of what is being observed on the objective and respond appropriately.

The individual who voluntarily shields terrorists loses his status as an innocent civilian and is therefore a legitimate military target. The operational consequence of this is that the individual who the soldier concluded was acting voluntarily may be killed by a military unit.[7] There is, accordingly, an extraordinary obligation on the unit to verify "voluntariness". This is extraordinarily difficult, if not all but impossible at times.

However, we are of the opinion that there is no choice but to engage in this debate; we are convinced not only of its appropriateness, but more importantly of its timeliness and relevance in the post 9/11 world. While we do not expect consensus, we do hope to foster debate. Senior military commanders, policy and decision makers, academics, the general public and those supporting terrorists must address this issue. Otherwise, the killing of innocent civilians is as inevitable as the tragic death of a soldier unequipped to determine "who is the enemy".

This article is divided into the following sections: Section II (Applicable Law), Section III (Human Shielding – Definitions and Historical Examples), Section IV (Exploiting the Asymmetrical Advantage – Why Unconventional Forces Engage in the Use of Human Shields) and Section V (Guidance for the Commander). The scenario with which we opened this article will be our "road map" in the following pages.

II. Applicable Law

A. *International Law*

The international law of armed conflict requires attackers and defenders alike to take precautions to reduce the risk of collateral damage and civilian injury.[8] Parties to an armed conflict must abide by the "principle of distinction" whereby the military is not to attack civilians and civilians are to stay out of the conflict. Article 48 of the Protocol Additional to the Geneva Convention provides:

> In order to ensure respect for and protection of the civilian population and civilian objects, the Parties to the conflict shall at all times distinguish between the civilian population and combatants and between civilian objects and military objectives and accordingly shall direct their operations only against military objectives.[9]

7 See Mark Thompson, 'Opening with a Bang' in *Time* (March 17, 2003). (While preparing for the 2003 invasion of Iraq, "[t]he Pentagon has made it clear that it would treat voluntary human shields differently from hostages forced to stay at military targets. Volunteers, a senior Pentagon official [said], are 'working in the service of the Iraqi government and may, in fact, have crossed the line between combatant and noncombatant.' That's another way of saying they could be legitimate targets, he adds.")

8 Hague Regulations Respecting the Laws and Customs of War on Land, Oct. 18, 1907, art. 22, 1 U.S.T. 647 [hereinafter Hague Regulations]. ("The right of belligerents to adopt means of injuring the enemy is not unlimited.").

9 Protocol Additional to the Geneva Conventions of 12 August 1949, and Relating to the Protection of Victims of International Armed Conflicts, art. 48, 16 ILM 1391 (1977).

In an effort to balance the demands of military necessity with humanitarian concerns, the international legal regime requires that attackers discriminate between combatants and noncombatants, and between military assets and civilian property.[10] In *Public Committee Against Torture in Israel v. The Government of Israel*, the Israeli High Court of Justice also addressed balancing military necessity with humanitarian concerns:

> The international law dealing with armed conflicts is based upon a delicate balance between two contradictory considerations [citation omitted]. One consists of the humanitarian considerations regarding those harmed as a result of an armed conflict. These considerations are based upon the rights of the individual, and his dignity. The other consists of military need and success [citation omitted]. The balance between these considerations is the basis of international law of armed conflict. Professor Greenwood discussed that, stating: 'International humanitarian law in armed conflicts is a compromise between military and humanitarian requirements. Its rules comply with both military necessity and the dictates of humanity' DIETER FLECK (ed.) THE HANDBOOK OF HUMANITARIAN LAW IN ARMED CONFLICTS 32 (1995) ... Indeed, 'like in many other areas of law, the solution is not found in 'all' or 'nothing'; the solution is in location of the proper balance between the clashing considerations. The solution is not in assignment of absolute weight to one of the considerations; the solution is in assignment of relative weights to the various considerations, while balancing between them at the point of decision' (citation omitted). The result of that balancing is that human rights are protected by the law of armed conflict, but not to their full scope. The same is so regarding the military needs. They are given an opportunity to be fulfilled, but not to their full scope. This balancing reflects the relativity of human rights, and the limits of military needs. The balancing point is not constant. 'In certain issues the accent is upon the military need, and in others the accent is upon the needs of the civilian population' (citation omitted).[11]

In every armed conflict there are three parties who have obligations: the defender, the civilian population and the attacker. Defenders cannot use the civilian population as a means of shielding their forces or military assets.[12] A civilian cannot engage in direct participation in hostilities if he or she wishes to retain civilian status.[13] As previously stated attackers must discriminate between combatant and civilian and direct their

10 See Emanuel Gross, 'Use of Civilians as Human Shields: What Legal and Moral Restrictions Pertain to a War Waged by a Democratic State Against Terrorism?', in *Emory International Law Review* Vol. 16, pp. 445, 450 (2002).

11 HCJ 769/02, *Public Committee Against Torture in Israel v. The Government of Israel*, (13 December 2006). Available at: http://elyon1.court.gov.il/Files_ENG/02/690/007/a34/02007690.a34.pdf (last viewed 18 January 2008).

12 See Protocol I, supra note 9, art. 51(7).

13 See Protocol I, supra note 9, art. 51(3).

attacks against combatants.[14] In short, each party is obligated to minimize collateral damage. However, this does not mean that civilian casualties are strictly forbidden.

Armed conflict is an inherently dangerous environment where the "fog of war" can be a difficult and formidable obstacle to contend with. Even when all precautions are taken, civilian casualties and civilian property damage are inevitable. As noted by Colonel W. Hays Parks, "[t]arget intelligence, planning times, weather changes and other factors may lead inadvertently to collateral damage."[15] There are also instances where objects, previously classified as civilian structures, lose their civilian status and become legitimate military targets. For example, an office building or residential neighborhood could become a legitimate military target if taken over by an armed force and if the location is used for the purpose of launching attacks.

In other words, the status of the person or property changes; in essence, immunity is lost. Article 51(4) of Protocol I prohibits attacks not directed at a specific military objective or which employ a method or means of combat that cannot be directed at a specific military objective.[16] The international legal regime further requires that attackers refrain from actions likely to cause civilian damage or injury disproportionate to the expected military gain.[17]

At the same time that it regulates the actions of combatants, the international legal regime prohibits a defender from deliberately increasing risks to its own population – for example, by co-mingling civilian and military persons or assets in an effort to shield military targets from attack.[18] Some parties may breach this restriction, creating dilemmas for war planners seeking to hold down the risk or level of civilian injury that results from military operations. Historical examples of such breaches are discussed in Section III (Human Shielding – Definitions and Historical Examples) of this article.

Article 28 of the Geneva Convention Relative to the Protection of Civilian Persons provides that: "The presence of a protected person may not be used to render

---

14 Supra note 9.

15 Colonel W. Hays Parks (Ret.), Address, *Displacement, Protection, of Civilians and the Law of Armed Conflict in the Current Middle East Crisis* (The Brookings Institution, Aug., 15, 2006) (copy on file at: http://www.brookings.edu/fp/projects/idp/20060815_ME_Report_FINAL.pdf last viewed June 27, 2007).

16 See Protocol I, supra note 9, art. 51(4).

17 See Protocol I, supra note 9, art. 35. (Parties to Protocol I are "prohibited [from] employ[ing] weapons, projectiles and material and methods of warfare of a nature to cause superfluous injury or unnecessary suffering."); See also Protocol I, supra note 9, art. 51(5)(b). ("An attack which may be expected to cause incidental loss of civilian life, injury to civilians, damage to civilian objects, or a combination thereof, which would be excessive in relation to the concrete and direct military advantage anticipated.").

18 See Protocol I, supra note 9, art. 51(7). ("The presence or movements of the civilian population or individual civilians shall not be used to render certain points or areas immune from military operations, in particular in attempts to shield military objectives from attacks or to shield, favour or impede military operations. The Parties to the conflict shall not direct the movement of the civilian population or individual civilians in order to attempt to shield military objectives from attacks or to shield military operations.").

certain points or areas immune from military operations."[19] Article 51(7) of Protocol I prohibits the parties from using the civilian population as a human shield or as a means of achieving immunity from military attack. Also, Article 58(b) requires the parties to the conflict avoid, insofar as possible, locating military objectives within or near densely populated areas.[20] Article 44 of Protocol I recognizes an exception in circumstances where, "owing to the nature of the hostilities, an armed combatant cannot so distinguish himself"[21] from the civilian population. In such cases, a combatant need only carry his arms openly "during each military engagement" and "during such time as he is visible to the adversary while he is engaged in a military deployment preceding the launching of an attack ..."[22]

In circumstances where one party breaches these prohibitions, the breach does not entitle the other party to kill civilians. Article 50(3) of Protocol I provides that the presence within the civilian population of individuals who do not come within the definition of civilians does not deprive the population of its civilian character.[23] Accordingly, Article 51(8) emphasizes that even if one party does hide or take refuge behind civilians, this does not release the other party to the conflict from its international humanitarian law obligations with respect to the civilian population.[24] However, when dealing with combatants hiding amongst willing participants – voluntary human shields – we are no longer dealing with accounting for civilians in the targeting assessment. In *Public Committee Against Torture in Israel v. The Government of Israel*, the Israeli High Court of Justice stated that:

> [t]he basic approach is thus as follows: a civilian – that is, a person who does not fall into the category of combatant – must refrain from directly participating in hostilities (citation omitted). A civilian who violates that law and commits acts of combat does not lose his status as a civilian, but as long as he is taking a direct part in hostilities he does not enjoy – during that time – the protection granted to a civilian.[25]

The Red Cross *Model Manual on the Law of Armed Conflict for Armed Forces* similarly supports the notion that civilians lose their protected status once they participate in hostilities.[26] The *Model Manual on the Law of Armed Conflict for Armed Forces* states:

---

19 Geneva Convention Relative to the Protection of Civilian Persons in Time of War, Aug. 12, 1949, art. 28, 6 U.S.T. 3538, 75 U.N.T.S. 308.

20 Protocol I, supra note 9, art. 58. (Parties to Protocol I are obligated to "endeavor to remove the civilian population, including civilians and civilian objects under their control from the vicinity of military objectives.").

21 *Id.* art. 44(3).

22 *Id.* art. 44(3)(a)-(b).

23 *Id.* art. 50(3).

24 *Id.* art. 51(8).

25 HCJ 769/02, *Public Committee Against Torture in Israel v. The Government of Israel*, (13 December 2006). Available at: http://elyon1.court.gov.il/Files_ENG/02/690/007/a34/02007690.a34.pdf (last viewed 18 January 2008).

26 *Model Manual on the Law of Armed Conflict for Armed Forces*, pg. 34 (ICRC, 1999).

"Civilians are not permitted to take direct part in hostilities and are immune from attack. If they take a direct part in hostilities they forfeit this immunity."[27]

Voluntary human shields have crossed the line between an innocent civilian and one who is actively engaged in hostilities. They have, in short, lost their immunity status. They are, in short, no longer innocent civilians. By virtue of crossing this line, we posit that voluntary human shields no longer share the protections afforded to civilians during times of armed conflict. The voluntary human shield is, in fact, an active participant in hostilities and therefore a legitimate target under the laws of armed conflict.

B. *Voluntary Human Shielding – An Issue of Aiding and Abetting*

Voluntary human shields provide aid to the forces they support because the natural consequence of their act of blocking likely targets would, if successful, encourage and advance the interests of the enemy.[28] They are, in a word, seeking to protect terrorists and their infrastructure. By attempting to protect weapons, infrastructure and terrorists voluntary human shields are attempting to enhance the survivability of assets essential to terrorism.

Human shields therefore take a direct part in hostilities, and are not entitled, *if voluntary*, to protection from attack. This interpretation is supported by the *Commentary on the Additional Protocols*, which states that direct participation in acts of war are those acts likely to cause actual harm to the personnel and equipment of the enemy armed forces.[29] The *Commentary on Additional Protocols* also states that

> [u]ndoubtedly there is room here for some margin of judgment: to restrict this concept [direct participation in hostilities] to combat and to active military operations would be too narrow, while extending it to the entire war effort would be too broad, as in modern warfare the whole population participates in the war effort to some extent, albeit indirectly. The population cannot on this ground be considered to be combatants[...].[30]

The drafters of the *Commentary on Additional* emphasize that "direct participation in hostilities" should be defined narrowly enough to protect civilians and maintain the meaning of the principle of distinction. However, the definition should be broad enough to meet the legitimate needs of the armed forces to effectively respond to the

27 *Model Manual on the Law of Armed Conflict for Armed Forces*, pg. 34 (ICRC, 1999).

28 *U.S. v. Al-Arian*, M.D. Fla. 2004, 329 F. Supp. 2d 1294 (the court held that the statute that prohibited providing material support or resources to a terrorist organization required the government to prove beyond a reasonable doubt that the defendant knew the organization was a Foreign Terrorist Organization (FTO) **or** had committed unlawful activities that caused it to be so designated, and what he was furnishing was material support, with the specific intent that the support would further the illegal activities of the FTO).

29 International Committee of the Red Cross, *Commentary on the Additional Protocols of June 1977 to the Geneva Conventions of 12 August 1949*, Yves Sandoz, Christopher Swinarski, and Bruno Zimmermann, eds., Geneva: Martinus Nijhoff Publishers, 1987, p. 618.

30 *Id.* at p. 516.

means and methods of warfare relevant to asymmetric warfare. Furthermore, the *Commentary* states that, "at least in the case of civilians, the term 'hostilities' covers both times when the person is using or carrying a weapon, as well as situations in which he undertakes hostile acts without using a weapon."[31] Direct participation in hostilities, therefore, includes not only activities involving the delivery of violence, but also acts aimed at protecting personnel, infrastructure or materiel.

Voluntary human shields aid the enemy by helping them protect their personnel and military assets from attack by acting as *innocent* civilians in and around important assets, thus shielding them from potential attack. Defining "aiding and abetting" in the international context can be augmented by examining the U.S. statutory definition. 18 U.S.C. § 2339B provides that anyone who:

> [K]nowingly provides material support or resources to a foreign terrorist organization, or attempts or conspires to do so, shall be fined under this title or imprisoned not more than 15 years, or both, and, if the death of any person results, shall be imprisoned for any term of years or for life. To violate this paragraph, a person must have knowledge that the organization is a designated terrorist organization ... that the organization has engaged or engages in terrorist activity ... or that the organization has engaged or engages in terrorism.[32]

We argue that the international community needs to clearly define voluntary human shielding as unlawful and thereby strip the voluntary human shields of any protected status as civilians. We posit that criminalizing the act of voluntarily shielding a legitimate military target by individuals masquerading as civilians by defining it as unlawful aiding and abetting will help to clearly distinguish the act as illegal from the perspective of the international community. Any ambiguities with respect to the status of voluntary human shields (combatant or civilian) could potentially be resolved by criminalizing voluntarily acting as a human shield of a legitimate military target. Voluntary human shields have abandoned their status as civilians; the state has the responsibility to duly inform them of the potential consequences of their actions. A bright line rule will bring immediate predictability to the status of voluntary human shields. The social and moral debates regarding the status of voluntary human shields will give way to practical, legally based consequences for engaging in the act of voluntarily shielding a legitimate military target. The practical consequences are clear – voluntary human shields are combatants.

---

31 Parrish, Richard. 'The International Legal Status of Voluntary Human Shields' Paper presented at the annual meeting of the International Studies Association, Le Centre Sheraton Hotel, Montreal, Quebec, Canada, 2004-03-17 Online ⟨.PDF⟩. 2007-05-21 (quoting from International Committee of the Red Cross, *Commentary on the Additional Protocols of June 1977 to the Geneva Conventions of 12 August 1949*, Yves Sandoz, Christopher Swinarski, and Bruno Zimmermann, eds., Geneva: Martinus Nijhoff Publishers, 1987, p. 619.) (internal quotes omitted).

32 18 U.S.C. § 2339B(a)(1) (2004).

III. Human Shielding – Definitions and Historical Examples

A. *Definitions*

There are three different classifications of human shields: (1) proximity human shields, (2) involuntary human shields/hostages, and (3) voluntary human shields.[33] Proximity human shields are human shields by their propinquity to legitimate military targets.[34] Proximity human shields have not been coerced to participate or have not volunteered to provide a shielding force.[35] Proximity human shields are present on the battlefield because a belligerent force has chosen to co-mingle with the civilian population in an effort to gain protective cover provided by a surrounding civilian population. Proximity human shields by virtue of their proximity to legitimate targets are, in many instances, collateral damage. Military planners have to consider collateral damage in assessing potential targets.[36]

Involuntary human shields (or hostages) are unwilling participants forced into service by an armed force or terrorist organization.[37] Saddam Hussein's regime in Iraq engaged in this practice.[38] During Operation Desert Shield, Saddam Hussein's regime held hundreds of non-Iraqi civilians at government and military facilities throughout Iraq and described them as "human shields".[39] The Central Intelligence Agency released a report stating that Saddam Hussein

33 See Captain Daniel P. Schoenekase, 'Targeting Decisions Regarding Human Shields', in *Military Review*, pp. 26–31 (September – October 2004). ("Human Shields are noncombatants whose presence protects certain objects or areas from attack.") Available at: http://www.au.af.mil/au/awc/awcgate/milreview/schoenekase.pdf (last viewed April 9, 2007).

34 *Id.* at 26.

35 *Id.*

36 Thompson, supra note 7 ("Civilian casualties are a political and military nightmare. Human-rights groups estimate that about 3,500 Iraqi civilians died in the 1991 war. U.S. officials refuse to estimate the numbers of civilian expected deaths in a second Gulf War. It could get extremely messy, with the carnage broadcast instantly around the world. 'What appears on al-Jazeera TV in the region is going to determine success maybe even more so than the actions on the ground,' says retired Marine General Anthony Zinni, who ran Central Command from 1997 to 2000. 'All the explanations afterwards won't counter those first images.'").

37 *Id*; For a sampling of reports or cases of recent involuntary human shields see *Hill v. Republic of Iraq*, 175 F. Supp. 2d 36 (D.D.C. 2001)(Americans used as human shields by Iraq during first Gulf War); *Ange v. Bush*, 752 F. Supp. 509 (D.D.C. 1990) (American citizens used as human shields by Iraq during first Gulf war); *Begzatowski v. Immigration and Naturalization Service*, 278 F.3d 665 (7th Cir. 2002) (Albanian seeking U.S. asylum, used by Serbians as a human shield); and J. Aglionby, *Rebels Use Children as Human Shields*, The Guardian, June 4, 2001, at http:// www.guardian.co.uk/international/story (n.d.).

38 *Putting Noncombatants at Risk: Saddam's Use of "Human Shields"*, Central Intelligence Agency (January 2003). Available at: http://ftp.fas.org/irp/cia/product/iraq_human_shields/index.html#01 (last viewed December 11, 2007).

39 *Id.* (In late 1990, Saddam held more than 800 Western, Japanese, and Kuwaiti nationals as involuntary human shields at strategic installations in Iraq and Kuwait to deter attack

> … regularly imposed involuntary service as human shields on Iraqi citizens by authorizing the placement of high-value military units and equipment in heavily populated civilian neighborhoods and near civilian facilities, such as mosques, markets, schools, and cultural sites. The tactic is designed to conceal these military assets but also to deter – or, failing that, to capitalize on – Coalition attacks on them through the high likelihood of collateral civilian casualties.[40]

Similar to proximity human shields, military planners have to consider involuntary human shields during the targeting process.[41]

The third type of human shields are voluntary human shields. Voluntary human shields are individuals who willingly assist the armed force or terrorist organization.[42] There has been much debate concerning whether voluntary human shields have become de facto combatants by their active participation in hostilities. Captain Daniel Schoenekase writes:

> Some scholars argue that voluntary human shields forfeit immunity … a group of law professors and attorneys wrote, '[d]eath or injury to human shields … who voluntarily take up positions at the site of legitimate military objectives, does not constitute civilian collateral damage, because those voluntary human shields have assumed the risk of combat and, to that extent, have compromised their noncombatant immunity.[43]

The argument that voluntary human shields are, in fact, belligerents and therefore stripped of any protections associated with a civilian status is analyzed in Section II of this article.

---

by the international Coalition being organized against Baghdad. Saddam refused to allow thousands of other foreigners, including women and children, whose countries had joined the Coalition to leave Iraq or Kuwait and announced that they also might be used as human shields.)

40 *Id.*

41 See *Israel bans use of human shields*, BBC News ("Israel's supreme court has banned the use of Palestinian human shields in arrest raids, saying the practice violates international law … The army cannot use civilians for its purposes, Israel's chief justice said. 'You cannot exploit the civilian population for the army's military needs, and you cannot force them to collaborate with the army,' Aharon Barak said.") Available at: http://news.bbc.co.uk/1/hi/world/middle_east/4314898.stm (last viewed 30 January 2008); See also Steven Erlanger, *Israel: Rebuke Over 'Human Shield'*, New York Times (October 19, 2007) ("The former Israeli commander of the West Bank, Brig. Gen. Yair Golan, was reprimanded after an investigation of a 'human shield' episode in Nablus, in the West Bank, in March, the army said.") Available at: http://www.nytimes.com/2007/10/19/world/middleeast/19briefs-general.html?_r=1&ref=middleeast&oref=slogin (last viewed 30 January 2008).

42 For recent examples of voluntary human shields, see AFP, *Activists to be Palestinian 'human shields,'* The Advertiser, at ⟨http:// www.theadvertiser.news.com.au/common/story_page⟩ (n.d.); Reuters, *After Smiles and Song, Sober Truth for Iraq Shields*, (March 19, 2003); IMRA, *Excerpts: Bulldozer death of human shield activist*, at http:// www.imra.org.il/story.php3? id=16203 (March 18, 2003); US Dept. of Defense, *News Transcript: Briefing on Human Shields in Iraq*, at: ⟨http:// www.defenselink.mil/news/Feb2003/⟩ (February 26, 2003); Human Rights Watch, *Human Shields in Iraq Put Obligations on U.S.*, available at: ⟨http:// www.hrw.org/press/2003/02/iraq022.htm⟩ (February 20, 2003).

43 Schoenekase, supra note 33.

B. *Historical Examples*

History has shown that enemy forces are willing to incorporate the tactic of human shields in an effort to gain an operational advantage. In adopting this technique, enemy forces or terrorist organizations hope that the potential for political backlash resulting from anticipated collateral damage will deter military intervention. The use of human shields aims to confront military (and political) planners with a dilemma – refrain from attacking (or attack under extremely restrictive rules of engagement) certain targets, therefore risking degraded military effectiveness, or attack the targets effectively and risk collateral damage.

By breaching their legal obligations to segregate military and civilian assets and persons, terrorists can deter operational counter-terrorism campaigns or compel military (and political) planners to choose between military effectiveness and the risk of collateral damage. Learning from the various historical examples of the use of human shields seems a suitable starting point for analyzing the operational and strategic implications of this tactic.

In Sri Lanka, the Tamil Tigers[44] have a long history of using involuntary human shields by forcing the civilian population to stand between them and government forces during active combat engagements.[45] This tactic has resulted in many civilian deaths.[46] The Tigers have attempted to gain an advantage over Sri Lankan government forces by exploiting the civilian deaths.[47] The Tigers have used the civilian deaths as a form of propaganda seeking to show Sri Lankan responses that lack careful and diligent targeting decisions frequently resulting in large numbers of civilian casualties.[48] The attempted exploitation, though, is failing. The mounting civilian casualties are causing the Tamil Tigers to lose popular support for their cause.[49]

The use of human shielding (proximity human shielding in this case) also occurred in the Second Lebanon War (summer, 2006) between Israel and Hezbol-

---

44 'Liberation Tigers of Tamil Eelam (Sri Lanka, separatists)', Council on Foreign Relations (August 2006), ("The Liberation Tigers of Tamil Eelam (LTTE) is a separatist terrorist group that seeks an independent state in areas in Sri Lanka inhabited by ethnic Tamils. (*Eelam* means homeland in Tamil.) The LTTE, also known as the Tamil Tigers, has used conventional, guerrilla, and terror tactics, including some 200 suicide bombings, in a bloody, two-decade-old civil war that has claimed more than 60,000 lives and displaced hundreds of thousands of Sri Lankans. The U.S. State Department lists the LTTE as a foreign terrorist organization.") Available at: http://www.cfr.org/publication/9242/ (last viewed 09 December 2007).

45 'Realities Behind Human Shielding: For a Few Days More', *Media Centre for National Security* (April 8, 2007). See also, 'LTTE holding IDPs as human shield, preventing them entering Government controlled areas', in *Asian Tribune*, (August 14, 2008), Available at: http://www.asiantribune.com/?q=node/12728 (last viewed 22 September 2008).

46 See generally 'Anger over Lanka Civilian Deaths', *BBC News*, (November 9, 2006). Available at: http://news.bbc.co.uk/1/hi/world/south_asia/6131566.stm (last viewed 01 January 2008).

47 'Realities Behind Human Shielding: For a Few Days More', in *Media Centre for National Security* (April 8, 2007).

48 *Id.*

49 *Id.*

lah. A New York Times article recounts Hezbollah militiamen bringing arms and munitions into a Sunni village on the Lebanese-Israeli border in an effort to "shield" their activity by using the civilian village as a form of cover and concealment.[50] The result of this incursion into the Sunni village was 23 villagers killed during an Israeli airstrike.[51] The civilian deaths led to harsh criticism of Hezbollah tactics by members of the village. This is significant because "[c]riticism of Hezbollah is rare in southern Lebanon, where the group exercises significant influence and economic power."[52] The residents of the village accused Hezbollah of using them as human shields.[53]

The villagers stated that when they fled the village, the Hezbollah militia did too.[54] This should be proof enough of the intent of the Hezbollah militia. One resident stated, "[w]e want the army and the United Nations to come in here and protect us," he said. "Israel is our enemy, but the problem is that Hezbollah gave them an excuse to come in and kill our children."[55]

Israel felt their own backlash from the international community for the number of civilian casualties during some of the confrontations with Hezbollah militants in Lebanon. The international community was quick to respond to the number of Lebanese civilian casualties by strongly criticizing Israel for their military targeting decisions.[56] Human Rights Watch executive director, Kenneth Roth, commented on the issue of Israel's targeting decisions against Hezbollah militants in Lebanon.

> Hezbollah fighters often didn't carry their weapons in the open or regularly wear military uniforms, which made them a hard target to identify, … [b]ut this doesn't justify the Israel Defence Forces' failure to distinguish between civilians and combatants, and if in doubt to treat a person as a civilian, as the laws of war require.[57]

Israel responded to the condemnation by emphasizing that Hezbollah flagrantly violated international law by deliberating using Lebanese civilian population centers to shield their munitions caches and to launch their rocket attacks from.[58] Israel made attempts to limit the potential civilian casualties.

---

50 Hassan M. Fattah, 'At Funeral, a Sunni Village Condemns Hezbollah's Presence', in *The New York Times* (August 25, 2006).

51 *Id.*

52 *Id.*

53 *Id.*

54 *Id.*

55 *Id.*

56 Dan Williams, 'Report Blames Israel for Lebanon War Civilian Deaths', in *Reuters* (September 6, 2007). Available at: http://www.reuters.com/article/worldNews/idUSL053893620070906?sp=true (last viewed 01 January 2008).

57 *Id.*

58 'Hezbollah's Human Shields', in *The Washington Times* (July 31, 2006). See also Dan Williams, 'Report Blames Israel for Lebanon War Civilian Deaths', in *Reuters* (September 6, 2007). ("Israel said its forces, which overran Hezbollah's strongholds, had acted lawfully. 'We conform with accepted norms in the conduct of military conflict and we conformed with the accepted norms in the conduct of the rules of war,' said Mark Regev, spokesman for Israel's Foreign Ministry. Regev cited U.N. relief coordinator Jan Egeland, who told CNN on July 26, 2006 that Hezbollah guerrillas were unlawfully 'shielding

> Israel Defense Forces [had] relinquished the element of surprise by dropping leaflets on Qana and many other Lebanese towns telling residents that they should leave the area because the IDF is preparing to conduct military operations against Hezbollah. Just as Israel tries to move Lebanese civilians out of the line of fire, Hezbollah does its best to put them in danger and peril.[59]

Human shields were also used during the Vietnam War. "Cambodian government forces used ethnic Vietnamese civilians as human shields as they advanced on Vietnamese positions."[60] The North Vietnamese also used proximity human shields by co-locating their forces and weapons with civilian populations near Hanoi.[61] The North Vietnamese accused the United States of flagrantly attacking civilian areas and causing massive suffering during December 1966 air strikes against railway targets near Hanoi.[62] These North Vietnamese tactics caused U.S. forces significant targeting[63] dilemmas. The targeting process required U.S. combatant commanders to balance between legitimate military targets and the risk of collateral damage.

Additional examples of human shields include Bosnian Serb tactics during Operation Allied Force in Kosovo.

> Yugoslav President Slobodan Milosevic has a history of putting civilians and other noncombatants in harm's way, said David Scheffer, U.S. ambassador-at-large for War Crimes Issues. In Bosnia between 1992 and 1995, Serb forces put hundreds of hostage U.N. peacekeepers and civilians at key military locations to deter attacks.[64]

In addition to the U.S. ambassador-at-large for War Crimes Issues, NATO also accused President Slobodan Milosevic of the widespread use of civilians as "human shields" around targets in Kosovo.[65] CNN recounted the following in an online news report:

---

themselves close to U.N. posts and close to the civilian population'. Egeland also condemned Israel's tactics. Regev said: 'Hezbollah had a clear pattern of behavior where it embedded itself among the Lebanese civilian population and exploited it as human shields. This is not just the Israeli understanding.'") Available at: http://www.reuters.com/article/worldNews/ idUSL0538936200709062sp=true (last viewed 01 January 2008).

59 *Id.*

60 Schoenekase, supra note 33.

61 Stephen T. Hosmer, *Constraints on U.S. Strategy in Third World Conflicts* (New York: Crane Russak & Co., 1987), p. 61; Pentagon Papers (Gravel Edition), Vol. IV (Boston: Beacon Press), p. 135.

62 *Id.*

63 Joint Publication 1-02, *DOD Dictionary of Military and Associated Terms*, pg. 537, April 12, 2001 (amended 17 October 2007). (The United States Department of Defense defines targeting as "[t]he process of selecting and prioritizing targets and matching the appropriate response to them, considering operational requirements and capabilities."). Available at: http://www.dtic.mil/doctrine/jel/new_pubs/jp1_02.pdf (last viewed 30 January 2008).

64 Linda D. Kozaryn, 'Serb "Human Shield" Ploys Are War Crimes, U.S. Envoy Says', in *American Forces Press Service* (May 19, 1999). Available at: http://www.defenselink.mil/news/newsarticle.aspx?id=42058 (last viewed 30 January 2008).

65 CNN.com, 'NATO says 'human shields' account for bombing deaths', May 18, 1999, Available at: http://www.cnn.com/WORLD/europe/9905/17/kosovo.03/ (last viewed 30 January 2008).

> NATO spokesman Jamie Shea told reporters in Brussels on Monday that the organization had documented dozens of reports of Kosovar Albanians being used as human shields. Shea mentioned three new reports: In mid-April, 500 young Albanians in the town of Presevo 'were pressed into military service, forced to wear the uniform of the Yugoslav army and told they would be used as human shields and I quote, 'as soon as a NATO troop offensive began.' In late March, 10,000 residents from the town of Cirez were 'forced to serve as human shields in the munitions factory at Srbica.' On April 6, Serb police rounded up 4,000 people in Doganovic and 'forced them to be human shields in a quarry.'[66]

Bosnian Serbs used human shields in an effort to thwart NATO bombing missions.[67] John Tirpak pointed out in more detail the Bosnian Serb tactic of using human shields in hopes of swaying public opinion on NATO bombing and NATO targeting:

> NATO pointed out that the Serbs had adopted a tactic of holding Kosovar hostages near targets of military significance, both in plain view and hidden. Those in plain view were intended to ward off attacks; those hidden were, if killed, to be displayed later as an example of NATO's reckless bombing of civilians. Both human-shield tactics were cited as violations of international norms by the International War Crimes Tribunal.[68]

The International Tribunal for the former Yugoslavia indicted Radovan Karadzic and Ratko Mladic for violations of international humanitarian law, including using hostages as human shields, in and around Srebrenica in 1995.[69] Zatko Aleksovski was

---

66 *Id.*

67 Schoenekase, supra note 33.

68 John A. Tirpak, 'Victory in Kosovo', in *Air Force Magazine*, Vol. 82, No. 7, (July 1999). Available at: http://www.afa.org/magazine/July1999/0799watch_print.html (last viewed 01 January 2008).

69 *The Prosecutor of the International Tribunal for the Former Yugoslavia v Radovan Karadzic and Ratko Mladic*, Case No. IT-95-5-I. (Part III, Counts 13–16 of the indictment states that "[a]fter seizing UN peacekeepers in the Pale area, Bosnian Serb military personnel, under the direction and control of RADOVAN KARADZIC and RATKO MLADIC, immediately selected certain UN hostages to use as "human shields," including but not limited to Capt. Patrick A. Rechner (Canada), Capt. Oldrich Zidlik (Czech Republic) Captain Teterevsky (Russia), Maj. Abdul Razak Bello (Nigeria), Capt. Ahmad Manzoor (Pakistan) and Maj. Gunnar Westlund (Sweden). From on or about 26 May 1995 through 27 May 1995, Bosnian Serb military personnel physically secured or otherwise held the UN peacekeepers against their will at potential NATO air targets, including the ammunition bunkers at Jahorinski Potok, the Jahorina radar site and a nearby communications centre in order to render these locations immune from further NATO airstrikes. High level Bosnian Serb political and military delegations inspected and photographed the UN hostages who were handcuffed at the ammunition bunkers at Jahorinski Potok." "RADOVAN KARADZIC and RATKO MLADIC, individually and in concert with others planned, instigated, ordered or otherwise aided and abetted in the planning, preparation or execution of the taking of civilians, that is UN peacekeepers, as hostages and, additionally, using them as "human shields" and knew or had reason to know that subordinates were about to take and hold UN peacekeepers as hostages and about to use them as "human shields" or had done so and failed to take necessary and reasonable mea-

also indicted and ultimately convicted for using detainees as human shields.[70] He was sentenced to seven years in prison.[71]

IV. Exploiting the Asymmetrical Advantage – Why Unconventional Forces Engage in the Use of Human Shields

Asymmetric warfare refers, in general, to tactics employed by states and non-state groups who strive to strike weak points in the social, economic, and political structures of militarily superior nations or forces in an effort to avoid direct confrontation with these stronger forces.[72] Asymmetric warfare encompasses "unorthodox, indirect, surprising, [unlawful] or even 'unthinkable' methods"[73] of challenging the military dominance of other nations.

Terrorists have conducted an assessment of their "centers of gravity"[74] and their "critical vulnerabilities,"[75] as well as assessing the centers of gravity and critical vulnerabilities of the United States and its allies. As stated in Marine Corps Doctrinal Publication 1, *Warfighting*, centers of gravity and critical vulnerabilities can be summed up as follows:

> Depending on the situation, centers of gravity may be intangible characteristics such as resolve or morale. They may be capabilities such as armored forces or aviation strength. They may be localities such as a critical piece of terrain that anchors an entire defensive system. They may be the relationship between two or more components of the system such as the cooperation between two arms, the relations in an alliance, or the junction of two forces. In short, centers of gravity are any important sources of strength. If they are friendly centers of gravity, we want to protect them, and if they are enemy centers of gravity, we want to take them away ... In battlefield terms, this means that we should generally avoid [the enemy's] front, where his attention is focused and he is strongest, and seek out his flanks and rear, where he does not expect us and where we can also cause the greatest psychological damage. We should also strike at a moment in time when he is vulnerable. Of all the

---

sures to prevent them from doing so or to punish the perpetrators thereof." "In regard to the UN peacekeepers used as "human shields" on 26 and 27 May 1995, RADOVAN KARADZIC and RATKO MLADIC, by their acts and omissions, committed: Count 15: a GRAVE BREACH as recognised by Articles 2(b) (inhuman treatment), 7(1) and 7(3) of the Statute of the Tribunal. Count 16: a VIOLATION OF THE LAWS OR CUSTOMS OF WAR (cruel treatment) as recognised by Articles 3, 7(1) and 7(3) of the Statute of the Tribunal.") Available at: http://www.un.org/icty/indictment/english/kar-ii950724e.htm (last viewed December 11, 2007).

70 Schoenekase, supra note 33.

71 *Id.*

72 Steven Lambakis, James Kiras, and Kristin Kolet, *Understanding "Asymmetric" Threats to the United States*, National Institute for Public Policy (September 2002). http://www.nipp.org/Adobe/Asymmetry%20%20final%2002.pdf (last visited April 09, 2007).

73 *Id.*

74 *Warfighting*, Marine Corps Doctrinal Publication 1 (1997), p. 46. Available at: http://www.dtic.mil/doctrine/jel/service_pubs/mcdp1.pdf (last viewed April 9, 2007).

75 *Id.* at pp. 46–47.

> vulnerabilities we might choose to exploit, some are more critical to the enemy than others. Some may contribute significantly to the enemy's downfall while others may lead only to minimal gains. Therefore, we should focus our efforts against a critical vulnerability, a vulnerability that, if exploited, will do the most significant damage to the enemy's ability to resist us.[76]

This is the essence of guerrilla tactics and asymmetric warfare. The terrorists know all too well that they cannot compete "mano y mano" with the superior technological capabilities or with the vast fiscal resources of the United States and its allies. Max Boot opined that

> [g]iven the size and scope of America's military advantage, it is doubtful that any country will mount a full-spectrum challenge to U.S. military capabilities in the foreseeable future. The entry barriers are simply too high, especially for air, sea, and space systems. Virginia-class nuclear submarines cost $ 2.4 billion, Nimitz-class aircraft carriers go for $ 6 billion, and the F-35 Joint Strike Fighter program will cost at least $ 245 billion. The U.S. spends around $ 500 billion a year on its military, almost as much as the rest of the world combined. In fact, the U.S. spends more simply on the research, development, testing, and evaluation of new weapons – $ 71 billion in 2006 – than any other country spends on its entire armed forces. (By way of comparison, the top three spenders after the U.S. are Russia, whose defense budget in 2003 was estimated at $ 65 billion; China, at $ 56 billion; France, at $ 45 billion; and Japan and the United Kingdom, at $ 42 billion. These are only estimates; the figures for Russia and China may be considerably higher.)[77]

As they cannot compete on a level playing field with the military strength and technological superiority of the U.S. and its allies, non-state actors have found at least one tool to use to their advantage – "human shields."[78] The use of human shields has become an effective weapon used by the weak to thwart the efforts of the strong. "Terrorists are fanatics, but they are not idiots. If the terrorist tactic of using human shields helps them achieve their goals, they will utilize it. If it undermines their goals, they will abandon it."[79] It is an important tactic employed in conflicts with militarily superior nations to influence targeting decisions, sway public opinion, and protect limited assets.[80]

---

76 *Id.*

77 Max Boot, 'The Paradox of Military Technology', *The New Atlantis*, Number 14, Fall 2006.

78 Schoenekase, supra note 33.

79 Yaalon, Moshe, *The Washington Post*, 03 August 2006.

80 Matthew Waxman, *International Law and the Politics of Urban Air Operations*, Rand Monograph Report (2000), quoting Louis Henkin, *How Nations Behave: Law and Foreign Policy* (New York: Praeger, 1968), p. 44. ("In adopting these techniques, adversaries hope that the potential for U.S. casualties or political backlash resulting from anticipated collateral damage will deter U.S. intervention. In the event that the United States intervenes, these techniques aim to confront U.S. planners with a dilemma – refrain from attacking (or attack under extremely tight operational restrictions) certain targets, therefore risking degraded military effectiveness, or attack the targets effectively and risk collateral damage or perhaps higher levels of U.S. casualties."). See also Lloyd J. Matthews, *Challenging*

Terrorists often understand that "[i]f excessive force is used against a civilian community where terrorist live and operate, the most moderate of people within that community may begin to sympathize with the terrorist causes."[81] As noted earlier in the article, civilian casualties resulting from terrorists deliberately co-mingling with the civilian population can backfire.[82] The civilian population can end up turning against the terrorists for putting the civilian population in a position that subjects them to the combatant force armed engagements.

However, history is also replete with instances where civilian casualties result in additional popular support for the terrorists.[83] Protecting civilians during counter-terrorism operations is paramount to the ultimate mission success. The United Nations has attempted to highlight the importance of accounting for the protection of the civilian population during combat operation. General Kofi Annan called for the establishment of a "culture of protection" during his 30 March 2001 report on the Protection of Civilians in Armed Conflict.[84]

> In such a culture, Governments would live up to their responsibilities, armed groups would respect the recognized rules of international humanitarian law, the private sector would be conscious of the impact of its engagement in crisis areas, and Member States and international organizations would display the necessary commitment to ensure decisive and rapid action in the face of crisis. The establishment of this culture will depend on the willingness of Member States not only to adopt some of the measures (outlined in the report) but also to deal with the reality of armed groups and other non-state actors in conflicts, and the role of civil society in moving from vulnerability to security and from war to peace.[85]

---

the United States Symmetrically and Asymmetrically: Can America Be Defeated?, Strategic Studies Institute, p. 7, (Army War College, July 1998). ("Enemies may perceive vulnerable asymmetries in what the West views as its virtues. While the mindset in the United States and the West sees, [omitted], the 'moral strengths' and the 'ethical standards' of its troops as keys to military power, adversaries willing to abandon Westernized legal and ethical regimes may well consider them as things to exploit and manipulate. Increasingly, opponents will seek to present Western militaries with moral and ethical conundrums.")

81 Aisha Sabadia and Greg Austin, *Protect! Civilians and Civil Rights in Counter-Terrorist Operations*, East West Institute (August 2007). Available at: http://www.ewi.info/pdf/PROTECTIONciviliansFINAL1.pdf (last viewed 11 December 2007); See also Hassan M. Fattah, 'At Funeral, a Sunni Village Condemns Hezbollah's Presence', in *The New York Times* (August 25, 2006).

82 *Realities Behind Human Shielding: For a Few Days More*, Media Centre for National Security (April 8, 2007).

83 See William M. *Arkin*, 'Lebanese Civilian Deaths May Embolden Terrorists', in *The Washington Post*, July 19, 2006, available at: http://blog.washingtonpost.com/earlywarning/2006/07/understanding_israeli_and_leba.html (last viewed 30 January 2008). See also Contra Costa Times, 'U.S. anti-terror sweep angers Iraqis', (June 18, 2005) ("But the head tribal sheik of the town, Osama Jadaan Dulaimi, said the American troops were only further inflaming the rage and sense of persecution among the nation's minority Sunni Muslim community, the backbone of the insurgency that's killed thousands.").

84 Id.

85 Id. Quoting from *Introduction to United Nations Office for the Coordination of Humanitarian Affairs: Protection of Civilians.*

States must take into account civilian casualties in the planning and execution of counter-terrorism operations. "Counterterrorist operations lack credibility and are self-defeating when states advocating freedom resort to disproportionate force."[86]

The conceptual challenge in the war on terror will be to transform the traditional strategic approach away from industrial-age military concepts that focus primarily on conventional, symmetrical threats and responses suitable to maneuver-style warfare. Instead, States will need to develop concepts that include the capability to deal with non-conventional, asymmetrical threats by employing new tactics, techniques and procedures. "The practical challenge will be to address existing weaknesses and gaps in strategy, adapt to fundamental changes in the national security environment as it transforms from the industrial age to the information age, and develop a grand strategy for success."[87]

"The United States [and its allies] generally benefits from status quo stability and international order, whereas its adversaries are often interested in overturning that order, '[s]ince law is generally a conservative force, it is more likely to be observed by those more content with their lot.' "[88] The adversaries of the United States and its allies recognize the tactical advantages they can gain by defying international legal norms. Utilizing tactics, such as the use of human shields, gives terrorist organizations an effective, albeit illegal, means of creating a dilemma for opposing forces.

Commanders are faced with many decision points once terrorist organizations or enemy forces introduce human shields into the equation. As the scenario at the beginning of this article alludes to, commanders must determine whether the human shield is friend, foe, or innocent bystander. After making this determination, the commander then must consider the impact of potential civilian casualties or the perception that civilian casualties occurred. These decisions often have to be made by the commander on the ground with little to no time to contemplate the pros and cons of the decision that is being made.

V. Guidance for the Commander

A. *The Critical Issue Associated With Voluntary Human Shields – Assessing Voluntariness*

A voluntary human shield should be considered a belligerent and therefore part and parcel of the opposition forces.[89] Claims can be made that voluntary shields are not direct participants because "[t]heir actions do not pose a direct risk to

86 Id. at pg 5.

87 Donald J. Reed, 'Why Strategy Matters in the War on Terror', *Homeland Security Affairs*, Volume II, No. 3 (October 2006). Available at: http://www.hsaj.org/pages/volume2/issue3/pdfs/2.3.10.pdf (last viewed December 11, 2007).

88 Matthew Waxman, *International Law and the Politics of Urban Air Operations*, Rand Monograph Report (2000), quoting Louis Henkin, *How Nations Behave: Law and Foreign Policy* (New York: Praeger, 1968), p. 49.

89 See William J. Fenrick, 'The Targeted Killings Judgment and the Scope of Direct Participation in Hostilities', in *Journal of International Criminal Justice*, Vol. 5 (May 2007) p. 332.

opposing forces" and they are not "directly engaged in hostilities."[90] Such an assertion ignores the fact that voluntary human shields are deliberately attempting to preserve a valid military objective for use by the enemy. "In this sense, [voluntary human shields] are no different from point air defenses, which serve to protect the target rather than destroy inbound aircraft. Voluntary shielding is unquestionably direct participation."[91]

The volitional participation in hostilities on the part of a voluntary human shield strips them of their civilian status and makes them legitimate targets for military operations.[92] The critical issue for the battlefield commander, though, still hinges on discriminating between combatants and noncombatants. Determining whether persons engaged in the act of human shielding are doing so voluntarily or involuntarily becomes an important assessment that could potentially dictate the course of action chosen by the battlefield commander.

> [M]ilitary authorities cannot afford to debate the issue with a human shield actually on the ground in a combat area, thereby putting troops in even greater harm's way by resulting delay or inaction. Unfortunately, a committed but intractable human shield might have to be taken out quickly by either persuasion at best or by weapons at worst.[93]

Many of the battlefield commanders' targeting decisions can become streamlined, though, if it is determined that the human shields located on or in the vicinity of the intended target are there voluntarily. The voluntary human shields are no longer a part of the civilian damage quotient of the proportionality calculus. Voluntary humans shields would be legitimate targets.

The difficulty for the battlefield commander remains in determining whether the human shields are there voluntarily or if they are there due to coercion, duress, or even unknowingly. Providing battlefield commanders with decision-making guidelines regarding the determination of whether or not the human shields on their objective are unknowing or unwilling civilians (non-combatants) or if they are indeed combatants is an important and critical tool that must be introduced during training.

The term "voluntary" is often used in the criminal law context to express the general conclusion that a defendant possessed sufficient free will to be blamed for

---

90 Human Rights Watch, Briefing Paper, *International Humanitarian Law Issues in a Potential War in Iraq* (Feb 20, 2003). Available at: http://www.hrw.org/backgrounder/arms/iraq0202003.htm (last visited May 20, 2007).

91 Michael N. Schmitt. 'Humanitarian Law and Direct Participation in Hostilities by Private Contractors or Civilian Employees', in *Chicago Journal of Int'l Law* Vol. 5 (2005) pp. 511, 541.

92 In many cases, it will serve no valid military purpose to directly target the voluntary human shields. The objective should be the target they are shielding, not the actual human shields. However, the fact that they are directly participating in hostilities and now belligerents means that their injury or death should not factor into the required proportionality calculation under international law.

93 Alfred J. Sciarrino and Kenneth L. Deutsch, 'Conscientious Objection to War: Heroes to Human Shields', *Bringham Young University Journal of Pub. Law*, Vol. 18 (2003) pp. 59, 106.

his or her conduct.[94] Oliver Wendell Holmes analogized a voluntary act as "willed" contraction of a muscle.[95] Pursuant to the Model Penal Code (MPC), criminal liability depends on one "fundamental predicate": A defendant's guilt must be based on conduct that includes a *voluntary* act or an omission to engage in a *voluntary* act that the defendant is physically capable of performing.[96] Under the MPC, liability cannot be based on "mere thoughts," involuntary acts, or physical conditions.[97] These MPC standards were written and designed to comport with key United States Supreme Court decisions.[98]

Unfortunately, the MPC never specifically defines the term "voluntary."[99] Instead, it provides four examples of acts that are ***not*** voluntary: "(a) a reflex or convulsion; (b) a bodily movement during unconsciousness or sleep; (c) conduct during hypnosis or resulting from hypnotic suggestion; (d) a bodily movement that otherwise is not a product of the effort or determination of the actor, either conscious or habitual."[100] Although the MPC explains that these examples emphasize "conduct that is within the control of the actor,"[101] it provides little additional guidance and is otherwise vague.

We argue that "voluntary", in the context of the actions of human shields, should be defined as an intentional act conducted without the influence of duress or coercion. Defining "voluntary" is something presumably easy to conceive on paper, as we have just done. However, developing a true understanding of what is happening in the operational environment on the ground becomes a much different issue. Attempting to understand if the human shields are on the battlefield voluntarily or due to coercion, duress, or undue influence becomes a critical intelligence requirement. Intelligence gathering efforts resulting in actionable intelligence will be essential to enabling the battlefield commander to determine whether or not the human shields are there voluntarily. Getting this intelligence information to the battlefield commander prior to any operation will be critical to enabling him to properly assess the situation on the ground.

---

94 George P. Fletcher, *Rethinking Criminal Law*, at 803 (1978).

95 Oliver Wendell Holmes, Jr., *The Common Law* at 54 (1881).

96 Model Penal Code § 2.01 explanatory note at 213; see also id. § 1.13(3) at 209 (defining "voluntary" under "General Definitions" by reference to Model Penal Code § 2.01). (Official Draft and Revised Comments, 1985) [hereinafter Model Penal Code 1985].

97 Id. at § 2.01 explanatory note at 213.

98 See id. at 217. The MPC Commentaries refer directly to *Robinson v. California*, 370 U.S. 660, 667 (1962) (holding that it is cruel and unusual punishment under the Eighth and Fourteenth Amendments to convict the defendant for the status of being a narcotics user without evidence that he had actually used narcotics within the jurisdiction). See also *Powell v. Texas*, 392 U.S. 514, 544 (1968) (Black, J., concurring).

99 See Model Penal Code 1985, § 2.01(2) cmt. 2 at 219 (noting that "voluntary" is defined "partially and indirectly by describing movements that are ***excluded*** from the meaning of the term" rather than defining voluntary by acts that would constitute volitional movements/acts).

100 Model Penal Code 1985, § 2.01(2) at 212.

101 Model Penal Code 1985, § 2.01 cmt. 1 at 215.

B. *Intelligence – Shaping the Battlefield and the Commander's Decisions*

A battlefield commander needs more than the vague standards of the MPC to draw from when making on-the-spot, potentially grave decisions on the battlefield. The battlefield commander needs to rely on an objective standard for determining whether or not the specific human shield is a legitimate military target or if harmed would qualify as civilian casualties. The battlefield commander requires a rational basis on which to make the determination of innocent civilian or enemy forces. The basis the commander requires is reliable/actionable intelligence information.

Intelligence information provided to battlefield commanders must include a history of enemy tactics, techniques and procedures. The history of enemy activity will provide some context for the battlefield commander. The commander can assess whether the current conduct he is witnessing is in conformance with known enemy tactics. The commander also needs to be provided discrete, real-time intelligence regarding the particular situation he is confronted with, if such intelligence is available. If reliable intelligence sources indicate that the local populace has made a knowing and voluntary decision to collaborate with enemy forces by acting as a shield to enemy strongholds, then this intelligence needs to be disseminated to the battlefield commanders.

C. *Strategic Communications*

One of the final requirements of a successful strategic plan for dealing with the issue of human shields on the battlefield is to let the world know what is really happening on the ground. "The presence of human shields on the battlefield is a manageable targeting situation for a commander; however, it is unique and challenging because of the media attention they receive and the political visibility involved."[102] Terrorists will continue the illegal use of human shields because "forces with little resources have little incentive to comply with international humanitarian law."[103] States countering such reprehensible tactics must employ an effective and proactive communication plan to ensure the fight to win "hearts and minds" is constantly engaged. The development of a Strategic Communication Plan to address enemy tactics is imperative to attaining future success. In 2004, the *Report of the Defense Science Board Task Force on Strategic Communication* summed up the importance of developing a Strategic Communication Plan in stating that

> [s]trategic communication requires a sophisticated method that maps perceptions and influence networks, identifies policy priorities, formulates objectives, focuses on "doable tasks," develops themes and messages, employs relevant channels, leverages new strategic and tactical dynamics, and monitors success. This approach will build on in-depth knowledge of other cultures and factors that motivate human behavior. It will adapt techniques of skillful political campaigning, even as it avoids slogans, quick fixes, and mindsets of winners and losers. It will search out credible messengers

102 Schoenekase, supra note 33.

103 Id.

> and create message authority. It will seek to persuade within news cycles, weeks, and months. It will engage in a respectful dialogue of ideas that begins with listening and assumes decades of sustained effort. Just as importantly, through evaluation and feedback, it will enable political leaders and policymakers to make informed decisions on changes in strategy, policies, messages, and choices among instruments of statecraft.[104]

The enemy cannot be allowed to shape public perception through the use of civilians. If civilians are voluntarily on the battlefield actively engaged in aiding and abetting the enemy, we posit that their civilian status ceases to exist under international law. The world needs to know that human shields are being encountered on the battlefield. The enemy's use of unlawful tactics also needs to be communicated to the appropriate audiences so that the enemy doesn't benefit from perceived civilian casualties. If the human shields are there voluntarily, then they no longer can be classified as civilian casualties. They now become enemy personnel killed in action. This fact and the basis for the cessation of the civilian status have to be appropriately articulated and effectively communicated to the identified target audiences.

VI. Conclusion

It is ultimately the commander who needs to determine whether what appears to be an individual voluntarily engaged in acting as a human shield is in fact doing just that. In the context of the rule of law, the significance is palpable – the individual becomes a legitimate target. That is, rather than enjoy the immunity accorded civilians, the individual voluntarily human shielding is as legitimate a target as the terrorist actually holding the weapon or wearing a suicide belt. From the commander's perspective, the categories are not distinguishable because the individual voluntarily human shielding presents as much a threat to the forces as do the other two individuals.

By standing in the midst of the shooter or in the vicinity of the suicide bomber the individual engaged in human shielding is granting both actors "cover" that potentially endangers commander and soldiers alike. An army that trains (and retrains) its soldiers the obligation to minimize collateral damage will "wait that extra second" before opening fire. That extra second may result in the death of a soldier. Conversely, if the commander is convinced that an individual is actively and voluntarily aiding and abetting a suspected terrorist and is therefore placing soldiers at risk then open fire orders may well be given

Herein lies the rub: if the individual is indeed voluntarily shielding the terrorist and thereby endangering the soldiers then an open fire order is legitimate. Conversely, if the individual is involuntarily shielding then an open fire order resulting in injury or death to that individual is a violation of international law and possibly of the military's standing orders which may result in court-martial.

How then is the dilemma to be resolved? Prior to addressing this question it is critical to understand combat realities – soldiers are under extraordinary stress,

104 *Report of the Defense Science Board Task Force on Strategic Communication*, September 2004, Office of the Under Secretary of Defense for Acquisition, Technology, and Logistics.

fatigue and anxiety. Commanders have repeatedly warned them regarding the Geneva Convention and the limits it places on their operational flexibility. Conversely, soldiers have learned from after-action reports that deception is an inherent part of terrorism and that what may appear to be an innocent individual is in actuality a combatant threatening a military unit and civilians alike.

The scenario suggested at this article's outset describes a real-life scenario. It expresses the dilemma as faced by soldiers on a daily basis; it also articulates the dangers faced by an individual forced to act as a human shield by terrorists who systematically violate international law and the consequences be damned. The decision the commander makes – in the final analysis – is determined by a combination of the following factors: 1) intelligence information; 2) the conduct of the specific individual; 3) field circumstances at the relevant time; 4) the commanders' prior experience; 5) the conduct of additional individuals in the surrounding area. The integration of formal intelligence assessment tools into all levels of operational planning that specifically address the issue of human shields will better enable our battlefield leaders to make the right call – engage or hold back. If the intelligence points to voluntary human shields, then our fictional Captain Smith from the scenario we described at outset of this article can follow through with the mission as planned and the actions of he and his unit will conform to international humanitarian law standards.

Will the commander always make the right decision? No. What is important – in the context of post 9/11 conflict – is applying the five-part test above to the opening scenario. Application of our proposed five-part test will enable the commander to honor international law obligations while minimizing collateral damage in the context of voluntary shields. While terrorist organizations will undoubtedly continue to use human shields for the reasons discussed in the paper, the ultimate responsibility is the commanders.

To that end, the proposal that is the essence of this paper seeks to articulate a workable model that enables the commander to complete his mission while respecting international law (minimizing civilian casualties) while not knowing if the seemingly innocent civilian is truly innocent or a voluntary human shield. By seeking to objectify the commanders' decision-making process, we are seeking to create checklist that balances between competing, powerful interests. It is our hope that this proposed model will serve as a basis for discussion on this most difficult of issues. The lives of innumerable individuals are resting on such a discussion.

Chapter 5

The Obligation to Remove and Destroy Anti-Personnel Mines and Explosive Remnants of War in Peace Operations

Kjetil Mujezinović Larsen

I. Introduction

Are military forces bound by a legal obligation to remove and destroy anti-personnel mines, unexploded cluster submunitions, and other explosive remnants of war, during international peace operations?[1] This is the issue that will be addressed in this study. Two factual incidents provide an introduction:

In 2006 Norwegian newspapers reported that Norwegian military personnel who were involved with removing and destroying anti-personnel mines in the American-led operation "Enduring Freedom" in Afghanistan allegedly omitted removing mines in order to protect American soldiers against attacks.[2] It was further alleged that Afghan civilians were killed by these mines.[3]

In May 2007 the European Court of Human Rights declared as inadmissible the application in the *Behrami* case concerning UNMIK and KFOR omissions in Kosovo.[4] The case concerned an incident where some children while playing found a number of undetonated cluster bomb units, which had been dropped during the NATO bombardment in 1999. When a cluster bomb unit exploded, one boy was

1 In this study, the term "unexploded ordnances" is sometimes used for the sake of brevity when referring to all these three categories collectively.

2 *Ny Tid* 3.2.2006, available (in Norwegian) at: http://www.nytid.no/index.php?sk=&id=3440 (accessed 20.10.2008).

3 The allegations were rejected by the Norwegian Armed Forces, see press release 3.2.2006 from Headquarters Allied Forces North Europe, available (in Norwegian) at: http://www.mil.no/start/aktuelt/pressemeldinger/article.jhtml?articleID=116285 (accessed 20.10.2008). In a follow-up report in *Ny Tid* 17.2.2006, available (in Norwegian) at: http://www.nytid.no/index.php?sk=&id=3450 (accessed 20.10.2008), a Lt. Col. in the US Marines, confirms – to a certain extent – the allegations.

4 European Court of Human Rights (hereinafter "ECtHR") Grand Chamber decision 31.5.2007, applic. no. 71412/01 *Behrami v. France*, and applic. no. 78166/01 *Saramati v. France, Germany and Norway*. The facts of the Behrami case are given in paras. 5–7 of the judgment.

Cecilia M. Bailliet (ed.), Security: A Multidisciplinary Normative Approach.
 ISBN 978 90 04 17296 8. pp. 117–136.

killed and another was seriously injured. It was alleged that UNMIK personnel were aware of the location of the units.[5]

This study addresses the concept of security in a very concrete manner. The examples illustrate that there is an inherent tension between the security of the civilian population and the security of military personnel. The security of military personnel is affected not only by the risks connected with the actual removal of unexploded ordnances, but also by tactical operational considerations, since the continued presence of such ordnances (in particular anti-personnel mines) can improve the security of the personnel. The study will examine to what extent demands for security of the civilian population result in legal obligations to the potential detriment of the security of international military personnel.

Section II describes the general framework under international humanitarian law for the removal and destruction of unexploded ordnances, and the applicability of this regime in international peace operations. For reasons that will be explained in section II.B.1, the discussion will also address briefly the legality of the *use* of these weapons. Section III describes human rights law, and inquires whether this regime provides any independent, relevant legal obligations in peace operations, and how these relate to the provisions of international humanitarian law. Section IV provides concluding remarks.[6]

II. Relevant Norms under International Humanitarian Law

A. *General Principles*

It is useful as an introduction to describe the application of the relevant general principles of international humanitarian law with regard to the issue at hand. Of particular importance is the fundamental relationship between military necessity and humanitarian considerations, which influences the whole body of international humanitarian law.[7] International humanitarian law allows States considerable freedom in the conduct of hostilities in accordance with the demands of military necessity, but it simultaneously places substantial restrictions on this freedom based on

5 The study does not address the legality of the alleged omissions in the cases, which serve only as an illustration.

6 The study does not discuss a possible obligation to *search* an area for the possible presence of unexploded ordnances. It does not distinguish between situations where the omission is founded on tactical reasons or on lack of available resources, time constraints, other priorities, etc. The study is concerned only with the applicability of the norms, and not with issues of responsibility and accountability for violations of the norms. It should also be noted that the legal framework of contemporary international peace operations is highly complex, and the norms must generally be reviewed in light of the operation-specific context, but this falls beyond the scope of the study.

7 See for example Yoram Dinstein, *The Conduct of Hostilities under the Law of International Armed Conflict* (Cambridge: Cambridge University Press, 2004) 16–20, or Christopher Greenwood, "Historical Development and Legal Basis" in Dieter Fleck (ed.), *The Handbook of International Humanitarian Law* (2nd ed., Oxford: Oxford University Press, 2008) 35–38.

humanitarian considerations.[8] The tension between these considerations is very evident with regard to the use of the ordnances that are relevant to this study. For example can the use of anti-personnel mines create significant advantages for the protection of military personnel, and the military necessity test will often be met: The mines can create security conditions for the benefit of military purposes that other means of conduct cannot create.[9] As for cluster weapons, these are by its advocates considered to be an effective weapon – both in terms of reliability and in terms of the time that is required to complete an operation – against certain targets, and they can therefore, arguably, satisfy the requirements of military necessity.[10] But the other side of the coin is that the weapons represent grave danger to the civilian population, and that this danger often remains long after the end of active hostilities. Critics of these weapons therefore argue that their use violates fundamental principles of humanity.

Equally important is the principle of distinction between combatants and noncombatants (civilians), which has been recognized by the International Court of Justice (ICJ) as a fundamental principle of international humanitarian law.[11] The principle is reflected in Article 48 of Additional Protocol I to the Geneva Conventions,[12] which states that the parties to a conflict "shall at all times distinguish between the civilian population and combatants and between civilian objects and military objectives". The principle is also expressly recognized in the ICRC's study on customary international humanitarian law.[13] A practical consequence of this principle is the general prohibition against non-discriminatory attacks. Attacks must be directed only against combatants or military objectives, and the parties to a conflict can never use weapons that are incapable of distinguishing between civilian and military targets.[14]

It is only for the purpose of combat against military objectives that customary international law recognizes military necessity as a legitimate justification for mili-

---

8 See Dinstein, *ibid*, p. 17.

9 Stuart Maslen, *Anti-Personnel Mines under Humanitarian Law: A View from the Vanishing Point* (Antwerp-Oxford-New York: Intersentia-Transnational Publishers, 2001) 202 ff. describes the military *utility* of anti-personnel mines, and concludes that the effectiveness of these mines is low, although it "is not possible to argue convincingly that anti-personnel mines have no military utility whatsoever" (at 208).

10 See for example Nout van Woudenberg, 'The Long and Winding Road Towards an Instrument on Cluster Munitions', 12 *Journal of Conflict & Security Law* (2008) 450, who describes some standard arguments for and against the use of cluster weapons.

11 ICJ Advisory Opinion 6.7.1996 on the Legality of the Threat or Use of Nuclear Weapons, paras. 78–79, see also Dinstein, *supra* note 7, p. 82.

12 Protocol Additional to the Geneva Conventions of 12.8.1949, and relating to the Protection of Victims of International Armed Conflicts (Protocol I), 8.6.1977, entry into force 7.12.1978 (hereinafter "GC AP I").

13 Jean-Marie Henckaerts and Louise Doswald-Beck (eds.), *Customary International Humanitarian Law (Volume I: Rules; Volume II: Practice)* (ICRC/Cambridge: Cambridge University Press 2005) (hereinafter "ICRC Customary Law Study"), volume I, rule 1 ("The parties to the conflict must at all times distinguish between civilians and combatants."), pp. 3–8.

14 The Nuclear Weapons case, *supra* note 11, para. 78, see also Maslen 2001, *supra* note 9, p. 188.

tary use of force.[15] If an attack is directed at civilian objects, or fails to respect the principle of distinction, the attack is illegal even if it can be said to comply with the test of military necessity. The prohibition against non-discriminatory attacks means further that attacks against military objectives shall be conducted with maximum precautions to protect the civilian population, so as to minimize collateral damage to civilians and civilian objects.[16] This is in turn one side of the general principle of proportionality, which in this respect results in the disallowance of attacks against military objectives if there can be anticipated disproportionate injury and damage to civilians and civilian objects.[17] This is reflected in Article 51.5(b) GC AP I, which prohibits "an attack which may be expected to cause incidental loss of civilian life, injury to civilians, damage to civilian objects, or a combination thereof, which would be excessive in relation to the concrete and direct military advantage anticipated".

The application of these principles to anti-personnel mines, cluster weapons and other weapons which may create explosive remnants of war is, however, subject to discussion. It is probably most defensible to conclude that *anti-personnel mines* do not fall within the category of inherently indiscriminate weapons,[18] which means that they are not prohibited on this ground alone. The situation may be different for *cluster munitions*, which arguably are prohibited already under Article 51.5(b) GC AP I.[19] Even if the weapons cannot be considered as inherently indiscriminate, their use may in specific circumstances be in violation of the principle of proportionality, if the risk to the civilian population is disproportionate to the military objective sought.[20]

These principles also apply (mutatis mutandis) to the *removal* and *destruction* of unexploded ordnances. As already mentioned,[21] one can argue that the time of attack with regard to anti-personnel mines is the moment when the mine endangers a person or actually explodes, in which case the mine must be removed if it at a given time no longer complies with the principles of military necessity and distinction. If the time of attack is considered to be at an earlier time, when active hostilities are still taking place, the presence of anti-personnel mines after the cessation of hostilities may be considered as a continuation of the attack, which means that their continued presence must still respect the general principles.

15 Stefan Oeter, 'Methods and Means of Combat' in Fleck 2008, *supra* note 7, p. 175.

16 Oeter, *ibid*, p. 189, Dinstein, *supra* note 7, p. 126.

17 Dinstein, *ibid*, p. 120.

18 See Maslen 2001, *supra* note 9, p. 193. A further problem for the application of the principles on anti-personnel mines is that there are doubts about at what point the use of anti-personnel mines in fact constitutes an attack (Maslen 2001 p. 190 with further references). If one considers the time of attack to be the time when the mine is *laid* or *armed*, the assessment of the principles may be different than it is if the time of attack is considered to be the time when a *person is endangered* by the mine or when the mine eventually *explodes*. The two latter circumstances may occur long after the cessation of active hostilities, and it is in that case difficult to argue that the principle of distinction is respected.

19 See Gro Nystuen's contribution in this volume.

20 Maslen 2001, *supra* note 9, 209.

21 Supra footnote 18.

The latter point arguably applies also to other unexploded ordnances. For cluster munitions do not the same doubts arise about the time of attack, since this obviously is the time when the cluster munitions are fired. But when undetonated cluster munitions remain on the ground this can, perhaps, be considered to represent a continuation of the attack, which clearly do not satisfy the requirements of military necessity.

B. *Specific Norms*

i. Anti-Personnel Mines

With regard to anti-personnel mines, the primary source of legal obligations is now the Anti-Personnel Mine Ban Convention.[22] This Convention provides absolute prohibitions against using, developing, producing, acquiring, stockpiling, retaining and transferring anti-personnel mines, or to assist, encourage or induce anyone to engage in such activities, cf. Article 1.1. The prohibition against the *use* of anti-personnel mines is of particular interest here. Does this prohibition only refer to the active deployment of new mines, or does it also prohibit tactical reliance on previously laid mines and the maintenance of existing minefields?[23] This may affect the assessment of whether an entity is under an obligation to remove and destroy the mines: If military forces in international operations are permitted to rely on and maintain existing minefields, it is more difficult to claim that they are simultaneously under a legal obligation to remove and destroy the same mines.[24]

These issues were discussed in the negotiations to the Convention. A disagreement existed between those States who wished to define "use" narrowly as referring only to the active emplacement of mines, and those States who argued that "use" is a wider concept and that "gaining benefits" or "taking military advantage of a minefield which it would have been feasible to remove" is included.[25] As a result, the term "use" was not defined more precisely. Subsequent State practice does not provide a clearer picture, but Maslen argues that the existing practice indicates that the term covers more than merely active emplacement.[26] He concludes by asserting that a State "is prohibited from taking operational or tactical advantage from anti-personnel mines that have been laid for its benefit or where it was in a position to choose not to take the

22 Convention on the Prohibition of the Use, Stockpiling, Production and Transfer of Anti-Personnel Mines and on their Destruction, 18.9.1997, entry into force 1.3.1999, hereinafter "the APM Convention". A commentary to the APM Convention is S. Maslen, *Commentaries on Arms Control Treaties, Volume I* (2nd ed., Oxford: Oxford University Press 2005).

23 See Maslen 2005, *ibid*, pp. 80–86.

24 This is, however, not logically impossible or absurd. One could claim that a possible obligation to remove mines is more limited in factual scope than the permission to rely on them, typically that a State is obligated to remove mines in areas under its jurisdiction and control, but at the same time permitted to rely on mines outside such areas.

25 Maslen 2005, *supra* note 22, at 84.

26 *Ibid*, p. 83.

benefit, for example where it could reasonably be expected to clear and destroy the emplaced mines".[27] For the purpose of the present study, it suffices to conclude that the Convention itself does not provide a clear answer, and the other relevant means of interpretation are not sufficient to establish beyond doubt the correct interpretation of the text.

While Article 1.1 governs the negative aspects of the legal obligations – *i.e.*, the obligation to refrain from performing a particular conduct – Article 1.2 is concerned with positive action. It provides that each State Party "undertakes to destroy or ensure the destruction of all anti-personnel mines" in accordance with the provisions of the Convention. Of particular relevance for the present study is Article 5, of which the relevant parts read:[28]

1. Each State Party undertakes to destroy or ensure the destruction of all anti-personnel mines in mined areas under its jurisdiction or control, as soon as possible but not later than ten years after the entry into force of this Convention for that State Party.
2. Each State Party shall make every effort to identify all areas under its jurisdiction or control in which anti-personnel mines are known or suspected to be emplaced and shall ensure as soon as possible that all anti-personnel mines in mined areas under its jurisdiction or control are perimeter-marked, monitored and protected by fencing or other means, to ensure the effective exclusion of civilians, until all anti-personnel mines contained therein have been destroyed.

A common feature of the two paragraphs is that the obligations apply in areas where the State exercises "jurisdiction or control". These are alternative requirements, not cumulative, and are not limited to areas within the State Party's territory. If a State Party exercises "jurisdiction or control" extraterritorially, the obligation applies.

But the interpretation of this phrase is not evident. What level of control is required? Does "jurisdiction" refer to the meaning of this term in general international law, or does it rather refer to the exercise of "authority" whether or not the State has jurisdiction under international law?[29] Does the obligation to destroy mines apply immediately when a State Party achieves control, or does the 10 year time limit in practice mean that the obligation does not apply during short-term control?

At the outset, the inclusion of the term "control" makes it unnecessary to adopt a wide interpretation of the term "jurisdiction". The latter term should be interpreted in accordance with its ordinary meaning,[30] which is the meaning the term is given in

27 *Ibid*, p. 85.

28 The remaining parts of the provision give more specific rules on the marking of mined areas and on the procedure for submitting and granting requests for an extension of the deadline in paragraph 1.

29 This is the common interpretation of the term "jurisdiction" in, for example, Article 1 of the European Convention on Human Rights, see, *e.g.*, Alexander Orakhelashvili, 'Restrictive Interpretation of Human Rights Treaties in the Recent Jurisprudence of the European Court of Human Rights', 14 *European Journal of International Law* (2003) 529–568. See section 3 below.

30 Cf. Article 31.1 of the Vienna Convention on the Law of Treaties.

general international law.[31] There are different categories of jurisdiction, commonly referred to as executive, judicial, and legislative jurisdiction.[32] Jurisdiction is primarily territorial, but there exist other bases of jurisdiction which applies extraterritorially.[33]

The "control" criterion extends the scope of the obligation, as this term also includes areas which are not under the State's jurisdiction but which are none the less under its control.[34] But "control" means different things in different contexts, and it is difficult to make accurate statements about the interpretation of the term in the APM Convention. It is, however, clear that it is a factual criterion rather than a legal one, it is *de facto* control rather than *de jure* control that is required. Maslen refers to areas where the State "exercises factual power or authority", and in particular occupied territories or areas.[35] Article 42 of the Hague Regulations[36] defines a territory as occupied if "it is actually placed under the authority of the hostile army", and states that "[t]he occupation extends only to the territory where such authority has been established and can be exercised". There are clear similarities between Article 5 APM Convention and Article 42 HagueReg, and it may be appropriate to interpret the provisions so that their scopes of application coincide. In the UK Manual of the Law of Armed Conflict it is stated that two requirements must be satisfied if an area shall be considered as occupied, namely

> First, that the former government has been rendered incapable of publicly exercising its authority in that area; and, secondly, that the occupying power is in a position to substitute its own authority for that of the former government.[37]

This appears to be an appropriate test also under Article 5 APM Convention, as it expresses a degree of control that places the State in a position to perform its obligations under the Convention. It can, however, not be required that a formal state of occupation has been recognized by the occupying (controlling) force. It is a contentious issue whether the United Nations can become an occupying force,[38] but the organization can certainly acquire factual control over a territory.

---

31 See for example F.A. Mann, 'The Doctrine of Jurisdiction in International Law', in the Hague Academy of International Law, *Recueil des cours* (vol. I, Leyden: A.W. Sijthoff 1964) 1–162, or Michael Akehurst, 'Jurisdiction in International Law', 46 *BybIL* (1972) 145–257.

32 For example Akehurst, *ibid*. See also Rosalyn Higgins, *Problems & Process: International Law and How We Use it* (Oxford: Clarendon Press 1994) 56, who instead refers to "jurisdiction to *prescribe* and jurisdiction to *apply*" (original emphasis).

33 See for example Higgins, *ibid*, p. 78.

34 Maslen 2005, *ibid*, p. 176.

35 *Ibid.*

36 Regulations annexed to the Hague Convention IV Respecting the Laws and Customs of War on Land (1907), hereinafter "HagueReg".

37 UK Ministry of Defence, *The Manual of the Law of Armed Conflict* (Oxford: Oxford University Press 2005), para. 11.3 at p. 275. See also Hans-Peter Gasser, "Protection of the Civilian Population" in Fleck 2008, *supra* note 7, p. 274.

38 See Daphna Shraga, 'Military Occupation and UN Transitional Administrations – The Analogy and Its Limitations' in Marcelo G. Kohen (ed.), *Promoting Justice, Human Rights*

Removal and destruction of the mines must be undertaken "as soon as possible but not later than ten years after the entry into force of this Convention for that State Party", see Article 5.1. This time limit also applies when a State (or a multinational force) acquires sufficient control over an already mine-contaminated area, but it is not clear how the provision should be interpreted when control is acquired after the entry into force of the Convention. If the Convention entered into force for State A on 1 March 1999, and State A acquired control over a mine-contaminated area in 2005, does this mean that State A only has until 1 March 2009 to clear the area? What if State A instead acquires such control after 1 March 2009, does this mean that State A at the very moment of acquiring control is in violation of the APM Convention? According to a literal interpretation of the provision, the answer to these questions is "yes". However, this would be an absurd interpretation, especially in the latter example. Common sense suggests that a State should have a reasonable period of time in which to fulfil its obligations. It is, however, difficult to interpret the provision so as to allow the State a full ten year period from the date on which control was acquired.

Leaving the APM Convention temporarily aside, some remarks should also be made about the amended Protocol II to the Convention on Certain Conventional Weapons.[39] The original Protocol placed restrictions on the use of mines,[40] but did not contain an explicit obligation to remove mines.[41] This has changed with the amended Protocol, where Article 3.2 provides that each State Party or party to a conflict is "responsible" for all mines employed by it and undertakes to "clear, remove [or] destroy them" as specified in Article 10, which in turn provides that "[w]ithout delay after the cessation of active hostilities, all minefields, mined areas, mines, booby-traps and other devices shall be cleared, removed [or] destroyed". The provisions allow, however, also for the maintenance of such areas, if the areas are properly marked and all feasible precautions are taken for the protection of civilians.[42] The responsibility to remove mines is placed on States with regard to mined areas

and Conflict Resolution through International Law – Liber Amicorum Lucius Caflisch (Leiden: Martinus Nijhoff, 2007) 479–498.

39 Convention on Prohibitions or Restrictions on the Use of Certain Conventional Weapons Which May be Deemed to be Excessively Injurious or to Have Indiscriminate Effects (hereinafter "CCW"), and Protocol II on Prohibitions or Restrictions on the Use of Mines, Booby-Traps and Other Devices, both of 10.10.1980, entry into force 2.12.1983. CCW Protocol II was amended 3.5.1996, entry into force 3.12.1998 (hereinafter "CCW Protocol II").

40 Article 3 stated that it is prohibited to direct mines against the civilian population or to use the weapons in an indiscriminate manner, and Article 4 placed restrictions on the use of mines in populated areas.

41 Under the original Protocol, the State Parties had an obligation under Article 7 to "take all necessary and appropriate measures ... to protect civilians from the effects of minefields [and] mines" after the cessation of hostilities, but this could be achieved by other means than the removal and destruction of the mines, for example by clear marking of minefields. Article 9 provided further that State Parties should endeavour to reach agreements "necessary to remove or otherwise render ineffective minefields [and] mines", but any obligation to remove mines would in that case stem from the mentioned agreements rather than from the Protocol.

42 See Articles 3 and 5.2 CCW Protocol II.

"under their control", see Article 10.2. As in the APM Convention, the existence of "control" determines the obligations of the States, and the control criterion should be interpreted similarly under the two regimes so as to maintain consistency in the legal regulation.

Some remarks should also be made about international customary law. With the controversies surrounding the use of anti-personnel mines in mind, it is not surprising that it is difficult to identify clear rules under international customary law about their use, and even more so about their removal and destruction. The ICRC Customary Law Study does nevertheless identify the rule that "[a]t the end of active hostilities, a party to the conflict which has used landmines must remove or otherwise render them harmless to civilians, or facilitate their removal".[43] This rule only applies, however, to the party who has in fact used landmines, and not to other States who temporarily or permanently exercise jurisdiction or control over the area. There is little State practice on the removal of mines in areas under the State's control, and what practice there is does not suffice to satisfy the requirements for obtaining the status of international customary law.

In summary, there are clear treaty obligations that require the removal of mines in areas under a State's control, but international customary law does not provide a corresponding rule, and such obligations therefore do not exist for States which are not a party to the treaties.

ii. Explosive Remnants of War

The term "explosive remnants of war" encompasses a wide range of ordnances, and can include any unexploded ordnance that is left behind in an area after the cessation of hostilities. In the recently adopted Protocol V to the CCW,[44] explosive remnants of war are given a rather complex definition, see Article 2. Of particular relevance for the present study is the category of unexploded ordnance, which are defined in para. 2 as an explosive ordnance that has been primed, fused, armed, or otherwise prepared for use and used in an armed conflict, and which may have been fired, dropped, launched or projected and should have exploded but failed to do so.

The main purpose of the ERW Protocol is to minimise the risks and effects of explosive remnants of war, and to reduce the serious post-conflict humanitarian problems that they cause.[45] The Protocol is not concerned with the *use* of explosive ordnances during armed conflicts, but rather with precautions to eliminate the risk to the civilian population in a post-conflict situation. Of particular importance in this regard is precisely the obligation to remove explosive remnants of war. Obligations concerning the clearance, removal or destruction of explosive remnants of war are provided in Article 3, which stipulates that each State Party and party to an armed conflict shall "mark and clear, remove or destroy explosive remnants of war in affected

---

43 ICRC *Customary Law Study*, *supra* note 13, volume I, rule 83, pp. 285–286.

44 Protocol V on Explosive Remnants of War, 28.11.2003, entry into force 12.11.2006. Hereinafter "ERW Protocol".

45 ERW Protocol, Preamble.

territories under its control", see paragraphs 2 and 3(c).[46] Again one sees the "control" criterion. The primary obligation to remove and destroy explosive remnants of war rests not with the user of the explosive ordnances, but with the State that controls the area after the cessation of hostilities. The obligation shall be carried out "[a]fter the cessation of active hostilities and as soon as feasible",[47] and the ERW Protocol shares the feature of the APM Convention that no exception is made for short-term control. If it is "feasible" for a State to remove the explosive remnants of war in the time when it controls the area, the State is under a legal obligation to do so regardless of whether the control over the area is scheduled to be transferred to another entity in the near or distant future.

The ERW Protocol has at present been ratified by relatively few States compared to the instruments on anti-personnel mines which are described above, but the number is rising.[48] The legal regulation of these ordnances is still of a new date, and it cannot realistically be claimed that there exists an obligation under international customary law to remove and destroy explosive remnants of war in areas under a State's control but outside that State's territory.

iii. Specifically about Unexploded Cluster Munitions

Unexploded cluster munitions are covered by the ERW Protocol as described above, see Article 2.1. However, the Cluster Munitions Convention[49] includes more specific provisions on the clearance and destruction of cluster munition remnants. Article 4.1 CMC provides that each State Party "undertakes to clear and destroy, or ensure the clearance and destruction of, cluster munition remnants located in cluster munition contaminated areas under its jurisdiction or control". The obligation is not limited to cluster munition that the State Party has originally itself used, but speaks instead broadly about the obligation to destroy remnants in areas under its "jurisdiction or control", regardless of who used it. This criterion is identical to the criterion in the APM Convention, and at the outset it should be assumed that the terms should be interpreted identically.

It is further noteworthy that the CMC provides the same time schedule as the APM Convention, with one significant amendment. Article 4.1 (b) CMC, which concerns the clearance and destruction of cluster munitions which become cluster munition remnants after entry into force of the Convention, states that clearance and destruction "must be completed as soon as possible but not later than ten years after the end of active hostilities". Thus, the ten year deadline should not be calculated from the entry into force of the Convention, as the case is for the APM Convention,

---

46 See also para. 1, which places obligations also on the user of an explosive ordnance which has become explosive remnants of war.

47 The ERW Protocol does not provide a ten year deadline (or any other fixed deadline) for the implementation of the obligation.

48 Per 21.4.2008, the ERW Protocol had 42 State Parties, while the APM Convention had 156 and the amended CCW Protocol II had 90. For reference, see the ICRC Treaty Database: http://www.icrc.org/ihl.

49 Convention on Cluster Munitions, 30.5.2008, not yet in force. Hereinafter "CMC".

but rather from the end of active hostilities. This provides a much more flexible and suitable obligation in situations where multinational forces acquire control over an area after entry into force of the Convention.

C. *Application of the Norms in International Peace Operations*

The previous section has shown that international conventions provide obligations on States to remove and destroy unexploded ordnances in areas under their control, but such obligations do not form part of international customary law. The issue in the present section is therefore whether the relevant conventions apply when States participate in international peace operations.

The applicability of international humanitarian law during peace operations has been discussed ever since the earliest United Nations operations.[50] The natural starting point for a discussion of the issue at present is the United Nations Secretary-General's Bulletin on Observance by United Nations Forces,[51] which sets out "fundamental principles and rules of international humanitarian law applicable to United Nations forces conducting operations under United Nations command and control".[52] The Bulletin can be described as a synthesis of fundamental rules and principles of international humanitarian law,[53] and within its scope of application it appears to settle the issue of whether international humanitarian law is binding for the forces. Its scope of application is, however, limited to situations where United Nations forces are actively engaged in an armed conflict as combatants, which means that it is "applicable in enforcement actions, or in peacekeeping operations when the use of force is permitted in self-defence".[54] Therefore it does not apply to a wide range of peace operations, namely those where the use of force neither is mandated nor becomes necessary in self-defence.

The Bulletin also states expressly that it is not an exhaustive document.[55] This has two consequences: Firstly, there may be supplementary applicable rules and principles in international humanitarian law even if the Bulletin is applicable, and secondly, there may be such applicable rules even in situations where the Bulletin is not applicable.

50 The issue cannot be discussed in detail here. See, inter alia, Daphna Shraga, 'UN Peacekeeping Operations: Applicability of International Humanitarian Law and Responsibility for Operations-Related Damage', *American Journal of International Law* Vol. 94 (2000) 406–412, Ray Murphy, 'United Nations Military Operations and International Humanitarian Law: What Rules Apply to Peacekeepers', *Criminal Law Forum* Vol. 14 (2003) 153–194, or Jaume Saura, 'Lawful Peacekeeping: Applicability of International Humanitarian Law to United Nations Peacekeeping Operations', *Hastings Law Journal* Vol. 58 (2007) 479–531.

51 ST/SGB/1999/13, 6.8.1999 (hereinafter "the Bulletin").

52 *Ibid*, introduction.

53 See for example Shraga, *supra* note 50, p. 408.

54 The Bulletin, *supra* note 51, section 1.1.

55 *Ibid*, section 2.

Certain rules and principles in the Bulletin are of particular relevance to this study. First of all, section 5.1 explicitly incorporates the principle of distinction:

> The United Nations force shall make a clear distinction at all times between civilians and combatants and between civilian objects and military objectives. Military operations shall be directed only against combatants and military objectives. Attacks on civilians or civilian objects are prohibited.

This is followed by a general obligation in section 5.3 to take all feasible precautions to avoid or minimize incidental loss of civilian life, injury to civilians or damage to civilian property. The removal of unexploded ordnances is precisely such a precaution, but it will depend on the particular circumstances whether this is "feasible".

Under section 6.2 the use of anti-personnel mines by the forces is prohibited. One can argue that the provision also prohibits United Nations forces from taking advantage from existing minefields, depending on the interpretation of the term "use" as described above, but the provision does not address removal and destruction of existing mines, and it cannot be interpreted to include an obligation in this regard. An obligation to remove and destroy unexploded ordnances is therefore difficult to deduce from the Bulletin.

Looking beyond the Bulletin, it would appear useful to take as a starting point the proposition that international humanitarian law is binding on United Nations forces whenever they are involved in armed conflicts, regardless of the application of the Bulletin.[56] However, this proposition does not assist us here. The United Nations is not a Party to any of the relevant Conventions, and cannot become so. The United Nations is – still according to the proposition – bound by international customary law, but it should be recalled that the obligation to remove and destroy unexploded ordnances cannot be considered as international customary law.

One must therefore turn to an examination of the obligations of individual Troop Contributing States. There is now widespread acceptance for the proposition that the obligations of Troop Contributing States remain in force when these States provide forces to international peace operations.[57] If so, this means that a State is obliged to remove and destroy unexploded ordnances during participation in a peace operation if the State is otherwise so bound. The particular situation of peace operations was also discussed during the negotiations of the APM Convention, where it was acknowledged that international forces can establish control over an area where another actor has deployed anti-personnel mines.[58] The Convention does not *per se* exclude international operations from its scope of application. Contemporary peace operations are very heterogeneous, and the degree of jurisdiction and control performed by an operation will depend on various elements such as the mandate, SOFA and other constitutive documents, but also on the facts on the ground.

The CMC implicitly recognizes that it is applicable in international peace operations, see Article 21.3. This is a provision on the interoperability between States Parties and States that are not parties to the CMC, and it is stated that States Parties "may

56 See *supra*, note 50.

57 See, for example, Greenwood, *supra* note 50, p. 17 or Saura, also *supra* note 50, p. 528.

58 Maslen 2005, *supra* note 22, p. 176.

engage in military cooperation and operations with states not party to this Convention that might engage in activities prohibited to a State Party". If it was assumed that the Convention would not apply in UN mandated peace operations, this provision would have a very limited reach.

It should be underlined that the primary obligation to remove and destroy unexploded ordnances must rest with the State on which territory the ordnances are situated. The wording of the relevant Conventions suggests, however, that if another State acquires control over an area inside the territory of another State, the obligation rests either with the former State alone or in concurrence with the latter State. This may be an undesired consequence for the Troop Contributing States.

However, a final, and significant, question remains. Is it the Troop Contributing State or the United Nations that should be considered to have "control" when such control is acquired by the forces? This question has not received an authoritative answer with regard to any of the relevant Conventions, and the scope of the present study allows only for an imprecise indication of the starting points. When the operation is established as a subsidiary organ of the United Nations (which is the norm), strong reasons suggest that the control is held by the United Nations. These operations are considered as a part of the organization, and the conduct of the forces is in principle attributable to the organization. The question is less clear for operations without this status. If the operation stands under national command and control, the present author has argued elsewhere that the conduct of the forces should be attributed to the individual Troop Contributing States.[59] This indicates that the forces' control over an area is also attributable to the State.

In conclusion, this author suggests that the relevant treaty obligations apply in full for States that participate in international peace operations, which means that a State is under an obligation to remove and destroy unexploded ordnances in areas over which the State acquires control during the operation.

III. Relevant Norms under International Human Rights Law

A. *Brief Introduction: The Relationship between International Humanitarian Law and Human Rights Law*

The relationship between international humanitarian law and human rights law raises many challenges, and the attention to these challenges has increased in recent years.[60] The core of the problem is that the two regimes provide different standards

59 Kjetil M. Larsen, 'Attribution of Conduct in Peace Operations: The "Ultimate Authority and Control" Test', *European Journal of International Law* Vol. 19 (2008) 509–531.

60 A comprehensive analysis of the systemic similarities and differences of the two regimes is René Provost, *International Human Rights and Humanitarian Law* (Cambridge: Cambridge University Press 2002). Shorter contributions from recent years include, for example, Hans-Joacim Heintze, 'On the relationship between human rights law protection and international humanitarian law', *IRRC* Vol. 86 (2004) 789–814, Anthony E. Cassimatis, 'International Humanitarian Law, International Human Rights Law, and Fragmentation of International Law', *International and Comparative Law Quarterly* Vol. 56 (2007) 623–640, and Alexander Orakhelashvili, 'The Interaction between Human Rights Law

for the protection of the civilian population, and that it is not clear how the inherent discrepancies should be tackled. The discussion has primarily focused on the application of human rights law in situations of armed conflicts, *i.e.*, situations where international humanitarian law is also applicable.

It is today commonly accepted that human rights treaties in principle remain applicable during armed conflicts, and that their application is not *per se* excluded in situations where international humanitarian law is applicable. A significant contribution to the clarification of this position was made by the ICJ in its two Advisory Opinions in the *Nuclear Weapons* case[61] and the *Wall* case.[62] In the latter case, the ICJ stated in general terms that it

> considers that the protection offered by human rights conventions does not cease in case of armed conflict, save through the effect of provisions for derogation of the kind to be found in Article 4 of the International Covenant on Civil and Political Rights.[63]

Even if one accepts this position, there exist different theories on how the relationship should be handled. The ICJ took the view that with regard to rights which are a matter of both human rights law and international humanitarian law, the latter must be regarded as *lex specialis*.[64] This can, however, be nothing more than a starting point, because it can not generally be proclaimed that a norm under international humanitarian law is more specific than a norm under international human rights law, nor that it is more suitable for regulation of a particular situation during armed conflicts (although this normally will be the case). For one thing, it is difficult to argue that international humanitarian law is lex specialis to human rights law in non-international armed conflicts, where only the limited norms in Additional Protocol II to the Geneva Conventions,[65] or alternatively only Common Article 3 of the Geneva Conventions, are applicable, as compared to the detailed and comprehensive set of norms that are found in human rights law. Many contributors are instead arguing that where diverging norms under human rights law and international humanitarian law govern a given conduct, one must assess each particular norm to determine which norm takes precedence. If there is indeed a presumption that the international humanitarian law norm should prevail, this presumption is in any case rebuttable. A variant of this approach is what Schabas has metaphorically described as a "belt

---

and Humanitarian Law: Fragmentation, Conflict, Parallelism, or Convergence?', *European Journal of International Law Vol.* 19 (2008) 161–182.

61 *Supra*, note 11.

62 ICJ Advisory Opinion 9.7.2004 on the *Legal Consequences of the Construction of a Wall in the Occupied Palestinian Territory*.

63 *Ibid*, para. 106.

64 *Ibid*. This refers to the maxim *lex specialis derogat legi generali*, meaning that a specific norm takes precedence over a general norm.

65 Protocol Additional to the Geneva Conventions of 12.8.1949, and relating to the Protection of Victims of Non-International Armed Conflicts (Protocol II), 8.6.1977, entry into force 7.12.1978.

and suspenders" theory, meaning that one applies the norm that in each situation provides the maximum protection of civilians.[66]

When addressing norms concerning the removal of unexploded ordnances; it is, however, also necessary to include another aspect of the relationship between human rights law and international humanitarian law. The relationship is ordinarily described from the perspective of applying norms belonging to human rights law in a situation of armed conflict, but the present study also involves the opposite situation, namely the application of norms belonging to international humanitarian law in a situation where there is no ongoing armed conflict. The obligations to remove unexploded ordnances are primarily aimed at peacetime or post-conflict situations, which are situations where human rights law undoubtedly is applicable. Unless derogated from, the norms belonging to human rights law apply in full. The argument that international humanitarian law is *lex specialis* to human rights law because it is specifically designed for a state of armed conflict, clearly becomes irrelevant. Nevertheless, it is still necessary to regard each particular norm to determine which norm prevails in case of a conflict between the norms.

B. *The Right not to be Arbitrarily Deprived of One's Life*

In discussions about the relationship between international humanitarian law and human rights law, it is often the individual's right not to be arbitrarily deprived of his or her life that is the focus of attention. The applicable norms under the two regimes are considerably different, and it is of great significance for the protection of civilians what regime is applied in a specific situation. International humanitarian law prohibits direct attacks against civilians, but permits the loss of civilian lives as long as all feasible precautions are taken for the protection of civilians and the fundamental principles of proportionality, distinction and military necessity are complied with. Human rights law protects everyone's right not to be "intentionally" or "arbitrarily" deprived of his life, see Article 2 of the European Convention on Human Rights[67] and Article 6 of the International Covenant on Civil and Political Rights.[68]

These provisions include an obligation for the State to take affirmative action for the protection of civilians' lives. The State must not only "respect" the right to life, but it must also "secure" this right.[69] The ECtHR has developed a doctrine that the State must take "appropriate steps" to safeguard the life of individuals within

66 William A. Schabas, 'Lex specialis? Belt and Suspenders? The Parallel Operation of Human Rights Law and the Law of Armed Conflict, and the Conundrum of jus ad bellum', *Israel Law Review* Vol. 40 (2008) 592–613.

67 European Convention for the Protection of Human Rights and Fundamental Freedoms (1950), entry into force 3.9.1953. Hereinafter "ECHR".

68 The International Covenant on Civil and Political Rights, 16.12.1966, entry into force 23.3.1976. Hereinafter "ICCPR".

69 The positive obligation to protect life is described by, for example, Clare Ovey and Robin C.A. White, *The European Convention on Human Rights* (4th ed., Oxford: Oxford University Press 2006) 62–65.

their jurisdiction.[70] There is no reason why the removal of anti-personnel mines and other unexploded ordnances should be excluded from this obligation. The ordnances represent a permanent, direct and immediate threat to civilians, and we are at the core of the scope of application of the provisions on the right to life.

The Court has on a couple of occasions in recent years dealt with cases that in various ways touch upon this issue, but it has not yet delivered a precise judgment on the positive obligation to remove unexploded ordnances.

The first specifically relevant case is *Evcil v. Turkey* from 2004.[71] The applicant complained that her husband died as a result of an explosion of a tracer bullet that had been abandoned by Turkish security forces. She argued that the national authorities had an obligation to ensure the security of the citizens by collecting mines and ammunition that had been used for military purposes and later left behind. The case was declared inadmissible as manifestly ill-founded, partly because the Court was unable to conclude that the security forces were responsible for the abandoned tracer bullet. This may perhaps indicate that the Court considered that the authorities is under an obligation to remove unexploded ordnances that it has used, but not ordnances that are used by others. However, the issue was not directly addressed.

The case *Albekov and others v. Russia* concerned the death and injury of several men in a village in Chechnya.[72] The facts of the case were disputed. The applicants claimed that military forces had placed anti-personnel mines around the village, while the Government claimed that the mines had been placed there by illegal armed gangs. The Court considered it unnecessary to establish who had laid the mines, since the Government did not deny that the authorities were aware of the mines. The Court therefore considered that the Government was under a positive obligation to protect the residents from the risks involved, and the key question for the Court was accordingly whether "the State has taken all necessary measures to protect the applicants' relatives and other villagers from being exposed to the danger constituted by the land mines".[73] The Court here observed that

> in the absence of efforts to locate and deactivate mines the State might have discharged its positive obligation under Article 2 of the Convention by marking and sealing off the area so as to prevent anybody from entering it freely, and by comprehensively warning the residents of the location of the mines and the risks involved.[74]

The Government had not made any efforts in this case to seal off the area, and the Court concluded that

> having regard to the State's failure to endeavour to locate and deactivate the mines, to mark and seal off the mined area so as to prevent anybody from freely entering it, and to provide the villagers with comprehensive warnings concerning the mines

70 *Ibid*. See, for example, ECtHR judgment 30.11.2004 (Grand Chamber), applic. 48939/99 *Öneryildiz v. Turkey*, para. 71.

71 Admissibility decision 6.4.2004, applic. 46260/99 *Evcil v. Turkey*.

72 Judgment 9.10.2008, applic. no. 68216/01 *Albekov and others v. Russia*.

73 *Ibid*, paras 85–86.

74 *Ibid*, para. 88.

> laid in the vicinity of their village, the Court finds that the State has failed to comply with its positive obligation under Article 2 of the Convention ...[75]

That the Court points to the "failure to ... deactivate the mines" may indicate that the State is under an obligation to deactivate mines in order to satisfy its positive obligations under Article 2. The preceding statement indicates on the other hand that the positive obligation can be satisfied by less extensive measures, such as "marking and sealing off the area". The case therefore does not expressly support the view that Article 2 places an obligation on the state to remove and destroy known anti-personnel mines. The case law nevertheless demonstrates that anti-personnel mines are not excluded from the scope of application of Article 2.

Important is also, however, the aforementioned *Behrami* case.[76] The applicants claimed that the death and injury to the boys was caused by the failure of French KFOR troops to mark and/or defuse the undetonated cluster bomb units which those troops knew to be present, and that this represented a violation of Article 2.[77] The Court considered that de-mining fell within UNMIK's, rather than KFOR's, mandate, and that conduct by UNMIK is attributable to the United Nations rather than to the individual Troop Contributing States.[78] The Court therefore declared itself incompetent *ratione personae* to examine the application.[79] The decision contains no statements about the substantive issue under Article 2.

I have elsewhere criticised the Court's decision with regard to the conduct by KFOR, as I believe that the Court has applied the wrong test in attributing conduct to the United Nations.[80] This criticism is less relevant with regard to the conduct by UNMIK. As a subsidiary organ of the United Nations, it is in accordance with general principles of the responsibility of international organizations to attribute conduct by UNMIK to the United Nations. The decision is nevertheless open for criticism: For one thing, the Court has not addressed the potential significance of the fact that the undetonated cluster bomb units were dropped by NATO – and thus, possibly, States that are parties to the ECHR – in air raids prior to authorization by the United Nations Security Council. And further, the Court has not addressed the possibility of dual attribution of conduct or the possibility of holding individual States responsible for acts carried out by an international organization.

Whether the human rights instruments can be interpreted so as to provide obligations to remove unexploded ordnances can from this not be given a definite answer, but the general obligation not to arbitrarily deprive individuals of their lives may in certain circumstances include this element. One must therefore consider the relationship between such a norm under human rights law and the relevant norms under international humanitarian law.

---

75 *Ibid*, para. 90.

76 *Supra*, note 4.

77 *Ibid*, para. 61.

78 *Ibid*, paras. 125–127 and 142–143.

79 *Ibid*, para. 152.

80 Larsen, *supra* note 59.

From one perspective, the issue at hand provides a "classic" illustration of the relationship between norms for the protection of civilian lives under international humanitarian law and human rights law: The APM Convention, the CCW Protocol II, the ERW Protocol and the CMC permit conduct that human rights law prohibits. With regard to the rules that are relevant for the present study, the contradiction is primarily found in the temporal aspects of the norms. The "right to life" under human rights law is undoubtedly an *immediate* right, in the sense that the State is under an obligation to respect and to secure the individuals' right to life immediately when the norm becomes binding on the State. The State cannot argue that it will improve the protection of the right over time, or that it will implement the right within reasonable time. The mentioned conventions, on the other hand, provide exactly such a time frame. Contaminated areas shall be cleared "as soon as possible" or "as soon as feasible", and some of the instruments even provide a deadline of ten years. This is clearly a more specific regulation, which has been adopted especially for the removal of unexploded ordnances. Also in other aspects is it clear that the relevant weapons conventions are more specific than the general provisions under human rights law. The conventions contain clear provisions, inter alia, about the assessment of the threat posed by the unexploded ordnances, and about how to reduce the risk until such time as the ordnances can be removed. If one subscribes to the *lex specialis* theory, it appears clear that the weapons conventions are *lex specialis* to human rights law on this issue, and therefore prevail. But even if one subscribes to the "belt and suspenders" theory, the end result would probably be the same. While the "right to life" undoubtedly is an immediate right, this does not mean that the State's obligation to take affirmative actions for the protection of the right is unlimited. Whether one says that the State must take "appropriate steps"[81] or one applies another norm, the reality is that the State must take such measures that are feasible and appropriate in relation to the specific risk, available resources, etc. It is difficult to imagine that the obligation to take "appropriate steps" under human rights law will place further demands on the States than the detailed measures that are provided in the weapons conventions.

C. *The Applicability of Human Rights Instruments in Peace Operations*

The *de jure* applicability of human rights instruments during international peace operations has not yet received the same attention as the applicability of international humanitarian law. It is commonly accepted that peace operations in fact perform important human rights functions, and that there exist clear moral or political obligations to protect the human rights of the civilian population. This is, however, clearly not the same as imposing legal obligations on the forces. In the recent "Capstone Doctrine" the UN Department of Peacekeeping Operations maintains that "[i]nternational human rights law is an integral part of the normative framework for United Nations peacekeeping operations" and that "United Nations peacekeeping personnel ... should act in accordance with international human rights law",[82]

81 *Supra*, note 70.

82 United Nations Peacekeeping Operations: Principles and Guidelines (approved 18.1.2008), section 1.2, p. 14.

but this does not in itself clarify the issue of whether human rights instruments apply as a matter of *law* or as a matter of *policy*. There are many obstacles that need to be cleared before legal obligations can be established, and these cannot be discussed in depth here. For the purpose of the present study, the following summary must suffice:

First, the *Behrami* case illustrates the perhaps greatest obstacle to the establishment of responsibility for alleged human rights infringements during peace operations. In the view of the ECtHR, conduct during peace operations is attributable to the United Nations and not to the individual Troop Contributing State, as long as powers are lawfully delegated by the Security Council and the conduct is performed in accordance with the delegation.[83] The ECtHR therefore declared itself incompetent *ratione personae* to examine the allegations, and this makes it difficult to hold individual States accountable for violations of the ECHR. However, the House of Lords in the United Kingdom held in the *Al-Jedda* case that conduct by British forces in Iraq is attributable to the United Kingdom and not to the United Nations, and this shows that the obstacle is not insurmountable.[84]

Second, the *Al-Jedda* case also illustrates that the application of human rights instruments can be qualified by the mandate which authorizes the operation. The UN Charter Article 103 states that obligations under the Charter prevail over other obligations under international law in case of conflict, and the House of Lords held that this provision also means that *authorizations* by the Security Council can qualify the rights under the ECHR.[85]

Third, the Troop Contributing States are operating outside their own territory when participating in peace operations, and it is accordingly the rules and principles on extraterritorial application of human rights instruments that determine the scope of the States' obligations. Extraterritorial effect has been recognized by both the ECtHR with regard to the ECHR and by the United Nations Human Rights Committee with regard to the ICCPR. In short, the legal position is that the human rights instruments may apply to extraterritorial conduct when the State exercises a certain authority or control over a territory or over an individual, and – as has been discussed above – the forces may acquire such control during the operation.[86]

---

83 See Larsen, *supra* note 59, pp. 520 ff.

84 R (on the application of Al-Jedda) (FC) (Appellant) v Secretary of State for Defence (Respondent), [2007] UKHL 58, House of Lords judgment 12.12.2007. See Larsen, *ibid*, p. 526, where I argued that it is difficult to reconcile the House of Lords' conclusion with the ECtHR's decision in the *Behrami/Saramati* case.

85 This interpretation of Article 103 is debatable. One can argue that the provision only concerns *obligations*, and not *authorizations*. One can argue that it only refers to obligations in the Charter itself, and not to resolutions, decisions etc. from Charter bodies. Rob McLaughlin, "The Legal Regime Applicable to Use of Lethal Force When Operating under a United Nations Security Council Chapter VII Mandate Authorising 'All Necessary Means'", *Journal of Conflict & Security Law* vol. 12 (2008) 398–402, provides an overview of the discussion.

86 There exists a large amount of literature on the extraterritorial application of human rights instruments, and the issue can not be pursued here. See, for example, Fons Coomans and Menno T. Kamminga (eds.), *Extraterritorial application of human rights treaties* (Antwerp: Intersentia, 2004), Morten P. Pedersen, 'Territorial Jurisdiction in Article 1 of

The obstacles have led me to conclude previously that the ECHR is in practice rendered irrelevant for international peace operations.[87] But, as a side note: The UN Human Rights Committee has for its part consistently maintained that the ICCPR remains binding on States Parties when they contribute forces to international operations.[88] The applicability of human rights instruments in peace operations therefore remains a contentious issue.

IV. Concluding Remarks

There exists a wide range of norms under international law that obligate States to remove and destroy anti-personnel mines, unexploded cluster submunition and other explosive remnants of war in areas within their control. The application of these norms is not excluded during international peace operations. The generally accepted principle that the international humanitarian law obligations of Troop Contributing States remain in force during participation in peace operations also imply that States remain bound by their obligations to remove and destroy such ordnances when they control an area during the operations, even when the ordnances have been used by other actors. However, this obligation has not (yet) acquired the status of international customary law, and is accordingly not binding for those States that have not ratified the relevant treaties. Nor is it binding for the United Nations as such, and it does not form a part of the organization's legal obligations under international humanitarian law. Whether the troops are bound by the obligation will depend on the operational structure, including the command and control structure, of the specific operation, as it must be determined which entity in reality exercises control over the specific area.

Regardless of the binding effect of norms under international humanitarian law, all actors involved in international peace operations are obliged to respect the civilian population's right under human rights law not to be arbitrarily deprived of their life, certainly as a matter of policy, and arguably as a matter of law. The affirmative actions required by this obligation may under certain condition include the removal and destruction of anti-personnel mines, unexploded cluster submunitions and other explosive remnants of war.

The presentation has shown, however, that the existence of legal obligations to remove unexploded ordnances in peace operations remains contentious. As these ordnances present a significant danger to civilians, the clarification of such a norm should be pursued further in order to improve the security of civilians in conflicts and in post-conflict situations.

---

the European Convention on Human Rights', *Nordic Journal of International Law* Vol. 73 (2004) 279–305, or Alexander Orakhelashvili, *supra* note 29.

87 Larsen, *supra* note 59, p. 531.

88 See the Concluding Observations to Germany (CCPR/CO/80/DEU, 4.5.2004, para. 11), Belgium (CCPR/CO/81/BEL, 12.8.2004), Poland (CCPR/CO/82/POL, 2.12.2004, para. 3), Italy (CCPR/C/ITA/CO/5, 24.4.2006, para. 3), and Norway (CCPR/C/NOR/CO/5, 25.4.2006, para. 6).

Chapter 6

A New Treaty Banning Cluster Munitions: The Interplay between Disarmament Diplomacy and Humanitarian Requirements

Gro Nystuen

I. Introduction

Weapons that leave unexploded remnants in large numbers represent a very concrete human security issue. In 1997, anti personnel mines were outlawed. In May 2008, a new treaty banning cluster munitions was negotiated and adopted in Dublin. This chapter describes the background for this recent humanitarian diplomatic undertaking, as well as the political aspects of the process towards a prohibition on cluster munitions. It discusses the scope of application of the principle of distinction to weapons that represent a threat to civilians long after their deployment. Moreover, it discusses the content of this newest addition to the body of international humanitarian law against the background of a discussion on whether there was a case for new law at all.

II. Background

Cluster munition is the categorisation of weapons that consists of a "parent" munition containing a number of *sub-munitions* or *bomblets*. The weapon is normally designed to be both anti vehicle and anti personnel. One key feature is the weapon's "area effect", in other words, that it is meant to cover a "footprint".[1] Because of its area effect, cluster munitions tend to hit objects randomly *during* an attack, and because of the large quantities of sub-munitions, the amount of unexploded sub-munitions remain a danger to the population in the area *after* an attack.

Cluster munitions have been used in several conflicts following World War II. They were used in Laos and Vietnam, in the Gulf War, in the former Yugoslavia, in Chechnya, in the war between Eritrea and Ethiopia, in Afghanistan, in Iraq and they were used by Israel in southern Lebanon in the summer of 2006. The use of cluster

1 Extensive deployment of air launched cluster munitions is often characterised as "carpet bombing".

Cecilia M. Bailliet (ed.), Security: A Multidisciplinary Normative Approach.
 ISBN 978 90 04 17296 8. pp. 137–153.

munitions in Lebanon was well documented in international media and was one of the reasons why the campaign against cluster weapons gained momentum.

A technical description of cluster munitions was given in a UK Working Paper at a governmental experts meeting in 2005:

> Cluster munitions are area effect weapons, which may be either air delivered or ground launched. In both cases a carrier munition releases a number of bomblets onto the battlefield to cause destruction, neutralisation or suppression of personnel or materiel.[2]

A more effect based description is provided on the website of the leading NGO in this field, the Cluster Munition Coalition (CMC):

> Air-dropped or ground-launched, they cause two major humanitarian problems and risks to civilians. First, their widespread dispersal means they cannot distinguish between military targets and civilians so the humanitarian impact can be extreme, especially when the weapon is used in or near populated areas.

Many sub-munitions fail to detonate on impact and become de facto antipersonnel mines killing and maiming people long after the conflict has ended. These duds are more lethal than antipersonnel mines; incidents involving sub-munition duds are much more likely to cause death than injury.[3]

The concrete and devastating effects on human security for those affected by cluster munitions have been described elsewhere.[4] Here, it will suffice to point out that these weapons kill and maim civilians, often for decades after their deployment. In addition, cluster munitions (or even the risk of presence of cluster munitions) can impede economic development because areas (for example agricultural) cannot be accessed until they have been cleared.

A. *Was There a Case for New Law?*

It has been pointed out by many legal experts that indiscriminate use of cluster munitions is already inconsistent with the obligation to distinguish between civilians and civilian objects on the one hand, and military objectives and combatants on the other, which is laid down in Additional Protocol I to the Geneva Conventions.[5] This reference to the principle of distinction has been used as an argument against regulating specifically the use of cluster munitions; it has been presumed that use of

2 Working Paper on the Military Utility of Cluster Munitions, distributed by the delegation of the United Kingdom at a meeting of the Convention on Prohibitions or Restrictions on the Use of Certain Conventional Weapons Which May be Deemed to be Excessively Injurious or the have Indiscriminate Effects, 1980, (CCW) Group of Governmental Experts in Geneva, March 2005.

3 http://www.stopclustermunitions.org/the-problem/.

4 See for example report on the effects of cluster munitions on Handicap International's website: http://www.handicap-international.org.uk/page_247.php.

5 See Articles 48–58 of Additional Protocol I (1977) to the Geneva Conventions (1949).

these weapons has normally been consistent with the requirements of IHL. New and more specific regulations, it has been argued, were thus not necessary. In an article from 2005, it was for example maintained by Boothby that

> The existing law of targeting in Additional Protocol I has the merit of applying to all conventional attacks. It does not appear to be helpful to seek to vary the wording of those well established rules in order to seek to cater for the particular issues identified in relation to cluster munitions.[6]

Article 51 (4) of Additional Protocol I to the Geneva Conventions (AP I) specifies that indiscriminate attacks are prohibited, and that indiscriminate attacks are defined as *inter alia* "those which employ a method or means of combat which cannot be directed at a specific military objective". Clearly, many cluster munitions would fall into this category. In fact, these rules were the basis for the conviction of Milan Martic by the International Criminal Tribunal for the Former Yugoslavia (ICTY) due to his responsibility for the deployment of cluster munitions. In this judgment from 2007, the defendant was found guilty of war crimes for having targeted Zagreb with cluster munitions of the type M-87 Orkan. The Orkan M-87 was a surface launched rocket, delivered from MLRS (Multiple Launch Rocket System) platforms, deploying 12 rockets at the time, each rocket carrying 288 sub-munitions, and each sub-munition carrying 420 pellets. Its firing range was 50 kilometres, ad the footprint of each rocket was 150 by 200 metres.[7] The Tribunal described this cluster munition[8] as follows:

> … the Trial Chamber notes the characteristics of the weapon, it being a non-guided high dispersion weapon. The Trial Chamber therefore concludes that the M-87 Orkan, by virtue of its characteristics and the firing range in this specific instance, was incapable of hitting specific targets. For these reasons, the Trial Chamber also finds that the M-87 Orkan is an indiscriminate weapon …[9]

In its decision, the Trial Chamber did not discuss the legal issues relating to unexploded ordnance, in spite of the fact that the dud rate[10] following this attack was a staggering 46 to 69 %, depending on how many rockets that were actually fired.[11] The arguments focused on the imprecision of the Orkan 87 *during* the attack.

One might, however, argue that the dud rate *following* an attack also represents a possible violation of the principle of distinction. Article 51 (5) (b) of AP I defines indiscriminate attacks as

6 William H. Boothby, *Cluster Bombs: Is There a Case for New Law?*, HPCR Occasional Paper Series, fall 2005, page 2.

7 Judgment of: 12 June 2007, Trial Chamber I, Prosecutor v Milan Martic, para 472.

8 See *Cluster Munitions – A survey of legal responses*, by Stuart Maslen and Vigil Wiebe, published by Landmine Monitor 2007, page 37, about this testimony in the Martic case.

9 Judgment of: 12 June 2007, Trial Chamber I Prosecutor v Milan Martic, para 463.

10 The percentage of the total number of sub-munitions that do not detonate on impact.

11 *Cluster Munitions – A survey of legal responses*, by Stuart Maslen and Vigil Wiebe, published by Landmine Monitor 2007, page 41.

> … an attack which may be expected to cause incidental loss of civilian life, injury to civilians, damage to civilian objects, or a combination thereof, which would be excessive in relation to the concrete and direct military advantage anticipated.

This provision tries to balance humanitarian concerns against the expected military advantage, and it represents an additional limitation to those already listed elsewhere in Article 51.[12] It seems clear that because the military advantage must be *concrete and direct*, it must also be immediate. The term "*expected … incidental loss of civilian life* …" does not appear to be subject to the same time limitation. Does "expected … incidental loss of civilian life …" refer to *immediately*, in a *few hours*, several *weeks* or even *years*, after the attack? If an attack continues to produce civilian harm for a lengthy time period after the attack, this would appear to have a direct bearing on whether or not such an attack would be "excessive". Use of cluster munitions may be expected to cause incidental loss of civilian life for years, even decades (if areas are not cleared) after the attacks. It seems unlikely that there will be any military advantage from damage that occurs after the conflict is over. In any case, as stated in the above mentioned provision, the military advantage must be concrete and immediate. One might therefore suggest that this provision implies that damage to civilians that occur after the attack itself is almost always excessive in relation to the military advantage when it comes to cluster munitions, because it is well known that they leave large amounts of duds.

This view has been subject extensive debate. Several writers have expressed the view that the general rules on proportionality and distinction in IHL are sufficient in order to regulate use of cluster munitions. This is not, however, because they necessarily agree that the general rules would normally outlaw the use of cluster munitions because of long term effects,

In a report, drafted on the basis of a questionnaire presented in the CCW Group of Governmental Experts context in 2005, professor McCormack concludes, on the basis of the responses from participating states, that "Protocol V to the CCW [on Explosive Remnants of War (ERW)] and the existing rules of IHL are specific and comprehensive enough to deal adequately with the problem of ERW *provided that those rules are effectively implemented*." (Emphasis added)[13] This observation begs the question of what is meant by the term "effectively implemented".

Professor Greenwood has stated that if cluster weapons "are used against military targets in an area where there are known to be civilians, then the proportionality test may require that account be taken both of the risk to the civilians from submunitions exploding during the attack and of risk from unexploded submunitions in the hours

12 ICRC Commentary to Article 51, para 1980: The idea has also been put forward that even if they are very high, civilian losses and damages may be justified if the military advantage at stake is of great importance. This idea is contrary to the fundamental rules of the Protocol; in particular it conflicts with Article 48 '(Basic rule)' and with paragraphs 1 and 2 of the present Article 51. The Protocol does not provide any justification for attacks which cause extensive civilian losses and damages. Incidental losses and damages should never be extensive.

13 CCW/GGE/X/WG.1WP 2, 8 March 2005.

immediately after the attack. It is an entirely different matter, however, to require that account be taken of the longer term risk posed by ERW, particularly of the risk which ERW can pose after a conflict has ended … The proportionality test has to be applied on the basis of information reasonably available at the time of the attack."[14]

The question arising from to this line of reasoning would be: what kind of information is *reasonably available* to the commander who decides to use cluster weapons in areas normally used by civilians? One might assume that expected dud rates ought to be known to persons in charge of choosing targets, but this appears not necessarily to be the case. Boothby, for example, argues that "To expect a military commander to agonise over remote philosophical chances is clearly unrealistic."[15] One might therefore conclude that the term *effective implementation* of the general rules on proportionality and distinction does not represent very specific guidance with regard to whether or not civilian harm caused by expected ERW should be taken into account in a targeting process.

From a legalistic point of view it is still fully possible to argue that the use of cluster munitions often will be in violation of Article 51 (4) because they cannot be directed at a *specific military objective*, and that such use in any event may constitute a violation of Article 51 (5) (b) because of the amount of unexploded ordnance left after attacks. From a practical point of view, however, it seems that the provisions of Additional Protocol I do not constitute sufficiently detailed regulations regarding cluster munitions. In an actual targeting process, chances are remote that the term "expected" in Article 51 (5) (b) will be analysed in light of the term "excessive".[16] The prohibition on cluster munitions represents recognition of the fact that it is unfeasible for the individuals who are responsible for targeting in a combat situation to engage in in-depth legal analysis before choosing targets. As van Woudenberg concludes in his article on cluster munitions, "The time when it could be asserted that the world has no need of a specific instrument dealing with cluster munitions and that general international humanitarian law provided an adequate answer would seem to be definitely past."[17]

The argument that the general principles of Additional Protocol I suffice to regulate means of warfare in all situations could also apply to a number of other weapons that are subject to specific prohibitions. Biological and bacteriological weapons have been outlawed since 1925.[18] Chemical weapons have been prohibited since

14 Christopher Greenwood, Legal Issues regarding Explosive Remnants of War, CCW/GGE/I/WP 10, 22 May 2002.

15 William H. Boothby, *Cluster Bombs: Is There a Case for New Law?*, HPCR Occasional Paper Series, fall 2005, page 28.

16 As Boothby describes the potential mindset of someone about to deploy cluster munitions: "'To expect a commander to agonise over remote philosophical chances is clearly unrealistic.', ibid. page 28.

17 Nout van Woudenberg, 'The Long And Winding Road Towards an Instrument on Cluster Munitions', *Journal of Conflict & Security Law* Vol. 12 No. 3 (2008), p. 483.

18 The "Gas Protocol" of 1925 and the Convention on the Prohibition of the Development, Production and Stockpiling of Bacteriological (Biological) and Toxin Weapons and on Their Destruction, 1972.

1993.[19] Anti personnel mines were outlawed in 1997.[20] All of these weapons were prohibited because of the expected violation of the principle of distinction. Undetectable fragments and blinding laser are examples of weapons outlawed because they cause unnecessary suffering.[21] Recognising the difficulties with respecting in practice the principle of distinction and proportionality as laid out in Additional Protocol I, certain means of warfare are not available at all. Against this background it does not seem out of place to specifically prohibit cluster munitions.

B. *The Process*

i. Background

The war in south Lebanon in the summer of 2006 led to an increased recognition that the use of cluster weapons was difficult to reconcile with the principle of distinction. In particular, the large amounts of unexploded sub-munitions which continued to kill and maim civilians after the hostilities had ceased, were subject to increasing concern.

Two other international humanitarian law processes have been instrumental when it comes to the Oslo Process on a total ban on cluster munitions: First, the *Ottawa Process* towards a total ban on anti personnel landmines through the Convention on the prohibition of the use, stockpiling, production and transfer of anti-personnel mines and on their destruction (Mine Ban Convention).[22] Second, the development of several instruments in the context of the Convention on Prohibitions or Restrictions on the Use of Certain Conventional Weapons Which May be Deemed to be Excessively Injurious or the have Indiscriminate Effects (Certain Conventional Weapons Convention, also called the CCW).[23]

When the CCW Convention was adopted in 1980, it had four protocols on specific weapons. As the title of the Convention indicates, these were all weapons that *may be deemed to be excessively injurious or to have indiscriminate effects*.[24]

19 Convention on the Prohibition of the Development, Production, Stockpiling and Use of Chemical Weapons and on Their Destruction, 1993.

20 Convention on the prohibition of the use, stockpiling, production and transfer of anti-personnel mines and on their destruction, 1997. Since the adoption of this convention, the decrease in numbers of new victims is considerable. Also, production and trade with anti personnel mines have practically ceased.

21 Protocols I and IV of the Convention on Prohibitions or Restrictions on the Use of Certain Conventional Weapons Which May be Deemed to be Excessively Injurious or the have Indiscriminate Effects, 1980.

22 Convention on the prohibition of the use, stockpiling, production and transfer of anti personnel mines and on their destruction, 1997.

23 Convention on Prohibitions or Restrictions on the Use of Certain Conventional Weapons Which May be Deemed to be Excessively Injurious or the have Indiscriminate Effects, 1980.

24 The CCW Protocol I prohibits the use of non-detectable fragments, CCW Protocol II lays down certain restrictions on the use of mines, booby traps and other devices, CCW Protocol III lays down restrictions on the use of incendiary weapons. CCW Protocol IV,

The Ottawa Process on anti personnel mines was initiated as a result of disappointment, not only among civil society, but also among a number of Governments, with the failure of the revision process of CCW Protocol II on mines etc., to adopt a strong ban on anti personnel mines. Amended Protocol II of 1996 under the CCW regime only regulates the use of anti personnel mines, it does not prohibit them. Likewise, one might point to the failure of Protocol V on Explosive Remnants of War to effectively address the cluster munitions issue, as one of several factors contributing to the Oslo process.

The CCW remains an important part of the body of treaty law which regulates and prohibits specific weapons because of their potential non-compliance with the general principles on distinction and proportionality laid down in international humanitarian law. The shortcomings of this forum, however, constitute certain obstacles when it comes to achieving prohibitions on categories of weapons that some states wish to retain. Since its initial diplomatic conference in 1980 the CCW has worked under a principle of consensus for adoption of instruments. The CCW Framework Convention itself states that protocols to the Convention shall "be adopted in the same manner as this Convention".[25] This has been interpreted to mean that all additional protocols must be adopted by consensus, which again means that it is difficult to get results with which certain States are uncomfortable.

ii. The Oslo Process

The Oslo Process started in Geneva. At the CCW Review Conference in November 2006, it seemed clear that it would not be possible to agree on another protocol which would effectively address the problems caused by cluster munitions. The mandate that had been given the expert group was to "negotiate a *proposal* to address urgently the humanitarian impact of cluster munitions ..." (Emphasis added). On the last day of the CCW Review Conference it was announced that all interested States were invited to a meeting in Oslo in February 2007 with the aim of initiating an alternative process to negotiate a treaty to ban cluster munitions.

On 22–23 February 2007, 49 States, several UN agencies, the International Committee of the Red Cross, the Cluster Munitions Coalition and other humanitarian organisations, met in Oslo. The Oslo Conference adopted a declaration which laid the foundation for the process towards a ban. The declaration described the problem and then set out the necessary course of action:[26]

> Recognising the grave consequences caused by the use of cluster munitions and the need for immediate action, states commit themselves to:

---

prohibiting the use of blinding laser weapons, was added in 1995, and in 1996, CCW Protocol II on mines, booby traps and other devices was amended. In 2003, CCW Protocol V on clearance of explosive remnants of war was adopted.

25 Article 8 (2) (b) of the Convention on Prohibitions or Restrictions on the Use of Certain Conventional Weapons Which May be Deemed to be Excessively Injurious or the have Indiscriminate Effects.

26 http://www.clusterconvention.org/oslo-declaration/.

> Conclude by 2008 a legally binding international instrument that will: prohibit the use, production, transfer and stockpiling of cluster munitions that cause unacceptable harm to civilians, and
>
> establish a framework for cooperation and assistance that ensures adequate provision of care and rehabilitation to survivors and their communities, clearance of contaminated areas, risk education and destruction of stockpiles of prohibited cluster munitions . . .[27]

At the time of the Oslo Conference, a Core Group of interested states had been established.[28] The actual sequence of conferences towards a diplomatic conference was agreed as follows: Lima 23–25 May 2007, Vienna 5–7 December 2007, Wellington 18–22 February 2008. The Diplomatic Conference was scheduled for 19–30 May 2008 in Dublin.[29] Before the conference in Lima in May 2007, the Core Group had worked out a strategy concerning the text proposal as well as the procedural aspects of the diplomatic conference. It seemed important to raise awareness about the humanitarian and other problems caused by cluster munitions, but it was also clear that the technical and legal aspects of this process were complex and needed to be raised and discussed thoroughly before actual negotiations on a convention text could start. While the definition of an anti personnel mine had been, in comparison, relatively straight forward, the actual definition of what kind of weapon would fall into the category of "cluster munition" was far less clear. Also, information concerning the actual functioning of many of the potential cluster munitions was disputed. The sequence of meetings was therefore aimed at generating discussions that would enhance the understanding of the complex issues that would have to be dealt with in the "legally binding instrument" referred to in the Oslo Declaration.

In order to facilitate such discussions, the Core Group drafted a "Chair's Discussion Text" for the Lima meeting.[30] The Lima Discussion Text was in many respects a blueprint of the Mine Ban Convention. The major difference pertained to the definition of the object of the prohibition; what would be classified as cluster munitions? This question remained the key question throughout the process. Would one get a definition that would not prohibit certain weapons because they had certain fail safe mechanisms, or would one get a prohibition that would take into account

27 Several of the States present at the Oslo Conference were uncomfortable with the idea of leaving the CCW forum and take the cluster munition process out of its established framework. In order to avoid a split at the conference, the following sentence was added to the declaration: "Continue to address the humanitarian challenges posed by cluster munitions within the framework of international humanitarian law and in all relevant fora."

28 It first consisted of Austria, Ireland, Mexico, New Zealand, Norway, Peru, and Sweden. Later, Sweden withdrew from the Core Group because of internal political issues. The Vatican (the Holy See) joined the Core Group relatively soon after the Oslo Conference.

29 In addition, there were regional conferences in support of the process in Cambodia in March 2007, Costa Rica in September 2007, Serbia in October 2007, Belgium in October 2007, Zambia in March 2008 and Mexico in April 2008.

30 http://www.clusterconvention.org/limatext/.

that even more sophisticated weapons could in fact represent serious humanitarian problems?[31]

At the Wellington Conference, 18–22 February 2008, there was heated debate concerning the content of the (then Wellington) discussion text. As a result of these discussions, all proposals for amendments of this text were attached as a compendium to the Declaration from that conference, and were also later submitted as formal text proposals to the Dublin Diplomatic Conference.[32] Thus, the Chair's Discussion Text for the Wellington Conference (dated 21 January 2008) became the *Basic Proposal* for the Dublin Diplomatic Conference as specified in Rule 30 of the Rules of Procedure for the Conference.[33]

The Wellington Declaration constituted the "entry ticket" for participation in the Dublin Diplomatic Conference. The Declaration stated that the essential elements of a treaty would be: ... a prohibition on the use, production, transfer and stockpiling of cluster munitions that cause unacceptable harm to civilians.[34]

As it was far from clear *which* cluster munitions that would be considered to cause "unacceptable harm to civilians", states that held very differing views on what ought to fall under the prohibition could all come to Dublin as participants.

The Ottawa Process was the blueprint for the Oslo Process. The existence of a core group of states driving the process, the close cooperation between States and key NGOs and civil society, the specific Rules of Procedure for the Diplomatic Conference which allowed for voting on controversial issues, were all key features of both the Ottawa Process in 1997 and the Oslo Process 11 years later.

iii. The M-85 Report

One of the important turning points of the Oslo Process was the distribution at the Vienna Conference of the so called "M-85 Report".[35] The report, which was written by technical experts with years of experience in mine clearance as well as

31 The Lima Discussion Text served its purpose; it did generate a number of discussions, which in turn was processed within the Core Group between the Lima Conference and the Vienna Conference. A new version of the "Chair's Discussion Text" was prepared and distributed in advance of the Vienna Conference in December 2007. This version of the text was changed again in advance of the Wellington meeting. The Chair's Discussion Text for the Wellington Conference was dated 21 January 2008, following Core Group discussions in the aftermath of the Vienna Conference. As it was still clear that the one large outstanding issue would be the definition of cluster munitions, the text was kept open ended on this point. On a number of other issues, not least on victim assistance, international cooperation and assistance and on stockpile destruction, the Wellington Discussion Text had been developed further and refined compared to the Lima text.

32 See Conference Documents CCM 4 – CCM 50 at http://www.clustermunitionsdublin.ie/documents.asp.

33 http://www.clustermunitionsdublin.ie/pdf/CCM52_001.pdf.

34 http://www.mfat.govt.nz/clustermunitionswellington/conference-documents/Wellington-declaration-final.pdf.

35 http://www.npaid.org/filestore/M85.pdf Report by: Colin King, C King Associates Ltd, Ove Dullum, Chief Scientist, Norwegian Defence Research Establishment, Grethe Østern, Policy Advisor on Cluster Munitions, Mine Action Unit, Norwegian People's Aid, Edited

experience with research on weapons technology, described recent research on the relatively modern cluster munition, M-85. This munition had been tested extensively in Norway, and had during tests showed a failure rate of slightly more than one per cent. The Norwegian Ministry of Defence had believed it to have a failure rate of slightly *less* than one per cent. This discrepancy between actual failure rates in tests and the assumption before the tests was considered unfortunate and disturbing. This specific ammunition constituted approximately 40 % of all stockpiled ammunition in Norway. The Norwegian Ministries of Defence and of Foreign Affairs thus decided to fund further research on the failure rates in actual use. The tests that had been carried out in Norway had taken place before the Israeli bombing of Lebanon in the summer of 2006. The very same cluster munitions (M-85) were used in bombing campaigns against Hezbollah, especially towards the end of the hostilities. The M-85 Report describes how, when in actual use, the M-85 cluster munitions have actual failure rates of between 9 and 12 %, in conservative estimates.

These findings were instrumental to the realisation by an increasing number of States that it would not suffice to have a definition of cluster munitions in the convention that was based on failure rates. The discrepancies between failure rates given by producers, by actual testing and not least by the findings in real usage, were so significant that they could not be ignored. After the publication of this report, fewer and fewer States argued for a definition that would allow cluster munitions of the M-85 category.

C. *The Diplomatic Conference*

The Draft Rules of Procedure for the Dublin Diplomatic Conference were based on rules of procedure for other diplomatic conferences such as the Oslo Diplomatic Conference on the Mine Ban Convention, the Diplomatic Conference for the Third Additional Protocol to the Geneva Conventions and several UN diplomatic conferences. The one aspect of these rules which made them substantially different from the agreed procedural system under the CCW[36] was that they allowed for voting.[37] Although there was no voting at the Dublin Diplomatic Conference, it seems beyond any doubt that the possibility for voting was instrumental in achieving consensus on the final text of the Convention.

One hundred and twenty seven states and a number of Intergovernmental- and Non-Governmental organisations met during the last two weeks of May 2008 in Dublin. Of these, one hundred and seven states were participants while twenty were observers. The Irish President of the Conference had Vice Presidents from Lebanon,

---

by: Richard Moyes, Policy & Research Manager, Landmine Action, Copyright © 2007 by Norwegian People's Aid, ISBN: 978-82-7766-071-4.

36 Article 8 (2) (b) of the Convention on Prohibitions or Restrictions on the Use of Certain Conventional Weapons Which May be Deemed to be Excessively Injurious or the have Indiscriminate Effects.

37 The adoption of a treaty at international conferences by a two-third majority of the States present and voting is laid down in Article 9 of the Vienna Convention on the Law of Treaties, and seems to be the prevailing procedural system at diplomatic conferences.

France, Chile, Mauritania, Norway, Mexico, Zambia and Hungary. While a large majority of NATO allies participated in the negotiations, the US did not. Neither did Russia, China and Israel, who are among past or current users or producers of cluster munitions. A number of states that had been at the "receiving end" of cluster munitions such as Afghanistan, Laos, Lebanon, Cambodia, Croatia, Serbia and Bosnia were also present.

The Irish Presidency and the eight Vice Presidents, in addition to the Conference Secretariat, constituted the formal structures of the Diplomatic Conference. As had been the case during the negotiations on the Mine Ban Convention, however, informal structures that were not laid down in the Rules of Procedure were also established. The President established a group of "Friends" who could take responsibility for difficult issues and try to negotiate solutions in informal groups during the Conference. These "Friends" were mostly members of the Core Group; New Zealand, who was given the very difficult task of working out a solution on definitions, Austria, who had responsibility for victim assistance, and Norway who was responsible for stockpile destruction. Switzerland, who was not in the Core Group, was given the task of working out an agreement on interoperability.

Intergovernmental Organisations (IGOs) and NGOs were allowed to take part in the Conference as observers. As such they could not submit formal proposals, but they could make statements, and circulate informal papers and take part in the discussions. The ICRC, with its undisputed competence in international humanitarian law, provided input to many of the discussions. The Cluster Munitions Coalition (CMC) had been one of the main driving forces for a strong convention for several years. Being an "umbrella" organisation for many humanitarian organisations and entities, they provided both technical and legal expertise with regard to the discussions on topics such as definition, stockpile destruction, and not least clearance of contaminated areas and victim assistance. With their large delegation of experts, campaigners and cluster munition survivors, they moreover provided the delegates with a constant reminder of why the Dublin Diplomatic Conference was taking place.

i. The Prohibition

The Convention on Cluster Munitions (CCM) was adopted by the Dublin Diplomatic Conference on 30 May, at 10.15 AM. It contains, in addition to a preamble, 23 Articles and is, in the English version, 18 pages long. It will enter into force six months after 30 states have become parties to it.

General obligations and scope of application

Article 1 a)–c) of the Convention reads as follows:

1. Each State Party undertakes never under any circumstances to:
   a. Use cluster munitions;
   b. Develop, produce, otherwise acquire, stockpile, retain or transfer to anyone, directly or indirectly, cluster munitions;
   c. Assist, encourage or induce anyone to engage in any activity prohibited to a State Party under this Convention.

It thus contains a prohibition, not only on *use*, but also on developing, producing, transferring, stockpiling, retaining and acquiring cluster munitions. It also contains a prohibition in Article 1 (c) on assistance etc. to use, stockpiling, transferring etc. This is the so called "complicity provision" that partly triggered the debate on interoperability which will be addressed below.

In the same manner as the conventions on biological weapons, chemical weapons and anti personnel mines, the Convention on Cluster Munitions applies in *all* situations, regardless of the intensity of a conflict or indeed whether there is an armed conflict going on at all. Article 1 specifies that Each State Party undertakes *never under any circumstances* to do any of the things prohibited by the Convention. This is a significantly much broader scope of application than that of international humanitarian law in general, as its main body of law only applies in international armed conflicts.[38] A more limited part of international humanitarian law applies also in non-international armed conflicts, as provided for in Additional Protocol II to the Geneva Conventions and Common Article 3 of the Geneva Conventions. The prohibitions and restrictions contained in the protocols to the CCW are only applicable in situations of armed conflict that at least reaches the threshold of Common Article 3 of the Geneva Conventions.[39] These instruments, as opposed to the Cluster Munitions Convention, would thus not apply for example in internal armed conflicts which are not recognised as such, for example in Chechnya; a situation not recognised by Russia as an armed conflict.

ii. Definition of Cluster Munitions

The Basic Proposal for negotiations at the Dublin Diplomatic Conference had been elaborated by a limited number of States (the Core Group), but was based on extensive discussions in a number of conferences and meetings. The most controversial part, a definition of cluster munition, was left open in the Basic Proposal.[40] The general approach was to define a specific category of munitions as *cluster munitions*. All such munitions would then fall within the prohibition. An alternative approach would have been to divide munitions into *prohibited* cluster munitions and *non-prohibited* cluster munitions. This approach was seen as politically unfortunate by many as it would be demanding to explain why certain types of a generally prohibited weapon should not be banned. It was thus decided early on in the process as an important point of policy that the approach would be that everything falling within the definition would be classified as cluster munitions and would thus be prohibited. Anything not captured by the definition would not be regarded as cluster munitions at all.

Throughout the Oslo Process, three basic approaches to a prohibition on cluster munitions emerged. The least ambitious would be to only prohibit cluster munitions

38 See Common Article 2 to the Four Geneva Conventions, 1949.

39 Convention on Prohibitions or Restrictions on the Use of Certain Conventional Weapons Which May be Deemed to be Excessively Injurious or the have Indiscriminate Effects, Article 1 (1) and (2).

40 Article 2 c simply read: "…."

with none (or low performance) fail-safe systems. This approach would capture the kind of weapons dealt with in the Martic case,[41] and thus a large part of existing stockpiled cluster munitions. The second approach would be to also prohibit the cluster munitions with more advanced or modern fail-safe mechanisms, such as the M-85, as well as other munitions containing sub-munitions that may cause humanitarian harm. This approach was the prevailing one, and is now reflected in Article 2 of the Convention. The third, and most radical, approach was to prohibit basically every weapon with more than one sub-munition, regardless of the potential humanitarian consequences. Such an approach would have resulted in a pure disarmament treaty. This had clearly not been the aim of the Oslo Process; there had to be a humanitarian justification for the prohibition.

The main part of the definition of a cluster munition in Article 2 reads as follows:

> For the purposes of this Convention:
>
> 2. *Cluster munition* means a conventional munition that is designed to disperse or release explosive submunitions each weighing less than 20 kilograms, and includes those explosive submunitions. It does not mean the following:
>
> a. A munition or submunition designed to dispense flares, smoke, pyrotechnics or chaff; or a munition designed exclusively for an air defence role;
> b. A munition or submunition designed to produce electrical or electronic effects;
> c. A munition that, in order to avoid indiscriminate area effects and the risks posed by unexploded submunitions, has all of the following characteristics:
>   i. Each munition contains fewer than ten explosive submunitions;
>   ii. Each explosive submunition weighs more than four kilograms;
>   iii. Each explosive submunition is designed to detect and engage a single target object;
>   iv. Each explosive submunition is equipped with an electronic self-destruction mechanism;
>   v. Each explosive submunition is equipped with an electronic self-deactivating feature;

Article 2 c) makes it clear that those munitions which carry less than ten sub-munitions, when each sub-munition weighs more than four kilogrammes, is designed to detect and engage single target objects, is equipped with an electronic self destruction mechanism and is also equipped with an electronic self deactivation feature, are not cluster munitions and therefore not prohibited under the Convention. The requirements in Article 2 c) are cumulative, in other words; all of them must be fulfilled. In practice this means that only sub-munitions that are large enough to contain sophisticated electronic fusing and fail-safe mechanisms, and which therefore do not hit targets indiscriminately and moreover do not leave undetonated duds after the end of hostilities, are allowed.

This prohibition captures also several so called sensor fused weapons, which were believed by many as advanced munitions that did not cause humanitarian problems.

41 See above in this article "Was there a case for new law?".

The far reaching scope of this definition thus exceeded the expectations of many delegations as well as many in the NGO community.

iii. Other Provisions

The Convention on Cluster Munitions contains relatively detailed regulations on stockpile destruction, which of course is crucial in order to prevent future use of cluster munitions. Also the obligation to undertake clearance and destruction of cluster munition remnants in the contaminated areas is vital in order for the treaty to make a difference. Both stockpile destruction and not least clearance are complicated and time consuming undertakings. The Convention therefore stipulates workable deadlines as well as, in specific circumstances, possibilities for extensions of these. Stockpile destruction must be carried out as soon as possible but no later than eight years after entry into force. Applications for extensions of this deadline must be accompanied with detailed information of why the original deadline could not be met.[42] A similar system is contained in the article on clearance of contaminated areas.[43]

Provisions on Victim Assistance are more prominent and detailed in the CCM than in the Mine Ban Convention. This was one of the areas where "lessons learned" over the past decade was reflected in the new convention. Another important feature of both the Mine Ban Convention and the CCM is the provision on International Cooperation and Assistance.[44] While there are no hard core financial obligations on certain states to provide assistance to other states, there is guidance to how states should exchange for example know-how and technical expertise with regard to for example clearance, risk reduction education, marking and protection of civilians.

Article 9, which deals with national implementation measures, is similar to the corresponding article in the Mine Ban Convention. It specifies that States Parties shall take all appropriate measures to implement the Convention, including the imposition of penal sanctions to prevent activities prohibited by the Convention. This provision was another stumbling block with regard to the issue of interoperability. It was feared that national legislation, penalising acts that would be prohibited under the Convention, could lead to criminal prosecution of military personnel of states not belonging to the Convention while participating with States Parties in military operations. This issue was also dealt with in Article 21, which is discussed below.

As is the case with the Mine Ban Convention, the Convention on Cluster Munitions does not allow any reservations.[45] The articles concerning reporting and compliance measures, national implementation measures, Meetings of States Parties and Review Conferences, constitute the framework for the actual implementation of the Convention.[46]

---

42 Article 3, CCM.

43 Article 4, CCM.

44 Article 5, CCM.

45 Article 19 of the CCM.

46 Articles 7–12 of the CCM.

III. Interoperability

Interoperability was, together with the definition of cluster munitions, the most difficult question at the diplomatic conference, and one which was only solved towards the very end. Interoperability is a term used to describe issues that arise when troops from various states cooperate in military operations. Restraints on interoperability are seen as potentially complicating military cooperation.

Interoperability restraints might typically arise when states participating in the same military operation have different legal obligations, either under national law or under international law. Within NATO, there are different obligations among the member states with regard to international humanitarian law (such as the Additional Protocols to the Geneva Conventions and the Mine Ban Convention) and even international human rights law. One example is the complex issue of accountability of international peace operations and recent developments in international law. International operations may be conducted under unified command and control of an international organisation, with the participation of both member and non-member states. Attribution of conduct under such operations potentially creates interoperability issues in the planning and setup of the operation. Likewise, not all states are parties to Additional Protocols I and II to the Geneva Conventions. This affects interoperability in many ways, for instance with regard to status of combatants and the treatment of detainees. The Statutes of the International Criminal Court establishes jurisdiction over war crimes. Not all contributing States are parties to the ICC statutes. Different interpretations of international human rights obligations (including the interpretation of the term "torture") have also proved to represent practical problems with regard to, for example, the transfer and treatment of detainees.

NATO allies have been in military operations together for decades regardless of such differences. Specific legal obligations for States Parties to a treaty do not, as a general rule, prevent them from taking part in international operations together with non-state parties. Such interoperability problems resulting from differing treaty obligations are typically solved through national *caveats* to Rules of Engagement for the individual operations.

In the run up to the Diplomatic Conference, there were nevertheless concerns that Article 1 (c) prohibiting assistance to any of the acts banned by the Convention, would potentially invoke responsibility for States Parties participating in military operations with non-state parties that might use cluster munitions. It was also alleged that Article 1 (c) together with Article 9 on individual criminal liability would entail that service personnel in international operations may be subject to unjustified criminal prosecution. As explained above, Article 9 deals with sanctions under national law, which would normally provide for penal provisions regulating issues such as command responsibility, effective control and individual culpability, in relation to international operations. Notwithstanding this, there was an increasing worry that states might be accused of assisting non-state parties through military cooperation, and that their individual soldiers might risk unwarranted criminal prosecution.

The US in particular, not participating in the Conference, worried that their allies through becoming party to the Convention could hamper common military operations. Being a very vocal non-participant in the process when it came to this issue, they demarched a number of states, including their NATO allies, in order to warn about the possible negative effects regarding future military cooperation this treaty might have if the interoperability issue was not solved. In essence they were in favour of the deletion of Article 1 (c), so that it would not be a violation of the treaty to assist someone else in doing what was prohibited. A deletion of Article 1 (c) would also solve the potential problem with individual criminal liability.

Several states, including NATO members, were of the opinion that Article 1 (c) would generate neither state responsibility nor individual criminal liability because of the mere participation in military operations, including planning and execution of such operations at the strategic, operational and tactical level, with non-state Parties. Both the Chemical Weapons Convention and the Mine Ban Convention had exactly the same prohibition against assistance, encouragement and inducement in Article 1 (c), and its potential deletion in this new convention would raise questions as to how states were to understand their previous obligations according to these treaties. Should "assistance" suddenly be interpreted differently and more extensively?

The result of the negotiations was a new Article 21 in the Convention. Paragraph 3 of this Article states:

> Notwithstanding the provisions of Article 1 of this Convention and in accordance with international law, States Parties, their military personnel or nationals, may engage in military cooperation and operations with States not party to this Convention that might engage in activities prohibited to a State Party ...[47]

The next paragraph specifies that:

> Nothing in paragraph 3 of this Article shall authorise a State Party:
>
> a. To develop, produce or otherwise acquire cluster munitions;
> b. To itself stockpile or transfer cluster munitions;
> c. To itself use cluster munitions; or
> To expressly request the use of cluster munitions in cases where the choice of munitions used is within its exclusive control.

Article 21 (4) thus specifies how *not* to interpret Article 21 (3), and has little bearing on the interpretation of the prohibitions laid down in Article 1.

Thus the issue if interoperability, having dominated much of the negotiations at the Dublin Diplomatic Conference, did give the necessary assurances to states that they could still pursue international military cooperation with non-state parties. At the same time, Article 21 did not potentially undermine any substantive part of the Convention.

IV. Conclusion

The diplomatic process towards a prohibition on Cluster Munitions was possible due to a number of factors. An essential element in generating enough political support for the process and to gain sufficient momentum was the partnership between civil society and governments. The blueprint had been one of the key exercises in the

47 Article 21 (3).

human security tradition, the Ottawa Process towards the Mine Ban Convention. The fact that once again thousands of campaigners and volunteers worked for a ban made it possible to generate sufficient political momentum for the process.

The Convention on Cluster Munitions[48] (although it will not enter into force until 2009 at the very earliest) has made it politically difficult to actually use any of the weapons defined as prohibited cluster munitions. This is true even for States not planning to become Parties. As was the case with anti personnel mines, the weapon will become increasingly stigmatised and many states, if not all, are likely to refrain from deploying it in military operations in the future.

In international military operations the overall political aim is often to secure peace and promote establishment of democratic structures. The use of weapons that cause long term civilian harm are not inductive to such aims. Long term political objectives may thus be seriously hampered by short term military considerations. This is probably one of the overriding reasons why it was politically possible to achieve a total ban on cluster munitions in a very short time span and with as many as 107 states participating in the adoption of the Convention.

48 http://www.clustermunitionsdublin.ie/pdf/ENGLISHfinaltext.pdf.

Part III

Conflicting Definitions of Security within the Realm of Ethics and Democracy

Chapter 7

Private versus Citizen-soldiers: New Mercenarism in a Just-War Framework

Lene Bomann-Larsen[*]

War is a legal condition which equally permits two or more groups to carry on a conflict by armed force. It is also (...) a moral condition, involving the same permissiveness (...) at the level of armies and individual soldiers.[1]

War can at once be viewed as a relation between persons and as a relation between super-personal collective entities. Every military action is ascribable to some kind of collective entity, but it is at the same time constituted by actions ascribable to particular persons.[2]

Not only are far more contractors operating in war zones than in the past, but they are now responsible for many tasks that used to be carried out exclusively by the military. One of the most controversial roles being outsourced is armed protection for convoys, government facilities and diplomats. According to the Private Security Company Association of Iraq there are more than 180 such companies in operation that now employ 70,000 armed private security contractors in the country, and that number is only growing. (...) The UN Working Group on the Use of Mercenaries has warned that these so-called "security guards" are "in fact private soldiers militarily armed," and that the companies that employ them in Iraq constitute "new expressions of mercenarism in the twenty-first century."[3]

* I am grateful for comments on earlier drafts of this paper from all participants at the conference *Security – A Multidisciplinary Normative Approach*, participants at the Ethics Programme research school, University of Oslo, the participants at the Nordic Network in Political Theory annual conference in Uppsala, and the audience at the Ethics Seminar at the University of Oslo 6 Nov 2008. I am particularly indebted to Andreas Brekke Carlsson, Jakob Elster, Amos N. Guiora, Gina Gustavsson, Robert Huseby, Christopher Kutz, Kasper Lippert-Rasmussen, Larry May, Torbjørn Tennsjø and Tatjana Valland for critical and helpful comments that have contributed to shape the argument I present here. Many thanks also to Cecilia M. Bailliet for the opportunity to write this paper.

1 Michael Walzer, *Just and Unjust Wars A Moral Argument with Historical Illustrations* (New York: Basic Books, 2000), 41.

2 David Rodin, *War and Self-Defense* (Oxford: Oxford University Press, 2002), 122.

3 http://www.privateforces.com; accessed on 22 July 2008.

Cecilia M. Bailliet (ed.), Security: A Multidisciplinary Normative Approach.
 ISBN 978 90 04 17296 8. pp. 157–173.

I. Introduction

New kinds of armed conflict and new security situations create "normative gaps" and legal vacuums. What is the standing of Taliban fighters, global terrorists, the prisoners at Guantanamo Bay, and finally, armed contractors working for private security companies in war zones? What are the rights and obligations of these new combatants; and to whom are they accountable when they commit war crimes and crimes against humanity? While perpetrators at Abu Ghraib who committed atrocities in US army uniforms were immediately court-martialed and punished, Blackwater Security personnel have not yet been prosecuted for the massacre of 17 Iraqi civilians in Falluja in 2007. Because of this normative gap and the problems related to accountability and prosecution it is possible to argue, on consequentialist and prudential grounds that armed contractors should be brought in under the same legal paradigm as ordinary soldiers. Legalization could help ameliorate current problems such as: under whose command are armed contractors? Who has the authority to prosecute them? What is their standing in combat? What is their standing if wounded or captured? If these gaps were filled, it is possible that some of the drawbacks of the current use of private forces could be avoided. There is therefore a presumption in favor of legalization.

The aim of this paper is to enquire some consequence-based and principled reasons which may count *against* such legalization. I will not draw an all-things-considered conclusion with regard to the legalization issue; my main aim is to point out the principled arguments against legalization that should be taken into account when facing the disregarded of the possible beneficial consequences.

In simple terms, there are two kinds of combatants recognized by international law, lawful and unlawful, whereof *mercenaries* (soldiers for hire) are considered unlawful fighters. I concentrate on the standing of a particular kind of mercenary, namely those armed contractors who are employed by security companies that operate in war zones where the state with which the company is on contract is also present with its own army. I will call these 'private soldiers', and assume that they can be classified – in accordance with the concern of the UN Working Group on the Use of Mercenaries – as a new form of mercenary.[4] I shall contrast these 'private soldiers' with ordinary soldiers, whom I call 'citizen-soldiers'. By 'citizen-soldier' I mean any soldier who is a member of the armed forces of a warring nation, either conscripted or professional. Today, only citizen-soldiers enjoy impunity for the 'mere fact of fighting' and secondary status as prisoner of war under international law.[5] I shall thus grant that there is, at present, a recognized distinction between ordinary soldiers and armed contractors, both in law and in moral theory, and go on to question on what grounds that distinction can be sustained.

---

4 Cf. n. 2.

5 "Whereas combatants may not be punished for 'the mere fact of fighting', persons who take a direct part in the hostilities without being entitled to do so (unlawful combatants) face penal consequences. They do not have the right to prisoner of war status. Unlawful combatants do, however, have a legitimate claim to certain fundamental guarantees, including the right to humane treatment and a proper judicial procedure." (Knut Ipsen, "Combatants and Non-combatants", in Peter Fleck, ed., *The Handbook of Humanitarian Law in Armed Conflicts*, Oxford: Oxford University Press, 1995, 68).

When all else is equal, what distinguishes a citizen-soldier from a 'private soldier'? In order to create the maximally favorable situation for the case of legalization, I will assume that the private soldier with whom we are dealing here is engaged by a company situated in the country in which he is a residing citizen, and which operates in a war zone where his residence country is also engaged with its own army – in addition to having engaged private companies on state contract.

Note also that in calling 'private soldiers' a *new* kind of combatant, I am not denying the historical fact that mercenaries have been widely used as well as widely discussed in the just war literature. What present itself as a distinctively *new* situation is the way private soldiers are formally incorporated in a business framework, and the way states commission the services of such corporations in terms of contract. As we shall see, this raises some particular issues that may not necessarily be relevant to all forms of mercenarism.

I will address two questions: first, is it permissible to be a mercenary? Second, is it permissible for states to use mercenaries? The first concerns the motivation of soldiers, the second concerns their representative function as instruments of the state. I will examine these two questions separately, though I will argue that they converge in a general discussion about the problem of serving two masters with conflicting aims.

II. Are Some Soldiers More Equal Than Others?

The question of 'lawful versus unlawful' combatants is a species of the general question concerning the moral equality of soldiers, which is on currently on the agenda in ethics of war. So far, the debate has mainly concerned the question of symmetrical permissions between lawful combatants on the *just versus unjust* side of a war. In legal terms, just and unjust combatants are equal in virtue of being subject to the same obligations with regard to respecting the immunity of non-combatants and prisoners of war, and in virtue of enjoying impunity for 'the mere fact of fighting'. However, critics have raised the question about whether the *legal* equality of combatants has a *moral* foundation, or whether it is merely a prudential (and perhaps even immoral) rule. Their main objection to the assumption that just and unjust combatants are morally equal is that it is hard to see how unjust aggressors can have a permission to kill defenders; that seems counterintuitive with reference to the underlying analogy with individual self-defense. From this objection, critics draw different conclusions with regard to the implications for international law; should it be revised in order to be brought into concord with morality, so that moral asymmetry is reflected in the law,[6] or should we for pragmatic reasons keep a bifurcated view on law and morality[7] and leave the legal equality of soldiers unrevised?

6 David Rodin, "The Moral Inequality of Soldiers: Why *jus in bello* Asymmetry is Half Right", in David Rodin and Henry Shue, *Just and Unjust Warriors*, (Oxford: Oxford University Press, 2008), 44–68.

7 Jeff McMahan, "The Morality of War and the Law on War" in *Just and Unjust Warriors*, 19–43.

Equality, then, is also an issue with regard to the distinction between lawful and unlawful combatants. Even though International Law does not recognize these as equal, or more precisely, perhaps, *defines* them as unequal, the question of their *moral status* still needs to be debated.

When dealing with the issue of legalizing private soldiers we must consider whether or not there is a principled difference between private soldiers and ordinary soldiers, with regard to their permission to exercise violence in war zones. More precisely, is there a good reason why 'private soldiers' should be denied the permissions that are granted 'citizen-soldiers'; that is, why they should not enjoy impunity for 'the mere fact of fighting'? If no good reason can be established, the distinction seems arbitrary and ought to be eliminated on that ground.

International law on armed conflict does not give explicit moral reasons for discriminating between mercenaries and citizen-soldiers, but some possibly morally relevant factors may be identified in the criteria demarcating a mercenary. According to International Law, mercenaries are regarded unlawful combatants.

> "Under art. 47, para 1 AP I, mercenaries are not entitled to the status either as combatant or prisoner of war. (...) a mercenary is defined as fulfilling six criteria: recruitment in order to fight in an armed conflict; actual and direct participation in hostilities; participation motivated by desire for private gain with payment that substantially exceeds that of normal combatants; lack of legal ties to the party to the conflict based on nationality or residency in a territory controlled by that party; lack of membership in the armed forces of the party to the conflict; and not being on official duty in the armed forces of the party to the conflict."[8]

How is this definition relevant for the *normative standing* of mercenaries? Recall that our main question is why private soldiers should not be exculpated for the 'mere fact of fighting'. To be exculpated for the 'mere fact of fighting' means that the state, not the soldier, is ultimately responsible for the ordinary acts of war (i.e. harming enemy combatants, military installations and the like). In order for the exculpation argument to get off ground, two conditions are required: (1) the individual soldier must be personally exculpated for becoming a fighter and fulfilling that role (in order for the state to be *ultimately* responsible for his war-acts); and (2) the soldier must represent the state (in order for the state to be ultimately *responsible* for his war-acts). I will tie these two dimensions of exculpation to the definition of a mercenary by asking (1) is there a relevant difference in the motivation for becoming fighters which justifies discrimination between citizen-soldiers and private soldiers, in terms of exculpating the former, and not the latter? (2) Can a state legitimately outsource its monopoly-right to use violence, making private soldiers proper representatives of the state, acting on its behalf? Having discussed these two issues – pertaining to whether it is morally permissible to become a private soldier on the one hand and whether it is permissible to contract them on the other hand – I will show how the issues of

8 Knut Ipsen, "Combatants and Non-combatants", 69. In addition, the fact that they fight motivated by private gain makes mercenaries illegitimate even if they do take part in hostilities on the side of a party to the conflict.

motivation and representation converge in the problem of 'serving two masters', and point out the implications of dual loyalty for the possibility of fighting on behalf of the state.

III. Moral Predicaments and Soldiers' Motives

One of the criteria of being classified as a mercenary in International Law is "participation *motivated by desire for private gain* with payment that substantially exceeds that of normal combatants".[9] What is the significance of *motivation* when it comes to participation in war? Soldiers' rights and permissions are generally not granted them in their personal capacity; to the contrary, they are granted them precisely *because* their personal capacity is not taken into consideration. Therefore the impunity enjoyed by soldiers for killing does not follow from the motives on which they fight. Soldiers are in an important way *instrumentalised*.

However, most contemporary philosophers working on the ethics of war agree that the view depicting the soldier as a pure instrument of the state is insufficient to justify or exculpate soldiers for the 'mere fact of fighting'. The argument from instrumentalisation – claiming that states carry the total responsibility for soldiers' acts of war – requires that we regard soldiers *only* in their collective capacity, and that we explain why human beings who are at the outset autonomous, responsible agents should not also be assessed in their individual capacity, as responsible at least for taking on the role of soldiering. The explanation we give must answer to the fact that the days of the truly coerced and victimised conscripted citizen-soldier – if that description has ever been correct – are gone.[10] Most citizen-soldiers today are part of professional armies, they are paid for their service, and being a soldier is by many regarded a rather attractive career choice. It is no longer true of the soldier's predicament that "from my mother's sleep I fell into the state".[11] Even in Norway, one of few countries which still operate with a conscripted army, the degree of coercion is so low that it can hardly be said to be irresistible. This is a fact that has encouraged many philosophers to rethink the idea that soldiers in general should enjoy impunity for the 'mere fact of fighting'. Philosophers like Jeff McMahan and David Rodin argue that there can be no permission to fight in an unjust war,[12] and since most soldiers are autonomous, educated human beings who freely take on a job, who have access to relevant information, and to whom ordinary exculpating factors such as coercion, invincible ignorance or duress therefore no longer apply, soldiers ought at least in theory to be held individually responsible for the 'mere fact of fighting'. They chose freely to become fighters, hence they should be held morally responsible for what they do as fighters.

---

9 My emphasis.

10 See Cheyney Ryan, "Moral Equality, Victimhood and the Sovereignty Symmetry Problem" in *Just and Unjust Warriors*, 131–152. See also Bomann-Larsen, Lene, *Reconstructing the Moral Equality of Soldiers* (Oslo: Acta Humaniora, 2007).

11 Michael Walzer, supra note 1 at 40.

12 See e.g. Jeff McMahan and David Rodin in *Just and Unjust Warriors*.

In reply to this, other philosophers – myself included – have argued that even though the soldiers' predicament can no longer be properly described in terms of 'victimhood',[13] there is still a moral case to be made for their impunity. My own argument to this effect is based on the soldier being called by a moral imperative, and that the existence of conflicting moral imperatives (i.e., "serve your country" versus "don't fight in unjust wars") entraps the soldier in a dilemma of a notably moral character, an entrapment which exculpates citizens for giving up their autonomy by becoming soldiers and subsequently exculpates soldiers for the 'mere fact of fighting'. The argument does not rule out that some soldiers may be personally culpable for their participation in an unjust war, but yields impunity on a *presumption of moral innocence*.[14]

Roughly, the argument for exculpation can be outlined as follows: The predicament of the non-coerced soldier should be understood as being called by a moral imperative. Within this frame of interpretation, patriotism, loyalty towards ones compatriots, community, and family are important moral concerns. Invoking the value pluralism[15] of Thomas Nagel and Bernard Williams,[16] we may say that the *value set* to which the moral-military duty appeals is that of *special obligations*, an important moral category which is not reducible to general moral obligations, such as respect for universal human rights. Still, it is a key point that being motivated by or appealing to special obligations *does not invalidate* other types of – more general – obligations like those that derive from universal human rights. These retain their moral force even though one chooses to act on a conflicting value set, or one is not moved by them or perhaps not even aware of them (in which case, of course, one's negligence might be culpable).

So, while it is morally permissible, perhaps even obligatory, to participate in the protection of one's community or nation, it is at the same time morally *impermissible* to take part in an unjust war where one risks killing the innocent and violate the human rights of more distant people. Objectively speaking, the existence of two incommensurable value-sets, on either of which one may be justifiably inclined to act, makes for a moral conflict, be it experienced or not. I have argued, though, that *precisely because* these sets are incommensurable and conflictual, one is not to blame for taking either course of action.[17] It is permissible to take part in the military activities of the nation by signing up to become a soldier, and it is permissible to refuse, on the basis of general moral concerns. Whether such a conflict of value is subjectively experienced as a dilemma, or the unrecognized value set is merely pointed out by the critical voices of others, both value sets retain their validity. Thus in one sense, both the soldier and the conscientious objector do something morally

13 Michael Walzer, supra note 1.

14 See Bomann-Larsen, supra note 10 at 190.

15 I.e., value pluralism as a normative theory, not as a descriptive theory about de facto value pluralism.

16 Bernard Williams, "Conflicts of Values" in Bernard Williams, *Moral Luck* (Cambridge: Cambridge University Press, 1981), 71–82 and Thomas Nagel, *Mortal Questions* (Cambridge: Cambridge University Press, 1979).

17 See Bomann-Larsen, supra note 10.

tainted, *pro tanto* wrong. In another sense they both do something for which they are not to blame. This predicament I have called *entrapment in a moral conflict*.[18]

Given value pluralism it seems justifiable to choose to become a soldier, to take on a role where one abandons one's autonomy with regard to the job, insofar as this role is defined in terms of important values. Once the role is taken on, the soldier is obligated and permitted to act according to political and military decisions that are not of his own making. Role obligations are precisely one kind of special obligation that may cut across the more general obligations that belong to all human beings.

To take on a role typically entails being granted certain permissions and obligations in virtue of that role. The role, in turn, is justified in terms of its being part of a legitimate institution in society, an institution which serves the public good and is therefore in itself legitimate. Now, the soldiering role entails certain permissions, such as the permission to kill, but also some obligations, such as not to question lawful orders. It is as such the soldier may be compared to the executioner, as some have done:[19] it is not permissible for the executioner to question the court's verdict and refuse to kill the condemned man, even if he believes him to be innocent. Thus the executioner does not act morally wrong when he executes the innocent man.[20] To the contrary, it is his duty to do what his role requires of him, because justice is better served in general when people fulfill their role obligations within legitimate institutions. Though of course, the executioner may refuse to be part of the system and resign, which is an option analogous to refusing military service, and refusing is a morally defensible act given the conflict of values in which one stands when choosing a role defined by role obligations which cut across ones general obligations as a human being.

Even if the executioner can be said to be entrapped in a, objectively speaking, moral dilemma between doing his legitimate job – serving justice – and the general obligation not to lend oneself to a practice that may entail killing the innocent, we know nothing about what motivated him personally to take on this job or what motivates him to keeping it. That is equally true of the soldier, whose objective entrapment in a conflict of values we may identify, but about whose subjective motivation we know nothing. We judge them based on the acceptability of what they do, acting according to their role obligations, not on the basis of their personal motives. However, it may be objected, and correctly, that in order for an identifiable moral reason (such as the duty to serve one's country) to be morally significant to our judgment of a person's action – i.e., to absolve someone of blameworthiness – it must be *internalised* as a reason capable of motivating that person to act.

Further, in the legal definition of a mercenary, motivation seems to be an essential mark of his standing as unlawful combatant. It is implied that the mercenary is not driven by a moral imperative (concern for the "common good"), but by his per-

18 Ibid.

19 See e.g. Cheyney Ryan, "Self-defence, Pacifism and the Possibility of Killing" in *Ethics* (1983), 93, 3: 508–524.

20 If one dislikes the analogy, I think the argument would work also with regard to imprisonment: the prison guard is not permitted to let out the convict who he believes to be innocent.

sonal interests; his desire for private gain. But given that we cannot really know what motivates any soldier, how can we use motivation as a demarcation criterion for differentiating between private soldiers and citizen-soldiers? Discerning people's true motives, let alone their *desires*, is of course epistemically extremely difficult, if not impossible, and that is why the moral equality of soldiers must be based on a *presumption* of moral innocence, not on *actual* innocence.[21] God at Judgment Day (as a term of art) may judge differently. But as epistemically imperfect beings, *we* need to point at objectively identifiable indicators on which we can base a plausible presumption of motives. We need to establish some objective criteria that give force to differentiating between professional soldiers who fight because it is their job to fight (a job which they have voluntarily chosen) and private soldiers who fight because it is their job to fight (a job which they have voluntarily chosen), but for a considerably larger amount of money – or we have to give up the distinction as being arbitrary.

Rather than asking what X's real motives are, we must delineate a class of motives available to X; i.e, what *can* motivate X, and what it is plausible to think motivates X. Now, it does not follow from his desire for private gain that the private soldier is not also morally motivated. It is perfectly possible to say that "I want to serve my country, but why not make some extra cash while doing it?" Still, does the fact of excessive payment suffice as an objective indicator of possible motivating factors for private soldiers? At least the fact that some soldiers are *excessively* paid gives us a reason to question whether they are truly moved by a moral imperative, a reason that does not obtain in the case of the citizen-soldier. Moreover, the fact that the citizen-soldier is not excessively paid gives us a reason to assume that his motives are morally more acceptable. One may ask what 'excessive' should refer to here, given that the excessive payment of the private soldier is defined in relation to the lesser payment of the citizen-soldier. But becoming a private soldier is an option open to the citizen-soldier, so it seems unlikely that he, when facing that possibility and not choosing it, should be motivated by private gain. The possibility of private gain always invokes suspicions about moral motivation. Amongst those who choose between two options whereof one involves private gain, it thus seems reasonable to sustain a justified doubt about the motives of those who go for the gain.

The importance of the presumption that the soldier at least *can* be motivated by a moral imperative – a concern for the common good or some common value that is the justification for his role – becomes clear when we compare soldiering with other kinds of participation in collective or organized violence. Without reference to a moral imperative, soldiers could not be exculpated for the 'mere fact of fighting', because then, they would be nothing but criminals. One reason why we distinguish between soldiers who fight and kill, and organized criminals who do the same, is precisely because we presume that soldiers do not act for private gain, or on their own behalf. Of course, the private soldier may also be acting according to a moral

21 This would be the case also for arguments that favour moral *inequality* of soldiers, that is, asymmetry on the basis of the justness of the war one fights; it is objective, not subjective, justification that is emphasized by asymmetry-theorists. Cf. e.g. Vitoria, who argued on a *presumption of guilt* for combatants on the unjust side. (See Bomann-Larsen, supra note 14 at 190).

predicament (serve his country). But the reasonable doubt, raised by the fact of excessive payment, about whether this is what ultimately moves him to participate in war, counts against his exculpation *ex ante.*

So far in this section I have tried to show how the moral predicament to serve exculpates citizens for becoming soldiers, and how excessive payment of private soldiers casts doubt upon whether they are really acting according to a moral predicament. If not, it seems we cannot grant special permissions (i.e., impunity for the mere fact of fighting) to private soldiers because they would come closer to organized criminals than to citizen-soldiers. If they fight for private gain, they fight in the capacity of being private persons, and private persons have no right to use force (This in fact is what makes criminals criminal; they use unauthorized force). However, it would be interesting to ask whether there could be something morally questionable about taking on the profession of being an armed contractor also in *the absence of* excessive payment. We can make the cases to be compared – private versus citizen-soldiers – even more equal if we bracket out private gain and focus narrowly on the different institutional roles the soldiers occupy. To take on the role of being soldier is justifiable because the role as such is a legitimate part of a legitimate institution, which at least in principle serves the common good. Can the private company be said in the same way to serve the common good, thus rendering the professional position of the private soldier a legitimate role to occupy? This raises the further question: can the state legitimately outsource its monopoly-right to use force to private soldiers by commissioning the services of a private company? If the state *cannot* legitimately outsource its monopoly-right to use force to a private company, soldiers working for such a company cannot be motivated by a role obligation defining them as servants of the state.

IV. Can a State Legitimately Outsource its Monopoly-Right to Use Force?

I have taken as my point of departure a general prohibition against the use of force, and in particular against the use of violent force. The exception from the rule is the state, which thus has a *monopoly-right* to use force.[22] The state monopoly-right to use force is granted – and justified – in virtue of the social contract between the state and its citizens to protect *their* basic rights from internal and external threats. The social contract is what ultimately grants the state its right – and duty – to use coercive force. Just as the police and the criminal justice system are delegated the authority to use coercive, and, when necessary and proportionate also violent, force against those individuals who trespass against other individuals, so is the military delegated authority to use force against those who trespass against the political community and its territorial boarders. As previously argued, taking on the professional roles that are defined within these institutional frameworks is thus justifiable to the extent that the state is minimally legitimate (i.e., fulfills its part of the social contract), that the institutions serve the state properly, and that the role as it is defined serves the institutions properly. Given this basic framework, then, ordinary soldiers have the

22 Though the right is of course severely constrained.

right to use violent force *in virtue of* being representatives of a state which has that right and which confers that right to the individual soldier.

The citizen-soldier acquires his war-rights (i.e., his permission to fight), in virtue of occupying a role representative of the state. Now, whether the private soldier whose employer is on a contracted mission for a state should also be regarded as authorised as the state's instrument in a way which absolves him of personal responsibility for 'the mere fact of fighting' depends on whether states can *legitimately* transfer its right to use force by commissioning the services of a *private company*.

Let me first set aside two pragmatic concerns that naturally arise at this point. For one, the question of outsourcing is not only raised in international affairs. A similar debate concerns outsourcing law enforcement tasks in *internal* affairs, i.e., by contracting private security firms to supplement police or prison authorities. This of course, governments do all the time. Politicians assess that the police simply do not have sufficient resources to secure public space; hence, private security guards are increasingly being used as a means of public protection. The *legitimacy* of such outsourcing is rarely questioned, however; instead the debate is centred on issues such as (mis)conduct of private guards, lack of proper training, recruitment of criminals, etcetera. These practical problems, we may assume, are rectifiable by simple means. Aside of that, I will raise, but not answer, the question of whether outsourcing public protection to private guards who are granted permissions that go beyond the permissions of ordinary citizens, is really legitimate.

Secondly, in both internal and external affairs, outsourcing creates a risk of losing control by decreased transparency. The legitimacy of using force requires control, and control requires transparency. Thus it seems paramount to discussing how outsourcing may be counter-productive to transparency. For example, it has been suggested that the excessive use of private security firms in Iraq is a way of disguising the losses of war; the public does not react as negatively to dead armed contractors – US citizens or not – as they do when soldiers return in a coffin draped in an American flag. Moreover, the public is not it the same way shamed by perpetrations committed by someone who are not associated with the nation. Thus a case can be made that the use of private companies deceives the demos in a way that does not facilitate democratic processes. Yet while this issue does have a bearing on the legitimacy of outsourcing, it is not an argument against legalisation of private soldiers, precisely because these problems may be solved by bringing private soldiers under state control.

Now, to return to the main issue; it is important to emphasize that the argument for the state monopoly-right to use force does not presuppose the *substantive* legitimacy of a given state, say, that the state in question be a democracy, or even a liberal democracy. The discussion about outsourcing should not be restricted to substantively legitimate states. Without making any assumptions about the substantive legitimacy of a given state (or what substantive legitimacy would entail), then, a minimalist conception of the *raison d'etre* of any state can be found in a Hobbesian style social contract. Citizens entrust to their rulers the power to protect them, in turn creating both a right and a duty on part of the rulers to do so. The means of protection consist in legislation and law enforcement. It follows that the state loses its reason for existence if it fails to protect its citizens by either of these means.

While we may grant that the monopoly-right to use force is not restricted to substantively legitimate states, we may also grant that it is restricted to sovereign states. Failed states or states where power is disputed (by civil war, occupation, revolution, etc) cannot have a monopoly-right to use force. It may therefore be that the argument here presented cannot be applied to states where sovereignty is challenged. But it will apply also to non-liberal, non-democratic states insofar as these are properly classified as sovereign. Beyond this, I will not make any assumptions about what makes a state legitimate.

Sovereign power entails that both legislation and law enforcement is in the hands of the ruling power alone. All law enforcing institutions, the military included, must be under the control of the sovereign power, or else the power is *ex hypothesi* not sovereign.

The issue of transferring the right to use violence (i.e., authorising violence) to individual soldiers is assumed unproblematic in the case of the citizen-soldier, who is a direct representative of the state (aka, sovereign power) in virtue of the role he occupies: "A [lawful] combatant does not act on his own behalf, but on behalf of the state. His war-acts are acts of service, for which the state is responsible."[23] Thus the state's authority to use force is conferred via the *role* the individual soldier occupies, and it is also this fact that grants the individual soldier impunity for his acts of war. His acts of war are not really *his* acts; he is acting on behalf of the state and the state is ultimately responsible for any harm he causes in that capacity.[24] But in which capacity does the private soldier fight? Who is ultimately responsible for his acts of war? On whose behalf does he kill? No one has the right to kill in their personal capacity. The only exception for private persons appears to be killing in self-defence,[25] but even that exception is merely apparent, since also for self-defensive killing one is answerable to the state *ex post*. So in order for the private soldier to be exculpated *ex ante* for fighting and killing in combat (and hence to not be answerable for 'ordinary killing or fighting'), his acts must also be acts of state. It does not suffice that they are *company acts*, because just as little as a private person has the right to use force, so has a private firm.

The private soldier's direct contract is not with the *state*, but with the *company* with which he is employed. The contract with the state is *indirect*, in the sense that the state enters into contract with the company. Is there, then, a difference *in terms of authorization*, between an ordinary soldier in direct service for his state, and an armed contractor who serves the state more indirectly, by being in service for a private company which in turn is on a contract with the state? As stated at the outset, in order to isolate the relevant factors by rendering all else equal, it is assumed that our private soldier is, say, a US citizen working for a US security company which is under contract with the US state department, who is on mission in a conflict zone were the US army is also present.[26] In spite of the indirect quality of the contract

23 Arne Willy Dahl, *Håndbok i militær folkerett* (Oslo: Cappelen akademiske forlag, 2003), 66. My translation.

24 The exception being his duty to oblige to the *jus in bello* rules, as expressed in the Geneva Conventions, and the violation of which is defined as war crimes.

25 I am excluding suicide, direct and assisted, from this discussion and focusing solely on killing people against their will.

26 In reality, of course, such companies operate on very different terms. Some are located

between the soldier and the state, is the link between the 'private soldier' and the state strong enough to determine his war acts as acts of the state, in the same way as we determine the acts of the citizen-soldier of the US army as acts of state?

V. Serving Two Masters

We may identify two lines of argument favouring scepticism about whether the state can legitimately outsource its monopoly right to use force. One line of argument pertains to the issue of state control over the exercise of force conducted by contractors. For power not to be formally divided, the state must be in control over the contractors' conduct: both in terms of the command chain (downwards) and in terms of accountability (upwards). In other words, state control over contractors requires a legal framework securing control, transparency and accountability. Thus this is not an argument against the *legalisation* of private security companies, only against their use as long as their legal status is unclear.[27] To the contrary, legalisation may be an effective means to securing formal control both in terms of downward command and upward accountability. However, another line of argument goes to the effect that outsourcing may not be legitimate even if the formal authorisation should be in place; namely that the private and public sector might have fundamentally different and incompatible aims.

Imagine a company offering highly trained (and highly paid!) judges under the slogan: "Independence and Impartiality Guaranteed!" Why would we, as I assume we would, be hesitant to accept outsourcing the state monopoly right to *punish* – a subset of the monopoly right to use force – to such a company? Note that is not a counter-argument that 'private judges' in some countries un-problematically serve in arbitration cases between consenting parties, because for *punishment*, one must assume that the use of force against the prosecuted is use of (justified) *coercive* force which implies that the prosecuted is non-consenting.

It seems that our hesitation is not mainly about the issue of *formal authorisation*. The state commissions the services of the judge, and the judge *judges in the capacity of representing the state*. The state confers that right on him, and the judge is accountable to the state. I will suggest that we are hesitant for a different reason: we would be doubtful about the independence and impartiality of such a judge because we could never be sure of his *loyalties*; and we would be unsure of them because the judge

---

nationally, some are international. (E.g., in 2007 Blackwater Securities went from Blackwater US to Blackwater International). Being private companies operating internationally, their employees may be of all nationalities, and they may in principle take on missions for anyone; states, other companies, aid agencies etcetera.

27 "The [UN]Working Group[on the Use of Mercenaries] warns that States that employ these services **may be responsible** for violations of internationally recognized human rights committed by the personnel of such companies. Such violations are furthermore attributable to those States if the private military and private security companies are empowered to exercise elements of governmental authority or are acting under governmental direction or control." (http://www2.ohchr.org/english/issues/mercenaries/index.htm; accessed on 11/3/08).

simultaneously serves the state and the company with which he is employed, and these two actors may have conflicting aims.

While the state is not to have any interest in a criminal case apart from that justice should be served, the private company *does* have an interest in the criminal case, namely, to earn a profit. The very simple fact of the internal logic of private companies – the drive to stay profitable – vouches for possible conflicting aims between the private and public sector. Thus even if the state in principle can be in control over the exercise of force by the private company and that power therefore is not necessarily divided on the formal account, the fact that the private company has a *raison d'etre* which turns its interests in a different direction than that of the state may establish a second master for the servant to serve. And whose aims does he then serve?

In this particular thought experiment, whether the aims of the two actors are in fact conflicting depends on what would be the success criteria for a company offering law enforcement services. What would give market advantages in an imagined competition between two companies offering this kind of services? "More convictions and longer sentences for the money?" Or: "Justice better served"? One can only speculate, so let us leave this question open and return to the case at hand, where it is easier to see how the aims of the two actors served by the private soldier may conflict with one another, thus establishing two masters.

VI. Private Soldiers in the Just-War Framework

It seems plausible to presume that belligerent states take an interest in restoring peace (in a non-moralised sense; i.e., by winning the war). Whether or not the cause of the war is just, a state has an interest in the conflict ending, not just because perpetual war is costly – financially and politically – but because every war has some *aim* for which it is fought. If the war is one of conquest, the won peace may be *unjust*, but it is still peace.

According to the just-war tradition, a just war is to be fought with a legitimate authority – the power in charge of the common good – and only in response to a wrong received (just cause). Under the contemporary "legalist paradigm",[28] the only just cause of war is defense or law enforcement against aggression. The additional (ethical) criterion of *right intention* states that the aim of the defense or law enforcement should be no more or less than rectifying the situation and restore peace as it was before the act of aggression occurred. Within a broader and more disputable interpretation of 'just cause' which includes preemptive and perhaps even preventive wars, forcible democratization or humanitarian intervention, the picture becomes more complicated, but given that the cause is presumed just, we can still identify the right intention as aiming only to rectify the situation which gave rise to the presumed just cause in the first place.

A just cause thus ensues from a wrong received. And fighting with a right intention is to fight with the aim of restoring the situation which has been disturbed

28 See Michael Walzer, supra note 1.

by this received wrong.[29] There are two senses in which we may interpret the meaning of 'right intention'; one thick and one thin. In the thin sense, an *actual* just cause does not seem to be required in order for the intention to be 'right'.[30] On this rather formalistic interpretation, nothing seems to rule out that one can have an unjust cause and still fight with the right intention. Even a war fought for an unjust cause can be fought with a narrow aim to restore peace. For instance, a preventive war against a potential threat may be defined as an unjust war of aggression, but it seems unproblematic to say that the aggressor acts with the right intention if the aim is narrowed down to merely pacifying the threat. That does not make the war just – which would require a just cause – but it makes the *intention* right. In a thicker sense, which I will not discuss here, 'right' intention is shaped by a just cause. The aim is not only peace, that is, war's end, but *just* peace. If the cause is unjust, say, if the war is one of conquest, then winning peace amounts to winning unjust peace.

Now, it can of course be objected that some states do have an interest in perpetual war. When invoking a Hobbesian account of sovereignty rather than a substantive theory of legitimacy, I render my argument especially vulnerable to this objection. This is because whereas leaders in legitimate democracies typically cannot afford perpetual war insofar as this will cost them their power, a dictator who is not in the same way accountable to the people does not need to take such concerns into account. Dictators who do not care about their people and who can dispose of them at no risk to themselves may prudentially endorse militarism in their external affairs. Hence, it is not true about sovereign states *per se* that they take an interest in restoring peace; that might only be true of substantively legitimate states. And if that is the case, we are back at the problem that outsourcing the right to use force is only impermissible for substantively legitimate states, which is a counter-intuitive conclusion.

I don't believe this objection limits the validity of my argument only to substantively legitimate states, but it suggests that the claim that belligerent states take an interest in restoring peace is merely conditional; it is not a conceptual truth. I am willing to bite the bullet by accepting this objection, but retain that it is empirically plausible that in most cases, a state takes an interest in winning the war in which it is engaged, even if the state is substantively illegitimate.

There is vast disagreement on what constitutes a just cause of war, but everyone except absolute pacifists agree that *some* causes of war are just. We can even grant as much as saying that on a realist interpretation of the use of military force, there is a presumption that some wars are *justified*.[31] In fact, there is a presumption that *all* wars are justified to the extent that they serve the interest of the state, but this only

29 E.g., a *wrong received* should not be used as a pretext for fighting for other purposes.

30 This argument rests on one particular and very thin interpretation of 'right intention', namely, that use of armed force should aim narrowly at the cause of the war. A preventive war against a potential threat may be defined be an unjust war of aggression, but it seems unproblematic to say that the aggressor acts with the right intention – in the thin sense – if aiming narrowly at pacifying the threat.

31 The subtle difference between *just* war and *justified* war dissolves to the extent that any just war is also justified war, and the latter suffices for the argument presented here.

broadens the *scope* of the number of wars that can be justifiably fought,[32] and changes the *content* of reasons given for resort to armed force (prudential rather than moral reasons). It does not change the *structure* of the argument: (1) there are just causes for resort to armed force, and (2) when resorting to armed force, one should aim narrowly at rectifying the situation that gave rise to the just cause in the first place.

Hence, even without a unified conception of what constitutes a just cause, anyone who resorts to the use of armed force justify their use of force with reference to the conceptual possibility of just(ified) war. The state, then, whether its cause is truly a just one, or merely ostensibly just or even disguised as a just one, aims to restore some form of peace. A private security company aims at staying profitable. Is this aim in conflict with the state's aim of restoring peace?

The internal logic of private companies yields a drive towards profits. Of course, companies may have plural aims, and they may be highly socially responsible in their operations. But the bottom-line is that if a company is not profitable, it will eventually go out of business. That is a fact. It is also a fact that private security companies profit from conflict, both as a consequence of security needs which radically increase in conflict zones, and because states commission them to supplement armies in war zones. Security companies' by their inherent drive for profitability thus feed on conflict and lack of security, and this can be seen as antithetical to the state's interest in winning peace.

Now, it can also be objected that it could give competitive advantages to security companies to market themselves as 'socially responsible' in the sense that they direct their aims towards reducing the need for their own services. The US state department, say, would not hire a security company which exacerbates the conflict and prolongs the war (despite the interest of the US government in keeping the war short and swift), or make the war more unpopular to the voters and more costly for the US state. Thus a security company may in fact profit from finishing the job effectively and making its services redundant, thereby building a reputation as a company that 'gets the job done'.

Still, if the security company "get's the job done", its' internal logic compels the company to seek another conflict in order to stay in business. A security company can, and must, move on to sell its services to some else, even the prior enemy, if that is where the money is. Therefore, a system permitting private companies to offer private soldiers contributes to global instability and more wars.[33]

Now, this consequence-based reply does not really address the objection against the "two masters" argument. But the objection only shows that they *can* be convergence between the aims of private companies and states; and we need more – we need a *guarantee* that soldiers always and necessarily fight on behalf of the state, sharing the state's aims.

---

32 '*Alters* the scope' is perhaps more correct, because the rational self-interest of states dictating political realists may create a very restrictive practice of resorting to armed force, while reference to moral causes of war may yield quite many wars against a great deal of injustices.

33 This was in fact Machiavelli's argument against using mercenaries: mercenaries were loyal to the wage and not to the Prince, and therefore unreliable. They could at any time turn against the Prince if someone paid them more for their services.

Another dimension to the objection that private security companies may be socially responsible aiming to fight clean and get the job done, turns on the *jus in bello*. I have previously fended off the objection that states might not be aiming narrowly at peace but rather seek perpetual war by accepting that states don't *necessarily* aim for peace, yet holding that in most cases it is plausible to assume that this is what they will do. However, what states aim at on the political level and what their representatives actually do in combat are two different things. Consider again the case of Abu Ghraib. It is not unreasonable to suggest that such atrocities may typically be conducted by citizen-soldiers and officers, precisely because they act with the self-conception that they are fighting on behalf of a state with a presumptively just cause; rendering the enemy *unjust* or even construed as evil. The moral stakes involved may easily lead to an ends-justify-the-means kind of reasoning; 'just war' may easily slide into "holy war". Private soldiers and their companies, on the other hand, do not have such moral stakes, and their incentives for fighting dirty may thus be weaker.

This hypothesis may be correct, but it is not an argument for legalisation of private soldiers. Rather, it is an argument for better training of citizen-soldiers and for command responsibility all the way up to the political level. Moreover, those who argue that private soldiers may properly represent the state by sharing its aims cannot at the same time consistently argue in favour of private soldiers that there is *dissociation* between the cause and the soldier. If the private soldier represents the state, there will no longer be dissociation between the soldier and the cause. And conversely, to hold that the private soldier does not represent the state after all only reinstates the argument that private soldiers serve two masters.

With regard to the right to fight of private soldiers (i.e., their exculpation for the 'mere fact of fighting') we have now returned to the question whether their acts can really be construed as acts of war for which the state is ultimately responsible. It seems the answer must be no. The two problems discussed in this paper can be seen as converging in Machiavelli's concern that mercenaries are "loyal to the wage, not to the Prince": whether the private soldier operates for private gain (loyal to the wage) or in loyal service of a company (established for profitability) will in either case yield the result that the state cannot count on the military power to subject to the state's aims. There will be conflicting aims when profitability is introduced as a second master; and the question will arise on whose behalf the soldiers are really fighting, who they represent. The just-war tradition has always ruled out war for private gain as a candidate for a just war[34] precisely because greed conflicts with the aim of achieving (just) peace, on which the legitimacy of using armed force is parasitic.

VII. Conclusion

I started out by asking if private soldiers should be legalised, i.e., whether armed contractors working for private security companies on state contract should be brought under the same legal framework as citizen-soldiers. The answer to this question hinges partly on whether private soldiers are morally equal to other soldiers in terms

34 Greg Reichberg, Henrik Syse and Endre Begby, *The Ethics of War* (Cornwall: Blackwell, 2006).

of being exculpated for taking on the fighting role. I suggested that the fact of *excessive payment* on the part of private soldiers (as for other mercenaries), cast doubts on their *moral* motivation, rendering them perhaps less distinguishable from organised criminals than from citizen-soldiers. It is thus suggested that mercenaries cannot have a right to kill, i.e. they cannot be morally exculpated for the 'mere fact of fighting.'

Can states still give them that right? I further asked whether states can have a right to employ private soldiers via contracting private security companies by raising the question of whether states can legitimately outsource its monopoly-right to use force. My reply here is that even though the formal authorisation may not be a problem, the fact that the private and public sector operate on different rationales can cause a problem. Soldiers representing two actors with conflicting aims will be serving two masters, and serving two masters challenges sovereign power of the state as well as creates a loyalty problem for soldiers.

Assessed within the just-war framework, both legitimate authority construed as the authority in charge of the common good, and 'right intention' construed as aiming at peace seem to conflict with the inherent drive towards profits of a private company which feeds on conflict.

The conclusion is therefore that while citizen-soldiers act on behalf of the state and its "common good" and thus acquire permissions to fight in that capacity, private soldiers cannot be said to act only in the capacity of representing the state and its "common good". They also represent the company and the company's good, and even though these goods need not always conflict, there is no guarantee that they won't.

Whether this is a decisive factor in an all-things-considered assessment of whether private soldiers still ought to be made lawful is a discussion for another paper.

Chapter 8

The "Unrule" of Law: Unintended Consequences of Applying the Responsibility to Prevent to Counterterrorism, A Case Study of Colombia's Raid in Ecuador

Cecilia M. Bailliet[*]

I. Introduction

In 2001 the U.N. Security Council issued Resolution 1373 which expanded the scope of state responsibility to address indirect situations, setting forth duties to "[r]efrain from providing any form of support, active or passive" to terrorists and to "[d]eny safe haven to those who finance, plan, support, or commit terrorist acts, or provide safe havens." It also called for states to "prevent those who finance, plan, support or commit terrorist acts from using their respective territories for those purposes against other states or their citizens."[1] There have been developments in theory and practice which indicate efforts to transform the normative content of this resolution into international customary law. This is pursued by seeking consensus as to its content, demonstrating legal applicability, and applying creative argumentation for effective implementation via traditional and new compliance mechanisms.[2] Furthermore, it

* The author would like to extend warm thanks to Arne Willy Dahl, Nobuo Hayashi, Bruno Demeyère, and Simon O'Connor for their corrections and suggestions. Any remaining errors are my own responsibility.

1 See also Declaration on Principles of International Law concerning Friendly Relations and Cooperation among States in accordance with the Charter of the United Nations, GA Res 2625 (XXV), UN GAOR, 25th Sess., Supp. No. 28, UN Doc A/Res/25/2625 (1970) 122: "Every State has the duty to refrain from organizing or encouraging the organization of irregular forces or armed bands including mercenaries, for incursion into the territory of another State. Every State has the duty to refrain from organizing, instigating, assisting or participating in acts of civil strife or terrorist acts in another State or acquiescing in organized activities within its territory directed towards the commission of such acts, when the acts referred to in the present paragraph involve a threat or use of force."

2 Georges Abi-Saab, 'The Security Council as Legislator and as Executive in its Fight against Terrorism and against Proliferation of Weapons of Mass Destruction: The Question of Legitimacy', in Rudiger Wolfrum & Volker Roben (eds), *Legitimacy in International Law* (Berlin: Springer 2008) p. 129.

Cecilia M. Bailliet (ed.), Security: A Multidisciplinary Normative Approach.
 ISBN 978 90 04 17296 8. pp. 175–229.

appears that violation of 1373 *itself* is increasingly being characterized as constituting a threat to international peace and security.[3]

It has been suggested that there are attempts to transfer the *Responsibility to Protect Doctrine (R2P)* (which originally conditioned the state's sovereign right to non-interference in domestic affairs to its own fulfilment of human rights duties) to the field of counterterrorism, becoming the *Responsibility to Prevent Terrorism.*[4] Under classic R2P, states have an *erga omnes* duty to protect and to prevent violations of human rights (genocide, ethnic cleansing, or crimes against humanity) and war crimes. Failure to do so would flag the responsibility of the international community to respond. There are numerous efforts to expand R2P's application beyond these specific criteria, for example in order to respond to harm caused by natural disasters.[5] Nevertheless, this has not yet been accepted by the UN Security Council. Similarly, as stated by Vincent Joel Proulx, one may evince efforts to support recognition of a state duty to prevent terrorism as another obligation *erga omnes*. Tal Becker buttresses this view:

> The duty of states to prevent, and abstain from any involvement in acts of terrorism is beyond question in international law. At a fundamental level, these obligations are a corollary of sovereignty and arise from the basic duty of the state to exercise due diligence in order to prevent harm to other states or their nationals emanating from its territory.[6]

---

3 Proulx asserts that the international community has moved toward a model of indirect responsibility, which has supplanted direct responsibility in the field of attribution. Vincent Joel Proulx, 'Babysitting Terrorists: Should States be Strictly Liable for Failing to Prevent Transborder Attacks' in *Berkeley Journal of International Law* vol. 23 (2005) pp. 615,629,637.

4 On R2P see the UN General Assembly, 2005 World Summit Outcome, paras. 138–139: ⟨http://www.responsibilitytoprotect.org/index.php/united_nations/398?theme=alt1⟩. The response is to first utilize peaceful means, then progressing to coercive measures, including the use of force, in the event of failure. The intervention must meet the criteria of just cause, right intention, last resort, proportional means, reasonable prospects and right authority (i.e., the UN Security Council). On the emergence of a duty to prevent, see Lee Feinstein and Anne-Marie Slaughter, 'A Duty to Prevent' in Foreign Affairs (January/February 2004); see also Ivo H. Daalder & James B. Steinberg, Preventive War, A Useful Tool, Brookings Institution (4 December 2005); see also Jose E. Alvarez, 'The Schizophrenias of R2P', Panel Presentation at the 2007 Hague Joint Conference on Contemporary Issues of International Law: Criminal Jurisdiction 100 Years After the 1907 Hague Peace Conference, The Hague, the Netherlands, (30 June 2007).

5 See France's invocation of the Responsibility to Protect in the context of a cyclone in Burma in May 2008. See: ⟨http://www.securitycouncilreport.org/site/c.glKWLeMTIsG/b.4130257/⟩.

6 Tal Becker, *Terrorism and the State: Rethinking the Rules of State Responsibility* (Hart Publishing 2006) p. 118. He cites the Declaration on Principles of International Law concerning Friendly Relations and Cooperation among States in accordance with the Charter of the United Nations, GA Res 2625 (XXV), UN GAOR, 25th Sess., Supp No. 28, UN Doc A/Res/25/2625 (1970) 122 which prohibits states from acquiescing or tolerating terrorist activity directed towards another state.

States which harbour and fail to prevent terrorist acts conducted by non-state agents against other states, may increasingly expect response by aggrieved states or other actors within the international community.[7] The failure to uphold the responsibility to prevent terrorism is interpreted by its proponents as entailing a loss of recognition of the sovereign right to non-interference, arguing that the situation may engage a claim of self-defence as well as constitute a threat to international peace and security.

This chapter presents the empirical study of Colombia's targeted strike of FARC leader Raúl Reyes in Ecuador on March 1, 2008. The methodology is a merger of International Affairs and International Law, as it combines review of academic literature with media reports and official statements made within the OAS Permanent Council and the Rio Group. This approach serves to examine the consequences of a state's concrete act coupled with resulting institutional discourses addressing the state's appeal for recognition of the emergence of an "instant" norm of a "Responsibility to Prevent Terrorism" as legitimising unilateral extra-territorial targeted killing. The central question is whether such norm may be regarded as compatible with the existing normative framework composed of the UN and OAS Charters, in particular the fundamental standards of non-intervention, territorial integrity, and peaceful dispute resolution. It is submitted that Resolution 1373 is prompting the articulation of juridical innovations that serve to promote an international state of exception founded upon an inverted concept of security, effectively piercing the veil of territorial sovereignty.[8] The issue of the legitimacy of the use of force is separate from consideration of protection due individuals during and after hostilities. Hence, this chapter also seeks to expose the impact of the inverted security paradigm on the interpretation of customary international humanitarian law, international human rights, and international refugee law.

II. Self Defence and the Measure of Complicity

According to Article 2(4) of the UN Charter, states are required to refrain from utilizing force against another state:

7 Proulx, supra note 3 at 650 referring to Articles on State Responsibility, Article 11. See also Philip Bobbitt, *Terror and Consent: The Wars for the Twenty-First Century* (Allen Lane 2008) p. 496, noting that the determination that a state intentionally harbours terrorists and is subject to lawful intervention should be made by the UN, a regional group, or "a concert of (democratic) states". He uses the term "states of consent" to refer to those who abide by Western, liberal norms including respecting democratic traditions and human rights (especially women's rights, minority rights, and the right of conscience).

8 One may suggest that we are witnessing the international variant of Boaventura de Sousa Santos' identification of "the emergence of a new state form, the state of exception, which, contrary to the old forms of state of siege or state of emergency, restricts democratic rights under the guise of safeguarding or even expanding them." Boaventura de Sousa Santos, 'Beyond Abyssal Thinking: From Global Lines to Ecologies of Knowledge' in *Eurozine* (19.02.2008), available at: ⟨http://www.eurozine.com⟩. See also Joan Fitzpatrick, 'Speaking Law to Power: The War against Terrorism and Human Rights', in *European Journal of International Justice* Vol. 14 No. 3 (2003) 241–264, discussing the "permanent emergency" of the war against terrorism.

> All Members shall refrain in their international relations from the threat or use of force against the territorial integrity or political independence of any state, or in any other manner inconsistent with the Purposes of the United Nations.

This is considered to be a peremptory norm under international law. There are two exceptions. The first is Article 51 of the Charter which permits states to act in self-defence in response to an imminent or actual armed attack:

> Nothing in the present Charter shall impair the inherent right of individual or collective self-defence if an armed attack occurs against a member of the United Nations, until the Security Council has taken the measures necessary to maintain international peace and security.[9]

This provision gives no definition of what may be considered an armed attack.[10] The second exception is pursuant to Chapter VII; the UN Security Council may authorize a military action. The use of force in counterterrorism operations tends to be characterized as self-defence actions.[11] Query arose as to whether terrorist attacks by non-state actors could be considered "armed attacks". In response to the terrorist action on September 11, 2001, the Security Council issued Resolutions 1368 (2001) and 1373 (2001) which characterized these acts as constituting an armed attack which supported a right of self-defence. This was also confirmed at the regional level by OAS Ministry of Foreign Affairs Resolution on the Terrorist Threat to the Americas which highlighted that regional collective self defence had been activated by the attack:

> That these terrorist attacks against the United States of America are attacks against all American states and that in accordance with all the relevant provisions of the Inter-American Treaty of Reciprocal Assistance (Rio Treaty) and the principle of continental solidarity, all States Parties to the Rio Treaty shall provide effective reciprocal assistance to address such attacks and the threat of any similar attacks against any American state, and to maintain the peace and security of the continent.[12]

Nevertheless, in the ICJ's Advisory Opinion on Israel's barrier in the Occupied Palestinian Territory, the Court held that the right of self-defence pursuant to Article 51 refers to armed attack by one state against another state.[13] Hence, the issue of attribution is considered a crucial element for justifying self-defence against terrorism.

---

9 States acting unilaterally in self-defence must report the action to the Security Council.

10 Terry D. Gill, 'The Temporal Dimension of Self-Defense: Anticipation, Pre-Emption, Prevention and Immediacy' in Michael Schmitt and Jelena Pejic, *International Law and Armed Conflict: Exploring the Faultlines, Essays in Honour of Yoram Dinstein*, (Martinus Nijhoff Pub. 2007) p. 121.

11 Craig Forcese, 'Demilitarizing Counter-Terrorism: Anti-Terrorism, Human Rights, and the Use of Force' in Nicole La Violette & Craig Forcese (Eds.) *The Human Rights of Anti-Terrorism* (Irwin 2008) p. 174.

12 OAS Twenty-Fourth Meeting of Consultation of the Ministers of Foreign Affairs, (21 September 2001) OEA/Ser.F/II.24, RC.24/RES.1/01. See also OAS Resolutions 1270 & 1273 (2001).

13 *Legal Consequences of the Construction of a Wall in the Occupied Palestinian Territory* (Advisory Opinion of 9 July) reprinted in (2004) 43 ILM 1009, at 10049–50.

There is a broad range of state involvement in terrorism from active sponsorship to toleration of bases, as well as variable degrees of absence of complicity or sheer inability to stop attacks from its territory.[14] In terms of attribution to a state for actions conducted by non-state actors, the ICJ set forth in the Nicaragua Case that the criteria of "armed attack" includes the deployment of armed groups to conduct armed actions (similar in scale and effects to those carried out by national armed forces), but not to cases of assistance to rebels such as provision of weapons or logistical or other support.[15] Further, the Court set forth a high standard of attribution of actions by non state actors to the state. Recognition of a state's substantial involvement in non-state actions constituting "armed attack" is possible only in situations where the state exercises effective control over the group.[16] This standard was codified in the International Law Commission's Draft Articles on State Responsibility (2001), Article 8: "The conduct of a person shall be considered an act of state if the person is acting on the instruction of or direction or control of the state."

The U.S. government articulated the Bush Doctrine which lowered the standard of attribution to include the harbouring of non-state actors and claimed justification of use of force against host states.[17] Hofmeister suggests that this presents a conundrum as it is unclear whether the standard of liability demands "harbouring" as opposed to "tolerating" or "encouraging", or whether there is a requirement that the state both "harbour and support" the armed group, or whether each element is sufficient by itself.[18] Further, he points to the problem of addressing whether the state "knows" a terrorist attack will occur, as oppose to "wills" such attack.[19] Similarly,

---

14 Jane Stromseth 'New Paradigms for the Jus Ad Bellum?' in George Washington International Law Review vol. 38 (2006) pp. 561, 568.

15 *Case Concerning Military and Paramilitary Activities in and against Nicaragua* (Nicaragua v. United States of America) (Merits) (1986) ICJ Rep 14 (195). See also *Congo v. Uganda* (2005) in which Uganda's use of force against rebels in DRC was rejected as constituting self-defence.

16 See also *Application of the Convention on the Prevention and Punishment of the Crime of Genocide (Bosnia and Herzegovina v. Serbia and Montenegro)*, (2007), ICJ Rep. 91 (406). But see *Prosecutor v. Tadic*, Case No. IT 94-1-A, ICTY AC 1999 (117) (145), lowering standard to "overall control", including planning and supervision of military operations.

17 Hannes Herbert Hofmeister, 'When is it Right to Attack So-Called "Host States"? An Analysis of the Necessary Nexus Between Terrorists and their Host States', in *Singapore Year Book of International Law* vol. 11 (2007) pp. 1–10, at 4 footnote 28, citing National Security Strategy of the United States, September 2002 at 5. See also President George W. Bush, Statement by the President in His Address to the Nation (11 September 2001). See also statement by Tom Farer: "States can experience a temporary and qualified loss of immunity from intervention by gross abuse of the nationals of other states or by failing to prevent use of their territories for activities gravely threatening other states' security." Tom J. Farer, Daniele Archibugi, Chris Brown, Neta C. Crawford, Thomas G. Weis & Nicholas J. Wheeler, 'Roundtable: Humanitarian Intervention After 9/11' in *International Relations* vol. 19 (2005), pp. 211 at 212.

18 Ibid at 5.

19 See International Court of Justice, *Corfu Channel Case* (U.K.V. Ireland) (1949), ICJ Rep. 4 p. 22, in which the Court held that every state has a duty "not to allow knowingly its territory to be used of acts contrary to the rights other states." See also International Court of Justice, *Diplomatic and Consular Staff (U.S. v. Iran) Case* (1980) at 12 in which the Court

Becker determines that identification of whether there has been an actual violation of the due diligence standard, mere acquiescence, or no violation at all is difficult.[20] Problems usually arise given the varying degrees of a state's ability or willingness to identify or neutralize terrorists due to lack of resources or inability to exert real control in their territories.

Garwood-Gowers suggests the lower standard of attribution is *lex specialis* to be applied only in situations of international terrorism prompting assertion of the right of self-defence.[21] Stromseth advocates promotion of norm evolution in this arena: "The US should work with friends and allies to forge greater consensus on a robust right of self-defence (including anticipatory self-defence) in response to terrorism."[22] She sets forth that normative consensus gradually emerges from practice and case-by-case decision-making.[23] There is a growing trend towards selection of the use of military force against insurgents (who use terrorist methods of attack) in "host" states. Justification claims are based on assertion of the right of self-defence, e.g. Israel in the Occupied Territories, Lebanon and Syria; the United States in Afghanistan, Sudan and Somalia, Syria, and Pakistan; Russia in Uzbekistan and Turkey in Northern Iraq.

One of the primary conditions of the original R2P framework is the expectation that peaceful avenues will be explored before resorting to coercive or forceful measures. It is of concern that this contingency is not strictly applied within the realm of counterterrorism, as the application of force appears to be pursued without full exhaustion of alternatives. The responsive framework for Responsibility to Prevent in the realm of counter-terrorism is actually vast, appearing in different forms, each with varying degrees of interaction and/or intervention between states, e.g.: 1) Shared intelligence to assist arrest, extradition and criminal prosecution of suspected terrorists, narco-traffickers, arms dealers, or their financiers, 2) Military/counterinsurgency/counter-narcotics/surveillance/border control aid, arms procurement and training, 3) Freezing of financial assets, 4) Proposed amendments to national counterterrorism legislation, and 5) The assistance/coordination of military strikes against terrorists in the host state or aggrieved state. One may suggest that there is need for a substantive assessment as to whether a targeted killing will actually further the interests of security or backfire upon review by the international community. The issue then becomes the cost of transference of R2P to counterterrorism, are we moving towards the "unrule" of law via increased reference to the indirect attribution of host states?[24]

---

held Iran liable for failure to protect the US embassy against seizure by students.

20 Becker, supra note 6 at 133.

21 Andrew Garwood-Gowers, 'Self-Defense Against Terrorism in the Post 9/11 World' in *Queensland University of Technology Law & Justice Journal* vol. 13 (2004) p. 4.

22 Stromseth, supra note 14 at 568. She sets forth that the regional self-defence alliances would be good places to commence such diplomacy.

23 Jane Stromseth, 'Rethinking Humanitarian Intervention: The Case for Incremental Change', in J.L. Holzgrefe & Robert O. Keohane, *Humanitarian Intervention: Ethical, Legal and Political Dilemmas* (2003 Cambridge) pp. 232–233.

24 The term "unrule" of law was coined by Paulo Sergio Pinheiro in reference to Latin

III. "Necessity" and "Proportionality" as Prongs of the Responsibility to Prevent Terrorism Analysis

Necessity requires examination of whether the use of force is necessary to repel the armed attack and whether there are any alternatives to use of force.[25] Limitations of military strikes by advocates of the Responsibility to Prevent within the realm of counterterrorism appear to place the burden on the host state to demonstrate its active battle against terrorists, consider Kimberly Trapp:

> In cases where a state is actively countering the terrorist activities of non-state actors operating from its territory to organize or launch attacks, a victim state's use of force against non-state actors in the territorial state (amounting to a violation of that state's territorial integrity) is simply not a necessary use of force. It is the substitution (and imposition) of the victim state's views on how to deal with the terrorist threat emanating from the host state's territory for those of the host state, which amounts to an illegal intervention.[26]

In cases where a state is considered to be combating terrorists, the issue is whether cooperative criminal law enforcement mechanisms are possible. Trapp suggests that where the host state is unwilling or unable to meet its obligation to prevent terrorists from using its territory as a base (thereby amounting to acquiescence or consistent failure to suppress terrorism) then the victim state may engage in a *limited, targeted action* against the source of attack in the host state territory, thereby meeting the criteria of necessity and proportionality.[27] Cassese rejects the argument that a state's failure to implement its counter-terrorism duties alone would justify use of force.[28] He highlights the UN Charter, Article 2.3, calls for States to settles international disputes peacefully. As confirmed by the 1970 Declaration of Principles of International Law concerning Friendly Relations and Co-operation among States (GA Resolution 2625 (XXV)), states may only resort to military force after every peaceful avenue has

---

America. See Juan E. Mendez, Paulo Sergio Pinheiro and Guillermo O'Donnell (eds.) *(Un)Rule of Law and the Underprivileged in Latin America* (South Bend, 1999).

25 See ICJ, *Case Concerning Oil Platforms (Islamic Republic of Iran v. United States of America)*, ICJ (6 November 2003) at para. 76, determining use of force as unnecessary.

26 Kimberley N. Trapp, 'Back to Basics: Necessity, Proportionality, and the Right of Self-Defence Against Non-State Terrorist Actors' in *International Comparative Law Quarterly* vol. 56 (January 2007) pp. 141–156 at 147, citing the non-intervention principle contained in the Declaration on Principles of International Law Concerning Friendly Relations and Cooperation among States in Accordance with the Charter of the United Nations, GA Res 2625 (XXV), 24 Oct. 1970.

27 Ibid. Trapp cites examples of cross-territorial military strikes by States against non-state actors and the resulting debate within the UN Security Council to argue in favour of recognition of the norms of necessity and proportionality as the criteria used for measuring the legitimacy of such actions.

28 Antonio Cassese, 'The International Community's "Legal" Response to Terrorism' in *International and Comparative Law Quarterly* vol. 38 (1989) p. 589 cited by Becker, supra note 5 at 160. Becker also cites ME O'Connell, 'Evidence of Terror' in *Journal of Conflict & Security Law* vol. 7 (2002) p. 19.

been explored.[29] Nevertheless, he notes that "States do opt immediately for forcible response to terrorist activity and receive no greater admonition from the rest of the international community than a verbal condemnation."[30] Cassese infers from recent UN Security Council reactions to state practice in the area of counter-terrorism that "attacks against states harbouring terrorists are a lawful form of self defence, subject to some stringent conditions: that the state actively assists terrorists or allows them to mount *serious, repeated, and large-scale terrorist onslaughts* on other states; that the forcible reaction is immediate and proportionate."[31] Stromseth highlights the need to assess the following factors when determining the justification of a forcible action in self-defence:[32]

1. The intent of the terrorist group and the probability of attack
2. Capacity of attack (danger of acquiring WMD)
3. Methods of attack (use of stealth and deception)
4. Gravity of Likely Harm
5. Urgency of Threat

This assessment is contingent on reliable intelligence addressing future acts and must also be combined with review of why the elimination of the target is deemed necessary as opposed to arrest.[33] It is notable that Dinstein concludes that "the absence of alternative means for putting an end to the operations of the armed bands or terrorists has to be demonstrated *beyond a reasonable doubt*."[34] The issue is whether it can be demonstrated that there are actually no other means of disabling the terrorists other than use of military force; thus indicating that the method is selected as a last resort rather than on the grounds of convenience. Dinstein points to a need to react to a past attack (immediacy), rather than anticipatory of a future threat, but with expectation of repetition of an attack (urgency).[35]

29 Antonio Cassese, *International Law* (Oxford, 2nd Ed. 2005) at 464.

30 Ibid at 465.

31 Ibid at 476. He cites UN Security Council Resolution 748 (1992), adopted on 31 March 1992, regarding Libya's responsibility for the Lockerbie terrorist attacks, stating that in accordance with article 2 (4) of the UN Charter every state "has the duty to refrain ... from acquiescing in organized activities within its territory directed towards the commission of such acts, when such acts involve threat or use of force." Cassese concludes that this view would permit military use of force in self-defence to such situation as it would be understood to constitute an "armed attack".

32 Stromseth, supra note 14. The UN High-Level Panel on Threats, Challenges and Change recognizes the right of states to thwart an imminent attack in self-defence.

33 Guiora, Amos N., 'Self-defense from the Wild West to 9/11-Who, What, Why, When', *Cornell Journal of International Law* vol. 41 (2008) p. 3.

34 Yoram Dinstein, *War, Aggression and Self-Defence* (Cambridge University Press 4th Ed. 2005) at 250. The protection of civilians is paramount in such actions.

35 Ibid at 249. Under customary standards, self-defence actions must meet the standards of proportionality, necessity (no other means to deflect) and imminence of attack. Regarding preventive defence, the response must be immediate, proportional and a means of last resort. The 1837 Caroline case, referring to anticipatory self-defence calls for criteria of "necessity of self-defence that was instant, overwhelming, leaving no choice of means and no moment for deliberation".

The criteria of proportionality require that the use of force may not be greater than needed to repel the armed attack. One must weigh the degree of threat presented by the target at the time. Garwood-Gowers asserts that the definition of "armed attack" has been amended to include the "cumulative effects of a series of attacks", thereby including an ongoing campaign of terrorist acts.[36] Cassese indicates that "to qualify as an armed attack, terrorist acts must form part of a consistent pattern of violent terrorist action rather than just being isolated or sporadic uses of violence."[37] He opines that "merely permitting insurgents or terrorists to sleep in disused huts in remote border areas, acquiescence which should not of itself engage the state's responsibility for an armed attack ... (I)t may safely be contended that in those instances where the assistance or acquiescence is not sporadic but *regular and consistent*, once may well conclude that the state involved is responsible for a breach of Article 2(4) and must hence be held accountable for terrorist attacks coming from its territory."[38] As pertaining states which are unable (as opposed to unwilling) to exercise control over terrorist groups in the territory, he suggests that the host state may not bear responsibility for the terrorist acts, but it may not oppose a foreign state's initiative to use lawful force against the terrorists.[39] Similarly, Dinstein suggests that states that are unable or unwilling to prevent terrorist operations should permit other states to send forces to eliminate the threat – "extra-territorial law enforcement".[40]

Thus, we are left to consider was the Colombian strike in Ecuador a legitimate act of self-defence? Was the post-facto evidence presented to attribute responsibility for terrorist presence in Ecuador sufficient to justify the use of military force? Was there any reasonable alternative? In terms of assessing proportionality and collateral damage, were those killed or wounded combatants, civilians participating in hostilities, or civilians not participating in hostilities? From a human rights perspective, were the killings of civilians extra-judicial executions? Of particular importance to the normative development of public international law: What are the implications of the resolutions emitted by the OAS and Rio Group in terms of assessing the customary evolution of the recognition of a responsibility to prevent terrorism? Is there regional recognition of a lower standard of attribution in the case of harbouring terrorists as grounding use of force?

36 Garwood-Gowers, supra note 21 at 231 refers to the policy of the United States and Israel. In addition, he cites the *Nicaragua Case* in which the ICJ refers to the gravity of collective attacks, as well as the *Case Concerning Oil Platforms (Islamic Republic of Iran v. United States of America)* (Merits) (6 November 2003) ICJ (64).

37 Cassese, supra note 29 at 469.

38 Ibid at 472.

39 Ibid.

40 Dinstein, supra note 34.

IV. Case Study: Colombia's Raid in Ecuador

A. *Facts*

The Colombian government has been engaged in an armed conflict against the Revolutionary Armed Forces of Colombia (FARC) since 1966. The FARC was originally formed to pursue internal self-determination of the people via reclamation of redistribution of wealth and agrarian reform. They established schools, health centres, and agrarian cooperatives while seeking to form an independent, communist state. During the nineties, they became involved in narco-trafficking, kidnapping, and extortion. This provides an estimated budget of USD 250–500 million a year. Their former linkage to social justice concerns has been eclipsed by their criminal activities; which in turn has fomented escalation of the military conflict, due to an endless infusion of modern weapons. The Colombian government refuses to grant political recognition of the FARC and is instead pursuing a policy of total military defeat.

Operation Fénix was conducted on March 1, 2008 by Colombian forces against FARC operatives camped within Ecuadoran territory. On February 25th the Colombian National Police intelligence operatives located Raúl Reyes (second in command of FARC) by tracking his satellite phone signature while he was negotiating the potential release of hostage Ingrid Bentancourt with French contacts. The attack was approved on February 27th but scheduled for the 29th due to weather conditions.[41] Because the camp was located inside Ecuadoran territory, President Uribe was requested to grant authorization. According to Jane's report, two Super Tucanos (night strike planes) dropped bombs on the camp at 0130 hours.[42] The sole Mexican survivor stated that there was a second bombing strike at 0300 hours. Colombian armed forces were sent by helicopter to retrieve Reyes' body and computer and assess the effectiveness of the strike. The survivor alleged that they fired their weapons, counted the dead, and gave orders to shoot the wounded and those who surrendered. At the sound of approaching Ecuadoran helicopters, the Colombians fled immediately, taking documents, a computer, and two of the bodies (one of whom was Raúl Reyes) with them. They left behind ca. twenty bodies, four wounded, and weapons.

Both Ecuador and Venezuela recalled their ambassadors and broke off relations with Colombia. Nicaragua followed suit, adding its direct condemnation of Colombia's actions. Brazil, Argentina and Paraguay also condemned the action, and Mexico and Uruguay denounced the violation of territorial integrity. President Chavez of Venezuela announced his full support of Ecuador and threatened that should similar action occur in Venezuela, this would be interpreted as an act of war. On camera, he immediately deployed 10 battalions to the border. Ecuador's troops were also deployed to the border.[43] President Correa contacted the OAS given its mandate in the area of regional peace and security, in an effort to attain efficient investigation as to the facts and prompt resolution of the conflicts.

41 "Analysis: Colombian Raid Hits a Raw Nerve", in *Jane's Report* (April 1 2008).

42 Ibid.

43 Chavez deployed 9,000 troops to the border, while Correa deployed 3,000.

B. *Multilateralism as the Path to Security*

Feinstein and Slaughter emphasize that "the duty to prevent should be exercised collectively, through a global or regional organization".[44] Hence, the legitimacy of the Colombian action was in part immediately questionable due to being outside the framework of the UN (specifically without authorization by the Security Council) or the OAS. Indeed, Ecuador's position was that the unilateral nature of the strike was subject to condemnation and sought affirmation of the principle of sovereignty and the inviolability of the territory of a state. Further, it requested the OAS to create a commission to produce a report and call a special meeting of the Permanent Council. Review of how the case was debated within the OAS and Rio Group is important for understanding how arguments for implementation of 1373 and recognition of a duty to prevent terrorism was pursued via cross-reference to regional norms. The articulation of the legality of the action by the governments of Colombia and the United States was met with strong counterarguments by other governments which sought to reject legitimization of the action as meriting recognition as a new ("instant") custom under international law. The primary concern was whether the attempt to confirm a new customary practice would sacrifice international legal standards pertaining to territorial sovereignty. The consequence would be an expansion of unilateral state counterterrorism powers partially justified by the interest in human rights protection/protection of society.

C. *Regional Instruments Addressing Terrorism*

There are various regional instruments which provide a normative framework for counter-terrorism. The Inter-American Convention against Terrorism (IACT) (2002) has three articles which address cooperation: Article 7 on Cooperation on Border Control, Article 8 on Cooperation among Law Enforcement Authorities, and Article 9 on Mutual Legal Assistance.[45] Its preamble reaffirms that the fight against terrorism must be undertaken with full respect for national law, international law, and democratic institutions in order to preserve the rule of law, liberties and democratic values in the Hemisphere. These are defined as the essential components of a successful fight against terrorism. Article 15 specifically addresses the principle of the rule of law and human rights as overarching counterterrorism actions, and further prohibits override of the rights and duties of both state and non state actors under international and regional public law, including the law of war and refugee law:

1. The measures carried out by the states parties under this Convention shall take place with full respect for the rule of law, human rights, and fundamental freedoms.

---

44 Feinstein & Slaughter, supra note 4. See also Daalder & Steinberg, supra note 4.

45 Ratified by Ecuador in May 2006, signed by Colombia 06/03/2002. See also Inter-American Convention against the Illicit Manufacturing of and Trafficking in Firearms, Ammunition, Explosives, and other Related Materials (1997), article III sovereignty, XIII exchange of information, XIV cooperation, XV exchange of experience and training, XVI technical assistance, XVII mutual legal assistance.

2. Nothing in this Convention shall be interpreted as affecting other rights and obligations of states and individuals under international law, in particular the Charter of the United Nations, the Charter of the Organization of American States, international humanitarian law, international human rights law, and international refugee law.

In retrospect, after Operation Fenix, this provision appears to have been laden with prophetic dimensions. As this chapter will discuss, much of the debates in the Permanent Council of the OAS and Rio Group centred on precisely whether or not Colombia had violated obligations under the universal and regional charters, as well as fundamental guarantees under International Humanitarian Law, Human Rights, and Refugee Law through invocation of a new security normative paradigm.

The OAS Declaration on Security in the Americas (2003) reaffirms the inherent right of all states to individual or collective self-defence and calls for a commitment to refrain from the use of force against the territorial integrity or political independence of any state.[46] Significantly, it recognizes terrorism as posing a serious threat to security. In like manner to the IACT, it calls for fighting terrorism with full respect for the rule of law and international law. It also highlights both the IACT and UN Security Council Resolution 1373, placing the latter at the same level as the conventions.[47]

> 22. We affirm that terrorism poses a serious threat to security, the institutions, and the democratic values of states and to the well-being of our peoples. We renew our commitment to fight terrorism and its financing with full respect for the rule of law and international law, including international humanitarian law, international human rights law, international refugee law, the Inter-American Convention against Terrorism, and United Nations Security Council resolution 1373 (2001). We will undertake to promote the universalisation and effective implementation of current international conventions and protocols related to terrorism.

It calls upon the countries to *prevent* terrorism and the international movement of terrorists. Of special significance, the OAS Ministers of Foreign Affairs issued two resolutions which state that those who harbour terrorists are responsible/complicit in those acts.[48] In 2003, the OAS Permanent Council expressed condemnation of ter-

---

46 Declaration on Security in the Americas, OEA/Ser.K/XXXVIII, CES/DEC.1/03 rev.1 (28 October 2003).

47 This was reiterated in the OAS General Assembly's Resolution AG/RES.2271 (XXXVII-O/07) Protecting Human Rights and Fundamental Freedoms While Countering Terrorism (June 5 2007) which sets forth:

> 1. To reaffirm that the fight against terrorism must be waged with full respect for the law, including compliance with due process and human rights ... as well as for democratic institutions, so as to preserve the rule of law and democratic freedoms and values in the Hemisphere. 2. To reaffirm that all member states have a duty to ensure that all measures adopted to combat terrorism are in compliance with their obligations under international law, in particular international human rights law, international refugee law, and international humanitarian law.

48 OAS, Convocation of the Twenty-Third Meeting of Consultation of Ministers of Foreign Affairs, OEA/Ser. G CP/RES 796 (1293/01) (2001) and OAS Res RC23/RES1/01

rorist acts in Colombia, reaffirming the commitment of member states to take steps to ensure strict observance of the provisions of UN Security Council resolution 1373 and the Inter-American Convention Against Terrorism concerning the obligation to refrain from providing any form of support or safe haven to entities or persons involved in terrorist acts.[49] In 2007, the OAS Permanent Council issued a Declaration on Strengthening Cooperation in the Fight against Terrorism and the Impunity of its Perpetrators which called for effective border controls and confirms the duty of prevention.[50] In addition, the OAS General Assembly adopted Resolution 2272 which called upon all states to implement the relevant conventions and UN resolutions specifically in order to deny safe haven to terrorists:

> To reiterate that it is important for the member states of the Organization of American States (OAS) to sign, ratify, implement, and continue implementing, as the case may be, the Inter-American Convention against Terrorism, as well as pertinent regional and international conventions and protocols, including the 13 international conventions and protocols and United Nations Security Council resolutions 1267 (1999), 1373 (2001), 1540 (2004), 1566 (2004), 1617 (2005), and 1624 (2005), in order to find, deny safe haven to, and bring to justice, on the basis of the principle of extradite or prosecute, any person who supports, facilitates, participates, or attempts to participate in the financing, planning, preparation, or commission of terrorist acts or provides safe havens.[51]

(21 September 2001).

49 Permanent Council of the Organization of American States, Condemnation of Terrorist Acts in Colombia, OEA/Ser.G, CP/RES/837 (1354) (12 February 2003): "*The unwavering commitment of the member states to deny refuge and/or safe haven to those who finance, plan or commit acts of terrorism in Colombia or who lend support to such persons, noting that those responsible for aiding, supporting or harbouring the perpetrators, organizers, and sponsors of these acts are equally complicit.*"

50 Permanent Council of the Organization of American States, "Declaration on Strengthening Cooperation in the Fight against Terrorism and the Impunity of its Perpetrators", OEA/Ser.G CP/DEC. 36 (1599/07) (28 May 2007). It cross-references OAS resolutions resolutions of the Organization of American States: AG/RES. 1840 (XXXII-0/02), "Inter-American Convention against Terrorism"; AG/RES. 1906 (XXXII-O/02), "Human Rights and Terrorism"; AG/RES. 1931 (XXXIII-O/03), AG/RES. 2035 (XXXIV-O/04), AG/RES. 2143 (XXXV-O/05), and AG/RES. 2238 (XXXVI-O/06), "Protecting Human Rights and Fundamental Freedoms While Countering Terrorism"; and AG/RES. 2249 (XXXVI-O/06), "Extradition of and Denial of Safe Haven to Terrorists: Mechanisms for Cooperation in the Fight against Terrorism". It also cross-references UN resolutions S/RES/1373 (2001), S/RES/1540 (2004), S/RES/1566 (2004), S/RES/1624 (2005), and S/RES/1737 (2006) of the United Nations Security Council; as well as resolutions A/RES/61/40 and A/RES/60/288 of the United Nations General Assembly.

51 OAS General Assembly AG/RES. 2272 (XXXVII O/07) Support for the Work of the Inter-American Committee Against Terrorism (June 5, 2007). It expressed the commitment to respect the rule of law and international law, including International Humanitarian Law, Human Rights, Refugee Law, ICAT and UN SC Resolution 1373 (once again placing the resolution at the same level as hard law). See also OAS General Assembly AG/RES. 2396 (XXXVIII-O/08) Support for the Work of the Inter-American Committee Against Terrorism (June 3, 2008).

Of special interest, the resolution establishes a link between counter-terrorism and democratic entitlement, and in the debate within the Permanent Council this provided a basis for creative argumentation when calling for cross-regime applicability of 1373:

> To reiterate its most vigorous condemnation of terrorism in all its forms and manifestations, as criminal and unjustifiable under any circumstances in any place, and regardless of who perpetrates it, and because it poses a grave threat to international peace and security, and to the democracy, stability, and prosperity of the countries of the region.[52]

Thus, OAS Resolution 2272 is the normative vehicle for implementation of UNSC Resolution 1373 at the regional level.

D. *Debate within the OAS Permanent Council*

The debate within the OAS Permanent Council on March 4, 2008 centered on whether Ecuador's demand that the traditional, prescriptive, peremptory norm of international law prohibiting intervention should prevail over Colombia's creative plea for recognition of a new, normative rule expressing an imperative to intervene in situations in which terrorists are being harbored. Specifically, Colombia attempted to legitimize the violation of territorial sovereignty by reference to its defence of its citizens (and other human beings) at risk of victimized by terrorist acts. Colombia presented a *lex ferenda* argument which in part relied on the *lex lata* norm relating to self-defence.

i. Presentation by Colombia

Colombia readily admitted its violation of territorial integrity and extended full apology to Ecuador, emphatically rejecting the incorporation of condemnatory language by the OAS Permanent Council. Further it presented an argument building on Article 51 of the UN Charter and UN Security Council Resolution 1373's identification of a duty to combat terrorism.[53] Ambassador Camilo Alfonso Ospina Bernal

---

52 This foreshadowed the advocacy of a "league of democracies" by John McCain, See 'America Must be a Good Role Model', in *The Financial Times*, 18 March 2008, available at: http://www.ft.com/cms/s/0/c7e219e2-f4ea-11dc-a21b-000077b07658.html?nclick_check=1. See also Philip Bobbitt's characterization of "states of consent", supra note 7, or Condoleeza Rice's reference to "well-governed, law-abiding states" as cooperating in the strengthening of democratic, secure and open international order against transanational terrorism. See Condoleezza Rice, "The New American Realism" in *Foreign Affairs* Vol. 87 n. 4 (August 2008) p. 2.

53 It should be noted that one may also find possible basis for support of such alternative interpretation by referring to the OAS Charter. Specifically, this would invoke reference to the right to self-defence as stated in Article 22: "The American States bind themselves in their international relations not to have recourse to the use of force, except in the case of self-defence in accordance with existing treaties or in fulfilment thereof". In addition, this is then linked to the view that the strike sought to uphold the security of the Colombian people as well as others affected by terrorism and narco-trafficking, pursuant to Article 23:

declared a national policy of "Democratic Security" and noted that they were committed to implementing UN and OAS principles and the Democratic Charter of the Americas. The primary argument was that they crossed borders in order to exercise the constitutional duty to guarantee security of Colombians against terrorists. Ospina Bernal emphasized that terrorism is transnational and thus not only violates Colombian sovereignty but that of its neighbors, thereby arguing that the action was in defense of regional security interests, not only national security interests. Hence, Colombia expressed support for two contrasting notions of sovereignty affected by human rights: the first is expansive as the state in which terrorist acts are committed is considered entitled to use force in response to violation of human rights of its citizens (conflating self-defense and threat to international peace and security), and the second is restrictive, limiting the host state's territorial integrity based on vicarious responsibility for the external violation of human rights.[54]

Ambassador Ospina Bernal was very clear in declaring that the FARC are "terrorists" and whoever protects them violates criminal law. He noted that terrorism (in all its forms and for whatever purpose) has been repeatedly condemned by the UN and the OAS because it constitutes a grave threat to peace, international security, democracy, stability and prosperity of the countries within the region. Ospina Bernal reminded the OAS members that they have repeatedly recognized the importance of cooperating to prevent terrorism and related crimes. He highlighted the universal and regional legal instruments supporting a duty to cooperate fully to deny safe haven to "terrorists" and to hold those who provide such safe haven being responsible, including UN Security Council Resolution 1373 (2001), 1368 (2001), 1456 (2003), 1624 (2005); OAS General Assembly Resolutions AG/2270 (2006) and AG/2272 (2007), as well as Interpol directives.

Ambassador Ospina Bernal stated that to permit terrorists to have camps in the border territory to plan terrorist acts is *itself* a criminal act and a clear violation of international treaties against terrorism as well as the sovereignty principle and other international obligations. He reiterated that Colombia loves peace, respects the UN Charter and international law, and has never been an aggressor nation. This insinuated that the targeted strike was not grave enough to amount to an act of aggression. In short, there appeared to be an appeal for comity in light of its identification as a democratic state. In his view, the targeted strike was a legitimate response to a situation in which a state violated the duty to deny safe haven to terrorists.

With respect to Venezuela, he cited evidence obtained from the FARC computers that President Chavez extended financial support (13 million USD) and small arms to the FARC, thereby violating the terms of UN Security Council Resolution 1373

"Measures adopted for the maintenance of peace and security in accordance with existing treaties do not constitute a violation of principles set forth in Articles 19 and 21." However, it is precisely the merger of the two concepts of self-defence and threat to security that has received criticism for being illegitimate for expanding the option for the use of force in imprecise situations.

54 See Vaughn Lowe, 'Security Concerns and National Sovereignty in the Age of World-Wide Terrorism', in Ronald St. John MacDonald & Douglas M. Johnston (eds.), *Towards World Constitutionalism*, (Martinus Nijhoff 2005) pp. 655–679.

(2001) as well as the Inter-American Convention Against Terrorism.[55] Hence, he announced the intention to denounce President Chavez before the International Criminal Court for the crime of financing terrorists. He called upon the governments of Ecuador and Venezuela to explain their relationship to the FARC, as well as the permanent presence of the FARC in the border territory.

Ambassador Ospina Bernal objected to the perception that the FARC somehow represented the interest of the people, and thereby merited recognition as belligerents or political actors. He stated that the FARC is a "narco-trafficking mafia" that does not represent the Colombian people, citing the March 14th march by the Colombian civil society against the FARC. He offered a description of Raúl Reyes as having 14 indictments and 121 penal charges for crimes against humanity and other criminal acts in Colombia and in other states, such as massacres, homicides, kidnapping, trafficking of children for sexual exploitation, drug-trafficking, terrorist acts, and organized crime. He queried:

> Why are we being condemned for an action which tried to free ourselves from a threat which we have been subjected to for 40 years? … Nobody talks about the thousands kidnapped and massacred by the FARC, nobody talks about the criminality of Raúl Reyes, and nobody talks about the right to liberty of the Colombian people. Why did they expel our ambassadors? I hope they expel the terrorists.

ii. Presentation by Ecuador

Ecuador's Minister of Foreign Affairs, Maria Isabel Salvador, rejected Colombia's account of the legitimacy of the action as self-defense. She noted that the criteria for measuring the legitimacy of a self-defense action are necessity, immediacy and proportionality; which she concluded had not been met. She stated that Ecuador had not engaged in any provocation, action or aggression against Colombia. On the contrary, Colombia was depicted as the aggressor. The action had been premeditated and planned in clear violation of the principles of sovereignty and territorial integrity, in particular violating Articles 15, 19, 21 and 28 of the Charter of the Organization of American States which set forth the criteria for sustaining hemispheric peace and security. These include the reflection of moral principles in the enunciation of a duty of states not to engage in harmful actions against another state in order to ensure its own survival, i.e. Article 15: "the right of each State to protect itself and live its own life does not authorize it to commit unjust acts against another State." This is concretized in the identification of legal categories for such violations, i.e. the prohibition of intervention and the recognition of the inviolability of the state. Article 19 prescribes that "No State or group of States has the right to intervene directly or indirectly, for any reason whatever, in the internal or external affairs of any other State." Article 21 states that "The territory of a State is inviolable; it may not be the object, even temporarily of military occupation or of other measures of force

55 The ICJ judgment in the *Case concerning Military and Paramilitary Activities in and against Nicaragua*, 1986, ICJ Reports 14, para. 195 established that provision of arms, financial and logistic support may be considered intervention in internal or external affairs of other states.

taken by another State, directly or indirectly, on any grounds whatever."[56] Article 28 defines violation of a state's borders as constituting a threat to the region: "Every act of aggression by a State against the territorial integrity or the inviolability of the territory or against the sovereignty or political independence of an American State shall be considered an act of aggression against the other American States."

The accusations against Ecuador for collaboration with the FARC were characterized as constituting an illegitimate attempt to distract attention from Colombia's actions. She declared that Ecuador emphatically rejects the presence of irregular groups and foreign troops in the territory as well as their pursuit of military operations. Furthermore, she attested to the government's generous reception of Colombian refugees and full engagement in counter-terrorism, counter-narcotics, and border patrol actions. Ambassador Salvador stated that the apology offered by the Colombian government was insufficient. Rather, she called for condemnation of the violation of territorial integrity, the creation of an investigatory commission, and an additional meeting by the Ministers of Foreign Affairs.

iii. Interventions by Permanent Council Members and Observer

The reactions of other states emphasized the need to preserve peace within the region and respect international law. The Nicaraguan Ambassador, Denis Ronaldo Moncada, asserted that Colombia had clearly violated norms pertaining to the inviolability of territorial integrity and non-intervention, contained within the OAS and UN Charters, as well as UN General Assembly Resolution 3314 (XXIX) (14 December 1974) on the Definition of Aggression and Resolution 2131 (XX) (21 December 1965) Declaration on the Inadmissibility of Intervention in the Domestic Affairs of States and the Protection of Their Independence and Sovereignty. He characterized the action as converting Colombia into a warrior state which posed a threat to the region.[57] In terms of attribution, Nicaragua asserted that the act of aggression corresponded to Colombia and that complicity was due to that state which financed the Plan Colombia, i.e. the United States. Further, both Colombia and the United States were characterized as nations respectively involved in internal and external wars that rejected the use of dialogue and negotiation to resolve conflicts. In conclusion, Nicaragua characterized Raúl Reyes as meriting recognition of status as a political actor due to his primary role in opening spaces for dialogue and negotiation for the release of hostages. In particular, the diplomatic negotiations conducted by Venezuela, Brazil, Uruguay, Argentina, Bolivia, Nicaragua, France, Ecuador, and Argentina with FARC were struck a severe blow by the targeted assassination of

56 See also UN Declaration on Principles of International Law concerning Friendly Relations and Co-operation among States in accordance with the Charter of the UN Resolution 2625 of the UN General Assembly (1970), noting that the territorial integrity and political independence of the State are inviolable.

57 All statements presented at the Special Meeting of the OAS Permanent Council to Treat the Situation between Colombia and Ecuador, March 4, 2008, are available at: http://www.oas.org/OASpage/videosondemand/home_eng/videos_query.asp?sCodigo=08-0064#.

Reyes. The position of the Nicaraguan government was clearly in favour of negotiation as the most appropriate means to achieve peace and a rejection of military actions.

The Bolivian Ambassador, Pablo Soló, stated that one cannot hide nor justify a grave violation by presenting arguments that seek to make the victim the aggressor. The French Observer affirmed the principles of sovereignty and territorial integrity. She indicated concern for the destabilization of the region, the damage to the diplomatic efforts for a humanitarian exchange of kidnapping victims, and firmly denounced Colombia's rhetoric. The Venezuelan Ambassador, Jorge Valero Briceño, warned that one cannot use state terrorism against terrorism and that the extension of Colombia's internal violence to the region posed a threat to peace.[58] The Peruvian representative, Mr. Gonzalo Gutierrez, called for an explanation, satisfaction, and guarantee of non-repetition by Colombia. He recognized that the situation in the border territory was complex and required immediate solution, upholding the importance of defence of the constitutional order, but indicated that the best mechanism was that of dialogue. He expressed concern that respect for the fundamental principles of Inter-American law pertaining to sovereignty, territorial integrity and non-intervention were being degraded dangerously in both words and actions. In his view, should such habits persist, the maintenance of regional harmony would be extremely difficult.

The Uruguayan ambassador to the OAS, Maria del Lujan Flores, reaffirmed their firm commitment to the principles of the inviolability of a state's territorial integrity and non-intervention. It was noted that Article 21 of the OAS Charter reflects a right of sovereignty which serves as the basis for international relations and Article 19 expresses a Latin American tradition rejecting intervention, requiring strict compliance. These provisions were cited as forming a fundamental constitution, setting vital standards for the rule of law within the hemisphere. Indeed, Argentina's Ambassador to the OAS, Rodolfo Hugo Gil, declared the argument that the argument that the presence of irregular armed groups in Ecuadoran territory was sufficient pretext for an illegal act in the name of self-defence was a dangerous doctrine. He emphasized that under no circumstance may a state engage in a unilateral action which violates the territorial integrity and sovereignty of another state. Response to actions by irregular armed groups must come in the form of bilateral or multilateral actions acting within the framework in international law. Argentina offered conditional support for security cooperation premised on legality: "*Dentro de la ley: todo; fuera de la ley: nada.*"

The general conclusion drawn by the unanimous Latin American governments was that Colombia had destabilized the region by breaching vital regional security guarantees contained within the principles of territorial integrity and non-intervention in favour of pursuing a national security end, thereby imperilling the framework of the OAS Charter. Venezuela's ambassador suggested that the credibility of the OAS was at stake, should it not respond to the blatant violation of fundamental principles of international law then there was little point to its existence. All states

58 Indeed, UNHCR estimates that there are ca. 200,000 Colombian persons "of concern" to UNHCR in Venezuela. http://www.unhcr.org/protect/PROTECTION/47060a7ca.pdf.

called for a return to dialogue, conciliation, and use of good offices as the mode to resolve the conflict.

iv. Presentation by the United States

In contrast, Colombia received solid backing from the United States which sought to support the view that that act of aggression was conducted by the non-state actor, the FARC. On March 4th, President Bush issued a statement indicating "... *that America fully supports Colombia's democracy, and that we firmly oppose any acts of aggression that could destabilize the region. I told him that America will continue to stand with Colombia as it confronts violence and terror and fights drug traffickers*."[59] The US Ambassador to the OAS, Robert Manzarnares, reiterated this perspective at the special meeting, seeking to redirect the discussion away from consideration of Colombia as an aggressor and instead placing the focus on the FARC as a threat to the region:

> It is the FARC, rather than any member state here that has undertaken repeated incursions and infringements of national sovereignty of several of Colombia's neighbours. The stated goal of the FARC is the violent overthrow of the government of Colombia. We fully support the efforts of the Colombian government and President Uribe to respond to this threat ... FARC has committed numerous human rights violations and other affronts to dignity while infringing upon the sovereignty of both Colombia and its neighbours ... We condemn terrorists irrespective of the cause they pretend to espouse ... We underscore the commitments all OAS members except one undertook through OAS GA Resolution 2272 calling for implementation of the UN Security Council resolutions referring to the duty to deny safe haven to terrorists.

This statement provides an overview of the attempt to evolve the notion of sovereignty as directly threatened by terrorism (both because of the attempt to overthrow the government and because the state is unable to protect its citizens against human rights violations caused by terrorist acts). The conclusion offered is that armed response in situations involving the harbouring of terrorists is permitted. The human rights interest of the citizens victimized by terrorism is placed above the sovereign interest in inviolability of its territory, granting Colombia extended sovereign powers and restricting that of Ecuador in light of attribution. It reiterates the duty to deny safe haven to terrorists defined in 1373 as being confirmed by OAS resolution 2272 and thereby requiring follow up by individual member states of the OAS. Nevertheless, it should be noted that OAS Resolution 2272 does not promote the use of force. Hence there is a conceptual gap between the recognition of a duty not to provide safe haven and the relinquishment of the right to territorial integrity.

From a political perspective, Colombia appeared isolated in terms of relations with its regional neighbours which rejected the legal reasoning behind the extraterritorial action. In addition, the strong support offered by the United States concerned many governments that are sensitive to prior interventions and influence

59 See: http://www.whitehouse.gov/news/releases/2008/03/20080304-3.html.

within the region (as well as the current action in Iraq), polarizing the debate further.[60] In contrast, Ecuador demonstrated sophisticated lobbying of support from its neighbours by rapidly contacting governments and clearly calling for fidelity to basic international public law principles.

E. *OAS Permanent Council Initial Resolution*

On March 5th, 2008, the OAS Permanent Council adopted a unanimous resolution which did not formally condemn Colombia; but recognized that the operation conducted without Ecuador's consent constituted a violation of the sovereignty and territorial integrity of Ecuador. The lack of state consent is precisely the greatest weakness of "instant custom", thereby complicating recognition of legitimacy.[61] The Permanent Council resolved: "To reaffirm the principle that the territory of a state is inviolable and may not be the object, even temporarily, of military occupation or of other measures of force taken by another State, directly or indirectly, on any grounds whatsoever."[62] Further, it created a commission headed by the Secretary General and four ambassadors (the Bahamas, Panama, Argentina, and Peru) to visit Colombia and Ecuador and submit a report to the Meeting of Consultation of the Ministers of Foreign Affairs.

F. *OAS Commission Report and Final Resolution*

The OAS Commission produced a report which classified the military strike as a violation of the sovereignty and territorial integrity of Ecuador and of principles of international law.[63] It cited concern for the serious damage to the trust between the governments of Colombia and Ecuador, the contradictory versions of the event presented by the governments, and the difficult situation in the border area because of geographical aspects, territorial control, communications, and the economic and social problems.[64] Ecuador's narrative included in the report alleged that some of the victims were shot in the back, questioned whether the bombing was actually launched from Colombian territory, and rejected that the camp had been localized via a human source. It was alleged that the high technology of the bombs indicated that they

60 See generally, Michael J. Sullivan, *American Adventurism Abroad: 30 Invasions, Interventions and Regime Changes since World War II* (Praeger 2004); Alan McPherson, *Intimate Ties, Bitter Struggles: The United States and Latin America since 1945* (Potomac Books 2006); Michael Grow, *US Presidents and Latin American Interventions: Pursuing Regime Change in the Cold War* (University Press of Kansas 2008).

61 Indeed, the number of state engaging in extraterritorial targeted killings is limited, although increasing. Furthermore, recent actions, such as the U.S. targeted strikes in Syria and Pakistan in 2008 were condemned by the governments as constituting acts of "aggression".

62 Convocation of the Meeting of Consultation of Ministers of Foreign Affairs and Appointment of a Commission, (OEA/Ser.G, CP/RES.930/1632/08) (5 March 2008).

63 Report of the OAS Commission that Visited Ecuador and Colombia, OEA/Ser.F/II.25, RC.25/doc.7/08 (16 March 2008).

64 Ibid.

were not those under Colombian stockpile. Colombia insisted that they had utilized conventional bombs, launched from Colombian territory. Upon entering Ecuador to retrieve the dead, they alleged to have been subject to attack, thus explaining the use of small arms. A serious problem was the inability to get an international team in quickly to retrieve evidence, and this hindered assessment of the alleged violations of customary international humanitarian law. The OAS did not issue a judgment on the contradictory versions.

As for recommendations, the Commission called for restoration of diplomatic relations and political consultation mechanisms, the establishment of an OAS mission for follow-up on border control (including a bilateral early-warning system), cooperation and integration programs. It also proposed support of civil society organizations, border-area trade, and border control consultations.

Delays within the OAS system were circumvented by the XX Meeting of Presidents of the Rio Group on March 7, 2008, which was able resolve the crisis and conclude a "Declaration of the Heads of State and Government of the Group of Rio on the recent events between Ecuador and Colombia" (discussed in section H). On March 17th, 2008, the OAS Meeting of Consultation of Ministers of Foreign Affairs issued a compromise resolution which reflected the interests of both Colombia and Ecuador because it reaffirmed the principles of sovereignty and abstention from the use of force, rejected (but not condemned) the action as violating of Articles 19 and 21, but also confirmed the commitment of states to combat security threats by irregular groups and criminal organizations:[65]

2. To reaffirm the full applicability of the principles enshrined in international law of respect for sovereignty, abstention from the threat or use of force, and noninterference in the internal affairs of other states, which are embodied in Article 19 of the Charter and are founding principles of the inter-American system – principles that are binding on all its member states in all circumstances.
3. To reaffirm the full applicability of the principle of territorial sovereignty, enshrined unrestrictedly and without any exception in Article 21 of the OAS Charter, as a vital principle for harmonious relations among the nations of the Americas.
4. To reject the incursion by Colombian military forces and police personnel into the territory of Ecuador, in the Province of Sucumbíos, on March 1, 2008, carried out without the knowledge or prior consent of the Government of Ecuador, since it was a clear violation of Articles 19 and 21 of the OAS Charter.
5. To take note of the full apology for the events that occurred and the pledge by Colombia, expressed by its President to the Rio Group and reiterated by its delegation at this Meeting of Consultation, that they would not be repeated under any circumstances.

65 Twenty-fifth Meeting of Consultation of Ministers of Foreign Affairs OEA/Ser.F/II.25 RC.25/RES.1/08 (17 March 2008).

6. To reiterate the firm commitment of all member states to combat threats to security caused by the actions of irregular groups or criminal organizations, especially those associated with drug trafficking;
7. To instruct the Secretary General to use his good offices to implement a mechanism for observing compliance with this resolution and the restoration of an atmosphere of trust between the two Parties.

The United States issued a reservation to point 4, noting that there was no mention of Colombia's right to self-defense. It was the only member of the OAS to support Colombia's argument that the action had been grounded in law:

> The United States supports this resolution's effort to build confidence between Colombia and Ecuador to address the underlying crisis. The United States is not prepared to agree with the conclusion in operative paragraph 4 in that it is highly fact-specific and fails to take account of other provisions of the OAS and United Nations Charters; in any event, neither this resolution nor CP/RES.930 (1632/08) affects the right of self-defence under Article 22 of the OAS Charter and Article 51 of the U.N. Charter.

In sum, the Permanent Council resolution did *not* demonstrate consensus as to recognition of a state's right to use unilateral force in response to a state's alleged failure to prevent the use of its territory as a safe haven. Indeed, the majority rejected this as illegitimate and in violation of the regional rule of law; the most relevant criteria being the right of territorial integrity and the duty of non-intervention. The OAS members agreed that there is a duty to act in a preventive and responsive manner to terrorism, but the scope of action is left open for other alternatives within a multilateral or bilateral framework.

G. *Institutional Weaknesses*

Ecuador's Minister of Foreign Affairs criticized the wieldy consensus structure of the Permanent Council as a weakness which affected its viability as a conflict resolution mechanism. President Correa also expressed disappointment with the OAS, questioning its viability as a conflict resolution mechanism by specifically pointing to the delays in achieving a resolution (although the lack of veto may have proved beneficial to Ecuador here). He reiterated the idea that the OAS should be replaced by the Rio Group (which does not include the United States) as the primary mechanism for dispute resolution in matters affecting peace and security.

Curiously, the UN Security Council remained silent with respect to the conflict. Colombia did not seek authorization by the UN Security Council prior to the mission, instead opting to conduct a unilateral action based on an expanded notion of self-defence against terrorism without seeking consent by the host state first. This would have been an excellent opportunity for thc UN Security Council to emit a statement indicating a duty to seek such authorization. Instead, the UN Secretary General expressed concern for the situation, urged restraint among the parties, and encouraged the pursuit of dialogue and cooperation.[66] He expressed deferential support of the regional institutional mechanism to attain a peaceful solution, thereby leaving a void in terms of asserting the UN's primary mandate in maintaining peace and security by determining the legitimacy of actions involving breaches of territorial integrity. A particular concern is that the lack of condemnation may be interpreted as acquiescence. On the other hand, the deference to the regional institutions may be viewed as a deliberate strategy to strengthen the collective security system as a whole by permitting the regional organizations which are more proximate to the actors to determine the legality of the mission.[67] It is beneficial to review the mode in which the dispute was resolved in the Rio Group.

H. *Dispute Resolution within the Rio Group*

The Rio Group was established in 1986 as a permanent body for political consultation and cooperation for regional integration. It is currently composed of yearly summit meetings of the Heads of State of Argentina, Brazil, Colombia, Mexico, Uruguay, Venezuela, Chile, Ecuador, Bolivia, Paraguay, Peru, Panama, Costa Rica, Honduras, El Salvador, Nicaragua, Guatemala, and the Dominican Republic. As the United States is not part of the group it serves as an alternative forum which is purely Latin American. In 1997, the Summit produced the "Statement about Adopting Unilateral Measures" which opposed the practice of unilateralism in handling diplomatic matters and reiterated the principle of adhering honestly to multilateralism, noting also in particular the principle of equality of sovereignty, lawful status and mutual respect.

i. Presentation of Post Facto Evidence at the Rio Group Summit

The issue of transparency is contentious in Responsibility to Prevent Terrorism cases. States often act on intelligence which is not subject to public review. Thus, the legitimacy of extra-territorial law enforcement is heavily dependent on post facto presentation of proof by the State to the international community. Hofmeister suggests a standard of "clear and compelling" evidence that a host state is harbouring "terrorists" who have conducted attacks or have definite plans to conduct an attack.[68] In the current case, this took on Hollywood dimensions, as Colombia captured Raúl Reyes' laptop computer, which somehow survived the bombing and shooting. It purportedly contained documents confirming FARC financial support of USD 20,000 to Correa's presidential election run. It also supposedly included evidence of President Chavez's financial support and provision of weapons to the FARC, as well as FARC

66 UN Secretary General statements of 3, 6 and 10 March 2008 addressing Colombia-Ecuador. The Security Council has had a tradition of not debating situations which are covered by the OAS. Christine Gray, *International Law and the Use of Force*, (Oxford 2008) p. 13 at footnote 43.

67 Alain Pellet, 'Legitimacy of Legislative and Executive Actions of International Institutions' in Rudiger Wolfrum & Volker Roben (eds.) *Legitimacy in International Law* 78 (Springer Berlin 2008).

68 Hofmeister, supra note 17 pp. 1–10 at 8.

plans to obtain uranium to make a dirty bomb. These and additional allegations that members of Correa's government had ties to the FARC spread in the international media like wildfire, requiring the embassies to launch immediate damage control.[69] It appeared to be a type of reverse causal link, in which the FARC's financial contributions to President Correa were supposed to impute his attribution for the FARC's cross border attacks. Nonetheless, it could also be interpreted to indicate the FARC's self-sufficiency and ability to conduct terrorist acts irrespective of whether or not they received any state support. The dissemination of the post facto evidence was used by the Colombia government to buttress its decision not to have consulted the Ecuadoran government prior to the raid. It suggested a potential relationship of agency or complicity between the Ecuadoran government and the FARC (as well as a lack of will to pursue the FARC). President Correa repeatedly requested access to the files for verification and response, but he did not receive the evidence immediately even though President Uribe claimed to have turned it over to INTERPOL. The Colombian government stalled in turning over the documents and hard drive to their Ecuadoran counterparts.

President Correa emphatically denied the accusations, characterizing them as "infamy", which he alleged proved more destructive than the bombs.[70] Furthermore, he stated that the contacts between Ecuadoran officials and FARC pursued good faith negotiations for the release of an Ecuadoran hostage (as well as other foreign nationals) held by the FARC. Upon receiving a copy of the FARC documents, he immediately published them on the government's website, confusing intelligence experts who assumed that publication would prove detrimental to his government.

ii. Self-defence v. Violation of Territorial Integrity

a. *Hot Pursuit*

President Uribe originally claimed that the action was one of "hot pursuit" in which the Colombian Army had engaged in combat with the FARC in Colombian territory and had pursued them into Ecuadoran territory. This transplanted the "hot pursuit" principle from its origins in the 1982 UN Convention on the Law of the Sea, Article 111, and the 1958 Convention on the High Seas, Article 23, referring to pursuit of criminals on the high seas to more questionable application on crossing ter-

69 The most contentious example of potential manipulative use of the media was the Colombian newspaper El Tiempo's publication of a photo in which it alleged that Ecuadoran Minister of the Interior, Gustavo Larrea was with Raul Reyes. This later proved to be false, as the man in the photo was actually the Secretary General of the Communist Party of Argentina, Patrico Echegaray. See 'Ecuador: Supuesta foto de ministro con líder FARC es de comunista agentino' in *El Comercio* (17.03.2008).

70 Of interest, a tally of news pieces on the conflict in the international press were largely in favour of Ecuador, resulting in Correa announcing that they had won the "media war". 'Ganamos la batalla informative', press release from the Ecuadoran National Government on 8 March 2008, tallying 2,199 pieces from CNN, Associated Press, Agence France, BBC, Prensa Latina, Miami Herald, etc. in favour, 450 against, and 1,900 neutral.

ritorial frontiers between countries.[71] The problem is that hot pursuit between two countries would normally require normal processes of notification, consultation, and consent.[72]

President Correa correctly determined that there was no situation of hot pursuit as the dead were photographed in their pyjamas/underwear, and thereby could not have retreated to their camp during a situation of conflict as claimed by Colombia. This was confirmed by the testimony of the Mexican and Colombian survivors. President Correa insisted that the action had been obviously premeditated and planned with the assistance of high technology from other allies (i.e. the US).[73] The conclusion appeared to be that action would have been appropriate had the Colombian military contacted the Ecuadoran military for assistance in locating the rebels and capturing them. As Correa demonstrated, the action was not one of hot pursuit, but rather extra-territorial law enforcement/targeted strike. President Uribe then switched tactics and asserted that the action was grounded in self-defence.

b. *R2Prevent Terrorism and Self- Defence*

President Uribe next stated that the action was pursuant to Article 51 of the UN Charter, as well as the duty to combat terrorism derived from UN Security Council resolution 1373. The fight against terrorism, in his opinion, was fully within the framework of democracy. He presented again the concept of "Democratic Security", characterized as being conducted on behalf of all Colombians, regardless of their economic or political position. He considered it an autonomous action conducted by the Colombian people in order to live in democracy and pluralism without terrorists. This recalls the theory of democratic entitlement and utilizes self-determination

71 United Nations Convention on the Law of the Sea, opened for signature on 10 December 1982 and entered into force on 16 November 1994, 1833 UNTS 397, *reprinted in* 21 ILM 1261 (1982) (http://www.UN.org/depts/los). Convention on the High Seas, Apr. 29, 1958, 450 U.N.T.S. 82. See also Reuters, "Somalis Protest After U.S. Missile Attack", in *The New York Times*, March 4, 2008.

72 Indeed, in the OAS Permanent Council, Ecuador's Ambassador Salvador cited the Colombian Ministry of Foreign Affairs press conference in 1996 in which the Colombian government had declared the notion of "hot pursuit" as being illegal under international law, there being no justification for the violation of territorial integrity. Christine Gray notes that South Africa pursued (unsuccessfully) a similar argument of "hot pursuit" when justifying its actions against terrorist operations in Botswana and other neighbouring countries. Gray, supra note 65 at p. 137, citing UN Security Council Resolution 568 (1985) denouncing the application of this doctrine in counter-terrorist operations.

73 President Correa indicated his displeasure at the possible collusion of the United States (which leased the Manta base in Ecuador to monitor narco-trafficking and FARC movement); given that if they had cooperated with Colombia to inform President Uribe as to the whereabouts of the FARC in Ecuador they failed to inform the Ecuadoran authorities, thus dismissing the alternative of a joint capture mission and in fact supporting a unilateral strike. Further complications arose after Correa fired one of his top intelligence officers due to concern that they were operating in cooperation with the CIA, which in turn shared intelligence with Colombia. He further changed the Minister of Defence, purged the intelligence agencies, and announced the intention not to renovate the lease of the Manta base to the U.S.

imagery to discredit the FARC by presenting them as tyrannical actors holding a society hostage through fear induced by terrorist acts. The aim of the action was to defeat the FARC and the targeted killing of Reyes was considered a necessary part of this mission. What is ironic is that in spite of the similarity in symbolism, this is exactly the opposite of the original R2P, which is contingent on the action being in defence of persons subject to atrocities who are *not* the citizens of the responding country. Pursuant to the responsibility to prevent terrorism, instead of liberating a foreign population from a despotic state leader, the state seeks to protect its own people from terrorist acts conducted by repressive non-state actors.

President Uribe offered a two-pronged approach to sovereignty. He agreed that sovereignty is violated by an incursion within the territory of a state, but suggested that it is also violated when the people are subject to attack. He indicated surprise that that the discussion revolved around Colombia's violation of territorial integrity, instead of the violation of sovereignty of the Colombian people and their right to security.

President Uribe testified as to forty attacks by FARC since 2004 on Colombian civilians and security forces; thereby indicating a collective approach to the cumulative effects of the FARC's operations in order to present the expanded notion of having experienced an actual "armed attack" under Article 51. The cumulative acts were cited as meeting the standard of "immediacy", in order to reformulate the proportionality analysis. In addition, the attacks were cited as indicating an expectation of repetition in the near future, thus pointing towards the criteria of "urgency". The repeated nature of the FARC's cross-border attacks were highlighted by President Uribe as suggesting that Ecuador had failed in its due diligence obligation under international law to prevent harm to Colombia, either due to a lack of will or ability to locate and dismantle FARC camps in Ecuadoran territory.[74] Under Proulx' liability mechanism, this would constitute a *prima facie* case of responsibility.[75] Hence, President Uribe embraced a notion of conditional sovereignty based on the state's *de facto* situation of harbouring "terrorists". President Uribe's arguments implied that states are required demonstrate effectiveness in counterterrorism. If not, there is a risk that the aggrieved nation will engage in extra-territorial law enforcement by running the counterterrorism operation itself or with other partners in spite of the violation of the territorial border.

The protection of the civilian population is considered an essential interest of the state which may ground the claim that the use of force was necessary against the grave and imminent peril presented by the presence of the FARC camp in Ecuador.[76] It is undeniable the elimination of FARC's second in command is considered to yield a concrete and direct military advantage to the Colombian Army and thus may be

---

74 Becker supra note 6 at note 311, citing the *Texas Cattle Claims* arbitration, 30 December 1944 in which Mexico was found responsible for raids in the US due to its toleration (and indeed some officials were implicated in the raids).

75 Proulx, supra note 3 at 656.

76 See Draft Articles on Responsibility of State for Internationally Wrongful Acts, Article 25 (International Law Commission 2001).

considered to satisfy the requirement of military necessity.[77] In order to satisfy the international public law concept of necessity, the Colombian government insisted that there was no alternative of arrest, ostensibly due to the excessive danger/risk of failure of such operation. As the mission was limited in duration and scope (with forces withdrawing immediately after accomplishing their mission) the action was presented as proportional to the risk of further terrorist attacks by the FARC. Additionally, Colombia had to demonstrate that the killing was not retributive but rather preventive. Support for the preventive view was provided by the revelations from the FARC computer documents that included alleged plans for future attacks on installations and acquisition of uranium to build "dirty bombs". The Colombian Ministry of Defence announced that based on the information contained within the computer, they were able to locate 30 kilos of uranium obtained by the FARC with supposed intention to sell on the black market, thereby linking the FARC to WMD and drawing the analysis clearly within Stromseth's paradigm to legitimize military action.[78] Nevertheless, the low grade quality of the uranium indicated that it was not of immediate threat.

iii. Rebuttal of the Presumption of Responsibility by Ecuador

According to Proulx, the "host" state is expected to have opportunity to refute the presumption of responsibility.[79] President Correa asserted that his government was willing to prevent FARC activities within Ecuador, but was unable due to lack of control of the border territories. He indicated that indeed the FARC's transgression of borders was a serious problem, one that Ecuador had to pay for in the form of costly maintenance of a large number of forces at the borders and loss of life. The government simply lacked knowledge of the presence of the FARC in that specific area, given the enormous size of the territorial border (720 km) rendering control difficult and costly.

President Correa rejected that he provided a safe haven for the FARC, as he claimed to have deployed 50,000 troops to the border for patrols and spent 100,000 USD per year on border control. Additionally, the rough and dense terrain and the limits of the Ecuadoran army indeed appeared to reduce the degree of culpa of the government. It faced significant challenges in effectuating border control which were not indicative of bad faith. Further, President Correa dismissed insinuations that his political ideology indicated a lack of will to dismantle the FARC's use of the border territory as a safe haven. He stated that in 2004 there was another regime in Ecuador that enjoyed a closer relationship with the US, but which similarly proved unable to prevent the FARC from entering the territory. Indeed, most of the cross-border raids occurred during his predecessor's regime. The FARC conducted attacks irrespective of which government was in power. State support appears not to be a decisive causal factor when considering the FARC attacks; hence it is difficult to hold Ecuador responsible.

---

77 See Nils Melzer, *Targeted Killing in International Law* (Oxford University Press 2008) pp. 397–398.

78 See: http://www.mindefensa.gov.co/index.php?page=181&id=6867.

79 Proulx, supra note 3.

As characterized by Dinstein, as long as Ecuador did not "knowingly" allow its territory to be used as a base for terrorism, it bears no responsibility for the FARC actions.[80] Furthermore, even if Ecuador is considered to have known about the FARC's use of its territory, it is excused from responsibility if it exercised due diligence (taking all reasonable measures) to prevent the attacks or to apprehend and punish the FARC after such attacks.[81] Becker sets forth that the due diligence standard in this area should be flexible, depending on the capacity of the State and the magnitude of the terrorist threat.[82] Indeed, the U.S. Department of State Country Report on Terrorism in Ecuador highlights that the government responded to the regular crossing of the FARC and the establishment of training camps in Ecuadoran territory by shifting troops to the northern border region for patrols which resulted in dismantling of over 30 FARC camps.[83] President Correa reiterated that they dismantled 47 FARC camps in 2007, thereby implying a fulfilment of a due diligence standard. The inability to prevent the use of Ecuadoran territory as a safe haven appears to be in spite of the Ecuadoran government's genuine efforts to pursue preventive measures and appears largely a result of the difficult topography of the border region and the limitation of resources, capacity, and even high-technology to locate the FARC. The government is described as strengthening its dialogue with Colombia and working closely with the US to promote lawful economic activity in the North. In short, the report provides a picture of a partner in counter-terrorism.

iv. Duty to Consult/Give Opportunity to Comply with the Responsibility to Prevent Terrorism

President Correa warned the President of the Dominican Republic (who was the host of the Rio Group Summit Meeting) to beware; should the FARC appear there, the Colombians would bomb the Dominican Republic. President Uribe quickly responded that they would not bomb; rather they would seek the cooperation of the Dominican authorities to apprehend the FARC. Indeed, Garwood-Gowers indicates that in cases in which a host state is willing but unable to prevent terrorist groups from seeking safe haven in their territory, the victim state should seek to obtain the host state's consent to intervene on its territory in order to target the "terrorists", thus "the weakness in the new attribution requirement is unlikely to pose significant problems in practice".[84] In like manner, Becker concludes that "respect for territorial integrity, as well as the principle of necessity, would usually demand that the host State be given the opportunity to comply with its obligations before a resort to defensive action."[85]

80 Dinstein, supra note 34 at 244 citing the *Corfu Channel* case (Merits) (1949) ICJ Rep. 4, 22.

81 Ibid.

82 Becker, supra note 6 at 142.

83 U.S. Department of State, Country Reports on Terrorism: Ecuador (Office of the Coordinator for Counterterrorism 30 April 2007).

84 Garwood-Gowers, supra note 21.

85 Becker, supra note 6 at 163. See also Michael N. Schmitt, 'Responding to Transnational Terrorism under the Jus ad Bellum: A Normative Framework' in Michael Schmitt & Jelena

Of particular significance is that President Correa emphasized that Colombia acted in bad faith when conducting the extra-territorial law enforcement. This is because President Uribe did not give Ecuador the option of cooperating in a joint operation, as President Correa was not consulted prior to the mission or given the intelligence regarding the presence of the FARC camp. President Correa was especially disturbed because he stated that he had actually spoken with President Uribe hours before the mission. Thus, there was clear opportunity for such consultation. Instead, President Uribe did not mention the plan throughout the conversation, but rather telephoned him again the next morning to announce the events *post facto*. President Correa noted that he had expressed condolences for any Colombian loss in the action and had immediately dispatched helicopters to the site to provide cover for Colombian agents who claimed that they were under attack. The helicopter personnel reported that when they arrived they assumed coverage positions, but there were no attacking forces. Rather, they felt duped into facilitating the withdrawal of Colombian personnel from the area. This was presented as proof that the government had been willing to collaborate in counter-terrorist operations if called upon, and in fact did so immediately.

President Uribe responded that he did not inform President Correa of the action because he was not sure it would succeed, that they had previously failed five times, and more seriously, that "they had not had the cooperation of the government of President Correa in the fight against terrorism."[86] In short, President Uribe implied that consultation would have jeopardized the entire operation. It was clear that the Colombian government considered consultation to carry a risk of leak to the FARC, thereby potentially enabling Reyes to escape before the raid was conducted. The irony for him is that had he not notified President Correa at all, there was little chance that he would have found out about the event given the dense topography in the border region. The entire crisis was a result of President Uribe's decision to provide notice to President Correa *post facto*.

v. Colombia's State Responsibility to Prevent Terrorism

President Correa insisted that the focus of state responsibility was misplaced as it was the *Colombian government's* failure to prevent the FARC from crossing from Colombian territory to its neighbours which was the root of the problem. Whereas Ecuador stationed 20% of its troops (7,000) in the Northern border, Colombia only had 2% of its troops (800) stationed in the North.[87] Ecuador has received over

Pejic, *International Law and Armed Conflict: Exploring the Faultlines, Essays in Honour of Yoram Dinstein*, (Martinus Nijhoff 2007) p. 182: "The victim State must make a demand on the 'host' State to satisfactorily cure the situation, and the latter must be afforded sufficient opportunity to do so, at least to an extent consistent with the realities the victim State's effective defence."

86 Speech of President Alvaro Uribe before the Heads of State of the Rio Group, March 7, 2008.

87 "Canciller ecuatoriana denuncia campaña mediática en contra de su gobierno", *La Hora* 18 March 2008.

40,000 Colombian refugees since 2000, signifying that it has the highest percentage of refugees in all of Latin America.[88] Ecuador called upon Colombia to assume its own responsibility in failing to contain the FARC along the borders and recognize that Ecuador is a victim, not a collaborator, in the Colombian conflict.[89] These arguments are sound and underscore the difficulty of assigning blame in responsibility to prevent terrorism in border areas. As responsibility may be joint, the appropriate solution would require cooperation.

vi. Towards Regional Rule of Law

The verbal exchanges between the Presidents of Colombia, Venezuela, Ecuador and Nicaragua grew heated, with Uribe being accused of being a liar, militarist, imperial puppet, paramilitary, and guilty of genocide and massacres. President Chavez was accused of providing refuge to the head of the FARC. President Uribe threatened to file a complaint against President Chavez with the International Criminal Court (ICC) on account of complicity with "genocidal terrorism".[90]

President Cristina Fernández de Kirchner of Argentina called for rejection of unilateralism from attaining legitimacy within the region, rather indicating that a restoration of multilateralism was the only path towards achieving real security. She recognized Colombia's right to fight the FARC but called for the rejection of a doctrine of unilateral action, indicating that no country could engage "*manu militari*" without consulting the other country.[91] Moreover, she called for respect for principle of legality in conjunction with recognition of Latin America as a unilateral-free zone, which she characterized as constituting the *patrimony* of Latin American foreign policy. Multilateralism was characterized as the key protection against vigilante justice. Of most importance, she emphasized that the pursuit of security is contingent on the use of legality to combat illegality, especially when such action is being conducted in the name of democracy, human rights, and the rights of peoples. This was a direct response to President Uribe's classification of the strike as being an example of "Democratic Security". She noted "Terrorism is not fought with massive violations of human rights; illegality is not fought with illegality, but rather with much more legality". Furthermore, she underlined that respect for the law leads to international, regional and national political legitimacy. President Fernández's speech was particularly noteworthy, given Argentina's history during the Dirty War against subversion

---

88 UNHCR, Country Operations Plan 2008–2009: Ecuador.

89 Indeed, in March 27, 2002 Ecuador protested Colombian cross- border incursions in which they killed persons identified by Colombia as "guerrillas". In addition, Ecuador filed a complaint in the UN Human Rights Council and in the ICJ against Colombia for its fumigation of Ecuadoran territory. See: http://www.icj-cij.org/docket/files/138/14629.pdf?PHPSESSID=c8c344f9d53f366a41535106a38b18bf.

90 On the possibility of qualifying terrorism as crimes against humanity, see Vincent-Joel Proulx, 'Rethinking the Jurisdiction of the International Criminal Court in the Post September 11th Era: Should Acts of Terrorism Qualify as Crimes Against Humanity' in *American University International Law Review*, vol. 19 (2004) p. 1009.

91 Speech by President Cristina Fernandez de Kirchner in the Summit of the Rio Group on March 7, 2008.

in the 70's and the sacrifice of the rule of law during that period in the name of "security".[92] According to Fernández, the fight against subversion requires greater adherence to the rule of law and the institutional structures which define it, i.e. the UN and the OAS.

vii. Resolution by the Rio Group

President Uribe expressed his country's commitment to peace and the OAS Charter. He asked for forgiveness for the deployment of helicopters into Ecuadoran territory and promised never to repeat such action. President Chavez and President Correa reaffirmed that they would combat terrorism and President Uribe promised not to file a complaint against President Chavez with the ICC. On March 7th 2008, The Heads of State and Government of the Rio Group issued a Declaration of the XX Summit meeting on the recent events between Ecuador and Colombia which denounced (but did not officially *condemn*) the violation of the territorial integrity of Ecuador:

> We denounce this violation of the territorial integrity of Ecuador, and we therefore reaffirm that the territory of a state is inviolable and may not be the object, even temporarily, of military occupation or of other measures of force taken by another State, directly or indirectly on any grounds.

It acknowledged the full apology of President Alvaro Uribe for the violations and his pledge of non-repetition, under any circumstances, in compliance with Articles 19 and 21 of the OAS Charter. It recalled the principles of respect for sovereignty, abstention from the threat or use of force, non-interference in the internal affairs of other states, and commitment to peaceful settlement of disputes. It also reiterated firm commitment to combating security threats emanating from irregular groups or organised criminal groups, in particular those linked to narco-trafficking, which Colombia considers to be terrorists. The Latin American leaders welcomed the peaceful resolution of the conflict and the apology, but expressed concern for the destabilization of the region. President Correa declared that this marked "a new era in Latin American diplomacy, in which an extremely grave problem was resolved in a peaceful, principled manner within a presidential summit … in which principles, justice and international law prevail."[93] Hence, the Rio Group confirmed the inviolability of territorial sovereignty, clearly declaring that counterterrorism initiatives are legitimate but may not trump the core principles of the international rule of law.

---

92 See *Nunca Mas*, report of the National Commission on the Disappearance of Persons, at ⟨http://www.nuncamas.org/index2.htm⟩. See Also Thomas C. Wright, *State Terrorism In Latin America: Chile, Argentina and International Human Rights* (Rowman & Littlefield Pub. 2007).

93 Nicaragua retains a maritime boundary dispute with Colombia and the case is being processed in the International Court of Justice. President Ortega asked President Uribe to remove his naval vessels. President Uribe refused, noting the importance of combating narco-trafficking in the region, but promised to respect the ICJ's orders and final decision, thereby permitting restoration of normal relations between the two states within a record-breaking 24 hours.

V. Assessment of Violations of International Human Rights and Customary International Humanitarian Law

Although the OAS and Rio Group issued resolutions denouncing the violation of territorial integrity, they did not address particular violations against persons. The restoration of diplomatic relations between Ecuador and Colombia was delayed, in part because of unresolved issues regarding the need for further investigation of allegations regarding specific acts of violence during the operation. The extra-territorial targeting of alleged "terrorists"/rebels presents a gray area in international law, as it is unclear whether the standards of human rights or international or non-international armed conflicts are applicable.[94]

A. *International Humanitarian Law*

According to the United Nations, the war in Colombia conducted between the National Armed Forces and the dissident FARC constitutes a non-international conflict in which Protocol II and Common Article 3 are applicable.[95] Protocol II, Article 1, describes a non-international armed conflict as occurring between a state's "armed forces and dissident armed forces or other organized armed groups which, under responsible command, exercise such control over a part of its territory as to enable them to carry out sustained and concerted military operations and to implement this Protocol." In this author's view, the FARC may be considered an organized armed group under responsible command which exercises control over sufficient areas of Colombian territory in order to conduct sustained military operations. However, it does not respect the provisions of Protocol II and it engages in terrorist acts.[96] As second in command of the FARC, Reyes may be considered a member of an organized armed group who may be targeted with lethal force. President Uribe supported recognition of classification of the FARC as "unlawful combatants" who were lawful targets for attack for the duration of the armed conflict between the FARC and the Colombian State.[97] Suffice is reference to the generic term "combatant" as

94 See W. Jason Fisher, 'Targeted Killing, Norms, and International Law', in *Columbia Journal of Transnational Law* vol. 45 (2007) 711.

95 U.N. Econ. & Soc. Council [ECOSOC], Commission on Human Rights, Report of the United Nations High Commission for Human Rights on the Situation of Human Rights in Columbia, [paragraph] 3, U.N. Doc. E/CN.4/2006/9 (May 16, 2006).

96 Pursuant to this standard, the targeting of Reyes may considered appropriate given the fact that as second in command of the FARC, Reyes was continually engaged in actions that constituted a direct threat to the Colombian Army as well as death or injury to the Colombian citizenry. Further his leadership may be considered as forming an integral part of the conduct of hostilities.

97 Article 13 (3) sets forth the standard for targeting of civilians directly participating in hostilities: "Civilians shall enjoy the protection afforded by this part, unless and for such time as they take a direct part in hostilities." If one were to consider Reyes a civilian, according to Cassese, he would only be able to be targeted while actually engaged in combat, while carrying arms openly during a military deployment preceding an attack, or (exceptionally) if he was manifestly concealing explosives that he intended to use against

included within the ICRC Study on Customary International Law (albeit noting that the FARC would not be recognized as enjoying the privileges associated with such status) or "fighter" as included in the San Remo Manual on Non-International Armed Conflicts.[98] The cross-border facet of the operation supports reference to customary international humanitarian law.

i. Proportionality, Distinction, and Precaution

Proportionality is a central element for the evaluation of the legitimacy of actions involving the use of force. The principle of proportionality is central within the law of war. It forbids striking even legitimate targets, if the attack is likely to lead to injury of civilians which would be excessive in relation to the concrete and direct military advantage anticipated. This principle is contained in article 51(5)(B) of *The First Protocol*, which according to the ICRC Study constitutes a customary rule and hence may be applied within the context of non-international conflicts as well.[99] The Inter American Court has held that the planning of a military raid should include safeguards to guarantee the proportionality and necessity of the force used.[100] Proportionality is complemented by the customary norms of distinction, which requires attacks to be directed only against combatants (codified in Articles 48, 51(2) and 52 (2) of *The First Protocol* & Article 13(3) *of the Second Protocol*), and precaution, which requires care to be taken to avoid incidental loss of civilian life or injury (codified in Article 57 (1) of the *First Protocol*).[101] The Inter-American Commission of Human Rights' Report

enemy civilians or combatants and did not comply with a summons to demonstrate his innocence. If Reyes was only planning or preparing an attack, he should have been subject to arrest for prosecution. Lethal force would be appropriate if there was no alternative and arrest was rendered impossible. Cassese, supra note 29 at 421–422. Others advocate recognition of a right to target individuals conducting, planning, or dispatching others to commit terrorist acts in order to negate the revolving door of individuals alternating between civilian and combatant status. See Fisher, supra note 94 at 725. See the Inter-American Commission of Human Rights, *Report on Terrorism and Human Rights*, OEA/Ser.L/V/II.116 Doc. 5 rev. 1 corr. 22 October 2002, at para 69, available at: http://www.cidh.oas.org/Terrorism/Eng/toc.htm. It suggests that once a person actively engages in hostilities he cannot revert back or alternate with civilian status.

98 Jean-Marie Henckaerts & Louise Doswald-Beck, *Customary International Humanitarian Law: Volume I: Rules* (Cambridge/ICRC 2005) p. 3, Rule 1. See also David Kretzmer, 'Targeted Killing of Suspected Terrorists: Extra-Judicial Executions or Legitimate Means of Defence?' in *European Journal of International Law* vol. 16 No. 2 (2005) p. 198. Similarly, according to the San Remo Manual on Non-International Armed Conflicts, for this discussion, it is sufficient to utilize the term "fighters", thereby highlighting the characterization of Reyes and the FARC as not being subject to protection accorded civilians when distinguishing targets for lethal attack. Michael N. Schmitt, Charles H.B. Garraway, & Yoram Dinstein, *The Manual on the Law of Non-International Armed Conflict* (International Institute of Humanitarian Law 2006).

99 Henckaerts & Doswald-Beck, supra note 98 at p. 46, Rule 14.

100 Inter American Court of Human Rights, *Case of Zambrano Vélez et al. v. Ecuador*. Merits, Reparations and Costs. Judgment of July 4, 2007. Series C No. 166 para. 77.

101 Henkaerts & Doswald-Beck, supra note 98 at p. 3, Rule 1, and p. 51, Rule 15. See also Inter-American Commission of Human Rights, *La Tablada* Case 11.137 (Argentina),

on Terrorism and Human Rights recommended the following standard regarding distinction and precaution within the context of armed conflict:

> In situations of armed conflict, member states should ensure that their armed forces comply with applicable rules and principles of international humanitarian law, in particular the requirements that armed forces distinguish between military objectives and civilians and civilian objects and launch attacks only against the former, and take precautions so as to avoid or minimize loss of civilian life or damage to civilian property incidental or collateral to attacks on legitimate military targets.[102]

As previously mentioned, the Colombian government deemed it risky to consult with their Ecuadoran counterparts for cooperation in a capture mission, given the apparent perception that the Correa government supported or acquiesced in the FARC's use of Ecuadoran territory for camps. The implication was that consultation would result in the escape of Reyes. Further, deployment of special forces without prior bombing in conjunction with orders to apprehend Reyes (as opposed to kill) would have likely resulted in more losses to those forces as well as possible failure. The choice of military strike indicates the selection of a more effective means of eliminating Reyes.

Nevertheless, bombs do not discriminate between civilians and combatants, and President Uribe was incorrect in assuming that there were no civilians. Colombia did not present evidence of exhaustion of non-forcible means of removing the FARC, rather arguing that military force was the only reasonable way of removing them. Thus, there is a grey area when determining whether an assessment is conducted on grounds of convenience as opposed to necessity. There is concern that Colombia may have failed to uphold the standard of precaution, if their intelligence failed to identify the presence of civilians.[103] On the other hand, it is possible that the Colombian authorities conducted a precautionary analysis, if they were aware of the presence of civilians, determined that Raúl Reyes was a high value military target, and concluded that the level of collateral damage was not excessive.

ii. Collateral Damage & Direct Participation in Hostilities

President Uribe insisted that they did not bomb the Ecuadoran people; rather they targeted a "terrorist camp" in the jungle in which there allegedly were no civilians. Hence, he opined that the attack was limited and proportional. Unlike targeted killings in other regions of the world, the action in Ecuador did not result in substantial civilian casualties. However, the claim that there were no civilians was later subject to dispute. Among the dead were four Mexican university students (Juan González, Fernando Franco, Natalia Velásquez and Soren Avilés) and one Ecuadoran

---

OEA/Ser/L/V/II.97, Doc. 38, (October 30, 1997) paras. 64, 133,443 and 810. See also Article 13 (1) of the *Second Protocol* granting the right of civilians to general protection against danger arising from a military operation.

102 Inter American Commission of Human Rights, supra note 97, chapter IV B 5.

103 Henckaerts & Doswald-Beck, supra note 98 at 51–62, Rules 15–19.

citizen (Franklin Aisalia). Under customary international humanitarian law, civilians enjoy protection against attack unless and for such time as they take a direct part in hostilities.[104]

There was also one Mexican survivor, Lucia Morett. It was unclear in what capacity the Mexicans were visiting the camps. Morett claimed that they had attended a Bolivarian conference in Ecuador and sought to visit the FARC in connection to their university studies addressing social movements. Some allegations arose that the students sympathized with the FARC ideology and may have been interested in disseminating this abroad. They suffered what Michael Schmitt would deem to be the price of mixing with targets.[105] Indeed Colombia's Minister of Defence Juan Manuel Santos declared that "a terrorist camp is a legitimate military objective" and "anyone who is in a terrorist camp … exposes oneself to the highest risk, irrespective of whether or not (s)he is a guerilla."[106] President Uribe classified the Mexicans as "terrorists"; President Calderon of Mexico rejected this, calling for further investigation.[107]

The Ecuadoran civilian was originally presented by the Colombian authorities as a member of the FARC, Julián Conrado, until Aisalia's parents recognized the footage of the body in the media and flew to Bogota to reclaim his remains. He is believed to have assisted the FARC in entering Ecuadoran territory and establishing the camp.[108]

---

104 Ibid at p. 19, Rule 6.

105 Schmitt calls for liberal approach to interpreting civilian participation stating that this would create "… an incentive for civilians to remain as distant from the conflict as possible – in doing so they can better avoid being charged with participation in the conflict and are less liable to being directly targeted" Michael N. Schmitt, 'Direct Participation in Hostilities and 21st Century Armed Conflict', in H. FISCHER (ed.), *Crisis Management and Humanitarian Protection: Festshrift fur Dieter Fleck* 505–509 (2004). Certainly, the raid made this point very clearly.

106 See 'La relacion de Ecuador con Colombia mas tensa' in *Rosario Net*, available at: http://www.rosarionet.com.ar/rnet/internacionales/notas.vsp?nid=37731.

107 See "Calderon pidió menos prejuicios por los mexicanos muertos en Ecuador", (16 April 2008) in AdMundo.com, available at: http://www.adnmundo.com/contenidos/politica/calderon-uribe-farc-terroristas-mexicanos-pi-160408.html. It should be noted that the Israeli Supreme Court has considered those who spread propaganda to be engaged in indirect participation, and hence should not be subject to a targeted killing. See HCJ 769/02, 14 December 2006: *The Public Committee against Torture in Israel & Palestinian Society for the Protection of Human Rights and the Environment* versus *The Government of Israel; The Prime Minister of Israel; The Minister of Defense; The Israel Defense Forces; The Chief of the General Staff of the Israel Defense Forces & Shurat HaDin – Israel Law Center and 24 others*, Judgment paragraph 35. Lucia Morett's father, a university professor, emphatically denied his daughter's classification as a terrorist, characterizing her as a university student of a particular ideology with obvious bad judgment. Nevertheless, a complaint against Morett on charges of terrorism (accused of being FARC's operative in Mexican) was filed by José Antonio Ortega, president of the *Consejo Ciudadano para la Seguridad Pública y la Justicia Penal*.

108 President Correa was outraged to find that his own intelligence officers were aware of the Aisalia's assistance to the FARC, but chose to share the information with their Colombian counterparts rather than the President. This prompted a full scale cleansing of the intelligence and defence agencies in Ecuador.

According the Inter-American Commission of human rights, "direct participation in hostilities" is defined as "acts of violence which pose an immediate threat of actual harm to the adverse party."[109] The establishment of direct participation in hostilities in this case is strained because although the action may qualify as supporting the FARC; it is arguable that it may not qualify as having an immediate or direct causal link to a concrete military threat to the Colombian army, or death, injury, or destruction to persons or property protected against direct act.[110] Nor may it necessarily form an integral part of hostilities so as to justify removal of protection rights.[111] Thus, it may fail in terms of meeting the criteria of threshold of harm and direct causality, because the action does not aim to carry out a concrete hostile act. Rather it may be viewed as general support, unless the camp is viewed as constituting a strategic position from which to carry out attacks, which is precisely Colombia's view.[112]

Furthermore, according to Cassese, should he be viewed as having participated directly in hostilities, then the use of lethal of force against him after he served his function as guide to the campsite may be viewed as illegitimate as he was no longer directly participating in hostilities at the time of the targeting.[113] Yet, this is an issue of intense debate within IHL, beyond the scope of this chapter.[114] It must be emphasized that attempts to expand the notion of direct participation to include non-confrontational acts, and similarly broaden the temporal application, narrows the range of civilians who are entitled to protection against deliberate, indiscriminate and disproportionate attacks.

An additional point is that President Correa raised an objection that Aisalia was allegedly killed with a knife wounds to the throat, rather than due to gun shots or projectile fragments from the bombs (as claimed by the Colombian government), thereby highlighting the specific violence on the part of the Colombians.[115]

Finally, there were two Colombian peasant women, Martha Pérez Gutiérrez and Doris Bohórquez Torres, who were injured but survived because they claimed to have been forced to sleep separately in the animal pens. They alleged to have been kidnapped from their villages and forced to cook and care for the animals. If

---

109 Inter-American Commission on Human Rights, Third Report on Human Rights in Colombia, (1999) at 811.

110 ICRC, Third Expert Meeting, on the Notion of Direct Participation in Hostilities, Summary Report, October 23–25, 2005, available at: http://www.icrc.org/Web/eng/siteengo.nsf/htmlall/participation-hostilitiesihl-311205/$File/Direct_participation_in_hostilities_2005_eng.pdf. But see *Public Committee Against Torture* case, supra note 106 at paragraph 37 including guides as direct participants subject to targeting.

111 Ibid.

112 The Israeli Supreme Court in the *Public Commitee* Case supra note 106 at para. 37 includes guides as direct participants.

113 Cassese, supra note 29 p. 421. See also Marco Sassòli, 'Use and Abuse of the Laws of War in the "War on Terrorism"' in *Law & Inequality* vol. 24 (2004) p. 195.

114 See *IHL and Civilian Participation in Hostilities in the OPT*, Policy Brief, Harvard University (October 2007), examining the specific acts approach, the affirmative disengagement approach, the membership approach, and the limited membership approach.

115 Mario Wainfeld, 'Ganar las elecciones no es ganar al poder', *Pagina 12* (22 June 2008), available at: http://www.forumdesalternatives.org/ES/readarticle.php?article_id=4959.

true, they would then be viewed as victims of the FARC, entitled to protection. The official position of the Colombian government at present is that they are "terrorists". It is essential to point out that even if the women chose to serve the FARC, their engagement in cooking and caring for animals would not serve to qualify them as directly participating in hostilities. This is because the activity of cooking would not meet the threshold of harm to the enemy or civilians, nor would cooking have a direct link to such harm, and finally cooking is not considered to be designed to negatively affect the enemy such that there would be a belligerent nexus.[116]

iii. Perfidy, Murder and Duties to Assist and Evacuate the Wounded

President Correa criticized the Colombian forces for not assisting the wounded. The eye-witness testimony of the sole Mexican survivor claimed that the soldiers called upon the FARC and the other persons present to surrender, promising them safety, only to shoot them.[117] Further, according to the testimony, those who called for help given their injuries were also allegedly shot under direct orders. This would constitute perfidy and, in relation to the injured persons, murder of persons *hors de combat*.[118] Indeed, the Mexican survivor stated that the only reason she was spared was her gender (although some women also died in the strike). Armed forces have a duty to protect all civilians, irrespective of sex. Lucia Morett described being threatened, interrogated, video-taped, photographed, and sexually harassed by the Army which allegedly also forced her to urinate on herself.[119] She indicated that they later cleaned her wounds and changed her soiled clothes. Upon hearing the sound of Ecuadoran helicopters, the Colombian army then abandoned Morett and escaped. Under customary IHL there is a duty to collect and evacuate the wounded, not to abandon them.[120] The Colombian forces alleged that they determined that the incoming Ecuadoran forces would be able to care for the wounded and transfer them to Ecuadoran hospitals. It is also possible that the Colombian forces were concerned about ensuring their safe withdrawal from Ecuador in order to avoid arrest by the Ecuadoran authorities. The seriousness of the alleged transgressions indicates that there exist grounds for further investigation.

116 See Michael N. Schmitt, *Civilians at War: Deconstructing the 21st Century Battlefield*, Summary Chatham House International Law Discussion Group (1 November 2007).

117 Video interview available at: http://video.google.com/videoplay?docid=683903971086669909.

118 Henckaerts & Doswald-Beck, supra note 98 at pp. 211–226, Rule 65 and p. 311, Rule 89. Perfidy is defined in Additional Protocol 1, article 37 (1) as "acts inviting the confidence of an adversary to lead him to believe that he is entitled to, or obliged to accord, protection under the rules of international law applicable in armed conflict, with intent to betray that confidence." See also Rome Statute of the International Criminal Court, Article 8, prohibiting killing of civilians.

119 Ibid at 315, Rule 90.

120 Ibid at 396, Rule 109.

B. *International Human Rights – Violation of the Right to Life*

President Uribe characterized Raúl Reyes as a "terrorist", thereby signalling the possible application of the law enforcement regime as opposed to international humanitarian law. The legality of law enforcement actions are measured within the framework of human rights.[121] All persons, including "terrorists" enjoy the right to life. The right to life is contained in Article 1 of the American Declaration of Human Rights and Article 4 of the American Convention of Human Rights and is considered jus cogens.[122] According to the Inter-American Court it may not be suspended or arbitrarily deprived even in a time of war, public danger or other emergency that threatens the independence or security of the state.[123] The use of force must reflect a balance between the means utilized and the legitimate aim of the state of achieving security for its population.[124] The Inter-American Commission of Human Rights has set forth a framework for measuring the legality of actions conducted to protect a population against the threat of violence:

> In situations where a state's population is threatened by violence, the state has the right and obligation to protect the population against such threats and in doing so may use lethal force in certain situations. This includes, for example, the use of lethal force by law enforcement officials where strictly unavoidable to protect themselves or other persons from imminent threat of death or serious injury, or to otherwise maintain law and order where strictly necessary and proportionate ... Unless such exigencies exist, however the use of lethal force may constitute an arbitrary deprivation of life or a summary execution; that is to say, the use of lethal force must be necessary as having been justified by a state's right to protect the

121 Indeed, President Uribe used the term "sinister terrorist" in reference to Reyes a total of thirteen times during his speech at the Rio Group.

122 American Declaration of Human Rights, Article 1: "Every human being has the right to life, liberty and the security of his person." American Convention of Human Rights, Article 4: "Every person has the right to have his life respected. This right shall be protected by law and, in general, from the moment of conception. No one shall be arbitrarily deprived of his life."

123 See Inter-American Court of Human Rights, *Case of the Pueblo Bello Massacre v. Colombia*. Merits, Reparations and Costs. Judgment of January 31, 2006. Series C No. 159 para. 119. See also *Case of Montero Arangueren et. al. (Detention Center of Catia) v. Venezuela*, Preliminary Objection, Merits, Reparations and Costs. Judgment of July 5, 2006. Series C No. 150 para 63. See also *Case of Baldeón-García v. Peru*. Merits, Reparations and Costs. Judgment of April 06, 2006. Series C No. 147 para. 82.

124 In comparison to the European Court of Human Rights, see also William Abresch, 'A Human Rights Law of Internal Conflict: The European Court of Human Rights in Chechnya', *European Journal of International Law*, Vol. 16 No. 4 (2005) pp. 741–767. The European Court has held that the lethal force should be a last resort, it must be no more than absolutely necessary and it must be strictly proportionate to the achievement of the permitted aims in Article 2(2) of ECHR. See *Isayeva, Yusupova and Bazayeva v Russia*, ECtHR, App Nos. 57947–49/00 (24 Feb. 2005) at 884 cited by Christine Byron, 'A Blurring of the Boundaries: The Application of International Humanitarian Law by International Human Rights Bodies', *Virginia Journal of International Law*, Vol. 47, (Summer 2007) p. 839 at 855.

> security of all ... In such circumstances, the state may resort to the use of force only against individuals that threaten the security of all, and therefore the state may not use force against civilians who do not present such a threat. The state must distinguish between the civilians and those individuals who constitute the threat. Indiscriminate uses of force may as such constitute violations of Article 4 of the Convention and Article 1 of the Declaration ... Finally as specified by the Inter-American Court and the Commission, the amount of force used must be justified by the circumstances, for the purpose of, for example, self-defence or neutralizing or disarming the individuals involved in a violent confrontation. Excessive force, or disproportionate force by law enforcement officials that result in the loss of life may therefore amount to arbitrary deprivations of the loss of life.[125]

As noted by the Inter-American Court of Human Rights: "[R]egardless of the seriousness of certain actions and the culpability of the perpetrators of certain crimes, the power of the state is not unlimited, nor may the state resort to any means to attain its ends."[126] The state's fight against criminality is to be conducted "within the limits and pursuant to the procedures that permit both the preservation of public security as well as the fundamental rights of human beings."[127] This necessitates review of whether the Colombian authorities planned and controlled the operation to minimize the risk to loss of life and whether they were negligent. It appears that Colombia determined that the presence of the camp in an isolated border region would minimize civilian casualties. Review of the planning requires an independent investigation recovery of probative material, interview of Colombian officials, the soldiers/police participating in the operation, identification and interview of witnesses, determination of the exact cause of death in autopsy, as well as examination of intelligence reports, photographs, and recordings.

The Inter-American Commission of Human Rights highlighted a strict necessity standard for use of force in law enforcement:

> In situations short of armed conflict, member states should ensure that law enforcement officials comply with the basic principles governing the use of force, including the requirement that lethal force may only be used where strictly unavoidable to protect themselves or other people from imminent threat of death.[128]

Proulx calls for an absolute ban on targeted killing, based on clear violations of due process norms and the right to fair trial, as well as denial of opportunity for

125 Inter-American Commission of Human Rights, supra note 97 at paras. 87–92. It cites its case *Juan Carlos Abella v. Argentina*, Case No. 11.137, Report No. 55/97, OEA/Ser.L/V/II .95 Doc.7 rev at 271 (1997) paras. 204,218, & 245 identifying the killing of individuals who have been involved in attacks on military barracks but surrendered a violation of Article 4.

126 Inter-American Court of Human Rights, *Case of Velasquez Rodriguez v. Honduras*, Merits Judgment of July 29, 1988 Series C, No. 4, 1, para. 154.

127 Inter-American Court of Human Rights, *Case of the Miguel Castro-Castro Prison v. Peru.* Merits, Reparations and Costs. Judgment of November 25, 2006. Series C No. 160 at para. 240.

128 Inter-American Commission of Human Rights, supra note 97 at Chapter IV B 4.

"unpriviled combatantants" to surrender or lay down arms.[129] This would hinder mistake, provide an opportunity to present a defence and prove one's innocence, respond to evidence, and seek judicial review.[130]

In sum, at the regional level, it is recognized that the use of force is to be limited by the principles of proportionality, necessity and humanity. The Inter-American Court has defined these criteria as such:

> Excessive or disproportionate use of force by law enforcement officials that result in the loss of life may therefore amount to arbitrary deprivation of life. The principle of necessity justifies only those measures of military violence which are not forbidden by international law and which are relevant and proportionate to ensure the prompt subjugation of the enemy with the least possible cost of human and economic resources. The principle of humanity complements and inherently limits the principle of necessity by forbidding those measures of violence which are not necessary (i.e. relevant and proportionate) to the achievement of a definitive military advantage.[131]

Doswald-Beck concludes that the Inter-American case law indicates that where there is a threat to life or link to serious offences, the use of force would not be considered a violation if the opportunity of arrest would be contingent on such use of force.[132] She relates that the regular practice of the Colombian army is precisely to bomb FARC camps even when the rebels are not actively involved in hostilities. Doswald-Beck points out that this is regarded as legitimate, even from a human rights perspective, as "it is understood that rebels who are organized, armed and assembled cannot be arrested."[133] Thus, the use of military force against Reyes may deemed legitimate given the perception of the FARC as constituting a threat to the Colombian armed forces and civilians.

Nevertheless, the alleged use of lethal force upon persons who surrendered or were injured may be considered unnecessary and disproportionate, if there was a lack of direct or imminent danger to the soldiers.[134] As confirmed by the Inter-American

---

129 Vincent-Joel Proulx, 'If the Hat Fits, Wear It, if The Turban Fits, Run For Your Life: Reflections on the Indefinite Detention and Targeted Killing of Suspected Terrorists', in *Hastings Law Journal. Vol.* 56 (May 2005) 801, 884 and 890.

130 Similarly, the Israeli Supreme Court called for arrest, interrogation and trial of a terrorist, where possible. The Court indicated that concern for the risk to the soldiers' lives would indeed be relevant in determining whether or not arrest is possible.*Public Committee Case*, supra note 105 at para. 40.

131 Inter-American Court of Human Rights, *Case of Zambrano Vélez*, supra note 100 at para. 85.

132 See Louise Doswald-Beck, 'The Right to Life in Armed Conflict: Does International Humanitarian Law Provide all the Answers?' in *International Review of the Red Cross* vol. 84 (December 2006) p. 886.

133 Ibid p. 885.

134 See Inter-American Court of Human Rights, *Case of the Miguel-Castro-Castro Prison v. Peru*, supra note 127. See also UN Basic Principles on the Use of Force and Fire Arms by Law Enforcement Officers, adopted by the Eighth Congress of the United Nations for the Prevention of Crime and Treatment of Delinquents, Habana, Cuba, August 27-

Court of Human Rights, the use of lethal force should never exceed the use of which is "absolutely necessary" in relation to the force or threat to be repealed.[135] The excessive character of the use of force would qualify the loss of life as arbitrary.[136] Indeed, the Inter-American Commission of Human Rights' Report on Terrorism and Human Rights confirms the protection due to those who have surrendered or are injured:

> Similarly, in their law enforcement initiatives, states must not use force against individuals who no longer present a threat as described above, such as individuals who have been apprehended by authorities, have surrendered, or who are wounded and abstain from hostile acts. The use of lethal force in such a manner would constitute extra-judicial killings in flagrant violation of Article 4 of the Convention and Article 1 of the Declaration.[137]

The Inter-American Court has confirmed that the state must prevent arbitrary executions by its forces.[138] The use of force by state agents is to be reasonable, restricted and controlled.[139] Furthermore, the Inter-American Commission of Human Rights has recognized that states may be held accountable for violation of the right to life when its agents exercise power and authority over a person, irrespective of whether it is outside of the territory of the state.[140]

September 7 1990, noting that police may use lethal weapons when it is strictly inevitable to protect a life and when less extreme measures result ineffective. See Also Case of the *Rochela Massacre v. Colombia*, Merits, Reparations and Costs. Judgment of May 11, 2007. Series C No. 163 at para. 127 qualifying the use of firearms against persons rendered defenceless as violations of the right to life.

135 Inter-American Court of Human Rights, *Case of Montero Aranguren et. al.* supra note 123 at para 68.

136 Ibid.

137 Inter-American Commission of Human Rights, supra note 97 at Chapter III para. 91.

138 Inter-American Court of Human Rights, *Case of Baldeon Garcia*, supra note 123 at para. 87, See also *Case of the Gómez-Paquiyauri Brothers v. Peru*. Merits, Reparations and Costs. Judgment of July 8, 2004. Series C No. 110 para. 128 and *Case of Myrna Mack-Chang v. Guatemala*. Merits, Reparations and Costs. Judgment of November 25, 2003. Series C No. 101 at para. 139.

139 Inter-American Court of Human Rights, *Case of Zambrano-Vélez et al. v. Ecuador*. Merits, Reparations and Costs. Judgment of July 4, 2007. Series C No. 166 at para. 76.

140 See Christina M. Cerna, *Out of Bounds? The Approach of the Inter-American System for the Promotion and Protection of Human Rights to the Extraterritorial Application of Human Rights Law*, Center for Human Rights and Global Justice Working Paper No. 6 (2006) p. 8 citing the Inter-American Commission of Human Rights, Case of *Armando Alejandre Jr. et al.*, (Cuba), September 29, 1999, Report No. 86/99, Case No. 11.589. This case concerned the downing of civilian aircrafts by Cuban military planes in 1996. See also *Salas et al.*, Decision on Admissibility (United States) October 14, 1993, Report No. 31/93, Case No. 10.573, addressing non-combatant deaths resulting from the US use of military force to remove Noreiga from power in Panama in 1989.

C. *Investigation and Compensation*

Within the Inter-American System, the State has an international obligation to determine if the force used was excessive in the event of death or injury:

> Upon learning that firearms have been used by members of its security forces and that such use had lethal consequences, the State has an obligation to initiate, ex officio and without delay, a serious, independent, impartial and effective investigation.[141]

In the case of a confirmed violation, it must punish the perpetrators and planners, as well as compensate the victims or their next of kin.[142] Failure to do so would incur responsibility for violation of the right to life in the Convention pursuant to the duty under Article 1(1) of the Convention to ensure free and full exercise of human rights which entails an obligation to investigate violations. In addition, it would be considered to have the general effect of promoting impunity. The investigation is to be "carried out with all available legal means and must be directed towards the determination of the truth and the investigation, pursuit, capture, prosecution and possible punishment of all the masterminds and perpetrators of the facts, particularly when State agents are involved."[143]

According to the President of Ecuador, the killing of an Ecuadoran citizen on Ecuadoran soil by foreign forces rendered the action particularly heinous, as an act of extra-judicial execution which requires compensation. In like manner, the Mexican government sought indemnification from the Colombian government for the injuries and loss of life suffered by the Mexicans. The Colombian government noted that it was conducting an investigation as to the Mexicans' relation to the FARC, because it disputed the notion that indemnification was due. The Colombian Minister of Foreign Affairs initially indicated that indemnification could be provided if ordered by a court or achieved via an administrative conciliation proceed-

141 Inter-American Court of Human Rights, *Case of Zambrano Vélez* supra note 139 at para. 88.

142 The Israeli Supreme Court supports the premise that in the event of a targeted killing there should be an ex post monitoring of the legality of the operation and duty of compensation. See *Public Committee* Case, supra note 106 at para. 21. See also Antonio Cassese 'Are "Targeted Killings" Unlawful? The Israeli Supreme Court's Response', in *Journal of International Criminal Justice* Vol. 5 (May 2007) at 344–345, discussing a customary standard of a duty to pay compensation within international humanitarian law. See also Roy S. Schondorf, 'Extra-State Armed Conflicts: Is There a Need for A New Legal Regime?' in *New York University Journal of International Law & Policy* Vol. 37 (Fall 2004) p. 67 discussing a duty to compensate as an element of proportionality. See also Doswald-Beck, supra note 132 at 887 citing the Inter American Court of Human Rights, *Case of Myrna Mack Chang v. Guatemala*, surpa note 138 at paras. 153–158 and *Case of Juan Humberto Sánchez v. Honduras*. Preliminary Objection, Merits, Reparations and Costs. Judgment of June 7, 2003. Series C No. 99 at paras. 107–113.

143 Inter-American Court of Human Rights, *Case of Zambrano Velez* supra note 139 at para. 123, citing *Case of the Pueblo Bello Massacre, supra* note 122, para. 143; *Case of the Rochela Massacre, supra* note 134, para. 148; and *Case of the Miguel Castro-Castro Prison, supra* note 126, para. 256.

ing.[144] In spite of this, President Uribe immediately issued a press statement which declared that "Colombia has no reason to pay indemnification on account of the Public Forces' legitimate actions against terrorist groups."[145] The categorical rejection of consideration of the claims based on the overarching security framework of counterterrorism places those injured or killed and their family members in a legal black hole in which the right to reparation is denied.

The controversy regarding the protection due the civilians prompted public reclamation within the Ecuadoran and Mexican societies. From the perspective of the people, recognition of state responsibility in the event of the loss of life of a national due to use of force is the core of "security". Hence, both the Ecuadoran and Mexican governments were under significant political pressure to pursue further investigation and attain reparation from the Colombian government. Yet, the Mexican families declared that they would refuse any indemnification offered apart from that provided via a judicial proceeding, signalling the possibility that they would seek recourse of an international tribunal.

The investigation of this case has been hindered, as access to the site for collection of forensic evidence was delayed, the collection of documentary evidence from the Colombian government was dominated by material allegedly derived from Reyes' computer, and the questioning of the actual soldiers/police and witnesses was not fully conducted. Furthermore, at the bilateral level, President Correa asserted that the Colombian government refrained from turning over additional information, including alleged recordings of the actual bombardment, which are essential for a full investigation.

In conclusion, although the Colombian government was willing to apologize for infraction of the international public law prohibition against territorial intervention, it was adamant in refusing to admit the possibility of a duty of indemnification of violations of *jus in bello* or human rights law. There a need for additional, independent efforts to establish the truth about the operation and whether reparation is due to victims and their families in the event of insufficient precaution taken in the planning or execution of the operation. The failure to uphold standards of state accountability would suggest further expansion of the state of exception to weaken ex post facto monitoring of precautionary, proportionality and necessity standards.[146]

---

144 See "Colombia propone indemnizar a Mexicanos" in CNNExpansion, available at: http://www.cnnexpansion.com/actualidad/2008/03/28/uribe-indemnizaria-a-familias-mexicanas.

145 Press release of 28 March, 2008, available at: http://web.presidencia.gov.co/sp/2008/marzo/28/11282008.html.

146 In November 2008, the UN High Commissioner for Human Rights, Navi Pillay, stated that the Colombian forces committed widespread extrajudicial executions which constituted a crime against humanity, hence she strongly supported government accountability initiatives. See: http://globalgeopolitics.net/ed/2008/11/04/rights-colombia-un-warns-of-civilian-killings-by-military/.

VI. The Promotion of Exceptions as the Rule: Defining Asylum and Negotiation as Acts of Aggression

The three women survivors sought asylum in Nicaragua. Within international law, asylum is classically characterized as a non-political humanitarian act and negotiation is viewed as the quintessential peaceful means of dispute resolution.[147] Ironically, both concepts were presented by the Colombian government as acts of "aggression" that minimized the impact of Colombia's targeted action in Ecuador and further weakened "the maintenance of the democratic order" within the region. The debate on these issues presented additional confusion as Colombia continued to present arguments expanding the concept of an international state of exception.

A. *Weighing Security and Aggression from the Perspective of Asylum*

The survivors of the strike gave testimony alleging violations composing "state terrorism". They called for prosecution of President Uribe in the Hague and voiced concern that their own personal security was at risk, thereby seeking and receiving asylum in Nicaragua.[148] Nicaragua's Attorney General, Hernan Estrada, announced provision of asylum to the Colombian women, Martha Perez Gutierrez and Doris Bohórquez Torrez to the National Assembly on 16 May 2008.[149] The power of the State to grant asylum to persons persecuted for political reasons is set forth in Article 5 of the Nicaraguan Constitution. According to Article 42, refuge and asylum protects those persecuted on account of fighting for democracy, peace, justice and human rights. The women were considered to have a well-founded fear of persecution on account of political opinion, in conformity with the definition contained within the 1951 Convention on the Status of Refugees.[150]

---

147 On asylum see UN Declaration on Territorial Asylum, adopted by the General Assembly Resolution 2312, (XX12) of 14 December 1967: "Recognizing that the grant of asylum by a State to persons entitled to invoke article 14 of the Universal Declaration of Human Rights is a peaceful and humanitarian act and that, as such, it cannot be regarded as unfriendly by any other State." On negotiation, see the UN Charter, Article 33 (1): The parties to any dispute, the continuance of which is likely to endanger the maintenance of international peace and security, shall, first of all, seek a solution by negotiation, enquiry, mediation, conciliation, arbitration, judicial settlement, resort to regional agencies or arrangements, or other peaceful means of their own choice.

148 Eduardo Marenco, 'Asilo a colombianas fue illegal', *El Nuevo Diario*, (28 May 2008), available at: http://www.elnuevodiario.com.ni/nacionales/16906.

149 "Procurador Estrada explica a diputados asilo politico legal a las mujeres FARC" in *La Gente* (4 June 2008), available at: http://www.radiolaprimerisima.com/noticias/general/30865.

150 The protection grounds in the 1951 Convention relating to the Status of Refugees include political opinion, race, religion, nationality, and social group. The political opinion consists of the women's comments *sur place* in Nicaragua against President Uribe. One may also consider the social group category, as the women have knowledge of alleged violations in Ecuador and this is immutable. They have expressed their knowledge of the event and may be targeted on account of it. See Mark R. Von Sternberg, *The Grounds of Refugee Protection in the Context of International Human Rights and Humanitarian Law* (2002).

Moreover, Estrada set forth a protection view which went beyond the traditional confines of political persecution to address victimization within the context of armed conflict, thereby linking the provision of asylum or refuge as directly evolving from humanitarian and human rights law:

> One should consider the humanitarian spirit within the doctrine and various international instruments on asylum or refuge, having the common element of when a person has been or is in danger, be it for political persecution, or social unrest (internal war) with attacks upon physical integrity, rendering extreme risk for his life. This circumstance is the essential motivation of human rights and humanitarian law. In both cases, there operates a principle of protection for persons in vulnerable situations.[151]

The Nicaraguan government deemed Colombia's intent on the day of the raid to eliminate all living persons in the camp, thereby pointing to a need for humanitarian protection. Essentially, the violations of international public and humanitarian law in the raid were depicted as additionally grounding the protection claim of the victims.[152] The fact that the women survived (and later denounced the violations and were willing to serve as witnesses) was considered to constitute a factual risk of persecution/harm meriting asylum.

Colombia protested Nicaragua's transport of the women by military plane from Ecuador across Colombian airspace as an unfriendly act. Specifically, the charges were "a flagrant abuse of the principle of good faith" and a violation of the International Convention on Civil Aviation, Article 3. This was because Nicaragua requested permission to cross Colombian airspace on May 11th due to "official business constituting an emergency". The Colombian government opined that the transport of the women could not possibly be considered official business, but rather a blatant ruse.

Nicaragua is party to the 1951 Convention on the Status of Refugees and its Protocol since 28 March 1980. Nicaragua also recognizes the Cartagena Declaration on Refugees (1984) which provides an expanded definition of a refugee to include persons who have fled their country because their lives, safety or freedom have been threatened by generalized violence, foreign aggression, internal conflicts, massive violation of human rights or other circumstances which have seriously disturbed public order.

151 Estrada set forth Nicaragua's ratification of the regional and international human rights and refugee instruments which set forth the right of all persons to seek and enjoy asylum including, the Universal Declaration of Human Rights, Art. 14 (1) and the non-refoulement guarantees in the American Convention of Human Rights, Article 22.7 and American Declaration of Human Rights, Article 22.8. Specifically the Convention on Territorial Asylum sets forth that states have the right to permit the entry of persons and other states may not protest this. The Nicaraguan Ambassador to the OAS, Dennis Moncada reiterated that the root of the events was a planned act of aggression against Ecuador. The provision of asylum to persons injured under the attack was characterized as a humanitarian act, a sacred act which Nicaragua valued because of the history of Nicaraguans seeking asylum as a result of experiencing state terrorism under Somoza and throughout the 80's.

152 Stéphane Jaquement, *Under What Circumstances Can a Person Who Has Taken an Active Part in Hostilities of an International or Non-International Armed Conflict Become an Asylum-Seeker* 26 (UNHCR DIP PPLA/2004/01) (June 2004), citing UN Security Council Resolution 1296 (2000).

This is debatable because the provision of asylum is indeed a sovereign act which may constitute official business. The Colombian government accused Nicaragua of failing to interrogate the women to establish whether and when they had been "recruited", implying that Nicaragua should have conducted an exclusion hearing prior to an inclusion finding.

i. Exclusion from Protection

Within the OAS Permanent Council, Ambassador Ospina Bernal denounced the provision of asylum as an act of aggression and abuse, defined as providing protection and promoting terrorist groups. He thereby expanded the notion of aggression to include the provision of legal protection under the refugee/asylum regime by interpreting it through the normative content of UN Security Council Resolution 1373 (2001), Resolution 1566 (2004), and Article 12 of the Inter-American Convention Against Terrorism which set forth the duty not to provide asylum to persons involved in terrorism.[153] Because "aggression" is not defined, this interpretation is possible and encourages reference to cross-regime enforceability of UN Security Council Resolution 1373 (3) which sets forth that attribution may encompass safe haven before and during attacks, but also afterwards:

f. Take appropriate measures in conformity with the relevant provisions of national and international law, including international standards of human rights, before granting refugee status, for the purpose of ensuring that the asylum seeker has not planned, facilitated or participated in the commission of terrorist acts;
g. Ensure, in conformity with international law, that refugee status is not abused by the perpetrators, organizers or facilitators of terrorist acts, and that claims of political motivation are not recognized as grounds for refusing requests for the extradition of alleged terrorists;

Under the 1951 Convention on the Status of Refugees, Article 1 F, a person may be excluded from refugee status if he has committed crimes against peace, war crimes, or crimes against humanity, as well as serious, non-political crimes outside the country of refuge, or he has been guilty of acts contrary to the purposes and principles of the United Nations (this would include terrorist acts). Nonetheless, UNHCR advocates inclusion prior to exclusion, and notes that ex-combatants may be entitled to seek asylum under the relevant circumstances.[154] Stéphane Jacquemet sets forth:

---

153 On the impact of counter-terrorism on asylum see UNHCR Background Paper on Preserving the Institution of Asylum and Refugee Protection in the Context of Counter-Terrorism: The Problem of Terrorist Mobility (October 2007) Online. UNHCR Refworld, available at: http://www.unhcr.org/refworld/docid/475fec412.html.

154 See UNHCR Guidelines on the Application of the Exclusion Clauses: Article 1F of the 1951 Convention relating to the Status of Refugees, HCR/GIP/03/05 (4 September 2003), available at: http://www.unhcr.org/publ/PUBL/3f7d48514.pdf. See also Rosa da Costa Maintaining the Civilian and Humanitarian Character of Asylum, PPLA/2004/02 (June 2004), available at: http://www.unhcr.org/protect/PROTECTION/40ebf51b4.pdf.

> Those who have been armed elements in such non-international armed conflict and have been disarmed and demobilized should be separated from asylum seekers, interned, and given an opportunity to establish that they have genuinely and permanently renounced military activities; if they have, they can then apply for asylum and be recognized as refugees if they pass the "double refugee test of inclusion and exclusion".[155]

Nicaragua has a duty to prevent the women from engaging in subversion against the Colombian government, and should the women be considered as engaging in subversion as opposed to expressing political opinions, the provision of asylum would be considered an unfriendly act against Colombia.[156] President Ortega himself adopted the same language as the Colombians, accusing President Uribe of engaging in state terrorism. Hence, should such statements be deemed illegitimate, this would apply to the Head of State himself as well as those receiving asylum. From the perspective of President Ortega, the statements denouncing the illegality of the raid in Ecuador are not subversive, but rather legitimate concerns that merit expression.

Because Nicaragua has a duty not to interfere in Colombia's internal affairs, it is expected to intern those who have "taken a direct part in hostilities."[157] The Colombian government suggested that the women were not victims of kidnapping, but rather voluntary recruits who merited prosecution (as opposed to persecution). However, it did not address the issue that the recruitment may have indeed been forcible in another manner than kidnapping and amount to human rights violations meriting protection. Nor did it address their alleged duties as cooks and caretakers of animals. If true, this would render their role in taking active part in hostilities/committing terrorist acts nil and would thus be a mitigating factor when applying the exclusion clauses. The Mexican survivor, Lucia Morett, was granted humanitarian protection, instead of asylum, because she was not considered to be under threat of persecution by the State of Mexico.

The 1951 Convention on the Status of Refugees, Article 33 (2) denies non-refoulement protection to a refugee whom there are reasonable grounds for regarding as a danger to the security of the country in which he is, or having been convicted by a final judgment of a particularly serious crimes, and constitutes a danger to the community of that country. The asylum seekers were deemed not to pose a threat to the security of Nicaragua. It should be noted that even confirmed terrorists are protected under customary and human rights treaty non-refoulement standards against return to a place where there would be a real risk of being subject to torture, or cruel, inhuman or degrading treatment (the Inter-American standard also includes threat to life and freedom on account of political opinion, etc.).[158]

---

155 Jacquemet, supra note 152 at p. iv. See also James C. Hathaway & Colin J. Harvey, 'Framing Refugee Protection in the New World Disorder', in *Cornell International Law Journal* vol. 34 (2001) 257.

156 Ibid at 36.

157 Ibid at 17. Jacquemet suggests that Article 11 of the 5th Hague Convention has attained customary status and thus applies to internal armed conflicts.

158 Sir Elihu Lauterpacht & Daniel Bethlehem, 'The Scope and Content of the Principle of Non-Refoulement: Opinion', in Erika Feller, Volker Turk & Frances Nicholson, *Refugee*

The dispute over the grant of asylum reflects challenges in interpretation of refugee law within the context of armed actions conducted under the rubric of self-defence and the "war against terrorism". Of particular concern are the political repercussions for what should be a humanitarian act in an environment in which the Responsibility to Prevent terrorism, as interpreted via UN Resolution 1373, is made applicable through the asylum regime. It clearly demonstrates the pressure to apply exclusion analysis before inclusion when determining the protection needs of persons fleeing armed incidents. There is a need for standard procedures to safeguard the overriding protection standards applicable to all persons. Politicization, in particular characterizing asylum as "aggression", within international forums and media was detrimental to the asylum system as a whole.[159]

B. *Negotiation as "Aggression"*

In the OAS Permanent Council, Ambassador Ospina Bernal offered another novel interpretation of international public law duties by alleging that President Ortega had violated the Inter-American Democratic Charter by offering to pursue a dialogue with the FARC to bring peace to Colombia. This was characterized by the Colombian government as constituting support of terrorist groups, amounting to aggressive and abusive conduct against the Colombian people. It was further described as constituting an attack on democracy, human rights and fundamental freedoms, as well as a threat to the entire region in violation of the OAS Charter articles, 1,2,3,11,13,15,17,19 and 20. The Colombian government issued a note of protest that President Ortega had acted in violation of the principle of non-interference

Protection in International Law: UNHCR's Global Consultations on International Protection 87 (Cambridge 2003). See Article 3 of the Convention Against Torture: 1. No State Party shall expel, return ("refouler") or extradite a person to another State where there are substantial grounds for believing that he would be in danger of being subjected to torture. See also the American Convention on Human Rights, Article 22 (7): Every person has the right to seek and be granted asylum in a foreign territory, in accordance with the legislation of the state and international conventions, in the event he is being pursued for political offenses or related common crimes and (8) In no case may an alien be deported or returned to a country, regardless of whether or not it is his country of origin, if in that country his right to life or personal freedom is in danger of being violated because of his race, nationality, religion, social status, or political opinions; International Covenant on Civil and Political Rights, Article 7: No one shall be subjected to torture or to cruel, inhuman or degrading treatment or punishment. See *Agiza v. Sweden*, Comm. No. 233/2003 CAT/C/34/D/233/2003 (24 May 2005) and *Alzery v. Sweden*, Comm. No. 1416/2005, CCPR/C/88/D/1416/2005 (10 Nov. 2006).

159 In June 2008, the Nicaraguan legislature approved a new refugee law which would establish a national commission to process claims. President Ortega's opponents stated that this body would prevent the Executive from granting asylum as had been done in the case of the Colombians, instead the commission would be in charge of such determination. See http://www.adnmundo.com/contenidos/politica/nueva_ley_refugiados_nicaragua-acn. Ley de Proteccion de Refugiados No. 655, published in La Gaceta, No. 130 (9 July 2008).

in internal affairs of the State and in violation of the letter and spirit of the Inter-American Convention Against Terrorism and UN Security Council resolutions 1373 and 1269.[160]

It is undeniable that the Colombian government did not consider the Nicaraguan government to have demonstrated neutrality given its provision of asylum to the survivors of the targeted strike, the statements against the legitimacy of the action, and the support of recognition of the FARC as belligerents. Ambassador Ospina emphasized that the Colombian government would not endorse the pursuit of a negotiation by President Ortega towards the FARC. Furthermore, he alleged that such negotiation would frustrate his government's policy of pursuing "democratic security". This effectively disqualified a classic public international law mechanism of dispute resolution considered to maintain peace and security in favour of military action.[161]

Of concern is that the adamant refusal to negotiate with the FARC actually renders the achievement of a non-violent resolution to the conflict more difficult.[162] The Colombian government ignored the impact of the deaths of the FARC leaders Raul Reyes, Ivan Rios, and Manuel Marulanda, as well as the surrender of Nelly Avila Moreno, as pointing towards non-violent resolution. Instead, it seemed to prioritize the high levels of desertions, dismantling of camps, and interference with financing as support for a policy geared towards total military defeat. The government effectively discarded the option of a cease-fire agreement which would accompany a negotiation in which the current FARC leader, Alfonso Cano, could present his social justice concerns for full discussion. It has been pointed out that FARC members are driven by conceptions of feeling socially excluded. Hence, their inclusion in peace talks to design social policies on behalf of the nation would be a large incentive towards renunciation of violence and demobilization.[163] This process would assist

160 Ambassador Ospina Bernal cited the preamble of Inter-American Convention Against Terrorism to emphasize the risk which President Ortega had exposed Colombia to: "Considering that terrorism is a serious criminal phenomenon, which is of deep concern to all member states; attacks democracy; impedes the enjoyment of human rights and fundamental freedoms; threatens the security of states, destabilizing and undermining the foundations of all society; and seriously impacts the economic and social development of the states in the region ..." See also Letter from Jaime Bermudez Merizalde, Colombian Minister of Foreign Relations to Samuel Santos, Nicaragua's Minister of Foreign Relations, 17 July 2008 (on file with the author).

161 See OAS Charter, Article 24: International disputes between Member States shall be submitted to the peaceful procedures set forth in this Charter. Article 25: The following are peaceful procedures: direct negotiation, good offices, mediation, investigation and conciliation, judicial settlement, arbitration, and those which the parties to the dispute may especially agree upon at any time.

162 See Harmonie Toros, '"We Don't Negotiate with Terrorists!": Legitimacy and Complexity in Terrorist Conflicts', in *Security Dialogue* vol. 39 (4) (August 2008) p. 407.

163 See Council on Hemispheric Relations, *Colombia: The Multi-faceted Motivation of the FARC and Prospects for Peace* (10:11:07) http://www.politicalaffairs.net/article/articleview/5981/1/289. See also Virginia Bouvier, *Colombia's Crossroads: The FARC and the Future of the Hostages* (United States Institute of Peace June 2008) at: http://63.104.169.51/articles/1011732.984/1.PDF.

the socialization of FARC towards real political participation, effectively choosing to include them, instead of isolate them, precisely to transform them via participation in conformance with the rule of law.[164] Cano has previously participated in peace talks and is considered a political actor, rather than military commander. Rejection of a rapprochement with Cano may actually radicalize other members of the FARC further.[165]

The pressure that Colombia is placing on Nicaragua, Ecuador and Venezuela is intended to ensure that they will not provide support to the FARC and thus promote the fragmentation of the FARC. Farah predicts that the FARC will implode into smaller criminal groups that will not pose a national threat, but rather a regional threat due to their engagement in narco-trafficking.[166] From a security perspective such fragmentation may not necessarily improve the consolidation of peace and democracy within Colombia. Pursuit of a peace agreement with full demobilization and genuine development guarantees for those who claim to have been socially excluded may be better than uncontrolled, fragmented drug gangs.

Ambassador Ospina Bernal sought to discredit the Nicaraguan government as repressing human rights (in particular freedom of speech and political association) and supporting terrorism, thereby calling for response by the OAS. In essence, this recalls Franck's "emerging right to democratic governance" in which the legitimacy of the state is contingent on the participation of its polity in open, competitive, fairly administered elections, as well as guarantees of freedom of expression, association, assembly, etc.[167] Democracy is presented as an entitlement which collective international institutions shall protect and promote. This is pursuant to Article 5 of the OAS Charter which highlights the duty of members to promote "the effective exercise of democracy" and the OAS General Assembly Resolution on Representative Democracy (OEA/Ser.P/AG/RES.1080) (XXI-0/91), para. 1.[168] In this case, Ospina Bernal applies the theory in the traditional manner, calling for response to authoritarian tendencies of the Nicaraguan president.[169] He challenged the OAS

164 Toros, supra note 162 at 414 and 422.

165 It is noteworthy that a recent RAND report reviewing the end of terrorist groups since 1968 concluded that the majority ended by either joining the political process or having key members arrested/killed by local police and intelligence agencies. Military force was rarely the reason for the end of the terrorist activity. Seth G. Jones & Martin C. Libicki, *How Terrorist Groups End: Lessons for Countering al Qa'ida* RAND 2008.

166 Douglas Farah, *The FARC in Transition: The Fatal Weakening of the Western Hemisphere's Oldest Guerilla Movement*, The NEFA Foundation (2 July, 2008).

167 Thomas Franck, 'The Emerging Right to Democratic Governance' *American Journal of International Law*, vol. 86 (1992) p. 46. See also Samuel Huntington, *The Third Wave* (U. of Oklahoma 1991).

168 Franck cites the OAS Ministers of Foreign Affairs as demanding replacement of the Somoza regime in 1979 and transfer of power by Noriega in 1989. The OAS Permanent Council also called for democracy in Haiti in 1987 and sanctions were adopted in 1991.

169 Ospina alluded to possibility of sanctions under Article 23, 28 and 29. The OAS pursued sanctions in 1960 against the Dominican Republic and against the Cuban government in 1962, both based on charges of promoting subversion in Venezuela. Cuba was later suspended from participation in the OAS. See M. Akehurst, 'Enforcement Action by Regional

to respond and queried whether the Charter was still in force.[170]

Ambassador Moncada retorted that President Ortega respectfully offered his services for mediation in search of peace. He noted that he did not have to ask for permission given the urgency of the situation because the absence of peace in Colombia constituted a regional security threat. The ambassador concluded that Colombia would never attain peace via war. He recalled that the Nicaraguan civil war was ended by way of peaceful negotiation promoted by the Contodora group, of which Colombia formed part of, instead of war, and that this was never denounced as intervention in internal affairs. Furthermore, he accused the Colombian government of believing that it may impose an absolute supremacy of its internal situation in violation of international law. In his government's view, Colombia had infringed the UN Charter and the OAS Charter by not seeking peaceful resolution of disputes and violated human rights and international humanitarian law in its actions.

Finally, the ambassador raised an additional issue: the transit of Colombian drugs through Central American land, waters, and airspace to the primary market, the United States, was negatively affecting their security and depleting their resources in the battle against trafficking of drugs. He protested the continuous presence of Colombian naval frigates in Nicaraguan territorial waters (engaged in surveillance of narcotics transport) purportedly in violation of the UN and OAS Charters. In conclusion, the ambassador denounced reference to counter-narco-trafficking and counter-terrorism or any other national security threat as a pretext to justify intervention and aggression against other states.

The US Ambassador, Hector Morales Jr., evinced a conciliatory tone in which he highlighted the regional security challenge of transnational terrorism and the importance of denying legitimacy to the FARC. He pointed out generous bilateral support for Nicaragua in the form of grants to fight poverty and promote development. This was in response to Moncada's implication that regional human security had been sacrificed by the diversion of resources to the wars against drugs and terrorism. He called for the OAS to be utilized as a forum for cooperation, not to sow discord. Curiously, the session ended silently without further debate. The silence underscored the complexity of achieving integration amidst a clash of different concepts of security that are perceived as being potentially incompatible.

VII. Dénoument

Domestically, the death of Reyes was a tremendous political victory for President Uribe. The choice to eliminate Reyes undeniably provided a short-term security gain in weakening the FARC. Further, the reaffirmation of the importance of combating terrorism by the neighbouring states served to strengthen the pressure on the FARC.

Agencies, with special reference to the Organization of American States' in *British Yearbook of International Law vol. 42* (1967) p. 175. In 2009, the OAS suspended Honduras from the OAS on account of a coup d'etat, citing the Inter-American Democratic Charter, Article 21, (AG/RES.2(XXXVIII-E/09)).

170 Ospina called upon the Nicaraguan national judicial authorities to investigate the President Ortega as his statements violated the language of the ICAT by protecting and promoting the FARC, and meeting with FARC could be direct violations of duties, as well as granting protection to alleged FARC members.

Nevertheless, the unilateralist measure taken by Colombia without consultation of Ecuador, the UN, or the OAS was deemed illegitimate by all of the Latin American nations – the decision lacked proper authority. The evidence of the failure of Ecuador to meet a due diligence standard in counter terrorism was not proved "beyond a reasonable doubt". The inability to prevent use of the border territory as safe haven was in spite of Ecuador's best efforts and its lack of capacity; hence it was entitled to notice prior to the action. It also revealed Colombia's shared lack of capacity in policing the borders.

The foreign relations fall-out stemming from the aerial strike was dramatic. The end result of the application of the Responsibility to Prevent to counterterrorism in the form of unilateral extra-territorial law enforcement is that it actually resulted in the immediate regional destabilization to brink of international war. Operation Fenix's impact was a breach of trust which prompted remilitarization and the hindrance of normalization of relations; thereby potentially weakening inter-state security. Colombia's adamant rejection of negotiation as a primary strategy to attain peace is questionable and may be interpreted as a blow to the dispute resolution mechanisms highlighted by both the UN and OAS Charters as constituting primary modes of maintaining peace and security.

On the other hand, the action also seemed to jump start regional, broader implementation of UN Security Council Resolution 1373 in the sense that Brazil, Peru, Costa Rica, Nicaragua, and even Venezuela and Ecuador immediately engaged in arrests of persons suspected linked to the FARC or narcotics rings (linked to FARC in terms of financing), thereby resulting in a flood of "due diligence" as pertaining the duty to prevent terrorism and narco-trafficking.

In essence, the region appeared to become enveloped in a spirit of cooperation seeking increase of bilateral trade, aid, and purchase of surveillance and armaments in pursuit of strategies to combat the spread of "narco-terrorists" and strengthen socio-economic development. Ecuador and Colombia both announced plans to purchase additional fighter jets, communication equipment, radars, etc. to improve border controls. Brazil signed an agreement with Colombia to share intelligence, purchase arms and conduct joint military exercises in order to better control the borders with respect to drug trafficking and FARC movement. It initiated the creation of a South American Defence Council to provide a forum for the Ministers of Defence to engage in consultation, cooperation and integration in security policy. This may serve to complement the UN Security Council, or assume primary regional responsibility. In short, one may define these events as leading towards regional development of an identity as a "subject" of 21st century security policy rather than an object of such.

VIII. Conclusion: Measuring the "Unrule of Law" and the Scope of the Responsibility to Prevent Terrorism

Compliance with UN Resolution 1373 was strengthened by regional affirmation of the importance of cooperating to prevent the spread of terrorism. In this sense the OAS and Rio Group resolutions demonstrated consensus and the subsequent elaboration of follow-up and monitoring mechanisms will promote effective implementation of the duty to prevent terrorism. Nevertheless, the regional resolutions confirm that unilateral use of force in the context of counter-terrorism, conducted without consultation of the host state, is *not* lawful. Thus, on a normative level, this case does not support a finding of consensus as to recognition of a "Responsibility to prevent terrorism" as legitimizing unilateral extra-territorial targeted killings. The "new" norm was not considered compatible with the normative framework contained within the UN and OAS Charters. From the regional perspective, the guarantees of territorial integrity, respect for sovereignty, abstention from the threat or use of force, non-interference in the affairs of other states, and peaceful settlement of disputes are the core standards of the rule of law. Appropriate response to terrorists seeking safe haven appears to be the alternatives of: improved coordination of surveillance and border control in joint operations, collaboration for arrest, extradition, and prosecution of criminals and their financiers and arms suppliers, as well as freezing of their financial assets, and shared intelligence.[171]

Allegations of transgressions conducted during the operation highlight the importance of recognizing a duty of states to pursue independent investigation and examination of the indemnification claims presented on behalf of the civilians injured or killed in extra-territorial targeted strikes. Categorical denial of state responsibility for harm on account of a tapering of the range of civilians who are entitled to protection precludes review of action pursuant to customary international humanitarian law or human rights law. Finally, the Colombian government's classification of President Ortega's grant of asylum and the offer to serve as a negotiator as acts of aggression reveals additional negative consequences of the expanded application of 1373 upon fundamental humanitarian and peaceful principles of international public law. The articulation of these juridical exceptions are dangerous because they invert

171 It would behove Colombia to exercise caution in its counterinsurgency actions given human rights reports identifying abuses by Colombian security forces. There is also information regarding violations by paramilitary groups linked to Colombian officials and members of the security institutions via collusion or acquiescence: extra judicial executions, massacres, forced displacement, eviction and expropriation of property, as well as linkage to narco-trafficking. Amnesty International's report on Colombia for 2007 states:

All parties to the conflict – the security forces and army-backed paramilitaries as well as guerrilla groups, mainly the Revolutionary Armed Forces of Colombia (Fuerzas Armadas Revolucionarias de Colombia, FARC) and the smaller National Liberation Army (Ejército de Liberación Nacional, ELN) – continued to abuse human rights and breach international humanitarian law. They were responsible for war crimes and crimes against humanity … There were further attacks on trade unionists and human rights defenders, mainly by paramilitary groups. Extrajudicial executions by members of the security forces, and selective killings of civilians and kidnappings by guerrilla forces continued to be reported.

Additional allegations of ties between paramilitaries and President Uribe's government and family (as well as members of Congress) complicated perceptions of legitimacy. Indeed, immediately after the raid, another FARC leader, Ivan Rios, was executed by his one of his own soldiers who delivered Rios's hand to the Colombian Army as proof in order to claim 2.5 million USD reward, thereby providing an example of a sanctioned assassination on top of the strike, leading some commentaries to question the validity of President Uribe's assertion that he pursued "Democratic Security".

the perception of what is legitimate in order to discard fundamental elements of the international rule of law, thereby weakening international security.

IX. Post Script: Operation "Jacque"

On July 2, 2008 the Colombian military conducted Operation "Jacque" in which they engaged in a ruse to convince the FARC groups holding high profile hostages (including Ingrid Betancourt) in three different places to be transported to another location to be visited by an international mission. The Army painted two helicopters white with red stripes to mimic a humanitarian agency. The military personnel were given clothing with "International Humanitarian Commission" lettering, and at least one actually wore an ICRC emblem. They freed 15 hostages and captured two FARC members within 22 minutes. There were no casualties, indeed not one shot was fired, leading Ingrid Betancourt to declare that it was a 'peace operation' not a war operation. President Uribe noted it was an operation which respected human rights. Nevertheless, there was criticism that the ruse of posing as a humanitarian agency placed real NGOs in danger. On the one hand, it was argued that because the mock operation sought to free the hostages from a camp and did not engage in violence, it could be considered legal because of the lack of the use of force during the operation.[172] Yet, because the operation succeeded in capturing two members of the FARC, then it is possible to suggest that the feigning of non-combatant status (and specifically the improper use of the ICRC emblem) to such end constitutes an act of perfidy.[173] Thus, the operation was not correct in terms of legality as opposed to legitimacy.[174] President Uribe acknowledged the violation and issued an apology, which was noted by ICRC.

---

172 Henckaerts & Doswald-Beck, supra note 98 at 221, Rule 65.

173 Ibid. See Additional Protocol I, Article 37:

1. It is prohibited to kill, injure *or capture* an adversary by resort to perfidy. Acts inviting the confidence of an adversary to lead him to believe that he is entitled to, or is obliged to accord, protection under the rules of international law applicable in armed conflict, with intent to betray that confidence, shall constitute perfidy. The following acts are examples of perfidy:
   a. the feigning of an intent to negotiate under a flag of truce or of a surrender;
   b. the feigning of an incapacitation by wounds or sickness;
   c. the feigning of civilian, non-combatant status; and
   d. the feigning of protected status by the use of signs, emblems or uniforms of the United Nations or of neutral or other States not Parties to the conflict.
2. Ruses of war are not prohibited. Such ruses are acts which are intended to mislead an adversary or to induce him to act recklessly but which infringe no rule of international law applicable in armed conflict and which are not perfidious because they do not invite the confidence of an adversary with respect to protection under that law. The following are examples of such ruses: the use of camouflage, decoys, mock operations and misinformation.

174 John C. Dehn argues that the wrongfulness of this act may be precluded due to the view that it was a minor violation of IHL which was used in response to war crimes in order to end them. John C. Dehn, 'Permissible Perfidy?' in *Journal of International Criminal Justice* Vol. 6 (2008) p. 651.

Politically, the mission was deemed a tremendous success because it was an intelligence operation which shed no blood. This served as a complete contrast to the Reyes action and appeared to restore credibility in the military pressure on the FARC. Indeed, within the OAS Permanent Council there was full celebration and congratulations offered by all, including the French observer. However, there exists a parallel between Uribe's extra-territorial targeted killing of Reyes and the use of a ruse to liberate Betancourt; both operations achieved desired ends but it is suggested that these operations should be considered exceptions rather than examples of legitimate practice because of the negative implications of validating them and prompting repetition. There are analogous "unrule of law" implications: violation of territorial integrity in the first operation and perfidy in the first and second operations.

Chapter 9

Democratic Security

*Christopher Kutz**

I. Introduction

In recent years, the story of contemporary political philosophy, as well as a fair measure of the practice of international development politics, has involved the convergence of liberal and democratic values. Democratic institutions have come to be seen as both shields of human well-being and rights domestically, and as means of avoiding violent international conflict. Moreover, this convergence has both conceptual and empirical roots. Conceptually, democracy honors human capacities of expression, deliberation, and sociability. Empirically, as the work of Amartya Sen and Jean Drèze has shown, democratic institutions provide bulwarks against forms of corruption and tyranny that themselves have terribly pernicious effects on human welfare. The result is that democratic values, and conceptions of state legitimacy rooted in democracy, have come to have a nearly bewitching force in contemporary theory.

My aim is not to question the strength of the connection between democracy and security in this regard. Rather, it is to point out that along with these profound connections between the two run connections pointing in the opposite direction, between democracy and *in*security. Understanding the full spectrum of the relation between these two values is important in two respects: first, by providing a basis for qualifying the resort to the rhetoric of democracy; and second, by restoring to political theory a broader range of values with which it might operate in modern thought.

My plan in this chapter is as follows. In Section II, I will discuss the important conceptual shift from a discourse centered on national security to one centered on human security – a shift that transforms the locus of normative concern from state to subject, and opens the field of legitimacy from a sovereignty-based conception to a rights-based conception. In Section III, I discuss the constitutive and instrumental contributions of democracy to human security. Section IV challenges the yoking of democracy to security, looking at the ways in which themes and values associated with democracy can present obstacles to human security. Section V takes up the

* I would like to thank Cecilia Bailliet, Andrew Guzman and Oona Hathaway for their advice, and the participants at the conference "Security: A Multidisciplinary Normative Approach" for their comments.

Cecilia M. Bailliet (ed.), Security: A Multidisciplinary Normative Approach.
 ISBN 978 90 04 17296 8. pp. 231–247.

broader theme of this essay, of the need to see democracy, and democratic institutions, as values with a significant but nonetheless delimited role to play in a broader conception of legitimacy.

II. From national security to human security

We are in the midst of an important shift in how we organize claims of political justification, from a notion of national security to one of human security. The shift is partly rhetorical, but also conceptual: it reflects a shift away from a state-centered organization of moral interests, to a person-centered view. As such, it changes the locus of normative concern in a fundamental way, from concern for an abstraction – the state – conceived as extending across time and independent of the identities of particular persons, to the interests of persons taken independently of the states to which they belong. The shift began as a concerted effort of progressive development experts, who wished to coopt the persuasive force of national security claims for a broader agenda focusing on overall social welfare. But the shift has conceptual significance of its own, and has led to an impressive research agenda.

I want here mainly to sketch the concept of national security, and to show how the shift to human security brings with it a natural bridge to the concept of democracy. Conceptually, claims of national security focus on two factors: the security of borders from outside interference, whether by states or individuals; and internal political order, understood in terms of the continuity of an existing regime. The language of Chapter VII of the U.N. Charter implicitly invokes both considerations, in the responsibility of the Security Council to "maintain or restore international peace and security."[1] This Janus-like focus, on order and borders, is simply a consequence of the understanding of the state as a territorially-defined political entity. Generic risks are considered threats to national security to the extent they implicate either borders or orders – many things beyond foreign armies and terrorist threats can present such risks – so the concept of national security is reasonably capacious. For instance, epidemic disease and environmental catastrophe, whether human- or naturally caused, can disrupt internal political order (or, at the limit, present a so-called existential threat to the continuing viability of the state), or threaten borders with an uncontrolled flow of refugees from neighboring states. Similarly, an under-employed or educated workforce can be seen as a threat to national security, through its effects on domestic economic power and so on the international muscle the state is able to exert.

While claims of national security are naturally made by those whose advantages are conferred by the existing state order (and territorial organization), especially the members of a political elite, the concept need not be self-serving. The normative interests of a state derive from the interests of its citizens, but they are not, as I noted above, identical with the interests of its current set of citizens. Arguably, a state's interests extend both backward in time, in safeguarding traditions, and forward in time, towards generations unborn. To the extent custom or political organization are

1 U.N. Charter, Chapter VII, Art. 39.

seen as having intrinsic value as exemplars of a distinctive culture, they may ground a legitimate claim for preservation independent of the claims of their members. More to the point, territorial integrity and political order are primary contributors to the goodness of the lives of current citizens. One need not accept a Hobbesian autocrat to accept his premise that civil order is a precondition of a life lived beyond mere survival. The moral stakes in national security are substantial, indeed.

At the same time, national security has two significant drawbacks: one conceptual, and one rhetorical. The conceptual drawback is linked to its advantage, namely the logical space between the interests of peoples and the interests of the states to which they happen to belong. While high degrees of inequality and exploitation may threaten civil order, civil order is demonstrably compatible with extensive inequality. More generally, the interests of persons are more sensitive to disruption than the interests of the state as a whole, and so focus on the latter category of threats lets more pervasive forms of social harm go unchallenged.

The rhetorical drawback is a direct consequence of the moral importance of national security. Because national security values are tied to questions of existential threat, a discourse of national security *dominates* other forms of reason and justification that might be offered to advance alternative policy goals. Threats to national security command resources and overcome objections made on behalf of subsidiary values, including values of both welfare and dignity. As a consequence of the Hobbesian (or Schmittian) logic of national security discourse, efforts to maintain the preconditions of political order can entail sacrifices to the substantive values of the political order – values like the Rule of Law and constitutional commitments to substantive freedoms. This might be reckoned the paradox of national security: threats to national security can appear to justify eviscerating the qualities that make the nation state worth preserving, under the guise of emergency powers or executive prerogatives.[2]

The rival concept of *human security* has been offered as a way to correct the conceptual problems with an excessive focus on state welfare, and to coopt the rhetorical force of national security discourse. The term came to prominence in the 1994 U.N. Human Development Report, where it named a set of concerns to be monitored and fostered by the international community. While human security is, in that sense, an oppositional concept, it has substantial positive content. At the most general level, it shifts the locus of normative concern from the state to the individual, thus rendering salient the significance of disease, poverty, hunger, and vulnerability to environmental damage even when those risks do not threaten the foundations of political order. From the perspective of human security, state security is valuable only instrumentally, as one tool among many for promoting the interests of persons. Claims made on behalf of the state must be redeemed in the currency of personal well-being.

There are two more conceptual advantages to human security, apart from the breadth of its concerns and the focus on personal well-being and dignity. First, by breaking the tight link between individual and state security, the concept of human

2 I have discussed this point extensively, in "Torture, Necessity, and Existential Politics," *California Law Review* 95: 235–276 (2007).

security is better able to reckon with the non- and supra-state level concerns that are proper focuses of policy, at both the national and international levels. To take the most obvious concern, while global climate change will affect states disparately, the nature of the threat requires coordinated international action. If the costs of global climate change are seen exclusively through the lens of national security, collective action problems loom large, for the threat to any given state's security may not be enough to justify costly response. When seen trans-nationally – as person-affecting – interstate response can be warranted. Similarly, questions of access to energy, and to sustainable nutrition, again require an awareness of borderless risks and coordinated international policies, with potentially large transfers of wealth and technology. A state-based perspective will fall short.

Most basically, a focus on human security implicates no state in particular; states are relevant only instrumentally, in virtue of the protections they offer their subjects. National security concerns, by contrast, presuppose the perspective of the particular state whose security is in question, and implicate other states in virtue of the threat they pose. In practice, this means that national security concerns come to be identified with the interests and claims of strong states, whose interests are most affected by other actors in their geo-strategic neighborhood. As a result, resources and attention simply fail to move in the direction of isolated states: non-oil or drug-producing states in Africa or Latin America simply fail to move U.S. policy, for example, except on the basis of much lower-ranking humanitarian concerns. A focus on human security corrects this bias towards the strong, by looking to the incidence of humanity. Policy makers guided by human security concerns thus look south and east rather than north and west, towards regions lacking the strong state institutions that ground national security. And they look towards international aggregations of power, such as the World Trade Organization (WTO), as both causes and possible cures to human insecurity.

The second advantage consists in the implicit dynamic dimension of human security. To be sure, national security is a forward-looking concept, but the object to be protected from risk is essentially static: the state. Threats to the state are one-off: an attack pierces a border, unrest undermines state or civil authority, a foreign armory reduces international leverage, etc. By contrast, a focus on human security looks not to the lives of persons conceived statically, in terms of a present set of interests, but to individuals' capacities to cope with the vicissitudes of fortune. Human security, that is, focuses on reducing volatility through institutions that protect access to food, medical care, shelter, and employment. Such institutions, which John Rawls calls the "basic structure" of a society, form an integrated fabric of social protection, not simply a defensive perimeter around the state. A corollary of this point is that human security cannot be reduced to any crude form of utilitarianism, because individual security can be threatened as directly by welfare-maximizing state policies that shift resources without attention to individual claims, as surely as it can be threatened by non-state dangers. A focus on human security is thus philosophically dense, by virtue of the institutions we call upon to protect it.

Now, the expansiveness and density of human security, which I have called a virtue of the concept, might also be thought a vice. If part of the point of introducing human security is to capture the dominating quality of national security discourse, that rhetorical advantage is lost to the degree the concerns become ill-focused, assimilable to a generic policy goal of social welfare maximization. To put the point another way, one might well be suspicious that the rhetoric of human security is simply a repackaging of welfare economics, with the units of welfare conceived as whole lives rather than life-slices. Certainly, the emergence of the discourse in the UNDP reports, and in the work of Amartya Sen in particular, points to the welfarist foundations of the concept.[3]

My point is not to decry welfarism in social policy, to be sure. Rather, the point is that if human security is to have comparable suasive force, we must be able to pick out a set of normative demands, and thus institutions meeting those demands, that can command appropriate priority. But while human security is not necessarily more protean than other basic concepts of political justification, its capaciousness makes it hard to see how it can meet this demand – to be something other than a portmanteau for the range of concerns already canvassed by sophisticated, distributionally-sensitive welfare economics.

III. From human security to democracy

One response to the concern that human security sweeps too broadly has been to link it tightly to a particular set of institutions: democratic institutions.[4] Spurred by the contemporary 1990s discussions of the so-called "democratic peace" – or the thesis that democracies tend to avoid military conflicts with one another – the discourses of human security and democratization have come to run together. In part this is a matter of happy coincidence: if the democratic-peace thesis is at least partly correct (as it seems to be, notwithstanding substantial debate about the basis and limits of the thesis), then democratic institutions might be thought to have a strongly instrumental relation to human security concerns.[5] Obviously interstate war threatens human security like nothing else. But internally as well, democratic institutions can promote civil understanding, or at least *modi vivendi*, among different groups, simply by offering paths to resources and power without resort to violence.[6]

The more interesting set of instrumental connections, however, stems not from the stabilizing effects of democratic governance per se, but from the support of the ancillary institutions typical of democracies – notably, a free press, free speech, and

3 See, e.g., *1994 U.N. Human Development Report*, Ch. 2, ttp://hdr.undp.org/en/reports/global/hdr1994/chapters/; Amartya Sen, *Development as Freedom* (New York: Basic Books, 2001).

4 See, e.g., United Nations, *Final Report of the Commission on Human Security* (2003), available at: http://www.humansecurity-chs.org/finalreport/index.html; and materials collected in IDEA (Institute for Democracy and Human Security), *Democracy, Conflict, and Human Security* (2006), available at: http://www.idea.int/publications/dchs/dchs_vol1.cfm.

5 For a recent review of the democratic peace literature with a region-based explanation, see Erik Gartzke, "The Capitalist Peace," *American Journal of Political Science* 51(1) pp. 166–191, available at: ⟨http://dss.ucsd.edu/~egartzke/publications/gartzke_ajps_07.pdf⟩.

6 Contrarily, if groups see democratic competition as hopeless, then democracy will not play this instrumental role.

market-based distribution of resources. As to the first, Amartya Sen and Jean Drèze have argued that famines are rare in states with free presses, for the reason that a free press protects against the sort of corruption and rent-seeking that tip the balance from a problem of food access to mass privation.[7] A free press also provides early warning of health and environmental risks, independently of government channels. Next, institutions of free speech, like democratic competitions, also enable monitoring of governmental misconduct, while party competition creates rival sources of power, breaking up governmental monopolies over resources. Third, while market systems can of course generate great inequality and unrest, they also prevent governmental aggregations of power, and hence can mitigate the victimization of vulnerable or disfavored groups by the state. Finally, the informal institutions of democracy – the barter and truck of political organization, conversation about elections – nurture a reserve of social capital that can be drawn upon for a range of welfare-enhancing ends.

These contingent, instrumental connections between democracy and security are important. But equally important are the constitutive connections between the two. Democracy can be conceived simply as one decision procedure among many, competing with dictatorships, aristocracies, and anarchies on the basis of its capacity to deliver maximum welfare. Indeed, classical treatments of democracy famously treat it as an erratic and essentially irrational decision procedure at that, with decisionmaking relegated to those least capable of exercising rational choice.[8] But, since at least the Enlightenment (and with traces in medieval and early modern political theory) democracy has been conceived in more ambitiously moralized terms: as a way of allocating decisional authority in accordance with individuals' equal moral worth. Democracy, in other words, is the political manifestation of a moral ideal, one that insists that the proper unit of respect is the individual, taken one at a time, without regard to rank or station. The ideal of democracy runs hand in hand with the rhetoric of human security, and in sharp contrast to the rhetoric of national security, insofar as both claim to honor the same value of equality. We might thereby come to take the connection's intimacy for granted, by recognizing a fused concept: that of *democratic security.*

IV. The limits of democratic security

We should, I have suggested, be impressed by the robustness of the connections between democracy and human security. Democratic institutions represent a convergence of moral and political thought, bringing together a range of ideals within

---

7 Amartya Sen and Jean Drèze, *Hunger and Public Action* (New York: Oxford University Press, 1989).

8 While theoretical concerns about the rationality of democratic choice date back at least to the Marquis de Condorcet, the modern formal treatment of the insufficiency of democratic institutions to provide a coherent form of social choice is Kenneth Arrow, *Social Choice and Individual Values* (New Haven: Yale University Press, 2nd ed. 1970); see also William Riker, *Liberalism against Populism: A Confrontation between the Theory of Democracy and the Theory of Social Choice* (Waveland Press, 1988).

a relatively coherent set of practices. We should therefore expect such happy coincidences. But I want now to offer some cautions as well. If the demand for democratic decisionmaking is one lesson of the Enlightenment, the plurality of values is another – the resistance of values like liberty, most famously, but also dignity, recognition, honor, and excellence, to be reduced to some common coin.[9] I turn now to the problems posed by plurality. I do not mean to question the robustness of these connections, both instrumental and intrinsic. It is precisely because democracy has become such a powerful value in modern thought, to the extent that it displaces complementary but occasionally rival political values, that we must seek the limits of those connections as well.

First, however, a brief note about my use of the term "democracy." I have been deliberately non-specific about what form of political regime counts as a democracy, and what institutions are democratic. At a certain level of generality or idealization, there is little dispute: democratic regimes are those in which political power is fundamentally directed through a mass electorate, reflecting a universal franchise, by means of the aggregation of expressed political preferences. Furthermore, it is a constitutive feature of democracy that preferences are weighted equally, a duke's no more than a squire's, in the aggregation of those preferences.

In practice, of course, derogations from the ideal do not necessarily forfeit a claim to the democratic label. A franchise restricted by sex, race, class, or literacy is distasteful and clearly imperfect in its democratic pedigree, but a state with such a system might still merit the label of a democracy, at least in contrast to dictatorial or oligarchic regimes. More vexing are questions whether systems with universal franchise but massive informal intimidation of voters, or without free presses or limited rights of assembly, or irregular elections, can be called democratic. And harder yet are questions about the compatibility of technocratic or administrative governance with some features of democratic decisionmaking; or whether systems of constitutional restraint, entrenched citizen rights, and judicial review are either demanded by or even consistent with democratic ideals. I do not want here to wade into those swamps. All I need for the present discussion is the loose ideal of decisionmaking by mass electorate.

There are a number of quite obvious misconnections between human security and democracy that I should like to get out of the way. Both, alas, are risks fully on the modern scene. I will call these the problem of outcomes and the problem of pretexts.

The problem of outcomes is, simply, "what if the bad guys win?" Since democracy is a procedural not a substantive concept, there is no guarantee that the victors in democratic competition will, in fact, honor the ends of human security. While those who wish to retain power in subsequent elections will, presumably, try to ensure adequate levels of well-being for those voters, actual electoral calculations can be more cynical. Resources can be exploited unsustainably, to boost the standard of living for the electorate immediately but threatening their food security later. Populist

---

9 This is a theme of Montesquieu, Constant, Herder, and Condorcet in the Enlightenment; and of Isaiah Berlin more recently.

land or industrial reforms can cripple productivity. Leaders can start wars to gin up nationalist fervor. And with victories in hand, democratic leaders can impose a range of restrictions on the press, or on personal liberties (liberty of conscience is a favorite target), all of which have the effect of reducing political voice, increasing cultural marginalization, or otherwise negatively affecting security. At the limit, leaders can be voted in who take their genuine democratic mandate as a justification for restricting the effective franchise, eliminating elections or vastly increasing the power of the head of state.

The problem of pretexts is different, although also generated typically by cynicism on the part of participants in the democratic process: the values of democracy itself can be an occasion for highly non-democratic interventions. Domestically, the preservation of "free and fair elections" can result in spurious charges of voter fraud or media manipulation, interfering with the communicative channels of democracy. Internationally, as we have seen too well, a "democracy-exporting" agenda can lead to foreign wars of "democratic liberation," or to other interference with foreign political processes, in the name of improving their democratic responsiveness. While in some cases this interference may be in good faith, in other cases it is patently a pretext for expanding the zone of influence of the exporting state. The use of pretexts in international Realpolitik is not novel. But access to the legitimizing frame of democracy makes the pretext harder to displace, putting it in line with a tradition of other pretextual traditions, notably the Christianization of the New World and the *mission civilisatrice* of France.

I do not want to belabor these points, but simply to indicate that democratic processes are consistent with a great deal of mischief, all of which can undermine the otherwise positive instrumental connections. All ideologies are subject to opportunistic manipulation. The goal of democraticization, or the mandate of democracy, is, if anything, more resistant than other ideologies, precisely because the concept can do critical work even as it is deployed opportunistically. It remains a fair question to the popular leader who seeks to expand his power whether such a move is really consistent with the democratic ideals he espoused – as Hugo Chavez recently learned. And lessons about the preparations necessary for a genuinely pro-democracy intervention – and the self-defeating nature of most of those interventions – can temper the enthusiasm of even good-faith proponents while also offering an obstacle to the opportunists.[10]

I now want, however, to focus on another aspect of democracy that can undermine human security more insidiously, because it is grounded in neither political naiveté nor opportunism. This is the way a conception of political legitimacy, as rooted in democratic processes, serves to undermine rule of law values and individual protections, by rendering such claims as non-democratic, matters of elite or foreign opinion.

10 In the U.S., the neo-conservative democracy-promotion agenda appears to be considerably chastened by the lessons of Iraq and Afghanistan.

V. Legitimacy and democracy

"Legitimacy," in its normative rather than sociological sense, has to do with the justifiability of political authority. It is sometimes conceived in terms of a "right to rule" or the justifiability of the exercise of political power; but both of these conceptions seem to me too restrictive to capture its full sense – at least the sense that needs to be captured in order to discuss international law. A "right to rule" only makes sense in the domestic context, where "ruling" involves extensive or total control over the lives of subjects. But whatever one might think about the legitimacy of the U.N. Security Council – which is legitimate if any international institution is – it neither claims nor exercises any general power to rule subject states, but only to fulfill the limited terms of its charter to keep the international peace. Similarly, defining legitimacy in terms of justifications for the exercise of political power is too narrow. If we understand power as an ability to enforce compliance with an order, then because many international institutions and agreements lack enforcement mechanisms and so lack power, they would not be able to make claims to legitimacy. The Convention against Torture is one such institutional agreement, for its "enforcement" system is limited to a power to demand reports of violations.[11] It prejudges debates about the justifiability of such agreements, especially given their complex effects through domestic incorporation, to look at them solely through the lens of power.

So the working definition of legitimacy I prefer focuses on the justification for an institution to declare an authoritative norm, whether or not it has the power to enforce that norm. Roughly, an institution, institutional process, or institutionally-defined agent enjoys legitimacy when its announcement of a norm gives actors subject to the norm substantial reason to comply with it. (Derivatively, a norm has legitimacy when it is issued by a legitimate institution, or by a legitimate institutional process.) The crucial part of this definition is that the announcement *gives* reason, in the sense that it adds substantially to the reasons the actors have to act (or refrain from acting) in compliance with the norm. Consider again the Convention on Torture and assume that the investigating Committee, created by Article 20, determines that U.S practices of interrogation, administered at Guantanamo, violated the Convention.[12] If the Commission is correct, then presumably the U.S. already has independent moral reasons to cease these practices, including the reason that it would be in breach of its obligations under the treaty. But if the Commission is legitimate to boot, then its declaration gives the U.S. an additional reason to cease, on grounds of deference to the authority of the Commission to define party obligations under the Convention. This is true even though the Commission lacks any enforcement power.

11 Convention against Torture and other Cruel, Inhuman, or Degrading Treatment or Punishment, Art. 20, http://www.unhchr.ch/html/menu3/b/h_cat39.htm.

12 Indeed, it is patently true that a Commission would find this. See Laurel Fletcher and Eric Stover, *Guantanamo and its Aftermath: U.S. Detention and Interrogation Practices and their Impact on Former Detainees* (Berkeley: Human Rights Center, 2008), http://hrc.berkeley.edu/.

Put aside for the moment what kinds of arguments can support claims of legitimacy, and look now to some facts about the term's usage. "Legitimacy" is a *challenge* term: it gets used in order to contest claims of authority. In the domestic context, the challenge is usually of the form, "who are you to do this to me?" And in the international, it is, often, "who are you to say this to me?" Legitimacy, in other words, functions contextually as the silent shadow of illegitimacy – as perhaps, as Judith Shklar famously suggested, justice is defined by the shadow of injustice.[13] My point is not that legitimacy is defined in terms of illegitimacy, however, for the opposite is true. It is just that what we need to take note of are the circumstances in which challenges to legitimacy do *not* arise. The absence of those challenges does not entail legitimacy; their absence just means that there is no practical pressure on the issue.

Consider, as an analogy, how a question of the meaning or point of life arises. While it might arise in the philosophy seminar, or while stretched on one's back, contemplating the stars in the wilderness, it arises poignantly only when something has happened to raise with urgent force the question whether to go on – the death of a loved one, the defeat of a goal. In those cases the question demands an answer, not mere speculation, and the demands on the sufficiency of an answer are very great, perhaps insuperable. What one seeks is to return to conditions in life where the question does not arise at all.

When political institutions are functioning well, or circumstances are providing no obstacles, the question of the legitimacy of those institutions simply does not arise. Of course it might arise in idle reflection, as for example someone might simply wonder about the grounds for the authority of the WTO. A quick reference to the WTO's origins in the Uruguay GATT round, for example will suffice, for its legitimacy was not really under challenge, just investigation. But sometimes the question of legitimacy arises with urgency, because a real challenge has been set, for instance the conflict of national health regulation with the terms of global free trade. Conflicting claims of democracy and local self-governance press on the claimed legitimacy of the institution, and we must enter the realm of normative argument for the authority of the WTO. And once we move down that path, we must be prepared to acknowledge the failure of the institution to meet norms that properly apply, even if they are rarely applied with their full force. The open question is whether, once the crisis has been put to the past through diplomatic finesse, we can return to reside in the unchallenged, and perhaps unsustainable, normal attitude of legitimacy.

I have already simply asserted the dominance of democracy as a legitimation concept. But it might be worth comparing the relevant alternatives. First, and most primitively, is *relational* or *natural* legitimacy: an institution, or person representing an institution, simply claims authority in virtue of its nature, origin, or relation to the subject of the norm. "Because I'm your parent," or "because I come from the house of Stuart" are claims of this sort, and ever since the Enlightenment they have had only marginally better rhetorical success in the household than they have in the nation-state. Second

13 Judith Shklar, *The Faces of Injustice* (New Haven: Yale University Press, 1988).

is "procedural" legitimacy, whereby questions of legitimacy are answered by reference to the outcome of some favored procedure, for instance free and fair balloting, or parliamentary decisionmaking, or entrail divination. Third, is *instrumental* or, as it is sometimes called, *performance* legitimacy.[14] On such accounts, institutions are legitimate if they produce or protect certain goods or interests, relative to some further specified baseline. Hobbes' conception of legitimacy is arguably performance-based, for the sovereign's warrant flows from his success in maintaining the civil peace; and so obviously are utilitarian or other welfarist conceptions. On a performance theory, nothing succeeds like success, and success in delivering the goods gives legitimate title. Fourth, is the dominant modern form of legitimacy argument: voluntaristic legitimacy. Subjectively voluntaristic legitimacy claims are grounded in the actual consent, assent, or acquiescence of norm subjects to the authority, while objectively voluntaristic claims are based in what parties would choose or could not reasonably reject, given their prior aims or evaluative commitments.

Clearly, reductions of some of these categories to others are both possible and necessary. Purely relational claims are empty unless they are grounded in other arguments, for instance an instrumental argument that restricting political authority to a single dynasty reduces political violence. Procedural claims beg the question why some procedures are favored over others, for instance as ways of maximizing subjective welfare or revealing popular will. They turn, ultimately, on the question of what factors they process into the currency of legitimacy. Instrumental theories, meanwhile, are only in part actually theories of legitimacy at all. If the institutions are delivering goods subjects actually want, then subjects have independent instrumental reason to comply with the institutions in question, so the claim to legitimate authority by the institution is redundant. It adds no significant reason of its own to their compliance. Alternatively, if performance measures are grounded in interests individual subjects do not think they actually have – for instance, an interest in maximizing aggregate welfare – then they beg the question why some particular goods or interests should be protected or promoted, rather than others. That question might be answered intuitionistically; but more frequently in contemporary theory it itself gets an objectively voluntaristic basis, in terms of what people would want, in the right deliberative circumstances with the right information.[15]

The upshot of this anatomy of legitimacy claims is that democracy starts to loom quickly once we reflect on the basis of legitimacy claims. If the question is what goods are to be promoted, and the initial answer is "the goods people show they need by what they try to do," we must still answer the further question of *which* people can do the showing, and how they can do so. While various forms of elitism are conceptually possible, political pressure pushes towards goods with broad audiences.

14 For the claim that EU legitimacy is best conceived in performance terms, see David Beetham and Christopher Lord, *Legitimacy and the European Union*, (London: Longman, 1998).

15 True, we may seem to be left with intuitionism in some form if we are pressed for why we concern ourselves with what people want or should want. But a fundamental insistence on this conception of the political good seems a reasonable place to declare one's justificatory spade turned.

Similarly, if consent or acquiescence is the basis for legitimacy, then the question of whose consent (real or hypothetical) arises. The question of the legitimacy of an international institution might be answered by reference to state consent in the treaty process. But, since states are artificial persons, this merely moves the question to the relation between state consent and citizen consent, and how that relation might be discerned. Again, pressure builds towards a broader conception of the consenting constituency, and a method of revealing and actuating that consent.

In the domestic context, where what is to be legitimated are institutions with extensive control over their subjects' lives, the pressures towards democracy are especially intense. The possibility of lethal coercion obviously raises the justificatory stakes in a general way, as does the broad domain of control. If political institutions restricted themselves to indicating salient points for coordination and providing requisite reassurance for cooperators, with perhaps a dash of jawboning thrown in, then few questions of legitimacy would arise. But domestic politics are not so easy: the state must arbitrate between competing claims on the same scarce resource, deter the free rider and punish the malefactor, or restrict the claims of the majority to domesticate the unruly minority. The contexts in which legitimacy challenges arise sprout like daisies, and so the justificatory stakes are raised.

More specifically, the problem of how to justify the subjection of a whole population, each with particular interests, to the control of a central authority makes some version of Rousseau's solution highly attractive. Provisionally, the forms of control exercised over the population will be illegitimate unless they capture both the assent and secure the common interests of all. Institutions that can credibly claim to represent that assent, such as robustly deliberative popular assemblies governed by consensus or, at worst, a preference for super-majoritarian decisionmaking, will be the standard form of practical solution to the theoretical problem. (Simple majoritarianism has its defenders as a legitimate system of governance, but not among the dissenting minority crushed underfoot.) Legitimation discourse quickly converges upon radical democracy once dogmatic or natural justifications are no longer on the table.

To the international context

I have hinted that matters might be different on the international front. This is not because the standards of legitimacy are lower or the institutions better, but because the crises are less frequently provoked. First, as I mentioned above, much of international law is toothless, either because the obliging treaties provide for no sanctions, or because the norms are embedded in so-called "soft law" voluntary undertakings that don't even rise to the level of obligation. Second, a great deal international law, perhaps unlike domestic law, represents forms of non-zero-sum coordination over the long-term, generating internal pressures of compliance. An obvious example are the treaties governing international air travel and currency exchange; more controversially, so might be the law of war, or international humanitarian law, which has over the long-term substantial benefits in the form of reciprocal treatment of prisoners and easier transitions from war to peace. Third, the international arena is – relative to the domestic arena – passive. There are relatively few formal disputes. Particular subject areas, notably trade, may generate a lot of disputes, but overall the workload of international legal institutions is a fraction that of their domestic analogues.[16] True, much of the business of international law is channeled through diplomatic systems rather than litigation, but precisely to the degree that inter-state diplomacy is at stake, the legitimacy of a third-party international institution is not.

Fourth, a lot of international law is treaty-based; there are roughly 50,000 treaties recorded as in current force. These are voluntary obligations and voluntary accessions to jurisdiction, whose force stems from freely-given consent. While it would be a mistake to see state consent as strictly parallel to personal consent in the domestic context – insofar as states can thereby bind nonconsenting individuals – explicit state consent displaces many legitimacy concerns. Fifth, it is a peculiar feature of international law that for customary international law, its validity depends upon its efficacy. I mean efficacy at the level of the individual norm, not the legal system as a whole. On the domestic side, a necessary condition of a legal system's existence is the general efficacy of the system in ensuring popular compliance with its norms.[17] But if the system (or its operators) is generally effective in securing compliance, then the validity (understood as an existence condition) of a given legal norm demands no special compliance. A new statute might be widely ignored or disobeyed, but would still count as valid law in the jurisdiction so long as it meets the relevant formal tests. But efficacy and validity are far more closely connected in the case of customary international law, where the existence tests involve the question of the scope of actual international compliance with the norm, arising out of subjective deference to the norm as a principle of law (the *opinio juris* test). An ignored customary norm is no norm at all; and when formally declared norms (or the canonical interpretations of those norms) come to be ignored, the law itself is seen to have shifted. What was illegal at Time 0 may, through force of intransigence in the face of the norm pass through to permissibility. Conversely, when a violation of international law succeeds in delivering clear gains to commonly recognized interests, the very efficacy of that violation redefines the governing norm.

What follows is that international legal institutions are rarely called upon to meet criteria of legitimacy – criteria they would likely fail if tested by. At most, they are generally tested by reference to performance, criteria which have only an intermediate bearing on the case for ultimate legitimacy. And yet, on the other hand, it is precisely these international institutions that are asked to do the hard work of furthering human security. Their democratic deficit undercuts the human security agenda, and shows the tension between the two. I will try to show this with two examples.

The first example is a recent decision by the United States Supreme Court, which declared the juvenile death penalty unconstitutional, on the grounds that the evolving standards of decency now condemn the practice.[18] Formally speaking, this was fully a decision of domestic law, governed by the terms of the U.S. Constitution. In fact, however, international law seems to have played a significant part in the decision.

16 For example, the current docket of the International Court of Justice reports just twelve pending cases, dating from 1993.

17 See H.L.A. Hart, *The Concept of Law* (2nd. ed., Oxford, 1994), p. 103.

18 *Roper v. Simmons*, 543 U.S. 551 (2005).

Justice Kennedy's majority decision rested on three legs. First, he claimed that a national "consensus" has come to exist on the question – not a real consensus, marked by unanimity, but a consensus by a majority, with indications of a trend in the abolitionist direction.[19] Second, he argued that psychological evidence showed cognitive immaturity among juveniles, which supported a hypothesis of mitigated culpability and poor risk assessment, which undermined both retributive and deterrent rationales for the punishment. And third, he referred to the extraordinarily isolated global position of the U.S. in executing juvenile killers, which was one of but eight countries to permit a practice outlawed by a large number of international treaties.

In fact, the international leg is the only one capable of bearing much of the weight of the opinion. As dissenting Justice O'Connor noted, evidence of any national trend (much less a consensus) is equivocal at best, given that a significant number of states have recently made explicit provision for the juvenile death penalty. And the empirical evidence best supports narrow tailoring of the penalty to the most culpable juvenile offenders, not the bright-line categorical rule. But the force of the international claim was substantial, where a real international consensus exists with such vigor that there is strong support for the claim that juvenile executions are a violation of a non-treaty-based *jus cogens* norm, binding even on those who – like the U.S. – have exempted themselves from treaty provisions on that point. International law, toothless as it is, was presumed to speak with authority to the U.S. case.

Justice Kennedy's invocation of the international community of opinion generated an explosive dissent from Justice Scalia. Scalia called into question the legitimacy of using international public opinion to rebut the deliberate policy choice of and decency standards of the citizens of Missouri, as well as the other five states permitting the practice. He wrote, "Though the views of our own citizens are essentially irrelevant ... the views of other countries and the so-called international community take center-stage."[20] Despite the hyberole, Scalia had a point – if one takes seriously the distinctive legitimating power of democracy. Since the force of the international norm is itself ostensibly established by the universal practice of nations, the Court is effectively holding that the muted reflection of democracy in that norm trumps the direct exercise of democracy in Missouri. And it is indeed hard to see how the practice, however universal, of other states restricting their own punitive practices could legitimately be brought to bear on what Missourians should do in their territory, especially given that the national political community has refused, on each opportunity, to join in the international consensus by treaty. While a paean to democracy in support of juvenile executions is less than compelling, Scalia's complaint rings true. We cannot simply presume that the international norm ought to apply to Missouri because of its moral truth, for its moral truth is precisely what is in question among the citizens to whom it has been made to apply. The dignity claims of human rights conflict with the dignity claims of democratic voters.

Here is a second example, from the domain of trade. As part of the WTO system, the state parties made a number of ancillary agreements governing, among other

19 Ibid at 13.

20 Scalia, J., dissenting, 543 U.S. __ (2005), at 16.

issues, health and safety. Article 3 of the Sanitary and Phytosanitary Measures (or SPS) Agreement formally permits nations to adopt health measures they see as necessary to protect their domestic constituencies, even exceeding international standards, but only insofar as the measures have an adequate "scientific justification."[21] The point of this test is to screen out ostensibly health-related measures that are in fact protectionist measures.

In 1996 the relation of domestic health norms to WTO authority was tested by the U.S. and Canada, when they brought a complaint against the European Union which had, in 1995, adopted a rule prohibiting the importation of cattle treated with various growth hormones.[22] The EU decision was taken under the guidance of the so-called "precautionary principle," which directs risk minimization in the face of scientific uncertainty and high stakes. In the abstract, one might well think that extreme risk-aversion concerning hormonal additions to beef would fall within the scope of reasonable judgments about the public health, whether or not one agrees with the merits. In fact the measure was rejected by the Appellate Body, not on the basis of its content but on the lack of any "reasonable support or warrant" for the measure.[23] This conclusion, which may accurately represent the scientific evidence put before the Appellate Body, also reflects what was at stake: an essentially normative, political judgment about how to manage health risks of unknown magnitude was supplanted by an expert, trade-focused body's essentially technocratic standard.

While the EU standard-setting process is no model of democracy, it is fair to say that resistance to genetically or hormonally-modified foodstuffs runs deep in the popular will. On the other side of the books is the mandate of the Appellate Body itself, which flows from the SPS and WTO agreements entered into and ratified by the legislative assemblies of the member states, and applying international standards set through the ostensibly über-democratic norm of consensus. And while one may easily be critical of the actual voluntariness of the decision by less developed states whether to accept the terms of the WTO, the concern about coerced consent hardly holds for the European and North American players. On this view, the Appellate Body simply enjoys power delegated to it by its members, who all seek the common good of trade harmonization. In principle, the democratic deficit of the Appellate Body doesn't seem different in kind than that enjoyed by U.S. Article III courts or their international equivalents, also mandated by statute and – at least in the U.S. – thereafter capable of rejecting seemingly reasonable health or environmental regulations on their own judgments of adequate empirical basis.[24]

So much is true, and can ground the legitimacy of the WTO institutions in ordinary business, below crisis point. But in the case of a real conflict between local and international standards, these considerations provide little comfort. Delegated

21 http://www.wto.int/english/tratop_e/sps_e/spsagr_e.htm.

22 See the the Appellate Body Report, EC-Hormones, WT/DS 26, 48/AB/R, http://www.worldtradelaw.net/dsc/ab/ec-hormones(dsc)(ab).pdf.

23 Judgment of the Appellate Body, Paras. 208–209.

24 Under U.S. law, federal courts can reject health and safety administrative regulations as "arbitrary or capricious" exercises of delegated judgment; and they can reject health and safety legislation as inconsistent with a limited constitutional mandate.

powers within a domestic system come with greater powers of popular revision, however balky the process, greater opportunities for political monitoring, as well as with a sense that a common cultural and political matrix will ensure a fair degree of harmony between regulation and adjudication. These formal and extra-formal considerations, which make direct or indirect democratic institutions mainstays of legitimacy, are significantly less present on the international stage, particularly within the WTO's secretive "green room" policy discussions and appellate decisions. When a crisis arises, the international institutions fail the comparative test of legitimacy.

VI. Reserving our enthusiasm for democracy

The two cases I have described feature conflicts between principles protecting fundamental aspects of human security – freedom from state violence, and access to the benefits of globalization – and basic principles of democratic legitimation. Nor are these conflicts incidental. Norms such as restrictions on execution, or protection of the benefits of a free trade system, are much likelier to arise from non-democratic institutions than from democratic ones, given the political economies of the relevant policy questions: local interests will almost always defeat global interests in a democratic match. In some cases, we outside observers might side with the international forum; in others with the local constituency. But the point is such conflicts are endemic, and they will inevitably sap the resources of the institutions the human security agenda depends on. Indeed, an argument from democratic premises is one of the central struts of a recent, influential critique of international law in the United States, Eric Posner and Jack Goldsmith's *The Limits of International Law*.[25] Posner and Goldsmith combine a descriptive thesis, that international law only appears to bind nations, who act in conformity with it only when they have separate, self-interested reasons to do so, with a normative thesis: that democratic states should not regard themselves as bound by international law unless and until it is legitimated through local, democratic incorporation.[26]

Put aside the merits of their descriptive thesis. Their normative thesis is essentially unchallengeable, so long as we cede the ground to democracy as a source of legitimate authority. The human security movement risks doing so by tying its agenda to democratization too closely. To put the point in broader perspective: treating democracy as a master value of political theory and institutional design not only aids those who would cloak policies of national or majoritarian self-interest in grander cloth. It also deprives us of the range of intellectual and policy tools necessary for solving the practical and moral problems of a complex international world. These problems range from climate change to access to health care and nutrition to protection of disfavored minorities to optimization of international trade. No single set of legitimating practices will fit all these problems. Within specific policy domains, for instance international credit or human rights, it may be that we need a frank nod to technocratic or intellectually authoritarian institutions bound to performance stan-

---

25 Eric Posner and Jack Goldsmith, *The Limits of International Law* (New York: Oxford University Press, 2005).

26 Ibid at 189–192.

dards, to guard against the short-horizoned temptations of popular politics. There will be a place for democratic direction of these institutions, but their democratic deficits must not be seen as immediately disabling. Similarly, attempts to impose direct democratic control on markets and information may well reduce the supplies of those crucial goods to ordinary individuals. By contrast, more democratic control over the institutions of national security or economic development is a valuable corrective to rent-seeking by insiders. We should be prepared to recognize and reap the human security gains brought by democratic institutions. But we must see democracy as an uneasy partner, working most fruitfully with a mixture of powers and limitations.

Chapter 10

Global Procedural Rights and Security

Larry May

Most of the recent literature on global justice in political philosophy has focused on substantive issues, such as claims of economic distributive justice of those in poor countries, or the right against persecution. Such rights are extremely important. But there is a class of issues that have been given little attention, namely procedural rights such as the right of habeas corpus or non-refoulement at the global level. These rights are arguably just as important for the security of peoples across the globe and yet there is little discussion of them and few global institutions that currently consider them. I will address this issue in the context of both human and state security in an increasingly interconnected world.

The debates about global justice typically concern economic distributive justice or criminal retributive justice. Both of these forms of justice concern substantive justice, namely the substantive rights that people have by virtue of either their economic need or their status as victims. I wish to discuss a different subject matter in the field of global justice, namely, the procedural rights that constitute an international rule of law. I will contend that procedural rights provide a moral core to any system of law, and even more so at the international level. Such procedural rights also provide at least minimalist protection concerning substantive rights as well. In this respect, the moral content of the law may very well be best exemplified in the institution of the international rule of law. Any substantive rights can be held hostage if the person who would claim these rights can be incarcerated unjustifiably.

I. The Value and Subjects of Security

Security is a value, but its extent is different for nearly each person or entity subject to it. At one end of a spectrum, security means not being attacked, or at least reducing the risk of attack until it is very low. At the other end of the spectrum, security means being able to flourish without interference, or at least with only a very small risk of interference. What lies in between the ends of this spectrum includes all of the liberties and rights that individuals may be said to have by virtue of our common humanity.

Security can be understood in three distinct ways: personal, collective, and national. The *jus ad bello* and *jus in bellum* considerations of the Just War tradition

Cecilia M. Bailliet (ed.), Security: A Multidisciplinary Normative Approach.
 ISBN 978 90 04 17296 8. pp. 249–260.

are aimed at each of these ways of understanding security. The *jus in bello* norms are primarily aimed at protecting the personal security of combatants and civilians in armed conflicts. The provisions of The Hague and Geneva Conventions, modeled on these Just War considerations, have become the gold standard of personal security protection during those most insecure times, namely when war is afoot. The *jus ad bello* norms are aimed at protecting States from aggression by other States. And the Security Council has been authorized, in Chapters VI and VII of the Charter of the United Nations to enforce the norm against aggression. There is also a sense that both sets of norms are aimed at protecting collectivities, especially social groups, from harm. Soldiers are treated as a group for some of the *jus in bello* considerations, as are civilian populations.

There are three subjects in need of security protection in armed conflict: States, especially those that have been unjustly attacked, civilians caught in the crossfire of wars, and combatants, especially those who have been captured. It is clear that atrocities like aggression and genocide harm the international community in that they destabilize security for many of those who are affected, individuals, social groups, and States alike. When NATO decided to send troops into Kosovo it was because of a concern that the ethnic cleansing campaign in the Balkans had already risked spreading into a wider European problem. The genocide in the Sudan is not merely a horrific humanitarian crisis for the people who are being starved to death; it is also a major factor destabilizing collective security of ethnic peoples and States, as well as individuals, in the region. Atrocities like genocide can thus be understood in terms of their effects on security: personal, collective, and national. Norms of armed conflict aim to protect each form of security.

The Universal Declaration of Human Rights (UDHR), in Article 3, says: "Everyone shall have the right to life, liberty, and the security of persons." The International Covenant on Civil and Political Rights sought to provide specificity to the provisions of the UDHR. Of special note are Article 9's provision against "arbitrary arrest or detention" and Article 13's provision against removal of an alien without review by "competent authority." But the specific provisions having to do with the treatment of those who are incarcerated, or who are subject to deportation, were not given the highest standing of being non-derogable. And there are no international institutions, on the order of the International Criminal Court, where someone can appeal. As a result these rights have not been generally recognized or protected internationally. Yet, these rights are crucial for the protection of most others.

I wish to call attention to two new directions in security having to do with norms of armed conflict. The first set of issues comes under the label of what I call "global procedural justice." Here I would mention two global procedural rights that need to be protected to secure individuals and populations: habeas corpus and non-refoulement. Habeas corpus rights, including the right not to be arbitrarily incarcerated, and non-refoulement rights, including the right not to be deported to a State where one's life will be put in jeopardy, are the cornerstones of procedural rights that protect security of individuals as well as those of social groups. The latter claim is most plausible concerning members of groups that are currently being persecuted in a given State. Such procedural rights take on added importance during situations of nontraditional armed conflict, such as the United States' war on terrorism, where special detention facilities were established in Guantanamo Bay, Cuba. Contrary to current international instruments, the United States has failed to provide hearings and has also employed extraordinary rendition of prisoners back to States that will torture them.

Habeas and non-refoulement are basic security rights but they are also procedural rather than substantive in that they set limits on a process, imprisonment in the case of habeas and deportation in the case of non-refoulement. For habeas, the limit is that there must be a publicly declared charge against the prisoner, and the imprisonment must be for a definite and relatively short period of time until a preliminary trial is held. For non-refoulement, the limit is that no one should be deported to a State where it is likely that the prisoner will be put in serious jeopardy of harm. These rights are procedural and negative; yet most of what is currently protected has to do with substantive matters and positive rights. This new global focus on such procedural matters is needed but lacking.

A second new direction, but one I will not say much about here, concerns the way that aggression is conceptualized. In a book I published in 2008, *Aggression and Crimes Against Peace* (Cambridge UP), I argue that the International Criminal Court should start prosecuting State leaders for waging aggressive war, just as was done at Nuremberg. And the reason to protect States according to *jus ad bellum* norms has to do with protecting human rights. If States are doing a good job protecting human rights, then all three types of security call for prosecuting the leaders of those other States that would engage in aggression against the rights-protecting State. But if a State is not protecting human rights, it should not be shielded from aggression, whether meted out by the United Nations or by other States. Such considerations would make it clearer that humanitarian intervention can be justified and even required in certain cases. Similarly, even targeted assassination could be justified on such grounds, namely to protect security of individuals, groups, and States, and strict procedural guarantees must be met here as well.

New global institutions should be established to guarantee basic procedural rights and existing global institutions, such as the International Criminal Court, should be reformed so they are given larger mandates in order to advance the rights I have discussed. Not only is there significant risk that denial of these rights will adversely affect individuals, and be used to persecute disfavored groups, but since human rights abuses can easily spread across borders, this is also a matter of security for States. So, there are good self-interested reasons for States to accept the greater protections of human rights I have indicated here. New forms of warfare and armed conflict require new norms and new enforcement regimes as well. It is time for a serious discussion of a new institutional regime to protect security in light of the problems I have addressed.

II. Magna Carta Today

This project is inspired by two events, 788 years apart. The first is the signing of Magna Carta in 1215 and the second is the establishment of a prison at Guantanamo Bay in 2003. It may seem odd to link these two events, but I don't think it is odd at all. Magna Carta established that any person is entitled to due process of law. Guantanamo Bay stands for the idea that certain prisoners can be denied due process if they fall through the cracks in the various extant legal regimes.

Both international law today and Magna Carta are law based on contract. Magna Carta was a covenant extracted from King John of England by feudal barons. Chapter 39 (normally referred to as Chapter 29, in the 1225 revised version of King Henry III) says:

> No freeman shall be taken or imprisoned or desseised or exiled or in any way destroyed, nor will we go upon him nor send upon him, except by the lawful judgment of his peers or by the law of the land.

There are at least four distinct rights in this document, which came to stand for the core of procedural due process, and all four were violated by the establishment of the prison at Guantanamo Bay.

The rights enshrined in Magna Carta are:

1. The right not to be arbitrarily imprisoned;
2. The right not to be sent into exile;
3. The right not to be removed from the protection of the law;
4. The right to trial by jury.

At Guantanamo Bay, all four rights were violated. The right of habeas corpus was denied to these prisoners. Several prisoners were sent from Guantanamo to countries that were known routinely to use torture. The prisoners were described as being in a "legal black hole" in that they were neither within the jurisdiction of US courts nor under the jurisdiction of the laws and customs of war, since they were unlawful, or "enemy," combatants. And the prisoners at Guantanamo were denied trial by jury of their peers.

The writ of habeas corpus predates the Magna Carta of 1215, but is thought to have been given support in that document, even if not named there. By 1230, Henry of Bracton clearly lists the writ in his **De Legibus et Consuetudinibus Angliae**, and specifies its form as follows:

> that he produce his body ["et nunc praecipietur vicecomiti quod habeat corpus"] on another day by a writ of this kind: The king to the viscount greeting. We enjoin you before our justiciaries &c. on such a day the body of A., to answer to B. concerning such a plea.[1]

Here we see the writ described as addressing the official who is detaining or jailing a person to produce the body of the prisoner and provide an answer concerning why the prisoner should continue to be deprived of his or her freedom. The writ of habeas corpus "developed as an instrument for judges to control arbitrary detention." And at least one legal theorist has persuasively argued that such rights were never thought to be restricted to just one jurisdiction.[2] I will argue that such rights are basic rights, on all fours with their better known economic and retributive concerns.

---

1 6 Bracton 474–477, Sir Travis Twiss, ed., Bracton, *De Legibus et Consuetudinibus Angliae* (London: Longmans and Co., 1883), quoted in William F. Duker, *A Constitutional History of Habeas Corpus*, Westport, CT: Greenwood Press, 1980, pp. 16–17.

2 Timothy Endicott, 'Habeas Corpus and Guantanamo Bay: A View from Abroad', draft in the possession of the author.

I will include other rights than habeas that are often not seen as procedural rights, but which I believe should be so considered. Here are the contemporary equivalents of Magna Carta's rights:

The right of habeas corpus
The right of non-refoulement
The right to be a subject of international law
The right to trial by jury

It is my contention that such rights are the backbone of a minimal respect for human rights generally and if recognized globally would provide equitable relief and significantly fill gaps in an international rule of law. I defend this thesis in what follows.

At the moment, the ICC has four substantive crimes as the basis of its jurisdiction: genocide, crimes against humanity, war crimes, and the crime of aggression (the last is currently not operational because of a lack of consensus on what constitutes aggression). The crimes other than aggression are very specifically defined and are only likely to be prosecuted when there has been a mass atrocity. In addition, the ICC is governed by the important principle of complementarity, which requires that the prosecutor can only take a case if the State that otherwise would have jurisdiction has refused or indicated that it cannot hear the case on its own. I see the global procedural justice rights as a corollary consideration to the substantive rights already protected at the ICC, but they are also gap fillers on the way toward a much more robust, and morally significant, international legal regime.

III. Preconditions for the Rule of Law

The rights contained in Chapter 29 (39) of Magna Carta are what are sometimes referred to as fundamental law. A number of historians, including Holdsworth, date the idea of habeas corpus to an earlier time than Magna Carta. And interestingly, the earliest uses of habeas corpus also do not stand for such a broad right as due process, but only for the right to challenge one's imprisonment, a purely procedural right, or perhaps a proto-procedural right. Such rights do not specify any right to a particular form of treatment or liberty that the State must protect. Rather these rights are simply what minimally must be done so that arbitrariness does not creep into the way that people are deprived of their liberty by being incarcerated, outlawed or exiled. What is not initially clear, but what I will explore in the next sections, is how procedural or proto-procedural rights could come to be thought of as fundamental or constitutional law.

These great rights in Chapter 29 (39) of Magna Carta can be seen as procedural rights. They are not themselves what people normally mean by "due process rights" and they are not those listed in the canonical treatment of the rule of law by Lon Fuller.[3] Fuller does mention habeas corpus in passing, as part of the congruence between official action and declared rule. He lists this right along with the right to

3 See Lon Fuller, *The Morality of Law*, New Haven, CT: Yale University Press, 1964, 1969, Chapter 2.

appeal, not as part of "procedural due process," but as rights "in part directed toward the same objective" as due process, in that lack of such rights can contribute to a broken or arbitrary system.[4]

Perhaps, the provisions of Magna Carta's Chapter 29 (39) should be seen as proto-procedural rather than procedural, but in any event, they are not substantive in the normal sense of the term since they do not secure any particular liberty. Proto-procedural rights would be those that are necessary for the efficacy of procedural rights, but do not have the normal features of being procedural themselves. Habeas corpus says only that there must be some ability of a prisoner to be made visible, to get his case reviewed, and this right can act in a way to deter the most egregious forms of arbitrariness. But it does not specify what that procedure should be. Nonetheless, I will generally continue to talk about these rights as procedural, but one should note that I do recognize the distinction between procedural rights that are a precondition even for other procedural rights, and procedural rights that are not a precondition for other rights.

When the great struggles over English sovereignty took place in the Seventeenth Century, the part of Magna Carta that people fixed on were these rights in Chapter 29 (39). Here is how a distinguished legal scholar characterizes this later development:

> Thus the Habeas Corpus Act [1679] provides heavy penalties against all who offend against its provisions: judges who refuse to issue the writ, officers who send a prisoner out of England. The right of the penalty is a private right, enforceable like any debt; and the King has no power to pardon, at any rate after the proceedings have been commenced. In other cases the right of action is given to the 'common informer,' that is, any member of the public who chooses to take proceedings; in others, again, to some corporation which represents professional interests, such as the Law Society or Goldsmiths' Company.[5]

The provisions of Chapter 29 (39) were seen as crucial for "enforcing the law" especially for making sure that the legal rights were not denied by spiriting a potentially complaining party away, either into jail or out of the country altogether. No rights would be secured without these rights of habeas corpus and other similar rights enforced.

Consider for instance the practice of basing conviction merely on the King's claim of "notoriety" of the deeds of the accused. Magna Carta was cited to show that there must be some kind of judicial proceedings, with the accused present, for conviction and execution to be lawful.[6] What transpired over the centuries after Magna Carta was "the long slow progression toward the 'rule of law.'" Even kings, such as King Edward II, would declare that they could not act "contrary to Magna Carta and the common law of the realm,"[7]

---

4 Ibid., p. 81.

5 W.M. Geldart, *Elements of English Law*, London: Thornton Butterworth, Ltd., 1911, 1933, p. 233.

6 See Faith Thompson, *Magna Carta – Its Role in the Making of the English Constitution 1300–1629*, Minneapolis, MN: University of Minnesota Press, 1948, p. 73.

7 Ibid at 84.

Henry Maine made an important point very clear indeed when he said:

> So great is the ascendancy of the Law of Actions in the infancy of Courts of Justice, that substantive law has at first the look of being gradually secreted in the interstices of procedure; and the early lawyer can only see the law through the envelope of its technical forms.[8]

The substantive rights of liberty, especially the right to be free in one's bodily movements, are indeed first approached in a system of law that moved beyond the purely local, in this somewhat surprising way. Perhaps, a similar kind of move can be made in international law today. Rather than focusing directly on substantive rights, perhaps it is such procedural rights, or proto-procedural rights, such as habeas corpus that we should turn to, since the substantive rights developed much more slowly in medieval English legal debates.

It is also true that many other types of early law, including Irish and Indian legal systems, give "an extraordinary prominence" to procedure.[9] When early legal systems focus on procedure they display an awareness that the most important "service to mankind was to furnish an alternative to savagery, not to suppress it wholly" by limiting but still partially allowing private remedies. As long as the appropriate procedures are followed, these private remedies were important since early tribunals often lacked the "power of directly enforcing their own decrees."[10] Procedures, like those that set limits on the arbitrary use of power, nonetheless allow a wide variety of enforcement mechanisms, something that is especially important when there is no centralized sovereign power, as is of course true of international law today.

Maitland tells us how the "forms of action" were absolutely crucial in determining whether there even was a wrong that had been committed. As Maitland put it, one didn't see a wrong and then look for a form of action, but one first had to find a form of action before there was anything that could be called a wrong that was legally actionable. Maitland also explains how the growing importance and consolidation of forms of action contributed to the gradual increase in sovereign power within England. Here is how he characterized the incremental move toward centralized sovereignty:

> Had the worst come to the worst, the king might have claimed these things: jurisdiction over his own immediate tenants, jurisdiction when all lords have made default, a few specially royal pleas known as pleas of the crown. To this he might have been reduced by feudalism … That his court should throw open its doors to all litigants … is a principle that only slowly gains ground.[11]

Magna Carta did not instantly transform English legal culture into a centralized system. Instead, procedural consolidation merely set the stage by restricting the form

---

8 Sir Henry Maine, *Dissertations on Early Law and Custom*, NY: Henry Holt and Company, 1886, p. 389.

9 See, ibid at 374 and 386.

10 Ibid. at 387.

11 F.W. Maitland, *The Forms of Action at Common Law* (1909), NY: Cambridge University Press, 1971, p. 11.

of law so that later a consolidation of substance could proceed. Indeed, the whole process took at least four centuries, and to a certain extent has not ended yet.

There is no doubt, though, that Magna Carta came to be seen as hugely important. One historian makes the point quite succinctly:

> Magna Carta had established itself as more than simply a venerable statute; by then it was fundamental law. In 1368, for example, a statute of Edward III commanded that the "Great Charter and the Charter of the Forest be beholden and kept in all Points; and if there be any Statute made to the contrary, it shall be beholden for none." Here we see Magna Carta treated as a superstatute, in other words as a constitution ... an obvious similarity ... to the language of the American Constitution ... and to the doctrine of judicial review.[12]

Parallels to the Rome Statute are also apt.

IV. Equity and Habeas

In the recently decided case of *Boumediene v. Bush*, Justice Kennedy, writing for the U.S. Supreme Court, discusses the role of the historical doctrine of habeas corpus I have outlined: "Remote in time it may be, irrelevant to the present it is not."[13] Kennedy cites *Schlup v. Delo* as holding that habeas corpus "is at its core an equitable remedy."[14] In this brief section I will say a bit about the various ways in which this statement can shed light on some of the issues I have been addressing. Equity has been a clear way to deal with unfairness in an otherwise proper legal proceeding, and when the laws are either silent or ambiguous. Indeed, since at least the time of Thomas More, the first lay official in England to be Lord Chancellor and to expand the reach of equitable relief, equity has been seen as the bridge between morality and legality in a system of law.

In his classic work, **Commentaries on Equity Jurisprudence**, Justice Joseph Story sketches the broad nature of equity:

> In the most general sense, we are accustomed to call that equity, which in human transactions, is founded in natural justice, in honesty and right, and which properly arises *ex aequo et bono*. In this sense it answers precisely to the definition of justice, or natural law, as given by Justinian ... Now it would be a great mistake to suppose that equity, as administered in England, embraced a jurisdiction as wide and extensive as that which arises from the principles of natural justice above stated .... But there is a more limited sense in which the term is often used, and which has the sanction of jurists in ancient, as well as in modern times ... Thus Aristotle has defined the very nature of equity to be the correction of the law ...[15]

---

12 A.E. Dick Howard, *Magna Carta: Text and Commentary*, U. of Virginia Press, 1964, 1998, pp. 24–25.

13 *Boumediene v. Bush*, 553 U.S. ____ (2008), p. 68.

14 Ibid., p. 50, citing *Schlup v. Delo*, 513 U.S. 298, 319 (1995).

15 Joseph Story, *Commentaries on Equity Jurisprudence* (1834), London: Stevens and Hayes, 1884, pp. 1–3.

Indeed, Aristotle said that equity is outside of legal justice, since it is a correction of it, but is also better than legal justice and one of the most important considerations of law.[16]

Equitable considerations have played an important, if controversial, role in habeas proceedings in the United States. Consider the circumstance addressed in the *Boumediene* case where new potentially exculpatory evidence arises after a trial has occurred. In *Boumediene*, the Court declared:

> There is evidence from 19th century American sources indicating that, even in States that accorded strong res judicata effect to prior adjudications, habeas courts in this country routinely allowed prisoners to introduce exculpatory evidence that was either unknown or unavailable to the prisoner.[17]

While controversial in some respects, *Boumediene* affirms this doctrine today:

> If a detainee can present reasonably available evidence demonstrating there is no basis for his continued detention, he must have the opportunity to present this evidence to a habeas corpus court ... The role of an Article III court in the exercise of its habeas corpus function cannot be circumscribed in this manner.[18]

As the Court recognized, these considerations make habeas an equitable remedy.

The habeas court, seen as an equity court, acts as the conscience of the republic by making sure, in these circumstances for instance, that no innocent prisoner remain incarcerated. Another way to think about it is that, as fundamental law, habeas and related rights bring basic moral considerations into the legal system. And just as the foundation is not always part of the structure itself, so habeas is equitable in that it is fundamental to but not necessarily a proper part of the legal system itself. As I said above, this gives us the conceptual space to see equity as a bridge between morality and law.

Seeing habeas as an equitable remedy also allows us to understand how such a simple proceeding could constitute a challenge to the legitimacy of an action by a properly authorized executive action. "Within the Constitution's separation-of-powers structure, few exercises of judicial power are as legitimate or as necessary as the responsibility to hear challenges to the authority of the Executive to imprison a person."[19] Just as the old courts of equity (as the Chancellor's court) acted to overturn abuse in either the common law or king's courts, so habeas is understood today to have the same equitable function. And this is to say that habeas brings in a certain set of basic moral considerations into a legal system. It also allows for equity to be a gap-filler for situations where the law is silent or where the law as applied would be unfair, and hence cause law and justice to separate.

16 Aristotle, *Nicomachean Ethics*, Book V, Ch. 10, 1137b10.

17 Ibid at 51.

18 Ibid at 61. Also see Larry May and Nancy Viner, 'Actual Innocence and Manifest Injustice', *St. Louis University Law Journal*, vol. 49, no. 2, 2004, pp. 481–497.

19 Ibid., *Boumediene*, p. 69.

V. Security and Habeas

In my reconstruction of the history, habeas corpus was initially thought of as a proto-procedural right, merely the right to be brought from the dungeon and told of the charges against one. At nearly the same time, the right also came to be seen as a right to have those charges assessed to see if there was a prima facie reason to think that they had any basis, and this was understood as the right not to be arbitrarily incarcerated. Later, habeas corpus came to stand for the right to due process in general. And later still habeas corpus was understood, as it is today in the American system of law, as a right to challenge a ruling on the basis of any of one's significant constitutional liberties. As the right expanded it became more than proto-procedural.

The history of habeas corpus incorporates at least three different ways to understand this right. In the first instance, habeas is proto-procedural since the right to be made visible and told of the charges against one does not address anything about the form of the charges or the eventual trial of the accused. In the second instance, the right becomes a procedural right, especially when it is associated with due process in general. Finally, habeas comes to be seen as a substantive right, to particular constitutional liberties, such as that one is secure in one's papers and other personal effects.

Something may be either a procedural or a proto-procedural right if it is necessary for ultimately securing a substantive right. If one is languishing in a dungeon and few know that one is there, this can indeed be a kind of inaccessibility of the law. But this is surely different from lacking standing, and even more dissimilar from being barred from appeal due to having filed the appeals papers a day late. The prefix "proto" captures the idea well that I am interested in: both first in time, in terms of being primitive, and also first in importance. Because habeas, and other such rights, are first in time, they are only primitive not yet full-blown procedural rights, but this does not detract from their being very important.

This analytical analysis gives us a beginning at understanding the normative importance of procedural matters. In particular, I would urge that we give great weight to the following two normative statements, one first declared by Grotius and the other by Blackstone:

> Procedures should "prevent the dangers to persons of particular eminence becoming excessive."[20]

> If once it were left in the power of any, the highest, magistrate to imprison arbitrarily whomever he or his officers thought proper … there would soon be an end of all other rights and immunities.[21]

For Grotius, one of the great evils to be avoided, especially in time of war, was the excessive acts of a sovereign. For Blackstone, habeas corpus was a shield against arbi-

20 Hugo Grotius, *De Jure Belli ac Pacis* (On the Law of War and Peace) (1625) translated by Francis W. Kelsey, Oxford: Oxford University Press, 1925, p. 656.

21 William Blackstone, *Commentaries on the Laws of England* (1765), facsimile of the first edition, Chicago: University of Chicago Press, 1979, Volume 1, p. 131.

trary use of executive power. And the more general normative principle, one which Blackstone called a natural right, was that persons should have their liberty, especially liberty of physical movement, respected at all times, and especially by the executive.

Obviously, good normative grounds can be given for restrictions of liberty, but it is the arbitrary restriction of liberty that has been so strongly condemned since Magna Carta. And to make sure that arbitrariness is not hidden, the four rights of Magna Carta are as important today as they were at the beginning of the thirteenth century. And Blackstone, writing in the 18th century, again put it quite well:

> But confinement of the person, by secretly hurrying him to gaol, where his sufferings are unknown and forgotten; is a less public, a less striking, and therefore a more dangerous engine of arbitrary government.[22]

It is fitting that what is secreted in the interstices of the proto-procedural right of habeas corpus is the moral principle against secrecy in confinement.

I propose the normative *principle of visibleness*[23] in detention and incarceration as a counter to the secrecy that masks arbitrary exercise of power in this domain. Habeas corpus stands for the proposition at its most minimal, but also at its most powerful, that no one can be hidden in jail or prison. And the reason for this is that such secrecy is too likely to hide mistreatment and abuse. In its first instance, habeas corpus means simply that the prisoner must be produced. The other rights memorialized in Magna Carta's chapter 29 (39), spell out what procedures must be in place to deal with the prisoner who has now been brought into the light and made visible.

It is part of the folk history of the right of habeas corpus that one of the first things to look at when the prisoner has been made visible is whether there are marks on his or body indicative of abuse. Before one looks for such marks of abuse of power, one must first be able to look upon the prisoner, to see that he is still alive and then to see what his body tells us initially about how he has been treated. Habeas is a proto-procedural right since it does not yet tell us what procedures must be followed in treating the prisoner once transported out of the secrecy of the dungeon. And the normative basis of this right has to do with counteracting the normal human tendency to do wrong when it is unlikely that anyone will know about it, as Plato famously indicated in the myth of Gyges.

Several of the other three procedural rights embedded in Chapter 29 (39) of Magna Carta move from proto-procedural to procedural more properly, and they have roughly the same rationale as that of habeas, namely, the principle of visibleness. The prohibition against arbitrary exile or outlawry is normatively grounded in the idea that a person's other rights cannot be secure if he or she can be rendered invisible by being sent overseas or sent outside of the visible protection of the courts. The right to trial by jury is not as easily seen as falling under the principle of visibleness, because in part it is not merely a proto-procedural right in any event. But even this right has to do with being brought before one's peers, and made visible to the jury, rather than in

22 Ibid at 132.

23 The OED lists, as one of the earliest uses of the term visibleness, a 16th century reference to the fact that the Catholic Church did not maintain open procedures.

a possibly semi-secret proceeding of jurists. Jury trials have historically functioned, among other things, as a protection against what Blackstone saw as a great scourge, the arbitrary treatment by magistrates.

The principle of visibleness does not guarantee that those who are detained or incarcerated will be treated fairly, but only that if they are to be treated unfairly it must not be done in secret. The principle of visibleness is then a protection of security, which "subsists, too, in fidelity to freedom's first principles."[24] This, of course, still leaves open vast avenues of abuse, at least in certain societies. But in those societies that are governed by law and not by tyrants, visibleness will be able to curtail quite a lot of abuse. And even in those societies where tyranny is rampant, visibleness may deter as well, insofar as the tyrants, as humans, care about what others care about, even those outside the society in question.

Is the most minimal of habeas rights, the proto procedural right to be removed from the dungeon and brought into visibleness, the normative core of the rule of law? It is in the sense that most executive or judicial decisions that are arbitrary or unfair simply won't withstand the light of day, with the possible exception of extreme tyrants. If one can be secreted away in prison or in rendition, Blackstone is surely right that to say that none of one's rights are secure. I have tried to indicate why the minimal sense of habeas is so important, especially for the security of persons.

Let us return to the earliest form that habeas took, according to Bracton: that the jailer "B" is merely to produce the body of "A." Aside from seeing that "A" is still alive, and whether his or her body has bruises, it is not obvious why this is so important. And the answer is that those in power generally feel pressured not to act arbitrarily when their actions are exposed to public view. Twenty-five hundred years ago Plato made this point in **The Republic**. In Book Two, Plato discusses the ring of Gyges, where the motivation to be just is said to turn on whether one is "put to the proof" in terms of "the fear of infamy." To be clothed in justice, it cannot be that one can escape by becoming invisible.[25] The seemingly innocuous right of habeas corpus is crucial for global security rights, putting those who would abuse such basic rights "to the proof."

---

24 *Boumediene v. Bush*, 553 U.S. ____ (2008), p. 68.

25 Plato, *The Republic*, Book II, Jowett translation.

Chapter 11

Women's Security/State Security

Naomi Cahn[*]

I. Introduction

State fragility is an omnipresent concern in contemporary global politics. The effects of a state's disintegration go well beyond its borders, and other countries may become involved in the effort to prevent further collapse. Indeed, fragile states have been involved in almost 80% of the international crises over the past sixty years.[1] Consequently, developing tools for accurately evaluating the risk of ongoing state insecurity is a significant project, because the evaluation then guides development and other efforts to stabilize the country. Existing state fragility measurements rely on extensive data concerning a country's security situation, including indicators of economic stability and political rights.

Yet these data typically do not include any measurements focused on gender or women's status. Although there are separate measurements of gender equity that are available for numerous countries in the development and human rights literature, explicit considerations of women's legal rights and ability to participate equally in the political, social, and economic realms are absent from generalized assessments of state fragility.[2] To evaluate the relationship between gender and the factors for assessing stability, this paper discusses the link between women's security, as demonstrated by their legal, social, political, and economic status, and state security/fragility, and examines how measurements of fragility account for gender equality. The paper shows that, although gender equality is integral to ensuring state security, gender issues remain peripheral to the evaluation of state stability. The paper suggests means for ensuring that gender really does become central or "mainstreamed"[3] to any analysis of state security. While gender has become increasingly important in the development world, it remains peripheral to the purview of state security. And even with

* Thanks to Christine Walz for superlative research assistance and for preparing the charts, and to Cecilia M. Bailliet, Tony Gambino, and Ingunn Ikdahl for their strong "indications" of support.

1 J. Joseph Hewitt, Jonathan Wilkenfeld, and Ted Robert Gurr, 'Executive Summary', *Peace and Conflict 2008* (Paradigm Publishers, 2008), 1, http://www.cidcm.umd.edu/pc/.

2 This chapter is focused on efforts in the United States to evaluate state fragility.

3 See infra note 15 for a discussion of mainstreaming.

Cecilia M. Bailliet (ed.), Security: A Multidisciplinary Normative Approach.

ISBN 978 90 04 17296 8. pp. 261–287.

the development world, donors have tended to have a narrow focus when it comes to integrating gender into their work with fragile states.[4] The dimension of gender is an often neglected element of societal conflict and post-conflict transition which should be – but is not yet – of importance to the extraordinary international efforts to assist post-conflict societies around the globe – an effort that involves numerous governments, different entities within the UN system, and thousands of local and international nongovernmental organizations

As an initial matter, and as illustrated by the scope of this conference and the other papers, "state security" is capable of multiple and overlapping meanings.[5] It might connote, for example, the state's level of threat from terrorism (the United States has varied, in a post 9/11 world, between orange and yellow) or the state's policing or military apparatus, each of which may serve to secure the state's integrity, or even the state's "self-confidence," that is, just what must the state prove to itself and internationally? For the purposes of this paper, I am examining security in the contexts of intra- and inter-state conflict, and the implications of state fragility and failure with respect to women's status. Conflict does not inevitably lead to state failure or even fragility, but conflict is a major cause of both,[6] so it is an integral part of a discussion focused on security. Moreover, when conflict ends, the reconstruction process can contribute to ongoing insecurity. On the other hand, if the reconstruction process succeeds, it can involve establishing a secure peacekeeping and transition process along with a stable political system[7] that endures beyond the immediate aftermath and ensures long-term stability.

Gender security is a rich concept that extends beyond physical security to include civil, political, economic, and cultural security for men and women, boys and girls.[8] It includes formal and enforceable legal rights as well as opportunities to participate in the economic and political life of the country. This may mean, for example, providing safe (and passable) roads so that women can sell agricultural or other products,[9] establishing battered women's shelters, building primary schools, and creating job

4 Stephen Baranyi and Kristiana Powell, 'Fragile States, Gender Equality and Aid Effectiveness: A Review of Donor Perspectives' (CIDA 2005), 1 passim, http://www.nsi-ins.ca/english/pdf/Gender_FS_Paper_Donor_Perspectives.pdf.

5 For a description of the other papers in this volume, see Introduction. For a discussion and critique of "human security", see Gareth Evans, *The Responsibility to Protect: Ending Mass Atrocity Crimes Once and For All.* (Wash., D.C.: Brookings Institution Press, 2008), 34–35; V.M. Hudson and A.M. den Boer, *Bare Branches: Security Implications of Asia's Surplus Male Population* (Cambridge, MA: MIT Press, 2004), 1–3.

6 See United States Agency for International Development (USAID), 'Fragile State Indicators: A Supplement to the Country Analytical Template' (2006), p. 3.

7 See Tracy Fitzsimmons, 'Engendering Justice and Security after War' in *Constructing Justice and Security after War*, ed. Charles T. Call (Washington, DC: U.S. Institute of Peace, 2007), p. 351.

8 For further analysis of differences in views of the meaning of women's security, see Fionnuala Ni Aolain, 'Women, Security and the Patriarchy of Internationalized Transitional Justice', __ *Human Rts Q.* __ (forthcoming 2009), draft at 4–12.

9 Elaine Zuckerman and Marcia Greenberg, 'The Gender Dimensions of Post-Conflict Reconstruction: An Analytical Framework for Policymakers', *Gender and Development*

opportunities for young men and women. Throughout, it is important to remember that, notwithstanding the frequency with which issues involving "gender" focus on women; gender (especially gender security) implicates both men and women.[10]

Although gender has not yet been adequately integrated into this discussion of security, there are promising signs that gender issues may slowly be moving to become more central to the discussion of conflict and post-conflict reconstruction, discussions that are critical to notions of state security. In 2000, the United Nations Security Council adopted Resolution 1325, which emphasized the critical importance of equal involvement of women in the peace process, and "the urgent need to mainstream a gender perspective into peacekeeping operations." In 2002, UNICEF published an evaluation of gender and conflict that was co-authored by Ellen Johnson Sirleaf, now the president of Liberia, which also assessed the implementation of 1325. Two years later, in 2004, the U.S. Department of Defense, the UN and NATO each adopted policies addressing the trafficking of humans in and around military deployments. In 2000, the United Nations proclaimed its Millennium Development Goals which include gender equality as one of 8 goals.[11] In June, 2008, the United Nations Security Council finally decided that rape should be treated as a war crime – but only after several countries questioned whether rape really was an appropriate topic for the Security Council.[12]

These are significant steps by the international community towards recognition of the importance of gender in conflict and post conflict issues. Of course, conflict disproportionately affects women: women and children are most likely to be displaced from their countries of origin and become refugees,[13] so the lack of state security significantly impacts women. Gender is also important to the existence of conflict; for example, young men who perceive no opportunities in their lives are more likely to join a militia.[14]

---

vol. 12, no. 3 (2004), http://www.genderaction.org/images/ez-mg%20oxfam%20g&d%20 gender-per.pdf. They note that Afghan women "require private road rest areas for their own and children's needs." (Ibid at 9).

10 Gender mainstreaming is discussed infra note 15.

11 See UN Millennium Declaration (2000), http://www.un.org/millennium/declaration/ares 552e.pdf; http://www.un.org/millenniumgoals/background.html; World Bank, *Global Monitoring Report 2007*, http://www-wds.worldbank.org/external/default/WDSContent Server/WDSP/IB/2007/04/11/000112742_20070411162802/Rendered/PDF/394730GM R02007.pdf.

12 'UN Classifies Rape a "War Tactic"', *BBC News*, June 20, 2008, http://news.bbc.co.uk/2/hi/americas/7464462.stm; UN Security Council Resolution 1820, http://daccessdds.un.org/doc/UNDOC/GEN/N08/391/44/PDF/N0839144.pdf?OpenElement.

13 Women and children constitute approximately 75–80% of the world's 35 million refugees and displaced people. Women's Commission for Refugee Women and Children, *Facts* (2008), http://www.womenscommission.org/about/facts.php.

14 E.g., UN Office for the Coordination of Humanitarian Affairs, 'Nigeria: No Shortage of Niger Delta Youth Ready to Join Militias', (Feb. 1, 2008), http://www.irinnews.org/report .aspx?ReportId=76521. The article reports: "With youth unemployment soaring in the Niger Delta and even university graduates struggling to find work, recruitment by the militias is one of the only way for young men to make their own way."

"Gender mainstreaming" is a phrase commonly employed in post conflict reconstruction, and it is critical to examine the existing international standards for mainstreaming gender and how they are being implemented. This results in three questions: first, what exactly does gender mainstreaming mean to the entities that employ the term?; second, how are programs developed and decisions made in order to accomplish it?; and third, has the articulation of the concept and its implementation, in fact, had a positive impact on the role and status of women in transitioning countries? The UN defines "gender mainstreaming" as involving the "assess[ment of] the implications for women and men of any planned action, including legislation, policies, or programmes."[15] This strategy aims to ensure women and men benefit equally from such programs through monitoring, reporting, training, and evaluation.[16] Notwithstanding these efforts towards gender mainstreaming and rhetorical movement within the United Nations system towards the recognition of the significance of gender, gender mainstreaming typically is seen as "primarily relevant to policy development in particular areas, such as development, human rights, and some aspects of labor markets,"[17] and is marginalized in discussions of state security. And, unless it challenges underlying structures of patriarchy and subordination, gender

15 Noeleen Heyzer, 'Gender, Peace and Disarmament', in *Women, Men, Peace and Security*, ed. Kerstin Vignard (Geneva: United Nations Institute for Disarmament Research, 2003), p. 7. Gender mainstreaming also involves ensuring that "men and women have equal access and control over resources, development benefits, and decision-making at all stages." United Nations Development Programme (UNDP)/United Nations Development Fund for Women (UNIFEM), 'Introductory Gender Analysis and Gender Planning Training for UNDP Staff (2001)', http://www.undp.org/gender/resources/Gender%20Mainstreaming%20Training%20Module.pdf. Similarly, the European Commission defines gender mainstreaming as: "the integration of the gender perspective into every stage of policy processes – design, implementation, monitoring and evaluation – with a view to promoting equality between women and men. It means assessing how policies impact on the life and position of both women and men." European Commission, "Gender Mainstreaming: General overview," http://ec.europa.eu/employment_social/gender_equality/gender_mainstreaming/general_overview_en.html.

There is a distinction between gender mainstreaming, which is the consideration of gendered perspectives, and gender balance, which focuses on the number of men and women in various positions. See Department for Disarmament Affairs, *Gender Mainstreaming Action Plan, Public Version* (April 2003), 7, http://disarmament2.un.org/gender/gmap.pdf.

The earlier approach to gender, the "Women in Development" strategy, focused only on women and girls. Zuckerman and Greenberg, supra note 9 at 5. Gender mainstreaming goes beyond this focus only on women's participation to examine gender roles, and men and women's participation. Ibid.

16 Consider that, in its strategic plan on gender mainstreaming, the United Nations' Department for Disarmament Affairs suggests a series of questions to ask in developing Disarmament, Demobilization, Reintegration (DDR) programs. For example, although a gender perspective might suggest developing programs specifically for women, integrating gender requires attention to all aspects of the DDR Project, and involving the experiences of women throughout the program. Gender Mainstreaming Action Plan, supra note 14 at 16.

17 Hilary Charlesworth, 'Not Waving but Drowning: Gender Mainstreaming and Human Rights in the United Nations,' *Harvard Human Rights Journal* vol. 18 (2005) p. 14.

mainstreaming can create additional problems through its acceptance of the status quo.[18] While the goal of gender mainstreaming is admirable when it comes to developing programs, gender must become central to the institutions themselves.

The paper first shows the relationship between state fragility and gender equity, establishing the utility of looking at gender as a category. Then, in order to show how gender remains outside the mainstream, the paper critiques the most prominent and recent evaluative tools for state security and fragility that are applied in the United States.[19] Finally, the paper suggests how assessments of state security should incorporate gender, providing a rubric for measuring gender equity. The paper seeks to develop tools for a more accurate assessment of a state's security in order to accomplish two other goals: to improve the situation of women by providing tools for making gender central and to reduce the fragility of states by increasing gender equity.

II. The Relationship between Gender Equity and State Stability

Gender equity is a good goal, in and of itself, for any country. Indeed, as a general matter, recognizing the equal citizenship of all groups provides a strong basis for security and development.[20] In recognition of the significance of gender, the third MDG is gender equity. International law supports gender equity through a variety of mechanisms. The most prominent mechanism is The Convention on the Elimination of All Forms of Discrimination Against Women (CEDAW), which guarantees various rights to women and has been ratified by 185 countries.[21] Article 2e of CEDAW requires that States Parties "take all appropriate measures to eliminate discrimination against women by any person, organization or enterprise."[22] The CEDAW Committee explains this further stating, "Under general international law and specific human rights covenants, States may also be responsible for private acts if they fail to act with due diligence to prevent violations of rights ..."[23] CEDAW's enforcement mechanisms provide few rights for individuals – aside from an optional

---

18 See, e.g., Sari Kouvo, *Making Just Rights? Mainstreaming Women's Human Rights and a Gender Perspective.* (Uppsala: Författaten och Justus Förlag AB, 2004) pp. 325–326; Charlesworth, supra note 16.

19 While other countries and various non-governmental organizations appear to be more cognizant of gender issues, there remain problems. See, e.g., Baranyi and Powell, supra note 4.

20 See, e.g., Ashraf Ghani and Clare Lockhart, *Fixing Failed States: A Framework for Rebuilding a Fractured World* (New York: Oxford, 2008) p. 144.

21 Convention on the Elimination of All Forms of Discrimination Against Women ("CEDAW"), Dec. 18, 1979, 1249 U.N.T.S. 13. Even the United States has signed, but not ratified. United Nations Division for the Advancement of Women, CEDAW: State Parties, http://www.un.org/womenwatch/daw/cedaw/states.htm.

22 The full text of CEDAW's Article 2 is available at: http://www.un.org/womenwatch/daw/cedaw/text/econvention.htm#article2.

23 General Recommendation 19, http://www.un.org/womenwatch/daw/cedaw/recommendations/recomm.htm.

protocol which allows for an inquiry and complaint procedure.[24] Instead, CEDAW is enforced through a reporting mechanism (countries must make reports to the Committee on the Elimination of All Forms of Discrimination Against Women),[25] international pressure for compliance, a suit before the International Court of Justice by another signatory,[26] or as claims in domestic courts. While a country's reports to the CEDAW Committee provide a mechanism for evaluating the country's approach to women's rights, CEDAW is perhaps most effective as a "basis for self-analyses and has been, in some countries, an impetus to reconfigure legal rules."[27] Rights-based documents do establish formally binding legal obligations, but, until those obligations are implemented and enforced, they provide insufficient help on the ground.[28]

A. *Gender's Relevance to State Stability*

Gender inequities are strongly correlated with state fragility. Because it is difficult to determine whether state instability causes gender inequity, or whether gender equity cause state fragility, this paper focuses on issues of correlation, which are far better understood. The relevant questions then become whether gender equity is useful in evaluating the stability and security of a country: and, the more fundamental issue is gender equity related to state insecurity? There are, as discussed in this section, correlations in several areas, such as wealth, economic growth, dispute resolution, military action, social instability, and non-compliance with international norms.

---

24 Optional Protocol to the Convention on the Elimination of All Forms of Discrimination against Women (A/RES/54/4), http://www.un.org/womenwatch/daw/cedaw/protocol/whatis.htm. Ninety countries had ratified the Protocol as of Nov. 2007. http://www.un.org/womenwatch/daw/cedaw/protocol/sigop.htm. For further discussion of CEDAW's enforcement and implementation, see S.D. Ross, *Women's Human Rights: The International and Comaprative Law Casebook* (Philadelphia: University of Pennsylvania Press, 2008), 11–24.

25 These reports are available at: http://www2.ohchr.org/english/bodies/cedaw/cedaws41.htm.

26 CEDAW Art. 29(1) provides for referral to the ICJ if states have a dispute "concerning the interpretation or application of the present Convention."

27 Judith Resnik, 'Foreign as Domestic Affairs: Rethinking Horizontal Federalism and Foreign Affairs Preemption in Light of Translocal Internationalism', *Emory Law Journal* vol. 57 (2007) p. 53. As the CEDAW Committee noted about its powers, "While it may have the power to pronounce a State Party in violation of the Convention, it has no quasi-judicial powers enabling it to order an appropriate remedy." Committee on the Elimination of Discrimination Against Women, Progress Achieved in the Implementation of the Convention on the Elimination of All Forms of Discrimination Against Women, Para. 56, U.N. Doc. A/CONF.177/7 (June 21, 1995), available at: http://www.un.org/esa/documents/ga/conf177/aconf177-7en.htm.

28 See Ingunn Ikdahl, Anne Hellum, Randi Kaarhus, Tor A. Benjaminsen, and Patricia Kameri-Mbote. *Human Rights, Formalisation and Women's Land Rights in Southern and Eastern Africa*. Studies in Women's Law No. 57, Institute of Women's Law, Univ. of Oslo (June 2005), p. 104, available at: http://www.jus.uio.no/ior/kvretten/kvrett_skriftserien/dokumenter/noradrapport.pdf ("unless a state has the political will and enacts municipal law to fulfill international obligations, its subjects are unlikely to benefit from such international obligations").

Amartya Sen has famously said that democracies do not experience famines; do stable countries experience gender inequity? We know that there is a positive relationship between wealth and women's rights, according to the United Nations Development Programme's Gender-Related Development Index[29] and other studies that have corroborated the result.[30] Countries with greater gender equity have higher life expectancies for women than for men,[31] and have literacy rates that are comparable for both men and women.[32] The movement towards gender equality in countries that are stable and democratic is well-documented, and many Western countries have identified this as a goal. For example, some Western European countries have addressed the problem of low birth rates that may result in an inability to replace the population by developing solutions that are fair to both genders: men's involvement in child care provides a basis for inducing more childbearing. Industrialized countries that have "more unequal gender systems" also have lower fertility rates.[33] As many countries have found, women's increased workforce participation results in higher fertility rates[34] which, in turn ensures population stability.[35] While the relationship between women and economic growth/poverty reduction is well established, this section explores the link between this nexus and conflict/state fragility.

Numerous international organizations point out this strong correlation between state fragility and various forms of the inequitable treatment of women. The World Bank's *Global Monitoring Report 2007*, which discusses the relationship between gender equality, poverty, and economic growth, notes that poverty incidence tends to be lower in countries with more gender equality, that economic growth is positively correlated with gender equality, and that female education has a larger impact on

29 Lan Cao, 'Culture Change', *Virginia Journal of Int'l Law* vol. 47 (2007) p. 357, citing the UNDP Gender-Related Development Index (2003), available at: http://hdr.undp.org/statistics/data/pdf/hdr05_table_ 25.pdf. For further discussion of the GDI, see infra.

30 *Ibid.*, citing Clair Apodaca, 'Measuring Women's Economic and Social Rights Achievement', *Human Rights Quarterly* vol. 20 (1998) p. 160.

31 USAID, "Fragile States Indicators: A Supplement to the Country Analytical Template" (May 2006), 29, http://pdf.usaid.gov/pdf_docs/PNADG262.pdf.

32 See Social Watch, "Gender Equity Index 2008 – Progress and Setbacks," (2008), http://www.socialwatch.org/en/avancesyRetrocesos/IEG_2008/tablas/losmejores.htm (nine of the ten countries that rank highest on the gender equity index received a score of 100 on the education indicator, which includes the male-female literacy rate.)

33 See Melinda Mills, Letizia Mencarini, Maria Letizia Tanturri, and Katia Begall, 'Gender Equity and Fertility Intentions in Italy and the Netherlands', *Demographic Res.* Vol. 18 (2008) p. 7. Ironically, and as discussed infra, women in less stable and less industrialized countries tend to have extremely high fertility rates, which serves as an indication of the lack of gender equity.

34 See Russell Shorto, 'No Babies', *The New York Times*, June 29, 2008, at Sec. MM, p. 34.

35 Of course, while Western European countries struggle with low fertility rates, some developing countries struggle with high fertility rates. Each is, of course, problematic.

growth than male education.[36] Gender-based violence is "an important development constraint that retards economic growth and poverty reduction."[37]

When it comes to how a country resolves disputes, Professors Terry Dworkin and Cindy Schipani have found that there is a correlative relationship between a country's ranking on the UN Gender Development Index and the level of violence involved in the country's resolution of disputes.[38] In their study, which compared information from the Heidelberg Institute for International Conflict Research[39] with the UN's Gender Development Index,[40] they found that increasing amounts of gender inequality were correlated with a country's likelihood of resolving conflicts by using violence.[41] Although the authors note that correlation is not causation, they hold out the "possibility" that enhancing gender equity "may relate to a reduction in violence."[42]

In a study of fifty years of international crises, Caprioli and Boyer found that states with higher percentages of women in leadership positions were less likely to act aggressively.[43] Based on an examination of political, social, and economic measurements of inequality, Mary Caprioli concluded that "higher levels of gender equality correlate with lower levels of military action to settle international disputes."[44] Where there is a high level of intrafamilial violence then there is also a higher level of violence in dispute resolution and an increasing likelihood of involvement in conflict.[45] When a country has an abnormally high proportion of men to women (such as in some

---

36 World Bank, 'Promoting Gender Equality and Women's Empowerment', in *Global Monitoring Report 2007* (Washington, D.C.: World Bank, 2007), pp. 107–108, http://siteresources.worldbank.org/INTGLOMONREP2007/Resources/3413191-1179404785559/Chp3-GMR07_webPDF-corrected-may-14-2007-6.pdf. These statements are based on data provided by the UN Millennium Project Task Force on Gender Equality 2005. *See ibid*, 145.

37 UN Millennium Project, 'Taking action: Achieving Gender Equality and Empowering Women', 110, http://www.unmillenniumproject.org/documents/Gender-complete.pdf.

38 Terry Morehead Dworkin & Cindy A. Schipani, 'Gender Voice and Correlations with Peace', *Vanderbilt Journal of Transnational Law*, vol. 36, (2003) pp. 531–533; 'Linking Gender Equity to Peaceful Societies', *American Business Law Journal* Vol. 44 (2007) p. 391.

39 See Heidelberg Institute for International Conflict Research, http://www.hiik.de/en/index.html.

40 See UNDP, *Human Development Report 2007–2008* (2007) p. 326 http://hdr.undp.org/en/media/HDR_20072008_EN_Complete.pdf. The GDI supplements the Human Development Index, and it assesses the inequalities between men and women in four different areas. Ibid at 356, 358. The GDI is discussed infra.

41 'Linking Gender', supra note 38 at 391–392.

42 Ibid. at 398–399, 414.

43 Mary Caprioli and M.A. Boyer, 'Gender, Violence and International Crisis', *Journal of Conflict Resolution*, Vol. 45, no. 4 (2001) p. 503. For one potential explanation, see Jedediah Purdy, 'The New Biopolitics: Autonomy, Demography, and Nationhood', *Bringham Young University Law Review* (2006) pp. 951–952.

44 Mary Caprioli, 'Gendered Conflict', *Journal of Peace Research*, Vol. 37, no. 1 (2000) p. 57. She speculates that domestic prejudice translates into international prejudice against states that are seen as unequal. Ibid at 66.

45 Ibid. at 65.

Asian countries, where sex-selection for boys occurs through abortion, infanticide, and other means), this is correlated historically with increased levels of social instability;[46] when there are too many young men, they may become involved in criminal activity that attacks individuals or the government.[47] Other researchers have found that the less likely states are to have laws and practices in conformity with CEDAW, then the more likely they are to be of concern to the international community based on their non-compliance with economic, political, and anti-violence international norms.[48]

The correlation of gender inequality and state fragility might rest on a variety of bases; in light of the movement towards gender equality in more developed countries, gender inequality in fragile states may simply reflect gaps in development in most of these states. Some feminists have suggested that it may be due to a difference in values between men and women. Relational feminists have made the experience of mothering central in their theorizings, resulting in the development of an approach could be termed "biological feminism." As one way of showing the differences between men and women, these feminists have emphasized the distinctive connection that women feel to their children, beginning while the fetus is in utero and continuing throughout the child's life, thereby influencing their capacity for connection.[49] Gender equality, the full inclusion of women in the policymaking process, would result in different policies that were less violent.[50] Or, it may be that gender stereotypes, rather than biological essentialism, result in men pursuing more aggressive and inegalitarian policies; dissolving gender stereotypes would allow the integration of more peace-based values into domestic and international policymaking.[51] Because of their vantage point in post-conflict countries, women may be more likely to address socioeconomic issues that are critical to establishing security.[52]

---

46 See Jedediah Purdy, 'The New Biopolitics: Autonomy, Demography, and Nationhood', *Brigham Young University Law Review* (2006) p. 893.

47 Mary Caprioli, Valerie M. Hudson, et al., 'Walking a Fine Line: Addressing Issues of Gender with WomenStats', (paper presented at the annual meeting of the International Studies Association 48th Annual Convention, Chicago, IL, February 28, 2007), 5, http://www.all academic.com/meta/p180717_index.html; see Valerie Hudson and Andrea Den Boer, 'A Surplus of Men, A Deficit of Peace', *International Security* Vol. 26, no. 4 (2002) p. 5.

48 Valerie H. Hudson and Carl H. Brinton, 'Women's Tears and International Fears: Is Discrepant Enforcement of National Laws Protecting Women and Girls Related to Discrepant Enactment of International Law by Nation-States?' (paper presented at the annual meetings of the American Political Science Association, Chicago, Illinois, 2007), http://www.womanstats.org/images/APSA07HudsonBrinton.pdf.

49 See Naomi Cahn, 'Birthing Relationships', *Wisconsin Women's Law Journal* Vol. 17 (2002) p. 194. For a critique of women's "special" contributions based on biology, see Dianne Otto, 'A Sign of 'Weakness'? Disrupting Gender Certainties in the Implementation of Security Council Resolution 1325', *Michigan Journal of Gender & Law* Vol. 13 (2006) pp. 135–136.

50 Caprioli, 'Gendered Conflict', supra note 44 at 65.

51 See Ibid at 55.

52 Evans, 'Crimes', supra note 5 at 171.

Whatever the source, the result is, as Fionnuala Ni Aolain charges, that "the masculinities that dominate in times of conflict" affect "the forms of accountability sought in the post-conflict/post-regime environment [because they] reflect the gender biases that manifest in the prior context."[53] Unless women are involved in policy making, and unless policy makers explicitly focus on gender, then the inequities will continue as a country moves towards stability. Inclusion is insufficient without challenging the paradigms which have maintained their inequality and exclusion.[54]

B. *Gender and Conflict*

A country's insecurity affects men and women differently, and men and women are differently situated when it comes to efforts to stabilize the country.[55] Where the insecurity has been caused by conflict, women face additional issues during wars that men do not, including, of course, sexual violence, forced impregnation, or forced abortion.[56] Gender inequality may even be useful in explaining the support of some women for militant opposition groups because they lack other opportunities

---

53 Fionnuala Ni Aolain, 'Political Violence and Gender during Times of Transition', *Columbia Journal of Gender & Law* Vol. 15 (2006) pp. 830–831. See Fionnuala Ni Aolain & Catherine Turner, 'Gender, Trust, and Transition', *UCLA Women's Law Journal* Vol. 16 (2007) p. 279.

54 Otto, supra note 49 at 136–137.

55 See, e.g., Stephen Baranyi and Kristiana Powell, 'Fragile States, Gender Equality and Aid Effectiveness: A Review of Donor Perspectives', supra note 3 at 2. Indeed, in her case study of Eritrean women's asylum claims, Cecilia Bailliet suggests that, "The gains won during the war appear to have stagnated or diminished in the post-conflict period. In part, there are claims of a backlash against women, in which men seek to restore the traditional division of labour and gender roles ..., perhaps the area of greatest concern pertains to the right of security of the person. Incidences of rape in Eritrea have escalated in the recent period, and this suggests that the backlash manifests itself in the form of physical and sexual violence." Cecilia M. Bailliet, 'Examining Sexual Violence in the Military in the Context of Eritrean Asylum Claims Presented in Norway', *International Journal of Refugee Law* Vol. 19 (2007) p. 477.

56 See Hilary Charlesworth, 'Feminist Methods in International Law', *American Journal of International Law* Vol. 93 (1999) p. 385; Judith Gardam and Hilary Charlesworth, 'Protection of Women in Armed Conflict', *Human Rights Quarterly* 22 (2000) p. 1. Some sexual violence during conflicts is committed against boys and men, but the overwhelming majority is committed against women and girls. See Kelly D. Askin, 'Prosecuting Wartime Rape and other Gender-Related Crimes under International Law: Extraordinary Advances, Enduring Obstacles', *Berkeley Journal of International Law* Vol. 21 (2003) p. 297 (other than sexual violence in prisons, sex crimes are committed "overwhelming[ly]" against women). Homosexual rape has been credibly reported as well, but is far less common that heterosexual rape; see also USAID, 'Women in Conflict', http://www.usaid.gov/our_work/cross-cutting_programs/conflict/publications/docs/cmm_women_and_conflict_toolkit_december_2006.pdf (the report is very general and has only a few direct citations, but it provides a general framework for understanding how conflict situations can positively and negatively impact women's status in a country).

Rape and batterer survivors often experience post-traumatic syndrome in a manner comparable to war veterans, compounded by women's subordination. Judith Lewis Herman, *Trauma and Recovery* (New York, Basic Books, 1992), 32.

for political engagement. For example, some young women supported the Maoist insurgency in Nepal because they "have been given a level of authority and respect that traditional political and social structures simply do not allow." The insurgency was also able to successfully recruit women through campaigns against domestic violence and alcoholism.[57] Or consider that Tamil insurgents are able to recruit young women in Sri Lanka who have no means of supporting themselves if their husbands are killed or drafted into the military.

Post-conflict, in a weak state, women are fundamentally affected legally, economically, and physically by the state's failure to provide basic services. Without access to the justice system and without laws reinforcing their status, women may be unable to assert their property rights, claim protection from domestic violence, or obtain credit. With a state unable to deliver basic education or health services, women's literacy rates decrease, and, when they seek maternity services or contraception, they have few options. To reduce fragility in the post-conflict process requires: (1) proceeding upon the recognition that sustainable development requires gender equity; (2) recognizing women's rights to participate in all aspects of the transition; (3) developing laws that respect and foster gender equity; and (4) implementing a justice component that ends impunity and ensures accountability for crimes committed against women and girls during the conflict.[58] Unless gender is included as a tool in assessing a state's fragility, none of these steps might be taken.

III. Measuring State Security and Fragility

This section examines six reports on state weakness to determine their approach to the use of gender equality as an indicator of state fragility or failure.[59] These six reports were issued between 2005–2008 by highly influential U.S. foreign policy institutions, including private and public agencies. While measures of gender equity are included in other assessments, such as the UNDP's Human Development Report,[60] or

57 USAID, *Conducting a Conflict Assessment: A Framework for Strategy and Program Development*, 24, http://www.usaid.gov/our_work/cross-cutting_programs/conflict/publications/docs/CMM_ConflAssessFrmwrk_May_05.pdf.

58 Gareth Evans notes that women "are often the key not only to preventing the reemergence of violence and resolving ongoing conflict, but to rebuilding societies once the guns go silent." Evans, supra note 5 at 171.

59
- CRS Report for Congress: *Weak and Failing States – Evolving Security Threats and U.S. Policy*
- The Brookings Institution: *Index of State Weakness in the Developing World*
- United States Agency for International Development: *Measuring State Fragility*
- Monty Marshall and Jack Goldstone of the George Mason University: *Global Report on Conflict, Governance and State Fragility 2007*
- The Fund for Peace: *Failed States Index*
- University of Maryland's Center for International Development and Conflict Management: *Peace and Conflict Instability Ledger*

The chart at the end of this Section provides a summary of the reports and their inclusion of gender issues.

60 UNDP, "Measuring Human Development: A Primer" (New York 2007), http://hdr.undp.org/en/media/Primer_intro.pdf.

Freedom House's evaluation of global freedom[61] – showing the integration of gender into development or civil liberties markers – these assessments are not self-conscious analyses of state security and fragility.

This section examines the six prominent US efforts to measure state fragility. The reports are fairly consistent when it comes to assessing the most fragile states: four of these reports actually provide rankings, and 7 states appear in the list of ten weakest states on at least 3 of these indices, while another 4 appear at least twice. Indicators can be important components in establishing state policies and practices;[62] consequently, the components that comprise each of these evaluative efforts are signs of what is considered critical to ensuring state stability. Donor agencies are increasingly using various indicators to help them evaluate country performance in order to ensure that their resources will be used most efficiently and effectively.[63] While indicators are imperfect – they are subject to errors in measurement, and they take thin slices of complex issues[64] – they are useful, within these limitations, for providing broad-brush pictures of a country's status. Chart I provides information on countries that ranked among the ten weakest states on the reports.

Chart 1: Country Ranking on Fragility Indexes and GDI

	The Brookings Institute	USAID	Marshall-Goldstone	The Fund for Peace	University of Maryland	GDI[65]	
Country	Index of State Weakness in the Developing World	Anecdotal Examples	State Fragility Index & Matrix	Failed State Index	Peace & Conflict Instability Ledger		No. of List
Afghanistan	2	Crisis State	3	8	1	n/a	4
Iraq	4	–	6	2	2	n/a	4
Somalia	1	–	2	3	–	n/a	3
Congo, Dem. Rep.	3	–	8	7	–	148/157	3
Sudan	6	Crisis State	1	1	–	130	3

61 Freedom House, "Freedom in the World" (2008 edition), http://www.freedomhouse.org/template.cfm?page=351&ana_page=333&year=2007.%20%20.

62 For a discussion of the development of a human rights indicator, see Philip Alston, 'Promoting the Accountability of Members of the New UN Human Rights Council', *Journal of Transnat'l Law & Pol'y* Vol. 15 (2005) pp. 83 85.

63 See, e.g., Daniel Kaufmann, Aart Kraay, and Massimo Mastruzzi, "Governance Matters IV: Governance Indicators for 1996–2004," World Bank Policy Research Working Paper 3630 (2005), 2, available through ssrn.com.

64 For example, Ibid. at 27.

65 UNDP, Human Development Reports, 2007/2008 Report Gender-Related Development Index, http://hdrstats.undp.org/indicators/268.html.

	The Brookings Institute	USAID	Marshall-Goldstone	The Fund for Peace	University of Maryland	GDI	
Country	Index of State Weakness in the Developing World	Anecdotal Examples	State Fragility Index & Matrix	Failed State Index	Peace & Conflict Instability Ledger		No. of List
Central African Republic	7	–	–	10	9	152	3
Liberia	9	–	10	–	5	n/a	3
Burundi	5	–	9	–	–	147	2
Zimbabwe	8	–	–	4	–	129	2
Chad	–	–	5	5	–	151	2
Cote D'Ivoire	10	–	–	6	–	145	2

A. *The Brookings Institution: Index of State Weakness in the Developing World*

In 2008, the Brookings Institution released its highly influential *Index of State Weakness in the Developing World*, examining the effectiveness of central governments in four different areas, including the ability to prevent conflict.[66] The goal of the paper, which was co-authored by Susan Rice, an adviser to the campaign of Senator Barack Obama and a former member of President Clinton's National Security Council, is to provide an easy-to-use tool for policy-makers to assess state weakness, or state inability to provide services essential to the public good.[67] While the Index does not target post-conflict issues, many of the countries analyzed have experienced significant external and internal conflicts, and the Report notes that, of the 28 critically weak states, almost 90% had been involved in conflict in the previous 15 years.[68]

This report ranks all 141 developing countries based on their performance in four areas – economic, political, security, and social welfare. It explains that its approach is unique because it focuses on all areas of state function, offering a new, more comprehensive description of state weakness. Each of the four main areas of state function is further subdivided into five subindicators. A state's strength or weakness in each area is determined based on its effectiveness, responsiveness, and legitimacy.

- The *economic indicators* take into account recent economic growth, the quality of existing economic policies, whether the environment is conducive

66 Susan Rice and Patrick Stewart, 'Index of State Weakness in the Developing World' (Washington, DC: The Brookings Institution, 2008), http://www.brookings.edu/reports/2008/~/media/Files/rc/reports/2008/02_weak_states_index/02_weak_states_index.pdf.

67 Ibid at 5.

68 Ibid at 17.

to private sector development, and the degree to which income is equally distributed.
- The *political indicators* access the quality of a state's political institutions and the extent to which its citizens accept the system of governance and consider it legitimate. The subindicators include measurements of government accountability, the rule of law, the extent of corruption, the extent of democratization, freedom of expression and association, and the ability of the state bureaucracy and institutions to function effectively, independently, and responsively.
- The *security indicators* evaluate whether a state is able to provide physical security for its citizens. They include measurements of the violence conflict and its effects, illegal seizure of political power, widespread perceptions of political instability, territory affected by conflict, state-sponsored political violence and gross human rights abuses.
- The *social welfare indicators* measure how well a state meets the basic human needs of its citizens, including nutrition, health, education, and access to clean water and sanitation.

None of the indicators or sub-indicators explicitly measures gender equality in developing states. The authors note that they had to omit several indicators that otherwise would have served as good measurements of state weakness because there was insufficient data to provide an accurate understanding of state performance. The listed examples of omitted data include unemployment and crime rates, quality of education, and tax-collection capacity, but even these do not include a measurement that focuses on gender equity issues. While gender does not appear in the report, it was relevant to at least one of the 20 sub-indicators: the Freedom Indicator, a political indicator, addresses a country's civil and political rights.[69] This particular sub-indicator was selected, the report explains, because states with fewer civil liberties and political rights tend to be more susceptible to destabilizing events. Although the *source* for this indicator, a score of civil liberties and political rights developed by Freedom House,[70] does in fact include gender issues, there is no other

69 Rice and Stewart, Index, supra note 66 at 31.

70 Freedom House, "Freedom in the World" (2008 edition), http://www.freedomhouse.org/template.cfm?page=351&ana_page=333&year=2007.%20%. Freedom House measures global freedom, rather than state stability and security.

The civil liberty score assigned by Freedom House considers whether a state ensures the freedoms expressed in its civil liberties checklist, including freedom of expression, assembly, association, education, and religion. States with the best scores are distinguished by an established and generally equitable system of rule of law, free economic activity, and progress toward equality of opportunity. States are evaluated based on a total of 25 civil liberties and political rights questions. Gender issues are specifically addressed within 2 different questions on the civil liberties checklist: a Rule of Law question concerning whether there is equal treatment of distinct groups of the population and a series of sub-issues within a question on personal autonomy and individual rights concerning whether there are "personal social freedoms, including gender equality, choice of marriage partners, and size of family." Ibid.

acknowledgement of these issues in the index itself. Indeed, throughout the Report's 47 pages, the words "women" and "gender" do not appear – even once.

B. *Monty Marshall and Jack Goldstone of the George Mason University: Global Report on Conflict, Governance and State Fragility 2007*

With funding from USAID, Monty Marshall and Jack Goldstone developed a "State Fragility Index and Matrix" to measure state capabilities.[71] The index is based on indicators measuring state effectiveness and legitimacy in four dimensions of state function: security, governance, economics, and social development. The index ranks 162 developed and developing countries in each of the four areas. In each of four areas, a country is assigned a score from zero (no fragility) to three (high fragility). Two scores are assigned – one for legitimacy and another for effectiveness. There is no separate indicator for gender equity. Of the four indicators used in this report, the "social indicators" of social effectiveness and social legitimacy appear to be the one most likely to include gender equity. The social effectiveness indicator is based on the human development index, which measures a country's achievements in health, knowledge, and maintaining an acceptable standard of living:[72] While each of these may be different for men and women, the index does not assign separate scores based on gender, but measures in the aggregate; for example, the "knowledge" factor includes literacy rates and school enrollments,[73] two highly gender-sensitive measures. The social legitimacy factor is based on the infant mortality rate.[74]

C. *The Fund for Peace: Failed States Index*

Even more telling is the non-existence of women and gender in the 28-page executive summary of another index, this one focused on conflict: Peace and Conflict 2008.[75] The Fund for Peace, which publishes a Failed State Index in Foreign Affairs, uses a Conflict Assessment Tool (CAST) that rates countries based on a total of twelve social, economic, political, and military indicators.[76] The goal of the index was to rank the states according to their potential vulnerability to conflict and further instabil-

---

71 Monty Marshall and Jack Goldstone, "Global Report on Conflict, Governance and State Fragility 2007," http://www.fpbmonitor.com/action/reader?head=scorecard&jid=FPB.

72 UNDP, "Frequently Asked Questions," http://hdr.undp.org/en/statistics/faq/question,68,en.html.

73 UNDP, "HDI Interactive Calculator," http://hdr.undp.org/en/statistics/data/calculator/.

74 Monty G. Marshall and Benjamin R. Cole, 'Global Report on Conflict, Governance and State Fragility 2008', *Foreign Policy Bulletin* (Cambridge University Press: Winter 2008) p. 19.

75 J. Joseph Hewitt, Jonathan Wilkenfeld, and Ted Robert Gurr, 'Executive Summary', *Peace and Conflict 2008*, http://www.cidcm.umd.edu/pc/.

76 Fund for Peace, 'Failed States Index 2008', *Foreign Policy Vol. 167* (2008), 64, http://www.foreignpolicy.com/story/cms.php?story_id=4350.

ity.[77] The *Social Indicators* are mounting demographic pressures, massive movement of refugees or internally displaced persons creating complex humanitarian emergencies, a legacy of vengeance-seeking group grievance or group paranoia, and chronic and sustained human flight. The *Economic Indicators* are uneven economic development along group lines and sharp and/or severe economic decline. The *Political Indicators* are criminalization and/or delegitimization of the state, progressive deterioration of public services, suspension or arbitrary application of the Rule of Law and widespread violation of human rights, the security apparatus operating as a "state within a state", the rise of factionalized elites, and the intervention of other states or external political actors. None of the indicators specifically looks at gender equality, and gender does not appear explicitly. Nonetheless, gender is relevant to many of the indicators: refugees (who are predominatly women) provide an important measurement criterion for a CAST rating,[78] and the Economic Indicator, which examines uneven economic development along group lines, could encompass gender equality.

D. *University of Maryland's Center for International Development and Conflict Management: Peace and Conflict Instability Ledger*

The Peace and Conflict Instability Ledger attempts to evaluate countries according to their risk of future instability. The goal is to help direct resources to prevent state failure. Countries are then ranked based on their vulnerabilities, with Afghanistan, Iraq, Niger, Ethiopia, and Liberia occupying the top 5 slots.[79] The risk estimate for each country is obtained using a statistical model based on five variables that the authors identify as strongly related to destabilizing events or armed conflict, and comparing these countries to the risk of instability in OECD countries.[80] Afghanistan, for example, is 39.3 times as like to become unstable as the average OECD member.

The five variables comprising the index include the incoherence of the governing regime (a democratic or autocratic regime receives higher marks than a regime in transition), a high infant mortality rate, a lack of integration with the global economy, the militarization of society, and the presence of armed conflict in neighboring states.[81] The use of infant mortality as one criterion serves "as a proxy for delivering services that improve social welfare in a country."[82] This factor measures issues that are also correlated with women's status, although the report does not explicitly address any issues involving gender. Even if this factor might be some indication of gender equity, it is incomplete: gender equity goes well beyond providing services, but also a government's responsiveness to human rights such as freedom from intrafamilial violence and workplace equity.

---

77 Ibid.

78 Fund for Peace, "Methodology Behind CAST," http://www.fundforpeace.org/web/index.php?option=com_content&task=view&id=107&Itemid=145.

79 Hewitt et. al. supra note 75 at 5.

80 Ibid. at 4–5.

81 Ibid. at 9–10.

82 Ibid. at 10.

The last two reports do not themselves set out rankings, but provide guidance to United States government agencies on how to assess fragile states and develop appropriate policies.

E. *CRS Report for Congress: Weak and Failing States – Evolving Security Threats and U.S. Policy*

This report, prepared by the Congressional Research Service, which provides policy analysis to the US Congress, surveys U.S. programs and initiatives that address threats arising from weak states.[83] It highlights issues in U.S. policy for Congress concerning the relationship between failing states and US interests. The report discusses the link between weak and failing states and U.S. national security threats, including terrorism, international crime, nuclear proliferation, and regional instability.

As an initial matter, the report provides an overview of U.S. government and NGO efforts to define weak and failing states. It summarizes these evaluative efforts as typically based on four overlapping elements of state function: (1) peace and stability; (2) effective governance; (3) territorial control and porous borders; and (4) economic stability.[84] The report summarizes 9 definitions of weak states from different organizations, ranging from the World Bank to the OECD. Some definitions limit the concept to physical security and control of land.[85] Other definitions, however, allow for a broader view of failing and weak states. The Organization for Economic Cooperation and Development (OECD) defines fragile states as those states lacking "either the will or the capacity to engage productively with their citizens to ensure security, safeguard human rights, and provide the basic function for development."[86] The OECD also characterizes fragile states as those possessing "weak governance, limited administrative capacity, chronic humanitarian crisis, persistent social tensions, violence, or the legacy of civil war."[87] The U.S. Commission on Weak States defines weak states as those with "governments unable to do the things that their own citizens and the international community expect from them: protecting people from internal and external threats, delivering basic health services and education, and providing institutions that respond to the legitimate demands and needs of the population."[88] The World Bank describes fragile states as those characterized by poor government, internal conflicts or tenuous post-conflict transitions, weak security, fractured societal relations, corruption, breakdowns in the rule of law, and insufficient mechanisms for generating legitimate power and authority.[89] While these broader definitions are

---

83 CRS Report for Congress: *Weak and Failing States – Evolving Security Threats and U.S. Policy* (updated Aug. 28, 2008), http://www.fas.org/sgp/crs/row/RL34253.pdf.

84 Ibid., at 4–5.

85 For example, the National Intelligence Council defines failed or failing states as those states having "expanses of territory and populations devoid of effective government control." Ibid at 23.

86 Ibid, at 24.

87 Ibid.

88 Ibid.

89 Ibid, at 24–25.

much more conducive to the use of gender equity as an indicator of state weakness, the CRS report does not mention gender-based equity at all.

While the report does not provide its own rankings of states, it includes information on the ranking efforts of several of the other reports discussed in this paper.

F. *United States Agency for International Development: Measuring State Fragility*

This report describes the United States Agency for International Development's (USAID) strategic approach for dealing with fragile states. The Department's approach has four elements: 1) analysis and monitoring of the internal dynamics of fragile states; 2) priorities reflecting the realities of fragile states; 3) programs focused on those priorities and the sources of fragility; and 4) an Agency business model that allows for timely, rapid, and effective response. The monitoring and analysis prong of the United States' efforts is based on a Fragility Framework, which is used to evaluate a country based on the state's "legitimacy" and "effectiveness" in four governance areas – security, political, economic, and social.[90] These areas are broad, and include sub-factors, such as equitable provision of military and police services and toleration of "diverse customs, cultures, and beliefs," but none is explicitly gender-based.[91] In its listing of "other important factors,"[92] the Report does acknowledge gender issues. It notes the utility of monitoring the different impact that state fragility has on men and women, because of the strong correlation between state fragility and inequitable treatment of women.[93] Based on this correlation, the Report recommends that programming in fragile states take these different impacts into account, although provides no details on how this might occur or on how it might change existing programs.[94]

USAID has supplemented this report with various tools for measuring fragility, and these tools are somewhat more expansive on gender issues when it comes to evaluating the state's weakness in the social area.[95] These supplemental tools measure gender in two areas: life expectancy and school enrollment/literacy.[96] The life expectancy of women in more developed countries is higher than the life expectancy for men, so lower rates for women than for men indicate lower levels of development.[97] Education is relevant to fragility in numerous ways: the Report notes: "First,

---

90 USAID, "Fragile States Strategy," (January 2005), Table 1, http://www.usaid.gov/policy/2005_fragile_states_strategy.pdf.

91 Ibid at 4.

92 Ibid at 4.

93 Ibid at 4.

94 Ibid at 6. The Report simply states: "The different impact of fragility on men and women should also be taken into account." Ibid.

95 USAID, "Measuring Fragility: Indicators and Methods for Rating State Performance" (2005), available at http://pdf.dec.org/pdf_docs/PNADD462.pdf.

96 USAID, "Fragile State Indicators", supra note 6; "Measuring Fragility," Ibid at 30 (literacy rate).

97 USAID, "Fragile State Indicators", supra note 6 at 29; "Measuring Fragility", supra note 95 at 30 (life expectancy).

educated workers have higher current and future opportunity costs of abandoning the formal economic … Second, high education levels indicate that the state is successful in delivering essential social services … Male secondary school enrollment gives a measure of how many potential young combatants are in school, and presumably, see education as an economically valuable investment."[98] Gender is also relevant with respect to the male/female literacy rate.[99]

Apart from USAID, as summarized in Chart 2, none of the other reports uses gender as an assessment tool.

Chart 2: Summary of "Gender" in Six Reports

Report	Was the term "gender," "female," or "women" used in the report?	If the terms were used, how many times were they used?	Pages on which the terms appeared	Context in which the terms were used
CRS Report	No	–	–	
Brookings Institute	No	–	–	–
USAID	Yes	Women – 3	4, 6	useful to monitor the different impact that state fragility has on men and women; notes strong correlation between state fragility and inequitable treatment of women. Recommends that programming take these different impacts into account. Gender not a primary indicator, although relevant in "social area".
George Mason University	No	–	–	–
Fund for Peace	No	–	–	–
University of Maryland	No	–	–	–

98 USAID, "Fragile State Indicators," supra note 6 at 24.

99 Ibid.

IV. Next Steps

Gender equity provides a useful measurement of state security. Nonetheless, its significance is virtually unrecognized in numerous evaluations of state fragility, thereby leading to the risk that gender will remain unrecognized in efforts to promote state stability. For gender equity to become meaningful, gender must become one of the central measurements of state stability. Given the increasing importance of evaluative tools in determining international aid, not addressing gender at this initial phase reflects, quite simply, bias. Making gender a central category is a good in itself and serves as a preventive measure for future societal instability; it not only results in increased recognition of the challenges to gender equity, but also may create incentives to reducing gender differences.[100] Moreover, women's rights provide a useful assessment of a country's development and stability. Failing to assess the multiple structures that create and enforce women's status, and overlooking the measures of men's and women's comparable positions in a culture, results in an inadequate measure of state fragility, and a failure of imagination when it comes to restructuring these states. Indeed, the need to integrate gender shows how the evaluation process is deeply patriarchal in the measures that it uses; integration may result in a fundamental re-thinking of how to measure state fragility.

A new category, "gender equity" should be central to any – and each – attempt to evaluate a state's fragility. This category would be composed of a weighted set of different factors, almost all of which are already available through international organizations or non-governmental organizations. While merely adding a category to assess gender equity may not initially have a direct effect on the stability of states, it should have two other effects: first, in the short-term, it increases awareness of the centrality of gender equity to state stability; and second, in the longer term, as consciousness is raised, this may result in greater efforts to comply with gender equity goals. Without continuous attention to gender issues, they may too easily disappear as other issues take priority. In Iraq, for example, immediately following US intervention, women's issues were repeatedly recognized as important but, as the national security situation deteriorated, gender was "considered an afterthought at best."[101]

Ensuring gender security requires both women-focused programs that attempt to eliminate discriminatory barriers to women's full participation, as well as gender-mainstreaming activities.[102] The limited nature of existing measurements may have a significant effect not just on the analysis of fragility, but also on the proposals for

100 See World Economic Forum, *Global Gender Gap Report 2007*, 3, http://www.weforum.org/en/initiatives/gcp/Gender%20Gap/index.htm.

101 Women to Women International, "Stronger Women, Stronger Nations: 2008 Iraq Report" (2008), 5 http://www.womenforwomen.org/news-women-for-women/files/IraqReport.03.03.08.pdf.

102 Elaine Zuckerman and Marcia Greenberg, 'The Gender Dimensions of Post-Conflict Reconstruction: An Analytical Framework for Policymakers', *Gender and Development* Vol. 12, no. 3 (2004), http://www.genderaction.org/images/ez-mg%20oxfam%20g&d%20gender-pcr.pdf.

restructuring existing institutions. Without an explicit focus on gender, "the matters that are framed as central issues for resolution ... may only peripherally impact many women's day-to-day lives."[103] And, in the absence of a specific gender equity indicator, analyses of state fragility remain incomplete. Segregating gender equity analysis into development or even civil liberties measurements continues the devaluation of these issues.

A. *What Gender Equality Indices are Available?*

There are numerous potential indicators of women's equality; indeed, there are almost 100 such indicators that are already used by the UN and related agencies.[104] The challenge is choosing measurements that are integrally related to state stability, that are capable of measurement in fragile states,[105] and that provide guidance for developing appropriate policies that improve state fragility and the status of women. Evaluations of gender equity must examine both the public aspects of gendered lives – e.g., governmental leadership – as well as equity within the private sphere,[106] such as household role allocations. Evaluation must include not just objective numbers measuring quantitative data, but must be supplemented by analysis of customs and the law in practice.[107] Measurements of the number of women in legislative bodies, or even in leadership positions, might obscure women's lack of power;[108] if women hold /3 of 10 cabinet-level positions, and they are ministers of women's issues, of family services, and of housing, while men are the ministers of departments such as defense, justice, and mines, then women may lack real power within the government. In the analogous

---

103 Aolain, 'Political Violence' supra note 53 at 831.

104 The World Bank, *Global Monitoring Report 2007* (2007), 147, http://siteresources.worldbank.org/INTGLOMONREP2007/Resources/3413191-1179404785559/Chp3-GMR07_webPDF-corrected-may-14-2007-6.pdf.

105 The World Economic Forum provides a useful measurement of the gender gap, but only includes countries that have at least 12 of 14 critical data points. World Economic Forum, "Measuring the Global Gender Gap" (2007), 6, http://www.weforum.org/pdf/gendergap/report2007.pdf Most often countries at highest risk of state instability are not included. For example, Afghanistan, Congo, Iraq, Somalia, and Sudan are not included. Ibid. 27 (App. B).

106 "Women experience both the public and private aspects of ... [a] conflicted society, and articulate the need to transform politics and practices in both contexts." Fionnuala Ni Aolain, "Women, Security" supra note 7, 44. Hilary Charlesworth, Christine Chinkin & Shelley Wright, 'Feminist Approaches to International Law', *American Journal of International Law* Vol. 85 (1991) p. 626 (discussing weight historically accorded to public and private spheres).

107 Caprioli, Mary, Valerie M. Hudson, S. Matthew Stearmer, Rose McDermott, Chad F. Emmett, Bonnie Ballif-Spanvill (2007) "Walking a Fine Line: Addressing Issues of Gender with WomanStats," (unpublished paper, 2007) p. 13, available at http://www.womanstats.org/images/ISA2007WomanStats.pdf. For example, laws may criminalize rape or domestic violence, but objective criteria do not measure the social consequences to a woman of reporting these crimes, such as being declared unfit for marriage. Ibid at 20–23.

108 Caprioli, Hudson, et al., supra note 47 at 13–14.

context of land reform, Ingunn Ikdahl and her colleagues have found that, quite frequently, "discriminatory customary practices overrule equal rights-based statutory laws."[109]

A comprehensive measurement tool could build on the Millennium Development Goals, specifically Goal 3 (Promote Gender Equality) and Goal 5, Reduce Maternal Mortality as well as the 14 indicators in the WEF Gender Gap report, the GDI index, etc. More specifically, the organization, WomanStats, is compiling data on women's status from more than 200 sources (ranging from the World Health Organization, Save the Children, UNESCO, and the US State Department) on nine different measurements of women's security, such as physical, maternity, family, and economic.[110] The tool needs to evaluate state effectiveness at service delivery as well as respect for human rights.

Data for a gender equity evaluative tool are available through several comprehensive databases, and several entities, including the UN and various non-governmental organizations, already provide gender equity rankings.

i. Databases

The UN reports raw data on gender issues through Wistat, the Women's Indicators and Statistics Database.[111] It provides comprehensive information in nine categories, such as health and marital status, and includes measurements on numerous items, ranging from rates of intrafamilial violence to number of female teachers at different educational levels to women's leadership in government. Through Genderstats, the World Bank reports data disaggregated by sex in approximately 20 areas, including fertility, life expectancy, employment, maternal mortality rates, and education.[112] While the site provides extremely useful data on a country or regional, there are no comparative rankings. Like WISTAT, this is a database, without rankings.

ii. Gender Equity Analysis

a. *The UN*

In order to monitor a country progress towards the third Millennium Development Goal (promoting gender equality and empowering women), the U.N. uses three indicators:

---

109 Ikdahl, et al, supra note 28.

110 Caprioli, Hudson, supra note 47, 20; see The WomanStats Project (2007). http://www.womanstats.org/images/WomanStatsOverview.pdf1. The variables are: "1. Women's Physical Security; 2. Women's Economic Security; 3. Women's Legal Security; 4. Women's Security in the Community; 5. Women's Security in the Family, 6. Security for Maternity, 7. Women's Security Through Voice, 8. Security Through Societal Investment in Women, 9. Women's Security in the State."

111 UN Women's Indicators and Statistics Database, http://unstats.un.org/unsd/demographic/gender/wistat/index.htm.

112 GenderStats, http://genderstats.worldbank.org/home.asp.

- The ratio of girls to boys in primary, secondary and tertiary education;
- The share of women in wage employment in the non-agricultural sector; and
- The proportion of seats held by women in national parliament.

Each of these is analyzed separately, and the U.N. does not calculate one score that can be used to assess a state's progress toward gender equality.[113]

UNDP provides perhaps the most widely used ranking of countries with respect to gender equality.[114] Within its Human Development Report, UNDP provides several distinct measurements of gender equality. The Gender-related Development Index (GDI) includes information on 4 indicators, broken down by gender:

- Life expectancy at birth
- Adult literacy rate
- School enrollment
- Estimated earned income

The Gender Empowerment Measure provides information on:

- Percentages of seats in parliament held by women
- Percentages of female legislators and senior offices
- Percentages of female professional and technical workers
- Ratio of female/male earned income[115]

In addition, the Report provides rankings based on gender inequality in education, economic activity, and political participation, as well as a summary of how time for men and women is allocated between market and various nonmarket activities, such as child care and free time.[116]

b. *Social Watch*[117]

Social Watch, a non-governmental organization that is hosted by the Third World Institute in Uruguay,[118] has developed a Gender Equity Index (GEI). It classifies 157 countries that represent more than ninety-four percent of the world's population.[119] The GEI 2008 ranks countries on three dimensions:

- Economic activity (based on income gap and the activity rate gap);
- Empowerment (based on the percentage of women in technical positions, the percentage of women in management and government positions, the

113 All of the UN data are available at http://mdgs.un.org/unsd/mdg/Data.aspx.

114 See supra note 60.

115 Human Dev. Report, supra note 40 at 330–333.

116 Ibid., Tables, 30–33.

117 For information about Social Watch, see http://www.socialwatch.org/en/acercaDe/index.htm.

118 http://www.socialwatch.org/en/acercaDe/index.htm.

119 Social Watch, Gender Equity Index, http://www.socialwatch.org/en/avancesyRetrocesos/IEG_2008/index.htm.

percentage of women in parliaments, and the percentage of women in ministerial posts); and

- Education (based on the literacy rate gap, the primary school enrollment rate gap, the secondary school enrollment rate gap, and the tertiary education enrollment rate gap).

Chart 3 Gender Equality Data for the Most Unstable and the Most Stable Countries

Country	Social Watch	World Economic Forum	U.N. Millennium Goal 3					Other U.N. Data	
	Gender Equity Index[120]	Global Gender Gap Score	Primary Educ. (Girls: Boys)	Sec. Educ. (Girls: Boys)	Tert. Educ. (Girls: Boys)	Employment: Non-agricultural sector	Seats Held by Women in Nat'l Parliament	Literacy 15–24 (Women: Men)	Maternal Mortality Rate(per 100,000 births)
Afghanistan	–	–	.59	.33	.28	17.8	27.7	.36	1800
Iraq	–	–	.83	.66	.59	21.3	25.5	.91	300
Somalia	–	–	–	–	–	21.7	8.2	–	1400
Dem. Rep. Congo	43	–	.78	.58	–	25.9	8.4	.81	1100
Sudan	41	–	.87	.96	.92	20.1	18.1	.84	450
Central Afr. Rep.	42	–	.69	.4	.28	46.8	10.5	.67	980
Liberia	–	–	.9	.72	.76	11.4	12.5	1.12	1200
Norway	84	.8059	1.01	.99	1.54	49.3	36.1	–	7
Finland	85	.8044	1.00	1,04	1.22	51.0	41.5	–	7
Sweden	89[121]	.8146	1.00	.99	1.55	50.3	47.0	–	3

c. *The World Economic Forum*[122]

The World Economic Forum's *Global Gender Gap Report*[123] ranks countries using an index that consolidates four categories of gender equality – economic participation and opportunity, educational attainment, political empowerment, and health and survival. Fourteen indicators are used to calculate each country's score and rank. The report scores and ranks 128 countries, covering over ninety percent of the world's population.

120 Yemen is at the bottom of the index with a score of 31, followed by Cote d'Ivoire and Sierra Leone, at 39, then Chad, Togo, and the Central African Republic at 41. http://www.socialwatch.org/en/avancesyRetrocesos/IEG/tablas/GEITheWorst07.htm.

121 Sweden had the highest score: http://www.socialwatch.org/en/avancesyRetrocesos/IEG/tablas/GEITheBest07.htm.

122 http://www.weforum.org/en/about/Our%20Organization/index.htm.

123 See *Global Gender Gap*, supra note 100.

These different databases and reports demonstrate some of the information that is already available. Of course, in developing any index, it is important to acknowledge that many forms of data may not be available for all countries. For example, the World Economic Forum index did not have a score for the seven weakest countries that are listed (above) in Chart 3. Nonetheless, (1) the data might become available if there was a level of importance placed on gender equity;[124] and (2) even if data are not available for some of the weakest states, they are available for more than 90% of states, which is a good starting point. Chart 3 shows some of the available types of data and rankings for the bottom 10 countries when it comes to gender equity, comparing the statistics for these countries with those rated the least fragile on the Fund for Peace Failed States Index (Norway, Finland, Sweden, Ireland, and Switzerland).

B. *A Gender Equity Indicator*

Integrating these various existing efforts, a new measurement tool should include the data discussed below. These data are comparative, and a county that, for example, has equal enrollment of girls and boys in school, but has a relatively low percentage of its population enrolled in school would score more highly in gender equity than a country with higher overall enrollment rates, but more of a disparity in gender enrollment rates. The indicators are designed to capture both the official and actual practices and policies concerning gender equity.[125]

First, *education*: This subindicator would include comparative literacy rates for boys and girls, men and women, and enrollment in primary, secondary, and tertiary schools. More stable countries have less disparity between men and women in literacy and enrollment.

Second, *health*: This would include items such as the maternal mortality rates and access to contraception. WHO already collects information on the maternal mortality rate, the proportion of births that are attended by skilled health workers, and on access to condoms. Women's reproductive health is highly correlated with gender equality on issues implicating women's access to social and economic assets,[126] and health is correlated with state effectiveness; failure to provide adequate health services makes a state less likely to develop[127] because of a fragile workforce, higher infant and maternal mortality rates, and younger ages of death. When it comes to the sub-category of women's reproductive health, criteria might include

124 UN Statistics Division, "The World's Women: Progress in Statistics" (2006), vii, http://unstats.un.org/unsd/demographic/products/indwm/ww2005_pub/English/WW2005_text_complete_BW.pdf (explaining that the collecting of statistics facilitates policy development, and may also provide support for additional resources to help with the collection effort).

125 See notes 107–109, supra; see also Kaufmann, Kraay, and Mastruzzi, supra note 63 at 28–32 ("De Jure vs. De Facto Measures of Governance").

126 Guang-Zhen Wang, 'Testing the Impact of Gender Equality on Reproductive Health: An Analysis of Developing Countries', *Social Science Journal* Vol. 44 (2007) pp. 515, 516.

127 USAID, 'Fragile State Indicators,' supra note 6 at 28.

contraceptive access, maternal mortality, availability of prenatal care, childhood immunization rates, etc.[128]

Third, *employment opportunity*: This sub-indicator would include employment opportunity laws, numbers of women-headed businesses, parental leave policies, pay gap disparity between men and women,[129] and related measures. This provides information on the hospitability of the workplace for women, and would capture women's contributions to the economy.

Fourth, *family law*: This would include child custody, divorce, inheritance and property rights.[130] WomenStats has already compiled data on equity under marital law, including property law.[131] The inheritance rights of women provide fundamental insights into the equality of women, given the significance of land ownership.

Fifth, *violence against women*: This subindicator includes the pervasiveness of rape and domestic violence, together with information about any applicable laws.

Finally, *female political participation and leadership*, including numbers of women registered to vote, in elected bodies, appointive offices. While formal representation in government does not necessarily indicate power within government, it has symbolic significance on the ability of women

The goal of the new evaluative tool is to ensure that gender becomes more central in assessing state fragility, and then, in response to these assessments, that gender becomes central in developing policy responses to improving state security. The rhetoric is already there.[132] Without a conscious and distinct analysis of gender,

128 See Wang, supra note 126 at 515–516.

129 See, e.g., Mary Jordan, '**In Affluent Germany, Women Still Confront Traditional Bias; Female Workers Employ 2006 Law for Pay Equity**', *Wash. Post*, Oct. 26, 2008, A20 (showing the problem even in developed countries such as German, where women earn between 76–88 % of what men do for the same work; and comparing the work culture in the former east and west Germany, observing that cultures in which women are expected to work provide more support for women who do work).

130 As the CEDAW committee notes, "There are many countries where the law and practice concerning inheritance and property result in serious discrimination against women. As a result of this uneven treatment, women may receive a smaller share of the husband's or father's property at his death than would widowers and sons." Gen. Rec. No. 21 (1994), http://www.un.org/womenwatch/daw/cedaw/recommendations/recomm.htm; see Human Rights Watch, "Women's Property Rights Violations in Kenya" (2006), http://www.hrw.org/campaigns/women/property/factsheet.htm. In many parts of Africa, women "usually can only access land and housing through male relatives, which makes their security of tenure dependent on good marital and family relations." Marjolein Benschop, 'Women's Rights to Land and Property' (2004), http://www.unhabitat.org/downloads/docs/1556_72513_CSDWomen.pdf.

131 WomanStats (May 2008), http://womanstats.org/mapEntrez.htm. The organization has also compiled data on a variety of measures, including access to divorce, in heritance rights of women, and child custody. http://womanstats.org/Codebook7.30.07.htm.

132 For example, the USAID Website Section on Women in Development provides a description for integrating a gender analysis into technical assessments used for program planning and design. Gender analysis is most effective if it is included as a part of each and every technical assessment used in program planning and design. 'Gender' is not a separate sector to be analyzed or reported on in isolation. Rather, technical assessment teams should integrate an analysis of how gender relations and differences in men's and women's

however, gender will maintain its peripheral role in the security sector. Existing institutions and practices are affected both by how they are structured and by who exercises power within them.[133] Unless the structure changes and gender becomes relevant to those exercising power, change will be extremely slow. It is through a combination of gender mainstreaming (which may include activities focused on either women or men), efforts to promote gender equality, and challenges to existing paradigms that *gender will become central.*[134] As this paper has argued, improving the situation of women and reducing the fragility of states requires the development of tools for a more accurate and gender-sensitive assessment of the security situation in a state.

---

roles may interact with or affect their broader findings and incorporate these gender considerations into their program designs and monitoring plans.

USAID, 'Gender Analysis Overview,' http://www.usaid.gov/our_work/cross-cutting_programs/wid/gender/gender_analysis.html.

133 See Helen Irving, *Gender and the Constitution: Equity and Agency in Comparative Constitutional Design* (New York: Cambridge University Press, 2008) p. 34.

134 For some of the justifications, see Zuckerman and Greenberg, supra note 9 at 4, 17.

Part IV

Environmental Security

Chapter 12

Security in a "Warming World": Competences of the UN Security Council for Preventing Dangerous Climate Change

Christina Voigt

Extensive climate changes may alter and threaten the living conditions of much of mankind. They may induce large-scale migration and lead to greater competition for the earth's resources. Such changes will place particularly heavy burdens on the world's most vulnerable countries. There may be increased danger of violent conflicts and wars, within and between states.[1]

I. Introduction

Without resolute counteraction, the effects of climate change are likely to exceed many societies' adaptive capacities to internal or external stresses within the coming decades. This could result in destabilization and violence, jeopardizing national and international security to a new and unknown degree.[2] Currently there still is a window of opportunity for avoiding dangerous anthropogenic climate change by adopting a dynamic and coordinated global climate policy. Yet, the outlook of getting an effective international climate treaty into place in time to avoid dangerous climate change is dim; the chances for stopping climate change at a non-dangerous level rapidly decreasing.

If not halted, the likelihood sharply increases that climate change will draw ever-deeper lines of division and conflict in international relations. It has the potential to trigger numerous conflicts between and within countries over the distribution of resources (especially water and land), over the management of migration, or over compensation payments between the countries mainly responsible for climate change and those countries most affected by its destructive effects.[3]

In giving recognition to this threat, on 17 April 2007, the Security Council held its first-ever debate on the impact of climate change on international peace and

---

1 Excerpt from the Nobel Committee's explanation for the award of the 2007 Nobel Peace Prize to the Intergovernmental Panel on Climate Change and Al Gore.

2 German Advisory Council on Global Change (WGBU), *Climate Change as a Security Risk* (2007) at 23.

3 Ibid.

Cecilia M. Bailliet (ed.), Security: A Multidisciplinary Normative Approach.

ISBN 978 90 04 17296 8. pp. 291–312.

security.[4] No concrete action or decision followed this debate. The main achievement was perhaps that of global awareness rising of the consequences of climate change rather than any concrete outcome.

Prior and during the debate there had been strong opposition from some countries to any suggestion that the Security Council play a role in the international response to climate change. At the same time, the ever-increasing urgency of decisive action to address climate change, combined with the challenge's scale and complexity, suggest that at this stage all options (including a more active role of the Security Council) ought to be examined.

The second part will give an overview over the controversial discussion about the link between climate change and security threats (part 2). The third part deals with the normative concept of peace and security in the UN Charter and its relationship to climate change as a (possible) non-military threat. Part four assesses the current multilateral climate regime for its effectiveness to prevent climate change related threats. The fifth part investigates the mandate of the Security Council with regard to addressing environmental threats. Of particular interest in this context are the Council's competences to impose sanctions, to 'legislate', and to condemn state actions or inactions.[5] Also, in this part, the competences of the Security Council to request of the International Court of Justice an advisory on opinion legal questions in relation to climate change will be analyzed in connection. Part six concludes this chapter.

II. The Factual Link between Climate Change and International Security

The risks posed by climate change are real and impacts are already tangible. The Intergovernmental Panel on Climate Change demonstrated in its Fourth Assessment Report that in order to avoid a temperature rise of 2°C above pre-industrial global mean temperature concentrations of CO2-equivalents in the atmosphere need to be stabilized. Such stabilization requires global greenhouse gas (GHG) emissions to be reduced by up to 85 per cent, peaking between now and 2015.[6]

4 UN Department of Public Information, News and Media Division, *Security Council Holds First-ever Debate on Impact of Climate Change on Peace and Security*, UN Doc. SC/9000, 17 April 2007.

5 The possibility of use of force is omitted from this chapter. See for an extensive analysis of this issue the chapter by Ole Kristian Fauchald and Jo Stigen in this book.

6 IPCC, 2007: Summary for Policymakers. In: *Climate Change 2007: Mitigation. Contribution of Working Group III to the Fourth Assessment Report of the Intergovernmental Panel on Climate Change* [B. Metz, O.R. Davidson, P.R. Bosch, R. Dave, L.A. Meyer (eds)], Cambridge University Press, Cambridge, United Kingdom and New York, NY, USA, Table SPM.5, at 15. This global reduction target (relative to 2000 emission levels) is indifferent to countries' capabilities or responsibilities. In order to comply with the principle of common but differentiated responsibilities, this target needs to be broken down to specific targets for different country groups. Such differentiation, if emission growth for developing countries is included, could in fact lead to 'carbon negativity' (not just carbon neutrality) for the most industrialized countries, meaning emission reduction targets above 100 per cent. See Stockholm Environment Institute, *Accounting for emissions from*

A temperature increase above 2°C is likely to trigger a number of tipping points that would lead to accelerated, irreversible and largely unpredictable climate changes. Such changes may lead to unprecedented security scenarios. In this context, the EU High Representative for the Common Foreign and Security Policy and the European Commission to the European Council demanded that 'investment in mitigation to avoid such scenarios, as well as ways to adapt to the unavoidable should go hand in hand with addressing the international security threats created by climate change; both should be viewed as part of preventive security policy'.[7]

If, by 2020, political efforts to limit temperature increases to 2°C have failed, the international community must prepare itself to deal with climate-related conflicts. If this temperature threshold is crossed, the likelihood of conflicts increases significantly. Such conflicts include conflicts over resources (based on reduction of arable land, widespread shortage of water, diminishing food and fish stocks, increased flooding and prolonged droughts), conflicts over loss of territory and border disputes,[8] situations of fragility and increasing instability in weak or failing states, and tension over energy supply.[9]

The greatest single conflict-prone impact of climate change could be environmentally-induced human migration. The UN estimates that there will be millions of environmental migrants by 2020 with climate change as one of the major drivers of this phenomenon.[10] Some countries that are extremely vulnerable to climate change

---

a consumption perspective (April 2008) available at: ⟨http://www.sei-us.org/climate-and-energy/CO2andTrade.htm⟩. Similarly, the International Energy Agency states in a recent report that the 450ppm concentration target implies that net greenhouse gas emissions have to turn negative (i.e. carbon absorption exceeding gross emissions) by the end of this century. IEA, *World Energy Outlook 2008*, 12 November 2008.

7 S113/08, 14 March 2008, *CLIMATE CHANGE AND INTERNATIONAL SECURITY*, Paper from the High Representative and the European Commission to the European Council, at 1.

8 In this context, the High Representative and the European Commission to the European Council note: 'Scientists project major changes to the landmass during this century. Receding coastlines and submergence of large areas could result in loss of territory, including entire countries such as small island states. More disputes over land and maritime borders and other territorial rights are likely. There might be a need to revisit existing rules of international law, particularly the Law of the Sea, as regards the resolution of territorial and border disputes. A further dimension of competition for energy resources lies in potential conflict over resources in Polar Regions which will become exploitable as a consequence of global warming. Desertification could trigger a vicious circle of degradation, migration and conflicts over territory and borders that threatens the political stability of countries and regions.' Ibid at 4.

9 S113/08, 14 March 2008, *CLIMATE CHANGE AND INTERNATIONAL SECURITY*, Paper from the High Representative and the European Commission to the European Council, at 2–5.

10 UN University's Institute for Environment and Human Security warned that the international community should prepare for 50 million 'environmental refugees' by 2010. (Adam, D., '50m environmental refugees by end of decade, UN warns', *The Guardian*, 12 October 2005). The UN Environment Programme (UNEP) argues that by 2060 there could be 50 million 'environmental refugees' in Africa alone. (UNEP, *Africa Environment Outlook, Past. Present and Future*, 2002) In 2007 Christian Aid suggests that nearly a billion

are already calling for international recognition of such environmentally-induced migration. It is, however, important to note that all current predictions about the exact number of 'climate refugees' are fraught with methodological problems. So far, scientists have focused on establishing the extent and nature of anthropogenic climate change and its physical impact on weather systems and coastlines. Much less focus has been directed to the empirical analysis of the impacts of climate change on the distribution human populations.[11] The simple fact is that nobody really knows with any degree of precision what climate change will mean for human population movement and distribution.[12] This is unsurprising; the science of climate change is complicated. In addition, the interconnections between environmental conditions, societies with widely differing resources and varied capacities to adapt to external shocks, and resulting conflict potential add a high degree of complexity.[13]

Finally, climate change impacts may also pose a threat to international governance. The multilateral system is at risk if the international community fails to address the threats outlined above. The High Representative and the EU Commission stated in this context that

> Climate change impacts will fuel the politics of resentment between those most responsible for climate change and those most affected by it. Impacts of climate mitigation policies (or policy failures) will thus drive political tension nationally and internationally. The potential rift not only divides North and South but there will also be a South – South dimension particularly as the Chinese and Indian share of global emissions rises. The already burdened international security architecture will be put under increasing pressure.[14]

In the absence of absolute scientific certainty about the social and political impacts of climate change, the phenomenon is best viewed as a threat multiplier which exacerbates existing trends, tensions and instability. Rather than rejecting the threat in lieu of exact numbers, the risk of climate related human displacement needs to

---

people could be permanently displaced by 2050: 250 million by climate change-related phenomena such as droughts, floods and hurricanes, and 645 million by dams and other development projects. (Christian Aid, *Human Tide: The Real Migration Crisis*, 2007).

11 Brown, O., 'The numbers game', 31 *Forced Migration Review: Climate Change and Displacement*, October 2008, at 8.

12 Ibid.

13 Studies on environmental security have had focus on either a locality or region or particular sector or medium, such as soil degradation, water scarcity and conflicts over resources. Moreover, empirical research has mostly been conducted *ex-post*. Considering the impacts of climate change, however, requires an extension of the analytical time horizon including the coming decades, when the security-relevant disruption that is to be expected as a result of climate change is likely to occur. Also, research on environment and conflict has been dominated largely by political science. Transdisciplinary or interdisciplinary research of natural sciences and other social sciences has so far occurred only tentatively or not at all. See WBGU, 2007.

14 S113/08, 14 March 2008, *CLIMATE CHANGE AND INTERNATIONAL SECURITY*, Paper from the High Representative and the European Commission to the European Council, at 5.

be acknowledged and precautions put in place. Climate change needs to be seen in the broader concept of human security, which focuses stronger on effects on the individual.[15] In line with this concept, it is clear that many issues related to the impact of climate change on international security are interlinked requiring comprehensive policy responses.

In any event, preventing dangerous climate change means reducing the likelihood of climate-related individual and international security threats. Therefore, a pro-active climate protection policy must be in place with the aim of keeping global warming as close to the 2°C limit as possible. At the same time strategies for adaptation to unavoidable climate change must be intensified and oriented towards the type of climate impact scenario that can be expected. The greater the delay in commencing efforts to mitigate climate change and to adapt to its impacts, the more expensive such efforts will become. Development that leads to missed opportunities to protect the climate will entail far higher costs than a reference scenario in which compliance with the 2°C target is achieved.[16]

III. Climate Change and the Normative Concept of 'International Peace and Security'

After we concluded in the previous paragraph that climate change increases the risk of conflict by functioning as a threat multiplier, the next question is whether this kind of threat can be linked to the normative concept of 'international peace and security' as entailed in the UN Charter or in other words, is climate change a 'Security Council issue'? This question begs for analysis of both the political responses to climate change as a possible security threat (multiplier) and the legal substance of the UN Charter provisions.

A. *Political Views*

Analysing the political link between climate change related threats and international peace and security is arguably best done by examining the Security Council debate on climate change on 17 April 2007. The debate was requested by the U.K. and chaired by British Foreign Secretary, Margaret Beckett. She was of the clear opinion that climate change was a security issue, but it was not a matter of narrow national security –

15 UNDP, *Human Development Report 1994: New Dimensions of Human Security*, Oxford 1994. For definitions of 'security', see Brauch, H.G., *Environment and Human Security*, InterSecTions, 2/2005 (Bonn: UNU-EHS); Brauch, H.G., *Threats, Challenges, Vulnerabilities and Risks in Environmental and Human Security* (Bonn: UNU-EHS) 1/2005; and Commission on Human Security (2003) *Human Security Now*, Commission on Human Security: New York http://www.humansecurity-chs.org/. See also Bogardi, J. and Brauch, H.G., (2005) "Global Environmental Change: A Challenge for Human Security – Defining and conceptualising the environmental dimension of human security", in: Rechkemmer, A., (ed.) *UNEO – Towards an International Environmental Organization* (Nomos: Baden-Baden, 2005), at 85–109.

16 *Stern Review on the Economics of Climate Change*, 2006 (available at: http://www.hm-treasury.gov.uk/stern_review_climate_change.htm; and WBGU, 2007).

climate change was about "our collective security in a fragile and increasingly interdependent world".[17] Yet, there was no unanimity among the 50 participating states as to this link and the possible role of the Security Council.[18]

Among those states who were in favour of dealing with climate change at the level of the Security Council were European states and a number of states most prone to the effects of climate change, i.e. some coastal states and least developed developing countries. Those states accepted a broad concept of security, including human and international security. The main argument was that severe environmental degradation and environmentally induced conflicts triggered by climate change can be regarded as a threat to international security and world peace and that the impacts of climate change constitute a particularly high potential risk in this context. Dealing with climate change as a security issue is therefore seen as a strategy to *prevent* conflict.[19] In the context of conflict prevention, climate change needs to be seen in conjunction with other global threats, such as poverty, water scarcity, energy insecurity and diseases.[20] In a sense the threat of dangerous climate change was seen as a positive driving force in stimulating concerned action. Margaret Beckett declared "[So] climate change can bring us together, if we have the wisdom to prevent it from driving us apart".[21] In line with this view, the role of the Security Council was seen as playing an advisory role, rather than taking enforcement action.

Some low-lying island states, however, saw the risk of inundation of their lands by rising sea levels as an immediate security threat that can be linked to climate change. Papua New Guinea's representative said that 'the impact of climate change on small islands was no less threatening than the dangers guns and bombs posed to large nations'.[22] They therefore expected a more active role of the Council by keeping the issue of climate change under continuous review and ensuring that all countries contributed to solving the problem and that those efforts commensurate with their resources and capacities. They also expected the Council to review sensitive issues, such as implications for sovereignty and international legal rights from the loss of land, resources and people.[23]

In stark contrast to these views were the positions of fast developing economies, such as China and India, who considered climate change a development issue, rather than a security threat. The reasons for keeping climate change out of the Councils programme of work are linked to a fear that developed countries might use the Security Council as a tool to influence the development strategy – and therefore impact on state sovereignty – of developing nations.[24] Others agree to climate change

---

17 See SC/9000.

18 See for an overview of the debate: Sindico, F., 'Climate Change: A Security (Council) Issue?', 1 *Carbon and Climate Law Review* (2007) at 29–34.

19 See SC/9000, Statement of Germany and France.

20 See SC/9000, Statement of Germany. Also WBGU, 2007.

21 SC/9000.

22 SC/9000, Statement of Papua New Guinea on behalf of the Pacific Island Forum.

23 Ibid.

24 SC/9000. Statements who addressed this fear included those of Qatar, Pakistan, Egypt, China, India and Brazil.

but suggest the issue be dealt with either by more general or more specialized UN bodies, such as the UN General Assembly, the UN Economic and Social Council, or the UN Commission on Sustainable Development.[25]

The political landscape is divided. While there seems to be a developing consensus on viewing climate change as a security issue, it does not lead to generally accepting a role of the Security Council – whether active or passive – in this context.

B. *The Legal Framework*

The Security Councils primary responsibility according to Article 24.1 of the UN Charter is the maintenance of international peace and security. The language of the UN Charter is informed by the post-Second World War situation in which it was drafted and concerns primarily military activities. The inclusion of non-military threats to international peace and security, such as infectious diseases[26] and terrorism,[27] is a rather recent phenomenon.[28] Environmental threats, however, have not yet been 'officially' included into the catalogue of threats to international peace and security.[29]

The powers of Security Council to take coercive, binding action to maintain or restore international peace and security against a threat (whether military or non-military) are defined in Chapter VII of the UN Charter. Whether the Security Council can take such action is contingent upon a "threat to the peace, breach of the peace, or act of aggression", according to Article 39. In practice, the Council has identified a 'threat to the peace' much more often than a breach of the peace, and has proven reluctant to ever identify an act of aggression.[30] A 'threat to the peace' does not necessarily mean a threat to use force. The Council has taken a wide interpretation of 'threat to the peace' and has included internal conflict and the refusal to act against terrorism.[31] The determination of whether an environmental threat amounts to a threat to peace is left to the Security Council with a wide margin of discretion.

---

25 See for a discussion of these views, Sindico, 2007, at 32–33.

26 See UN Doc. UN/S/RES/1318 (2000), On Ensuring an Effective Role for the Security Council in the Maintenance of International Peace and Security, 7 September 2000.

27 S/RES/1373 (2001).

28 For an overview see Knight, A., 'Global Environmental Threats: Can the Security Council Protect our Earth?', *New York University Law Review* (2005) at 1565–1566.

29 The only exception being the recognition of Iraq's responsibility for compensating the environmental damages inflicted on Kuwait during in the 1990–1991 Gulf War. Security Council Resolution 687 (1991) states that Iraq is "liable under international law for any direct loss, damage, including environmental damage and the depletion of natural resources, or injury to foreign Governments, nationals and corporations, as a result of Iraq's unlawful invasion and occupation of Kuwait." S/RES/687 (1991) para. 16.

30 Gray, C., 'The Use of Force and the International Law Order' in: Evans, M.D., *International Law*, 2nd ed. (2006) at 606.

31 Ibid.

The Security Council has so far taken a somewhat cautious approach in this regard. Yet, a number of legal arguments can be listed, which allow the inclusion of climate change under the ambit of Article 39. In the following, three arguments will be explained in more detail: (i) dynamic or evolutionary interpretation of Article 39, (ii) protection of human rights, and (iii) breach of an essential international environmental obligation.

i. Dynamic Interpretation of Article 39 UN Charter

First, although there is no explicit mentioning of environmental protection – or the prevention of environmental threats – in the Charter, this does not mean that an inclusion of environmental objectives cannot be derived from a broader interpretation of the provisions of the Charter. It could further be argued that environmental protection lies within the implied powers of the UN. Article 1.1 states as one purpose of the UN the maintenance of international peace and security and calls for taking effective collective measures for the prevention and removal of threats to peace, while Article 1.3 requires international cooperation in solving international problems of an economic, social, cultural or humanitarian character. It can be argued that the protection of the environment and prevention of environmental threats can be essential elements in solving international problems of economic or social character.[32] Yet, while the debate around of 'environmental security' has been contentious for more than a decade, it has recently gained momentum.[33] Following an initiative by former UN Secretary General Kofi Annan in 2004 a High-Level Panel assessed 'new' threats to international security.[34] The assessment, which identified environmental degradation as one of the major threats, was explicitly approved by the Secretary General.[35] The assessment makes explicit mentioning of climate change as a driver in the context of disaster related conflicts.[36] As the climate change crisis has intensified, have the security implications been investigated with much greater intensity outside the UN. In the last two years alone there have been a number of reports and books published

---

32 See Simma, B., *The Charter of the United Nations: A Commentary* (Oxford, 1994).

33 See Birnie, P., and Boyle, A., *International Law and the Environment* (2002) at 48, with further references. See also the chapter of Ole Kristian Fauchald and Jo Stigen in this book for a more detailed discussion.

34 High Level Panel on Threats, Challenges and Change, *A More Secure World: Our Shared Responsibility*, U.N. GAOR, 59th Session, U.N. Doc. A/59/565 (Dec. 2, 2004).

35 The Secretary General, Report of the Secretary-General, *In Larger Freedom: Towards Development, Security, and Human Rights for All*, delivered to the General Assembly, U.N. Doc. A/59/2005 (Mar. 21, 2005).

36 "53. Environmental degradation has enhanced the destructive potential of natural disasters and in some cases hastened their occurrence. The dramatic increase in major disasters witnessed in the last 50 years provides worrying evidence of this trend. More than two billion people were affected by such disasters in the last decade, and in the same period the economic toll surpassed that of the previous four decades combined. If climate change produces more acute flooding, heat waves, droughts and storms, this pace may accelerate." *A More Secure World: Our Shared Responsibility*, 2004.

by think tanks, non-governmental organizations and universities identifying climate change as a threat to individual, national and/or international security.[37]

The conclusions of the assessments have yet to find repercussion in a Security Council resolution. However, the door has been 'pushed open' for justifying the legality of a climate change related action of the Security Council based on an evolutionary interpretation of the Charter. The assessment of the High Level Panel makes clear that the significance of the Charter term has changed over time and with the evolution of science and the law. It is therefore of importance to give legal recognition to this change and to ensure necessary dynamism of the UN, its laws and its organs.

ii. Protection of Human Rights

The second legal argument for the inclusion of climate change related threats into the ambit of the determinations made by the Security Council can be derived from the commitment of the UN to the promotion of universal respect for human rights and fundamental freedoms in Article 55 (c) UN Charter. The link between climate change and human security, outlined above, also has repercussions for the protection of human rights. The direct and indirect effects of climate change can affect some of the most fundamental human rights.

In order to highlight this link between climate change impacts and human rights violations we can look at the example of impacts on people living in Arctic regions. Average annual temperatures in the Arctic have increased by approximately double the increase in global average temperatures.[38] The direct impacts of global warming include higher temperatures, sea-level rise, melting of sea ice and glaciers, increased precipitation in some areas and drought in others. Indirect social, environmental, economic and health impacts will follow, including increased death and serious illness in poor Arctic communities, decreased crop yields, heat stress in livestock and wildlife, and damage to coastal ecosystems, forests, drinking water, fisheries, buildings and other resources needed for subsistence. If global warming continues unchecked it threatens to destroy the culture of Arctic peoples, to render their land uninhabitable, and to deprive them of their means of subsistence. The harm caused to their way of life has already been claimed serious enough so as to violate some fundamental internationally recognised human rights.[39] International human rights

37 See, *inter alia*, Abbott, C., *An Uncertain Future: Law Enforcement, National Security and Climate Change* (2008); Paskal, C., 'How climate change is pushing the boundaries of security and foreign policy' Chatham House Energy, Environment and Development Programme EEDP CC BP 07/01; Brown, O., Hammill, A. and McLeman, R. 'Climate Change as the "new" security threat: implications for Africa' 83 *International Affairs* (2007), at 1141; Busby, J.B., *Climate Change and National Security. An Agenda for Action* (2007); and Smith, D., and Vivekananda, J., *A Climate of Conflict. The Links between climate change, peace and war* (2007).

38 Arctic Council and the International Arctic Science Committee, *Arctic Climate Impact Assessment* (ACIA), 2004.

39 On March 1, 2007, the Inter-American Commission on Human Rights (IACHR) of the Organization of American States held a hearing to investigate the relationship between

that can be affected include the right to life, the right to residence and movement, the right to inviolability of the home, the right to preservation of health and to well-being, the rights to benefits of culture, and the right to work.

As exemplified by this scenario, it can be argued that human rights violation as a consequence of climate change could trigger a more active role of the Security Council in addressing inaction of the most polluting states and their contribution to climate change. Massive and egregious infringements of human rights can under certain circumstances lead the UN Security Council to decide on collective counter-measures or to authorize or recommend sanctions.[40] The Council has on occasions of human rights violations decided or recommended economic sanctions such as breaking off economic relations, embargoes on imports and exports, the blocking of financial operations or the suspension of co-operation in the scientific and technical fields.[41] Such economic or political sanctions are a public condemnation of the states that are disrespecting human rights caused by continuing massive greenhouse gas emissions. They are primarily intended to condemn a certain form of behaviour and thereby 'delegitimize' it. *Cassese* suggests that these sanctions could be used 'to prove to the world public opinion that the responsible State was wrong inasmuch as it acted contrary to internationally accepted standards.'[42]

iii. Breach of an Essential International Environmental Obligation

Thirdly, the argument has been made, that a breach of an international environmental obligation of 'essential importance' may qualify as a threat to peace and security.[43] Such environmental obligation will normally arise out of a treaty or a customary obligation. The UN Framework Convention on Climate Change (UNFCCC) is particularly relevant in the context of climate change impacts.[44] The central question is whether it contains obligations for States that can be breached.

global warming and human rights. The hearing was in response to a petition filed by Ms. Sheila Watt-Cloutier, the elected Chair of the Inuit Circumpolar Conference (ICC), in December 2005. The petition sought relief from violations of the human rights of Inuit resulting from global warming caused by greenhouse gas emissions from the United States. The IACHR rejected the petition on November 16, 2006.

40 See for a discussion of the link between safeguarding human rights and the competences of the Security Council: Cassese, A., *International Law*, 2nd ed. (OUP, 2005) at 347–348, and 373–374. He notes that massive and egregious infringements of human rights can under certain circumstances trigger competences of the Security Council under chapter VII of the Charter.

41 See Conforti, B., *The Law and Practice of the United Nations*, Kluwer Law International (2000) at 185–194.

42 Cassese, 2005, at 312.

43 Herbst, J., *Rechtskontrolle des UN-Sicherheitsrates* (1999) at 416.

44 The relevance of the Kyoto Protocol is limited in the context of establishing an international environmental obligation of 'essential importance', whose breach can amount to a threat to peace. The quantifiable emission reduction obligations in the Protocol amount in sum to less than 5 per cent below 1990 levels of 37 States. These almost insignificant

It can be claimed that the ultimate objective of the UNFCCC is to provide a duty of prevention with regard to dangerous climate change. The ultimate objective of the Convention is:

> to achieve, in accordance with the relevant provisions of the Convention, stabilization of greenhouse gas emissions at a level that would prevent dangerous anthropogenic interference with the climate system. Such a level should be achieved within a time-frame sufficient to allow eco-systems to adapt naturally to climate change, to ensure that food production is not threatened and to enable economic development to proceed in a sustainable manner.[45]

It is possible to interpret Article 2 UNFCCC as containing the duty of preventing dangerous interference with the climate system on the basis of current scientific and legal standards of protection.[46] Moreover, Article 4.2 (a) UNFCCC can be interpreted as entailing a concrete obligation for Annex I – industrialized – Parties to reduce their greenhouse gas emissions, which complements the objective. According to Article 4.2

> Each Annex I Party shall adopt national policies and take corresponding measures on the mitigation of climate change, by limiting its anthropogenic emissions of greenhouse gases and protecting and enhancing its greenhouse gas sinks and reservoirs. These policies and measures will demonstrate that developed countries are taking the lead in modifying longer-term trends in anthropogenic emissions consistent with the objective of the Convention.

Article 4.2 UNFCCC when interpreted in a teleological way in the light of the objective according to Article 31 Vienna Convention on the Law of Treaties (VCLT) sets forth an 'obligation of conduct' to reverse the long term trend of ever-increasing greenhouse gas emissions. This conduct is required in order to stabilize atmospheric concentrations. Article 4.2 UNFCCC in conjunction with Article 2, therefore, obliges parties to take action to adopt policies and measures to secure the stabilization of atmospheric concentrations of greenhouse gases. These Articles together could, therefore, be understood as a primary rule that can be breached. Such a breach is committed where a state is taking no or insufficient measures to modify upward emission trends. If an Annex I Party has increased its emissions continually since its ratification of the UNFCCC, this could amount to a breach of an international environmental obligation of 'essential importance'.[47]

Moreover, customary international law also clearly prohibits states from knowingly allowing their territory to be used to cause harm to other states. In environ-

---

emission reduction targets with regard to halting dangerous climate change and the limited number of obliged States lead to the conclusion that a breach of obligations under the Protocol cannot be considered a 'threat to peace'.

45 Article 2 UNFCCC.

46 See, in particular, Verheyen, R., *Climate Damage and International Law: Prevention Duties and State Responsibilities* (Martinus Nijhoff, Leiden, 2005) and Voigt, C., *Sustainable Development as a Principle of International Law – Resolving Conflicts between Climate Measures and WTO Law*, Leiden: Martinus Nijhoff Publishers, (2009) at 67–70.

47 For further discussion, see Voigt, C., 'State Responsibility for Climate Change Damages', *Nordic Journal of International Law* 77 (2008) at 1–22; and Verheyen, 2005.

mental law, this obligation has been translated into the obligation to not cause harm to the environment of other states and to areas beyond any jurisdiction.[48] While the early formulation of this rule focused on avoiding transboundary pollution between neighbouring states, the no-harm rule now extends to relations between all states, however distant, and has also extended its scope to areas beyond a state's jurisdiction. The no-harm rule is also enshrined in Principle 21 of the Stockholm Declaration and Principle 2 of the Rio Declaration. It has frequently been referred to by international courts and tribunals and forms the foundation of international environmental law. The International Court of Justice in *Nuclear Weapons* and *Gabcikovo-Nagymaros* confirmed the 'general obligation of States to ensure that activities within their jurisdiction and control respect the environment of other States or of areas beyond national control is now part of the corpus of international law relating to the environment'.[49] Establishing a breach of this obligation is still facing a number of legal problems, such as establishing causation and defining the due diligence standard.[50] To overcome this challenge, it has been suggested, that the Security Council 'interprets' the content of that customary legal rule as 'prohibiting cross-border environmental harm, recognizing the long-term threat posed to all states by irresponsible use of national territory resulting in excessive greenhouse gas emissions'.[51] Excessive emissions of greenhouse gases from a state's territory could therefore amount to a breach of the customary no-harm rule, which is an obligation of essential international importance and could – as such – comprise a threat to international peace.

Finally, as mentioned above, scientific uncertainty remains as to the concrete local or regional extent of climate change impact. Preventive action is warranted where science is readily available. In the context of climate change, however, risk scenarios linked to different emission paths are the basis for determination of consequences. Risk in this context is defined in terms of probability of a certain harm to occur and the magnitude of such harm. Where there is high risk of harm, either because probability of harm to human welfare is high or the harm is significant and potentially irreversible, or both – such as with climate change impacts as a result of atmospheric greenhouse emission concentrations above 450 ppm – a lower degree of scientific certainty needs to suffice in order to allow for action which lowers the threat. This is in line with the precautionary principle, as elaborated in principle 15 of the Rio declaration: 'Where there are threats of serious or irreversible damage, lack of full scientific certainty shall not be used as a reason for postponing cost-effective

48 The arbitral decision in the *Trail Smelter* case had a strong influence on the formulation and content of the no-harm rule. The tribunal concluded 'Under the principle of international law ... no State has the right to use or permit the use of its territory in such a manner as to cause injury by fumes in or to the territory of another state or the properties or persons therein, when the case is of serious consequence and the injury is established by clear and convincing evidence.' *Trail Smelter* (*USA* v. *Canada*), Award of 1941, III RIAA 1911, at 1965.

49 *Nuclear Weapons* ICJ Report 241, 1996, para. 29; re-stated in *Gabcikovo-Nagymaros Project*, ICJ Report 7, 1997, p. 41.

50 See Voigt, 2008.

51 Penny, C.K., 'Greening the Security Council: Climate Change as an Emerging "Threat to International Peace and Security"', *International Environmental Agreements* (2007) at 60.

measures to prevent environmental degradation'. The legal importance of this principle is consolidating and strong arguments can be made that it reflects a principle of customary international law.[52] In the context of threat determination by the Security Council it could be used as a means to define international tolerance of risk of climate change related damage.[53] A determination of climate change as a threat to international peace can therefore be founded on the risk of harm that might occur, i.e. the magnitude of such harm or its probability (there could be a rather low probability of disastrous harm or a high probability of serious harm), even in the absence of scientific certainty. This is of essential importance when it comes to climate change impacts. By the time science can deliver clear, empirical data, time will have run out for preventing climate change-related threats.

Presumably, therefore, the Security Council could legally and legitimately be authorized to take preventive action under Chapter VII of the United Nations Charter in cases of climate-related threats to international peace and security and where grave violations of human rights obligations and international environmental law have occurred. Specific measures to address this threat would therefore fall within the scope of competences of the Security Council.

IV. UN Responses so far: Multilateral Climate Treaties and the Failure to Take Effective Action to Mitigate Climate Change

Climate change is a global phenomenon and calls for a collective response in the form of global partnerships.[54] Solutions, in order to be effective, need to be based on a global consensus for global action. Measures of the Security Council, especially coercive ones that can be imposed against the will of States, should therefore be envisaged as the last resort only.

It is thus necessary to determine whether the current form of international climate governance, the climate regime consisting of the UN Framework Convention on Climate Change and the Kyoto Protocol, provides a sufficient and effective approach to the prevention of climate change-related threats.

The purpose of this part is not to describe the climate change regime in detail, but to focus on some if its weak aspects in avoiding or addressing climate change conflicts.

The first shortcoming in this aspect is the general and vague language in the UNFCCC. Being a framework convention, inspired by creating broad consensus rather than establishing concrete, quantifiable emission reduction obligations, it has the downside of missing legal concreteness and, as a consequence, enforceability. A breach of the legal obligation that has been identified above will meet significant procedural and substantial obstacles if claimed in an international court.[55]

52 See Sands, P., *Principles of International Environmental Law* (2003) at 179.

53 See Knight, supra note 28 at 1580.

54 UNDP (2004) *Reducing Disaster Risk: A Challenge for Development*. Geneva: UNDP, Bureau for Crisis Prevention and Recovery: http://www.un.org/special-rep/ohrlls/ldc/Global-Reports/UNDP%20Reducing%20Disaster%20Risk.pdf.

55 For a discussion of these legal challenges see: Voigt, 2008.

Second, both the UNFCCC and the Kyoto Protocol, fall short when it comes to setting up effective mechanisms that aim to oblige States to significant reductions in their greenhouse gas emissions. While the UNFCCC does not contain any quantification of emission reductions, the Kyoto Protocol sets a specific target of reducing the overall emissions of the gases listed in its Annex A by at least 5 per cent below 1990 levels in the commitment period 2008 to 2012.[56] This overall target applies exclusively to those States listed in Annex B of the Protocol. Both the limited geographical scope and brief duration of commitment (5 years) make this target already highly insufficient for halting temperature changes within the global 2 degree centigrade limit. Major emitters, such as the USA, but also fast growing economies with steep upwards emission trends, such as China, are not included. Moreover, even if all emitters were included, the 5 per cent reduction goal remains insignificantly small compared to the substantial emission cuts of up to 85 per cent required for stabilizing emission concentrations at 450ppm between 2100 and 2150.[57]

In addition to these shortcomings come loopholes in the design of the Protocol which further reduce the effectiveness of the regime. Because developing countries are not bound by reduction targets, there is the danger that these countries omit implementing climate policies and respective laws, a result which is often referred to as 'free-riding'. The absence of stringent environmental regulation could lead to so called 'pollution havens', an accumulation of highly emitting industries in non-capped countries. It also may become economically feasible for companies from countries with emission reduction targets to relocate to non-capped countries.[58] Such 'carbon leakage' affects the environmental integrity of the climate regime by increasing overall greenhouse gas emissions.

Even more, so far there is no indication that those countries which have committed themselves to greenhouse gas reduction targets are complying with their obligation. One reason for this is missing political willingness and fear of losing economic competitiveness to those States that have no emission reduction obligation. Another reason is linked to the weakness of the compliance mechanism established under the Protocol. Non-compliance with the emission reduction obligations can be met by hard sanctions imposed by the Enforcement Branch of the Compliance Committee.[59] If the Enforcement Branch has determined that a party is not in compliance with its emission reduction commitment under Article 3.1 of the Kyoto Protocol it shall – inter alia – deduce from this party's assigned amount in the second commitment period a number of tonnes equal to 1.3 times the amount in tonnes of excess emissions. Yet, while such hard enforcement measure would

56 Article 3 Kyoto Protocol.

57 See IPCC, AR 4, WGIII, *Summary for Policymakers*, at 15.

58 For an assessment of heavy industry's vulnerability to carbon leakage, see: Reinaud, J., *Competitiveness and Carbon Leakage – Focus on Heavy Industry*, International Energy Agency Information paper, OECD/IEA, October 2008.

59 For an overview over the Kyoto Protocol compliance system see: Schram Stokke, O., Hovi, J. and Ulfstein, G., *Implementing the Climate Regime-International Compliance*, Earthscan, 2005.

sanction non-compliance,[60] its teeth are lacking because there is to date no successive agreement to the Kyoto Protocol and thus no second commitment period.

This links to the final, major shortcoming of the present climate regime with regard to preventing climate change impacts from becoming a threat to international peace: the missing post 2012 agreement. The international climate negotiations are expected to lead to a new global agreement by the end of 2009.[61] While expectations are high, the stakes for failure are so as well. The complexity of the negotiations is historically unparalleled. The significant reduction cuts required to stop global warming at 2 degrees centigrade need to be met in a relatively short time period (until 2050). They can only be met if all major emitters are included. This demands differentiation of commitment between developed and developing countries and among developing countries, who are no homogenous group. Finding effective and equitable differentiation criteria, however, proves to be a major challenge.[62] Moreover, future commitments by developing countries will depend on compliance of Annex I States with their Kyoto Protocol targets[63] and on their readiness to pay for significant emission cuts in developing countries.[64] As said above, little indicates that Annex I countries have made demonstrable progress in this direction. Demands for financial and technology transfers to the developing world (i.e. to countries, like China, which are already seen as economic competitors), financing of adaptation to climate impacts which will happen despite any mitigation action and concerns about international competitiveness of affected industries are only adding to the complexity of the negotiations. International climate negotiations show that States still negotiate in their economic self-interest without recognizing the fact that avoiding dangerous climate change mitigation is in every state's self interest.

These short-comings of the present climate regime (and the fact that steep emission cuts are necessary in a very short time frame) indicate the need for external measures, such as those that can be imposed by the Security Council, for 'putting

60 See Ulfstein, G., and Werksman, J., 'The Kyoto Compliance System: Towards Hard Enforcement' in: Schram Stokke et al., 2005, at 54–55.

61 Decision 1/CP.13 (FCCC/CP/2007/6/Add. 1) Bali Action Plan. Also: The Road to Copenhagen Initiative, information available at: http://unfccc.int/files/press/backgrounders/application/pdf/the_road_to_copenhagen.pdf.

62 Rajamani, L., 'Differentiation in the Post-2012 Climate Regime' 4(4) *Policy Quarterly* 48 (November 2008).

63 Article 3 UNFCCC ('developed country Parties should take the lead in combating climate change and the adverse effects thereof') and Article 4.7 UNFCCC ('The extent to which developing country Parties will effectively implement their commitments ... will depend on the effective implementation by developed country Parties of their commitments ...').

64 Chinese Premier Wen Jiabao said rich nations must abandon their "unsustainable lifestyle" to fight climate change and expand help to poor nations bearing the brunt of worsening droughts and rising sea levels. Specifically, he suggested that wealthy nations should divert as much as 1 % of their GDP to help developing nations tackle climate change. See: Reuters 'China tells rich nations to pay up on climate change', *New Scientist*, 7 November 2008. For a discussion of India and Chinas climate policy expectations of developed nations see: Rajamani, L., 'China and India on Climate Change and Development', in: Bernstein, Brunnée, Duff and Green (eds.) *A Globally Integrated Climate Policy for Canada* (University of Toronto Press, 2008) at 104.

the world on the right track'. This is not to say that we can do away with multilateral climate treaties. A strong and efficient climate regime is urgently needed to tackle the roots of the problem.[65] Yet, in order to 'push and pull' States to the negotiation table – and an effective climate agreement – the Security Council could be assigned a more active role.

V. UN Security Council Competences with Respect to Preventing Dangerous Climate Change

As we have explored in the previous paragraphs, the UN Charter provides the Security Council with clear legal authority to respond to climate change related threats to international peace and security. Chapter VII of the UN Charter opens for measures to prevent dangerous climate change. According to Article 39 UN Charter, action taken by the Council in response to a 'threat to the peace, breach of the peace or act of aggression' must aim 'to maintain or restore international peace and security'. The term 'maintain' serves to emphasize the fact that the Council can take preventive actions and does not need to wait for the peace to be disturbed before taking action. More challenging than the question of the legal authority of the Council to respond to climate change is the question of what would be effective actions for the Security Council to take.[66]

In the following we will assess some of the possible actions of the Security Council to address the causes of climate change. From this assessment the possibility of use of force is omitted.[67] The reason for this omission is based on the understanding that use of military force to counter climate change related threats would be in stark contrast to the general spirit of cooperation and peaceful settlement of disputes that informs public international law in general and international environmental law in particular.[68]

A. *Coercive Measures*

If according to Article 39 UN Charter the determination of a 'threat to peace' has been made, several options are available to the UN Security Council. We will briefly examine (i) the Council's competences to impose targeted sanctions and suspension

65 See Sindico, F., 'Ex-Post and Ex-Ante [Legal] Approaches to Climate Change Threats to the International Community', *New Zealand Journal for Environmental Law* Vol. 9 (2005) at 209–238.

66 Resolution 1625 (2005) expressed the determination of the Council to enhance the effectiveness of the United Nations in preventing conflict. UN Security Council Resolution 1625 (2005), adopted on 14 September 2005. S/RES/1625 (2005).

67 See for a discussion of this possibility with regard to environmental security the chapter by Fauchald and Stigen in this book.

68 International environmental law is based on the idea that environmental threats are best met by cooperative multilateral responses. Principle 7 of the 1992 Rio Declaration states that 'States shall cooperate in a spirit of global partnership to conserve, protect and restore the health and integrity of the Earth's ecosystems' and Principle 26 demands accordingly that 'States shall resolve all their environmental disputes peacefully.'

of diplomatic ties (Article 41), (ii) the legislative competences in response to an identified threat, and (iii) the possibility to condemn certain action or inaction by states.

i. Sanctions and Suspension of Diplomatic Relations

Article 41 opens for binding economic or political coercive measures, such as the complete or partial interruption of economic relations, of various means of communication and the severance of diplomatic relations. Such sanctions could be imposed in very short time and are thus of importance to halt environmental threats, such as dangerous climate change, where time is running out. Article 41 measures could be used to compel states to take certain actions. So could, for example, states with high GHG emission records be targeted with the aim of forcing them to constructively negotiate an international climate accord or to implement effective domestic emission reduction measures in compliance with an existing treaty or customary obligation. Economic sanctions, such as freezing of funds, blocking of financial operations, or imposition of embargoes of imports and exports, would put political as well as economic pressure on these states, when exposing their destructive behaviour to the international community. The political embarrassment that comes with being the addressee of a Security Council sanction combined with the message that the international community will not tolerate the state's contribution to a threat to peace might exert a strong force on the targeted state/states. More specifically, *Knight* suggests that the Security Council under Article 41 could impose targeted sanctions against all states exporting products that are created or extracted using a particular environmentally harmful practice.[69] Such suggestion might become particularly relevant in preventing dangerous climate change by attempting to address specifically climate-damaging activities, such as clear cutting of forested areas with a high carbon intake or highly emitting industrial activities. *Knight* notes that 'Countries who continually impose negative externalities on a regional or global scale might be induced to reform their practices, come to the negotiation table, or abide by existing treaties if the spectre of the Security Council's enforcement power were looming overhead.'[70]

Moreover, targeted sanctions could be imposed on individuals and private entities which are considered by the Council a threat to global security and peace.[71] The Security Council's sanctions after September 11 is not directed solely toward member states, but also against individuals and private entities. The concept of targeted sanctions as an alternative to embargoes and other kinds of state sanctions is fairly new. Targeted sanctions are intended to impact directly on leaders, political elites, and segments of society believed responsible for objectionable behaviour, while reducing

69 See also Knight, supra note 28, 1561 1563.

70 Ibid, at 1562.

71 See, for example, S/RES/1390 (2002) imposing travel bans on individuals associated with Al-Qaida and the Taliban, S/RES/1737 (2006) imposing targeted financial sanctions on individuals associated with Iran's nuclear program, and S/RES/1718 (2006) imposing targeted financial sanctions and travel bans on individuals associated with Korea's nuclear program.

collateral damage to the general population and third countries.[72] This development marks a stark difference from the Security Council's previous practice.[73] Yet, in a climate context, sanctions targeted on private entities might be an effective means to stop particularly damaging activities, where the state can't or won't act. Most emissions of greenhouse gases are the result of industrial activities by private companies. The Council could, for example, target national or multinational companies that emit high amounts of GHG during production processes or are responsible for the massive destruction of forested areas via, for example, the imposition of import or export bans.[74]

ii. 'Legislative' Competences

Another way of attempting to prevent the threat of climate change related threats from realizing are Security Council measures that require all states to take or omit certain actions. Fairly recently, the Council has commenced to address security threats not confined to a particular country, time and geographical location. Resolution 1373 (2001)[75] on terrorism and Resolution 1540 (2004)[76] on weapons of mass destruction identified threats to peace and required *all* states to take or not to take certain actions.

In Resolution 1371 (2001) the Security Council laid down a set of stringent obligations for all states concerning steps that they must take within their domestic legal system to prevent and repress terrorism. The Council *de facto* legislated on national action against terrorism.[77] Resolution 1540 (2004) contained explicit non-proliferation obligations to all states, regardless of their membership to existing multilateral treaties addressing the issue of prohibition of weapons of mass destruction.[78]

---

72 See Fitzgerald, 'Managing Smart Sanctions Against Terrorism Wisely', 36 *New England Law Review* (2002) at 957.

73 For a critical discussion of sanctions targeted at private entities, see Zemanek, K., 'Is the Security Council the Sole Judge of its Own Legality? A Re-Examination' in: Reinisch A., and Kriebaum U., (eds.) *The Law of International Relations – Liber Amicorum Hanspeter Neuhold* (Eleven International Publishing, 2007) at 484–489; and Fassbender, B., *Targeted Sanctions and Due Process*, Study commissioned by the United Nations Office of Legal Affairs, Humboldt-Universität zu Berlin 2006.

74 Examples of such commodity bans are diamond and timber bans, S/RES/1521 (2003). Other targeted sanctions on corporate entities could include financial, travel, aviation, arms and commodities restrictions with the objective of applying coercive pressure on transgressing companies and entities that support them.

75 S/RES/1373 (2001), adopted on 28 September 2001.

76 S/RES/1450 (2004), adopted on 28 April 2004.

77 Cassese, 2005, at 468.

78 The Security Council required *inter alia* of member states to refrain from providing any form of support to non-State actors that attempt to develop, acquire, manufacture, possess, transport, transfer or use nuclear, chemical or biological weapons and their means of delivery; to adopt and enforce appropriate effective laws in this respect. It futher required States to take and enforce effective measures to establish domestic controls to prevent the proliferation of weapons of mass destruction, for example, border controls and national export and trans-shipment controls. This includes appropriate laws and

In addition, under both resolutions committees were established to monitor the implementation of the resolutions and the fulfilment of those obligations. Both committees were to receive reports from states on their implementation of the resolutions. The mandate of both Committees was subsequently extended by later resolutions.

This new legislative approach adopted by the Security Council has been met with criticism. Concerns were raised that the Council may be acting *ultra vires*.[79] Others argue that in passing legislative resolutions the Council was upsetting the balance of power between the Security Council and the General Assembly and weakening the fundamental principles of sovereign equality and consent in international law.[80]

Yet, council legislation of this kind could play a potential role in addressing climate change related threats. The Council could require of all UN Members the implementation of immediate, effective mandatory climate change mitigation measures. In order to monitor the implementation of and the compliance with those obligations, the Security Council could cooperate with existing UN bodies under the present international climate regime. The UNFCCC Secretariat and the Compliance Committee under the Kyoto Protocol could, for example, continue to play important roles with respect to monitoring and reporting requirements of Members States and facilitating implementation of climate change mitigation obligations.[81] Moreover, in order to gain the necessary technical knowledge and capacity, it would be advisable that the Security Council sets up a special committee on climate change matters, which could require periodic state reporting on legislative implementation and actual emission reductions. Such 'Climate Security Committee' could work in conjunction with other bodies to set the standards and establish and to monitor compliance with those standards.[82]

In spite of almost two decades of international diplomacy on climate change no international agreement adequate to the significant mitigation task has been produced. Urgent and strong mitigation action is of the essence in relation to climate change. In this context it was suggested that '[W]hat is needed is an investment internationally of political imagination … [T]he window of opportunity is rapidly

regulations to control export, transit, trans-shipment and re-export and controls on providing funds and services related to such export and trans-shipment such as financing, and transporting that would contribute to proliferation. It also called for establishing end-user controls and establishing and enforcing appropriate criminal or civil penalties for violations of such export control laws and regulations.

79 So Joyner, D., 'Non-proliferation Law and the United Nations System: Resolution 1540 and the Limits of the Power of the Security Council' 20 *Leiden Journal of International Law* (2007) at 489.

80 See for a discussion: Rosand, E., 'The Security Council as "Global Legislator": *Ultra Vires* or Ultra Innovative?' 28 *Fordham International Law Journal* 542 (2004–2005) at 544.

81 See Sindico, 2005, at 226–229.

82 See discussion in Penny, Ch.K., 'Greening the security council: climate change as an emerging "threat to international peace and security"' 7 *International Environmental Agreements* 35 (2007), at 61. Penny suggests an 'Environmental Security Council' as a subsidiary body of the UN Security Council. He notes that such a committee 'could even be vested with the binding legal authority and practical capacity necessary to conduct intrusive examinations on the territory of particular states to monitor their compliance', at 61.

closing.'[83] Because with regard to climate change the dilemma is time connected – the longer the delay, the more extreme the response that will be needed – effective and immediate action could be triggered by a 'legislative' Security Council resolution.

B. *Condemnations*

A further, though less coercive, means to gather international momentum behind climate change mitigation action are condemnations of certain state behaviour or inaction with regard to climate change mitigation without imposing sanctions or requiring specific measures to be taken. While arguably condemnations lack teeth compared to the two previously mentioned alternatives of Security Council action, they are important means to bring climate related threats to the attention of the international community. The Security Council could, for example, condemn 'the massive pollution of the atmosphere' and express the clear link to a threat to peace and security.[84] Such measure may heighten state concern for climate change and exert a deterrent effect with regard to continuing destructive behaviour. Moreover, treating climate change as a security issue in this way may clear the road for more constructive state action for meeting the climate challenge. Although mere condemnation does not have any binding effect, the public exposure as such could as well impress upon the delinquent state or states and may eventually lead to discontinuation of the deviant behaviour. States increasingly endeavour to avoid public strictures, such as being the target of repeated moral chastisements.[85] Condemnations pronounced by the Security Council could magnify the gravity of climate related threats and the need to respond to these threats effectively and urgently in a collective way.

C. *Request to the International Court of Justice*

One final avenue open to the Security Council, which has not been discussed in any detail in legal literature, is the possibility to engage in international adjudication. The Security Council has the competence to seek an advisory opinion from the International Court of Justice on any question of international law.[86] Possible legal questions that the Security Council might ask could relate to the legal consequences for states that are not complying with their obligations under the UNFCCC or the Kyoto Protocol. As mentioned above, the prospect of a number of Annex B States not complying with their quantified emission reduction targets is increasing. While no post-Kyoto agreement is in place yet, the enforcement measures that could be employed by the Compliance Committees' Enforcement Branch remain without coercive force. Yet, an advisory opinion on the consequences of non-compliance,

---

83 John Ashton, 'World's most wanted: climate change' *BBC News Viewpoint*. http://www.newsvote.bbc.co.uk/mpapps/pagetools/print/news.bbc.co.uk.

84 This would be similar to Security Council condemnations of the use of force: see for example S/RES1177 (1998) and S/RES/1227 (1999).

85 See Cassese, 2005, at 343.

86 Article 65 Statute of the International Court of Justice and Article 96.1 UN Charter.

breach of a treaty obligation and the possibility of imposing countermeasures[87] might be a means of deterring states from non-compliance. Other legal questions, which the Security Council might request the International Court of Justice to answer, could concern the legality of a massive pollution of the atmosphere by the emissions of greenhouse gases or the legality of causing significant damage to the stability of the global climate system, including the liability for compensating resulting harm to people and ecosystems. Such requests would be in line with the UNGA and WHO requests for an advisory opinion on the *Legality of the Threat or Use of Nuclear Weapons*.[88] The ICJ could further be requested to answer the contentious question about the status of the no-harm rule in international law in the context of causing dangerous climate change or the status of rights established under the UN climate regime.[89]

Although advisory opinions of the International Court of Justice are not binding in law upon the requesting body, they arguably carry just as much authority as a judgement in interstate proceedings.[90] Making use of advisory opinions would be an adequate means for the Security Council for drawing international attention to the dangers of climate change and the legality or illegality of states actions or inactions in effectively addressing it.

VI. Conclusion

In this chapter we found that climate change impacts have the potential to amount to a threat to peace in the normative sense entailed in Article 39 of the UN Charter. Such determination is, however, subject to the discretion of the Security Council. Yet, no legal obstacles exist that would prevent the Council from linking climate change to a security issue.

We found that various options exist for the Security Council to act once a determination in this respect has been made. These options include the imposition of economic or political sanctions or the severance of diplomatic bonds according to Article 41 UN Charter. Further, in line with recent developments the Council could fill the gaps left by the current climate change regime. As was highlighted in part 4, the current multilateral treaty regime falls short of providing an effective and timely remedy to climate change related threats as it is – per today – unable to compel states to mitigate dangerous global climate change. The Security Council could thus adopt a binding 'legislating' resolution, which demands of all States adequate, effective

87 For a discussion of the relationship between non-compliance and the general law on state responsibility, see: Koskenniemi, M., 'Breach of Treaty or Non-Compliance? Reflections on the Enforcement of the Montreal Protocol' 3 *Yearbook of International Environmental Law* (1992) at 123–163; and Fitzmaurice, M.A. and Redgwell, C., *Environmental Non-Compliance Procedures and International Law* 31 Netherlands Yearbook of International Law (2000) at 35–65.

88 *Advisory Opinion Concerning the Legality of the Threat or Use of Nuclear Weapons*, ICJ Reports (1996) 66 and 226.

89 See Sands, P., *Principles of International Environmental Law*, 2nd edition, CUP, 2005, at 189 and 212 ff.

90 Birnie and Boyle, 2002, at 222.

and immediate climate change mitigation action. A weaker form of coercion would be condemnations by the Security Council of certain actions or inactions of states with regard to mitigating climate change. Finally we found that the Security Council could raise international awareness of the legal implications of climate related state behaviour by requesting the International Court of Justice to give an advisory opinion on that matter.

The Security Council possesses sufficient legal authority to address climate change. Whether or not the Council will make such a determination and consequently act in order to effectively address the challenges posed by climate change depends on the political will of individual Council members. In order for the Security Council to make a decision on non-procedural matters an affirmative vote of nine members including the concurring votes of the permanent members is required.[91] In particular the votes of the P5 are of decisive importance and build the main obstacle. Not only would the US need to dramatically alter its position on climate change; the US would also need to come to some political arrangement with China and Russia on the issue. Complicating in this context is the fact that the US and China not only view each other as economic competitors, they are also engaged in competition for access to the world's remaining oil resources.[92] It can only be hoped that in the nearest future China and the US abandon their divergent views of the nature of the action needed to address climate change and to find a way to collaborate on the expansion of alternative energy technologies.

Reform of the Council's decisions making procedures may be another means for overcoming political obstacles. Discussions around this issue have been contentious for a long time.[93] There certainly is room for improvement of decision making procedures in the Security Council. The urgency and important of the task may help to overcome existing shortcomings and obstacles. Yet, the crucial issue is whether there is enough time for such reform. With regard to preventing dangerous climate change the answer is probably to the negative.

Much therefore depends on creating political consensus. The political obstacles are not insurmountable. When facing the dangerous impacts of climate change, the P5 may be able to overcome their political differences and consent to taking action. Such leadership role adopted by the Security Council might be exactly what is needed for facilitating the far-reaching global changes necessary to mitigate and adapt to what might well be the greatest global threat of the twenty-first century. It is also a unique chance to address the complex and interlinked challenges of poverty, climate change and political instability through the promotion of globally sustainable development.[94] Rather than despair and confrontation, this situation warrants, in the words of UN Secretary General Ban Ki-moon, 'a perspective of cautious but resolute optimism'.[95]

---

91 Article 27.3 UN Charter.

92 See, Leverett, F., and Bader, J. 'Managing China-US Energy Competition in the Middle East', 29 *The Washington Quarterly* (2005–2006) at 187.

93 For an overview, see: Penny, 2007, at 62–68.

94 See, Voigt, C., 'Sustainable Security', 19 *Yearbook of International Environmental Law* 2008 (forthcoming in 2010).

95 Ban Ki-moon, 'The Right War', *Time*, 16 April 2008.

Chapter 13

Environmental Security and the UN Security Council

Jo Stigen & Ole Kristian Fauchald

I. Introduction

For obvious historical reasons, international security was originally understood as connoting the protection of the state and its vital interests from military attacks by other states.[1] Originating as a narrow concept focusing on military security, "international security" has expanded in various directions.[2] The general view that international security has broadened to include threats to individual citizens and to our way of life, as well as to the integrity and interests of the state, resonate with statements in the UN Charter that it reaffirms "faith in fundamental human rights, in the dignity and worth of the human person … [and] promote[s] social progress and better standards of life in larger freedom".[3] An important step was taken by the adoption

---

1 Paragraph 1 of the United Nations Charter preamble notes the determination to "save succeeding generations from the scourge of war". See also e.g. Joseph S. Nye Jr. and Sean M. Lynn-Jones, "International Security Studies: A Report of a Conference on the State of the Field", in *Security Dialogue 12* (1988), 5–27.

2 According to Redclift "[s]ecurity has begun to be understood at different levels of political analysis, rather than exclusively at the level of the nation state". Among new threats to what Redclift refers to as "social stability", he lists "rapid population growth, natural resource scarcity, economic vulnerability and environmental degradation", and he notes that "human security" can be seen as "referring to the degree to which human beings are protected from environmental degradation, resource scarcity and environmental hazards by their own social institutions and processes", see Michael Redclift, "Addressing the Causes of Conflict: Human Security and Environmental Responsibilities", in *Review of European Community and International Environmental Law 9* (2000), 44, at 44, referring to J.B. Opschoor, "The Concept of Environmental Security: A Historical Introduction", Proceedings International Workshop, *Dutch National Research Programme on Global Air Pollution and Climate Change*, RIVM, Bilthoven, 1996. An oft-quoted definition of the term "security" is that of Wolfers, according to whom "security, in an objective sense, measures the absence of threats to acquired values, in a subjective sense, the absence of fear that such values will be attacked", see Arnold Wolfers, *Discord and Collaboration: Essays on International Politics*, Baltimore, Johns Hopkins University Press, London, 1965, at 150.

3 Paragraphs 2 and 4 of the preamble. Paragraph 1 states the purpose "[t]o maintain international peace and security", and several scholars have discussed whether the order of the purposes suggests a hierarchy; i.e. whether international peace and security should

Cecilia M. Bailliet (ed.), Security: A Multidisciplinary Normative Approach.
 ISBN 978 90 04 17296 8. pp. 313–342.

of the Helsinki Final Act of the Conference on Security and Co-operation in Europe in 1975. The Act contains a section on environmental cooperation focusing on the role such cooperation can play in establishing and maintaining peaceful relations among states. It does not, however, focus on the threats to international security that may follow from environmental degradation. The latter issue has received increased attention in more recent years, in particular after the end of the "Cold War"[4] and in the context and aftermath of the Rio Conference on Environment and Development in 1992.[5] Upon a plain reading of the UN Charter it remains unclear to what extent the coercive powers of the UN Security Council (UNSC) in Chapter VII extend to such threats.

A different approach to environmental security can be found when studying the development of international environmental law from the perspective of sovereignty over natural resources. Access to natural resources has throughout the history of mankind been a source of conflict.[6] In recent decades, in particular in the period

---

be prioritized over fundamental human rights; see e.g. Christopher J. Le Mon and Rachel S. Taylor, "Security Council Action in the Name of Human Rights: From Rhodesia to the Congo", in *U.C. Davis Journal of International Law and Policy 10* (2004), 197, at 202–203. Page notes that writers who want to include environmental threats as a security issue "can be divided into two camps depending on the account they offer of the *scope* of security discourse. The first camp seeks to include non-military threats in the discussion of security, but only insofar as these threats undermine the security of states; the second camp seeks to include non-military threats in the discussion insofar as these threats undermine the security of both states and other entities. The key difference between these camps, then, is that members of the former camp retain the traditional rubric of *national security*, whereas members of the latter embrace the more radical rubric of *human security*", see Edward Page, "Theorizing the Link Between Environmental Change and Security", in *Review of European Community and International Environmental Law 9* (2000), 33, at 36.

4 See S/23500 (1992) at 3: "The absence of war and military conflicts amongst States does not in itself ensure international peace and security. The non-military sources of instability in the economic, social, humanitarian and ecological fields have become threats to peace and security. The United Nations membership as a whole, working through the appropriate bodies, needs to give the highest priority to the solution of these matters."

5 See, *inter alia*, Alexandre S. Timoshenko, "Ecological security: Response to Global Challenges", in Edith Brown Weiss (ed.), *Environmental change and international law. New challenges and dimensions*, United Nations University, 1992, at 424–431, Ken Conca & Geoffrey D. Dabelko, *Environmental Peacemaking*, Washington DC, Woodrow Wilson Center Press, 2002, at 1–8 with further references, and Sverre Lodgaard and Anders H. af Ornäs (eds.), *The Environment and International Security*, International Peace Research Institute, Oslo (PRIO) Report No. 3, 1992.

6 See Nils Petter Gleditsch, "Armed Conflict and the Environment: A Critique of the Literature", in *Journal of Peace Research 35* (1998), 381, at 381–384. Ullman has noted that in the early 1980s there was a decrease in the number of territorial conflicts, and instead he suggested that "as demand for some essential commodities increases and supplies appear more precarious" there would be more resource-related conflicts between neighbouring states which would "take the form of overt military confrontations whose violent phases will more likely be short, sharp shocks rather than protracted wars", see Richard H. Ullman, "Redefining Security", in *International Security 8* (1983), 129, at 139–140. Other scholars who have concluded that struggle over access to and control over natural resources has been an important cause of tension or conflict include Lothar

after the Stockholm Conference on the Human Environment (1972), the issue has resurfaced in a broader context. From being an issue related to state sovereignty, imperialism and colonialism, the issue has been extended to overexploitation and destruction of resources of "common concern",[7] such as high sea fish stocks, a stable climate and the ozone layer. From this perspective, discussions on "environmental security"[8] can be related to what kind of measures, including measures decided by the UNSC, are needed in international law to secure sufficient protection of those elements of the environment that are essential to long term international security.

A third approach to environmental security, which is closely linked to the UNSC, is related to environmental concerns in times of armed conflict. While environmental destruction has been part of armed conflict from time immemorial, our current ability to inflict serious and long-term or even irreversible environmental damage means that the need to address the issue has changed fundamentally. Hence, the use of environmental modification techniques and certain kinds of environmentally destructive weapons have increasingly been regulated in international law.[9]

This chapter addresses the role of the UNSC in cases concerning environmental security. We use the term "environment" in a broad sense, including access to natural resources, but not including "fight over territory", i.e. disagreements on where to draw international borders. The main issue to be addressed concerns the criteria for UNSC decisions under Chapter VII of the UN Charter. In which situations can the state of

---

Brock, "Peace through Parks: The Environment on the Peace Research Agenda", in *Journal of Peace research 28* (1991), 407–423; Gro Harlem Brundtland *et al.*, *Our Common Future. World Commission on Environment and Development*, Oxford University Press, Oxford, 1987; Johan Galtung, *Environment, Development and Military Activity. Towards Alternative Security Doctrines*, Oslo, Norwegian University Press, 1992 (noting at 99 that "destruction of the environment may lead to more wars over resources"); J.B. Opschoor, "North-South Trade, Resource Degradation and Economic Security", in *Bulletin of Peace Proposals 20* (1989), 135–142 (noting at 137 that "ecological stress and the consequences thereof may exacerbate tension within and between countries"); and Michael Renner, Mario Pianta and Cinzia Franchi, "International Conflict and Environmental degradation", in Raimo Väyrynen (ed.), *New Directions in Conflict Theory. Conflict Resolution and Conflict Transformation*, London, Sage (in association with the International Social Science Council), 1991, 108–128 (noting at 109 that "throughout human history, but particularly since the system of sovereign nation states, struggles over access to and control over natural resources … have been a root cause of tension and conflict").

7 See, *inter alia*, Timoshenko 1992, *supra* note 5, at 416–418 and Patricia W. Birnie & Alan Boyle, *International Law and the Environment*, 2nd edition, Oxford University Press, Oxford, 2002, at 97–99.

8 Literature frequently uses the concept "ecological security", which, from the perspective of natural science and current environmental challenges, no longer appropriately reflects the underlying issues.

9 See UNGA res. A/RES/62/28 (2008) Observance of environmental norms in the drafting and implementation of agreements on disarmament and arms control, with further references. See also e.g. Jay E. Austin and Carl E. Bruch (eds.), *The Environmental Consequences of War: Legal Economic and Scientific Perspectives*, Cambridge University Press, Cambridge, 2000; Annotated Biography, First International Conference on Addressing Environmental Consequences of War, Washington, DC, Environmental Law Institute, 1998.

or threats to the environment be characterised as a "threat to the peace, breach of the peace or act of aggression" according to Article 39 of the UN Charter?

Article 39 lists three alternative criteria, each of which may trigger the UNSC's powers under Chapter VII: there must be a "threat to the peace", a "breach of the peace" or an "act of aggression". A crucial difference between the two latter and the first criterion is that the latter refer to situations where a breach of the peace or an act of aggression already exists, while the former only requires a threat, i.e. a certain risk that there will be a breach of the peace. The UNSC's competence to address environmental issues will be discussed from both perspectives (sections 3 and 4 respectively).

A meaningful discussion of the competence of the UNSC under Chapter VII must build on the premise that the UNSC is bound by the relevant provisions of the UN Charter as interpreted according to general principles of treaty interpretation. It must thus observe the limits that follow from a reading of the provisions of the Charter in light of their context, their object and purpose, relevant customary law and general principles of law, as well as subsequent practice of the UN and its members.[10] It is a widely held view that the UNSC must observe these constraints.[11]

One element of this legal framework that needs to be addressed initially is the term "peace". Does it refer exclusively to interstate armed conflict, or does it also cover internal situations, such as internal armed conflicts or even the protection of certain human rights, regardless of the international implications?[12] And are all factors that may contribute to the disturbance of peace covered, including in particular environmental factors?

---

10 See Article 31 of the Vienna Convention on the Law of Treaties which here must apply *mutatis mutandis*.

11 For instance, Frank concludes, in an assessment of *Libya v. United States*, Request for Provisional Measures, Order of 14 April 1992 (ICJ Reports 1992, 3), that the "majority and dissenting opinions [of the Court] seem to be in agreement that there are such limits and that they cannot be left exclusively to the Security Council to interpret. The legality of actions by any UN organ must be judged by reference to the Charter as a 'constitution' of *delegated* powers"; Thomas M. Frank, "The 'Powers of Appreciation': Who is the Ultimate Guardian of UN Legality?", in 86 *American Journal of International Law* (1992), 519, at 522–523. Also, former ICJ judge Bedjaoui notes that "all the principal organs of the United Nations must respect not only the Charter but international law itself, if only because the founding States did not invest them with any function as international legislators or creators of new rules"; Mohammed Bedjaoui, *The New World Order and the Security Council: Testing the Legality of its Acts*, Martinus Nijhoff, Dordrecht, 1994, at 32. The Institute for International Law and Justice, New York University School of Law, has adopted the following recommendation: "The Security Council should emphasize the importance of the rule of law in dealing with matters on its agenda. This embraces references to upholding and promoting international law, and ensuring that its own decisions are finally rooted in that body of law, including the Charter of the United Nations, general principles of law, international human rights law, international humanitarian law, and international criminal law", see *Final Report and Recommendations from the Austrian Initiative 2004–2008*, 2008, Recommendation 1.

12 For an analysis of UNSC resolutions addressing human rights concerns, see Le Mon and Taylor 2004, *supra* note 3.

II. The Scope of the Term "Peace"

The term "peace" may be viewed from the perspective of what constitutes threats to the peace and from the perspective of what may contribute to the establishment or maintenance of peace. Our main focus is on the former perspective as our aim is to analyse whether the UNSC has power under Chapter VII of the UN Charter where environmental situations can arguably threaten the peace.[13] However, in many cases it cannot be distinguished between measures taken to prevent threats to the peace and measures taken to establish or maintain peace, as a measure taken to establish or maintain peace would also constitute a measure to prevent future conflict.

It may be useful to distinguish between "peace" referring to the absence of armed conflict, and "peacefulness" referring to a situation in which there are harmonious, calm and quiet relations between relevant states and institutions.[14] It can be noted that the term used in relation to the UNSC in Art. 39 is "peace", and the term used in relation to the ECOSOC in Art. 55 is "peaceful". Even if both organs are expected to contribute to the fulfilment of the objectives listed in Art. 1 of the Charter, including in particular the maintenance of international peace and security, it can be assumed that the UNSC has a narrower focus than the ECOSOC when it comes to which situations it can address. Hence, while the core competence of the UNSC is to address urgent situations involving hostilities between states, the ECOSOC has a broader mandate to prevent armed conflict and secure long-term peaceful development. The functions of the institutions overlap significantly, and it is to be expected that the UNSC take into account and contribute to long-term peacefulness in the relations between states. Moreover, it can be argued that the less there is a need for the UNSC to focus narrowly on urgent and serious breaches of or threats to the peace, the more it is likely that it will focus on long-term peacefulness and thus overlap with the ECOSOC.[15]

Against this background, it must be observed that the term "peace" remains vague. It has for decades proved technically and politically infeasible to define the concepts "breach of the peace" and "aggression".[16] Some observers, including even some states, operate with a broad concept of "peace" according to which a genocide

13 Conca and Dabelko 2002, *supra* note 5, focuses on the latter, see in particular 9–11.

14 Cf. the different definitions of the term "peace" in *The Oxford English Dictionary.*

15 For an analysis of the relationship between the mandates of the ECOSOC and the Security Council, see Claire Breen, "The Necessity of a Role for the ECOSOC in the Maintenance of International Peace and Security", in *Journal of Conflict and Security Law 12* (2007), 261.

16 The 1945 Conference noted that "[t]he progress of the technique of modern warfare renders very difficult the definition of all cases of aggression", see *Documents of the United Nations Conference on International Organization*, 1945, Vol. 12, 505. In response to a Soviet proposal to provide a definition, the ILC Rapporteur noted that aggression is a "natural notion" a "concept *per se*, which is inherent to any human mind and which, as a primary notion, is not susceptible of definition", see YBILC 1951, vol. 2, at 68. As for the term "breach of the peace", Kelsen has suggested that "[a]ny serious violation of international law … could be interpreted as breach of the peace", see Hans Kelsen, "Economics and Political Science", in *The Canadian Journal of Economics and Political Science 12* (1946), 429, at 433.

situation in a state falls within the UNSC's mandate not just when the situation threatens interstate peace, but because certain fundamental human rights *per se* are protected by Art. 39. This view was expressed when a group of Pacific states in an open UNSC debate on climate change remarked that the Council was "charged with protecting human rights and security of States".[17] Along similar lines, it is possible to argue that environmental damage *per se* is covered by Art. 39, i.e. that it does not only fall within the UNSC's mandate because of a potential inter-state armed conflict, but also because certain essential elements of the environment are protected by Art. 39.[18]

On the other hand, it can be argued that the UNSC is positioned to address extreme internal situations only when such situations may cause international armed conflicts. As will be elaborated below, when the UNSC has addressed internal situations, it has been careful to stress the international implications, e.g. by pointing to the risk associated with mass cross-border movements of people. So far, there is no convincing practice or other evidence that the power of the UNSC reaches beyond situations where environmental threats or damages are linked to international armed conflict. Accordingly, if the UNSC is to protect the environment *per se* under Art. 39, regardless of the implications for international armed conflicts, it would be appropriate to seek to amend the Charter.[19]

III. A "Breach of the Peace" or an "Act of Aggression"

The two criteria, "breach of the peace" and "act of aggression", both refer to certain levels of interstate conflicts, although the more precise meanings are continuously debated among international lawyers and politicians.[20] It is conceivable that environmental damage as such may amount to a breach of the peace or an act of aggression. Birnie and Boyle, who have written extensively on international environmental law, note:

> It is possible to … equate environmental threats with aggression contrary to Article 2(4) of the Charter, thus giving the Security Council power to take mandatory action under Chapter VII, but the language of the Charter, not to speak of the clear record of the original meaning, does not easily lend itself to such an interpretation.[21]

---

17 Record of the UNSC's meeting 17 April 2007, S/PV.5663, at 29.

18 Most scholars conclude, however, that environmental damage *per se* is not covered. Knight notes, for instance, that "some link to human security would have to be shown", see Alexandra Knight, "Global Environmental Threats: Can the Security Council Protect our Earth?", in *New York University Law Review 80* (2005), 1549, at 1570.

19 See Articles 8 and 9 of the UN Charter.

20 See, *inter alia*, Art. 5(2) of the Rome Statute of the International Criminal Court which recognises that the prohibition against aggression as of today cannot be an operative crime as no authoritative definition of the crime exists. The provision also recognises the UNSC's role in making such a definition. For a brief history of the attempts of the international community to agree on a definition of the crime of aggression, see Elisabeth Wilmhurst, "Definition of Aggression", in *United Nations Audiovisual Library of International Law* (2008), available at http://untreaty.un.org/cod/avl/pdf/ha/da/da_e.pdf.

21 Birnie & Boyle 2002, *supra* note 7, at 48.

The Rome Statute of the International Criminal Court criminalises as a war crime the:

> Intentionally launching [of] an attack in the knowledge that such attack will cause incidental loss of life or injury to civilians or damage to civilian objects or widespread, long-term and severe damage to the natural environment which would be clearly excessive in relation to the concrete and direct overall military advantage anticipated.[22]

In addition, paragraph 3 of the preamble to the Rome Statute recognises that "such grave crimes threaten the peace, security and well-being of the world". The recognition of intentional and qualified environmental damages as war crimes clearly indicates that such acts can, under the circumstances, also be seen as acts of aggression and breaches of the peace.

A breach of the peace or an act of aggression could for example occur where state A deliberately conducts activity on its territory which causes serious environmental damage on the territory of state B, or where state A pollutes part of state B's territory with toxic gas in order to subsequently occupy the same area. The most extreme example would include the use of nuclear weapons with their highly destructive effect on the environment. Here, environmental destruction would be the consequence of the use of weapons as part of an act of aggression. One illustrative case was brought before the ICJ on 31 March 2008 by Ecuador against Colombia.[23] The case concerns aerial spraying of herbicide by Colombia as part of its efforts to combat the production of narcotics. Ecuador maintains that the spraying has violated its territorial sovereignty, partly because some of the spraying has taken place directly onto its territory, and partly because some of the spraying in Colombia has had significant effect across the border to Ecuador. While there is nothing in the case indicating that Colombia has acted with aggressive intent, Ecuador argues that it has been impossible to convince Colombia to stop activities causing harm to Ecuador through negotiations. One question that can be raised in relation to such a case is whether the UNSC could intervene, arguing that the acts of Colombia must be regarded as acts of aggression or breaches of the peace. One main question would be whether the purpose of combating production of narcotics would rule out the possibility of regarding the acts as acts of aggression or breaches of the peace.

Where a breach of the peace or an act of aggression has already occurred, the UNSC's powers are already triggered. Then, the Council may address a broad range of issues, including environmental damage, when it finds relevant implications for the restoration of international peace and security. It may, for instance, address environmental damage caused by one belligerent on the territory of another.[24] In

22 Article 8(2)(b)(iv) of the Rome Statute. See Lawrence and Heller, "The First Ecocentric Environmental War Crime: The Limits of Article 8(2)(b)(IV) of the Rome Statute", in *Georgetown International Environmental Law Review 20* (2007), 61–96.

23 See Application of the Republic of Ecuador, available at http://www.icj-cij.org/docket/files/138/14474.pdf.

24 For a discussion of the obligations under international law of belligerents to protect the environment during conflict, see Michael N. Schmitt, "Green War: An Assessment

that sense, the environment is protected by Art. 39, but it is not the environmental damage as such that triggers the powers; the powers are triggered by the breach of the peace or the act of aggression. In 1991, the UNSC confirmed that it can address such damage when it reaffirmed "that Iraq ... is liable under international law for any direct loss, damage, including environmental damage and the depletion of natural resources ... as a result of Iraq's unlawful invasion and occupation of Kuwait".[25]

IV. A "Threat to the Peace"

A. *Introduction*

It is unclear whether and when an environmental situation can be considered a "threat to the peace" under Article 39. Applying this label to a situation involves complex analyses relating to causality, probability and timing, resulting in more or less uncertain predictions about the future. Studies indicate that there are few situations in which environmental change is likely to be regarded as a main direct cause of a breach of the peace, but that it "is best understood as a potential catalyst for conflict".[26] A report from eleven retired US generals on national security and climate change concluded, *inter alia*, that:

> Environmental degradation can fuel migrations in less developed countries, and these migrations can lead to international political conflict.[27] ... Numerous African

of Environmental Law of International Armed conflict", in *Yale Journal of International Law 22* (1997), 1. See also Huang, "The 2006 Israeli-Lebanese Conflict: A Case Study for Protection of the Environment in Times of Armed Conflict", in *Florida Journal of International Law 20* (2008), 103; Roman Reyhani, "The Protection of the Environment during Armed Conflict", in *Missouri Environmental Law and Policy Review 14* (2007), 323; Andy Rich, "The Environment: Adequacy of Protection in Times of War", in *Penn State Environmental Law Review 12* (2004), 445.

25 UNSC res. 687 (1991) para. 16. See also the competence of the UNSC under Art. 13(b) of the Rome Statute to refer environmental damage to the International Criminal Court for individual prosecution.

26 Conca and Dabelko 2002, *supra* note 5, at 5. At 1 they observe that: "Most scholars remain sceptical of the idea that environmental change has been, or is soon to be, an important cause of war between nations. But several have argued that there is a dangerous and growing connection between environmental change and violent outcomes on a local or regional scale; these outcomes include episodes that can spill across borders".

27 Homer-Dixon notes that "[t]here is substantial evidence to support the hypothesis that environmental scarcity causes large population movement, which in turn causes group-identity conflicts", pointing *inter alia* to the huge number of people who, in recent decades, have moved from Bangladesh to India, "producing group-identity conflicts in the adjacent Indian states". But he also notes that "we must be sensitive to contextual factors unique to each socio-ecological system" and that "[t]hese are the system's particular physical, political, economic, and cultural features that affect the strength of the linkages between scarcity, population movement, and conflict", see Thomas F. Homer-Dixon, "Environmental Scarcities and Violent Conflict", in *International Security 19* (1994), 5, at 20–21. In a later article, Percival and Homer-Dixon note that "[h]igh levels of grievance does not necessarily lead to widespread civil violence. At least two other factors must be present: groups with strong collective identities that can coherently challenge state authority, and

> countries and regions already suffer from varying degrees of famine and civil strife. Darfur, Ethiopia, Eritrea, Somalia, Angola, Nigeria, Cameroon, Western Sahara – all have been hit hard by tensions that can be traced in part to environmental causes. … [A]s more people migrate from the Middle East because of water shortages[28] and loss of their already marginal agricultural lands, … the social and economic stress on European nations will rise. … [T]he critical factors for economic and security stability in the twenty-first century are energy, water, and the environment. … When [these three factors] are not in balance, people live in poverty, suffer high death rates, or move toward armed conflict.[29]

Of interest in this context is in particular the efforts undertaken by the Environment and Security Initiative in order to identify, examine, and provide a basis for dealing with environmental threats to international security in Eastern Europe and Asia.[30]

To list exhaustively all possible types of threats to the peace is for all practical purposes impossible. Our understanding of the complex nature of conflicts and the diversity of their causes is constantly changing and, one hopes, improving.[31] As technology develops, conflicts take on new forms. As scientists present new theories on complex interrelations, our understanding of what might threaten the peace improves. Threats previously not existing or thought of are recognised along a factual and conceptual learning curve. Consequently, the "threat to the peace" criterion for UNSC decisions must be dynamic and be interpreted and applied in light of current insights and practices.[32] The content of the criterion must be determined in relation to the specific issues at stake in the relevant situation, i.e. on a case-by-case basis.

---

clearly advantageous opportunities for violent collective action against authority", Val Percival and Thomas Homer-Dixon, "Environmental Scarcity and Violent Conflict: The Case of South-Africa", in *Journal of Peace Research* 35 (1998), 279, at 280. Hauge and Ellingsen note that "most research on environmental degradation and domestic armed conflict fails to take into consideration other conflict-generating factors", see Wenche Hauge and Tanja Ellingsen, "Beyond Environmental Scarcity: Causal Pathways to Conflict", in *Journal of Peace Research* 35 (1998), 299, at 300 (footnote added by the authors).

28 Homer-Dixon notes that "it seems reasonable to conclude that water scarcity and its consequent economic effects contributed to the grievances behind the *intifada* both on the West Bank and in Gaza", see Homer-Dixon 1994, *supra* note 28, at 14. It may, in this context, be noted that some scholars make a distinction between conflicts resulting from environmental degradation and conflicts resulting from simple environmental resource scarcity; see e.g. Stephan Libiszewski, "What is an Environmental Conflict?", ENCOP Occasional Paper No. 1, Zurich/Bern: Center for Security and Conflict Research/Swiss Peace Foundation, 1995 (footnote added by the authors).

29 Gordon Sullivan et al., *National Security and the Threat of Climate Change*, Center for Naval Analyses, 2007, at 18, 20, 29 and 35, available at http://securityandclimate.cna.org/report/.

30 See http://www.envsec.org/index.php.

31 See e.g. Stephen Van Evera, *Causes of War: Power and the Root of Conflict*, Cornell Studies in Security Affairs, 2001.

32 Former United Nations Secretary-General Javier Perez de Cuellar has noted that the Charter's "Principles are by no means frozen; their scope and the manner of their application is determined by changing global conditions … A rigid interpretation that fails to take human realities into account would ossify international law … and diminish its

The discussion below seeks to clarify whether and when an environmental issue may constitute a "threat to the peace" by discussing which factors might threaten "peace" properly understood. The conclusions will be based not only on a narrow interpretation in light of the ordinary meaning of the terms used, their context and the underlying object and purpose, but also on the practices of the UNSC, the UN General Assembly and states.

B. *"Threat to the peace"*

In order to constitute a "threat to the peace", a situation must, unless it is addressed, with a certain degree of probability develop into a breach of the peace or an act of aggression. We may distinguish between two types of situations; an environmental situation may itself develop into an act of aggression or a threat to the peace, or an environmental situation may trigger a reaction from one of the states concerned that can be classified as a breach to the peace or an act of aggression.

In order for an environmental situation itself to develop into an act of aggression or a threat to the peace, it seems appropriate to assume that the situation must be caused by a state or a group of states, and that it must concern or be directed against a state or a limited range of states.[33] Hence, if the environmental situation is the result of natural development, for example the threat of a volcanic eruption, or if no particular state(s) can be identified as responsible for the environmental situation, either directly or indirectly, such as in the case of emission of greenhouse gases, it cannot be assumed that the situation as such may develop into a breach of the peace or an act of aggression. Moreover, where the environmental situation represents a threat to all countries or to a broad and undetermined group of countries, such as in the case of depletion of the ozone layer, the situation itself can hardly develop into a breach of the peace or an act of aggression.

Against this background, the following factors seem particularly important when considering whether an environmental damage or a threat to the environment in itself constitutes a threat to the peace: the urgency of the environmental damage or threat; the nature of the act creating the environmental damage or threat, in particular the extent to which it can be regarded as an aggressive act; and the nature of the link between the act causing the environmental damage or threat and the states in question.

---

contemporary relevance ... We cannot ... regard the Charter as immutable", see *Report of the Secretary-General on the Work of the Organization*, U.N. GAOR, 46th Session UN Dok. A/46/404, reprinted in 1991 Yearbook of the United Nations, 3, at 13–14.

33 In its 1974 "Definition of Aggression" the UN General Assembly adopted the following: "Aggression is the use of armed force by a State against the Sovereignty, territorial integrity or political independence of another State, or in any other manner inconsistent with the Charter of the United Nations, as set out in this Definition." The following explanatory note is added: "In this Definition the term 'State': (a) Is used without prejudice to questions of recognition or to whether a State is a member of the United Nations; (b) Includes the concept of a 'group of States' where appropriate", A/RES/29/3314, 14 December 1974, Art. 1 (the 'Definition' includes seven other articles regarding the interpretation and application of Art. 1).

In cases where a "threat to the peace" is to be established on the basis of the probability that the environmental situation will trigger a reaction from a state that can be qualified as a breach of the peace or an act of aggression, we must assume that it will be possible to identify one state or a group of states as responsible for the environmental situation. On the other hand, it does not seem appropriate to limit the range of relevant situations to those where only one state or an identifiable group of states is suffering from the environmental situation. Hence, it can be argued that a state might undertake an act of aggression or breach the peace if the environmental situation is sufficiently serious and if the state can identify one or a limited number of states as responsible for the situation, even if a broad and undetermined range of states suffer or are likely to suffer from the same situation.[34]

Against this background, the following factors seem particularly important when considering whether one state's act endangering the environment is likely to trigger another state's breach of the peace or an act of aggression: to what extent are the states in question clearly identifiable, to what extent would it be possible to address the situation through diplomatic means, how urgent is the situation, to what extent can the act in question be regarded as aggressive, and how likely is it that the act of aggression or the breach of the peace may contribute to avoid or alleviate the environmental situation.

In order to conclude whether environmental situations might trigger the UNSC's chapter VII powers, we must first ask whether it is within the exclusive discretion of the UNSC to determine whether a given situation amounts to a threat to the peace. There are three possible answers to this question: 1) the UNSC has exclusive discretion, 2) the UNSC has exclusive discretion provided that it has considered factors of relevance to the determination, or 3) the UNSC does not have exclusive discretion. As indicated above, the UNSC is bound by the provisions of the UN Charter, and this must also apply to the provisions defining the scope of the powers of the UNSC. This means that answer 1) above can be excluded. The choice between answers 2) and 3) depends on an interpretation of Art. 39. The wording of the provision may indicate a preference for answer 2) due to the use of the phrase "[t]he Security Council shall determine ..." This can be read to indicate that the determination of the existence of a threat to the peace in individual cases is left to the UNSC alone. Such interpretation is supported by the view that the concept "threat to the peace" must be regarded as a dynamic concept, and that the existence of a threat to the peace thus must be determined on a case-by-case basis. Nevertheless, it remains uncertain whether answer 3) can be ruled out.

Against this background, we will distinguish between two main issues. The first is the extent to which the UNSC has freedom to determine which factors to take into account when determining whether there is a threat to the peace. The second is the extent to which the UNSC has freedom to determine whether the threat in question

34 Page notes the following characteristic of the environmental threat posed by anthropogenic GHG emissions: "No one state is responsible for the majority of the anthropogenic GHG emissions which, it is alleged, drive global climate change, and no single state is the sole recipient of the predominantly bad effects of climate change", see Page 2000, *supra* note 3, at 37.

is sufficiently serious to qualify as a threat to the peace. This latter question is only of interest if the UNSC does not have exclusive discretion. In the following, we will consider how these issues have been addressed in the practice of the UNSC (section 4.3), in the practice of the UN General Assembly (section 4.4), in case law of the ICJ (section 4.5) and in the practice of other UN organs of interest (section 4.6), before we turn to the practice of states and international organisations (section 5).

C. *Practice of the UN Security Council*

While the practice of the UNSC hardly will provide any definitive or clear answer, it may indicate how the UNSC views its powers.[35] It may *inter alia* indicate which factors it considers must be taken into account when determining whether an environmental situation constitutes a "threat to the peace". A recent declaration of the UNSC, adopted through res. 1625 (2005) on Strengthening the Effectiveness of the UNSC's Role in Conflict Prevention, Particularly in Africa, arguably sets the stage for the future practice of the UNSC. The following passages of the declaration are of particular interest:

> *Reaffirming* the need to adopt a broad strategy of conflict prevention, which addresses the root causes of armed conflict and political and social crises in a comprehensive manner, including by promoting sustainable development, poverty eradication, national reconciliation, good governance, democracy, gender equality, the rule of law and respect for and protection of human rights, ...
>
> 2. *Affirms* its determination to strengthen United Nations conflict prevention capacities by: ... (g) helping to enhance durable institutions conducive to peace, stability and sustainable development;
>
> 6. *Reaffirms* its determination to take action against illegal exploitation and trafficking of natural resources and high-value commodities in areas where it contributes to the outbreak, escalation or continuation of armed conflict;
>
> 9. *Encourages* also African countries to continue to work closely with the United Nations Secretariat and United Nations regional offices in the implementation of measures aimed at securing peace, security, stability, democracy and sustainable development consistent with the objectives of the New Partnership for Africa's Development;

The references to the "root causes of armed conflict and political and social crises", to promotion of "sustainable development", and to the need to control "illegal exploitation and trafficking of natural resources" signals the UNSC's willingness to take into account other causes of war than the most direct and obvious. It indicates an open approach to what might constitute a "threat to the peace", arguably including a will

35 Le Mon and Taylor note that "because several key Charter terms are not therein defined, the Council has been able to develop the meaning of these words through its practice. These ambiguities in the Charter have allowed the United Nations to remain viable, leaving its boundaries open to reinterpretation as new issues have arisen and new trends have emerged", see Le Mon and Taylor 2004, *supra* note 3, at 198–199.

to accept a low level of probability with respect to time and causality. The resolution recognises the potential relevance of a broad spectre of factors, arguably including environmental threats, despite the lack of an explicit reference to such threats.[36] However, the importance of the declaration for the determination of the powers of the UNSC under Chapter VII can be questioned, as it concerns the role of the UNSC in relation to conflict prevention, as opposed to more urgent situations, and as it emphasises the relationship between the UNSC and other organs of the UN.

In 1992 the President of the Security Council made a statement on behalf of the Council noting that:

> The absence of war and military conflicts among States does not in itself ensure international peace and security. The non-military sources of instability in the economic, social, humanitarian and ecological fields have become threats to peace and security. The United Nations membership as a whole, working through the appropriate bodies, needs to give the highest priority to the solution of these matters.[37]

This statement implicitly recognises that factors such as environmental degradation may threaten the peace. It also indicates, however, that the UNSC might not be the most appropriate institution to address such threats.

A survey of UNSC resolutions shows that the UNSC has approached environmental issues from two main perspectives.[38] The first perspective, which has been present in a number of resolutions adopted since 1997, is based on the link between sustainable development and international peace and security. Resolutions that focus on sustainable development are related to preventing threats to the peace, and to post conflict peace building. Those resolutions that relate sustainable development to the prevention of armed conflict are all of a general nature, i.e. they do not address specific situations.[39] These resolutions stress the need to address the root causes of armed conflict in a comprehensive manner, and point to the promotion of sustainable development as an essential factor. The references to sustainable development in these resolutions are not specified, and it must be assumed that the UNSC uses the concept in its generally recognised manner, as covering environmental, social and economic aspects of sustainable development.[40]

---

36 With regard to the Council's tendency to view human rights concerns as threats to the peace, Le Mon and Taylor note that this "has been made possible by two important factors: namely, the ambiguity of the charter itself, and the Council's willingness to incorporate changing notions of state sovereignty and human rights into its mandate ...", see Le Mon and Taylor 2004, *supra* note 3, at 198.

37 S/23500 (1992), *note by the President of the Security Council.*

38 The below findings are based on a survey of UNSC resolutions from 1992 until the autumn of 2008.

39 See UNSC res. 1265 (1999), 1674 (2006) and 1738 (2006) on the protection of civilians in armed conflict; 1327 (2000) on the implementation of the report of the Panel on United Nations Peace Operations; 1170 (1998), 1209 (1998) and 1318 (2000) on the situation in Africa; 1625 (2005) on threats to international peace and security (UNSC Summit in 2005); and 1366 (2001) on the role of the Security Council in the prevention of armed conflict.

40 See Brundtland *et al.* 1987, *supra* note 6.

Those resolutions that relate sustainable development to post conflict situations mostly address specific situations.[41] In addition, the mandate of the newly established Peacebuilding Commission states:

> *Recognizing* the need for a dedicated institutional mechanism to address the special needs of countries emerging from conflict towards recovery, reintegration and reconstruction and to assist them in laying the foundation for sustainable development …
>
> 2. *Also decides* that the following shall be the main purposes of the Commission: … (b) To focus attention on the reconstruction and institution-building efforts necessary for recovery from conflict and to support the development of integrated strategies in order to lay the foundation for sustainable development; …
>
> 22. *Recommends* that the Commission terminate its consideration of a country-specific situation when foundations for sustainable peace and development are established or upon the request by national authorities of the country under consideration[.][42]

A main purpose of these resolutions is to establish the mandate of and objectives for institutions that are assisting countries in achieving lasting peace in post conflict situations. The resolutions frequently stress the importance of assistance promoting sustainable development. In light of the generally accepted definition of "sustainable development", and given the increasing recognition of the role of exploitation of natural resources in armed conflict,[43] such resolutions can be regarded as references to environmental aspects of sustainable development. The extent to which sustainable development is identified as the ultimate objective of bodies dealing with post conflict situations, indicates that it should be regarded as relevant also when designing measures to prevent breaches of the peace and acts of aggression.

The second perspective from which the UNSC has approached environmental issues is based on the role that natural resources play for international peace and security. Most of the references to natural resources can be found in resolutions addressing specific conflict situations, starting with a resolution on the situation in Congo in 2000.[44] Reference to natural resources in UNSC resolutions is thus a fairly recent phenomenon. In addition to Congo, exploitation of and trade in natural resources have been main issues in UNSC resolutions concerning situations

41 See UNSC res. 1123 (1997), 1141 (1997), 1212 (1998), 1608 (2005) and 1780 (2007) on the situation in Haiti; 1230 (1999) on the situation in the Central African Republic; 1272 (1999), 1573 (2004), 1599 (2005) and 1745 (2007) on the situation in East Timor; and 1483 (2003), 1511 (2003) and 1770 (2007) on the situation in Iraq.

42 UNSC res. 1645 (2005) and UNGA res. A/RES/60/180 (2005) concerning post conflict peace building (see also paras. 97–105 of UNGA res. A/RES/60/1 (2005)). See also UNSC res. 1318 (2000) on the situation in Africa.

43 See e.g. Michael A. Lundberg, "The Plunder of Natural Resources during War: A War Crime", in *Georgetown Journal of International Law* 39 (2008), 495.

44 The issue has been dealt with in numerous resolutions concerning the situation in Congo, starting with UNSC res. 1291 (2000). See in particular UNSC res. 1457 (2003) and 1698 (2006).

in Liberia,[45] Côte d'Ivoire[46] and Sierra Leone.[47] While there is hardly any reference in UNSC resolutions to issues concerning natural resources as a threat to international peace and security,[48] there has been a significant focus on the role of natural resources during conflicts and in post conflict situations.[49] For example, the UNSC frequently refers to the "Kimberley Process" concerning diamonds.[50]

Most of the focus on natural resources has been on the role that exploitation of and trade in such resources play in funding belligerent groups. In addition, there is a certain focus on recruitment of fighters as a consequence of illegal exploitation of resources. In a series of resolutions on children in armed conflicts, emphasis has been on how illicit exploitation of and trade in natural resources can aggravate the impact of conflict on children.[51] Environmental issues related to such exploitation and trade have been almost totally absent in UNSC resolutions. Moreover, no explicit link has so far been established between such exploitation and trade and the goal of sustainable development. The only trace of environmental issues seems to be in the call for governments to assume control of the exploitation of natural resources and the encouragement that such resources be controlled and operated in a "proper", "transparent", "effective" and "legitimate" way.[52] Hence, so far the UNSC resolutions have only addressed the direct effects of exploitation of natural resources for the fuelling, aggravation and human effects of conflict.[53]

Against this background, it can be observed that there has so far been little focus on environmental issues in the resolutions of the UNSC. This is the case where the UNSC deals with threats to the peace, when they address specific conflicts, and when they decide upon measures in a peace building context. The only resolutions that may possibly be interpreted as indicating an important role for environmental issues are those referring to sustainable development in the context of post conflict situations.

45 See in particular UNSC res. 1343 (2001), 1521 (2003) and 1750 (2007).

46 See UNSC res. 1643 (2005).

47 See UNSC res. 1343 (2001) and 1346 (2001).

48 The only UNSC resolution of interest is 1625 (2005) concerning threats to international peace and security, in which the UNSC: "6. *Reaffirms* its determination to take action against illegal exploitation and trafficking of natural resources and high-value commodities in areas where it contributes to the outbreak, escalation or continuation of armed conflict".

49 There has been a significant focus on natural resources in post conflict situations, including in relation to re-emergence of conflicts, in Congo, Liberia and Sierra Leone.

50 See in particular UNSC res. 1459 (2003). The Kimberly Process has been a significant topic in UNSC resolutions concerning Sierra Leone, Liberia and Côte d'Ivoire.

51 See UNSC res. 1314 (2000), 1379 (2001), 1460 (2003), 1539 (2004) and 1612 (2005). See also UNSC res. 1674 (2006) on the protection of civilians in armed conflict.

52 See, *inter alia*, UNSC res. 1346 (2001), 1457 (2003), 1607 (2005) and 1756 (2007).

53 This is also reflected in literature on the role of natural resources in armed conflict, see, *inter alia*, Macartan Humphreys, "Natural Resources and Armed Conflicts: Issues and Options", in Ballentine and Nitzschke (eds.), *Profiting from Peace. Managing the Resource Dimensions of Civil War*, Lynne Rienner Publishers, London 2005, at 25–44.

Despite the scarcity of references to environmental issues in resolutions, environmental issues have clearly been brought onto the UNSC's agenda. The most significant debate on environmental issues so far occurred in 2007 when the UNSC committed a full day of discussions to the issue of climate change. The debate was held at the initiative of the United Kingdom which had provided the Council with a letter which served as the agenda for the debate.[54] In an annex to the letter the United Kingdom noted that "[r]esearch on the wider implications of climate change is exploring its potential impact on issues closely associated with threats to international peace and security".[55] As examples of security risks which might be exacerbated by climate change, the annex listed border disputes, migration, energy supplies, other resource shortages, societal stress and humanitarian crises.[56] The annex asked in particular: "How can the Security Council play a part in a more integrated approach to conflict prevention as foreseen in Security Council resolution 1625 (2005), including greater emphasis on climate-related factors?"[57]

The debate was open to all UN members, and 55 states made statements. The debate represents the most comprehensive survey of the extent to which states recognise threats linked to climate change as falling within the scope of Art. 39. With some notable exceptions,[58] the states participating in the debate can easily be classified as either favouring or opposing climate change as an issue to be placed on the agenda of the UNSC. While many European states, small island states, Canada, Ghana, Japan and Panama were in the former category, all other states were in the latter category. Those states that favoured a role for the UNSC emphasised the need for the Council to address new threats, in particular threats that can be labelled "conflict-drivers".[59] Moreover, many states emphasised the need for an integrated approach to security issues.[60] Climate change was linked to the occurrence of civil wars,[61] to uncontrollable migratory flows,[62] to increased instability in "conflict-prone" regions,[63] and to

54 Letter dated 5 April 2007 from the Permanent Representative of the United Kingdom and Northern Ireland to the United Nations addressed to the President of the Security Council, S/2007/186.

55 *Ibid.*, Annex para. 7.

56 *Ibid.*, (a)-(f).

57 *Ibid.*, para. 11(c). Relevant passages of the declaration adopted by UNSC res. 1625 (2005) are quoted above.

58 See in particular S/PV.5663 at 10–11 (USA).

59 See the statements in the record of the UNSC's meeting 17 April 2007, S/PV.5663 at 5–6 (Belgium), 19–20 (Germany on behalf of the EU), 21 (Netherland), 25–26 (Switzerland) and 29 (Japan), and S/PV.5663 (Resumption 1) at 14–15 (Denmark), 29 (Liechtenstein) and 33 (Canada).

60 See in particular S/PV.5663 at 7 (Ghana), 11–12 (France) and 29 (Papua New Guinea on behalf of small island states).

61 S/PV.5663 at 15 (Panama).

62 S/PV.5663 at 11–12 (France).

63 S/PV.5663 at 13–14 (UN Secretary General Ban Ki-Moon). See also p. 4 (Slovakia) and 29 (Japan).

terrorism.[64] One state proposed that the UNSC should "formally recognize that climate change is a threat within its mandate" and "then have the Secretary-General identify regions at risk and the potential impact on peace and security, as well as appropriate responses, in line with Article 99 of the Charter".[65]

Many of the states that argued against bringing climate change on the agenda of the UNSC were of the view that climate change was outside the scope of competence of the UNSC.[66] It was also suggested that dealing with climate issues in the UNSC would be against the principles and purposes of the UN Charter.[67] In addition, many countries argued that issues relating to climate change could more appropriately be addressed by other international institutions than the UNSC.[68] Some countries also mentioned the lack of expertise in the UNSC,[69] the need for the UNSC to give priority to its core issues,[70] and concerns related to the narrow membership of the UNSC.[71]

The opinions expressed during the debate were coloured by the broader political issues surrounding climate change and the ramifications that bringing the issue on the agenda of the UNSC could have. The relationship between energy production, energy consumption and environmental threats is a contentious issue. First, some states will be more affected than others by the environmental harm generated by climate change. Second, there is an obvious tension between western states bearing the greatest responsibility for today's situation, and developing states wanting to rely on the principle of common but differentiated responsibility.[72] Some of the latter states are thus reluctant to place the issue on the agenda of the UNSC, as they fear western states will seek to transfer the costs of addressing climate change to developing states through adoption of resolutions to reduce energy consumption and avoid deforestation.[73] Third, there may be concerns that western states want to

---

64 S/PV.5663 at 4 (Slovakia).

65 S/PV.5663 (Resumption 1) at 25 (Micronesia). See also the proposal of Tuvalu to review Charter obligations at 8–9.

66 S/PV.5663 at 12–13 (China), 16–17 (South Africa) and 18 (Peru), and S/PV.5663 (Resumption 1) at 9 (Bangladesh), 10 (Venezuela), 17 (Philippines), 20 (Mexico), 20–21 (Brazil), 21–23 (India), 23 (South Korea), 26 (Argentina) and 27 (Cuba on behalf of the non-aligned countries).

67 S/PV.5663 at 24 (Pakistan stating that "[t]he ever-increasing encroachment by the Security Council on the roles and responsibilities of other principal organs of the United Nations represents a distortion of the principles and purposes of the Charter; it also infringes on their authority and compromises the rights of the general membership of the United Nations.") See also S/PV.5663 (Resumption 1) at 12 (Sudan on behalf of the African group).

68 S/PV.5663 at 10 (Qatar), 14 (Indonesia), 17 (Russia), 23 (Maldives), 24 (Pakistan) and 31 (Namibia), and S/PV.5663 (Resumption 1) at 3 (Ukraine), 5–7 (Australia), 7 (New Zealand), 20–21 (Brazil), 31–32 (Costa Rica) and 35 (Comoros).

69 S/PV.5663 at 12–13 (China) and S/PV.5663 (Resumption 1) at 21–23 (India).

70 S/PV.5663 (Resumption 1) at 4–5 (Egypt) and 32–33 (Israel).

71 S/PV.5663 (Resumption 1) at 12 (Sudan on behalf of the African group).

72 See Principle 7 of the UN Declaration on Environment and Development (Rio, 1992).

73 Redclift notes that "[f]rom the viewpoint of a dispassionate observer, greenhouse gas emmissions are so much lower in the South, on a *per capita* basis, that developing

transfer the issue to the UNSC in an attempt to avoid other international mechanisms over which they have less control. Fourth, it cannot be ruled out that some states might want to use the issue of climate change as a bargaining chip in relation to other issues that are on the agenda of the UNSC.

This political backdrop to the debate is reflective of the political setting that will frequently be present when the UNSC considers measures under Chapter VII, namely a split between countries that want to extend the powers of the UNSC, and countries that are sceptical about such extension. The debate on climate change revealed a strong division between states, with no decisive majority in any direction. Yet, it is significant that a number of states, including some of the permanent members, expressed willingness to include climate change on the Council's agenda, and that a similarly important number of states, also including some permanent members, are clearly opposed to such ideas.[74]

As states experience increasingly serious consequences of climate change, their reluctance to placing the issue on the agenda of the UNSC might lessen. With more acute environmental harm related to climate change, the risks of international armed conflicts may become more obvious, thus outweighing the concerns against bringing the issue on the UNSC's agenda. On the other hand, it can be argued that as long as climate change is caused by emissions from all countries, and as long as most countries can be expected to suffer negative consequences, acts causing climate change are unlikely to constitute direct threats to the peace. It is the environmental situation as such, i.e. an unstable climate, which may increase the likelihood that a situation will develop into an armed conflict.

The practice of the UNSC and the opinions expressed by states in the UNSC indicate that the Council will use its power under Chapter VII cautiously where environmental conditions are such that they may only represent indirect threats to international peace. On the other hand, where there is a threat to the peace, the UNSC seems willing to address environmental issues that may be of relevance to preventing breaches of the peace or acts of aggression. Hence, while environmental conditions as such are unlikely to trigger the UNSC power under Chapter VII, the UNSC is likely to address such conditions once it has determined that there is a threat to the peace for other reasons.

Returning to the issues identified at the end of section 4.2 above, it can be concluded that the practice of the UNSC indicates that it approaches the inclusion of factors that are not directly related to a potential armed conflict with cautiousness when determining whether there is a threat to the peace. Nevertheless, the UNSC demonstrates a certain interest in approaching conflict prevention from a broad perspective in some resolutions addressing general issues, taking into account factors that are more indirectly related to the potential for armed conflicts. This is also a

countries should have more room to increase their emissions, while developed countries reduce theirs", see Redclift 2000, *supra* note 2, at 49.

74 The absence of any reference to the debate or activities of the UNSC in UNGA res. A/RES/62/86 (2007) on protection of global climate for present and future generations of mankind indicates the significance attributed to the disagreement between states within the UN.

significant element in resolutions addressing peace-building. The practice seems to indicate that the UNSC perceives itself to have a wide margin of appreciation when determining whether a threat to the peace is sufficiently serious to trigger its powers.

In the following, we will take a closer look at how the issue of environmental security has been addressed outside the UNSC, with a view to provide a more complete assessment of how the UNSC may approach the issue in the future.

D. *Practice of the UN General Assembly*

An exhaustive examination of the practice of the United Nations General Assembly (UNGA) concerning the relationship between environmental damage and threats to international peace and security goes beyond the scope of this chapter. A review of the practice of the UNGA limited to the past five years reveals that its approach to the relationship between security and environmental issues in general echoes that of the UNSC. Where the UNGA addresses cases which are also addressed by the UNSC, the UNGA emphasises the same perspectives as the UNSC, i.e. the objective of sustainable development and the problem of illegal exploitation of and trade in natural resources.[75] There is no specific focus on the environmental perspective in these contexts.[76]

One feature that distinguishes the UNGA from the UNSC is an explicit reference to the "need for continued collaboration between the Economic and Social Council and the Security Council in generating a coherent approach to the challenges of conflict prevention, conflict resolution and post-conflict reconstruction in Africa".[77] This indicates that one should avoid distinguishing clearly between the competences of the UNSC and ECOSOC in cases concerning security issues. While the UNGA thus focuses on general issues, there have been individual situations in which the UNGA has emphasised the role of environmental issues in relation to security.[78]

The UNGA addresses annually a number of environmental issues that can at least indirectly be linked to security, including climate change, desertification, exploitation

75 See UNGA res. A/RES/62/275 (2008), which, however, refers to "global warming and climate change" in para. 25, A/RES/61/230 (2006), A/RES/60/223 (2005), A/RES/60/180 (2005), A/RES/59/255 (2004), A/RES/59/59 (2004), A/RES/58/239 (2003), and A/RES/58/10 (2003), which, however, explicitly addresses issues of environmental protection and pollution in its preamble.

76 This is particularly noteworthy in relation to the annual resolutions adopted in the context of the Kimberley Process, where environmental issues related to mining for diamonds remain unaddressed. See the annual resolutions adopted since 2000, referred to in UNGA res. A/RES/62/11 (2007). See also Ian Smillie, "What Lessons from the Kimberley Process Certification Scheme?", in Ballentine and Nitzschke (eds.), *Profiting from Peace. Managing the Resource Dimensions of Civil War*, Lynne Rienner Publishers, London 2005, at 47–67.

77 See UNGA res. A/RES/59/255 (2004) Implementation of the recommendations contained in the report of the Secretary-General on the causes of conflict and the promotion of durable peace and sustainable development in Africa, para. 9.

78 See UNGA res. A/RES/60/216 (2005).

of natural resources and natural disasters. However, none of the resolutions adopted in the period examined explicitly address the issue from the perspective of international security.

The UNGA has in a number of resolutions addressed environmental issues related to warfare. In 1992 the UNGA expressed the view that environmental considerations constitute one of the elements to be taken into account in the implementation of the principles of the law applicable in armed conflict. It noted that "destruction of the environment, not justified by military necessity and carried out wantonly, is clearly contrary to existing international law".[79] Subsequently, the UNGA has annually since 1995 adopted resolutions on "Observance of environmental norms in the drafting and implementation of agreements on disarmament and arms control".[80] The content of the resolutions varies from specific recommendations in the early resolutions to more general recommendations and requests for information in the recent resolutions.

Against this background, it seems appropriate to conclude that countries have much of the same attitude to dealing with environmental aspects of security issues in the UNGA as in the UNSC. This is so despite the fact that the UNGA has a broader mandate and role than the UNSC, and that it thus could be expected to be a frontrunner when addressing the links between environment and security.

E. *Case law of the International Court of Justice*

The main case before the ICJ focusing on security issues from an environmental perspective was the advisory opinion concerning the legality of the use of nuclear weapons.[81] In the first of the two cases, brought by the World Health Assembly, the request was formulated as follows: "In view of the health and environmental effects, would the use of nuclear weapons by a State in war or other armed conflict be a breach of its obligations under international law including the WHO Constitution?"[82] The Court rejected the request on the basis that it was not related to a question which arose "within the scope of [the] activities" of the World Health Organization, according to Art. 96 (2) of the UN Charter.[83]

The request was resubmitted by the UNGA, and the link to environmental issues was removed from the text: "Is the threat or use of nuclear weapons in any circum-

---

79 UNGA res. A/RES/47/37 (1992).

80 See UNGA res. A/RES/62/28 (2008) with further references.

81 For a study of international obligations as well as international decisions relating to nuclear activities, including the use of nuclear weapons, see Ved P. Nanda, "International Environmental Norms Applicable to Nuclear Activities, with Particular Focus on Decisions of International Tribunals and International Settlements", in Heinz Stockinger *et al.* (eds.), *Updating International Nuclear Law*, Berliner-Wissenschafts-Verlag, Berlin, 2007, 185–203.

82 World Health Assembly res. WHA46.40.

83 *Legality of the Use by a State of Nuclear Weapons in Armed Conflict*, advisory opinion, ICJ Reports 1996, at 66.

stance permitted under international law?"[84] Nevertheless, the ICJ considered potential environmental effects from the use of nuclear weapons as part of its lawfulness assessment. The ICJ based its findings in this respect on "the general obligation of States to ensure that activities within their jurisdiction and control respect the environment of other States or of areas beyond national control", and noted that this rule "is now part of the corpus of international law relating to the environment".[85]

The ICJ also recognised the relevance of environmental considerations as a possible limit to a state's right to exercise self-defence in the sense that certain environmental damages might make an act of self-defence disproportionate:

> ... States must take environmental considerations into account when assessing what is necessary and proportionate in the pursuit of legitimate military objectives. Respect for the environment is one of the elements that go to assessing whether an action is in conformity with the principles of necessity and proportionality.[86]

The Court further referred to Articles 35(3) and 55 of Additional Protocol 1 (1977) to the Geneva Conventions (1949) and principle 2 of the Rio Declaration (1992) and concluded that:

> ... together, these provisions embody a general obligation to protect the natural environment against widespread, long-term and severe environmental damage; the prohibition of methods and means of warfare which are intended, or may be expected, to cause such damage; and the prohibition of attacks against the natural environment by way of reprisals. These are powerful constraints for all the States having subscribed to these provisions.[87]

While this case does not directly concern the issues addressed in this paper, its statements on the role that environmental degradation may play in armed conflicts are interesting. When the Court underlines the importance of environmental considerations during armed conflict, this can be read to indicate a willingness to regard environmental factors as significant for post conflict peace building, and possibly also when determining whether a situation qualifies as a "threat to the peace". As a consequence, it can be argued that the ICJ's advisory opinion in this case supports the suggestion that environmental damage may constitute a threat to international peace.

F. *Other UN initiatives of interest to environmental security*

It is not our ambition to examine how the link between environment and security has been addressed in all organs of the UN. Here, it is of particular interest to address those statements that are closely related to the work of the UNSC.

---

84 UNGA res. A/RES/49/75 K (1995).

85 *Legality of the Threat or Use of Nuclear Weapons*, at 226, para. 29. See also *United States v. Canada*, Award of 11 March 1941, *RIAA*, Vol. III, op. 1957; *Trail Smelter Arbitration Tribunal (US v. Canada)*, 33 *AJIL* 182 (1939) and 35 *AJIL* 684 (1941).

86 *Ibid.*, para. 30.

87 *Ibid.*, para. 31.

In its 1987 report, the World Commission on Environment and Development noted that "poverty, injustice, environmental degradation, and conflict interact in complex and potent ways".[88]

In an address to the UNSC in 2003, then Secretary-General Kofi Annan urged the UNSC to expand its agenda to "soft-threats", including environmental change and degradation. He noted that

> ... while some consider these threats [terrorism and proliferation of weapons of mass destruction] as self-evidently the main challenge to world peace and security, others feel more immediately menaced by ... so called 'soft-threats' such as the persistence of extreme poverty, the disparity of income between and within societies, and the spread of infectious diseases, or climate change and environmental degradation. ... In truth, we do not have to choose. The United Nations must confront all these threats and challenges – new and old, 'hard' and 'soft'. It must be fully engaged in the struggle for development and poverty eradication, starting with the achievement of the Millennium Development Goals; in the common struggle to protect our common environment; and in the struggle for human rights, democracy and good governance.[89]

Moreover, in a report to the UNGA in 2005 the Secretary-General stated that:

> The threats to peace and security in the twenty-first century include not just international war and conflict but civil violence, organized crime, terrorism and weapons of mass destruction. They also include poverty, deadly infectious disease and environmental degradation since these can have equally catastrophic consequences. All of these threats can cause death or lessen life chances on a large scale. All of them can undermine States as the basic unit of the international system.[90]

He further noted that "[w]here threats are not imminent but latent, the Charter gives full authority to the Security Council to use military force, including preventively, to preserve international peace and security".[91] He also advocated a dynamic interpretation of the Charter.[92] The report concluded by urging states to:

> Affirm and commit themselves to implementing a new security consensus based on the recognition that threats are interlinked, that development, security and human rights are mutually interdependent, that no State can protect itself acting entirely alone and that all States need an equitable, efficient and effective collective security system; and therefore commit themselves to agreeing on, and implementing, comprehensive strategies for confronting the whole range of threats, from international

88 See Brundtland *et al.* 1987, *supra* note 6, at 291.

89 Kofi Annan, The Secretary General Address to the General Assembly, 23 September 2003, available at www.un.org/webcast/ga/58/statements/sg2eng030923.htm. See also the Report of the UN Secretary-General to the UNGA in A/60/891, para. 22.

90 UNGA in A/59/2005, *In Larger Freedom: Towards Development, Security and Human Rights for All*, 21 March, 2005, para. 78.

91 *Ibid.*, para. 125.

92 *Ibid.*, paras. 153 and 154.

> war through weapons of mass destruction, terrorism, State collapse and civil conflict to deadly infectious disease, extreme poverty and the destruction of the environment.[93]

Despite these efforts, in the UNGA resolution on the 2005 World Summit Outcome, states omitted any reference to peace or security issues in the paragraphs on sustainable development, and to environmental issues in the part on peace and collective security.[94]

Nevertheless, the statements of Kofi Annan were followed up by the current Secretary-General, Ban Ki-Moon, who has emphasised that "climate change can have implications for peace and security. This is especially true in vulnerable regions that face multiple stresses at the same time – pre-existing conflict, poverty and unequal access to resources, weak institutions, food insecurity and the incidence of diseases such as HIV/AIDS."[95] However, as has been shown in section 4.3 above, there was no general agreement among states to bring the issue on the agenda of the UNSC.

The opinions expressed by the Secretary-Generals must be understood on the basis of the findings of the Secretary-General's High Level Panel on Threats, Challenge and Change. The High Level Panel opened by stating that:

> ... we know all too well that the biggest security threats we face now, and in the decades ahead ... extend to poverty, infectious disease and environmental degradation; war and violence within States; the spread and possible use of nuclear, radiological, chemical and biological weapons; terrorism; and transnational organized crime. The threats are from non-State actors as well as States, and to human security as well as State security.[96]

The High Level Panel further remarked that

> Poverty, infectious disease, environmental degradation and war feed one another in a deadly cycle. Poverty ... is strongly associated with the outbreak of civil war. Such diseases as malaria and HIV/AIDS continue to cause large numbers of deaths and reinforce poverty. Disease and poverty, in turn, are connected to environmental degradation. ... Environmental stress, caused by large populations and shortages of land and other natural resources, can contribute to civil violence.[97]

This statement illustrates well the causal relationship between environmental degradation and disease and, in turn, these factors and violence.[98] One scholar has illustrated the complex causality by noting that "[c]ountries experiencing chronic

93 *Ibid.*, p. 57, para. 6.

94 UNGA res. A/RES/60/1 (2005) paras. 48–56 and 69–118 respectively

95 S/PV.5663 at 14.

96 The Secretary-General's High Level Panel on Threats, Challenge and Change, *A More Secure World: Our Shared Responsibility*, United Nations 2004 (book format), Synopsis, at 9.

97 *Ibid.*, at 15, para. 22.

98 See also *ibid.*, at 26, paras. 53–55.

internal conflict because of environmental stress will probably either fragment or become more authoritarian".[99] In its conclusions on a possible reform of the UNSC, the High Level Panel stated that:

> ... the challenge for any reform is to increase both the effectiveness and the credibility of the Security Council and, most importantly, to enhance its capacity and willingness to act in the face of threats. This requires ... a firm consensus on the nature of today's threats, on the obligations of broadened collective security, on the necessity of prevention ...[100]

Apparently, the need to broaden the security concept to include environmental issues was supported by the Secretary-General, but it has largely been met by scepticism among states. The evolvement of this debate shows that the security concept under Chapter VII may possibly be expanded to a broader range of environmental issues in the future, but it also indicates that such a development will take substantial time and is likely to take place in response to specific needs or situations.

One means for addressing specific situations is provided for in Art. V (3)–(5) of the Convention on the Prohibition of Military or any Hostile Use of Environmental Modification Techniques (ENMOD Convention, 10 December 1976), according to which a state can make a formal complaint before the UNSC if it considers that another state has violated its obligations under the Convention. The Council can investigate and adopt the measures it finds appropriate. To our knowledge, no complaints concerning violations of the ENMOD Convention has so far been presented to the UNSC. In the Iraq-Kuwait situation, however, the UNSC addressed environmental aspects of the conflict even if none of these two states were parties to ENMOD.[101] The UNSC established the UN Compensation Commission to deal with compensation for damages inflicted on Kuwait and other countries,[102] and according to Decision no. 7 of the Governing Council of the Compensation Commission, environmental damage of a broad range was to be covered by the compensation scheme, including:

a. Abatement and prevention of environmental damage, including expenses directly relating to fighting oil fires and stemming the flow of oil in coastal and international waters;

99 Homer-Dixon notes that "[g]overnments of countries as different as the Philippines and Peru have lost control over outer territories; although both cases are complicated, it is nonetheless clear that environmental stress has contributed to their fragmentation. Fragmentation of any sizeable country will produce large outflows of refugees; it will also hinder the country from effectively negotiating and implementing international agreements on collective security, global environmental protection, and other matters", see Homer-Dixon 1994, *supra* note 28, at 36. He also notes that internal environmental problems may turn a state into a "hard" regime which is "more prone to launch attacks against neighbouring countries to divert attention from internal grievances".

100 *A More Secure World* (2004), *supra* note 96, para. 248.

101 See paras. 16–19 of UNSC res. S/RES/687 (1991).

102 See UNSC res. S/RES/692 (1991).

b. Reasonable measures already taken to clean and restore the environment or future measures which can be documented as reasonably necessary to clean and restore the environment;
c. Reasonable monitoring and assessment of the environmental damage for the purposes of evaluating and abating the harm and restoring the environment;
d. Reasonable monitoring of public health and performing medical screenings for the purposes of investigation and combating increased health risks as a result of the environmental damage; and
e. Depletion of or damage to natural resources.[103]

Against this background, it can be observed that despite the general reluctance against the engagement of the UNSC in issues concerning environmental security among a significant number of states, there seems to be little opposition against involvement of the UNSC in relation to environmental issues in specific cases, in particular at the post conflict stage.

V. Other Elements of Practice

Environmental threats are today viewed as an integral aspect of the overall security strategy of several states and intergovernmental organisations, including the United Kingdom, the United States, the European Union and NATO. The United Kingdom's security strategy notes that its scope and approach:

> … reflects the way our understanding of national security has changed. In the past, the state was the traditional focus of foreign, defence and security policies, and national security was understood as dealing with the protection of the state and its vital interests from attacks by other states. Over recent decades, our view of national security has broadened to include threats to individual citizens and to our way of life, as well as to the integrity and interests of the state. That is why this strategy deals with transnational crime, pandemics and flooding – not part of the traditional idea of national security, but clearly challenges that can affect large numbers of our citizens, and which demand some of the same responses as more traditional security threats, including terrorism. The broad scope of this strategy also reflects our commitment to focus on the underlying drivers of security and insecurity, rather than just immediate threats and risks.[104]

The United States' security strategy notes that:

> Globalization has exposed us to new challenges and changed the way old challenges touch our interests and values, while also greatly enhancing our capacity

103 *Criteria for additional Categories of Claims*, Decision no. 7 of the Governing Council, S/AC.26/1991/7/Rev.1, para. 35.

104 *The National Security Strategy of the United Kingdom. Security in an Interdependent World*, Cabinet Office March 2008, at 3–4, para. 1.5. In a footnote it is noted that: "The wider scope of issues to be addressed within this strategy is not to be taken as affecting the legally understood meaning of national security". The document is available at http://interactive.cabinetoffice.gov.uk/documents/security/national_security_strategy.pdf.

> to respond. Examples include: … Environmental destruction, whether caused by human behavior or cataclysmic mega-disasters such as floods, hurricanes, earthquakes, or tsunamis. Problems of this scope may overwhelm the capacity of local authorities to respond, and may even overtax national militaries, requiring a larger international response. These challenges are not traditional national security concerns, such as the conflict of arms or ideologies. But if left unaddressed they can threaten national security. We have learned that: Preparing for and managing these challenges requires the full exercise of national power, up to and including traditional security instruments. … The times require an ambitious national security strategy, yet one recognizing the limits to what even a nation as powerful as the United States can achieve by itself. Our national security strategy is idealistic about goals, and realistic about means.[105]

The European Union's security strategy states that:

> Large-scale aggression against any Member State is now improbable. Instead, Europe faces new threats which are more diverse, less visible and less predictable. … In contrast to the massive visible threat in the Cold War, none of the new threats is purely military; nor can any be tackled by purely military means.[106]

Finally, the 1999 NATO Summit endorsed the following in The Alliance's Strategic Concept:

> The Alliance is committed to a broad approach to security, which recognises the importance of political, economic, social and environmental factors in addition to the indispensable defence dimension. This broad approach forms the basis for the Alliance to accomplish its fundamental security tasks effectively, and its increasing effort to develop effective cooperation with other European and Euro-Atlantic organisations as well as the United Nations.[107]

In following up this reorientation, NATO has established a Science for Peace and Security Committee. This Committee has an Advisory Panel on Environmental Security which considers those environmental issues that pose risks to security and may lead to regional or cross-border disputes. Among the issues considered by the Panel are eco-terrorism, management of water resources, pollution of waterways, desertification and land erosion.[108]

105 *The National Security Strategy of the United States of America*, The White House, March 2006, at 47 and 49, available at http://www.whitehouse.gov/nsc/nss/2006/.

106 *A Secure Europe in a Better World: European Security Strategy*, Brussels, 12 December 2003, at 3 and 7, available at http://www.consilium.europa.eu/uedocs/cmsUpload/78367.pdf. See also *Climate Change and International Security*, S113/08, 14 March 2008 from the High Representative and the European Commission to the European Council, noting the security implications of various environmental incidents, available at http://www.consilium.europa.eu/ueDocs/cms_Data/docs/pressData/en/reports/99387.pdf.

107 See Press Release NAC-S(99)65, para. 25, available at http://www.nato.int/docu/pr/1999/p99-065e.htm.

108 See http://www.nato.int/science/about_sps/framework.htm.

The close relationship between the UNSC and regional arrangements, as provided for in Chapter VIII of the UN Charter, indicates that the regional and national approaches of key actors may affect the approaches to be taken by the UNSC. If states address environmental threats in a national setting but deny the UNSC a role at the international level, this might weaken the UNSC and strengthen regional arrangements. On the one hand, in the Council's 2007 debate on climate change, Venezuela advocated a "nationalisation" of the security concept by holding "the multidimensional character of security to mean that each sovereign and legitimate State defines its priorities in this area on the basis of its own national needs and interests, as has been recognised in various international instruments".[109] On the other hand, if the UNSC is reformed to include a broader representation and to follow more transparent procedures, states may more easily accept a broad interpretation of Art. 39 that covers environmental threats.

VI. Conclusion

In this article we have taken as a starting point that environmental issues constitute an increasingly important conflict driver.[110] This is supported by the fact that such issues form an integral aspect of the security strategy of several states and intergovernmental organisations. We have discussed whether the UNSC has the competence to address such issues under Chapter VII of the UN Charter. Our conclusion is that even with a conservative understanding of the term "peace" in Article 39, implying only the absence of interstate armed conflict, environmental issues may constitute a "threat to the peace", a "breach of the peace" or an "act of aggression".[111] Besides, environmental damage may be an essential element in an interstate conflict, automatically bringing it within the UNSC's mandate. Thus, while the environment as such is not protected in article 39, there will be situations where the UNSC may address environmental issues.

Despite the above, our study of UNSC practice has revealed that the Council so far only rarely has addressed environmental issues. And when it has, it has largely been to promote sustainable development in general resolutions or in post conflict situations, or to address the role that exploitation of and trade in natural resources play in funding belligerent groups. There are, however, indications that both states and the UNSC are gradually taking a more positive attitude towards bringing envi-

109 Record of the UNSC's meeting 17 April 2007, S/PV.5663 (Resumption 1), 10.

110 It should be noted that the body of empirical studies on which we base this starting point still seems to be in its infancy. Gleditsch has, ten years ago but still pertinently, noted that "[a] striking feature of the existing empirical studies is the problem of gathering valid and reliable data on the environmental behaviour of nations or smaller geographical units. Environmental accounting is miles behind national economic accounting", see Gleditsch 1998, *supra* note 6, at 396.

111 Such conservative understanding also seems to resonate with the current trend in international security studies. St. Jean notes that "there has been somewhat of a vindication of the traditional notion that international security should be primarily concerned with violence towards states", see C. Elisabeth St. Jean, "The Changing Nature of 'International Security': The Need for an Integrated Definition", in *Paterson Review 8* (2007), 22, at 23.

ronmental issues onto the Council's agenda. The most explicit signs of this can be found outside the UNSC, in organs appointed by the Secretary-General, in particular the High Level Panel on Threats, Challenge and Change. It was, however, also important when the UNSC held its 2007 debate on climate change. Although the majority of states in this debate expressed reluctance against placing climate issues onto the UNSC agenda, quite a few states expressed a positive or at least an open attitude.

While we recognise the concerns expressed by many states when discussing an expanding role for the UNSC, we still believe the arguments in favour of expanding the Council's agenda to more specific environmental situations are compelling. Environmental degradation is an indisputable indirect, and also more and more direct, cause of devastating conflicts, the UN Charter seems to allow such expansion, and such expansion resonates with the Charter's purposes and the Council's expressed intention to act more preventively. More importantly, such expansion could offer a long needed opportunity to address effectively environmental threats to our collective security. While there seems to be a widespread recognition among states of the threats posed by environmental deterioration, including but not limited to climate change, states have failed time and time again to establish effective regimes for addressing these threats.

Environmental threats typically imply long term damage. In theory, states should be able voluntarily to implement the measures needed to remedy many of the environmental threats they face, but states tend to prioritise short term interests at the cost of dealing with long term problems. One key to remedy tendencies towards "tragedies of the commons" may well lie in the UNSC's power to adopt binding measures.

The UNSC is the sole international organ with a permanent competence to address any threat to international peace and security and to dictate states in that respect. International agreements and custom already form a legal framework between states, aiming to avoid and remedy environmental threats. What the international community still lacks, in particular where non-compliance is the result of lack of will and not the result of lack of ability, is effective enforcement. As noted by one commentator, the UNSC could "add teeth to the enforcement regime where the soft measures internal to the environmental treaty regime have failed".[112]

In order to effectively protect the environment, and thus minimise the risk that environmental situations will occur and develop into interstate conflicts, some key aspects must be observed. First, an understanding among states – most notably including the Council's permanent members – must be established to the effect that no threat to international peace and security is, by its nature, outside the Council's mandate. In that sense, Article 39's broad formulation of the mandate is an advantage. We are of the opinion that the UNSC has exclusive discretion to determine the existence of a threat to the peace for the purpose of Article 39 provided the UNSC has sufficiently considered factors of relevance to the determination.

Second, states need to reach a general consensus that addressing environmental threats may be an appropriate task of the UNSC. Such a consensus is most likely to develop gradually on the basis of a case-by-case approach.

112 Knight 2005, *supra* note 18, at 1561.

Third, in the process of establishing such consensus, the UNSC must adapt its working methods accordingly. It may need to increase the transparency of its deliberations.[113] Moreover, it must ensure that it stays informed of environmental situations which may potentially lead to interstate conflict,[114] and it must creatively explore viable methods for addressing environmental situations adequately. Faced with threats that are fundamentally different from the traditional ones, the Council must update its toolbox with new tools, including new types of sanctions or pressure, which would effectively deal with environmental threats. The UNSC will need expertise to determine whether a given environmental situation meets the criteria in article 39, and to predict the likely effect of possible measures. The establishment of the Expert Panel that assessed the issue of resource exploitation in the DRC and the Compensation Commission that assessed compensation claims related to the Iraq-Kuwait conflict are examples of such expertise.

Arguably, before adopting any measure, the UNSC must (i) assess the seriousness of the threat; (ii) make sure any measure is for a proper purpose; (iii) decide whether a measure is the least intrusive effective measure; (iv) assess whether the burden on the targeted subject is proportionate to the expected gain from the measure; and (v) decide whether there is a reasonable chance of the measure being successful, with the consequences of action not likely to be worse than the consequences of inaction.[115]

One particularly interesting aspect of the UNSC's powers under Chapter VII is that the adopted measures do not have to be directed towards a "guilty party". Kelsen has noted that:

> The Charter does not … prescribe that the enforcement measures shall be directed only against the member guilty of a threat to the peace, breach of the peace, or act of aggression. The charter simply authorizes the Security Council to take, such measures after having determined the existence of any threat to the peace, etc. without binding the Security Council with respect to the state [or any other subject that the Council might instruct] against which these measures shall be directed. … Even if it is assumed that the Security Council is bound to conform its enforcement actions with 'the principle of justice and international law', the Council has the choice between 'justice' and 'international law'. The Security Council may consider it to be just to direct enforcement action against the party which legally, that is from the point of view of international law, is not wrong[.][116]

113 For a short comment relating to transparency of the procedures of the UNSC, see Anthony Aust, "The Role of Human Rights in Limiting the Enforcement Powers of the Security Council: A Practitioner's View", in Erika de Wet and André Nollkaemper (eds.), *Review of the Security Council by Member States*, Intersentia, Antwerpen, 2003, at 31–32.

114 In the 2007 debate on climate change, India noted that the UNSC "does not have the expertise … to make an uncertain long-term prospect a security threat", see Record of the Security Council's meeting 17 April 2007, S/PV.5663 (Resumption 1), at 23.

115 These factors are borrowed from the report *A More Secure World* (2004), *supra* note 96, para. 207, in the context of measures involving the use of force under article 42 of the Charter.

116 Kelsen 1946, *supra* note 16, at 434–435.

This brings us to another point which we believe can be of crucial importance in the context of environmental threats. A development seems currently to take place with regard to the group of subjects targeted in UNSC resolutions. It seems to be increasingly recognised that the Council has, when international peace and security is threatened, the power also to curb corporate activity.[117] Some of the activities of transnational corporations (TNCs), including but not limited to the exploitation of natural resources, are notorious conflict-drivers. When the UNSC adopted resolutions targeting TNCs operating in the DRC, the purpose was not to protect the environment as such, but to avoid the devastating effect on regional peace and security that the exploitation had. Another new category of subjects potentially exposed to UNSC measures are individuals, due to the possibility to establish international criminal tribunals or refer a situation to the ICC.[118]

The "international peace and security" label applied to any situation that the UNSC addresses, carries recognition with it. To the extent the UNSC addresses environmental threats, this will signal the significance of such threats. Regardless of how one interprets the Charter, it seems pertinent to ask whether environmental threats to the peace are any less dangerous than traditional threats or other threats that the Council has demonstrated increased willingness to address, such as gross human rights violations.

The most decisive challenge for the UNSC, if it is to address environmental issues, is to look beyond politics. Environmental issues can have huge political and economical ramifications. Combined with the permanent members' veto power this might be the main reason why so many states are reluctant to let the Council address such issues. The lack of democratic and transparent procedures represents another challenge. If the UNSC manages over time to carry out its mandate consistently and *bona fide*, the reluctance will probably lessen. The importance of mutual trust among states was aptly illustrated in the 2007 debate on climate change. Sudan noted, on behalf of the African Union, that to place climate change onto the UNSC's agenda represented an attempt to "shift matters of interest of all Member States to a body where a few members of the United Nations have been vested with the power to take final decisions".[119] While reform of the UNSC through expansion of its membership may detract from the expediency with which it will adopt measures, such a reform is likely to increase the acceptability and thus also the ultimate effectiveness of such measures.

117 For a discussion of the competence of the UNSC to address corporate activity which threaten or damage international peace and security, see Ole Kristian Fauchald and Jo Stigen, "Corporate Responsibility before International Institutions", forthcoming in *George Washington International Law Review*.

118 That the UNSC's establishment of the ICTY was lawful under Chapter VII of the UN Charter was confirmed by the ICTY Appeals Chamber in *Prosecutor v. Tadic*, IT-94-1, 2 October 1995, decision on the defence motion for interlocutory appeal on jurisdiction. According to article 13(b) of the Rome Statute, the UNSC may refer a situation, as opposed to an individual case, to the ICC.

119 Record of the Security Council's meeting 17 April 2007, S/PV.5663 (Resumption 1), at 12.

Part V

A Practitioner's Perspective

Chapter 14

Pragmatic Law for International Security

Sean Kanuck[*]

"The only relevant question about the future is not whether something will happen, but what we would do if it did happen." — *Arie de Geus*

I. Introduction

Multiple voices inform the global dialogue on international law and security; however, the various commentators do not always recognize that their professional disciplines ineluctably color their legal opinions. Government practitioners – including foreign policy makers, military commanders, and law enforcement officers – have now joined the jurists and academics in proffering interpretations of the law, usually in the service of their own professional interests. This matter is further complicated by other entities, such as nongovernmental organizations (NGOs) and the media, which also pursue their own political agendas through the modern legal discourse. It should come as no surprise then that legal practitioners, academics, and the rest – each with a unique set of priorities and objectives – apply different value judgments and risk assessments to arrive at disparate conclusions regarding the same points of international law.

Nowhere is that disparity more evident than in discussions regarding international security. Having been solicited to provide the practitioners' perspective for an academic conference on that topic, this article will adopt a multidisciplinary approach to explain how government policymakers think and why they arrive at legal conclusions which may differ from their peers working in other capacities. It will be neither an apology for, nor a critique of, those decisions; rather, the objective herein is merely to elucidate the epistemological biases and cognitive processes that may predetermine public officials' answers to legal questions before they are even posed.

---

* Fellow, National Security Council, USA. The views expressed herein do not necessarily represent the official position of the United States Government or any of its subdivisions; accordingly, they should be attributed solely to the author. The author wishes to thank Cecilia M. Bailliet of the Law Faculty at the University of Oslo for both the invitation to participate in this conference and her editorial comments. He also acknowledges the formative contributions of David Kennedy, Christopher Coker, and Arne Willy Dahl to his thinking on strategic issues in international law.

Cecilia M. Bailliet (ed.), Security: A Multidisciplinary Normative Approach.
 Printed in The Netherlands. ISBN *978 90 04 17296 8. pp. 345–365.*

In that respect, this paper is predominantly a study in human psychology, for only in the latter sections will normative suggestions be offered for improving the efficacy of public international law through increased pragmatism. By way of final caveat, the following discussion primarily addresses the mindset of political and military leaders responsible for crafting foreign policy decisions (vice government aid workers, human rights officers, etc.); moreover, it will remain generic in nature and not specific to the practices of any particular country or administration.

In order to develop an international legal system that can effectively constrain sovereign actions, one must first understand the context from which policy decisions emerge. Toward that end, this paper will offer four hypotheses for future consideration and verification by other researchers. Upon examining the impact of incomplete information, time constraints, and bureaucratic incentive structures on government practitioners – as opposed to professors, judges, or other international lawyers – one soon realizes that their perceived divergences from legal treatises or prior jurisprudence may be accounted for more by a special combination of uncertainty and professional responsibility than by any deep-seated, normative disagreements. Discussions concerning security – and the very definition of the word itself – are unavoidably affected by one's public duties, or lack thereof, because practical considerations and resource limitations often do not permit the adoption of a preferred course of action.

Furthermore, the inherently reflexive nature of international law, coupled with its reliance on state actors for its enforcement, mandates a full awareness of the participants and their competing professional responsibilities in order to transcend adversarial viewpoints and undesired outcomes. A truly collaborative and strategic approach to making international law would result in more pragmatic and uniformly enforceable rules – even if they were to fall short of the idealized norms that are currently espoused but too often honored in the breach.

II. Defining Security

There are at least two competing conceptions of the term *security*. One relates primarily to preventing physical harm and the mitigation of external threats. For purposes of this paper, we will equate that notion of security with the term *safety*. A second formulation of the term security concerns itself with one's quality of life (i.e. the promotion of human rights, satisfaction of popular needs, and fulfillment of individual desires). Hereinafter, that alternative notion of security will be equated with the term *welfare*. Whereas safety is a negative construct that seeks to protect against potential adversity and thereby permit freedom of thought and action, welfare concerns the positive realization of those values for human benefit.[1] Clearly, some level of safety is

1 Both conceptions are well established in public international law. For examples of the safety norm, see Article 3 of the Universal Declaration of Human Rights, which states "Everyone has the right to life, liberty and security of person" (UN General Assembly Resolution 217 A(III), 10 December 1948, hereinafter Universal Declaration); and Article 9, paragraph 1 of the International Covenant on Civil and Political Rights, which states "Everyone has the right to liberty and security of person" (16 December 1966). Alternatively, the welfare norm is represented in the Preamble to the Charter of the United Nations, which seeks "to promote social progress and better standards of life in larger

a precondition for welfare; however, where one stops and the other begins is a subjective determination. In fact, an excess of the former can even limit the latter, as with the imposition of martial law.[2] Moreover, a governmental regime can itself harm both the safety and welfare of its own subjects (e.g. if it tortures the citizenry), so the classification of certain human rights concerns as matters of safety versus welfare may depend on one's professional perspective.[3]

Much of the debate concerning security and public policy reflects a fundamental difference between how commentators define security and what they seek to achieve through policy measures. There is an inherent tension between the values of liberty and entitlement, as well as between the security of individual persons, the collective security within a polity, and the national security of the sovereign state itself. Normative judgments about how to resolve those tensions are often dependent on the professional role of the commentator at that time, as well as his or her cultural background, which helps form one's expectations of government.[4]

The United Nations (UN) has a stated objective "to maintain international peace and security" which requires the elimination, reduction, or management of any "threats to the peace."[5] This is the same context in which the classical and realist schools of international relations theory have considered the issue of security.[6] In the international arena, safety also takes on an institutional dimension through collective security agreements. Most notably, the UN Charter provides that "nothing in the present Charter shall impair the inherent right of individual or collective self-defense if an armed attack occurs against a Member of the United Nations, until the Security

freedom" (26 June 1945, hereinafter UN Charter); and Articles 2, 11, and 12 of the International Covenant on Economic, Social and Cultural Rights, which goes much further towards "achieving progressively the full realization of the rights recognized" by ensuring adequate standards of living and enjoyment of the highest attainable standard of health (16 December 1966, hereinafter ICESCR).

2 An analogous continuum is observed regarding the concept of *equality* in political science: equality of opportunity is often a necessary but insufficient prerequisite for equality of condition. Although in that case, excessive efforts to mandate the latter can limit the former.

3 From the government practitioners' perspective discussed herein, individual human rights concerns arising from actions taken by the state against its own subjects or those from another state would not qualify as safety issues because they are the result, and not cause, of security measures aimed at ameliorating external threats. Foreign or lay observers may be less likely to either (a) distinguish between the external and internal sources of harm to individuals within the polity, or (b) discount the negative impacts of the government's own actions.

4 Even within the practitioners' arena, the exact definition of security – and the role of government – differs between political cultures. For instance, the social democratic tradition of many European nations includes welfare systems that are not considered legal entitlements in other countries. Compare, for example, the rights and entitlements enumerated in the Constitution of the Federal Republic of Germany versus that of the United States of America.

5 See UN Charter, Article 1, paragraph 1.

6 The classical school is well represented by Thucydides' historical work entitled *The Peloponnesian War*, while the realist school comprises such renowned authors as Kenneth Waltz, Stephen Walt, and Robert Jervis.

Council has taken measures necessary to maintain international peace and security."[7] Those systemic alliances are meant to deter foreign threats and successfully rebuff those that are not effectively deterred. But at the end of the day, most collective security arrangements speak only to defeating or strategically restraining outside influences, which is an inherently negative role.

On the other hand, the crux of welfare is contained in other weakly enforceable covenants and declarations, such as the ICESCR.[8] It is undeniable that the safety conception of security still predominates among sovereign nations and the legal practitioners within their official ranks; otherwise, one would experience a very different atmosphere in international organizations (IOs) and multilateral negotiations. The UN paradigm was created by sovereign, victor states and remains in force to primarily serve the interests of those state actors, and only derivatively or residually, their citizens.

Originally, public international law also dealt primarily with the interactions of sovereign states, with a decided emphasis on the conditions of war and peace.[9] Not until the 20th Century did the role of the individual become a central concern for international legal theorists; however, many of today's debates regarding human rights and the laws of armed conflict are premised on concerns for the individual as opposed to the state.[10] That shifting focus brings difficulty and seeming inconsistency. The academic substance of international law is evolving faster than effective procedures of implementation can be realized due to political impasses in diplomatic negotiations. Developments in international law are challenging the very authority of the same sovereign states upon which it relies for enforcement, and some statesmen are reluctant to cede power to supranational and multilateral bodies for fear of selling out their national interest. Yet, that disconnect is partially owing to the competing interpretations of security as safety vice welfare. If one ignores economic and social gains in the security calculus, then a *realpolitik* approach to foreign relations is much more tenable. Conversely, if one questions the primacy of sovereignty, then general welfare considerations become much more relevant.[11]

7 UN Charter, Article 51.

8 Socio-economic rights are, however, beginning to receive increased effect through judicial enforcement in both domestic and international tribunals, as well as proceedings under the international mandates of entities like the UN Commission on Human Rights and the Office of the UN High Commissioner for Human Rights. See e.g. Michael C. Tolley, "The Judicial Enforcement of Socio-Economic Rights in Comparative Perspective" (paper delivered at the annual meeting of the American Political Science Association, Boston, Massachusetts, August 2008) (available online at: http://allacademic.com/meta/p_mla_apa_research_citation/2/8/0/3/7/p28037_index.html).

9 See generally Antonio Cassese, *International Law*, 2nd ed. (New York: Oxford University Press, 2005), 3–4, 22–34.

10 See generally Ian Brownlie, *Principles of Public International Law*, 6th ed. (New York: Oxford University Press, 2003), 529–533.

11 United States (US) President Franklin Delano Roosevelt's famous four freedoms speak directly to welfare rather than mere safety. As embodied in the Universal Declaration, the freedom of expression, freedom of religion, freedom from want, and freedom from fear

From a practical standpoint, the contrasting objectives of safety and welfare are perhaps most easily illustrated in the impoverished and politically troubled areas of the world. Many residents of the Levant, for example, support the local Hamas or Hezballah factions because they are able to provide social services despite their arguably destabilizing paramilitary activities. The Lebanese government, Fatah administration, and Israeli Defense Forces focus on the safety aspects of the local conflicts, while many aid workers, journalists, and affected individuals in the region look primarily to which entity can best deliver welfare. Development programs are also once again receiving increased attention among scholars and practitioners alike as a potential foreign policy tool for achieving economic stability and politico-military security.[12]

The qualitative experience of life – rather than its mere preservation – has taken on a new precedence among scholars. Academics now utilize terms like *human security* and *biopolitics* to expand a *security dispositif* that addresses critical issues of risk management and human welfare that are not captured by the simpler notion of safety.[13] But, for a legal practitioner, this expansion broadens the dialogue and does more to depict how security considerations impact living conditions and societal transaction costs than it does to redefine what security means to government officials. Of course, that oversight – or rejection, as the case may be – is premised on the same bias that was already identified above. Law professors and philosophers are more likely to consider the totality of an abstract subject matter, including the deeper sources of social conflict that threaten security, in a way that policy makers simply do not. Practical considerations of time and exigency usually do not permit such an exhaustive review of issues or the adoption of far-reaching strategies with uncertain outcomes. That realization is not meant to serve as a justification for the practitioners' view, but rather, as a simple recognition of reality. What remains to be explored in later sections of this paper is why policy makers are unwilling or incapable of adopting the more holistic approaches of their learned brethren in the ivory tower and international tribunals.

Thus far, the predilections of government and military practitioners have mainly been contrasted with those of academics. It is worth noting, however, that such individuals represent only two contingents from a much wider array of legal commentators that also includes international jurists, philosophers and ethicists, journalists, employees of IOs as well as NGOs, and many others. As David Kennedy has aptly pointed out, today's legal discourse involves many varied voices that engage on a

constitute positive objectives that go well beyond neutralizing external threats to physical safety or national security.

12 See J. Brian Atwood, M. Peter McPherson, and Andrew Natsios, "Arrested Development: Making Foreign Aid a More Effective Tool," *Foreign Affairs* 87, no. 6 (November/December 2008): 123–132.

13 Recent examples of this literature include: Marlies Glasius, "Human Security from Paradigm Shift to Operationalization: Job Description for a Human Security Worker," *Security Dialogue* 39, no. 1 (2008): 31–54; and Michael Dillon, "Underwriting Security," *Security Dialogue* 39, no. 2–3 (2008): 309–332.

common plane as never before.[14] He writes that "law has increasingly become the vocabulary for international politics and diplomacy, it has become the rhetoric through which we debate."[15]

The quintessential issue regarding the competing definitions of security is really general disagreement about the appropriate breadth of discourse. Government practitioners strive to resolve specific issues and manage risks within the purview of their public mandates, particular departments or agencies, and terms of office. Lawyers in academia or NGOs, on the other hand, can often take a broader approach which analyzes security concerns within their larger political, demographic, and sociological contexts. That critical distinction, coupled with the foregoing historical analysis, suggests the first hypothesis of this paper, namely that: *government practitioners adhere to a safety-oriented notion of security.*

III. Risk Assessment

If one accepts that safety is the central concern of government lawyers who bear a responsibility for the security of their constituents, then their practical considerations readily become: (i) what kind of measures should be adopted to protect citizens from potential hazards, and (ii) how should collective resources be applied to best mitigate those hazards. In light of those queries, policy makers will be immediately faced with two philosophical challenges. First, they must choose between deontological and utilitarian methodologies; and second, they must implicitly quantify the value of human life within their society. As counter-intuitive as it may sound, those two quandaries of moral philosophy are indirect factors in myriad policy decisions. In the real world, there are always policy trade-offs and opportunity costs that must be considered, whether explicitly or implicitly.

Let us begin with the first of those challenges. For centuries, philosophers have pondered whether the means and methods by which events come to pass are relevant, or if mankind is only to be concerned with the ultimate consequences?[16] Should there be normative limitations on the exercise of government power vis-à-vis individuals – even if it is exercised in good faith for the common benefit – or are certain actions to be prohibited under all circumstances?[17] Does the source or cause of harm matter for a victim, or are all hazards producing equivalent effects to be considered similarly by public officials? These seemingly pedantic questions take on practical import for the

---

14 See David Kennedy, *Of War and Law*, (Princeton, New Jersey: Princeton University Press, 2006).

15 Ibid. at 5.

16 The respective works of Immanuel Kant and John Stuart Mill represent premier arguments on behalf of the two competing schools of thought.

17 These age-old questions have preoccupied jurists and philosophers for millennia. Among the various learned opinions offered over the years is William Blackstone's famous adage that it is better that ten guilty persons escape than that one innocent suffer. It is worth noting that his Kantian perspective on criminal law matters stands at odds with the utilitarian justification for the sovereign right to expropriate real property (also known as *eminent domain* or *compulsory purchase*) in common law jurisdictions.

policy maker on a daily basis. If the legislatures of most developed countries sought merely the statistical safety (i.e. prevention of injury or death) of their citizenry, then the most appropriate answer to questions about terrorism and other foreign or transnational threats could easily be: "wear a seatbelt."[18] But the notion of security goes far beyond mere statistics, and how one dies does seem to matter for the policy makers in many countries. That is why most people can offer a much better approximation of the number of terrorist deaths in their country each year than the number of deaths attributable to tobacco use, even though the latter is likely several orders of magnitude greater.[19]

The second philosophical challenge is quantifying human life. In order to determine the appropriate level of state funding for certain safeguards, as well as the tolerable imposition of additional transaction costs on an economy, government practitioners must balance safety against other objectives. Among the possible ways that one could approximate the value accorded to human life in a society are: (a) by examining the financial awards in tort cases for wrongful death or product liability claims, or (b) by comparing the amount of public money spent on traffic safety with the number of annual highway deaths.[20] One could even perform a similar analysis of the number of victims in terrorist attacks versus official expenditures directed at eliminating such threats. The purpose herein is not to determine the absolute value of human life in any particular society, but rather to illustrate the complex considerations that are implicit in even the most seemingly mundane policy decisions. We must, however, also note two probable inconsistencies: (i) the valuations obtained

18 According to the World Health Organization (WHO), road traffic accidents were the only non-disease related cause of death to rank among the top twelve causes in 2002, accounting for over two percent of all global mortality. See WHO, *World report on road traffic injury prevention*, edited by Margie Peden et al. (Geneva, 2004), 33–34, 176, Table A.3 (available online at: http://whqlibdoc.who.int/publications/2004/9241562609.pdf). Similarly, another WHO report from 2007 showed road traffic injuries to be a leading cause of death among young people under the age of 25; in contrast, war casualties, terrorist attacks, and other traditional national security concerns did not rank among the top ten causes of mortality for youths. See WHO, *Youth and Road Safety*, edited by Tami Toroyan and Margie Peden (Geneva, 2007), 3, Table 1 (available online at: http://whqlibdoc.who.int/publications/2007/9241595116_eng.pdf).

19 See generally George Thomson and Nick Wilson, "Policy lessons from comparing mortality from two global forces: international terrorism and tobacco," *Globalization and Health* 1, no. 18 (15 December 2005), (published online at: http://www.globalizationandhealth.com/content/1/1/18). According to that study, the annualized ratio of tobacco-related deaths to international terrorism-related deaths for the period 1994–2003 in the US was 1,731 to 1, and in the United Kingdom (UK) it was 35,625 to 1. The ratios for France, Greece, Russia, and other European countries were also five orders of magnitude in difference. See Thomson and Wilson, 2, Table 1.

20 For a more extensive discussion of such valuations by government agencies in the US, see David A. Fahrenthold, "Cosmic Markdown: EPA Says Life Is Worth Less," *Washington Post*, July 19, 2008. Fahrenthold explains that the US Environmental Protection Agency (EPA) lowered its official estimation from $ 8.04 million to $ 7.22 million in 2008. In comparison, Fahrenthold states that the US Department of Transportation's 2008 value was $ 5.8 million.

by different measures within a society will not necessarily be equivalent, and (ii) the quantified value of life within a society may bear little or no relation to the value that that same society places on human life in other societies. That second discrepancy is the result of parochialism that will be discussed further under the rubric of national interest.[21]

How governments allocate the finite resources at their disposal reflects their assessments of security threats. For example, the decision to focus countless professional hours and resources on combating terrorism or trying to prevent the proliferation of weapons of mass destruction is illustrative of either (a) the deontological nature of foreign policy considerations for many countries, or (b) risk assessments that dramatically diverge from existing actuarial data.[22] Maintaining international security is viewed as something that must be done by those public officials entrusted with preserving our safety, even if it is not in our greatest microeconomic advantage. As will also be discussed below, none of these considerations occurs in a vacuum either; instead, they are part of the organic body of politics that spans many interconnected – as well as unrelated – topics.

The benefit of explicitly acknowledging this mathematical irrationality is to highlight the imprecise and subjective nature of policy calculations. Significant probability estimates are involved, in addition to emotional and political factors (such as national pride, preferences for specific forms of government, etc.). If one looks beyond those non-quantitative factors, then the core metrics that drive counter-terrorism and counter-proliferation efforts are the expected probability and number of future casualties that would ensue if such threats came to fruition, contrasted with the perceived likelihood of successfully averting such events through government action. Whether or not they realize it, any policy makers and legal practitioners engaged in such transnational security efforts have either made (perhaps subconsciously) a philosophical decision that the cause of death is supremely relevant to human safety or else concluded a risk analysis that runs contrary to most actuarial tables. To argue on purely rational grounds, one would have to presume that al-Qaeda is either capable of precipitating a large-scale war or else causing terrorist casualties several orders of magnitude greater than witnessed thus far in order to mathematically warrant the level of prophylactic counter-terrorism expenditures that we see today. By way of comparison, avoidance of another even more costly world

21 In economics terminology, that inconsistency represents the difference between *statistical* and *identified* lives. The cost-benefit calculations that people apply vary greatly between situations that involve numerical representations of hypothetical or unknown human lives versus situations that involve specific, known persons – especially if those persons are related to or confer other utility on the evaluator. See e.g. James K. Hammitt and Nicholas Treich, "Statistical vs. identified lives in benefit-cost analysis," *Journal of Risk and Uncertainty* 35, no. 1 (August 2007): 45–66.

22 If politicians were not partial to how people died, they would likely apply public resources pursuant to the same statistical calculations that insurance professionals use. For a broader discussion of risk perception and risk-management policy, see Paul Slovic, "Perception of Risk," *Science* 236, no. 4799 (17 April 1987): 280–285; and George M. Gray and David P. Ropeik, "Dealing With The Dangers Of Fear: The Role of Risk Communication," *Health Affairs* 21, no. 6 (November/December 2002): 106–116.

war is presumably what American theorists such as George Kennan felt they were accomplishing during the Cold War and its repeated conflagrations in Korea, Vietnam, Nicaragua, and elsewhere.[23]

The preceding discussion about threat reduction is only further confounded by the fact that human beings are notoriously bad at calculating probabilities.[24] Unfortunately, national and international security decision making hinges largely on risk assessments that must translate uncertainty into action. In many instances, the information available to make those determinations is not only *incomplete* but also *imperfect*.[25] Inherent in any security strategy is also an assumption about what constitutes the policy goal: it could be to (i) minimize threats to safety, (ii) maximize welfare, (iii) minimize the maximum harm among the possible outcomes, (iv) maximize the minimum welfare among the possible outcomes, etc.[26] Each competing approach relies on different assumptions and interpretations of what security requires, yet the implications of those different cognitive foundations are rarely considered in foreign policy circles. For example, most counter-proliferation decisions reflect a concerted *minimax* logic that seeks to prevent low probability but high impact events (i.e. worst case scenarios).

So, one critical distinction between practitioners and theorists in international law is the cliché of "where you sit determines where you stand." Unshared professional

---

23 For a theoretical explanation of that rationale, see generally George F. Kennan, *American Diplomacy*, Expanded ed. (Chicago: The University of Chicago Press, 1984). One could also envision counterfactual scenarios that not only avoided the human loss of those proxy conflicts but also averted the even greater costs of a direct war between the US and the Soviet Union.

24 That phenomenon has been well documented by psychologists and economists, such as Daniel Kahneman, Amos Tversky, Richard Thaler, and Peter Bernstein. "The most notable aspect of the estimates is that [people] significantly underestimated the probabilities for natural causes [of death] and vastly overestimated the probabilities for unnatural causes. This indicates that probably people give more attention to worrying about the unnatural dangers and not enough to the natural dangers." Thayer Watkins, "Kahneman and Tversky's Prospect Theory," San José State University (posted online at: http://www.sjsu.edu/faculty/watkins/prospect.htm). The behavioral economics research of Kahneman and Tversky goes well beyond just comparing subjective probability assessments to objective statistics, for it analyzes the apparently inconsistent risk-averse and risk-seeking strategies of individuals based on the context of their personal situations at the time a given decision is to be made.

25 In game theory parlance, players with *incomplete information* lack knowledge about the structure or context of the environment within which they are competing (e.g. the objective probabilities of natural events). Players with *imperfect information*, on the other hand, lack knowledge about the strategic actions of other players at one or more decision nodes. For more technical definitions of these terms, see Ken Binmore, *Fun and Games: A Text on Game Theory* (Lexington, Massachusetts: D.C. Heath and Company, 1992), 100–101, 501–502; and Eric Rasmusen, *Games and Information: An Introduction to Game Theory* (Cambridge, Massachusetts: Basil Blackwell, 1989), 51–54.

26 Pursuing efforts to minimize the maximum potential harm from any number of uncertain outcomes is referred to as adopting a *minimax* strategy. Conversely, pursuing efforts to maximize the minimum potential gain from any number of uncertain outcomes is referred to as adopting a *maximin* strategy. For additional explanations of these concepts, see Binmore, supra note 25 at 219–220; and Rasmusen, supra note 25 at 103–104.

responsibilities could actually provide the cognitive basis for differing probability estimates and decision strategies. To wit, if it is not substantive disagreement about legal norms – but rather the human psychology of risk analysis – that accounts for divergent views, then how one evaluates security situations will be highly dependent on one's own professional function. When individuals are charged with preventing terrorist attacks or foreign invasions, they attach higher probabilities to undesirable situations, for they would rather be overly safe than sorry. The mantra "not on my watch" echoes repeatedly through the corridors of power in many nations, even though such risk-aversion leads to inefficient policy calculations.

Other commentators on matters of law and security have the benefit of not being held responsible for what actually does happen. While journalists strive to accurately report on events, they will rarely if ever be criticized for what does transpire in the political or military spheres. Academics can take solace in an even more removed position that permits them the opportunity to forward non-refutable or counterfactual claims on a theoretical basis.[27] It is much easier to contemplate a wider array of options when one does not have immediate concern about them being tried and disproven in practice. That is especially true if one's legal analysis can be temporally deferred from the uncertainties and pressures of the moment. Consider, for example, a policy option which purportedly had a 33 percent chance of significantly increasing general welfare but simultaneously a 25 percent chance of decreasing public safety … and a decision had to be made before further studies could be conducted. One could speculate that a philosopher might seek to realize the former gain, but that a homeland security advisor would be more concerned about the latter risk. Those without public responsibility can be more innovative and risk seeking, whereas practitioners must try to focus on the expected utilities of various outcomes, which they (unfortunately) often miscalculate.[28]

When one extrapolates that predisposition to multiple government practitioners in different organizations or countries, then the emerging problem is only exacerbated. Edwin Jaynes studied how such loss functions operate in human society.[29] In his commentary on cognitive efforts to maximize expected utility and minimize expected loss, he explains that even where different individuals might agree on the likelihood of specific factual outcomes, it is their divergent analyses of potential implications which produce opposing opinions. "In fact, prior probabilities

27 The philosopher Karl Popper considered *falsifiability* to be a key feature of scientific reasoning. "According to Popper, the mark of a scientific theory is whether it makes predictions which could in principle serve to falsify it" through physical experiments or empirical observations. Philip Stokes, *Philosophy: The Great Thinkers*, (London: Arcturus Publishing, 2007), 211.

28 *Expected utility* refers to the probability of an outcome's likelihood multiplied by its resulting benefit (or cost) to the decision maker.

29 A *loss function* is akin to an expected utility equation, but for minimizing outcomes of negative value. See generally, Edwin T. Jaynes, *Probability Theory: The Logic of Science*, Fragmentary ed. (March 1996), 1303 (incomplete manuscript published posthumously online at: http://www-biba.inrialpes.fr/Jaynes/prob.html).

are usually far more 'objective' than loss functions, both in the mathematical theory and in everyday decision problems of 'real life'."[30] Jaynes continues:

> We note the sharp contrast between the roles of prior probabilities and loss functions in human relations. People with similar prior probabilities get along well together, because they have about the same general view of the world and philosophy of life. People with radically different prior probabilities cannot get along – this has been the root cause of all the religious wars and most of the political repressions throughout history.
>
> Loss functions operate in just the opposite way. People with similar loss functions are after the same thing, and are in contention with each other. People with different loss functions get along well because each is willing to give something that the other wants. Amicable trade or business transactions, advantageous to all, is possible only between parties with different loss functions.[31]

That defining feature of human sociology is ominous for foreign relations and international law; not only are government practitioners going to differ from their academic counterparts regarding prior probabilities (based on disparate threat perceptions due to their professional duties), but those same practitioners will also have nearly identical loss functions to their foreign counterparts in other governments. Such a realization does much to explain both the perceived disconnect between national security professionals and the rest of society as well as their hawkishness towards other sovereign competitors in the same field. Hence, it becomes clear that several adverse results stem directly from the second hypothesis of this paper, namely that: *government practitioners are primarily risk averse.*

IV. Institutional Incentives

The same type of risk aversion can be observed on systemic levels within bureaucratic organizations. Government workers, be they international lawyers or otherwise, have their own personal and professional ambitions. Success in government, which is usually associated with achieving high office and public recognition in lieu of monetary compensation, is most often predicated on avoiding pitfalls and diligently implementing the policies of one's superiors. Those factors are most clearly institutionalized in the military; however, they permeate all of the public sector. Personal success in the civil service can often be achieved through perpetuating inertia and obeying hierarchy. Conversely, the single worst thing to do in government is to be innovative and unsuccessful – either on the merits or due to the reigning politics of the day.

By comparison, academia rewards innovative thinkers who resist intellectual inertia and transcend established hierarchies. Acclaim as a professor frequently requires risk-seeking behavior to promote novel ideas. Accurate predictions can lead to success, but ample opportunities also exist to downplay inaccuracies through

30 Jaynes, supra note 29 at 1319.

31 Ibid at 1320.

nuanced discourse, revision, and near certainty that an adequately controlled experiment will never be performed on anyone's theories in the social sciences. Academics are subjected to rigorous peer review but not always public scrutiny. Moreover, a common interest in the pursuit of continued intellectual discourse usually precludes academia from the partisan vitriol that is so commonplace in politics nowadays.

Many NGOs have also been specifically organized to pursue concerns that are not being adequately addressed by IOs or governments.[32] Those efforts to improve human welfare pick up where the basic government service of providing physical security leaves off. The legacy of activists is measured in lives saved and quantifiable improvements in the international standard of living (i.e. positive results). The legacy of governmental security professionals is measured in lives lost (i.e. negative results), with the expectation being that any value other than zero reflects failure. Those incentives and measures of responsibility clearly contribute to the sense of risk aversion among practitioners.

Just as previous sections of this paper have drawn upon scholarship from the fields of philosophy, microeconomics, and human psychology to explain the cognitive behaviors of individuals, political science and international relations theory will be relied upon to explore their behavior within government organizations and on behalf of nation states, respectively. In his book entitled *Essence of Decision: Explaining the Cuban Missile Crisis*, Graham Allison described three different models for national decision making.[33] His second model discussed organizational processes, complete with their parochial priorities and uncertainty avoidance.[34] The former tends to produce suboptimal outcomes at the systemic level (if all organizations within a domestic or international system operate in a similar fashion), while the latter lends support to this paper's conjecture that policy makers are risk averse – whether taken as individuals or aggregated within government departments and agencies. Allison's third model concerns governmental politics. It is there that he addressed the ubiquitous conflict between strategic decision making and extraneous objectives:

> In contrast with Model I, the Governmental (or Bureaucratic) Politics Model sees no unitary actor but rather many actors as players – players who focus not on a single strategic issue but on many diverse intra-national problems as well; players who act in terms of no consistent set of strategic objectives but rather according

32 See generally Claude Bruderlein, "People's security as a new measure of global stability," *International Review of the Red Cross* 83, no. 842 (June 2001): 353–366.

33 Graham T. Allison, *Essence of Decision: Explaining the Cuban Missile Crisis* (Boston: Little, Brown, 1971). The three models respectively dealt with rational actors, organizational processes, and governmental politics.

34 "Primary responsibility for a narrow set of problems encourages organizational parochialism .... Promotion to higher rungs is dependent on years of demonstrated, distinguished devotion to a service's mission." Ibid. at 81. "Organizations do not attempt to estimate the probability distribution of future occurrences. Rather, organizations avoid uncertainty." Ibid. at 84.

> to various conceptions of national, organizational, and personal goals; players who make government decisions not by a single, rational choice but by the pulling and hauling that is politics.[35]

Allison's observations not only appear valid from empirical analysis, but his core criticism of decision making by political organs is supported by deductive logic. Kenneth Arrow has proven a key paradox of voting systems, namely that they cannot simultaneously satisfy a set of reasonable conditions of fairness and logic.[36] One of those conditions is that irrelevant alternatives (i.e. other possibilities not germane to a specific issue at hand) should not impact the decision making process or its outcome.[37] Nothing could be less true in the world of politics. Arrow's Theorem, as it is now called, provides the theory and analytic rigor to help explain why the competing priorities of organizations undermine strategic decision making. Moreover, even if they harbor the best of intentions, politicians are in fact forced to consider irrelevant alternatives when apportioning a centralized budget or voting on bills with unrelated amendments attached (as is possible in the US Congress).

Political incentives and the constant diatribes generated by adversarial systems of government, such as in the US or the UK, seem to mandate continued responsiveness to both the loyal opposition and the media.[38] In order to secure future electoral victories in a media culture, most practitioners feel obliged to take some action in response to every adverse situation. It is unsurprising then that the risk aversion of the public sector is complemented by a fear of inaction; incumbents feel a need to show that they are always doing something – even if it is ill-formed – lest they be accused of not defending the country.[39] This is further compounded by the contracted time horizon of most politicians. Western societies are impatient and seek immediate results, even in areas of foreign policy that do not lend themselves to short-term solutions. With elections for the chief executive occurring every four or six years, and legislative elections even more regularly, it may be difficult for many nations to pursue the most strategically beneficial course of action in foreign affairs. This is another contributing influence to the preoccupation with safety over welfare. Failures to protect are immediately registered in voters' minds, while improvements in welfare very often inure to the benefit of one's successor – even if he or she is from an opposing political party.

Idealized solutions become another casualty of that race against time for political legacy. Most bureaucrats have heard the maxim "the perfect is the enemy of the good."

35 Allison, supra note 33 at 144.

36 For a complete discussion of Arrow's mutually incompatible criteria, see William H. Riker, *Liberalism Against Populism: A Confrontation Between the Theory of Democracy and the Theory of Social Choice* (Prospect Heights, Illinois: Waveland Press, 1982), 116–119.

37 See Ibid. at 129–130.

38 The negative implications of such a media-centric political culture are described well in Neil Postman, *Amusing Ourselves to Death: Public Discourse in the Age of Show Business* (New York: Penguin Books, 1986).

39 Few Americans likely weighed the expected net casualties of a war in Afghanistan versus that from continuing terrorism by al-Qaeda. Emotional and nationalistic tendencies also play a large role in policy formulation.

In a culture of praxis and risk aversion, incremental stopgap solutions are preferred to wholesale, strategic visions.[40] That is partially due to the allocation of finite resources. Ideal solutions are beyond the realm of possibility for most governments which view any allocation of resources in one area as a zero-sum game with the resources to be applied in other (related or unrelated) areas. Whether in the application of political, monetary, or human capital, security decisions must take competing priorities into account.

Although academics regularly expand the realm of discourse to take account of many more contextual issues than practitioners, they rarely invoke completely unrelated decisions. Politicians, especially legislators, are notorious for horse trading, proposing pork barrel amendments, and linking multiple domestic and foreign policy issues that have no immediate bearing on each other. When one is forced to link non-security related issues with security decisions, the policy outcome can never be as pure or effective as one might desire. The third, and perhaps most damning, hypothesis of this paper is that: *modern political systems encourage, if not require, government practitioners to consider unrelated factors.*

V. National Interest

Having analyzed the influences and predispositions that dictate how statesmen consider security issues, it is now appropriate to acknowledge that the actions and declarations of sovereign states – which are intended to safeguard their own political and economic interests – are among the principal sources of customary international law.[41] Furthermore, both the Statute of the International Court of Justice and the Vienna Convention on the Law of Treaties directly incorporate state practice into their interpretive mechanisms.[42] The role of state practice as a necessary condition for establishing viable international law is illustrated by the general disregard for Articles 43 through 47 of the UN Charter, which were originally intended to create a Military Committee and a force analogous to a standing army at the UN Security Council's disposal. Those treaty provisions have been largely ignored by politicians and, in turn, legally reinterpreted to be non-binding articles. International law ultimately derives its legitimacy and force from sovereign states and relies on them for its effective implementation.

Thus, state practice plays a dual role in the legal realm because policy decisions are not only often predicated on legal rules, but those actions themselves also serve

40 It is true that fundamental changes are sometimes realized, but they are the exception rather than the rule. In the US, the Goldwater-Nichols Act, which reorganized the military forces into holistic combatant commands, represents one of those rare landmark changes. See *Goldwater-Nichols Department of Defense Reorganization Act of 1986*, Public Law 443, 99th Congress (1 October 1986).

41 See Cassese, supra note 9 at 156–157.

42 Article 38 of the Statute of the International Court of Justice lists "international custom, as evidence of a general practice accepted as law" as an interpretive source (26 June 1945). Article 31 of the Vienna Convention on the Law of Treaties stipulates that "any subsequent practice in the application of the treaty which establishes the agreement of the parties" must be considered in its application (23 May 1969).

to help formulate customary international law. According to the international jurist Rosalyn Higgins, "The preferable emphasis is on international law as a continuing process, a flow of legal decision-making."[43] Her dynamic view of international law places it within the larger context of international politics and provides ample opportunity for strategic action. Juxtaposed with Kennan's view that "the legalist approach to international affairs ignores in general the international significance of political problems and the deeper sources of international instability," one can see the potential disconnect between practitioners and other legal commentators.[44] For, if the law itself can be influenced by states, then it can also be manipulated for parochial objectives.

From a legal perspective, the security environment is quite ambiguous: not only are states regularly choosing to either honor or breach international law for strategic purposes, but such adherence or lack thereof, actually serves to alter those same legal norms. In this way, strategy assumes a multi-layered characteristic, and today's strategist becomes as much a legal innovator as a political or military tactician.[45] While many jurists and legal theorists view the strictures of public international law as inviolable, many practitioners view them as malleable. Cassese has noted that if a new practice "does not encounter strong and consistent opposition from other states but is increasingly accepted, or acquiesced in, a customary rule gradually crystallizes."[46] Some policy makers view the dynamic nature of law as an invitation to push new boundaries, and others simply feel that certain security interests cannot defer to international legal rules.[47] Of course, even their decision of whether or not to violate accepted international norms is likely made pursuant to skewed probability calculations and atypical loss functions.

One could describe international law as a collective, organic project of the world community. By championing the rights of individuals and non-self-governing communities, modern legal theorists espouse new legal principles to the equal detriment of all sovereign nations. Unfortunately, the same lack of discrimination is not observed among nation states in the legal and security arenas. In practice, national security is a parochial pursuit aimed at garnering strategic advantage and disproportionate spheres of influence. Decision makers may consider the unrelated policy

---

43 Rosalyn Higgins, "Intervention and International Law," in *Intervention in World Politics*, ed. Hedley Bull (New York: Clarendon Press, 1984), 29.

44 Kennan, supra note 23 at 99.

45 See generally Kennedy, supra note 14 at 36–39, 125. Kennedy states: "As humanitarian and military professionals work with the law of armed conflict, they change it." Kennedy at 37.

46 Cassese, supra note 9 at 157. Consider, for example, that Israel's 1981 military attack on an Iraqi nuclear reactor and its more recent destruction of a nuclear facility in Syria in 2006 both went unpunished by the UN Security Council. Even though the proposed right of anticipatory self-defense is not officially recognized under current international law, those events have certainly set a political – and possibly legal – precedent in international relations.

47 The realist school would argue that "there follows 'that iron law of international politics, that legal obligations must yield to the national interest.'" Louis Henkin, *How Nations Behave: Law and Foreign Policy* (New York: Frederick A. Praeger, 1968), 262–263 (quoting Hans J. Morgenthau).

implications of a proposed action – such as constructing impassable fortifications along the border of the occupied territories of Palestine or the southern border of the US – but they do so from a nationalist rather than cosmopolitan perspective. Policy debates in the US Congress about such a barrier might consider domestic civil liberties, the economic ramifications for specific industries, etc., but they are unlikely to concern themselves with the international human rights of Mexican citizens who reside – legally or illegally – on either side of the border.

The pursuit of national interest can also be analyzed from a microeconomics approach, where a distinction is made between stable equilibria, efficient outcomes, and socially optimal outcomes.[48] The first refers to situations where each party has taken its most individually advantageous action in light of others' actions; the second describes scenarios where no party can improve its situation without adversely affecting another party (e.g. when all of the benefits have been fully allocated in a zero-sum game); and the last concerns maximizing the total benefit to all parties involved (usually through redistributive mechanisms that effectively transfer value between participants). As alluded to in the preceding discussion regarding loss functions, national security often takes the form of a zero-sum game, with practitioners competing to promote their national interest at the expense of others' and regularly arriving at inefficient stalemates (i.e. equilibria). Impartial academics, on the other hand, can more easily seek cooperative solutions that protect mutual interests through more efficient and, sometimes, systemically optimal solutions.

The collective inefficiency of national security policies stems, of course, from state practices that are planned and executed with only the benefit of specific countries in mind. Few, if any, public officials are elected by their constituencies to promote the general welfare of the world community, and non-democratic regimes offer even less hope of fulfilling such global objectives.[49] One could argue, however, that the establishment of systemically optimal rules and procedures is the appropriate pursuit of public international law. Academics, journalists, and the like are permitted to evaluate security issues from a universal or disinterested perspective. In essence, they are free to operate from behind a Rawlsian veil of ignorance and determine the most desirable paradigm for international law itself. Meanwhile, government practitioners are literally paid to seek the greatest economic, political, or military advantage for their respective countries.[50] This last distinction between government practition-

48 A *Nash equilibrium* is reached if each player's strategy maximizes his payoff given the other players' strategies. See e.g. David Laidler and Saul Estrin, *Introduction to Microeconomics*, 3rd ed. (Hemel Hempstead, Hertfordshire: Philip Allan, 1989), 286. A *Pareto efficient* outcome exists when the resources available have been allocated in such a way that no party can increase its welfare without another party's welfare being reduced; however, such efficiency does not logically imply that the resources have been distributed in a fair fashion, or that the system in question has yielded the maximum aggregate welfare possible. Laidler and Estrin at 408–410, 423–425.

49 Even those countries which purport to serve the general welfare are usually promoting their own religious, philosophical, or political conceptions of what constitutes the greatest good for mankind.

50 One practical result of such professional mandates is the unequal valuation of human life and its impact on military rules of engagement. Parties to an armed conflict almost always

ers and other lawyers leads to the fourth and final hypothesis of this paper, namely that: *government practitioners pursue national interests in lieu of systemic equality.*

VI. Pragmatic Law

In today's security environment, practitioners regularly produce systemically undesirable decisions that are the product of inherently biased risk assessments and parochial interests. Accordingly, an international legal framework that is designed to assume otherwise is doomed to either failure or marginalization. In order to be more effective, public international law must conscript and constrain state actors better, since any system or process derives both its validity and utility from its own efficacy.[51] In the case of international law, however, that validation is dependent on external and often competing interests; absent an effort to reconcile state practice with postulated norms, academic theorists and government practitioners will continue to operate independently and exert inconsistent influences on the law. By explaining the underlying cognitive drivers that influence practitioners, this paper hopes to identify how progress could be made towards developing a more coherent legal paradigm.

Perhaps, the current schizophrenia in international law can be partially attributed to another cliché: "If you are not part of the solution, then you are part of the problem." Idealized versions of international law which mandate compliance without effective enforcement mechanisms, or worse yet, academic treatments of the subject which ignore the reality of widespread non-compliance, do a disservice to the collective project.

> All law, of course, is political: nations make law (rather than leave a matter unregulated) from a political judgment that it will be in their respective or common interests. How existing law would be interpreted, whether it should be violated, what kind or degree of violation should be perpetrated, are also political decisions subject to the constraints of law and the costs of violation in international society.[52]

Only by understanding the proclivities of political and military leaders, and adapting incentive structures to guide them, will the theory and practice of international law be unified in the security arena.

---

demonstrate higher concern for the safety and welfare of their own nationals than those of the enemy, whether combatants or civilians. Such trade-offs occur implicitly in decisions about the proportionality and discriminate nature of military attacks (e.g., in determining the required altitude from which pilots should conduct bombing sorties in order to limit collateral damage in the face of enemy anti-aircraft fire).

51 According to the pragmatic philosopher William James, "The truth of an idea is not a stagnant property inherent in it. Truth *happens* to an idea. It *becomes* true, is *made* true by events. Its verity is in fact an event, a process: the process namely of its verifying itself, its veri-*fication*. Its validity is the process of its valid-*ation*." William James, *Pragmatism*, Dover Thrift ed. (New York: Dover Publications, 1995), 77–78.

52 Louis Henkin, comment in *The Cuban Missile Crisis: International Crisis and the Role of Law*, by Abram Chayes (New York: Oxford University Press, 1974), 149–150.

Many of the norms of international humanitarian law (IHL) – such as proportionality and necessity – are open to subjectivity.[53] If one knows that different lawyers will apply disparate value structures and risk assessments, then there can be no single, binding interpretation. It is understandable that issues of fact may have to be determined before judgment can be passed on specific actions, or that the subjective *mens rea* of individuals may have to be proven, but there appears to be no persuasive argument in favor of establishing a legal regime where the norms themselves are continuously dependent on the practices of interested parties. For then, by definition, the law no longer serves as an external constraint.

Security is about eliminating uncertainty, doubt, and fear. The private sector either hedges against risk (e.g. through insurance contracts, offsetting investments, etc.), or strives to identify and quantify its impact; the public sector seeks to overcompensate in the face of uncertainty to prevent all adverse possibilities instead of just significant probabilities; and academia tends to either overstate or ignore the attainability of theoretical outcomes that it favors. Pragmatic laws would instead acknowledge the pervasive uncertainty and channel national interests into a viable system that was self-enforcing. As long as the current paradigm permits intransigence without repercussion, then government practitioners will avail themselves of its benefits.

William James has claimed, "*True ideas are those that we can assimilate, validate, corroborate and verify. False ideas are those that we cannot.*"[54] Unfortunately, if he is correct, then the proverbial fly on the wall would conclude that, when it comes to security matters, many of the provisions of international law as stated by academics and jurists are simply false from the practitioners' perspective. They cannot be assimilated with or verified by the actual behavior of sovereign actors within the international system. From a pragmatic viewpoint, unenforceable and oft disobeyed rules probably do more to undermine than advance the cosmopolitan project of international law.

A more pragmatic approach to international law can be illustrated in relation to two contemporary dilemmas in the field of security. First, today there exists no binding, international legal definition of *terrorism*. Despite sixteen international conventions against specific terrorism-related activities, multiple regional conventions, and increasingly common domestic legislation in many UN member states, it has not been possible to achieve international consensus on a legal definition.[55] Drafting of the Comprehensive Convention on International Terrorism has been stalled in the UN General Assembly's Sixth Committee for several years now due to disagree-

---

53 "Indeed, strange as it may seem, there is simply more than one law of armed conflict, as enforced by different jurisdictions and as viewed by different participants." Kennedy, supra note 14 at 38.

54 James, supra note 51 at 77.

55 See generally, the UN Security Council's Counter-Terrorism Committee website and related links at: http://www.un.org/sc/ctc/laws.html. For examples of regional anti-terrorism conventions, see the UN Treaty Collection website and related links at: http://untreaty.un.org/English/Terrorism.asp.

ment over two main points: (a) whether certain actions taken by the military forces of nation states should be subject to such a definition and its attendant prohibitions or punishments; and (b) whether certain motivations (such as the desire to achieve self-determination or liberation from an occupying power) could ever justify actions that would otherwise constitute terrorism.[56] Both of those impasses are rooted in the strongly held political objectives of competing nation states, and neither side is willing to compromise at this juncture.[57]

Space does not permit this paper to explore all of the intricacies of the various legal and diplomatic arguments that have been forwarded to date, but suffice it to say that no treaty solution is imminent. That said, the fact that a legal impasse exists due to political disagreements between sovereign states at least partially supports the foregoing discussion. An observer might turn to analyzing the underlying political objectives rather than the legal arguments themselves; for, most if not all of the actions considered to be terrorist in nature would also constitute war crimes under existing IHL if they were committed by combatants.[58] A disinterested, pragmatic lawyer would suggest that the issue here rests less on the semantic definition of terrorism than on its implications for ongoing political conflicts. He or she would instead seek a legal resolution that would provide the desired consequences for all parties. To debate the status of international legal rules purely in the abstract is only productive to a certain point.

Regarding the specifically contested topic of whether or not an international definition of terrorism would apply to sovereign military forces, for example, it might be more constructive to ensure that the existing penalties for war crimes committed by such forces under IHL were punished with similar attentiveness and severity as corresponding acts of terrorism by non-combatants. It should not matter what

---

56 See UN General Assembly, 62nd Session, Working Group of the Sixth Committee on Measures to Eliminate International Terrorism, "Oral report of the Chairman of the Working Group," prepared by Rohan Perera (26 October 2007); and UN General Assembly, 62nd Session, Working Group of the Sixth Committee on Measures to Eliminate International Terrorism, "Statement by Ms. Maria Telalian (Greece) on the bilateral contacts concerning outstanding issues relating to the draft comprehensive convention on international terrorism," delivered by Maria Telalian (18 October 2007).

57 For example, the US has long been opposed to exposing its military forces to the mandatory jurisdiction of an international criminal tribunal. Conversely, some members of the Organization for the Islamic Conference seek to retain the alleged right of individuals to resist unlawful occupation through violent measures aimed at what are commonly held to be civilian targets.

58 Both treaty law and customary IHL already prohibit (i) all measures of intimidation and terrorism (including the taking of hostages) against non combatant, civilian populations; (ii) the intentional or indiscriminate targeting of civilians; and (iii) the feigning of non-combatant civilian status by combatants (i.e. perfidy) by the armed forces of countries party to an international armed conflict. See Articles 3, 33, and 34 of the Geneva Convention Relative to the Protection of Civilian Persons in Time of War (12 August 1949); and Articles 37, 51, and 57 of the Protocol Additional to the Geneva Conventions of 12 August 1949, and Relating to the Protection of Victims of International Armed Conflicts (8 June 1977).

epithet we assign to the willful targeting and execution of a civilian, provided that anyone who commits such an act can be effectively prosecuted, and that all such perpetrators receive similar sentences.[59]

A second area of current concern is the legality and use of new space technologies. As with so many other areas of international law, the definitional question of what constitutes a *space weapon* must be closely considered. But for our purposes here, let us stipulate that the term covers any entity or activity that can damage, disrupt, or disable another country's assets beyond the Earth's mesosphere.[60] As competition for terrestrial resources increases and scientific research identifies new uses (both civilian and military) for space-based platforms, the so-called last frontier is becoming the focus of new political debates.[61] Security concerns about a multi-polar world with increasing national interests to exploit the heavens are at strategic odds with the previously agreed legal status of outer space as a peaceful commons for all mankind.[62]

Pragmatic law would begin by ascertaining the functional utility of space in the modern era and then tailoring itself to confront the likely practices of sovereign states, rather than presuming a legal conclusion based on analogies to the high seas or territorial airspace. How government practitioners decide to use and compete for space resources will have a profound impact on the future, and as one saw with the remote sensing debates of the 20th Century, internationally proscribed laws may defer to state practice where national security is involved. By identifying where the stakes are highest and which common fears prevail among nations – as with the potential vulnerability of communications and geo-location satellites that increasingly form the backbone of both civil society and military infrastructure – lawyers could propose a normative regime that recognizes strategic conflict but still furthers moderation in space. The Geneva Conventions remain the best example of such a pragmatic yet virtuous endeavor to date. However, just as government practitioners are reluctant to cede national prerogative, legal theorists will likely resist pragmatic deference to such practitioners' instincts. Unfortunately, it is the credibility of international law – and not the will of states – that usually suffers when mutual accords cannot be reached.

---

59 This rationale is consistent with several proposed definitions of *terrorism* that are indifferent as to the identity or status of the perpetrator. One can argue that the necessary (and sufficient) components of the developing norm against terrorism are: (1) a criminal act, (2) non-combatant targets, (3) the reasonable likelihood of serious physical injury to persons or significant damage to property, and (4) a secondary intent of compelling action by another entity (i.e. the political analogue of extortion).

60 The *Kármán Line* at an altitude of 100 kilometers is widely used as the dividing line between the Earth's atmosphere and outer space.

61 See e.g. Ashley J. Tellis, "China's Military Space Strategy," *Survival* 49, no. 3 (Autumn 2007): 41–72; and the several responses to that article published in the ensuing forum entitled "China's Military Space Strategy: An Exchange," *Survival* 50, no. 1 (February – March 2008): 157–198.

62 See Treaty on Principles Governing the Activities of States in the Exploration and Use of Outer Space, including the Moon and Other Celestial Bodies (10 October 1967).

VII. Conclusion

Despite cross-fertilization between the multiple professional disciplines involved with international law and security, one continues to see a dramatic gap between the theory and the practice. It seems curious that while legal theorists and practitioners are trained in the same law schools, they produce such different analyses of the same legal issues. This paper does not accept that personal opinion alone can account for such inconsistency; rather, it has been posited here that several epistemological and institutional factors drive the professional judgments of government and military practitioners. Those factors include (i) a pre-occupation with threat reduction (i.e. a focus on safety vice welfare), (ii) widespread risk aversion, (iii) the unavoidable consideration of unrelated political priorities, and (iv) an indifference to systemically optimal outcomes (i.e. the pursuit of exclusive, national interests). All of those characteristics of the government practitioner can be directly traced to the incentive and reward structures of public office, the civil service, or the military profession. If the four hypotheses offered in this paper are valid, then the practitioners' mindset itself is likely to govern his or her legal analysis on security issues. Pragmatism urges that these peculiarities be factored into the creation of rules that states are then hoped to obey in practice.

The essence of the government practitioners' predicament comprises significant uncertainty, compressed time horizons for decision making, and distinctive responsibility for actions or omissions. No other subset of legal commentators faces those same three constraints simultaneously – not judges, law professors, NGO workers, or journalists – and the resultant predisposition for biased risk assessments has systemic consequences. In light of those cognitive influences on practitioners, the legal intelligentsia would be well served to alter its idealized approach to international law in order to co-opt more sovereign support. By recognizing and even leveraging the known attributes of government representatives, the world community could garner additional respect for an improved legal regime. As long as international security depends on the might of sovereign nations to enforce collective rules, those enforcers will remain both the *de facto* legislators and final arbiters of justice.

List of Contributors

Cecilia M. Bailliet is Professor of Law and Director of the Masters Program in Public International Law at the University of Oslo, Norway. Her teaching, research, and publications combine cross-field perspectives, including International Public Law, Human Rights, Humanitarian Law, and Refugee Law. She serves as consultant to international and national actors engaged within the field of Refugee Law.

Lene Bomann-Larsen is Post-doctoral Fellow at the Department of Philosophy, Classics, History of Art and Ideas, University of Oslo, Norway. She is affiliated with the Ethics Programme and the Centre for the Study of Mind in Nature. Her publications span ethical dilemmas arising within the context of war to corporate social responsibility. Her current research concentrates on responsibility attribution and the issue of revisionism within legal and political philosophy.

Naomi Cahn is the John Theodore Fey Research Professor of Law, George Washington University Law School, USA. She is co-chair of the Women in International Law Interest Group of the American Society of International Law, and lived in Kinshasa, Congo, from 2002–2004. She has published numerous articles on issues relating to gender and international law, and co-taught one of the first International Women's Rights courses offered in the United States from 1992–1993 at Georgetown University Law Center. She served as a consultant to Global Rights for a report on domestic violence in Afghanistan that was released in March 2008.

Matthew Ezzo is Assistant Prosecuting Attorney at the Cuyahoga County Prosecutor's Office, Willowick, Ohio, USA. He was an infantry officer in the USMC. He participated in security operations in Haiti, humanitarian operations in Albania, as well as peacekeeping and combat operations in Kosovo. Mr. Ezzo has also worked on antiterrorism requirements for the Navy.

Ole Kristian Fauchald is Professor of Law at the University of Oslo Law Faculty, Norway. He worked as a legal adviser in the Norwegian Ministry of Environment for two years. He created the International Masters Program in Public International Law at the University of Oslo. He teaches Public International Law, Environmental Law and International Economic Law. His experience and publications are within the fields of International Trade Law (WTO), International Investment Law, Human Rights, and International Environmental Law, with a particular focus on biological diversity.

Amos N. Guiora is Professor of Law at the S.J. Quinney College of Law, University of Utah, USA. He served for 19 years in the Israel Defense Forces Judge Advocate General's Corps (Lt. Col. Ret.). He held a number of senior command positions, including Commander of the IDF School of Military Law, Judge Advocate for the

Navy and Home Front Command, and the Legal Advisor to the Gaza Strip. He teaches Criminal Law, Criminal Procedure, International Law, Global Perspectives on Counter-terrorism, and Religion & Terrorism. He writes and lectures extensively on issues related to terrorism and counterterrorism.

Ulf Häußler is a member of the Legal Service of the German Armed Forces since 2002. He is currently 'on loan' to NATO and holds his present position as Assistant Legal Advisor Operational Law at Allied Command Transformation since 2 January 2009. He has been deployed to KFOR (2006) and SFOR (2004) and has also served on secondment in the Legal Office, NATO International Staff (2006). His publications address peacekeeping operations.

Sean Kanuck is an international lawyer who has served the US Government as a national security analyst, diplomat, and policy adviser. He holds advanced degrees from Harvard University, the London School of Economics, and the University of Oslo.

Christopher Kutz is Professor of Law in the Jurispridence and Social Policy Program at U.C. Berkeley School of Law, USA, and the Director of the Kadish Center for Morality, Law, and Public Affairs. Kutz's work focuses on moral, political and legal philosophy, and he has particular interest in the foundations of Criminal, International, and Constitutional Law. His current work centers on: democratic theory, the law of war, the metaphysics of criminal law, and the nature of political legitimacy.

Larry May is W. Alton Jones Professor of Philosophy and Professor of Law at Vanderbilt University in Nashville, USA, and Professorial Fellow at the Centre for Applied Philosophy and Public Ethics, Charles Sturt and Australian National University Canberra, Australia. He has worked on conceptual issues in collective and shared responsibility, as well as normative issues in International Criminal Law. He has published over 80 articles and 21 books, the last four with Cambridge University Press.

Kjetil Mujezinović Larsen is Research Fellow at the Norwegian Centre for Human Rights, University of Oslo, Norway. He previously worked as Legal Adviser in the Norwegian Ministry of Justice. He teaches human rights law and international humanitarian law. His research focuses on human rights law in peace operations.

Gro Nystuen is Associate Professor of International Humanitarian Law at the Norwegian Centre for Human Rights, University of Oslo, Norway. She worked for the Norwegian Ministry for Foreign Affairs from 1991 to 2005. She has extensive experience addressing human rights, international humanitarian law and arms issues, including the Mine Ban Convention. She was legal adviser at the Yugoslavia Conference (ICFY) (1995), and for the High Representative in Bosnia (1995–1997). Her publications address peace agreements, International Humanitarian Law, international terrorism, corporate social Responsibility and jus ad bellum issues. Since 2005, she has been Chair of the Council on Ethics for the Norwegian Government Pension Fund – Global.

Marco Odello is a Lecturer at Aberystwyth University, UK, where he teaches International Law, Human Rights and Public Comparative Law. He is Fellow of the Higher Education Academy (UK), Member of the International Institute of Humanitarian

Law, and General Editor of *The Cambrian Law Review*. His research and publications concentrate on Public International Law, International Organisations, International Human Rights, International Humanitarian Law, Collective Security and Use of Force.

Marco Sassòli is Professor of International Law at the University of Geneva, Switzerland and Associate Professor at the universities of Quebec in Montreal and of Laval, Canada. He worked 13 years for the International Committee of the Red Cross at the headquarters and in the Field. His publications address Public International Law, International Humanitarian Law, and Terrorism.

Jo Stigen is Post Doctoral Research Fellow at the Department of Public and International Law, University of Oslo, Norway. He previously worked for the Ministry of Justice and the Prosecutor's Office. In 1996–1998 he served as a member of the Norwegian delegation to the conference establishing the Rome Statute. His teaching, research, and publications focus on International Criminal Law and International Public Law.

Christina Voigt is Post Doctoral Research Fellow at the Department of Public and International Law, University of Oslo, Norway. She teaches International and National Environmental Law, Climate Change Law and policy as well as International Public Law. Her current post doctoral research focuses on 'Safeguarding the Environmental Integrity of the Global Carbon Market'.

Index

International Humanitarian Law Series

1 Michael J. Kelly, *Restoring and Maintaining Order in Complex Peace Operations: The Search for a Legal Framework*, 1999 ISBN 90 411 1179 4

2 Helen Durham and Timothy L.H. McCormack (eds.), *The Changing Face of Conflict and the Efficacy of International Humanitarian Law*, 1999 ISBN 90 411 1180 8

3 Richard May, David Tolbert, John Hocking, Ken Roberts, Bing Bing Jia, Daryl Mundis and Gabriël Oosthuizen (eds.), *Essays on ICTY Procedure and Evidence in Honour of Gabrielle Kirk McDonald*, 2001 ISBN 90 411 1482 3

4 Elizabeth Chadwick, *Traditional Neutrality Revisited: Law, Theory and Case Studies*, 2002 ISBN 90 411 1787 3

5 Lal Chand Vohrah, Fausto Pocar, Yvonne Featherstone, Olivier Fourmy, Christine Graham, John Hocking and Nicholas Robson (eds.), *Man's Inhumanity to Man: Essays on International Law in Honour of Antonio Cassese*, 2003 ISBN 90 411 1986 8

6 Gideon Boas and William A. Schabas (eds.), *International Criminal Law Developments in the Case Law of the ICTY*, 2003 ISBN 90 411 1987 6

7* Karen Hulme, *War Torn Environment: Interpreting the Legal Threshold*, 2004 ISBN 90 04 13848 X

8 Helen Durham and Tracey Gurd (eds.), *Listening to the Silences: Women and War*, 2005 ISBN 90 04 14365 3

9* ** Marten Zwanenburg, *Accountability of Peace Support Operations*, 2005 ISBN 90 04 14350 5

10 Hirad Abtahi and Gideon Boas (eds.), *The Dynamics of International Criminal Law*, 2006 ISBN 90 04 14587 7

11 Frits Kalshoven, *Belligerent Reprisals*, 2005 ISBN 90 04 14386 6

12 Pablo Antonio Fernández-Sánchez (ed.), *The New Challenges of Humanitarian Law in Armed Conflicts: In Honour of Professor Juan Antonio Carrillo-Salcedo*, 2005 ISBN 90 04 14830 2

13 Ustinia Dolgopol and Judith Gardam (eds.), *The Challenge of Conflict: International Law Responds*, 2006 ISBN 90 04 14599 0

14* Laura Perna, *The Formation of the Treaty Law of Non-International Armed Conflicts*, 2006 ISBN 90 04 14924 4

15 Michael Schmitt and Jelena Pejic (eds.), *International Law and Armed Conflict: Exploring the Faultlines, Essays in Honour of Yoram Dinstein*, 2007 ISBN 978 90 04 15428 5

16 Ola Engdahl, *Protection of Personnel in Peace Operations: The Role of the 'Safety Convention' against the Background of General International Law*, 2007 ISBN 978 90 04 15466 7

17 Frits Kalshoven, *Reflections on the Law of War: Collected Essays*, 2007 ISBN 978 90 04 15825 2

18 Héctor Olásolo, *Unlawful Attacks in Combat Situations: From the ICTY's Case Law to the Rome Statute*, 2007 ISBN 978 90 04 16200 6

---

* Winner of the ASIL Francis Lieber Prize.
** Winner of the 2006 Paul Reuter Prize.

19 José Doria, Hans-Peter Gasser and M. Cherif Bassiouni (eds.), *The Legal Regime of the International Criminal Court: Essays in Honour of Professor Igor Blishchenko*, 2008 ISBN 978 90 04 16308 9

20 David A. Blumenthal and Timothy L.H. McCormack (eds.), *The Legacy of Nuremberg: Civilising Influence or Institutionalised Vengeance?*, 2008 ISBN 978 90 04 15691 3

21 Omar Abdulle Alasow, *Violations of the Rules Applicable in Non-International Armed Conflicts and Their Possible Causes: The Case of Somalia*, 2008 ISBN 978 90 04 16475 8

22 Ola Engdahl and Pål Wrange (eds.), *Law at War: The Law as it Was and the Law as it Should Be – Liber Amicorum Ove Bring*, 2008 ISBN 978 90 04 17016 2

23 Pablo Antonio Fernández-Sánchez (ed.), *International Legal Dimension of Terrorism*, 2009 ISBN 978 90 04 17053 7

24 Rob McLaughlin, *United Nations Naval Peace Operations in the Territorial Sea* ISBN 978 90 04 17479 5

25 Ian Henderson, *The Contemporary Law of Targeting: Military Objectives, Proportionality and Precautions in Attack under Additional Protocol I* ISBN 978 90 04 17480 1

26 Cecilia M. Bailliet (ed.), *Security: A Multidisciplinary Normative Approach*, 2009 ISBN 978 90 04 17296 8

brill.nl/ihul